D1565015

THE PATRON STATE

THE PATRON STATE

Government and the Arts in Europe, North America, and Japan

Edited by

Milton C. Cummings, Jr.
Richard S. Katz

New York Oxford
OXFORD UNIVERSITY PRESS
1987

Oxford University Press
Oxford New York Toronto
Delhi Bombay Calcutta Madras Karachi
Petaling Jaya Singapore Hong Kong Tokyo
Nairobi Dar es Salaam Cape Town
Melbourne Auckland

and associated companies in
Beirut Berlin Ibadan Nicosia

Published by Oxford University Press, Inc.,
200 Madison Avenue, New York, New York 10016

Oxford is a registered trademark of Oxford University Press

Library of Congress Cataloging-in-Publication Data
The Patron State.
1. Art patronage. 2. Federal aid to the arts. 3. Art and state.
I. Cummings, Milton C., Jr. II. Katz, Richard S.
NX720.P37 1987 700'.79 86-19186
ISBN 0-19-504364-2

2 4 6 8 9 7 5 3 1
Printed in the United States of America
on acid-free paper

Preface

It is now twenty-two years since Frederick Dorian's magisterial study of public support for the arts in nine countries of western Europe first appeared. In that time, there has been an astonishing growth in the scope of government cultural programs and in the number of countries which pursue them. We thought it would be of interest to see what has happened since Dorian wrote his book, in the countries which have had a long tradition of public arts support. We also thought it would be equally important to look at developments in the countries that more recently have begun to support the arts. This book is a study of the development of cultural policy since World War II in thirteen countries in Europe, North America, and Japan.

Both of the editors wish to thank the Political Science Department of the Johns Hopkins University for financial assistance which helped to defray the costs of translating chapters not originally written in English and paid the massive postage bill inevitable in a trans-Atlantic collaboration. Milton Cummings also wishes to thank the Ford Foundation and the John Simon Guggenheim Memorial Foundation for financial support which enabled him to work in the area of government and the arts.

We also wish to record our gratitude to a number of people who assisted us with the preparation of this book. Catherine Grover typed much of the manuscript, catching many of the errors and inconsistencies which escaped our notice. Evelyn Scheulen and Evelyn Stoller also provided secretarial assistance which was of great help. Chris Laurson, Kate Forhan, and Gian Falcone provided skillful translations of the German, French, and Italian chapters. Judith Katz helped us in many ways—as adviser, editor, and critic, and with her unflagging optimism that a book of this scope would in fact get done. We are particularly grateful for the support, encouragement, and assistance of our editors at Oxford University Press, Sheldon Meyer, Rachel Toor, and Stephanie Sakson-Ford. Finally, we wish to thank the sixteen authors of the chapters on thirteen countries. They collectively have provided a rich mosaic of the policies governments have been pursuing for the support of culture in much of the industrialized world.

Baltimore, Maryland
1987

M.C.C.
R.S.K.

Note

One of the problems in cross-national studies of public spending is that the relative values of national currencies vary over time. There is no fully satisfactory solution to this problem. To convert everything into a single currency, like American dollars, runs the risk of confusing changes in exchange rates with changes in real levels of spending. To leave everything in terms of local currency makes comparison across nations difficult. Since funds are appropriated and spent in local currencies, we have left the figures in each chapter in the original currency. The following table, showing the value of $1 (US) at five-year intervals should facilitate cross-national comparisons.

	1950	*1955*	*1960*	*1965*	*1970*	*1975*	*1980*	*1985*
Canada	1.06	1.00	1.00	1.03	1.01	1.02	1.19	1.40
Denmark	6.92	6.91	6.91	6.90	7.59	6.18	6.02	8.97
France	3.50	3.50	4.90	4.90	5.52	4.49	4.52	7.56
German Federal Republic	4.20	4.22	4.17	4.01	3.65	2.62	1.96	2.46
Great Britain*	2.80	2.80	2.80	2.80	2.39	2.02	2.39	1.44
Ireland*	2.80	2.80	2.80	2.80	2.39	2.02	1.90	1.24
Italy	625	625	621	625	623	684	931	1679
Japan	361	361	358	361	358	305	203	201
Netherlands	3.80	3.83	3.77	3.61	3.60	2.69	2.13	2.77
Norway	7.15	7.15	7.15	7.15	7.14	5.59	5.18	7.58
Portugal	28.9	28.9	28.8	28.8	28.8	27.5	53.0	157.5
Sweden	5.18	5.18	5.18	5.18	5.17	4.39	4.37	7.62

Source: International Monetary Fund, *International Financial Statistics*

*Dollars per pound.

Contents

List of Contributors

Marianne Andrault — Chargée de Mission, Ministry of Industry, France

Marit Bakke — Associate Professor, Institute of Political Science, University of Aarhus, Denmark

Mie Berg — Institute for Social Research, Oslo, Norway

Guido Clemente di San Luca — Ricercatore, University of Naples, Italy

Milton C. Cummings, Jr. — Professor of Political Science, Johns Hopkins University, Baltimore, Maryland

Philippe Dressayre — Senior Consultant, Bernard Julhiet Conseils, France

Pim Fenger — Deputy Director Policymaking, Higher Education and Research, Ministry of Education and Science, The Netherlands

Thomas R. H. Havens — Professor of History, Connecticut College, New London, Connecticut

Alice E. Ingerson — Managing Editor, Journal of Forest History, Durham, North Carolina

Wolfgang Ismayr — University of Bamberg, Federal Republic of Germany

Richard S. Katz — Professor of Political Science, Johns Hopkins University, Baltimore, Maryland

Anne Kelly — Department of Ethics and Politics, University College, Dublin, Republic of Ireland

Carl-Johann Kleberg — Swedish National Council for Cultural Affairs

JOHN MEISEL
Sir Edward Peacock Professor of Political Science
Queen's University
Kingston, Ontario

KEVIN V. MULCAHY
Associate Professor of Political Science
Louisiana State University
Baton Rouge, Louisiana

GIUSEPPE PALMA
University of Naples
Italy

F. F. RIDLEY
Professor of Political Theory and Institutions
University of Liverpool
United Kingdom

JEAN VAN LOON
Department of Political Studies
Queen's University
Kingston, Ontario

THE PATRON STATE

1

Government and the Arts: An Overview

Milton C. Cummings, Jr., and Richard S. Katz

It is common for many citizens of Canada, Great Britain, and the United States, as well as citizens of some other countries, to think that government programs to support the arts are quite new. Insofar as the kind of systematic programs of support that are now in place are concerned, and from a limited time perspective and within the confines of their own countries, they are right. Substantial concerted and direct government expenditures to benefit the arts and culture in these countries generally date only from the decades after World War II, although a number of indirect subsidies, such as tax exemptions for cultural institutions and reduced postage rates for periodicals, have existed for many years.

From a broader perspective, however, state support of the arts is not new at all. Instead, it is the continuation of a tradition that fostered the flowering of Western culture. In addition to commissioning artists' work for the decoration of public buildings—and we must recognize that in earlier times the distinction between artist and artisan was not drawn as sharply as we would draw it today—the democracy of ancient Athens was an active patron of drama as part of the state religion. Indeed, theater was so important to the Athenians that the Treasurer of the Theater Fund was one of the few officials—along with the generals—elected by vote rather than chosen by lot.[1] Many of the greatest works of Renaissance art were commissioned by princes and popes. In Italy, Germany, Austria, and France, there has been a tradition of public support for the arts that made possible the work of Raphael, Wagner, Haydn, and Molière, to name only four.

In feudal Europe, there was no real distinction between the Prince as sovereign, or between a duke or baron as lord (and therefore governor), and the same individual as a person. In particular, in financial terms there was not yet a distinction drawn at any level. In addition, where the local feudal lord was a bishop or an abbot, no clear lines were drawn among the institution of the church, the institution of the state, and the person of the incumbent. Nonetheless, all of these feudal governors were supported at least in part by levies which we would clearly recognize as taxes ostensibly raised for the public good. So when a prince or a bishop commissioned a painting, employed a court composer or *Kapellmeister,* or built a theater, he was engaged in what can only be called government patronage of the arts.

Of course, not every princeling supported the arts, and not every artist who received public patronage was a Mozart, a Michelangelo, or a Racine. Nor was every great work of

Renaissance art the product of a public commission. At the same time that Duke Christian Ludwig of Brandenburg was commissioning Bach's *Brandenburg Concerti,* King Frederick William I of Prussia forbade all forms of artistic life as being of "no practical value." For every Mozart, Schiller, or Caravaggio, there were countless other composers, poets, and painters receiving state largess who, if technically competent, still created nothing of transcendent value. Even when true geniuses were the beneficiaries of princely or ecclesiastical commissions, the works actually commissioned may have been pedestrian, produced to appeal to the patron's taste, while giving the artist the financial freedom to experiment and create to satisfy himself.

The consolidation of royal power in Europe left a class of nobles in command of what were truly private fortunes. At the same time, the growth of cities and the rise of commerce and manufacturing led to the creation of a prosperous merchant class. As a result of these developments, by the eighteenth century, private patronage also came to loom large in the artistic world. Nevertheless, for some art forms, especially opera, some form of public patronage remained virtually indispensable, and it continued to be significant for the other arts as well. Even if some artists, like Shakespeare, could support themselves without government assistance, it is not too much to say that without government support in one form or another many of the greatest artistic creations of Western civilization would not exist. It is only appropriate that the masterpieces housed in the Uffizi ultimately were willed to the people of Florence or that the collections in the Louvre now belong to the citizens of France; the taxes of their ancestors paid for them.

From this perspective, contemporary government programs to support the arts are not new in principle. However, especially since 1945, these programs have expanded tremendously: geographically, as more countries, particularly those in the Anglo-Saxon world, have joined (or rejoined) those countries with long-standing traditions of governmental support for the arts; in breadth, as more forms of cultural expression have been brought under the aegis of public arts programs; and in size, as the monetary commitment of national governments to preserving the cultural heritage of the past, facilitating cultural participation in the present, and fostering the development of new cultural achievements for the future has mushroomed. Although these programs often have been substantially reorganized, reflecting the transition from aristocratic or bourgeois government to mass democracy, the professionalization of all areas of endeavor characteristic of modern societies, and more general reforms or restructurings of the national bureaucracies of which they are a part, public support for the arts has deep historical roots.

It is principally modern programs to assist the arts as they have evolved in the postwar industrial democracies of western Europe, Canada, the United States, and Japan that form the subject of this book. If such programs are common in the sense that all Western countries now support the arts to one extent or another, the ways in which they provide support to the arts and artists are diverse. There is great variety—limited only by the number of countries—in cultural policies and in the institutions set up to implement them. And this variety reflects not only differing national traditions in the organization of public functions and the delivery of public services, but differing philosophies and objectives regarding the whole area of culture and the arts.

In some cases, it is possible to trace the institutions or policies of one country to an explicit borrowing from the experience of another. For example, the Irish Arts Council and, only slightly less directly, the American National Endowment for the Arts are based on the Arts Council of Great Britain. More perversely, the structure of the British Broadcasting Corporation was based in large measure on a decision to *avoid* the chaotic experience of radio broadcasting in the United States. In general, however, policies evolved without reference to, and often in ignorance of, developments in other countries. Calls for reforms in a nation's arts policies are still made in apparent ignorance of the results of similar policies in other countries. Thus, one task of this book is simply to describe for citizens and policy-makers of one country the development and current state of cultural policy and administration elsewhere.

Beyond this, however, comparison of these cases will enable us to *evaluate* as well as to describe cultural policies. Are some strategies for gaining and maintaining support for the arts, for deciding among policy alternatives and among competing applicants, for organizing an arts bureaucracy, more successful than others? And in what respects are they more successful? As these chapters show, in many cases the initial expansion of cultural policies appears to have been triggered by a unique combination of events. Often, for example, a fortuitously placed individual was given the opportunity to indulge his or her own taste for reasons that had little to do with a general governmental desire to support the arts. Nevertheless, once the process began, a "politics of cultural support" emerged that was quite similar from one country to another.

In this study we also will be addressing a more general problem of public policy. All policy problems can be considered as the conjunction of two types of questions: questions of taste (What is better than what? What goals ought to be pursued? Which trade-offs imposed by limited resources ought to be accepted and which rejected?); and questions of technical expertise (What are the possible trade-offs? What are the likely consequences of particular policy options?). One of the obvious tendencies in modern politics is for participants who can claim some special expertise (which often means everyone except members of the general public) to attempt to convert questions of taste, on which they would in a democratic society have no claim to special consideration, into questions of technique, on which they can claim a privileged position for their own opinions. The special standing given to physicians in deciding how medical care should be financed or to chemical company engineers in deciding tolerable levels of pollution are just two examples. This trend has been apparent in the field of cultural policy as in other fields, yet cultural policy is preeminently a matter of taste. Thus, examination of cultural policy provides an especially good opportunity to analyze this phenomenon.

Although our principal focus is on contemporary politics and policy, an understanding of modern developments requires at least a general acquaintance with their historical roots. In the broadest terms, one can distinguish two overall patterns that form the background against which twentieth-century arts policies have evolved. On the one hand, there were the royal absolutist states, typified by Austria and France. On the other hand, there were the more plutocratic, mercantilist states with more limited monarchies, such as England or the Netherlands. With the German and Italian proto-states (neither Germany nor Italy was united until the second half of the nineteenth century) showing mixed traits, these two polar types differed not only in their form of government, but in their economic and social development (with trade and industry and the commercial class to which they gave rise far more important much earlier in the mercantilist states than in the royal absolutist), and in religion (Protestant in the mercantilist, Catholic in the absolutist) as well. All these factors conspired to produce different patterns of support, and in turn different patterns of artistic development.

While earlier examples of royal support can, of course, be found, major royal patronage of the arts began roughly in the second half of the seventeenth century in both France and Austria, in both cases after the consolidation of royal power. In both, traditions of public support were established that continue to the present day, although their royal character ended with the end of the monarchies. The specific nature of royal patronage was in part idiosyncratic and in part reflective of national traditions. The Hapsburgs were heirs to an established musical tradition in Austria that had been sponsored mainly by the church, but they were talented in the musical field themselves, with many creditable compositions of their own.[2] The Bourbons were attracted more to theater.

In general terms, however, Hapsburg and Bourbon patronage had much in common. Both were typified by the establishment and support of major institutions on a grand scale. In Austria, Emperor Joseph I in 1705 paid for a large opera house in Vienna and in 1708 for the building of the *Theater am Kärnthner-Thor*. In 1776, the *Burgtheater* was opened, with the Emperor Joseph II as its first manager. In the same vein, one of the greatest legacies of the reign of Louis XIV was the *Comédie Française*. During the reigns of his two successors, the Paris *Opéra* and the *Opéra Comique* were established as beneficiaries of royal largess.

Although it would be unfair, especially in the case of the Hapsburgs, to attribute royal patronage of the arts solely to a desire for self- or national glorification, there is no doubt that this played a role. The content of the art commissioned often reflected the theme of royal power and grandeur (as had, indeed, many works of Michelangelo commissioned by the Medici over a century before). Nothing epitomizes this trend better than Louis XIV's palace at Versailles, but the trend runs through much of the artistic production of this period. Patronage of recognized creative geniuses also reflected credit on their supporters.

Along with creating massive opportunities for artists to find employment and laying the foundations for institutions that survive today, the third great achievement of these royal patrons was to establish an atmosphere in which support of the arts became widespread, both among those at the apex of society and among those who aspired to be. This included patronage by burghers and members of the nobility, as well as by municipalities, as when in 1767 the city of Paris decided to make an annual subvention to the *Opéra,* and by organizations, such as the prototypical *Gesellschaft der Musikfreunde* (Society of the Friends of Music) in Vienna.

The attitude that support of the arts was a virtue was particularly important because it survived the overthrow of the monarchies. Moreover, the regimes that succeeded the monarchies, far from destroying the former objects of royal largess, continued to support institutions established by the dynasties they replaced. Even during the Terror, the Jacobin Republic in France gave substantial support to the lyric stage, and if for a time the content of the work produced was more propagandistic then artistic, the tradition of public financial support for major musical and theatrical institutions was maintained.

In the Netherlands, and especially in England, things were quite different. In the first place, there were no absolute kings in a position to spend lavishly in order to glorify their reigns; instead, limited monarchs avoided the conspicuous consumption of the Bourbons and the Hapsburgs, both as a matter of policy and as a matter of necessity. Second, the austerity of Calvinist and Puritan Protestantism did not allow for the kind of artistic life that was flourishing in Austria and France. As Frederick Dorian noted, "Calvin envisioned the entire world as a convent; the ritual should offer no opportunity for appreciation of the beautiful art works which adorned Christian churches."[3] While the Church of England did not follow the Dutch Reformed Church in opposing instrumental (including organ) music in the liturgy, other Protestant sects went at least as far in regarding the arts, as well as other forms of enjoyment, as frivolous if not positively sinful. Theaters, in particular, came to be regarded as dens of iniquity and temptation, little better than bawdy houses. Third, power shifted to the new classes of burghers and merchants in whose liberal ideology that government was best which governed least.

In the Netherlands, there was often significant support of the arts from the towns. The city of Leyden, for example, began a regular series of organ recitals, while the City Theater of Amsterdam (*Amsterdamsche Schouwburg*) was founded in 1637. In England, however, while there were concerts, plays, and operas, these were purely commercial ventures, operating perhaps with royal license or patent but without public financial support. In this environment, it was only natural that the arts which flourished were the more "private" arts. Painting, in particular, offered the patron something tangible for his money; something with which he could decorate his town house or country seat, and something he could perhaps sell at a profit later on.

Ultimately, the "public" arts, such as opera and ballet, were endowed, in some cases on a grand scale, by private donors of great wealth. Particularly in the nineteenth and early twentieth century, these were often members of the industrial *nouveaux riches* anxious to enhance their own social standing. In this respect, they were not unlike the earlier aristocratic patrons of the arts in France or Austria.

One further general characteristic of pre-twentieth-century support of the arts, both public and private, and in both mercantilist and royal states, deserves mention. Almost never was a leisure class of subsidized artists created (although there were some movements in this direction in Scandinavia). Patronage rarely consisted of unconditional support for the artist to create. Rather, patronage meant employment for a particular period or on a particular product that the patron wanted, and if the patron was not satisfied he had the option of all buyers to take his business elsewhere. Even when patronage consisted of outright gifts, the flow of largess could be cut off at the whim of the patron. Only the most famous geniuses, such as Beethoven in his old age, were likely to receive unconditional pensions. Freedom for the artist came from the fact that there were many potential patrons. Still, an artist whose work pleased no one but himself could lay no claim to either public or private support.

The various systems of public and private support that evolved in many countries were adequate to maintain a vital cultural life into the twentieth century. In other countries, there simply was little domestic cultural life. With the period between the world wars as, perhaps, the decisive turning point, by the second half of the twentieth century, nineteenth-century patterns of support were obviously inadequate everywhere, and the role of government in financing the arts burgeoned. While the relative importance of the various factors contributing to this development depended on the previously existing scheme for financing the arts and on the particular social and economic trends in each country, the general story was much the same throughout the Western world.

First, a number of major developments altered the financial position of the arts. With the dramatic increase in rates of taxation engendered by the First World War, and especially with the avowedly redistributive income, wealth, and inheritence tax policies of many governments, the relative magnitude of private fortunes declined. Coupled with this were the effects of the industrial revolution, finally brought to fruition in the consumer societies of the post-World War II era. Mechanization vastly increased the productivity, and standard of living, of workers. Ironically, however, this increase in prosperity in some ways actually hurt the arts. It takes nearly as many man-hours to produce an opera today as it did in the eighteenth century. But since hours spent in manufacturing are so much more productive, and correspondingly so much better paid in terms of goods that can be bought for an hour's wage, than they were two hundred years ago, the relative cost of the arts has increased. Like domestic service, this labor-intensive activity has become progressively more expensive in real terms in capital intensive economies.

Another set of developments involves the tremendous expansion of the general role of the state that occurred in the twentieth century. This tendency was already noticeable in the nineteenth century, but it exploded in the years between World War I and World War II. Particularly with regard to culture, one can identify four major changes. The earliest was the expanded role of the state in the field of education. Education and the arts have always been related, so that once the government began to play a major role in education, it was a short step for it to begin playing a role in the arts as well. The second change was the emergence of radio as a major, perhaps *the* major, medium of cultural dissemination. Originally, radio was perceived as an advance on the telegraph as a medium of personal communication. Government control of radio in Europe, therefore, was a natural extension of European governmental monopolies on postal and telegraphic communication. This was only furthered by the chaos that developed in the early—essentially unregulated—days of American commercial broadcasting. With many hours of air time to fill, European state broadcasters became major consumers and patrons of the arts.

A third change was the idea that the state should play an active role in bringing the "good life" to average citizens, providing for the working class on a collective basis what the upper and middle classes had been able to provide for themselves individually. Access to culture is analogous in this respect to access to medical care. Once seen as luxuries to be provided only insofar as the individual could afford them, they are now increasingly seen as necessities that must be provided for all, regardless of ability to pay. Finally, there was the expansion of government responsibility in the field of public welfare brought about by the Great Depression of the 1930s. The forerunners of contemporary arts programs in the United States, for example, were the artists' programs of the New Deal, in which artists were just one more group of unemployed for whom work had to be created.

A third major class of developments were social changes that vastly increased the demand for the arts. One of the most important of these has been the tremendous growth of public education. Education has always been associated with the arts in at least two ways. As just suggested, countries that have been active in one field generally have been active in the other (beginning, perhaps, with the Empress Maria Theresa's introduction of compulsory education in Austria in 1774). In addition, individuals with higher levels of education generally have been more artistically interested and aware.[4] Particularly in the twentieth century, as public education beyond the level of basic literacy has become widely available, it has usually included some introduction to the arts in its curriculum. It has also contributed to a leveling of class differences and the establishment of interpersonal networks that cut across old class lines. These trends have expanded the range of people who have been introduced to the arts and who regard attendance at a concert or museum as appropriate "for people like themselves." And from the other side, the lessening of class differences has encouraged arts institutions to pursue actively programs of "out-reach" to attract patrons who in previous decades would have been considered "beyond the pale."

To this trend must be added the spread of the electronic media of mass communications. When during the Second World War, for example, the British Committee for the Encouragement of Music and the Arts sent musical groups on tour around the country, they found, somewhat to their surprise, that a "large and genuine" audience familiar with and anxious to hear serious music had already been developed by the broadcasts of the BBC.[5] Similarly, in the United States, many people who originally would never have thought of buying a ticket to an opera or ballet have been converted into patrons of these art forms after seeing them for the first time quite by accident on television.

Finally, there is the social consequence of mechanization—vastly increased amounts of leisure time. It is not surprising that many people who had to perform manual labor 12 or 14 hours a day, six or even seven days a week, had little interest in art or culture. With the five-day, 40-, 37½-, or 35-hour work week, filling up the remaining free time has become a serious social problem. The same concern is magnified for the mushrooming army of retired people, a group that in general has less money to spend and even more time to fill.

All of these economic, political, and social trends have combined to create strong pressures for government intervention in the field of culture. With the exceptions of Canada and the United States, most Western governments that had not already established significant programs to support the arts before the Second World War did so in the years immediately after. Even if the pressures for support did not grow dramatically stronger, the world-wide economic boom of the 1960s then contributed to these programs' rapid expansion in Europe and their introduction into North America. With both tax revenues and personal incomes growing, it became harder for conservatives to resist the arguments for the government to contribute to any worthwhile project. In many countries, this was also an era of governments by parties (for example, the Democratic party in the United States, 1961–1969, Labour in Britain, 1964–1970) that were generally committed to a more activist role in the improvement of society.

These trends have contributed to reducing the differences among nations in the relationship of government and the arts. Every major industrial nation now has a significant cultural or arts policy which involves the expenditure of significant sums of money and is able to have a real impact on cultural development and distribution. Yet, as the chapters which follow show, if countries are alike in having cultural policies, they are very different in the kinds of policies they have adopted. They differ with regard to the specific goals which are pursued, with regard to the ways in which they are organized, and with regard to the policy tools, especially the forms of support, which are available. Yet, in recent years, spurred in part by the economic downturn of the late 1970s and early 1980s and in part by experience, there has been some convergence in the content of the policies as well. The recession hit the arts hard, forcing them to turn increasingly to government just as governments felt themselves forced to retrench. One result has been a trend toward diversification of forms of support, no matter where the primary support formerly came from.

The experience that governments have had with various administrative devices has revealed some of their shortcomings in addressing the problems inherent in the field of cultural policy. Various "pure types" of programs have been bastardized, and diversification and movement toward a hybrid approach to arts programs have been common. These tendencies as well will appear in the chapters about individual countries. Before moving on to them, however, it will be useful to review the overall variety of forms of support and methods of organization possible in the cultural field, as well as to take an advance look at some of the major problems and dilemmas of arts policy.

Underlying the differences among national cultural policies are national differences in situation, tradition, and motivation. Cultural policy often has an important nationalistic objective, but what this means in practice depends on whether the country has a strong national tradition to defend or still feels the need to develop its own cultural identity. The magnitude of programs to preserve a nation's cultural heritage will depend on both the size of the artistic patrimony and its form (architecture needs more preservation than music).

Governments may have many other objectives when they enter the cultural field. The economic benefits of a vital cultural sector are often cited as a rationale for government programs designed to assist the arts. "Cultural industries" may promote tourism, and thus the restaurant, hotel, and allied industries, and may serve as magnets in schemes of urban or regional development. Sometimes government arts programs are justified in terms of their contribution to the general welfare—a lively arts life, it is argued, will raise the quality of life generally for a nation's citizens. Finally, governments may decide to support the arts because influential groups or individuals want them to, or because politicians hope to improve their public images or to leave their mark on history.

There are many measures governments can take to aid the arts and culture financially. The simplest is to be a consumer of the artist's work. When a government buys paintings or pieces of sculpture to decorate its buildings, or hires musicians to play at public ceremonies, it provides employment for artists as well as (one hopes) improving the environment of its citizens. This was, of course, precisely the kind of patronage provided by the Hapsburgs and the Bourbons; they employed artists to decorate their palaces and to perform for their pleasure. On a small scale, a government's purchases in the arts for its own use are of little consequence for the overall level of artistic employment, although in some cases—monumental sculpture, for example—a single commission can have a significant effect on the career of the artist involved. In other circumstances, however, the government, or government agencies, may be among the most significant "customers" that a nation's artists have. This has been the case for music in Britain, for example, where for many years the BBC was the country's principal employer of musicians playing "serious music."

This form of support also becomes important when a government develops large-scale programs to buy artists' works irrespective of any direct use for them. The make-work programs of the New Deal in the United States provide a partial example of this, although a large number of public buildings were decorated and numerous performances given. An even better example is the current Dutch program to buy paintings. Originally, these were to decorate public buildings, but the program has expanded to such a degree that now most of the works purchased go directly to warehouses.

When the government becomes a major consumer of a particular form of art, its patronage has indirect effects as well. As with any product, a major increase in demand will lead to an increase in price for all consumers, at least in the short run. In any case, if the government buys art in essentially unlimited quantities at a particular price, that becomes in effect the floor below which no one will be able to buy and the program of government art purchases becomes exactly analogous to the American program of farm price supports. If the program continues over time, artifically inflated prices can be expected to lead to an artificially high supply, i.e., more people will be attracted to become professional artists than would otherwise be supported by the market. In addition, if the government's purchases are not indiscriminate, its buying power can be expected to distort the quality as well as the quantity of supply, as artists are led inexorably to produce more of whatever kind of art the government is buying.

Indiscriminate buying comes close to being a direct subsidy, although something tangible still is exchanged for government money. Another strategy for government support of the arts, however, is the direct subsidy itself. Generically, the government gives money (or some other goods or services such as technical assistance or use of facilities) without a direct return. The return to the government, or more generally to society, is that some desired activity goes on, goes on more extensively, or is available to individuals more cheaply than would otherwise have been the case.

Subsidies or grants can take a variety of forms. Here we need only list a few of the many possibilities. A grant can simply be a lump-sum payment, or a match in some ratio to funds raised from other sources (as are American "challenge grants"). A subsidy can be a cost-sharing arrangement (as with Dutch orchestras), or a guarantee against loss. Subsidies can be granted for general operating expenses, for special projects of limited duration, or as "seed-money" for programs that are expected eventually to become self-supporting. Subsidies may be accompanied by numerous conditions and restrictions, or they may be outright gifts. Government subsidies may be given to cultural institutions, to individual artists, or to intermediate organizations that re-grant them.

Subsidies also can have many different objectives and effects. They can, of course, simply increase the total amount of money available for the arts. They may also, or alternatively, be designed to reduce the dependence of the arts on some other sources of income. For example, one possible objective of a program of subsidies would be to insulate the arts from the commercializing pressures of corporate donors. A third possibility would be to reduce the risk of experimental or avant-garde activities. Of course, different policy instruments are appropriate to different goals. The guarantee against loss, for example, encourages risk-taking but does not encourage a diligent search either for economies or for other sources of funds, since any reduction of the deficit only reduces the subsidy. Many European arts programs, which are lavish in their support but which treat museum admission charges or profits from museum-shop sales as income to the national treasury, or deduct outside funds raised from the government's grant, discourage searches for additional sources of support. Matching grants, on the other hand, while encouraging aggressive fund-raising, may also encourage excessive catering to the tastes of those who can afford to make large donations.

One set of indirect subsidies that deserve special mention consists of so-called "tax expenditures," that is, revenue forgone as a result of special tax provisions to benefit the arts. One form these subsidies may take is the exemption of the cultural institutions or artists themselves from various forms of taxation. Theaters and museums may be excused from real property or entertainment (ticket) taxes, or some forms of art-related income may be exempted from income tax. Provisions of this sort can also be used to influence the behavior of arts institutions as well as to give financial relief, as, for example, the Italian policy of taxing ticket receipts at a lower rate if there is an adequate proportion of cheap seats. A second form, particularly important in the United States, is to allow donations to cultural institutions to be deducted from income subject to individual taxation. The effect is to subsidize contributions—since the real cost to the donor is the value of the donation *minus the reduction in income tax it produces*—and thus to encourage giving. A final possibility, found in Great Britain, is for the treasury to refund to the *recipient* of a contribution the income tax paid on its value by the donor. Instead of making donations less costly to the giver, this provision makes them more valuable to the receiver.[6]

Finally, we should mention that the arts may also be beneficiaries of more general social policies which nonetheless create a climate favorable for culture or for those who work in the cultural field. The expansion of systems of public education is one example of such a policy. Provision of unemployment insurance is another; many performing artists depend on this and other social welfare programs when they are between engagements. (This pattern of regular dependence on social insurance is also typical of many occupations outside the arts, e.g., pattern makers in the garment industry.)

Protection of intellectual property through the system of copyrights has proven invaluable to the creators of music and literature. Indeed, the impact of the copyright system was underscored by the situation in the United States before foreigners became eligible for protection. Works by foreign artists frequently were pirated, not only denying them compensation for their work but also giving their material an unfair competitive advantage over the work of American authors and composers who would have to be paid royalties. Even elements of postal policy can have a sizable impact on the climate vis-à-vis culture. The stimulation given to magazines, and hence to the short story, by the American second-class postage rate greatly expanded the market for American writers.

In addition to the variety of policy instruments which are available to governments in the cultural field, there are many ways in which the administration of these policies can be organized. In this regard, it is important to remember that government may have many objectives beyond simple "support" of the arts, and that to achieve these objectives government may deploy a range of regulatory policies in addition to the "bribery" of subsidies. In gross terms, one can distinguish four major organizational forms which are in common use. The first two are variants of the normal public administration approach. Provision or encouragement of culture is regarded simply as one more public function to be run by the regular public service according to normal established procedures. One of these variants is the so-called "French Ministry of Culture Model"—although, as will be seen in Chapter Two, not even the French follow this model completely. Here a single ministry, headed by a cabinet minister, would be in charge of all cultural policies, ideally providing both comprehensive coordination and planning and high-level advocacy for cultural programs. With the other variant, responsibility for cultural programs is divided among several ministries, as has been the case, for example, in Italy. In either case, funds are allocated through the regular budgetary process and their spending is subject to the same political and bureaucratic controls as are found in any other government ministry. Likewise, the minister or ministers in charge of cultural departments are politically accountable for the programs and decisions of their ministries.

A third organizational form that governments may use to pursue cultural policy goals is the quasi-public foundation. The model here is the private philanthropic foundation, and examples of this type include America's National Endowment for the Arts and the Arts Councils of Great Britain and of Ireland. These have been established to remove arts policy, or at least direct support of the arts, from the normal government agenda, in the hope of "insulating" the arts from politics. Ideally, the government decides on a level of expenditure, and then passes the funds to the foundation which disperses them as it sees fit. The objective is to remove the details of allocation, and responsibility for the results of particular projects, from the sphere of partisan politics, thereby allowing judgments to be made on more artistically relevant grounds. Of course, there are limits to the insultation from politics which are possible with any public agency. Members of arts councils are appointed by politicians; governments can react to policies they dislike by threatening to cut the council's appropriation for succeeding years, and councils usually anticipate this possibility, making overt threats unnecessary; and despite the principle of autonomy, governments may impose restrictions on appropriations, such as the NEA's required 20 percent pass-through to the states. Nevertheless, in countries that use the quasi-public foundation model, the architects of cultural policies were trying to minimize the intrusion of politicians and bureaucrats in the cultural policy process.

The fourth organizational form for government arts programs casts the government directly in the role of impresario. Rather than supporting cultural institutions, the government simply runs them itself. The most common examples of this sort of arrangement in the United States are public museums, but other examples include the British Broadcasting Corporation and the Swedish regional orchestras. In some cases, employees are regular civil servants, while in others the institution is set up like a private corporation, although the directors are appointed by the government.

Although not precisely a method of administrative organization, one further possibility deserves mention. In some cases, particular museums and performing arts organizations may receive subsidies as direct line-item appropriations in the government's budget. Such organizations usually covet this procedure because it insulates them from competition with other arts organizations for funds *within* the cultural arena. On the other hand, if a significant portion of the cultural budget is earmarked in this way, there may be little left over to fund new or experimental ventures.

In addition, systems for administering cultural policies differ in the degree to which they are centralized, decentralized, or devolved. In a centralized administration all decisions are made at the national level. Most funds are appropriated at the national level, and where local funds are involved, the local governments have little discretion either as to how much they contribute or how their contribution is spent. Indeed, generally in these systems local government tends to be regarded more as a branch of national administration than as an opportunity for local diversity.

In a decentralized administration, the national government continues to be the focus of basic policy-making, but more diversity in local implementation is allowed. Local governments may have independent authority, or the national administration may simply allow some measure of autonomy to its local representatives.

With devolution, there is real local autonomy in the making of basic policy decisions as well as in their implementation. (The term itself suggests a strong central government relinquishing some of its powers, but is used here to refer as well to federal systems in which subnational governments retain substantial autonomous powers.) Not surprisingly, the federal systems of Canada, Germany, and the United States show the strongest evidence of devolved administration.

In part, the diversity in administrative forms found in the cultural field simply reflects different national traditions and varying constitutional structures. In addition, however, it reflects diverse attempts to deal with a number of difficult problems inherent in any government cultural policy. We conclude this introductory chapter by raising some of these general issues. The chapters which follow will indicate how the governments in a large number of countries have attempted to deal with them.

Perhaps the first problem that comes to mind in any discussion of government involvement in culture, whether as patron or as regulator, is the danger of censorship. In its extreme form, of course, censorship is incompatible with democracy, although several of the countries surveyed in this volume have had experience with censorship under nondemocratic governments (either their own, or German occupation governments) within the last half-century. Nevertheless, even in democratic systems, the question of censorship is a serious and recurring concern. It arises in several contexts. One concerns sexually explicit work, or work that is in some other way offensive to a significant element of the community. The dividing lines among avant-garde shock value, social statement, and pornography often are far less clear than either artists or prudes believe. In the countries surveyed here, constitutional norms, whether written or understood, usually protect artists from having their works banned.

When government is actively supporting the arts, however, the question of censorship takes on additional dimensions. In previous times, an artist whose work did not satisfy one patron could look elsewhere for support. When the government is the overwhelmingly dominant patron, there may be no other place to go. Often, a government's refusal to subsidize a project is equivalent to preventing its realization. Especially when funds are limited, choices must be made. Do these amount to censorship? Once the government has purchased a work of art, is it censorship if the work is not displayed? Must the government support "bad art" if it is to avoid censorship? And what is "bad art," anyway? Work that is technically deficient? Work that is morally dangerous? Work that is intellectually or esthetically vacuous? And who is to say? It is knotty problems like these which explain why, in many countries, liberals and conservatives alike have been afraid of government becoming overwhelmingly dominant as a source of arts support.

Seen in this light, the question of censorship opens into the broader questions of how the government decides what to support and how it apportions its funds among the projects supported. On the most basic level, there is the problem of defining art and culture in the first place. This is more than an academic debate, since it defines the types of activities that are eligible for support; unless total funding is increased, when more activities become eligible for support, those that were eligible before will get less. Most government arts programs began as programs in support of the fine arts, narrowly and conventionally understood. Music meant orchestral music or opera, not jazz or rock and roll; dance meant ballet, not folk dancing. More recently, these programs have expanded, in some cases, as in Sweden, tremendously. At one level, this has allowed the government to avoid some normative choices, although this itself was a normative choice; and in any case it only redefines the question of the value of these new "arts" from one of eligibility to one of allocation. It has also meant that, while some funds may have been diverted from the traditional arts, the constituency for arts support in general has been multiplied and the entire enterprise made more secure politically.

When one considers the problems of *allocating* government funds for the arts, the same problem reappears in several guises. One question is the balance to be struck between quality and equality. Is it better, for example, to pour resources into one world-class orchestra, or to support five orchestras, none of which will be truly great? This choice is closely related to the problem of geographic distribution. Five orchestras can be located in five different cities. How much weight should be given to geographic considerations, either for their own sake or for the sake of political constituency-building?

Alternatively, if some art forms are "better" than others (opera better than musical comedy, for example), should government policy aim to stimulate demand for the "better" activities, or ought it merely to support satisfaction of whatever demands currently exist? Indeed, should government attempt to stimulate new demand for the arts and culture no matter how broadly defined?

Within each art form, choices must be made between preservation of the existing cultural heritage and institutions and stimulation of new creative efforts. It is in the nature of the arts that most new work will fail, at least if it is judged by the standards of the masterpieces of the past. On the other hand, a cultural life that allowed no room for development would be virtually a contradiction in terms. The balance struck depends on many factors. In some cases, Ireland for example, a positive decision may be made to foster the development of a new national culture, with support channeled especially to creators rather than preservers. In another case, rapid social upheaval may make preservation of links with the past appear to be particularly important. Japanese support of its traditional art forms exemplifies this. In still another case—Italy is a prime example—there may be so rich a cultural heritage that merely to maintain the national patrimony strains the resources available.

Related both to the question of quality and to the question of preservation is the choice between support of professional artistic activity and the support of amateur participation in the arts. On one hand, the pursuit and maintenance of true excellence requires training and the commitment of time, not to mention talent, beyond the capacity of most people. On the other hand, the experience of actually playing music, acting in a play, or making a painting or sculpture is qualitatively different from going to a concert, theater, or museum. One aspect of this question is the relative value of those different experiences. A second is whether the intended beneficiary of a cultural program is to be the arts per se or the citizens. A third aspect is whether the objective is the discipline of excellence or the enjoyment of a pastime.

Although each of these questions has technical aspects—one can investigate and in principle determine, for example, the effects of concentrating support on a few recipients versus a wide diffusion of small grants—they are all basically questions of values, judgments, tastes, and preferences, rather than facts. They are also all inescapable. While none is necessarily an either/or choice (one can support both amateurs and professionals at the same time), with limited resources, decisions must be made. At the very least, those who are involved with government arts programs must decide how much support will go to amateurs and how much will go to professionals. And who is to make those decisions?

One possibility is that they be made by politicians. Although the dangers to the arts of becoming objects of partisan debate are only too obvious, one must remember that public money is being spent and that partisan politics is the way collective decisions are made in democracies. It is precisely in order to resolve disputes about preferences that elections are held and decisions are made by officials who are responsible to the people through the electoral process. In fact, the big ''framework'' decisions—those that shape the broad contours of policy—are generally made by politicians in the form of legislation or ministerial decrees.

Politicians are ill-suited by training and temperament, and ill-situated in the government apparatus, to make decisions about individual arts projects. Moreover, the political risks involved in having directly supported funds for what turns out to be a public eye-sore or a public scandal make the idea of being responsible for such decisions unattractive to politicians, some of whom realize that the effects of their own esthetic conservatism would be detrimental to the arts. Instead, decisions at this level are generally made by bureaucrats, whether technically in the civil service or not. This is not to say that bureaucrats themselves are not engaged in politics or subjected to political pressures. Often bureaucrats are powerfully influenced by ''expert'' opinion in the fields for which they have responsibility, by the internal politics of the bureaucracy, and by the ministers and legislative committees to whom they are responsible.

In any event, bureaucrats are not well prepared to make value decisions. Of course they can, like anyone else, indulge their own tastes, but they have no real ground to claim that their preferences deserve greater consideration than those of anyone else. To protect themselves from the claim that they are making arbitrary decisions, cultural bureaucracies have tended to surround themselves with so-called expert advisors. When questioned in parliament, or before a congressional committee, or in the press, they can claim they were only following expert advice. The use of expert panels has been widely hailed by many (including some of the authors of this book) as a way of avoiding the dangers of political or bureaucratic decision-making in the arts.

It should be observed, however, that delegation of authority to experts has its own dangers. Indeed, in many respects it merely returns us to the starting point. Granted that experts may be better able than politicians, or bureaucrats, or average citizens to judge the technical merit of an art work or proposal, there is far more to art than technique. Who is to say that the taste of experts actually is superior? Who decides who are the experts? Generally, it is other experts, but this may lead to an inbreeding of taste. It is likely to lead to old-boyism in decision-making as well. An experimenter or iconoclast may fare better before a board of bureaucrats than before a board of established artists or directors of mainstream institutions. Decisions made by a self-perpetuating board need be no less arbitrary or potentially stultifying because its members are artists who approve of one another. In fact, panels of experts may be little different from the juries of the nineteenth-century academies, and academic art certainly was not noted for its innovativeness.

In this situation, the injection of politics into the arts is inevitable. Judgments sometimes will have to be made on political as well as esthetic grounds. And, in the conduct of government programs for the arts, the mobilization of political support sometimes will loom as important as the problems of esthetic justification.

The fact that these and other problems have no easy solutions does not mean that government cultural programs and policies should be abandoned, only that no policy is likely to be unambiguously good. If judgments are to be made intelligently, one should be aware of the costs and the dangers of policies as well as their potential rewards. It is toward the understanding of these questions that this book is directed.

Notes

1. Aristotle, *Constitution of Athens,* chap. 43, 1.

2. Frederick Dorian, *Commitment to Culture* (Pittsburgh: Univ. of Pittsburgh Press, 1964), 12.

3. *Ibid.*, 319.

4. Contemporary survey research has shown that level of formal education is strongly linked to the likelihood that a person will be interested and involved in the arts. See William J. Baumol and William G. Bowen, *Performing Arts—The Economic Dilemma,* a Twentieth Century Fund Study (New York: Twentieth Century Fund, 1966), 453–67.

5. Benjamin Ifor Evans and Mary Glasgow, *The Arts in England* (London: The Falcon Press, 1949), 16.

6. For many years, Great Britain has provided some tax incentive for the arts by giving a refund to the *recipient* of a contribution. But until recently, Britain did not allow arts contributors to take deductions for donations to the arts that would reduce their own income tax liability. In 1986, however, a new incentive for charitable giving was added to British tax law. Since April 1986, corporations can deduct charitable contributions from their income up to a limit of 3 percent of dividends paid. In addition, a proposal to allow individuals to make tax deductible charitable contributions through payroll deduction plans was being seriously considered in Great Britain in 1986. See J. Mark Davidson Schuster, "Tax Incentives as Arts Policy in Western Europe," in Paul Di Maggio, ed., *Nonprofit Enterprise in the Arts: Studies in Mission and Constraint* (New York: Oxford Univ. Press, 1986).

2

Government and the Arts in France

MARIANNE ANDRAULT AND PHILIPPE DRESSAYRE

Since World War II, government intervention in the domain of culture and the arts in France has developed considerably. However, no other cultural policy had such an ambitious design as the one implemented after the presidential election of May 1981: "to be at the service of a collective endeavor, civilization's endeavor serving the changing of life."[1]

Nonetheless, it is traditional in France for the State to play an important role in artistic and cultural life. Under the *Ancien Régime,* the arts were to reflect the glory and the grandeur of the monarchy. Public patronage of the arts, allied with the "generosities" of the Court, assured the allegiance of official artists to royal authority. Thus, many of the most prestigious theatrical institutions were born during one of the most autocratic reigns, that of Louis XIV. Dating from this period, for example, are Molière's *Troupe du Roi* (1665) which became the *Comédie Française,* the *Opéra Comique* (1715), and the *Académie Royale de la Musique* (1672) which became the *Opéra.* The French Revolution of 1789 could not overturn the inherited structures of the *Ancien Régime:* the cultural and artistic life of France has been characterized, until recently, by an extreme "Parisianization," a reflection of the centralization of the political and administrative organization of the country.

At the beginning of the Revolution, the Convention proclaimed freedom of artistic expression (13 January 1791). The succeeding regimes undertook a gradual "nationalization" of the majority of cultural institutions. Thus we have the creation, for example, of the *Théâtre National de l'Opéra Comique* under the period of the *Directoire* (1801), the reorganization of the *Comédie Française* by a decree of Napoleon (Moscow, 15 October 1812), the discontinuation of all private subsidies for the *Opéra* and the *Opéra Comique,* and the creation of the National Union of Lyric Theaters, a public organization placed under the supervision of the Ministry of National Education (14 January 1939).

It is only with the Fourth Republic that we see an attempt to react against the excessive concentration of artistic activities in Paris and the cultural underdevelopment of the rest of France, the "French desert." The majority of cultural policies adopted by governments since 1945 have had as their primary goal to redress the imbalance between the cultural resources of the nation's capital and the cultural poverty of the provincial regions. During this period the development of State intervention in new policy areas, the growth of cultural expenditures in the public sector, and the provision of a great deal of material have characterized a more and more diverse government activity. Were these efforts futile? The balance sheet examined by the new leadership in 1981 has in any case underlined the urgent character of the cultural situation in France—absence of overall policy, phantom decentralization, inequities in the treatment of the arts, etc.

A new "imperative" was decreed, which formed the core for public action in the cultural sphere up to the legislative elections of March 1986. The policy of the Minister, Jack Lang, is still too recent for a thorough evaluation to be proposed. One should, nonetheless, in a presentation of the development of cultural affairs in France since 1945 and of the balance struck in 1981, trace the principal characteristics of the policies of the Mauroy and Fabius governments in the fields of art and culture.

Cultural Policy in France until 1981

The creation in 1959 of a Ministry of Cultural Affairs, entrusted by the French president to André Malraux, marked an important stage in the construction of an extensive cultural bureaucracy in France. Previously, the offices of the Secretary of State for Fine Arts had very limited responsibility and were content to administer a few prestigious institutions as well as a number of "cultural events" that were normally the province of other ministries.

André Malraux's actions expressed without doubt a "certain idea" of culture and of the role of the State in cultural activities, but had he a policy? Certainly, because of his initiative, many important projects were undertaken: the restoration of some great historical monuments, the creation of *maisons de la culture,* the implementation of a music policy, etc. But only a global conception of the country's cultural development would ensure the coherence of these different activities. Nor did the Minister have the necessary means—the department was until recently among the poorest of the ministries. (The budget for culture always represented less than 1 percent of the national budget until 1981.)

Spheres of Government Activity

Since the Second World War governmental activity in the cultural sphere has been very uneven. Early efforts were directed successively toward the theater (at the beginning of the 1950s), local activities (with the creation of *maisons de la culture*), music (with the adoption of a ten-year plan in 1966), and the protection of the national artistic inheritance. Other spheres were by contrast the object of no particular attention, such as literature, fine arts, crafts, and the cinema. The national budget reflects these inequities. See Table 1. In 1979, for example, the appropriations designated for historic preservation and museums (28.8%), for music (17.4%), and for theater (10.8%), represented more than half the total of the budget for cultural affairs. Literature (7.5%), fine arts and crafts (6.8%), the cinema (1.4%), constituted only a small fraction.

1. Museums. The protection and improvement of the national inheritance has become the central concern of government for the last few decades. Three laws mark this increase in interest in the preservation of the cultural inheritance of the nation (31 July 1962, 28 December 1967, and 11 July 1978). These laws, which include substantial financial provisions, contributed to the protection of national monuments but also, in the sphere of art, to the modernization of museums.

In France the first museums were created during the revolutionary period. In 1793,

TABLE 1. Budget of the Ministry of Culture (By Spheres of Activity in Percent of Total Budget)

	1979	*1981*
Music-Dance	17.4	18.8
National Monuments	17.2	17.9
Museums	11.6	14.9
Cultural Development	11.1	10.0
Theater	10.8	10.4
Literature	7.5	6.7
Artistic Creation	6.8	5.4
Archives	2.9	2.4
Cinema	1.4	0.7
General Administration	12.5	12.4
TOTAL (in millions of francs)	2370	2975

Source: U.N.E.S.C.O., *La Politique culturelle en France* (Paris, 1981), p. 19. "Repères budgetaires pour la culture," *Développement Culturel,* No. 48, September 1981, p. 11.

the "Museum of the Republic" was created at the *Louvre,* and a bill from the *An VII* confirmed the existence of ten museums in provincial cities. However, the growth of the French people's interest in public or private museums is a very recent phenomenon and as yet not well established (a poll conducted by the I.N.S.E.E. in 1967 found that 82 percent of the population had never visited a museum). At the end of the 1970s, an unprecedented effort was conducted by the government. Its objective was especially to enliven and to increase access to establishments often more inclined to stress conservation of art than presentation of their collections to the public.

In addition to the law of 16 April 1895 creating the Association of National Museums, the most important legislation concerning museum organization is the ordinance of 13 July 1945. This established:

1. a national museum administration charged with the direction of national museums and the supervision of other important museums;
2. three general categories of museums:[2]
   a. national museums (31 in number), such as the *Louvre* or the *Jeu de Paume;*
   b. city museums staffed by curators from the national civil service;
   c. museums owned either privately, by local groups, or by public establishments.

The program law of 11 July 1978 was the first to establish a financial "charter" for museums. Establishing a schedule of payments from 1978 to 1982, the law allocated a total of one billion four hundred million francs, allowing a chance to catch up on accumulated delays from preceding years. However, the balance remains a very modest sum, for two reasons:

First, the working budget given to the museums by the government was not as great as the ambitions expressed would have indicated. The authorities seemed to prefer the excitement of spectacular measures (such as the creation of the Pompidou Center or of the

Museum of the Nineteenth Century at the *Gare d'Orsay*), at the risk of ignoring their administrative responsibilities and some promising future projects.

Even more significantly, the State appeared, at least in the case of museums, to hesitate between a policy of conservation and a policy of exhibition. In a changing cultural environment, the very purpose of museums seemed in fact to be evolving very quickly.

Long a synonym for "boredom," the "cemetery of the arts" according to Lamartine, the museum has become an important place for the meeting between the public and its culture. This new French taste for the past and the attraction of an aesthetic escapism have aroused sufficient demand to upset the practices of museums, long reserved for the narrow circle of a social and intellectual elite. Given this movement, the responsibility of the government is immense. The Jacobin tradition has conferred on the State direct responsibility for institutions, often costly and poorly adapted to their new community functions. Could not too rapid a disengagement on the part of the State to the benefit of private or local initiative dangerously compromise the current renewal of French museums?

2. *Theater and the Dramatic Arts.* Among the traditional spheres of government intervention, theater is one of the oldest and best known; the current *Comédie Française* was placed at its birth under the protection of the King, endowed by statute in 1680, and for a long time was the sole publicly financed company. Since the beginning of the present century, many other theater companies have been distinguished by their quality and have benefited from public support. Government activity to support the theater has, in fact, been strongly emphasized and diversified since the 1950s thanks to the initiative of both enlightened advocates (Jeanne Laurent, André Malraux) and of talented persons of the theater (Jean Daste, Maurice Sarrazin, Gaston Baty, Jean Vilar).

The policy conducted under the Fourth Republic and followed by its successors was animated essentially by the desire to decentralize theatrical activity. The stimulus was given by Jeanne Laurent, in the Secretariat of Fine Arts from 1947 to 1952. This dramatic decentralization movement led to the establishment of professional groups of actors in certain large provincial cities (the *Comédie de l'Est* in Strasbourg, the *Grenier* in Toulouse), which were soon recognized and subsidized by the government as dramatic centers. After a slowdown during the 1950s, this movement restarted with the creation in 1958–59 of the Ministry of Cultural Affairs. A new category of groups was thus institutionalized, that of permanent theater companies.

The government's financial contribution quickly became the determining factor in dramatic arts, since it was the guarantee of the existence as well as of the quality of theatrical activity. Indeed, the organization of the present-day French theater can be classified by the size of this contribution. First, there is a strongly dependent sector—the national drama centers and theater companies. In France there are five national companies and twenty national drama centers, to which the six centers for children and youth must be added. All these centers are subsidized in varying proportion by the national government, regions, departments, and municipalities.

Second, there are a certain number of independent theater companies that are subsidized. Among some 300 private companies, about 150 receive some slight governmental financial aid. Forty receive exceptional government-financed subsidies, sometimes for large sums, due to the recognized quality of their work (for example, *la Compagnie Renaud-Barrault* and the *Théâtre de la Cartoucherie*).

Third, a basic support, provided in part by government funds, can indirectly aid private theater in Paris (forty-five theaters) for production costs or for equipment and supplies for the actual theater building. The *Théâtre de la Ville,* for example, used about 50 percent of the time for theater production, is in part subsidized by the municipal government of Paris.

The fragile economic condition of the theater, due to the decrease in public attendance and the increase in production costs, has had important consequences on theater activity. First, it has changed the kind of shows produced since only national theater companies have the resources to mount costly productions. Second, the situation of playwrights has worsened since few companies can take the risk of producing the work of an unknown. These difficulties for dramatic creation are further reflected in the employment conditions of actors. Nonetheless, despite the gravity of these problems, the situation seems less worrisome than that of music and dance.

3. Music. There are numerous indicators of a rebirth of interest in music on the part of the French people. One can cite, for example, the spectacular growth in the distribution of recorded music (record sales quadrupled between 1960 and 1974), the increasing success of concerts and the operatic season, and the development of music festivals and music education (the number of students has increased from 40,000 in 1966 to 800,000 in 1979).

The government has traditionally been involved in music. Considered as an important factor in social cohesion, music has often benefited from particular attention, as justified by Napoleon: "Of all the fine arts, music is that which has the most influence on the passions, thus is that which the legislator must most encourage." However, the music situation became particularly disastrous at the beginning of the 1960s, with loss of employment, the growing importance of foreign orchestras, and the absence of new musical compositions. To end the backwardness that characterized the institutions of French music, a ten-year plan was established in 1966 by Marcel Landowski to promote a coherent and decentralized music policy. At the same time André Malraux created a department of music, which became in 1970 the Department of Music, Lyric Arts, and Dance.

The Landowski plan was based on the idea that improvement and visibility in the quality of French professional music would depend on the widest possible practice of music. Thus, a long-term policy was necessary. This meant organizing "musical regions" which would each possess a conservatory, a lyric theater, and a coordinator. Toward this goal, new administrative structures (educational inspection, regional music committees, regional coordinators) were established and professional training and distribution structures were reorganized or even created. In education, the objective was to create a network of specialized local establishments. In distribution, the goal was to reorganize certain orchestras, to facilitate their integration into regional life, to develop regional choirs, and to carry out an auditorium program.

Continued nearly fifteen years, this policy began to bear fruit. The Paris *Opéra* began to regain an uncontested international reputation, and the French organization of city lyric theaters, created in 1964, now numbered thirteen establishments. In addition to the Paris Symphony, the *Ensemble Contemporain,* and the two orchestras of Radio France, there are thirteen permanent regional orchestras, to which must be added subsidized but private training. Moreover, more than one hundred festivals are aided by the government. As of 1 January 1979, there were twenty-six national conservatories in the different regions, forty-one national schools of music, and eighty-two accredited schools (of which twenty-nine are subsidized). The planned objectives were not only achieved by and large, they were sometimes surpassed.

This could only have been achieved by large budgetary increases in music, notably between 1974 and 1979. From 173 million francs in 1974, the budget was over 413 million in 1979. By the latter date, 53 percent went to vocal music of which 45 percent went to the Paris *Opéra,* 8 percent to provincial groups, and 2 percent to choreography. Twenty-five percent was allocated to music distribution and coordination. Nineteen percent was devoted to specialized training in music and dance, primarily the *Conservatoire National Superieur de Musique,* regional conservatories, and national schools of music. To this budget must be added those funds that come from other ministries, for example, National Education.

However, the music budget was still insufficient. Even adding the funds from other ministries, the total was only 800 million francs in 1979 or, as François Mitterand remarked in 1981, about one-fifteenth of the music budget of the Federal Republic of Germany.

4. Fine Arts and the Plastic Arts. More than twenty years ago, the former Department of Fine Arts became the independent Ministry of Cultural Affairs. This change both of structure and of name symbolizes a deep transformation in the intervention of the government. Arts and letters are no more than one of the components of an infinitely more ambitious policy—to assure the cultural development of the country.

In the sphere of plastic and fine arts, the tradition of aid from the public sector is very old. And, as in the past, it is essentially effected by government commissions and financial aid to artists.

The government has three buying agencies for the work of living artists: the *Réunion des musées nationaux,* the *Délégation à la création aux métiers artistiques et aux manufactures* (DCMAM), and the Georges Pompidou National Center for Art and Culture. Their total annual budget is currently around 12 million francs. Their purchases are a response not to a concern for assistance to needy artists, but to a desire to enrich the national artistic inheritance, to decorate public buildings, and more generally to promote artistic development.

One part of these acquisitions forms the National Fund of Contemporary Art which gives or lends works to provincial museums, exhibits, and to certain cultural organizations. The government buys, and commissions as well from certain artists, works destined to decorate particular buildings. Thus, Masson was commissioned to paint the ceiling of the *Odéon* theater and Chagall, that of the *Opéra.* The so-called "one percent" represents another very important form by sheer volume of state commissions. One percent of monies budgeted for the construction of public buildings must be allocated for their decoration. Established first by the Ministry of Education in 1951 for new buildings it was having built, this procedure has been successively enlarged to include the building plans of Defense, Cultural Affairs, and, since 1979, all other ministries.

In addition, to improve the living conditions of artists, the government has provided different forms of aid based on place of work, distribution of works, and the social circumstances of artists.

In addition to these different forms of aid, many organizations and establishments contribute to the training and assistance of artists. Created in 1979, the DCMAM was charged with the development of contemporary creative activity in all spheres of artistic expression, to improve its public dissemination and to facilitate appropriate training and teaching. Regional artistic councils associated with regional directors of cultural affairs extend the activity of the DCMAM to the regions. Their role consists in directing decorative projects for public buildings, informing artists of government measures that concern them, and facilitating the circulation of exhibits.

In addition, in 1976, a National Fund for Graphic and Plastic Arts was created in order "to favor and facilitate by every means, financial and other, all activities aiding and assisting the plastic arts as well as all activities aiding and encouraging research and creativity in this domain."

Finally, the teaching of the plastic arts as well as specific training in artistic skills are ensured jointly by the public and private sectors. Local communities and the national government assume responsibility for public education in the arts. This training includes the plastic arts, decorative arts, arts and crafts, and the design professions. As for other specialized training, the government has sole financial responsibility for the two national superior schools, the seven national schools of art, and the scholarship program for national, regional, and city schools. The government contributes 3 to 5 percent of the expenses of city and regional schools and gives more aid to the fourteen accredited schools.

Alleviating the shortcomings of practically non-existent private patronage in France, the government has to date been content to preserve the material conditions of artists by public commissions and to better their situation by financial assistance. This intervention has remained limited since the government felt it had other responsibilities than freeing the artist from financial constraints.

5. Literature. Reading habits have evolved considerably within the French population during the last twenty years. The proportion of non-readers (i.e., reading no books in the year) is currently 25 to 30 percent, rather than 60 percent as in 1960. But book purchasers represent only about half of the population over fifteen, and eight million people who buy at least one book per month accounted for 65 percent of the market. In 1978, book sales represented only 0.4 percent of total household consumption.

However, unlike other facets of the cultural industry (the cinema, for example) the sphere of literature is prospering. In 1978, publishing reached a gross income of 12.5 billion francs for wholesale and retail combined, and since 1960 has grown faster than national industry as a whole.

For some time, then, literature and books have not been a real priority for the Ministry of Culture. Since 1959, decisions in favor of other spheres such as theater have relegated literature to second place. Only one interministerial committee on literature (in 1967) submitted a report which was not tabled. The creation of a Department of Literature in 1975 furnished the Ministry of Cultural Affairs with an administrative tool it had desired for a long time. Transferred to the new Department were functions hitherto a part of other ministries: the export of books (Foreign Affairs), publishing (Industry), and public reading (Universities). The Ministry is not the only public organization concerned with books. Since 1973 the National Literary Center has had broad responsibilities on the subject of literary copyrights, writing, and publishing. Yet for the last few years, measures concerning books, notably those directed toward public reading, have become very rare and often are delayed.

Until 1945, the traditional conception governing public libraries contributed to making them an enclosed world within the general context of French publishing. For the last twenty years, public policy has been directed toward the need for a deepened view of public culture. But libraries have scarcely benefited from measures taken to support theater, dance, and music. Insufficient material, financial problems, long-established neglect of librarian training are the principal witnesses of policy (or lack of policy) in this sphere.

In fact, the first great public debate on the position of literature is recent, dating from 1975. After the Granet Commission formulated many proposals to better the publishing and distribution of quality books, many initiatives were undertaken. A bill was passed granting to writers the protection of the national health services. The National Literary Center was strengthened and a Department of Books and Libraries was created. But the most important measure was taken several years later: it concerned the prices of books.

Until 1976, book prices were governed by two categories. Free prices were allowed for new books and, under certain conditions, new editions. Prices were frozen for other categories of works. In 1976, paralleling commitments to moderation in other economic sectors, the President of the Republic requested a unified plan on the problems of the publishing industry in order to reduce the fears of professionals possibly intimidated by the appearance of modern forms of business.

Within a general policy of free-market pricing under Prime Minister Barre, Economic Minister Monory decided in favor of a net price on 10 January 1979: the labeling "recommended price" was not allowed; all discounts were abolished, with only the retail price available to the public. The Minister decided that a legally fixed price, combined with the absence of retail discounts, would both stabilize the book market (allowing the re-establishment of profits for small booksellers) yet lower overall book prices.

But as Giscard d'Estaing put it, books cannot be considered "a product like any other." In the aftermath of the 1981 elections Jack Lang, the new Minister of Culture, decided that books were cultural before being commercial. Book policy has since then rested on this assumption. Books thus remain an essential part of the totality of cultural development policy.

6. *Cinema.* Since the 1930s, the government has concerned itself with the condition of French cinema, trying both to support its activity and to organize a very divided profession. This willingness to encompass the cinema industry was later manifested more clearly under the Vichy government, which established a Department of Cinema and the Committee of the Cinema Industry. State intervention was reinforced after Liberation with the creation in 1946 of the *Centre national cinématographique* (CNC), the principal governmental policy instrument in this sphere, and of the Fund to Aid the Cinematographic Industry, which became in 1953 the Cinema Industry Development Fund.

Through these institutions, the government both regulates and stimulates the cinema. The CNC has, in fact, relatively important regulatory power and intervenes in professional organization (via professional licensing), in economic protection (most notably against foreign productions), and in maintaining a certain equilibrium among the different parties involved—producers, distributors, and workers.

The financial aid given by the government to the cinema industry stems from a tax on cinema theater tickets purchased by audiences and is administered by the CNC. Thus, it is closely allied to the behavior of cinema audiences. But the government financial contribution takes other forms: production subsidies, technical help, public events (Cannes film festival), or education (Institute of High Cinema Studies), advances against future sales, subsidies for distribution (building or modernization of movie theaters).

One of the weaknesses of this mechanism is that the tax on tickets contributes directly to lowering audience attendance and thus the returns. Moreover, cinema subsidies are relatively weak in France compared with those of other European countries. As much a cause for concern as the disaffection of the public are the structural changes in the cinema industry in the last few years that make government intervention more difficult. These include the multiplication and modernization of movie theaters (the increase in multi-theater complexes and more frequent showings), resulting in fewer owners owning more theaters. The theater owners who have remained independent of the large firms practice scheduling agreements. This integration and concentration, especially noticeable in the distribution of films of the cinema industry, has had consequences on the commercialization and scheduling of films (which demands a fairly high profit threshold) as well as on the creation and production of cinema products, which have become simply commercial products.

For several years another element has tended to modify the cinema context—the development of video cassette recording. The influence that television has had on the production and distribution of film is well known. The recent evolution of video recording constitutes a possibly similar threat as well as necessitating some kind of integration into a larger cultural context. This fact has been taken into account by the government since 1981. Established policy reserves a large area of flexibility in the definition of the relationship between cinema and audio-visual communications.

7. Radio and Television. Among all the Western countries, the radio and television industry has become the leader of the culture industry because of the size of its audience, the number of its "products," and its influence on the rest of the audio-visual sector. For example, in France, the average weekday audience was 70.2 percent for television and 63.9 percent for radio in 1977.[3]

The proportion of radio and television programming that could be considered "cultural" is difficult to establish. However, there is scarcely any doubt that the radio-television media make up an essential base for the production and spread of culture. In France, the circumstances that established a state monopoly in radio and television gave the government a dominant position in both the production and the distribution of programming.

The often passionate debate over the 1974 reform concerned the role of these communication media at the heart of society. Article I of the 1974 law defined the public service role of French radio and television. They were "to respond to the needs and aspirations of the population, for information, communication, culture, education, entertainment and the totality of civilized values." In evaluating the French communication media by this standard, the debate centered on the following principal defects:

1. The nearly total government stranglehold on radio and television news. "Speaking in the name of France," as then President Georges Pompidou put it (2 July 1970 press conference), radio and television were understood by the government less as an "eighth art" and more as a "fourth power" that had to be dominated. This is perhaps the only way to understand the government's gradual efforts to become the principal shareholder, either directly or indirectly, in broadcasting companies near, but outside, French national borders.
2. According to the majority of observers, the distressing vulgarity of programs is the result of trading the cultural and educational dimensions of radio and television for a conception of radio and television as pure entertainment.

After the 1981 presidential elections and during the first months of the new Socialist government, the future of French radio and television was once again at the center of political debate. Two questions were raised concerning the problems discussed above:

First, does a state monopoly mean in practice a monopoly for the current government? Can it guarantee respect for freedom of information and expression, the twin foundations of any pluralist democracy?

Second, can a public service be satisfied to provide only entertainment programs, most of foreign origin, or should it contribute to the birth and transformation of a new form of cultural activity? In trying to be more "cultural," does television risk becoming less popular and reinforcing social inequalities by addressing itself to the needs of an intellectual and social elite?

Public Expenditures in the Cultural Sector

The means and forms of governmental cultural activity vary from one sphere of intervention to another. In certain cases, financial aid can be very large, for example in the restoration of monuments and for prestigious projects. In others, it may be particularly limited, or even non-existent as, for example, in the cinema.

Public expenditures in the cultural sector were 11.2 billion francs in 1980, but nearly half of this total came from regional or local sources. Participation by the Ministry of Culture represented about 40 percent of government funds.

In examining the budget for the Ministry of Culture, we can see that despite an increase of more than 40 percent between 1960 and 1980, the percentage is still a modest 0.5 percent of the total government budget (the part of the budget earmarked for culture before 1972 was less than 0.45 percent of the total budget). From 1973 to 1978, it increased to 0.55 percent, reaching a peak in 1974 of 0.61 percent. By 1981, it had decreased to 0.48 percent. This regular decline since 1979 was preceded by a period of stagnation despite the reorganization of 1976 which incorporated literature and libraries into the Ministry of Cultural Affairs.

However, if one includes all government expenditures for cultural activities, the proportion of the total government budget that goes to culture increases to 1.4 percent. Other ministries combined spend more on culture than the Ministry of Culture does alone. The Ministry of Education has since 1976 spent the most. It organizes the teaching of the arts within the educational system and provides teachers for cultural associations. The Ministry of Youth and Sport spends large sums for socio-cultural activities. The Ministry of Universities is responsible for the *Ecole des Chartes,* the School of Library Science, the *Bibliothèque Nationale,* and many museums. The Secretary General of the Government directs diverse services (aid to the press, documentation) and the Commission on the French Language. The Ministries of Foreign Affairs and Cooperation finance artistic exchanges between France and foreign governments.

The establishment of the Fund for Cultural Support in 1971 was an attempt to deal with the consequences of the differing financial influences of ministries other than the Ministry of Culture. Created by the Commission on Cultural Affairs as part of the VIth Governmental Plan, the Fund is meant to encourage innovation and coordination among all government departments that affect cultural activities. Its funds can be spent only for operating costs and some material. The Fund's major goal over the last three years has been to act as a catalyst: to aid the growth of amateur cultural activities and to encourage cultural pluralism, especially by fostering the search for cultural identity. (This might be accomplished by restoring a cultural inheritance that properly belongs to a particular region, social milieu, or ethnic group, or by encouraging access to cultural activities by underprivileged groups.) The Fund also attempts to encourage implementation on the local level of national cultural policy goals. Examination of its budget shows that since 1959 government aid primarily has benefited people (artistic production, schools, cultural stimulation) rather than stone (ancient monuments). The decade of the 1970s accentuated this tendency, as is illustrated by the opening of the Pompidou Center and the reorganization of the Ministry of Culture to include public libraries.

This slighting of the national inheritance was slowed, however, by the launching of both a priority program of the VIIth Plan favoring historical monuments and the program law of 1978 for museums. The evolution of the budget reveals the level of funding directed toward conservation and distribution of the national patrimony. Since the creation of the Ministry of Culture, these functions have absorbed the greater part of the credits for capital expenditures. Operating costs have not grown significantly, except for the addition of the libraries.

For artistic production, which includes aiding the creation and distribution of works of art to the public, notably theater, opera, and music, operating costs have quintupled. The decentralization of drama, the creation of regional orchestras, and the *Orchestre de Paris* are the principal causes of this growth. In capital expenditures, the construction of two concert halls in Paris and Lyon, the renovation of the *Comédie Française* and the *Théâtre National de Chaillot* accounted for the bulk of the expenditures in recent years.

The operating budget for cultural activity has grown regularly, independent of the addition to the national budget of that vast cultural institution, the Pompidou Center. The wave of *maison de la culture* construction culminated before 1968. It was slowed by the tendency toward municipal management of arts centers, as well as a tendency to build less prestigious centers. The costs of the Pompidou Center dominated the 1970s. Finally, administrative costs grew as the willingness of the government to intervene in cultural affairs grew and was institutionalized in regional administrative offices.

In 1981 the presidential transition commission noted that the cultural budget had three inflexible aspects. First, a third of the budget was earmarked for conservation and distribution, i.e., primarily for national monuments and museums; second, three prestigious establishments (the Pompidou Center, the *Comédie Française,* and the *Théâtre National de l'Opéra*) situated in Paris received over 60 percent of the operating expenditures budget; and third, up to half of operating expenditures went to "cultural workers" in the form of salaries or transfer payments—unlike the pattern in the majority of cultural affairs budgets in other countries.

Inertia, combined with the weaknesses of this budget, characterized government intervention until 1981. But the State never had a monopoly on the financing of culture; regional, local, and departmental intervention, not negligible before 1981, is likely to predominate in the future. In 1974 only eleven regions intervened in cultural activity. Since 1976 all regions have been concerned and three devote more than 9 percent of their budget to financing cultural operations. Four areas dominate: historical monuments, music, theater, and assorted activities. But regional public establishments finance only capital costs and thus the intervention varies greatly from one year to the next.

Cultural expenditures represent about 1 percent of local budgets, but large differences appear among *départements.* Two-thirds of these expenditures are for operating costs, often in the form of subsidies to public establishments or associations. One-third are capital expenditures. Eight percent of the expenditures are directed toward the conservation and distribution of the national inheritance and activities, but these efforts vary considerably from one community to another. Towns and cities also spend a great deal for culture. They devote 6 to 9 percent of their total budgets to it, and this may rise to as much as 20 percent. Thus, cities and towns spend nearly four times more than the national government for public libraries (1975 estimate), and provide nearly two-thirds of all public aid to theater (1979 estimate).

Although national government aid to the decentralization of the theater remains twice that of local communities, community action, given a new political context, will rapidly grow and diversify.

Forms of Intervention

The forms of governmental intervention in cultural affairs are very diverse. In the last thirty years, two forms in particular seem to have been stressed. The first, traditional in France, has stressed the multiplication of large-scale prestigious projects. The second has emphasized local activity. Even though, in many cases, these two forms are very different from each other, they can be either complementary or antagonistic.

1. Large-Scale Prestigious Projects. Apart from certain "venerable" exceptions (the *Comédie Française, Opéra,* and *Théâtre de l'Odéon*), the great government cultural institutions are most often recent creations (for example, the Pompidou Center or the Museum of the Nineteenth Century at the *Gare d'Orsay*). In France, it seems that it is traditional for the government to undertake these grandiose projects.

Even in periods of budget restrictions and austerity, government seems irresistibly attracted to grand projects, often very costly and of questionable utility. In this area, political initiative at the highest level is predominant, and the "will of the prince" is always a determining factor. Every French President wants to associate his name with a large project. This concern to leave a mark appears even when the central goal of an administration is to favor decentralization and pluralism in cultural affairs. In the time of André Malraux, the cultural centers were seen as "modern-day cathedrals" spread across the countryside.

But it is in the capital where this tendency is most often manifested. Centralization has affected the French countryside even, perhaps especially, in the domain of culture. This weighty tradition has never been changed and the government continues today to concentrate its financial efforts in Paris, where the greatest cultural institutions of the country are found. That this tradition can systematically upset all attempts to decentralize scarcely seems to move the government. However, expenditures devoted to the creation or the administration of these great institutions drain funds that might otherwise have gone to the regions and local communities.

The budgetary figures are eloquent: in 1966, the Office of Music (Ministry of Cultural Affairs) directed 77 percent of its operating budget to the Paris *Opéra*. Projects such as the Pompidou Center, the Museum of the Nineteenth Century, and the Museum of La Villette have gravely compromised the capacity to diversify and to redeploy government cultural investments.

"In 1974, the Pompidou Center (Beaubourg) required 10 percent of the cultural expenditures of the central administration, that is, of the entire sum the government gave to cultural development."[4] That same year, this sum represented more than 30 percent of capital expenditures for culture and more than 15 percent of the budget of the Ministry of

Culture. In 1978, the operating subsidies for the Pompidou Center in the government budget were three times higher than those for all *maisons de la culture* and other cultural centers combined.

In 1978 the museum program law provided 1,407 million francs for the period 1978–82 for the equipping and renovating of French museums. But more than one-quarter of this sum was used by the Museum of the Nineteenth Century at the *Gare d'Orsay* alone (the total cost of this project considerably surpassed the forecast). In 1982, the one-year provisional budget was increased to 1,078 million francs, or an increase of 700 million francs at the 1979 value.[5]

Only the impact of the government's actions and accomplishments on the cultural development of the entire country could justify such undertakings. However, the effect of these prestigious institutions on France's international position and its halo effect for all of French life seemed incontestable. The success of the Pompidou Center tends to support this view. Opened in February 1977, the Georges Pompidou National Center for Art and Culture had welcomed more than twenty million visitors by the end of 1979, a daily average of more than 20,000 visitors. More than one thousand persons are employed by the Center. In 1979, its total budget was 161.3 million francs, of which more than 142 million francs came from government subsidies.

The success of the Pompidou Center, as well as what some critics have called its superficiality, rests on the extreme diversity of its goals and activities. The Center includes: a national museum charged with the presentation of permanent collections, the preparation of exhibits and diverse shows, and the distribution of specialized information on twentieth-century art; a center for industrial design which has as its goal "to understand relations among individuals, spaces, objects and signs" through the presentation of everyday objects; a workshop for advanced technical research, oriented toward micro-computer use; and an institute for research and music/acoustics coordination and their contemporary interconnections.

Thanks to the sum of these activities, the Center has been instrumental in the opening up of forms of cultural expression. However, since its creation, it remains at the crossroads: "a grand showplace, a bit extroverted and polished" as well as "a privileged place allowing a deepening, and an internalization of understanding of contempory creativity."[6] The polemics surrounding the Center rest on the ambiguity of this double vocation. One must admit, however, that the "Beaubourg" incontestably has become "a great hall of culture at the heart of the people's Paris. It is a place where those who haven't the habit of crossing the threshold of a museum, a theater or a library, can enter without impediment" (Le Corbusier).

Similar to the attraction to grand cultural centers, such as the Pompidou, is the French tradition of prestigious events. Some festivals are organized each year. On the other hand, some are non-recurring events, for example, "National Inheritance Year." The Avignon (theater), Cannes (cinema), and Aix-en-Provence (music) festivals are three important milestones in the annual cultural calendar of France. The impact of these prestigious events is difficult to measure with respect to more everyday cultural activities; they are a part of French cultural tradition. Some observers recognize, for example, a double role for Avignon as a meeting place for the exchange and expression of ideas between creators and as a crucible of innovation and imagination. Others, however, feel that the "festivalization" of theater is more detrimental than beneficial to regular and permanent activity in this field.

"National Inheritance Year" in 1980 was another example of "spotlighting," pointing up government activity in cultural affairs. At that time, the prompt provision of extra funds permitted intervention of a spectacular kind in a politically sensitive area within a few months of a presidential election. Such actions would doubtless be extremely beneficial if they led to an active program for succeeding years. Unfortunately, they are more often mere distractions, "dust in the eyes," an occasion of promises and pious wishes without a future.

Since 1981 the new government has shown no signs of discontinuing this tradition, which demands that government devote a large part of its means to prestigious cultural actions or projects. Recently, many grandiose projects have been adopted, but again on the initiative of highly placed government officials. All were intended for Paris. They include a vast Museum of Science, Technology, and Industry, a vast music center (the Villette project), and the great world's fair planned for 1989 (the bicentennial year of the French Revolution). However, as of early 1983, the partisan conflict between the national government and the Paris City Council, as well as hard financial realities, caused the abandonment of the latter monumental project.

2. *Cultural Activities at the Local Level.* Early efforts to decentralize cultural activity were succeeded in the 1960s by an even more extensive project of decentralization, the purpose of which was to encourage cultural activity at the local level. Thus, although the goal has remained identical over the years, government policy has evolved considerably in its ideas and ways of acting. The initial concern with cultural decentralization was followed by a preoccupation with cultural democratization. Its form was made more precise during the preparatory work on the VIIth Plan: "The imperative of democratic cultural policy is less in sharing culture than in assuring effective conditions of expression, promotion and recognition of specific cultural identities." This willingness to reanimate local cultural life is seen in two types of activity. The first is the creation of *maisons de la culture* and other establishments of cultural activity within the context of a decentralization movement strongly encouraged by the State. The second is the support given to the initiatives of the local partners (regions, *départements,* or local communities), either as one-time grants or within a long-term contractual framework (charters and cultural agreements).

Even though their name dates from 1936 and they have some aspects in common with the "people's universities" of the nineteenth century, the *maisons de la culture* are, above all, the result of the visionary policy of André Malraux. In 1982, there were sixteen (with six on the drawing board); they represented for the State a budget of about 40 million francs. According to Malraux's vision, a *maison de la culture* was a local project of the city and the State working together. After the inauguration of the *maison* at Grenoble on 3 February 1968, he explained that "the first *raison d'être* for this cultural center is everything that goes on in Paris also goes on here in Grenoble." At the beginning, the individuals and groups who ran the centers came for the most part from the theater. However, the *maisons de la culture* had been envisioned as more pluralistic. Today, in addition to the theater, they welcome cinema, orchestras, dance, and stage shows; they organize exhibitions or presentations in plastic arts, provide centers for the discussion of current problems, and seek to be as educational as they are artistic. Home of libraries, music collections, meeting rooms, video studios, they are intended to encourage creativity.

In fact, their legal status assigns to them three fundamental missions: creation, distribution, and development. The activity of artistic creation and distribution is linked to the ambition of making these "cathedrals of culture" places of nationally recognized quality. One motivation is a concern for local social cohesion: "the cultural centers equally must take account of the active participation, the invention, the adaptation, the creation, that culture requires of each individual, a practice that is at once individual and collective." The democratization of culture is a function of an active community at the local level. It rests also on a financial effort clearly expressed within the legal text. "The *maison de la culture* must be open to all, we cannot substitute a desire to make a profit at any price for our initial desire to assure activities that are accessible to all social levels."

Some have seen within the *maisons de la culture* "a new and pluralistic means of widespread cultural activity," as the Commission on Cultural Material and the Artistic Inheritance of the Vth Plan put it. In fact, between 1960 and 1968 the government considered these centers as "the cornerstone of the cultural edifice." But this understanding of the centers has since become a problem. In November 1968, the same year in which the capital expenditures were effected, André Malraux spoke of a "crisis of the *maisons de la culture*." It was not only that Malraux had recognized the failure of a building program that had planned one cultural center per *département* (by 1968 only eight had been built), or even the defects of these institutions, which had been detailed in the Raison Report of 1965 (uncongenial and constraining architecture, inconsistent geographical placement, excessive operating costs). It was the principle itself on which they had been founded that was challenged. The centers had never achieved their anticipated goals in numbers or heterogeneity of attendance. The *maisons de la culture* have attracted those whose education and social class had already prepared them for cultural activity.[7]

A new conception of cultural activity was necessary, one less ambitious in its actions and more open to local concerns. After 1968, more modest centers (the *centres d'action culturelle*—C.A.C.) were created. About twenty in number, these establishments were conceived according to the same principles as the *maisons de la culture* but, often without a permanent artistic organization, they were less costly and they answered more closely the needs of medium-sized cities.

After 1974, concern for decentralized planning in cultural subjects led to contractual agreements between the State and communities. These "cultural charters" were multi-annual agreements, revised each year, by which the State and the city, the *département,* or the region agreed on the planning and financing of diverse cultural projects.

This attempt to encourage local cultural activity took a new turn in 1981 with measures taken emphasizing administrative and financial decentralization. An Office of Cultural Development was created and an ambitious project announced. Two of its principal points were the restoration of minority regional cultures and the development of cultural activity within the workplace. These new priorities are within the framework of a larger cultural plan, the scope of which can only be appreciated within the context of cultural policies conducted since the beginning of the Fifth Republic.

Toward a New Cultural Policy: 1981–1986

In 1981, one of the first decisions of the new President was directed toward establishing a commission of experts to analyze critically the legacy bequeathed by the "*ancien régime*." The commission report was presented as "The Situation of France" in 1981. One of its chapters was on the cultural life of the French.[8] Almost simultaneously, a report was written by the working committee on "long-term culture" within the framework of preparation for the IXth Plan (1984–88). Its goal was to define major forms of state activity as part of a new "cultural imperative."[9]

"The Legacy" of Cultural Neglect

All reports given to the President of the French Republic or to the Ministry of Culture in 1981 and in 1982 reached the same conclusion: since the beginning of the Fifth Republic the overall state of cultural policy had been negative. During these years government action never was able to democratize access to culture, but, even worse, it contributed in certain areas to the reinforcement of inequalities. The primary cultural institutions have not been adapted to the needs of the population. The absence of a comprehensive cultural policy was, moreover, the principal defect of the legacy of previous administrations.

1. Cultural Inequality. French cultural life today is dominated by radio and television. Other cultural activities reach only a very small part of the population. With the exception of the cinema, which is attended by one individual in two, the audience for other kinds of performances is never more than 15 percent.[10] Music-hall and variety shows reach greater numbers than the theater and the circus, and outdraw musical activities such as concerts, ballet, and opera. Only visits to museums and historical monuments reach a larger public. (See Table 2.)

Individual cultural practices at home are nonetheless widespread. The average daily time spent listening to the radio is 2½ hours. Television is watched for about 2 hours per day by two out of three individuals. However, among the different kinds of programs, cultural programs such as opera, light opera, concerts, ballet, and artistic or literary programs rarely represent more than 30 percent. Reading and listening to music concern 69 percent and 50 percent respectively of the population.

TABLE 2. Cultural Activity Away from Home (1979)

	%
Shows	
Visited at least once in previous year:	
cinema*	45
nightclub show	15
theater	14
circus	12
classical music concert	7
jazz or pop music concert	6
ballet	4
opera	3
Visits	
Visited at least once in previous year:	
an historical monument	32
a museum	27
a painting or sculpture exhibition	19

Source: Ministère de la Culture, Des chiffres pour la culture (La Documentation Française, 1980), p. 333.

Note: All figures are based on population over 15 years of age.

*79 percent see at least one film per week on TV.

The last few years have seen an increase in the numbers of households with audio-visual equipment to facilitate cultural activities. Radio is found in nearly 100 percent of households, whereas TV has grown from 45 percent in 1965 to 87.5 percent in 1977, of which 22 percent have color sets. Stereo and hi-fi equipment are found in two out of three households (61 percent).

However, there are great differences among the French population with respect to cultural consumption. In fact, the intensity and nature of cultural practices vary considerably in terms of time, budget, and demographic criteria, such as age, socio-economic status, or living conditions:

First, cultural behavior significantly reflects age. In general, the practice of most cultural activities reaches its maximum between 15 and 25 years of age, and decreases progressively to the age of 60, an age at which disaffection tends to accelerate. Certain practices, very important between 15 and 25 years of age, decrease significantly with entry into professional life and marriage. Principally, they include cinema, pop and jazz concerts, and certain leisure activities such as fairs, public dances, and attendance at sports events. Other activities, if habitual in adolescence, continue until about 35 to 40 years of age, and only diminish gradually, such as visits to historical monuments, museums, theater, and, among home-based cultural practices, reading.

Moreover, the cultural behavior of those who live in small towns or in rural areas is clearly different from that which one observes in Paris. Television, fairs, public dances, sports events, and daily newspaper or magazine reading take a larger place the farther one is from major cities. This tendency is reversed for attendance at cultural activities. The gap between the rate of participation in small and large cities is 1-to-2 for the cinema, 1-to-3 for concerts of classical music, and reaches a maximum of 1-to-5 for the theater. Except for the cinema, these activities involve less than 15 percent of those who do not live in Paris. Visits to museums and historical monuments also decrease with the size of cities, but in less striking proportions.

Amateur cultural activities do not escape this general pattern. They are enjoyed by only a minority of individuals and tend to decrease with age. Music is the most common of these activities. Eleven percent of the French play a musical instrument. Following in importance are the plastic arts and the crafts (4.5 percent paint, draw, or sculpt, 2.5 percent are involved in pottery or ceramics), whereas the other arts are practiced by scarcely more than one percent of the French (dance 1.5 percent, theater 1 percent). One important difference is that amateur practitioners and participants in culture are as active outside of as in Paris. Unlike professional cultural creativity, these activities are not concentrated physically in Paris. In this sense, amateur activities in specified areas can contribute to the rediscovery of identity or the renaissance of local creativity.

But cultural differentiation is essentially social differentiation. The practice of a cultural activity does not come out of a vacuum and in fact important differences exist in the cultural awareness among different social groups. These differences are greater or lesser depending on the type of practices discussed. The gap between upper- and lower-class activities is widest for theater, opera, and concerts, ranging from 1-to-5 or even 1-to-10. For home-based cultural activities, such as reading or listening to music, the gap is from 1-to-2 to 1-to-3. The gap in participation disappears with the mass media: radio, newspapers, and books. Everyone participates in these activities, even though one finds differences in the quality of books, the kinds of newspapers and journals read, the quality of programs, and above all, a difference in the assiduity with which one watches television.

Thus, belonging to a particular social milieu is the principal variable in cultural participation. In general, the rate of participation decreases as one descends the socioeconomic ladder.

2. *Inflexibility of Institutions and the Absence of a Comprehensive Policy.* In France the State is not only endowed with a large Ministry of Culture, it controls, subsidizes, and even administers a great number of cultural institutions. Operating costs for these institutions and their role in the cultural development of the country have been a problem for many years. But successive increases in state subsidies and the nomination of prestigious individuals to those institutions often led to the disguising of the nature of these problems. It was necessary to wait for the political change of 1981 in order to have the government question the nature of its legacy.

At this point there are those who have expressed a fundamental doubt as to even the idea of institutionalization in the sphere of culture. Are not, they ask, cultural creativity and an institution fundamentally incompatible? Do not institutions in and of themselves suffocate instead of facilitate different kinds of expression? Thus according to the Dumayet Commission, these large cultural organizations become a kind of "machine" imposing their own logic on the rest of society. "They define the legitimate cultural arena and devalue any practices which do not belong within organizations. The organizations tend to conserve established values. Finally, organizations place the contemporary cultural arena between two poles—on the one hand a mass culture, on the other hand a tamed, sifted, sorted-out culture." But this framework must be rejected. Institutions must not be allowed to exercise legitimizing and selecting powers nor should "cultural facts be submitted to the functional logic of organizations."[11]

Most of the criticisms offered were, however, less radical. One criticism, for example, was that with a few exceptions, such as the *Comédie Française,* the Paris *Opéra,* and the *Théâtre de l'Odéon,* the great cultural institutions of France were of recent creation, either in successive waves (theaters under the Fourth Republic, *maisons de la culture* at the beginning of the Ministry of André Malraux, the Conservatory of Music at the end of the 1960s), or in a specific and very political manner (the Pompidou Center, the Museum of the Nineteenth Century, and the Museum of La Villette). Responding to different goals, cultural institutions become a very heterogeneous collection, not only in what their mission is but also in their juridical and financial status. The results that they achieve are equally uneven. The causes of any difficulties that they encounter differ from one institution to another. However, some of the most frequent are:

imprecision, or even errors, in the definition of their objectives;
the inevitability of budget deficits;
inflexibility in the subsidiary relationship with the State;
a certain carelessness and lack of dynamism in administration.

For these reasons, it does not seem that institutions have, at least until the present, contributed effectively to the reduction of inequalities between Paris and the provinces, nor to the democratization of culture and the support of creativity.

But for most observers, the principal cause of this situation is not to be found in the administration of the institutions themselves; it is the result more of the absence of a comprehensive government policy toward the arts. Certainly there have been numerous policies in this area, both elaborated and put into practice. But there has never been coherence in these actions and concern for comprehensive policy never seems to have constituted a real preoccupation of government. Two obstacles have hindered the emergence of a comprehensive cultural policy:

> The first results from the extreme fragmentation of responsibility within the government on this problem. In 1978, the budget of the Ministry of Culture was only 43.7 percent of the cultural budget of the government as a whole, and numerous offices played an important role in the conservation and distribution of research. As in other areas, coordination among the different government offices and their responsibilities has never been systematic.
>
> The second obstacle is linked to the progressive decrease in long-range planning in France. The IVth Plan, prepared in 1960, was the first to have a chapter entitled "Culture." It was notable for launching the program for *maisons de la culture* and for the restoration of some important historical monuments. But as of the VIIth Plan (1977–81), the idea of planning in the cultural domain began to be disputed. The VIIIth Plan (1981–85) avoided culture almost completely. Only the demands for distribution of scientific and technical information and for the development of some sort of community effort to support French cultural products were discussed.

The first few months of the new Socialist administration were marked by real change on this subject. The Minister, Jack Lang, had in fact made known his intention to endow France with "a grand cultural policy." With the solid support of the French President, Lang was to launch a campaign the objective of which was the expression of "a new cultural imperative."

Perspectives and Realities: The New "Cultural Imperative"

Since 1982, the Ministry of Culture has benefited from an unprecedented growth in its budget. However, two years later, the expected profound reform of government cultural activity had not taken place. For example, the governmental means of intervention—without doubt more "generous" than those of the past—seemed to conserve essentially the same characteristics and thus the same faults. Along with the decentralization, could a

TABLE 3. Government Cultural Expenditures 1978

Central Administrative Offices	*Cultural Expenditures (millions of Fr.)*	*Percent of State "Cultural Budget"*
Culture	2,395.9	43.7
Education	950.9	17.3
Youth and Sports	818.4	14.9
Universities	349.5	6.4
General Secretary of the Government	265.6	4.8
Foreign Affairs	203.9	3.7
Cooperation	116.7	2.1
Defense	73.4	1.3
Other Ministries	312.2	5.8
Total	5,486.5	100.

Source: A. Holleaux, "La politique culturelle de la France," *Revue Française d'Administration Publique*, no. 22, avril-juin 1982, p. 243.

new cultural policy become part of the "important business" of the presidency of François Mitterand?

1. The Government and Cultural Crisis. In 1981 the Dumayet Commission was to define long-term cultural policy. Their conclusions reflect very faithfully the cultural philosophy of the new Socialist government. According to the report, the crisis of western European countries, and France in particular, is not only economic but also cultural.

The symptoms of this crisis arise from the weakened models of mass consumerism, the search for new attitudes to work, and the rejection of large institutions in favor of diverse local ones that encourage autonomous action. In the field of culture, the crisis is reflected in a more obvious failure of cultural institutions to adapt, the rejection of an overly narrow definition of culture that favors a cultivated and "official" culture, as well as a growing deficiency in the credibility and legitimacy of the entire social and economic system. Faced with this "cultural crisis," what would become of the goals and modes of action of cultural policy?

For the new administration, a concept which does not place culture at the heart of all the practices and efforts of industrial society would be a refusal of modernity and would only reproduce the errors of the past. It appears necessary to encourage all possible coordination between economic necessity and cultural dynamism in all areas and in all social groups. To this end, public cultural institutions must have two essential objectives: the encouragement and support of creativity and the conservation and distribution of the creations of both the past and the present. At the level of civil society itself the State must limit itself to making possible the conditions that allow all its members to express, to keep alive, and to develop their own cultural practices wherever they are found, at work, at school, in lifestyles, and in institutions. Thus, as the new Minister put it, "to make culture both a daily experience and a pluralistic one."

Certainly such a strategy is ambitious because it is extended to areas generally considered outside of culture. But it also implies a kind of State and local government retreat. In fact, within the framework of these new demands, the State will only be able:

> to administer cultural institutions with particular attention to the relation between art and culture and to the necessity for cultural democratization;
>
> to create the conditions that allow the emergence of cultural diversity in substituting a "distribution strategy" for a "strategy of appropriation";
>
> to be, within the context of decentralization, "a place of assistance and of arbitration," in order to reduce the risks of cultural conformity and State direction at the local level.

These changes in orientation necessitate a profound modification of the forms of State intervention. First, they must be based on a broad association between government and its partners, whether new or traditional (business, cultural industries, communications media). They must encourage citizen participation and expression stemming from the development of firm-sponsored activities and from trained cultural facilitators. Moreover, creation of an agency of cultural development responsible for advising local communities and social groups in achieving their goals would allow the facilitation of experimentation and the integration of administrative intervention. Finally, the defense of the "cultural imperative" must necessarily count among the priorities in national, regional, and local planning.

Responsible for translating into action this important change in the government's role in cultural matters is Jack Lang, the new Minister of Culture (the new administration has separated culture from communication in creating two distinct ministries, whereas under the preceding administration these fields were within the competence of a single government office). In 1981, the new Minister asserted that he did not have at his disposal a central office able to implement a "great cultural policy." Set up in 1959 as a separate ministry, the domain of the former Secretary of State for Fine Arts was characterized by inefficient, overly centralized, and ponderous structures using outmoded work methods. As Bernard Gournay remarked recently, "France is in a peculiar situation in this regard. The Minister of Culture is responsible for a much larger domain than elsewhere. The administrative tasks indirectly exercised by the office have no equivalent in any other liberal democracy."[12]

Under the Fourth Republic, the Secretary of State for Fine Arts supervised numerous institutions (national theaters, operas, conservatories, historical monuments). Since 1959, the considerable expansion of these tasks had created new offices. Thus in 1969 two management offices, that of the theater and that of music, lyric arts, and dance, replaced the former Office of Art and Letters. An Office of Books and Reading was instituted in 1975 and an Office of the National Inheritance was substituted in 1978 for the old Office of Architecture.

One of the first tasks of the new Minister in 1981 was to put into action a reorganization of the Ministry which, despite valuable initiatives, often amounted to only personnel changes. Today, the offices at the rue de Valois have more than 13,000 employees of which about 4,000 are in different establishments under its supervision. The central service of the Ministry is composed of:

Six management offices. Four are concerned with the national inheritance (Archives, Museums, Books and Reading, National Inheritance). Two are oriented toward artistic creation and distribution (Music and Dance, Theater), to which must be added a representative of plastic arts and the National Center of Cinematography.

Two other offices are charged with coordination and maintenance (General Administration Office and Cultural Development Office). Before 1981, the function of cultural development had an ephemeral existence. Transformed into a separate agency in 1982, it has today been charged with the promotion of a cultural policy which is both global, thus integrating all of the fields in which the government intervenes, and decentralized, thus encouraging local initiatives. These structures are completed by a number of offices of multidisciplinary activity (the Pompidou Center, the General Secretary of the Cultural Intervention Fund) and by the offices of general inspection, information, and communication.

At the beginning of the 1970s the Ministry was expanded to include outside services in the form of regional administrative offices of culture. These offices were added to the numerous public establishments under Ministry supervision, such as the Paris *Opéra,* the *Comédie Française,* the National Cinema Center, and so on. Those responsibilities toward culture that in other countries are generally exercised by private associations or foundations are assumed in France by large national public entities. One would imagine that a large centralized administrative apparatus would constitute an asset for putting into action a new and ambitious policy. Sometimes, however, the facts revealed a different reality. The "machine" of the State seemed often in fact paralyzed by an extraordinary inertia and thus was susceptible to the "banalization" and rapid annihilation of even very audacious efforts.

2. *Change and Continuity: Le temps d'une législature . . .* Reflecting the new cultural ambitions of the Socialist government, budgetary growth of the Ministry since 1981 has raised as many hopes as criticisms. Measures taken since 1982 to double the sums allocated for culture were not challenged during the years that followed despite the tightening of the budget by the government. Thus the budget of the Ministry of Culture was 2.97 billion francs in 1981, 5.99 billion francs in 1982, and 6.99 billion francs in 1983. The proposed budget for 1984 presented to the National Assembly in October 1983, which limited most increases to 6.5 percent, provided nonetheless for an increase in the culture budget of 15 percent, from 7 to 8 billion francs in 1984. The provision for culture in the general budget of the State, which was never more than 0.5 percent until 1981, continues to grow. It represented 0.75 percent in 1982 and 0.78 percent in 1983. This growth was confirmed in 1984 in spite of the effort to economize and moves toward budgetary austerity.

Among the spheres of cultural action which benefited from this growth in budgetary means, principally figured the "plastic arts," the cinema, music, the protection of the national patrimony, and books. Although these changes seemed quite exceptional in both means and ends, they turned out to be less in reality. The weight of tradition added to the difficulty of implementing even ambitious policy changes:

(1) In the field of "plastic arts," the cultural policy in effect since 1981 has without doubt contributed most to the dynamization of artistic creation. All the same, not everything has been accomplished. In multiplying support and in promoting—above all by rhetoric—contemporary art, the Minister has sought to restore confidence to a field that has suffered for many years from "sinistrosity":

> no art form was forgotten, at the risk of an ineffective scattering of public intervention: photography, animation, crafts, design, fashion, and even cooking were the objects of often spectacular promotional actions;
>
> in material terms, the funds were tripled between 1981 and 1985; a plan of revival was elaborated and two hundred works were, in 1986, in progress for the parks of Paris, the railway stations, the *Métro,* and the highways. But it is above all by the creation of Regional Funds for Contemporary Art (FRAC) and Acquisitions by Museums (FRAM), started in 1982 and jointly financed by the State and by the regions, that a new movement in favor of creation was launched;
>
> numerous large projects have been realized in Paris, such as the creation of the Picasso Museum, the restructuring of the National Museum of Modern Art of the Georges Pompidou Center, and the opening of the Museum of the Arts and Fashion.

(2) The reform of cinema policy announced in April 1982 by the Ministry of Culture was to "redefine the fundamental mechanisms of the cinema economy." It was put into action by laws and regulations and by budgetary augmentation; the cinema budget, in constant francs, went from 219.4 million for the 1977–81 legislature to 1,562.5 million in 1981–86. The goals of this new policy were essentially to restructure the production and distribution apparatus of cinema and cinemagraphic activity within a more global policy favoring communication and audio-visual media. The measures turned on five fundamental points:

> to re-establish diversity, pluralism, and competition in the cinema economy;
>
> to strengthen the potential for creation and production in French cinema, notably with the help of a large endowment to the Committee on Advances from receipts on

full-length films (the advance on receipts rose, in constant francs, from 42.7 million between 1977 and 1981 to 358.05 million for the period 1981–86);

to regain a large mass public (in 1983, the State allotted 45 million francs to the modernization of cinema theaters, and, moreover, the funds allocated to local cinema projects doubled between 1980 and 1982);

to preserve and make known the cinema heritage (with the elaboration of a five-year plan for the restoration of films); the cinema heritage saw its budget grow, from the one legislature to the other, from 65.5 million to 224.5 million (constant francs);

finally, to accentuate the presence of French cinema in foreign countries through the institution of a system of export aid.

Presented by Jack Lang during a press conference in January 1983, the new cinema policy was fairly well received in professional circles. However, uncertainties continue to exist, most notably concerning the impact of measures taken in the fight against cartels and aid to exportation.

In the last few years the French cinema has experienced a growing movement toward concentration of movie-theater ownership, threatening both the activity and diversity of independently owned theaters. The most obvious and almost symbolic result of the effort to increase competition is the dissolution of economic agreements associating the two large chains of French movie theaters, Gaumont and Pathé. Beyond this first result, the attempt to establish certain business ethics stands little chance of overcoming the obstacles that will multiply over the next few years due to the powerful interests at stake.

Proposals to increase the presence of French cinema in foreign countries were shown to be very limited. The sale of French films, already low, decreased by 11 percent in 1982. A program of aid for the export of French products in numerous industries was proposed. But in the case of cinema, the quality of cinematographic works is definitely challenged.

Even if the role of the State in film production increases (the Fund for Film Advances was multiplied by a factor of eight in five years), it seems difficult to foresee significant changes in the future. Until the present, the percentage of successful films (judged by their increase over advance receipts) has never been as high as that of commercial production but is about 10 percent. But as some have noted, "one cannot construct a cultural industry on 90% rejects."[13]

Despite the uncertainties expressed by the profession on the new cinema policy, they were probably important reforms and were within an ambitious comprehensive project concerning cultural industries. It is important to recall that budgetary plans for cultural industries allocate 21 billion francs over five years and thus culture ranked among the twelve priority programs of the IXth Plan.

(3) In the field of music, there is still the considerable progression of the Ministry's budget which constitutes without doubt the most marked feature of the Socialist program: funds for music and dance have gone in effect from 3,525 million francs in 1977–81 to 8,363 million in 1982–86, an increase of 137 percent in constant francs. The increase in funds has allowed the realization of numerous new initiatives, such as the inauguration of a Day of Music and the development of festivals (+25%) on the national as well as local level, the institution of a *Conseil Supérieur pour la Musique,* the beginning of construction of new conservatories in Paris and Lyon, and, above all, the construction of a new *Bastille Opéra* (deferred by the Chirac government after March 1986).

The action undertaken under the leadership of Jack Lang has not overturned the previous mode of public intervention in this field; following the policies of his predecessors the Minister encountered—like them—the same difficulties and, notably, the inertia of the national education administration, which was incapable of offering to music the place that belongs to it in the curricula offered in schools, high schools, and colleges.

(4) "The heritage, from 1981 to 1986, will have been one of battle horses most voluntarily supported by the opposition, which was made nervous by the priority given to creation . . . ," Frédéric Edelmann wrote recently.[14] The action of the Minister of Culture since 1981 nevertheless shows a pattern of continuity in a number of areas: funds earmarked for repairs and maintenance of historical monuments have remained equivalent; the reforms (like those of the commission charged with advising on projects of classification or protection) have been purely institutional. Despite a new effort to aid archaeology, recent policy has without doubt lacked a more ambitious plan for the addition of contemporary work to the body of the nation's architectural heritage. The lively polemic to which the project for the pyramid at the *Louvre* has given rise proves, if there was any need, the lagging French conception in this field.

(5) In keeping with campaign promises made by the French President in 1981, policy toward books and reading has constituted one of the priorities of the new Ministry of Culture. There, as in other domains, the activity of the new government was in fact characterized by a highly symbolic "primary measure," administered without provision for coordination with other cultural activities of the government.

Thus, in the month of August 1981, a law was passed instituting a single price for books, running counter to the "deregulation" begun by the Ministry of the Economy two years earlier. Promised by François Mitterrand, this measure was passed even before the commissions charged with defining principles for a new cultural policy had submitted their reports and conclusions. If this strongly symbolizes the fact that books cannot be considered an industrial product like any other, it remains nonetheless incompatible with the objective of cultural democratization and modernization of distribution otherwise desired. The commercial centers and the FNAC could not continue their policy of discounting, and this has resulted in a general realignment of prices that are higher as a consequence. Thus, for one individual in four, the reform has meant paying 25 to 30 percent more for books than he did previously.

Faced with a *fait accompli,* the Pinguaud-Barreau Committee, responsible for defining new policy on books and reading, wrote a second report after having stated that "the single pricing system, even if it remedies the bookstore crisis, will not resolve today's basic problems of writing and publishing."[15]

It would be premature to analyze the results of State intervention since 1981 in this domain. Nonetheless, if the objective of the protection of the book distribution network in order to assure the promotion of new works seems to have been achieved, the principal setback of Jack Lang in this field is not to have been able to replace a distribution system that is particularly heavy, complex, and therefore very slow.

After an initial measure announced with fanfare (the single price policy), government action quickly ran out of steam. In fact, the decisions adopted by the government have been limited to a widespread financial scatter-shot approach. The funds of the Office of Books have gone from 163 to 677 million francs between 1981 and 1986; from 1981 to 1982, ordinary expenditures and authorizations for programs on books increased by 131 percent,[16] subsidies to city libraries by 887 percent,[17] and aid to the central lending libraries by 140 percent. However, this considerable growth in the book budget is neither accompanied by a guarantee of coordination of activities nor by any procedure for evaluating its results. Moreover, it is not certain that the increase in the number of public libraries can lead directly to an increase in reading. This multiplication of infrastructures must be complemented by advertising campaigns promoting reading and education for the non-reading public.

Thus, there is an absence of an overall strategic plan and even of simple goals in government projects on reading. It is important to recall in conclusion that this lacuna is more serious today given the fact that only one individual in six says that he has entered a library at least once, one in four reads not at all (that is, has not opened a book in the preceding year),[18] and that, since 1986, responsibility for the field has been transferred to the localities in the process of decentralization!

3. Cultural Policy and Decentralization. In 1981, at the time of the presentation of his Ministry's program before the National Assembly, Jack Lang defined cultural policy in two words: creation and decentralization. The latter has become since then a framework around which government action has been oriented in all of its spheres (in the institution of regional centers of cinematographic creation and production, aid to the functioning of regional orchestras and music, measures encouraging departmental lending libraries, and that of books, etc.). The budget reflects this evolution: In ordinary expenditures, financial effort supporting local communities was 80 million francs in 1981, 630 million francs in 1982, and more than 650 million in 1983. In capital expenditures, 95 million francs were authorized in 1981, 450 million francs in 1982, and 550 million francs in 1983.

In conformity with the principle defined in the law relative to the rights and liberties of local townships, *départements,* and regions, on 2 March 1982, a provisional cultural allocation was instituted: the Special Fund for cultural development, endowed with 150 million francs at its creation in 1982. This subsidy permits the reimbursement of certain local community expenses (the functioning of city libraries, of national conservatories and national schools of music, of city and regional schools of art) and encourages new projects, notably within the framework of "cultural development agreements" negotiated between the State and the regions.

The idea of negotiating agreements and conventions with the regions on cultural subjects is not a new one. These "cultural charters" were already signed with certain regions under the presidency of Giscard d'Estaing. But the essential difference is in the new status conferred on the region by the law of decentralization. Having become a territorial community, it is recognized as having an important role in the life and cultural activity of the country; hence it is the responsibility of the region to "promote the economic, social, sanitary, cultural and scientific development and the improvement of its territory and to ensure the preservation of its own identity with respect to the integrity, autonomy, and the characteristics of the *départements* and local communities."

In this sense, the desire to establish contractual relations with the regions on cultural subjects proves to be the determining factor. Contrary to the cultural charters in which the content is relatively limited, the new "cultural development agreement" must be written on a global cultural project and presupposes a definition by each region of an innovative policy in the cultural sphere as well as involving important financial transfers. The setting up of this contractual policy has already imposed an adaptation of ministerial structures in the sense of rapprochement with the regional authorities and of an effort at coordination at the national level. At the level of the outside services of cultural affairs, delegates are responsible for encouraging coordination with the regions. At the ministerial level, the cultural development office has been given three objectives: launching new decentralizing activities, putting them into effect, and following up on relationships with local communities.

The first agreement was signed in March 1982 by the Languedoc-Roussillon region, followed in June 1982 by the region Nord-Pas de Calais. Since then, all the regions have made agreements of this kind with the State, permitting the definition of cultural activity in a concentrated way and determining what priority to give State intervention in different regions. Making cultural development agreements thus represents an important innovation in the decentralization of cultural administration. It has enlarged the field of intervention for the regions, increased the adaptability of the administration in its relations with territorial communities, and substantially augmented the funds allocated for culture within a regional context. The realization of these objectives, however, remains to be seen. This policy will work only if the agreements give rise to a desire for regional activity and a mobilization of the means, particularly the financial means, to do it. In this respect, one can reasonably wonder whether, in the context of the current economy, cultural development will appear as a peripheral issue rather than as a priority. Although, as Jack Lang underlined, "a region without intellectual and artistic life dies economically," the concerns of those responsible for policy, whether on the national or local level, will without doubt set the priorities of the nation on problems of employment, economic, and industrial difficulties. The uncertainties which weigh on the capacity of regional institutions to take charge of cultural development in their territories exist equally for other forms of local government—*départements* and local communities—with which the State has attempted to establish a similar relationship.

Linked to the multiplication of demands, the tendency to scatter-gun initiatives is real. It risks compromising the policy aimed at by government because of a possible lack of coordination between the actions undertaken at each level of government and a possible waste of means (a situation which rarely favors creativity). Because if, as the President said, "It is the will of France to take a position on the capacity to create, to transform, and to use all the forms of individual and collective human invention," such an ambition, particularly in the arts, obviously calls for a concentration of forces and of means difficult to reconcile with the multiplicity of current activities. In this respect, decentralization both of means and of initiatives at the local level seems to present not only a risk of deviation toward a kind of regionalism (which is, of course, different from the search for a regional cultural identity), but, above all, a risk of politicization of the administration of cultural activities.

After decades, France had a centralized cultural administration unlike that of most other Western countries. Those aspects of cultural activity that were publicly administered had progressively become the sole province of the national government. Despite financial limitations, the Ministry of Culture administered most French cultural institutions directly.

One of the essential characteristics of the new cultural imperative was its challenge to this tendency. Cultural decentralization and political and administrative decentralization in effect have been announced by the new President himself to be "the important business of [his] term." The ambition was in fact a considerable one. It entails at least an attempt to oppose the "multisecular effort at centralization" which, for General De Gaulle, characterized the modern history of France.

[Translated by K. Forhan]

Notes

1. J. Lang, Ministre de la Culture, *France: une ambition nouvelle pour la culture,* Publication du Ministère de la Culture, 1981, p. 1.

2. There are about 1200 museums (including private museums) in all in France. In addition to the 1945 statute, certain museums have their own legal status, such as the Modern Art Museum at the Pompidou Center. Some have no official status, for example, the "eco-museums."

3. These figures indicate the percentage of persons over 15 years of age who have listened to the radio or watched TV at a specified moment of the day. (1% = c. 400,000 persons.) Chantal Lacroix, Marc Petit, François Rouet, "Les industries culturelles," *Notes et Etudes Documentaires,* Paris: La Documentation Française, no. 4535–36, Nov. 1979, pp. 45–46.

4. Odile Timbard, "Les dépenses culturelles des administrations centrales," *Futuribles,* no. 17, Sept.–Oct. 1978, p. 586.

5. The Budget Court in its 1983 report underlined that "such disparities whether due to increased costs or delays can only be explained by poor planning, insufficiently competitive bidding, numerous modifications and poor choice of contractors and architects." ("Rapport de la Cour des Comptes pour l'année 1983," *Journaux Officiels,* no. 4018, June 1983.)

6. Claude Mollard, "Le second souffle du Centre Pompidou," *Futuribles,* no. 16, Sept.–Oct. 1978, p. 647.

7. P. Bourdieu, "L'école conservatrice," *Revue Française de Sociologie,* July–Sept. 1966.

8. Commission du Bilan, *La France en mai 1981.* Paris: La Documentation Française, 1981 (5 volumes).

9. Ministère du Plan et de l'Amenagement du Territoire, *L'impératif culturel,* Rapport du groupe de travail "Long-Terme-Culture," Paris: La Documentation Française, 1983.

10. Percentages calculated on number of persons stating that they attended at least one show during the previous 12 months.

11. *L'impératif culturel,* pp. 29–30.

12. Bernard Gournay, "Un ministère pour la culture: l'expérience française," *Revue Française d'Administration Publique.* no. 22, April–June 1982, p. 52.

13. *Le Nouvel Observateur,* 21/27 Jan. 1983.

14. *Le Monde,* 13 March 1986.

15. *Pour une politique nouvelle du livre et de la lecture,* Paris: Dalloz, 1982, p. 22.

16. This increase takes into account the transfer of the *Bibliothèque Nationale* from the Ministry of Universities to the Ministry of Culture.

17. Including the special cultural endowment for local communities, *départements,* and regions.

18. Supplement to the "Lettre d'information du Ministère de la Culture," no. 1, June 1982.

Bibliography

Blum, S. *Vie culturelle et pouvoirs publics* (Paris: La Documentation Française, 1972).

Breerette, G. Les aides publiques à la création artistique en France, *Notes et Etudes Documentaires,* no. 4273–4272 (Paris: La Documentation Française, 1976).

Cabanne, P. *Le Pouvoir culturel sous la Vème République* (Paris: Olivier Orban, 1981).

Gourney, B. Un ministère pour la culture: l'expérience française, *Revue Française d'Administration Publique,* no. 22, avril/juin 1982, pp. 51–64.

Holleaux, A. La politique culturelle de la France, *Revue Française d'Administration Publique,* no. 22, avril/juin 1982, pp. 7–50.

Lacroix, C., M. Petit, F. Rouet, Les industries culturelles, *Notes et Etudes Documentaires,* no. 4535–36 (Paris, La Documentation Française, novembre 1979).

Mesnard, A.H. *La Politique culturelle de l'état* (Paris: P.U.F., 1974).

Ministère de la culture, Connaissance du Ministère de la Culture (Document de travail pour les concours), Edition 1983.

Ministère de la culture, Développement culturel, Bulletin d'information du Service des Etudes et Recherches.

Ministère de la culture, Les pratiques culturelles des Français (évolution 1973–81) (Paris: Dalloz, 1982).

Ministère de la culture et de la communication, Service des Etudes et de la Recherche, Annuaire statistique de la culture, Données de 1960 à 1970 (Paris: La Documentation Française, 1972).

Ministère de la culture et de la communication, Service des Etudes et de la Recherche, Annuaire statistique de la culture, Données de 1970 à 1974, (Paris: La Documentation Française, 1977–78).

Ministère de la culture et de la communication, Service des Etudes et de la Recherche, Des chiffres pour la culture (Paris: La Documentation Française, 1980).

Ministère du plan et de l'amenagement du territoire, L'impératif culturel, Rapport du groupe de travail ''Long-Terme-Culture'' (Paris: La Documentation Française, 1983).

Puaux, P. Les établissements culturels, Rapport au Ministère de la Culture (Paris: La Documentation Française, juillet 1982).

Queyranne, J.J. Les régions et la décentralisation culturelle—Les conventions de développement culturel règional, Rapport au Ministère de la Culture (Paris: La Documentation Française, juillet 1982).

Timbard, O. Les dépenses culturelles des administrations centrales, *Futuribles,* no. 17, septembre–octobre 1978.

U.N.E.S.C.O., La politique culturelle en France (Paris: L'action du Ministère de la Culture, 1981).

3

Cultural Federalism and Public Support for the Arts in the Federal Republic of Germany

WOLFGANG ISMAYR

The Tradition of Decentralized Cultural Politics

The demands of UNESCO and the European Community for stronger state support of cultural activities are bound up with the expectation of a "decentralization of facilities, activities and decisions."[1] Accordingly, the Bremen Declaration of the European Community of May 1983 called upon the governments "to pursue a consistent policy of cultural decentralization and to ensure that local and regional authorities have adequate powers and resources to play their vital role in the provision of artistic and recreational facilities and the promotion of cultural activities."[2]

Historical tradition as well as the constitutional order of the Federal Republic of Germany provide strong foundations for decentralized public support of culture and the arts. This, however, does not mean that the claims to support of "art and culture" relative to other areas of public concern are uncontested. Neither does it mean that the balance of responsibility among the federal, *Land,* and municipal levels is beyond challenge, nor that financial support to match the growing importance of the arts is assured.

The eighteenth- and nineteenth-century struggle of the liberal middle classes against the absolute State did not lead to the exclusion of the State from the cultural arena. The State not only undertook responsibility for schools, universities, and science, but also for the support and promotion of institutions for the arts and culture, such as theaters, orchestras, museums, and libraries. The quality of cultural institutions contributed significantly to the reputations of countless small German states.

The overwhelming share of governmental authority relating to internal affairs, especially educational and cultural policies, remained with the member states after the establishment of the German Reich in 1871. Cultural relations with foreign states were the concern of the Reich. Within Germany, the government of the Reich supported and enlarged—although without express constitutional authority—several cultural institutions of national significance, such as the German National Museum in Nuremberg, and historical-philological institutions.[3] Nevertheless, since then, cultural and educational policies, and especially support for the arts, have been the responsibility of the *Länder* and also of the municipalities. The Weimar Republic (Weimar Constitution, 1919) preserved the federal structure, in spite of a considerable expansion of the powers of the central government, particularly with respect to support for the arts. The countless princely theaters and museums which originated in monarchical times were taken over by the succeeding republics and also by cities. After the years of cultural "coordination" under National Socialism, the Western allies renewed the principle of cultural federalism in 1945.

As the name indicates, the Federal Republic of Germany that originated in 1949 is a federal state; it consists of eight territorial states and the two city states of Hamburg and Bremen. Close political ties exist between West Berlin and the Federal Republic, especially in cultural matters.[4] The federal structure of West Germany corresponds to the German constitutional tradition and takes into account the democratic, power-spreading principle of decentralization.[5] According to Article 30 of the Basic Law, the fulfillment of national tasks is the responsibility of the *Länder,* where the law does not provide otherwise. Besides the legislative authority that is reserved exclusively to the Federation (Art. 73 of the Basic Law), the Federation can be active in legislating for matters of concurrent legislation, as long as a need for federal legislation exists (Art. 72 of the Basic Law). The Federation has made very productive use of this opportunity (to be sure, usually with the consent of the *Land* governments represented in the Bundesrat).[6] Consequently the *Länder* kept as an area of independent regulation primarily the realm of cultural policies (education, science, support of arts and culture). A marked trend in the whole of western Europe toward regionalization and decentralization confirms these efforts.

Cultural politics in the *Länder* was and is, of course, above all the politics of schools, universities, and scientific investigation. For these, the *Länder* spent 53.8 billion DM in 1980, but during the same year only 2.3 billion DM for the support of the arts and culture.[7] The following are counted as support of the arts and culture: theater, opera, ballet, orchestras, museums and art exhibitions, music schools and other support of music, and also such areas as the protection of monuments and the support of artists, literature and films, and the promotion of cultural associations, initiatives, and urban neighborhood work. In these areas of cultural development, the cities and municipalities dominate with their manifold activities, among which are cultural institutions supported by the municipalities, activities originated by the municipalities, and a wide variety of initiatives by citizens that, if necessary, also are supported by the municipalities.[8]

The municipalities devote more than twice as great a share of their budgets to culture as do the *Länder*. In 1981, the *Länder* spent 1.1 percent, the municipalities 2.4 percent, and the Federation 0.1 percent of their total budgets for the support of the arts and culture. Since 1976, the proportions have risen slightly.[9] The whole expenditure amounted to 4.8 billion DM which is approximately 1 percent of all national (public) expenditure; the municipalities provided 56 percent of these expenditures, the *Länder* provided 42 percent, and the Federation provided 2.4 percent.[10] The *Deutscher Städtetag* (the association of the bigger cities and municipalities) likes to state that cultural politics in the Federal Republic is in the first instance municipal politics;[11] this statement gains weight especially from the fact that the initiative for cultural institutions, etc., comes overwhelmingly from the municipalities and approval of subsidies from the *Länder* is based on commitments and activities at the municipal level.

A more precise analysis of cultural expenditures shows that the cultural commitment of the municipalities varies widely, depending, among other things, on the size of the municipality and on its relation to the surrounding countryside.[12] The *Städtetag* and other associations of local governments (*Deutscher Städie- und Gemeindebund*) emphatically demand that the municipalities not regard cultural expenditures as "voluntary payments" that can be reduced more than other expenditures when budgets are cut. Since the cities and municipalities have laid a claim to a special competence for cultural programs, they have a duty to maintain them.

Cultural Support as a Public Duty

An explicit mandate for cultural support is not to be found in the Basic Law,[13] although freedom of art and science are expressly guaranteed in the catalog of basic rights (Art. 5, Sec. 3). This constitutional provision articulates a basic value concerning the relation of art to the State. It also guarantees a right of liberty for individuals. Participation in art, including not only artistic creation but also the performance and dissemination of artistic works, is protected as well. This article of the Basic Law stresses liberal guarantees that cannot be limited by ordinary laws, and that, according to judgments of the Federal Constitutional Court, may not be undermined by narrow definitions of art or State interference.

Actual government practice, as well as the current tendency to describe the Federal Republic of Germany as a "culture state," reflects the Federal Constitutional Court's interpretation of Article 5, Paragraph 3 as providing an active guarantee of artistic freedom: "As an objective value decision for the freedom of art, the modern state, which understands itself in terms of a national goal of being a culture state, at the same time sets itself the duty to maintain and support a free artistic life."[14] Freedom of art means not only protection against state interference, but also demands certain actions from the state. From that notion is derived the duty of government at all three levels to maintain artistic freedom and to support art and culture in the interest of the participation of the greatest possible number of citizens. In this sense, one should speak of "cultural democracy" rather than of the "culture state," in order better to express the state's duty to support a "culture for all, with and by all."[15]

According to a commission, installed by the Federal Minister of Justice, it should be incorporated in the Basic Law (Arts. 20 and 28) that the Federal Republic should defend and cultivate "culture and the natural foundations of life."[16] Such provisions are found already in most of the constitutions of the *Länder*. It is expressly stated in the constitutions of Bavaria (Art. 140) and North Rhine-Westphalia (Art. 18) that art, culture, and science are to be supported by the *Land* and the municipalities. The municipal constitutions (regulations) contain provisions that can be interpreted correspondingly. While the *Länder* maintain their "cultural sovereignty" vis-à-vis the Federation, the municipalities stress their cultural independence and cultural-political competence vis-à-vis the *Länder*, using similar arguments. For years, the municipalities have been defending themselves against the growing encroachment upon their decision-making powers through detailed legal regulations and orders tied to goal-oriented allotments of provincial aid. For this purpose they cite Article 28, Paragraph 2 of the Basic Law, according to which the municipalities regulate "on their own responsibility all matters of the local community within the scope of the laws." In view of this, distinguished constitutional lawyers recently have called special attention to an equally justified basis for local governments to claim "original" jurisdiction on cultural matters. Through local activities, cultural variety (and thus in certain ways also artistic freedom) and cultural participation are best guaranteed.[17] The

Städtetag, in view of the cut-back debates in the municipalities, emphatically pointed out to its members that corresponding duties go along with this competence.[18]

The *Länder* still do not regulate most cultural work; the associations of local governments justifiably want this situation to remain as it is. A stimulating municipal cultural policy that makes it possible to develop a many-sided and innovative cultural life presupposes a special measure of organizational freedom. In the view of the *Städtetag,* interference through legal regulation from the *Länder* can only be prevented in the long run if the municipalities are ready to commit themselves to continuous art and cultural policies: "Cultural work is a typical exercise of self-government and one of the few areas in which the cities can still have relatively wide decision-making and organizational freedom. This freedom from legal regulation will only be maintained if the cities themselves take appropriate responsibility for cultural affairs."[19]

The notion that community support of art and culture is not a duty, but simply a "voluntary exercise of self-government" appears to exist not only in the legal literature, but also among many community leaders.[20] Where this view prevails, cultural support and cultural activities can be treated as of lesser importance than are other functions and thus can be seen by many community leaders "as an unnecessary extra, as a very beautiful flower, but not especially important for life," as a former chief of the *Städtetag,* D. Sauberzweig, put it in 1973.[21] When funds are limited, then, the danger exists that cuts will be made here first. The *Städtetag* opposed this attitude in their latest position: cultural support is only a very limited burden on the budget and therefore is "not fat to be trimmed in lean years." Cultural support today is one of the unrenounceable tasks of the community. "The existing variety of theaters, orchestras, museums, libraries, and adult education courses has become much more of a central part of the basic services provided by the community. It should not be tampered with, even in times of financial difficulties."[22] This view was echoed by, among others, the German Trade Unions Federation in its "Principles of Cultural Policies and Cultural Work" (1981). The exercise of self-government, it has been argued, can become a duty even without specific legal provisions, if it corresponds to the common opinion of the municipal citizenry.[23] In fact, since the 1970s, there has been an undeniable growth of interest among many citizens in the availability of cultural institutions as well as a growing demand for artistic-cultural activities. This is shown by the rise in attendance at museums, exhibitions, libraries, and music theaters, and also by the many citizens' initiatives in the socio-cultural field.[24]

According to this understanding of support for the arts as "the exercise of a duty," the decision as to where and how their main effort is to be made is left to the municipalities. However, they are required to observe the principle of cultural diversity in accordance with democratic principles and in the interests of artistic freedom. Only through a variety of offerings and support measures can one guarantee not only that the interests of all groups are given attention, but that the range of those who take advantage of cultural offerings and are active themselves is widened. The *leitmotif* of "culture for all, with and by all" (*Städtetag,* 1983) permeates this cultural activity.[25] Concretely, this means that in accordance with the size and financial strength of the community, independent initiatives and associations, and cultural education and "animation" should be supported as well as various traditional and new cultural institutions. For many years the *Städtetag* has been striving to convince the cities of the importance of communal cultural support of a variety of activities. Without doubt, it has influenced the cultural consciousness and activities of many cities and municipalities and has generally stimulated social and political interest in art and cultural affairs.[26] Recently, other associations of local governments such as the *Deutscher Städte- und Gemeindebund* (municipalities) and the *Deutscher Landkreistag* (rural districts) also have made corresponding recommendations.[27] To be sure, a number of cities and municipalities have been very much less open to these suggestions than others have been.[28] A more positive and wider view of support for art and culture can be identified in the positions of parties, politicians, trade unions, and other associations, as well as in the news reports of the media.

Changes in the Understanding of Culture

By "culture" one understands, especially in the German tradition since the nineteenth century, "higher" activities removed from ordinary daily life. The word "civilization" applies to all other areas of life, as well as to the sphere of politics.[29] Accordingly, in the 1950s and 1960s, the important aim of cultural policy was the building or rebuilding and maintenance of "institutions of arts and culture"—theaters, museums, libraries, and orchestras. The building that resulted "in spite of great economic deprivation," and which already was promoted by the "principles of community cultural work" in 1952, has been referred to proudly by the cities in today's debates over budget cuts.[30]

In the 1970s, it increasingly was recognized that substantial initiatives could not be limited to the preservation of these institutions if a decline in the quality of life in the cities and municipalities was to be prevented. In the 1950s and 1960s, interest focused predominately on reconstruction and quick economic growth. This had great disadvantages for the development of cities and municipalities as human living space. City planners and architects subscribed to the now much criticized, but at least in practice not yet obsolete, pure functionalism. Now criticism of the "inhospitality of our cities" (A. Mitscherlich) in industrial mass society—the more they grew, the more inhumane they became—began.[31]

In fact, the cultural-ecological balance of many cities was upset. Driven by a desire for fast economic and technological development, they risked losing the quality of a humane living environment. At least since the appeals of the *Städtetag* in the early 1970s, a return to humane standards and the recovery of the cities' lost identities were demanded.[32] The *Städtetag* emphatically stressed the consequences for its member cities, and the other associations of local governments followed by taking similar positions. A precondition for the development of mankind in the city would be the creation of an environment that, through proportion and basic structure, stimulates the imagination and at the same time guarantees the identification of the inhabitant with his city. The city must be a place where socialization, communication, and creativity are possible.

Similar to the cultural resolutions of the Council of Europe (e.g., 1976, 1983) and UNESCO (1976) and in the statement of principles of the *Kulturpolitischen Gesellschaft* (Association for Cultural Policies)—founded in 1976—the various areas of human life are seen from the viewpoint of their interaction, thus paving the way for new cultural perspectives.[33] "Culture" in this sense is not just one aspect of society, but the whole variety of expressions of the life of a people. According to the intentions of these resolutions, insights from modern cultural anthropology and ethnology (to which the broader understanding of culture in these resolutions is oriented) can became normative. The trans-cultural significance of the creative integration of the environment, of experiencing one's identity—also emotionally—in structured living spaces, and of giving meaning to the accomplishments of daily life for all classes has been recognized. (Participation in cultural life means an "assertion of identity, authenticity, and dignity," according to the UNESCO recommendation. Nevertheless, the assertion of cultural identity should not lead to the isolation of groups, but should bring with it a fruitful mutual enrichment through frequent interchange.[34]

In addition to the development deplored in many cities and municipalities, still other social experiences have challenged cultural perceptions to change: the deterioration of the natural environment, along with the simultaneous growth of the life-threatening armaments industry;[35] and a trend toward the managerial state and the consequent encroachment upon the space free for individual action. A considerable number of citizens' initiatives have appeared since the early 1970s. These activities express the strengthened political commitment of many citizens outside the established parties, and are in part opposed to the policies of the established parties. Their activities and goals express a noteworthy orientation toward primarily ''non-materialistic'' values and a renunciation of a policy of economic growth at practically any cost.

The increase of leisure time and also the great number of unemployed people offer another challenge for cultural policy. In addition, new cultural policy problems have arisen because of the great number of foreigners whose children grow up in Germany. These problems include the preservation of cultural independence and cultural integration.[36] The growth of leisure time has spawned a flourishing commercial leisure and media entertainment industry with corresponding consumer demand. The fast-growing video market of the last few years has been dominated by violence and pornography. Nevertheless, it is to be expected that the government parties will carry through their media policy ideas. This means that along with the radio and television programs under public ownership, a wide offering of commercial programs will be offered soon, which, judging from the experience in other countries (Italy, the United States, Great Britain) not only should raise the amount of television viewing (especially among children), but also will lead to a decline in standards of all programs offered. Politicians of all parties concerned with cultural policy as well as the associations of local government confronted with proposed cuts in the cultural budgets often have drawn attention to the fact that, faced with these problems, public support of culture is challenged to greater efforts. These problems also show, however, the degree to which efforts in the area of art and cultural support in the narrow sense can be affected by decisions in other culturally relevant areas, such as entertainment policies. Cultural policy-makers of the Social Democratic Party (SPD) and the ''Green'' party (*Die Grünen*) have been more and more attentive to this relationship in parliamentary debates in the *Länder*.[37]

At the municipal level, the meaning of a widened understanding of culture is becoming especially evident. Correspondingly, the *Städtetag* understands culture in a democratic polity as a communal responsibility: ''Cultural work must serve the expansion and development of the social, communicative, and aesthetic potential and needs of all citizens.''[38] ''Culture for all, with and by all'' is the goal, from which we are still clearly far removed.

Public support for the arts and culture should prevent commercial domination of the lives of citizens in their increasing free time, especially since the attitude of the passive consumer also endangers the further development of a participatory democratic political culture. Thus the principles of cultural activity were recalled at the last meeting of the *Städtetag* in 1983. Cultural activity must stimulate the reflectiveness and contemplativeness of people, promote communication, and support the development of creativity. Especially apparent here is the duty to create and ensure space for leisure and play and for communication and action for the cultural self-development and achievement of identity of individuals, groups, and institutions.

In view of the interrelationship among various political spheres, and in view of the recognized problems of the future, the cultural policy-maker has the duty to ensure that politics in general supports the development of collective cultural interests, and to foster a change in orientation. These are prerequisites for the progressive development of cultural democracy.[39] Support for the arts and culture cannot be limited to the narrow view of maintaining and promoting the traditional institutions of theater, museums, libraries, and orchestras. Support also must be given to a variety of initiatives and groups for neighborhood-centered artistic and cultural educational vitality. The variety of artistic and cultural activities in many communities clearly shows that these recommendations have had an effect and correspond to the changing interests of many citizens.

A growing interest in political questions pertaining to art and culture is shown in the opinions of parties, politicians, and trade unions at countless meetings, in parliamentary interpellations and debates, and in reports of the government. In 1983, the Social Democratic Party created a "Cultural Forum for Social Democracy" to serve as a "bridge between politics and culture" and to which leading personalities from political and cultural life belong as associated members or as members of the board of trustees.[40] One of the working groups associated with the Christian Democratic Union (CDU) joined current discussions with its propositions for a "communal cultural politics" (1981).[41] And the German Trade Unions Federation (DGB) published in 1981 a statement on cultural policy in order to stimulate cultural programs, although they seem rather narrow compared with those of the Weimar Republic. Regional committees of the trade unions were called upon to strengthen their commitment to cultural programs, and to create appropriate working groups.[42]

To be sure, politicians concerned with art and culture usually are relegated to a subordinate role even today. But, on the whole, their place has improved since the 1950s and 1960s. Correspondingly, work in the cultural administrations of the cities usually is regarded more highly than it was in earlier years.

Federal Support for Art and Culture

Programs for the support of culture by the municipalities in particular, but also by the Federation and the *Länder,* became more varied in the 1970s. (The proportion allotted to "alternative culture" is still modest.) The question of possible versus necessary commitment of the Federation, the *Länder,* and the municipalities is always contested.

According to the Basic Law, the Federation has only a few spheres of jurisdiction in the area of cultural policy. It deals with cultural issues involving foreign countries (Art. 32 and Art. 73, Nr. 1 GG), but it also works closely with the *Länder* because of their internal jurisdiction. The Federal Republic also has concurrent legislative authority to protect "German cultural goods against being taken out of the country" (Art. 74, Nr. 5 GG) and for the cultural affairs of refugees and the expellees. It enacts the outline law for the general legal relations of the press and of film (Art. 75, Nr. 2) and for the protection of the environment and the cultivation of land. The authority of the Federal Republic over copyright and contract law (Art. 73, Nr. 9) and also its jurisdiction in the realms of tax law, labor law, and social insurance, are significant for cultural policy. For example, the

"Law for the Social Insurance of Self-employed Artists and Publicists" came into effect on January 1, 1983, after a tough political struggle. The possibility of using the tax laws to support the arts has not yet been exploited adequately. The German Cultural Council (*Deutscher Kulturrat*) recently pointed to the latter in its recommendation "For a Culture-Friendly Tax Law" (1983).[43] In sessions of the Standing Conference of the *Länder* Ministries of Education and Culture, critics representing the viewpoint of the *Länder* contended that the Federation gave preference to its own priorities in support of the arts.[44] The total expenditures of all the federal ministries for the support of art and culture—excluding external cultural programs—amounted to about 356 million DM in 1984.

In fact, the Federation has not limited itself to those areas in which it has explicit constitutional jurisdiction (Basic Law). Since the government declarations by the SDP-FDP coalition of 1973 and 1976, the Federation has made an increasing commitment to art and culture, especially with respect to shared financing of various institutions. The coalition program of the Christian Democratic Union (CDU), the Christian Social Union (CSU), and the Free Democratic Party (FDP) from March 1983 included a declaration that the federal government would "strengthen the support of art and culture in the framework of its constitutional rights and in the interest of national representation."[45]

The federal parliamentary parties also have shown a growing interest in cultural policy through parliamentary interpellations, although so far such initiatives have been supported by only a very small proportion of the deputies.[46]

There is a growing interest of the federal republic in cultural policy areas that do not fall within its express jurisdiction. It has justified its involvement in these areas by appeal to its responsibility for general national cultural representation or by appeal to customs which in part reach back to the nineteenth century. These initiatives have not been accepted without opposition by the *Länder*. In the 1950s, a controversy over the creation of the "Foundation for Prussian Cultural Property" through a federal law (1957) led to a complaint by a few *Land* governments before the Federal Constitutional Court. This Foundation has the duty to maintain and develop "the tradition of the appropriate national institutions" of prewar Prussia. It includes fourteen important museums, as well as a national library and archives, and is "the greatest and most varied but interrelated complex of public cultural institutions in Germany."[47] The Federal Constitutional Court approved the law on the ground that it concerned the consolidation and development of the prewar Prussian collections in Berlin as a "general German duty," representative of the nation.[48] The Foundation is now supported by the Federation and (since 1975) all eleven *Länder* collectively, with the Federation and the *Länder* sharing the cost on a 60 : 40 basis. In 1984, the share of the Federation is approximately 99 million DM.

With respect to the manifold support activities of the Federation, the criterion of the exercise of national tasks with reference to their "general national cultural representation" has been more controversial and also more significant than the criterion of "general German duty." Thus, according to an entry in the budget plan, projects are supported that serve "the preservation of the cultural rank of the nation as well as the presentation of German culture in its totality."[49] The various forms of financial aid given by the Federation and accepted by the *Länder* were not the least important justification given by the Federation for the *fait accompli* of its long-time practice of support.[50]

Primary responsibility for the domestic cultural policy of the Federation lies with the Federal Minister of the Interior, although other ministries have competence for their specific specialties. (External cultural policy is a matter for the Ministry of Foreign Affairs.) In this respect, considerable problems can arise at the federal level concerning consideration of the cultural dimension of politics as well as in coordinatng and effecting the interests of art and culture. These difficulties manifest themselves particularly in relations with the Ministry of Finance and the domestic budget committee of the federal parliament (Bundestag) and they also arise because of the special interests of the individual departments and their correspondingly motivated members of parliament. The difficulties are exacerbated by the fact that there is no organized lobby for the cultural area comparable to those in most other policy fields. The general advocacy of overlapping cultural interests at the federal level has begun to improve since the cultural associations formed the *Deutscher Kulturrat* (German Culture Council) working group in 1982.[51]

Coordination problems among the Federation, the *Länder,* and the municipalities are even more evident. To be sure, a most salutary cooperation of cultural administrations takes place in countless specific projects. Nevertheless, there are still no satisfactory regulations for concretely planned overlapping cooperation.[52]

The Federation sponsors special cultural activities in Bonn and Berlin (Foundation for Prussian Cultural Property) because of the special status of these cities. More than 50 percent of the support monies of the Federal Ministry of the Interior go to Berlin. According to an agreement of 1980, the Federation underwrites 70 percent of cultural expenditures in the capital city of Bonn. This support is especially heavy for theater and concerts. Only a few cultural institutions are supported solely by the Federation. These include the German Library in Frankfurt (1984 budget: 23.4 million DM) and the Federal Archives in Koblenz.[53]

In most cases, however, the Federation shares the financial support of cultural projects[54] that also are supported and operated by the *Länder,* municipalities, associations, and foundations. For example, the Federation shares in the research work of several museums of inter-regional significance (like the German National Museum in Nuremberg and the German Museum in Munich). A group of non-state, public utility institutions that joined together in 1967 as the "Working Group of Independent Cultural Institutions" also receives federal funds. Such important institutions as the Schiller National Museum and the German Academy for Language and Poetry belong to the Working Group. Also supported are inter-regionally important exhibitions and festivals (Bayreuth Festival), artists' associations (for example, the German Music Society [*Deutscher Musikrat*], the Museum Society [*Museumsrat*], etc.), artists' studies abroad, film projects, and, not least, the preservation of monuments.[55] (The Federal Ministry of Education and Science shares the cost of projects for the "cultural education" of youth.) The following measures are important for the support of artists: 2 percent of building costs may be used for the artistic decoration of federal public buildings; in addition, according to a cabinet decision (1976), federal ministries are supposed to spend at least 1 percent of their procurement budgets on contemporary art for exhibition in their offices.[56]

Since 1980, "general nationally significant projects" in the area of art and culture are supposed to be supported under a new budget title with a present allocation of 5.5 million DM. These monies are allotted via two institutions, the "German Literature Fund, Inc." and the "Art Fund, Inc.," that were founded in 1980 by art and literature associations, although two officials of the Federal Ministry of the Interior sit on their boards. These two support commissions are relatively independent, within the guidelines determined by the boards of curators. The German Music Society also receives funding for programs for the promotion of music. The distribution of monies without political strings can be taken as a model for a future "German National Foundation." The Federation created this budget title in reaction to the temporary running aground of efforts to create such a national foundation. After its establishment, the present budget title is meant to cease. The *Länder* have criticized what they regard as a pretension on the part of the Federation.

The concept of a national foundation has been viewed favorably since it was suggested in Federal Chancellor Willy Brandt's government declaration in 1973. However, differing views of the respective jurisdictions of the Federation and the *Länder* prevented any settlement. In June 1984, the Minister-Presidents of all the *Länder* agreed among themselves and with the federal government on a plan, the "Agreement for the Institution of a Cultural Foundation of the *Länder,*" and on an administration agreement between the Federation and the *Länder.*[57] As the name of the Foundation suggests, the *Länder* have maintained successfully their views of their sovereignty in the cultural arena.

The primary duty of the Foundation will be to support significant inter-regional artistic and cultural projects, especially those that until now have been supported by the Federation and via which the Federation has the opportunity to distinguish itself in the cultural sphere. The Federation wanted to provide 13.5 million DM in 1985. The Foundation is expected to seek contributions from other sources, as well, and to be supported by an association of private patrons.

Decision power will be held by the foundation council, consisting of one representative from each of the *Land* governments and—when the federal government is sharing the cost—three representatives of the Federation. Decisions must be unanimous. Also in view of the growing cultural activity of the *Land* parliaments, the dominance of the *Land* governments is not unobjectionable. One must hope that the board of curators appointed by the Foundation Council will in reality be as influential as the Minister-Presidents of the *Länder* assure. This board will consist of twenty experts: ten private patrons, and ten who can be nominated by cultural associations. Involvement of patrons in the allocation of public resources is controversial. (The associations of local governments have not been included in these deliberations about a cultural foundation; their available professional expertise thus has been snubbed.)

Despite many doubts about the plan, the establishment of a national foundation seems convenient in order to improve cooperation in supporting important inter-regional cultural initiatives. In addition, the new foundation could prevent future jurisdictional disputes between the Federation and the *Länder* that might impair their commitment to cultural policy.

The Organization of Cultural Policy

The division of duties and expenditures between *Länder* and municipalities in the individual federal *Länder* varies, partly according to history. Bavaria and Baden-Württemberg have taken over former princely cultural institutions (theaters, musical theaters, galleries, museums) more than the other *Länder*. In Bavaria, 59.7 percent of net expenditures for cultural affairs fell to the *Land* and 40.3 percent fell to the municipalities in 1979. In Baden-Württemberg the percentages were 51.5 percent and 48.5 percent. In contrast, in North Rhine-Westphalia, the municipalities dominated with a share of 80.3 percent.[58]

Support of the arts and culture in the *Länder* is under the jurisdiction of the Ministries of Public Education and Culture, although sometimes the most important responsibilities are divided between two ministries. Some responsibilities of relevance to art and cultural policy also are assumed by some other ministries.

The ministries have advisory commissions for the support of the arts (whose advice the ministers usually follow—in order to save themselves work). Control of policy for art and culture is naturally a matter for the *Land* parliament as a whole, and its cultural policy committee is especially concerned. In recent years, for the first time, a growing interest is recognizable among members of the parliaments, although interested members are still relatively few in number.[59]

Although by the beginning of the 1970s the *Städtetag* already was taking the lead, the *Land* parliaments showed little interest in cultural policy. School and university issues dominated. Only in recent years have *Land* governments and parliaments explored basic conceptual considerations concerning the support of the arts and culture. (The "Artistic-Cultural Education" supplement to the general education plan, which the "Federation-*Länder* Commission for Education Research and the Support of Research" [*Bund-Länder Kommission für Bildungsforschung und Forschungsförderung*] submitted in 1977, was, of course, important for cultural policy as well as for beginning a wider discussion.)

It has become ever more difficult to place political accents in the areas of universities and schools because of the budget cuts in the past few years. Above all at the *Land* level, interest in art and culture is growing due to the rapid growth in the field of microelectronics and the trend toward a leisure society. Rising unemployment also is a factor in this growing interest.

There are discussions at the *Land* level about the development of new electronic media (such as cable and satellite television, video, etc.) and their influence on the leisure time and consumer interests of citizens. These discussions in West Germany are likely to continue in the context of demands by the parties (CDU/CSU and FDP) for development of private television.

In addition, reduced public funding for the arts has alarmed cultural policy-makers, and has challenged them to establish basic principles for public support. Such principles are aimed at preventing cutbacks demanded by other departments, especially the finance ministries. Members of parliament interested in cultural policy, members of the government, and ministry officials can in many cases be presumed to have cooperated in this effort. This common interest unites them despite all ideological differences and party and faction lines.[60]

By a series of questions and interpellations from the *Land* parliaments, several *Land* governments have been prompted to table comprehensive reports, containing accounts of the manifold cultural activities as well as basic cultural principles and guidelines.[61] Questions of support for the arts and culture also have greater weight in budget debates. The most important organ for the cooperation of the *Länder* in cultural politics is the "Standing Conference of the *Länder* Ministers of Education" (abbreviated as KMK). Of course, school and university policies overwhelmingly predominate in the work of the KMK. The conclusions of the KMK have the character of recommendations and must be unanimous. The KMK has a permanent office in Bonn which is run by a secretary general.

In the committee for art and adult education of the KMK, questions of inter-regional significance concerning the support of art and culture are discussed and contacts with the corresponding departments of the federation and the associations of local governments and their committees for the support of culture are established. Very recently, the KMK again made a special recommendation in favor of strengthening this cooperation.[62]

The organization of city and municipal governments is regulated by the local government laws passed by the *Land* parliaments. They vary in the different federal *Länder,* but there are general structural similarities in cultural policy-making processes. Once allowance is made for the historically developed cultural structures, the kind and volume of the commitments of the cities and municipalities depends strongly on the personalities of the heads and leading officials of the cultural administration—their creativity and perception of art, and above all their ability to give attention to a variety of cultural interests and concerns and to represent them competently in the city council.

Cultural administrators are elected officials. According to the size of the city municipality, more or fewer areas of responsibility are grouped under the cultural administration; thus the head of a cultural administration can be responsible not only for the city's cultural institutions (theaters, museums, music schools, libraries) and the support of initiatives, cultural associations, and so forth, but also for adult education, schools, sports, leisure, and youth. The grouping together of several cultural areas in one department that is then divided among different offices also can have the advantage of preventing the isolation of cultural work in a narrow sense.

The ability of a cultural administrator to appear as the spokesman for the interests of all citizens in encouraging recognition of the importance for the city of support for the arts and culture is of crucial importance. Naturally, this is especially important when representing the interests of the arts before the city council which is responsible for granting financial support. According to a widened scope of cultural perception, it is also a matter of integrating the cultural dimension into the general process of formation of political will in the municipalities. The administrator must articulate a widened understanding of culture that highlights the cultural dimension of all city policies. This presupposes an overcoming of departmental egoism in the administrative departments and a correspondingly wide view of culture on the part of the city council and government.

A committee for cultural policy is responsible for the support of the arts and culture in the city council; according to some municipal constitutions, citizens with appropriate expertise can become members of this committee. Moreover, art advisory boards can be established as well.[63] As a whole, the experience in the Federal Republic demonstrates that artistic quality, innovation, and cultural variety can be much better assured by a system of public support for the arts and culture than would be possible with a purely commercial system of support.[64]

The slogan of the *Städtetag,* "culture for all and from all" should not be misunderstood as a leveling down to the standards of a commercial consumer culture. Radio stations as well as the commercial sector profit from public support for the arts.[65]

However, public support for the arts and culture also creates dependencies. Especially where there are small box-office receipts, governmental decision-makers, if subject to insufficient control, may succumb to the temptation to tie the size of their grants (for example, to the theater) to expectations of political good conduct. Spectacular interference with cultural institutions by politicians and administrative officials is an exception. It is hardly possible to trace, however, where convenient adaptations to (supposed) expectations are made. The multiplicity of support channels and political control organs as well as the watchfulness of the mass media are still the best guarantee for the assurance of artistic freedom, especially for positions critical of the establishment.

The dependency of cultural institutions on political decision-making institutions varies. Museum and library heads are officials or employees and subject to supervision and direction. Appeals to the guarantee of freedom of art will not be granted to a museum chief because his work usually is not artistic. "However, the authorities respect the decisions of museum chiefs that demand a special expert knowledge of art, and refrain from taking direct influences."[66] In the city state of Hamburg, a model of wider sharing of decisions is practiced: a museum council, on which professional personnel predominate, decides all important affairs of the museum.[67]

Public theaters are managed by directors who are allowed by temporary limited contracts the freedom to form a program, hire personnel, and produce individual works. Of course, they must "inform" the authorities as to their programs.[68] Thus, the *Städtetag* concluded that cooperation between the director and the democratically elected local government should be encouraged, since even the question of the financial soundness of the program can be raised. Also, the director, especially in the smaller cities, must pay attention to box office considerations—whether his program will appeal to the subscribers and the generally more traditionally oriented audience organizations. The line between necessary cooperation and artistic freedom on one hand, and accommodation and acceptance of influence that limits readiness to take a risk in social criticism on the other, is hard to draw.

Since the end of the 1960s, more participation, especially from those actively involved in the process of artistic creation, has been demanded in connection with discussions about democratization. Barely half of the theaters possess a mechanism for participation (such as an ensemble assembly or a theater advisory council), according to an enquiry of the German Theater Association in 1980. Participation usually is practiced in an informal way without legal grounding. In any case, the artistic production of a theater vitally depends not only on the commitment and creativity of the director and stage managers, but also on that of all participating artists. It follows that some form of participation is necessary.[69]

Advisory commissions have been formed by the ministries involved in various aspects of national support for the arts. The final decision remains with the respective minister in office, but as a rule he follows the advice of his expert commissions, in order to avoid taking sole responsibility for the decisions. In individual cases, nevertheless, different decisions sometimes are made, and if cultural associations (lobbies) and the (parliamentary) opposition enter the scene this can lead to a fight or in some cases to strong public controversies. In important cases, such as appointments to top jobs in the artistic institutions, the minister or the responsible decision-making body of the municipality must publicly justify its choice.

Changes in the Federal Ministry of the Interior's guidelines for the support of filmmaking made by Minister of the Interior F. Zimmermann (CSU) on March 1, 1984, provoked strong opposition as well as public debate on basic issues. The choice of films that are worthy of support is made by a selection committee and its subcommittees, and its advice had been followed strictly by the liberal Minister of the Interior Gerhard R. Baum (FDP): "The state supports; it is not the supervisor and not the controller."[70] The 1984 change, however, made the Minister of the Interior the chairman of the selection committee and its subcommittees (Sec. 21). Strong resistance from the public and the parliamentary opposition allow one to hope that such measures will not be imitated, and also that the watchfulness of the public will prevent more subtle attempts to usurp power.

Traditional and New Forms of Support for the Arts and Culture in the *Länder* and Municipalities

As has been shown, the *Länder* and municipalities assume different shares of the support for the arts in the different federal states. (In the city-states a distinction between *Land*

and municipal duties is hardly relevant.) Basically, municipal cultural programs stem from local needs, and the *Länder* are responsible for general cultural efforts that apply to more than one area.[71] Since the larger cities also provide the inhabitants of the surrounding countryside with cultural offerings, especially cultural institutions such as theater, orchestra, museums, and adult education, they claim financial support from the *Land*. As long as goal-oriented allotments to certain cultural institutions or activities of the communities (such as support for museums) are tied to detailed instructions for their use, associations for local governments criticize them. Papperman argues that making grants "for community cultural work" is a sufficiently detailed mandate, but the acceptance of this idea has become more difficult in the context of contemporary cut-back debates.[72] More than other federal *Länder,* and for historical reasons, Bavaria and Baden-Württemberg support many cultural institutions on their own. Because of the policy of centralization pursued by the House of Wittelsbach, most of the Bavarian *Land* arts institutions (museums, theaters) are found in the *Land* capital, Munich. In Bavaria, a greater measure of decentralization of *Land* efforts now has been pushed for and begun, in order to equalize access to the arts in other parts of Bavaria and to improve the participation of the population of the entire *Land* in cultural life (corresponding to the development program of the *Land*). Accordingly, *Land* support for community theater and orchestras has risen markedly since the 1970s.

According to the museum development program of the Bavarian *Land* government (1979), access to the arts should be spread more equally throughout Bavaria by establishing a larger number of branches of the Munich state museums. In order to approach this goal of improved decentralized offerings, higher subsidies for local and non-state museums were made available (1978:100,000 DM; 1984: 4.6 million DM). Also, scientific and educational advisory services for the non-state museums from a division of the Bavarian National Museum are planned to be further improved.

There is also a rich museum landscape in the other *Länder* of the Federal Republic of Germany: art museums and exhibitions, museums of ethnology and of cultural history, museums of technology and industry. The need "to collect and preserve the material evidence of industrialization, technology, commerce, politics, industry, and everyday culture"[73] is recognized increasingly. Concern with industrial culture as part of the history of everyday life that is especially close to us should strengthen democratic-republican identity.[74]

Museums are operated and financed in the first instance by the *Länder* and municipalities, but also by the Federation. Beyond that, there are museums belonging to foundations that receive the majority or a part of their financial support from public sources, as well as a large number of private art galleries. The municipalities, especially the larger cities, spent 459 million DM in 1981 for museums, and the *Länder* spent 320 million DM.[75] After World War II, the reconstruction of destroyed museum buildings was given special priority. In the 1950s and 1960s, exhibitions without educational concerns were common; in the 1970s, in connection with a changing perception of culture, more value was placed on opening up museums through improved outreach programs and museum educational services.[76] This process is by no means complete and must be continued.[77] Growing interest in visiting museums and exhibitions confirms cultural policy-makers in this view (54 million visitors in 1981).

Public libraries are important cultural centers in the cities and municipalities, and often have been developed further as meeting places via additional cultural offerings. In 1973, the "Plan for a Comprehensive Library Network for the Federal Republic of

Germany'' (Library Plan), the goals of which may seem utopian today, but which certainly caused excitement, was submitted to a congress of all library branches and associations. Since then, existing libraries have been enlarged and improved and many new and attractive libraries have been established. This occurred not only in the big cities, but especially in the remaining 8,438 towns and municipalities with their 40 million inhabitants: the number of libraries run on a full-time employment basis by communities or churches has risen from 411 in 1973 to 674. Total expenditures have grown fourfold.[78] Economy measures since 1981 nevertheless have endangered this positive development. Monies for book acquisition have been cut drastically especially often. (''Cutbacks in acquisition monies of the library'' were cited 53 times in a study of 86 cities by the *Städtetag*.) In the case of severe cuts in the acquisition budgets, the libraries rapidly lost their currency and thus their attraction for those who are interested in reliable information and career advancement.[79] In an appeal to the *Land* government and parliament in North Rhine-Westphalia, where allotments to the communities had dropped from 8.1 million DM in 1980 to 2.6 million DM in 1983, it was established that the information value of the libraries would diminish substantially by the end of the 1980s if such measures continued.[80]

The theaters are centers of cultural life in many cities, and they naturally play a role in the cities' competition for prestige. In 74 municipalities, there are at present 84 public theater organizations with their own ensembles, offering performances at 258 places.[81] Most of these theaters offer not only plays, but also opera, ballet, musicals, operetta, and concerts in their repertoire. The orchestras of the musical theaters have prominent significance for many cities, not only through concerts, establishing chamber music circles, and so forth, but also through the sideline music education activities of many of their members. (Independent opera houses are found in some metropolises, such as the Bavarian National Opera in Munich.) Municipalities and towns that do not have their own theater organizations often have stages to offer to publicly supported traveling theater groups (the *Land* theater organization) and also to commercial touring theater groups.

Although the overwhelming number of theater groups are run by the municipalities, there are 18 state theater organizations. In the 1982–83 season, over 19 million visitors attended the public theaters. There were 32,224 performances, of which 15,307 were plays (9,272 musical theater, 1,624 ballets, 3,307 children's and youth theater). The sale of tickets covers only a small proportion of the total cost—at present, 16.7 percent. In all, public allotments amount to 1.59 billion DM for the fiscal year. The share devoted to the theater in cultural expenditures of cities with over 20,000 inhabitants dropped from 41.5 percent in 1975 to 36.4 percent (1982), but it is still considerable.[82] In small cities, the theater budget accounts for between two-thirds and three-quarters of the total cultural budget, which is why readiness to erect new theaters is scarce.

According to the *Städtetag,* responsibility for the support of a local theater should not be established in the future by *Land* law, but rather it will be produced, at least for larger cities (over 150,000 inhabitants), by the expectations of the citizens and the cultural perception and self-consciousness of the cities.

In the face of scarcer financial resources, cultural policy-makers and administrators of the municipalities and the *Länder* have come under political pressure, which naturally comes especially from finance ministers and treasurers. The question of the cultural significance of playhouses, opera houses, and other artistic-cultural institutions, the influence of cutbacks on the continuation and quality of the offerings, and finally the question of what financial support is to be expected from the *Länder* all play a role in this. In discussions of cultural policy, the question of the effects of cutbacks is to some extent being linked to arguments pertaining to well-known structural problems (participation, flexibility, etc.).

The financial commitment of the *Länder* to the support of the theater varies, depending most importantly on whether the *Land* maintains its own state theater. Altogether, on average, the *Länder* at present assumes 43 percent of the running costs, with the contributions of Bavaria and Lower Saxony being above average (52 percent and 58 percent, respectively), while North Rhine-Westphalia contributes only 12 percent. The cities also share to different extents in the financing of the state theater. Community theater receives *Land* subsidies from all the *Länder*. In Bavaria, which spends at present 125.5 million DM, mostly, however, for the benefit of the state theaters, support for community theater fluctuates between 30 and 40 percent of subsidy requirements. The parties in the *Land* parliament have successfully prevented further cutbacks.

In North Rhine-Westphalia, with reference to higher general allotments, the financing of the theater was left largely to the cities. Stronger commitment came as late as 1975. In 1982, however, funds were cut drastically and since then have not been restored. This increased the tendency for existence-endangering cuts in municipal theater budgets.[83] Not least because of a resolute comment of the *Städtetag,* the *Land* parliamentary parties have agreed that support monies should be raised step by step back to the level of 1981.[84] Supported by public protests, cultural policy-makers from the *Länder* and the municipalities resist, not without some success, attempts to search for cutback possibilities especially in the support of art and culture. The monies previously assigned to the support of individual artists and alternative cultural activities have been particularly endangered. Cultural policy-makers, however, can argue plausibly that proposed short-term cutbacks in cultural institutions lead to rapid loss of substance and observable loss of quality. With theaters, this is the case with respect to apparently minor cutbacks of 5 to 10 percent in one year. Since the greater part of personnel costs (administration, choir, orchestra) are fixed by collective salary contracts, in the short run the cutbacks can be made only by not renewing the mostly short-term contracts with solo artists (actors, singers, etc.). (Thus the director of the state theater in Kassel calculated that mandated cutbacks of 4 million DM from a budget of 33 million DM would lead to the discharge of almost all soloists.[85])

Since the beginning of the 1970s, a large number of citizen initiatives have been generated.[86] This citizen initiative movement has been sparked especially by environmental problems, city development problems, and recently also by the peace movement. It articulates a growing interest in political participation and is the expression of a change in cultural consciousness. A large proportion of these initiatives are active in "sociocultural" areas.[87] With these manifold cultural initiatives in many different areas, independent groups and associations perceive themselves as "alternative" in the sense that they develop their communicative and creative abilities free from political and institutional supervision and want to participate in the formation of their environment. Their cultural significance is recognized increasingly by the municipalities, and thus in many places already existing groups (for example, music clubs, lay choirs, etc.) are newly "discovered." Viewed as a whole, since the 1970s artistic work independent of institutions (art and music associations, independent artists) and also "alternative cultural offerings," such as neighborhood festivals, jazz and rock music, cultural and communications centers, film clubs, etc. have been supported more strongly. Of course, the cultural-political commitment of the municipalities varies greatly. In some, there are signs that, in the existing financial difficulties of the municipalities, funds for these programs will be cut first, although the share for new cultural projects in the general cultural budget is usually very small (1 to 2 percent). (The share for private theaters and independent theater groups together makes up only 3 percent of the general public subsidy for the theater.[88]) Little by little, some cities are changing and establishing a budget title for the support of initiatives and associations in order to provide continuing and flexible support. Since support presupposes self-commitment and follows the principle of "helping them to help themselves" (e.g., through guarantees against loss), in many cities varied activities could be supported and encouraged with comparatively limited funds. Cultural administrations in some cities provide important help through information and procurement activities, such as providing administrative support for groups and non-public institutions.

When initiatives and associations require direct subsidies for performances, for example, there are understandably problems of evaluation and political dependency. The usual practice of granting subsidies according to the number of members has been criticized by the cultural committee of the *Städtetag* in its suggestions for "The Support of Cultural Associations by Cities." Instead, the *Städtetag* argues that support should depend on qualitative criteria; minimum standards should be established. "Thus, for example, associations that largely or usually have come forward in public with good performances and also those that in special measure demonstrate creativity should be supported."[89] Nevertheless, general criteria are lacking. In practice, evaluations of worthiness for support are made according to different and often subjective criteria. Not to infringe on self-government, it is necessary here that substantive instructions be avoided and assistance follow as unbureaucratically as possible, in order to avoid (self-) limitation, like that which can be observed repeatedly in public artistic-cultural institutions. In the last analysis, this can be avoided only via the control exercised by the public and the local press. The fear that such initiatives can fall into dependence and be pressed by financial difficulties to prove themselves worthy of support through appropriate political conduct is certainly not unfounded. (Some initiatives thus renounce public subsidies of their own will.)

Therefore, among other things, other forms of support besides direct subsidies are preferred and received from the *Kulturpolitischer Gesellschaft* (Association for Cultural Policies), for example, provision of musical instruments, video and film projectors, etc., and especially practice and performance spaces. (See note 33.)

In the bigger cities, such efforts are associated with increasing insight into the significance of decentralized cultural work. Meanwhile, in many cities, there are cultural and communications centers that have been established in empty workshops, warehouses, and run-down dwellings. Small cultural centers especially have proven their value in the neighborhoods (sections). They sometimes are run by the municipalities, but usually by associations that may have resulted from citizen initiatives and in some cases are supported by the city. Thus, the city of Hamburg created a budget title for "support of social-cultural neighborhood centers" in 1979. A series of cultural houses has appeared since then. As support criteria the following were named: the planned measures should enrich the cultural life of the city; the independent initiative of the group should already be evident; communication among individuals and groups in the neighborhood should be encouraged by the activities; and, above all, the activities should not be limited to members of the group or association, but should be open to the public in the urban neighborhood.[90]

The cultural administration of Hamburg draws a positive conclusion: "State support has meant that citizens in unexpected numbers have liberated their creative and organizational abilities and developed a brisk cultural life everywhere, with two effects:

> art in the sense of cultural production is decentralized; people who until now have been denied access to art for different reasons can participate more widely in communally created cultural wealth;
>
> out of their daily relations in the neighborhood, people together form their environment and create from it an identifiable cultural milieu."[91]

From such cultural houses ("culture shops"), groups and initiatives can obtain practical help and qualitative stimulation. Here also cooperation with central artistic institutions is sought: with mobile productions (for example, children's theater), people are reached who do not decide to visit the central institutions. (This should be adopted especially to support participation and creative independent activity.[92])

Although in the early 1970s demands for an alternative culture were directed against the traditional cultural institutions, such confrontations have become rarer. "The traditional institutions need the impulse to 'freer, more varied,' and better supplementary cultural expression, as much as independent groups must accept being measured against the productions of the existing institutions," according to the statement of the *Städtetag*.[93] In discussions of cultural policy and in part also in practice, the relationships among qualified artistic work, musical-cultural education ("animation"), and creative and communicative development of lay persons are emphasized increasingly. In fact, the more the variety of cultural places in a community, the more professional artistic performances can serve as a sensitizing and creative stimulus, in which creative development, communicative experience, and cultural learning are possible and actually take place.[94]

Arrangements for cultural-pedagogical assistance and motivation are as important as many forms of cooperation. Cooperation and reciprocal stimulation of cultural institutions, and also among cultural institutions, independent creative artists, and cultural initiatives, have been improved in many places, and proved, for example, in neighborhood festivals and cultural theme days (such as peace weeks); but in many municipalities it is still below expectations. In the context of the cutback debates, it is also suggested that the traditional cultural institutions put more material means, space, and personnel at the disposal of independent groups and artists.[95] Also because of cultural-pedagogical efforts, as suggested by the plan of a Federal-*Länder* Commission and the *Städtetag* for "artistic-cultural education," many of these institutions have opened their doors to a wider public. Libraries and, above all, museums have improved their presentation and public relations work and, partly in cooperation with schools and adult education schools, have built up their cultural education services.

The theater has a central significance for cultural education. Offerings of children's theater and youth theater expanded in the 1970s, although they are threatened again in part by cutbacks. Various forms of cooperation between schools and theaters are practiced, but the theater experience is still sporadic for most school children. Curricula of music schools, in which over 600,000 young people are taught, have been expanded considerably.[96] Adult education schools serve an important function in cultural education, with their often plentiful offerings. (In 1982, adult education schools numbered 404 with 2,496 external locations.[97])

In order to enhance the importance of culture in city development, and to assure long-term financing on the basis of an established cultural policy, since the mid-1970s some cities have established cultural development plans.[98] Through forward-looking planning, a framework for cultural activities designed for several years is created. In it, the cultural associations and initiatives as well as the respective offerings of the churches, trade unions, etc. should be considered. The close relationship of culture to other areas of communal policy (education, sports, recreation)—and thus also consideration of the cultural dimension of general development in the municipality—should be assured through incorporation in the process of city development planning. In this context, the increasing importance of protection and preservation of monuments is reflected. For the latter, since the 1970s, more, though not yet sufficient, public resources have been made available.[99]

[Translated by J. C. Laursen]

Notes

1. UNESCO, *Recommendation on Participation by the People at Large in Cultural Life and their Contribution to It.* Nairobi. 26 Nov. 1976. According to this recommendation, "the Member States or the appropriate authorities . . . [should] encourage, extend and strengthen the network of cultural and artistic institutions not only in large towns but also in smaller towns, villages and urban neighbourhoods."

2. Council of Europe, Standing Conference of Local and Regional Authorities of Europe and Council of Europe's Council for Cultural Cooperation, "Town and Culture—New Responses to Cultural Problems." Bremen Declaration, Strasbourg, 27 May 1983.

3. Cf. M. Abelein, *Die Kulturpolitik des Deutschen Reiches und der Bundesrepublik Deutschland* (Köln, 1968), 252.

4. The senators (ministers) from West Berlin who are responsible for schools, science, and art and culture are, for example, members of the Standing Conference of the *Länder* Ministers of Education (KMU).

5. According to Art. 79, para. 3 of the Basic Law, the political foundation of the Federal Republic may not be abolished even through a change in the constitution.

6. E. Benda, W. Maihofer, H.-J. Vogel (eds.), *Handbuch des Verfassungsrechts der Bundesrepublik Deutschland* (Berlin/New York, 1983), 809–949.

7. Sekretariat der Kultusministerkonferenz (ed.), *Kulturpolitik der Länder, 1979–1981* (Bonn, 1982), 304. (An example from Bavaria: of a total state budget for the year 1984 of 36.8 billion DM, 11.34 billion were designated for cultural affairs in the wider sense, within the responsibility of the Minister for Education and Culture, of which 0.43 billion DM were for "art and culture.")

8. See below, "Changes in the Understanding of Culture," for an expanded understanding of culture.

9. "Öffentliche Ausgaben für Kunst und Kulturpflege," *Veröffentlichungen der Kultusministerkonferenz,* Oct. 1983.

10. *Ibid.*

11. "Kultur in unseren Städten unverzichtbar," in: Deutscher Städtetag, *Unser Land braucht starke Städte* (Köln, 1983), 141. In the *Deutscher Städtetag* roughly 500 cities are represented with their 31 million inhabitants. Membership is free. These cities include the city states (Berlin, Hamburg, Bremen), all bigger cities, and about 530 municipalities. Regional associations have been established in all *Länder.* The headquarters is in Köln with approximately 100 employees working in 11 departments; further, 13 expert committees have been set up. The meeting of the delegates takes place every two years.

12. J. Grabbe, ''Finanzierung kultureller Aufgaben,'' in: E. Pappermann, M. Mombaur, J. -Th. Blank, *Kulturarbeit in der kommunalen Praxis* (Köln, 1984), 14; G. Kreissig, H. Tressler, J.v. Uslar, *Kultur in den Städten—eine Bestandsaufnahme* (Köln, 1979).

13. Clearly no cultural-political abstinence on the part of the State can be derived from this, since it appears opportunely under the demand for a guarantee of artistic freedom of Art. 5, par. 3, of the Basic Law; cf. among others, U. Steiner, D. Grimm, *Kulturauftrag im staatlichen Gemeinwesen* (Berlin/New York, 1984), (Veröffentlichungen der Vereinigung der Deutschen Staatsrechtslehrer, 42), 7–80.

14. BVerfGE 36, 321 (331).

15. ''Kultur in unseren Städte unverzichtbar,'' 141. W. Ismayr, ''Perspektiven einer kulturellen Demokratie,'' in: *Aus Politik und Zeitgeschichte,* B 40/79, 6 Oct. 1979, pp. 29–46.

16. U. Steiner, 38.

17. For example, P. Häberle, *Kulturpolitik in der Stadt. Ein Verfassungsauftrag* (Hamburg, 1979); F. Hufen, ''Kulturauftrag als Selbstverwaltungsgarantie,'' in: *Neue Zeitschrift für Verwaltungsrecht,* no. 9, 1983, p. 520.

18. Deutscher Städtetag, *Starke Städte—lebendige Demokratie* (Stuttgart, 1979), 261.

19. *Unser Land braucht starke Städte* (*Deutscher Städtetag*), 144–45.

20. For a critique, see E. Pappermann, ''Grundzüge eines kommunalen Kulturverfassungsrechts,'' in: DVBl., 1/15 Sept. 1980, p. 705.

21. *Deutscher Städtetag, Wege zur menschlichen Stadt* (Köln, 1973), 124.

22. *Unser Land braucht starke Städte,* 144–45.

23. E. Pappermann, 705; see ''Vorstellungen des DGB zur Kulturpolitik und Kulturarbeit'' (Düsseldorf, Oct. 1981).

24. See below, ''The Organization of Cultural Policy.''

25. See *Unser Land braucht starke Städte,* 141; E. Pappermann, ''Grundzüge''; H. Hoffmann, *Kultur für alle* (Frankfurt, 1981[2]); H. Glaser, K. H. Stahl, *Bürgerrecht Kultur* (Berlin, 1983).

26. See notes 11 and 18, and especially: ''Bildung und Kultur als Element der Stadtentwicklung'' in *Wege zur menschlichen Stadt* (Köln, 1973), 97–113.

27. *Hinweise des Deutschen Städte- und Gemeindebundes zur Kulturarbeit,* 1980. ''Empfehlungen des Deutschen Landkreistages zur Kulturarbeit der Kreise,'' in: *Der Landkreis,* 1980, p. 528.

28. See J. Grabbe, 14; H. Hoffmann, in: *Die Deutsche Bühne,* no. 6, 1984, pp. 17–21.

29. See I.-M. Greverus, in: W. R. Langenbucher, R. Rytlewski, B. Weyergraf, *Kulturpolitisches Wörterbuch* (Stuttgart, 1983), 344; I.-M. Greverus, *Kultur und Alltagswelt* (München, 1978).

30. ''Leitsätze zur kommunalen Kulturarbeit'' (1952), in: *Kulturpolitik des Deutschen Städtetages* (Köln, 1979), 62.

31. *Wege zur menschlichen Stadt;* W. Kücker, *Architektur zwischen Kunst und Konsum* (Frankfurt, 1976), 12.

32. *Wege zur menschlichen Stadt,* 91–102; ''Kultur durch Kommunikation?,'' *Loccumer Protokolle,* no. 1, 1976.

33. *Ibid.;* see notes 1 and 2; Council of Europe, *Ad hoc Conference of European Ministers with Responsibility for Cultural Affairs* (Strasbourg, 1976). The Kulturpolitische Gesellschaft (Association of Cultural Policies) consists of artists, politicians, administrators, and scientists, all engaged in cultural affairs.

34. UNESCO, ''Recommendation,'' *op. cit.,* III A.

35. See, among others, E. Eppler, *Wege aus der Gefahr* (Hamburg, 1981).

36. See, for example, D. Fohrbeck, *Türkische Kulturarbeit in der Bundesrepublik Deutschland,* Kulturpolitische Gesellschaft, Dokumentation 17 (Hagen, 1983).

37. See the interim report of the inquiry commission, *Neue Informations- und Kommunika-*

tionstechniken, Deutscher Bundestag, Drucksache 9/2442, pp. 123–25; Bürgerschaft der Freien und Hansestadt Hamburg, Plenarprotokoll 11/25, 15 Nov. 1983, p. 1477; Landtag von Baden-Württemberg, Plenarprotokoll 8/76, 9 Nov. 1983, p. 6268.

38. *Wege zur menschlichen Stadt,* 99.

39. *Ibid.,* p. 91; W. Ismayr, 1980; and W. Ismayr, "Von der Neuorientierung zu neuen Perspektiven. Kulturpolitische Verpflichtungen der öffentlichen Hand," in: *Das Parlament,* no. 37/38, 1980.

40. R. Schattenfoh, "Ziele und Aufgaben eines Kulturforums der SPD," in: *Die Neue Gesellschaft,* no. 5, 1983, pp. 468.

41. Arbeitskreis "kommunale Kulturpolitik" beim Institut für Kommunalwissenschaften der Konrad-Adenauer-Stiftung e.V., *Kommunale Kulturpolitik (Thesen),* Sankt Augustin, 1981.

42. *Vorstellungen des Deutschen Gewerkschaftsbundes zur Kulturpolitik und Kulturarbeit,* edited by DGB-Bundesvorstand (Düsseldorf, 1981), 21.

43. Für ein kulturfreundliches Steuerrecht. Steuerpolitische Vorschläge des Deutschen Kulturrates (Bonn, 1983).

44. Position of the Standing Conference of the *Länder* Ministers of Education, 212th plenary session, 18–19 Nov. 1982.

45. See the interpellation of the governing parliamentary parties (CDU/CSU, FDP): "Kulturförderungspolitik der Bundesregierung" of 7 Dec. 1983, Deutscher Bundestag, Drucksache 10/785.

46. *Ibid.* and interpellation of the Social Democratic Parliamentary Party (SPD), Deutscher Bundestag, Drucksache 10/382, 9/14/83. The subcommittee for "art and culture" of the Committee for the Interior (with Freimut Duve as the dedicated chairman) which was established in the ninth voting period was not reinstituted in the tenth voting period because of the protests of the CDU/CSU parties.

47. W. Knopp, in *Der Bund und die Künste* (Bonn, 1980), 44.

48. BVerfGE 10, 20; W. Maihofer, in *Handbuch des Verfassungsrechts,* 979–80.

49. Federal budget, Einzelplan 0602, explanations of title 68122.

50. H. Hieronymus, in *Der Bund und die Künste,* 12.

51. Deutscher Kulturrat—working group of the sections of music, theater, literature, arts, architecture, design, film/audiovision, sociocultural activities.

52. S. von Köckritz, in *Der Bund und die Künste.*

53. Information from the Federal Ministry of the Interior (BMI).

54. Kulturförderung des BMI, Arbeitspapier des Bundesministeriums des Inneren, p. 3.

55. *Ibid.* and *Der Bund und die Künste.* The 1984 budget (EPl. 06) includes, among others, the following estimates: museums, 14.3 million DM; festivals, 9.7 million DM; preservation of monuments, 10.2 million; music, 14.7 million; film, 9.6 million DM.

56. Appendix 2 to EPl. 06, p. 443.

57. Entwurf eines Abkommens zur Errichtung der Kulturstiftung der Länder (6 June 1984); Entwurf eines Abkommens über die Mitwirkung des Bundes an der Kulturstiftung der Länder (6 June 1984).

58. *Kulturarbeit in der kommunalen Praxis,* 14.

59. See note 61.

60. For example, Landtag Nordrhein-Westfalen, Plenarprotokoll 9/90, 8 Feb. 1984, p. 5233; Bayerischer Landtag, Plenarprotokoll 10/15, 24 March 1983, p. 687, and Concluding Recommendation of the Budget Committee, Drucksache 10/472. W. Ismayr, "Kulturförderung zwischen Neuorientierung und Sparzwängen," in: *Aus Politik und Zeitgeschichte,* B 27, 7 July 1984, pp. 3ff.

61. For example, interpellation of the Social Democratic Parliamentary Party (SPD), Landtag Baden-Württemberg, Drucksache 8/2636; answer of the *Land* government, Drs. 8/2839; and the plenary debate, Plenarprotokoll 8/76, 9 Nov. 1983; Bayerischer Landtag, Interpellations of the Free Democratic Party (FDP) (Drucksache 9/9668) and the Christian Social Union (CSU) (Drs. 9/10377)

and the plenary debate, Plenarprotokoll 9/111, 26 Jan. 1982; Interpellation of the SPD parliamentary party in Niedersächsischen Landtag, Drs. 10/1812; answer of the *Land* government, Drs. 10/2346; and the plenary debate, Plenarprotokoll 10/42, 15 Feb. 1984.

62. *Kulturpolitik der Länder,* 311.

63. See B. Dieckmann, in: Pappermann et al., 173.

64. See *Kultur für die Stadt—Chancen und Grenzen bei knappen Kassen.* Gespräche im Konrad-Adenauer-Haus, 8 Dec. 1982.

65. See W. Ismayr, *Das politische Theater in Westdeutschland (1977)* (Königstein, 1985[2]); K. Fohrbeck and A. J. Wiesand, *Musik, Statistik, Kultur* (Köln, 1982).

66. *Unser Land braucht starke Städte,* 149.

67. Kulturbehörde Hamburg: *Kulturbericht 1982,* p. 45; F. Ossenbühl, "Mitbestimmung in der Kunst," DÖV, no. 19, 1983, p. 786.

68. Intendanten-Mustervertrag des Deutschen Bühnenvereins: *Unser Land braucht starke Städte,* 149.

69. Deutscher Bühnenverein, *Umfrage über Mitsprache und Mitbestimmung an den Theatern und Orchestern,* 1980; W. Ismayr, *Das politische Theater in Westdeutschland,* 425–61.

70. Aktuelle Stunde, Deutscher Bundestag, Plenarprotokoll 10/57, 24 Feb. 1984, p. 4042 (G. R. Baum).

71. E. Pappermann, *op. cit.,* and J. Grabbe, 22.

72. E. Pappermann, "Grundzüge eines kommunalen Kulturverfassungsrechts," 710.

73. Instructions of the cultural committee of the Deutscher Städtetag for "Städtische Museumsförderung," 27 Dec. 1983.

74. See H. Glaser, "Industriekultur und demokratische Identität," in: *Aus Politik und Zeitgeschichte,* B 41–42/1981.

75. Kultusministerkonferenz, *Öffentliche Ausgaben für Kunst und Kulturpflege 1976 bis 1983,* Oct. 1983.

76. V. Plagemann, in Pappermann et al. *Kulturarbeit in der kommunalen Praxis,* op cit., 95–103.

77. Instructions of the Deutscher Städtetag for "Städtische Museumsförderung," op. cit.

78. "Bibliotheksplan 1973, Eine Bilanz nach zehn Jahren," in: *Buch und Bibliothek,* no. 7/8, 1983, p. 556.

79. "Mut zur Zukunft?," in: *Buch und Bibliothek,* no. 7/8, 1983, pp. 575ff.

80. Position taken by the North Rhine-Westfalia Städtetag on 4 Nov. 1983; thanks to a concerted effort by the cultural politicians of the government and opposition parties in the *Land* parliament, the expenditures were raised somewhat again.

81. Deutscher Bühnenverein. *Theaterstatistik 1982/83.* Edited by F.-H. Köhler.

82. *Ibid.;* items from F.-H. Köhler.

83. Concluding recommendations of the budget committee of the Bavarian *Land* parliament, Drucksache 10/472; Bayerischer Landtag, PlPr 10/15, 24. 3. 1983; Stellungnahme des Städtetages Nordrhein-Westfalen zur Haushaltsplanung 1984 des Landes Nordrhein-Westfalen, Theaterfinanzierung (Nov. 1983).

84. Landtag Nordrhein-Westfalen, Drucksache 9/3090.

85. M. Beilharz, in: *Unser Land braucht starke Städte,* 162–63.

86. See U. Kempf, B. Guggenberger, *Bürgerinitiativen und repräsentatives System* (Opladen, 1984[2]); H. Klages, P. Kmieciak (eds.), *Wertwandel und gesellschaftlicher Wandel* (Frankfurt/New York, 1979).

87. See, for example, the documentation of the foundation, "Die Mitarbeit," Heiligenhaus.

88. Deutscher Bühnenverein, *Theaterstatistik 1982/83;* J. Grabbe, Loccumer Protokolle, *Kultur für alle—von allen? Zwischenbilanz der Alternativ-Szene,* no. 6, 1980.

89. *Kulturpolitik des Deutschen Städtetages* (Köln, 1979), 197.

90. Kulturbehörde (ed.), *Stadtteilkultur in Hamburg* (Hamburg, 1982), 4.

91. *Ibid.,* 1.

92. Important initiatives have come from Hermann Glaser, the cultural administrator of the city of Nuremberg; H. Glaser, K. H. Stahl, *Bürgerrecht Kultur* (Berlin, 1983).

93. *Unser Land braucht starke Städte,* 151.

94. W. Ismayr, "Perspektiven einer kulturellen Demokratie," 41.

95. E. Pappermann et al., *Kulturarbeit in der kommunalen Praxis.*

96. *Statistisches Jahrbuch Deutscher Gemeinden* (Köln, 1982), 172.

97. *Statistisches Jahrbuch Deutscher Gemeinden* (Köln, 1983), 216.

98. E. Kloberg, T. Mirbach, *Kulturentwicklungsplanung in Grosskommunen und Stadtstaaten in der Bundesrepublik Deutschland* (Hamburg, 1981); D. Baacke, P. Wolters, N. Sievers, *Kulturentwicklungsplanung III,* Kulturpolitische Gesellschaft, Dokumentation 16 (Hohenhof, 1981); W. Ismayr, "Kulturpolitik und demokratische Kultur," in *Die Mitarbeit, Zeitschrift zur Gesellschafts—und Kulturpolitik,* no. 213, 1979, pp. 207–73; W. Ismayr, "Perspektiven einer kulturellen Demokratie," 44–46.

99. Deutsches Nationalkomitee für Denkmalschutz, *Zur Lage des Denkmalschutzes und der Denkmalpflege in der Bundesrepublik Deutschland,* Memorandum (Bonn, 1983).

4

State Intervention in the Arts in Italy from 1945 to 1982

GIUSEPPE PALMA AND GUIDO CLEMENTE DI SAN LUCA

Italy is a country rich in artistic traditions and endowed with an immense historical heritage. Italian public intervention in the so-called *traditional arts* (painting, sculpture, architecture, poetry, and literature) has been concerned primarily with the preservation of this existing patrimony. Its mere maintenance absorbs all the public resources currently available, and in fact even these are insufficient. Other than expenditures for artistic education and for the encouragement of writing, public intervention designed to sustain artistic "production" in the traditional arts is almost totally absent. For these disciplines, therefore, the discussion in this chapter is focused primarily on the administrative organization and related activities of the responsible agency (currently the Ministry of the Cultural Heritage). Here, the main focus is on maintaining the existing heritage.

A different approach must be taken regarding the so-called *representative arts* (cinema, theater, music). These disciplines benefit from a system of articulated support, although the qualitative, but above all the quantitative, inadequacy of the means employed is lamentable. For these art forms, the chapter focuses on the organization and activities of the Ministry of Tourism and Entertainment, and outlines the system of governmental aid to the arts for which this Ministry is responsible.

First of all, however, it is important to emphasize briefly that the complexities of the Italian system of public administration, especially the so-called "plurality of public administrations,"[1] is reflected also in the various sectors of the arts field. Within them, in fact, the agencies of the central government are not the only "public" authorities. In addition there are the so-called "parallel administrations" and the administrations of the "autonomous territorial agencies." The difficulty, if not the impossibility, of surveying all of the relevant activities of these many agencies means that this study is necessarily incomplete. Its subject is more precisely "State intervention" rather than "public intervention" *tout court*.

After a brief review of the Fascist period, from which the current Italian system, either as a continuation or as a repudiation, descends, and a sketch of the guidelines set forth on the subject by the Constitution of 1948, this study is divided into three parts. First, the evolution of the administrative apparatus from 1945 to the 1980s. Second, the evolution of public activities for the arts in the same period. And third, an analysis of ministerial expenditures in the various sectors of the arts.

Public intervention in the arts was not an unfamiliar topic to Italian juridical thought even at the turn of the century. In a 1906 memorandum, Raggi, with far-reaching insight, proposed to "demonstrate the relevance that art can and does assume in public law, [and] the necessity and multiplicity of its relations with public administration."[2] Taking for granted that art fulfills an eminently social function, Raggi distinguishes among several reasons why it is necessary for art to become a subject for administrative action: "State involvement is especially useful, positive, and preferable, and therefore obligatory: when one is dealing with interests that are too abstract, primarily non-economic in nature, not amenable to prompt economic reward and whose pursuit cannot obey the laws of the marketplace; when the benefits are attained only after a long delay; when their promise may only be fully appreciated by future generations; and for which individual resources are insufficient." All of the forgoing conditions, which for Raggi constitute "the standard by which the need for administrative intervention is measured,"[3] hold in the field of the arts.

Without wishing to enter into the controversy regarding the wisdom of "cultural politics" or, even more, concerning the difference between "cultural politics" and the "politics of culture,"[4] one still cannot avoid touching briefly on the relationship between Fascism and culture,[5] since the basis for public intervention in the arts was first institutionalized during the Fascist period. There is no doubt that the historical and political motivations for involvement by the Fascist State went far beyond those that inherently propel all modern States toward cultural activism.[6] Furthermore, Fascism expressly sustained the concept of a hierarchy between politics and art,[7] and this might be taken as a reason to pass over this period since the pathology of such an attitude is evident. Nonetheless, it is imperative to discuss the subject briefly because of the considerable impact left by the regime on the contemporary institutional structure.

In the absence at the beginning of century of any distinctively Italian cultural policy, Fascism presented a revolutionary face, theorizing on the need for intervention in the cultural sector. The involvement was essentially due, on the one hand, to the need to remedy the crisis which followed the assassination of Matteotti in June 1924 (which had widened the scope of opposition to the regime, especially among intellectuals). This led to development of a scheme to reattract intellectuals to the channels of "official" culture (the Italian Royal Academy was established for this purpose).[8] On the other hand, involvement was related to Mussolini's conviction that it was necessary to pass from the phase of "agitation" to one of "cultural integration" of the conscience of the various groups in Italian society (this was to be attained through the National Institute of Fascist Culture).[9] Even though these two were the actual goals of the regime, our primary concern is with the effects that the pursuit of such objectives produced: the growth of Fascist consciousness within cultural agencies;[10] the incremental growth of the Ministry of Popular Culture (MINCULPOP);[11] the resistance of the Ministry of National Education which sought to retain control over the artistic patrimony and which went so far as to try to extend its mandate to modern art.[12]

This resistance had the virtue of denying the nation's historical artistic patrimony to MINCULPOP's "loving care," and to MINCULPOP's attendant devotion to the repression of every cultural expression that was not perfectly attuned to Fascist doctrine. But, it also may have contributed decisively to the definitive separation between "traditional art" and "representative art" in so far as organizational schemes are concerned. The continued existence of this separation[13] produces no small hardship today in the definition and pursuit of a comprehensive cultural policy.

The ideological and political justifications for Fascist intervention in the cultural sector obviously vanished with the republican Constitution of 1948. The Constitution asserts both that "the Republic promotes the development of culture" (Art. 9, co. 1), and that "art and science are free as is their teaching" (Art. 33, co. 1). As has been claimed, "the two constitutional propositions . . . do not create an antithesis, but indicate that an equilibrium between public powers and culture must be sought."[14] The Constituent Assembly's choice, in its support of public promotion, nevertheless was for the "negation of the ideological-cultural monism inherent in the totalitarian fascist State."[15] One cannot help but agree with this observation, especially if one thinks of Article 22, co. 1 as bolstering the freedom of art and science beyond the more general principle of freedom of expression expressed in Article 21 of the Constitution. The special consideration given to the freedom of art and science can be explained by "opposition to the totalitarian regime which had been notoriously distinguished by its attempt to enslave the arts to the dictates and exclusive ends of the regime."[16]

There is a question of constitutional doctrine that has arisen concerning the involvement of the Republic with the arts. It focuses especially on the competence of regional and local governments to act in the cultural sphere, and revolves around interpretation of the term "Republic" as used in Article 9 of the Constitution.

With regard to this question, at first the prevailing interpretation was that the word "Republic" referred to the institutions of the State as a discrete entity,[17] thus excluding the Regions from any authority in the cultural sphere. Even at this time, however, there were indications of a wider interpretation. Indeed, it was noted that although conservation of the countryside (and analogously of the historical artistic patrimony) was not included in the list of subjects for regional legislation and administration (Arts. 117, 118), there was nothing to prevent the State from delegating authority in additional areas to other public agencies.[18]

Later it was clearly asserted that the goals set by Article 9 did not constitute an interest taken on by the State apparatus alone, but rather a "goal taken on by the entire republican order as a whole."[19] "The term republic," in short, "represents the *stato ordinamento* in all its possible articulations,"[20] and therefore "the other representative agencies that make up the *stato ordinamento* [Communes, Provinces, Regions, sectoral agencies] have the obligation to adopt appropriate policies for the attainment of the goals indicated by the aforementioned norm."[21]

With the progressive development of the regional system, individual regions have extended the scope of their activities, progressively claiming competence in areas traditionally the province of the national government (environmental matters, historic centers, promotion of cultural activities, etc.).[22]

The most recent conception of culture further strengthens the trend toward an enlarged regional role in cultural policy. Cultural activity adheres "to each community, whatever may be its size, as an undeniable expression of its own constitution as an organized community."[23] This is all the more true for Italy, where "for many centuries of her history, the localization of an artistic phenomenon often has been the greatest guarantee of its high quality. . . . It is only in the microcosm that the seminal spark, which makes up larger experiences, can be read usefully."[24] Thus, culture is unintelligible outside of a precise territorial context within which it is rooted and only from which can it draw prospects of growth. In this light, culture is the filter through which every territorial policy should be planned, and we have to recall that "urban planning" is one of the subjects included in the list of regional legislative functions in Article 117 of the Constitution.

While the conclusion drawn for culture can also be extended to art (which is, of course, one of its aspects), it still remains to be investigated what on a legal plane is intended by art.[25] Is anyone engaging in casual artistic activity deserving of public support or, on the contrary, should such aid go only to those who have reached a subjectively determined standard? Is it fair to have such skills evaluated by an expert (even if a collegial body) who could prevent an artist (or alleged artist) from obtaining vital assistance?

It is not possible to answer such questions without recognizing that each society and age assign different values and contents to art,[26] so that art which is unintelligible today could, in a year or so, appear to be an absolutely admirable expression of human artistic genius. Therefore, if on the one hand it is imperative to provide support for artistic production to rescue both art and man's spiritual needs[27]—which otherwise would be crushed in today's society—on the other hand, it is necessary to refrain from making such support conditional on skill or success, because to do so would deprive art of its essential characteristic: freedom, without which art loses its *raison d'être* and its possibility of exhibiting itself.[28] But, if one wishes to make such liberty accessible to all (Art. 3, Const.), it is necessary that consent for artistic expression be granted, theoretically, to all and therefore that the "neutrality" of public intervention be ensured. The activities of public authorities, in other words, must not favor one form of art or another, nor this trend or that, but should be guided toward an ever-growing concern for art itself; and it should be an interest that is not necessarily intent on the mere output of artistic works but rather an interest in the establishment of environmental conditions within which the artist (or alleged artist) can express himself.[29] Basically, this means, on the one hand, opening access to the instruments of artistic production to the largest possible number of candidates, while on the other hand also actively seeking to establish the socio-cultural environment that is most suited for creative work.

Public Organization in the Artistic Sector from 1945 to the Present

The present-day Ministries of Public Instruction[30] and of the Cultural Heritage derive from the Fascist Ministry of National Education. Truly, until the birth of the Ministry of the Cultural Heritage in 1975, all that pertained to the care and exploitation of the historical artistic patrimony was entrusted solely to the Ministry of Public Instruction (the direct heir of the Ministry of National Education) by virtue of the notion that educational and cultural matters are intimately linked and should be administered by a single entity.[31] In 1937 the Ministry of National Education (and therefore successively the Ministry of Public Instruction) was given responsibility for "guardianship of the archaeological, historic, monumental, literary, bibliographic, artistic, and linguistic heritage of the Nation; oversight, from the point of view of the arts, of the development of urban centers; and promotion of the diffusion of Italian art, culture, and science."

In the years that followed the enactment of the Constitution, there was a lively debate concerning the overhaul of the entire system (both organizationally and operationally). The first basic contribution, however, came only in 1966 when the Franceschini Commission (appointed to examine the proposed revision of the system of cultural guardianship) made its final report.[32] Subsequently, the issue was the subject of the two Papaldo Commissions, of which only the first, installed on April 9, 1968, made a report, which was presented to Parliament on March 11, 1970.[33]

The main conclusions of this series of studies were as follows. Above all else, the urgent need for public intervention to rescue the Italian cultural patrimony from its "dramatic state of impoverishment and decay" was definitively emphasized.[34] The need for a coherent approach toward reform of the system of guardianship and its related organizational structure was stressed. Such reforms had to move beyond the traditional idea of public action merely to preserve the nation's cultural patrimony, to embody a more dynamic approach, aiming toward its full appreciation, and therefore to its use as an instrument for the advancement of civilization.

In practical terms, reform of the system of guardianship has remained on the back burner and provision has been made only for the reorganization of the administrative structure. In 1974, the new Ministry suggested by the Papaldo Commission was established instead of the autonomous administration of antiquities and the material patrimony proposed by the Franceschini Commission. The process displays the obvious defects inherent in reforms only partially carried out. The new structure, due to the failure to rethink the basic regulation of the historical artistic patrimony is the outcome of a sterile, unproductive effort; in essence, "the choice of instruments was allowed to precede the identification of objectives."[35] "The birth of the new ministerial structure is not, indeed, the terminal point and the organizational translation of a reform of the principles for guarding the nation's cultural material patrimony."[36]

The organization of the Ministry of the Cultural Heritage consists of one central and one peripheral structure. There are four administrative offices at the core:

> The Central Office for the environment, architecture, archaeology, the arts, and history;
> The Central Office for archives;
> The Central Office for patrimony in the form of books and cultural institutes;
> General Directorate for general administrative affairs and personnel (and including the Office of Research).

There are also four technical institutes:

> The Central Institute for cataloging and documentation;
> The Central Institute for the master catalog of Italian libraries and bibliographic information;
> The Central Institute for book preservation;
> The Central Institute for restoration.

Alongside these agencies is the National Council for the Cultural Heritage, an auxiliary body whose composition assures technical competence (university professors, scientific and technical experts employed by the Ministry, and renowned outside experts) and institutional participation (representatives of Ministries, Regions, Provinces, and Communes). This seems to guarantee the quality of the advice which it must continuously furnish to the active agencies. This ranges from opinions on general regulatory and administrative acts and on arrangements with university institutes and research organizations, to opinions concerning the design of programs and the oversight of their implementation. The National Council is organized into five sectoral Committees (environment and architecture; archaeology; history and arts; archives; libraries and cultural institutes). These Committees have the power to propose programs for their respective areas.

Naturally, Central Offices and Central Institutes perform different tasks. Central Offices "coordinate the activities of the peripheral agencies and of the Central Institutes; arrange what is required for the functioning of the National Council and the sectoral Committees; and carry out the decisions of the Minister." The Central Institutes, which apart from personnel expenditures enjoy administrative and budgetary autonomy, "maintain functional contact with the peripheral agencies; where possible, coordinate joint programs of research on cataloging and conservation; and correspond with Italian and foreign research institutes."

Merely to recite the further subdivision of the Central Offices would probably be unproductive and certainly would be boring. It is worthwhile, however, to describe briefly the organization and functions of the Central Office for the environment, architecture, archaeology, the arts, and history. This currently consists of nine Divisions. Enforcement of preservation regulations and revocation of restrictions is the responsibility of the Division of protection, legal affairs, and the environment. The Division of budget and programming is concerned, among other things, with making payments to private owners of cultural items to enable the owners to restore those items, or with restoring the items itself. The Division of guardianship of items of archaeological, architectural, artistic, and historical interest is responsible for authorizations to demolish, modify, or restore architectural or monumental objects, permits for archaeological research, sanctions against violators, export and import of works of art, authorization to locate State-owned artwork in branches of governmental agencies in Italy and abroad, and art in public buildings. The Division of acquisition, inventory, cataloging, and statistics is responsible for the acquisition for the public domain of archaeological, architectural, artistic, and historical items, for the exercise of the right of pre-emption, and for the expropriation and cataloging of the same items.

Two of the Central Institutes also deserve further examination. The Central Institute for cataloging and documentation is divided into *services* (for archaeological, historical artistic, ethnographic, architectural, and environmental items) which develop programs for cataloging of items, promotion and coordination of executive cataloging activities, and preparation of the national plan for cataloging and documentation; *laboratories* that carry out survey tasks (photographic, aerial photography, etc.) of the data required for cataloging and documentation; *services* for the arrangement and utilization of information acquired; an *Administrative Office* that arranges and extends the execution of the Instititute's actions; and a *Technical Office* that provides technical consultations, maintains instruments and apparatus, and keeps up with technical and scientific advances.

The Central Institute for restoration is concerned with "scientific research oriented toward preservation, protection, and restoration of cultural items which are of archaeological and historical artistic interest." It consists of *laboratories* (chemistry, physics, and environmental controls, biological investigations, materials testing), which study the causes of deterioration and techniques for preservation and restoration; *services* for protective action (archaeological, historical artistic, architectural, and environmental); a *service* for teaching and information; an *Administrative Office;* and a *Technical Office* that monitors the operation and maintenance of the Institute's instruments and apparatus, purchases new equipment, and manages the storage and movement of items to be restored.

Throughout Italy, the peripheral structure of the Ministry's administration consists of several different agencies which oversee the custody of the items with which they are entrusted: the *Superintendencies* (archaeological, historical artistic, environmental and architectural, archival); the *State Archives; state public libraries.* The appointed heads of these agencies in each Region meet for regular conferences to plan coordination, study proposals, and share information.

Like the central one, this peripheral organization has an auxiliary structure: the Regional Committee for the cultural heritage in each regional capital. This Committee, "composed of the heads of the offices that constitute the regional conference . . . and by an equal number of representatives of the regional government," has the task of advancing national and regional initiatives and of liaison and coordination.

The Superintendencies, with the exception of archival holdings, are subordinate to the Central Office for the environment, architecture, archaeology, the arts, and history. They deserve further attention. Their geographic distribution does not necessarily follow regional boundaries, but evolved as circumstances warranted. Thus, if there is a single archaeological Superintendency for two regions (Veneto and Friuli Venezia Giulia), one can also find in a single region more than one Superintendency of the same type. One can also find *mixed* Superintendencies which are concerned with all (e.g., Molise) or almost all (e.g., Umbria) fields. Each modification of a Superintendency's authority or location requires the Minister's decree.

As has been noted, the reform accomplished with the establishment of the Ministry of the Cultural Heritage suffers from a basic flaw, because it took place without the necessary legislative reform concerning supervision of the nation's cultural patrimony. Failure to settle the central issue of cultural policy has fundamentally compromised organizational reform.

As the Giannini study group (to prepare the text for the Ministry's legislative organizational decree) observed, "Given the current state of protective legislation concerning cultural and environmental items, each structural modification would lead to disjunction between the modified organizational structure and the procedures to realize tasks to be carried out, which would remain unaltered."[37] Consequently, an administration which "displays no novelty" has been created; "the Ministry is shaped by throwing together existing units drawn from other Ministries."[38] To be sure, this has helped at least to resolve "the problem of illogical assignment of responsibility among the different offices for archives, works of art, landscape, and the state record library," but this does not mitigate the final negative judgment that "an outdated bureaucratic model" was reproduced and "the opportunity to introduce a new model was lost"[39]—either because the political skills required to decentralize tasks and organization were lacking, or because it was not desired.

On another level, the design to create a true Ministry of Culture was lost; "jurisdiction over performances was not given to it."[40] On the other hand, "the new ministerial apparatus seems so scantily equipped with personnel and resources as to restrict its activity to the mere conservation of the existing Italian cultural patrimony without any opportunity for growth."[41] This echos the opinion of those who maintain that the new Ministry "basically remains a ministry of restoration, museums, libraries, and exhibitions. It has not enabled cultural policy to take giant steps on the organizational plane."[42]

As has already been noted, during the Fascist period the State attempted to control all intellectual, and therefore all artistic, expression. This policy was limited with regard to the historical artistic patrimony by the Ministry of National Education's strong tradition of continuity (including the liberal culture which history had nourished). The same limitations did not apply to sectors dealing with entertainment (and especially the newest sector—cinema) which were progressively subordinated to the patronage of MINCULPOP, which had been created with the intention of guiding cultural developments.

After the war, with the collapse of Fascism and the promulgation of the Republican Constitution, MINCULPOP was suppressed and its responsibilities passed to the Office of the Prime Minister. Initially, an Undersecretariat was established; later, a General Directorate for Entertainment, an Information Service, and an Office of literary, artistic, and scientific copyright were created, all within the Office of the Prime Minister.

In the years that followed, two bills were introduced to relieve the Prime Minister of a number of tasks burdening him, and to make the administration of the sectors of entertainment, tourism, and sports autonomous. Neither attempt yielded concerete results. The idea of pairing the administration of entertainment with that of antiquities and fine arts (which was then entrusted to the Ministry of Public Instruction) was already present, and would resurface later, only to be cast aside again.

The Ministry of Tourism and Entertainment was established in 1959 and was organized into three General Directorates—for tourism, for entertainment, and for general affairs and personnel. The idea of consolidating the cultural sector was, therefore, "set aside since the Ministry of Public Instruction had too many tasks to carry out and the administrative effort in the field of entertainment would have become inefficient."[43] So, "with the customary system of concentrating structures and powers already present in the administration,"[44] the new Ministry inherited the Commissariat for Tourism and the General Directory for Entertainment and took over jurisdiction in sports.

The establishment of the Ministry was not—nor is it now—free from criticism. The subjects entrusted to it cannot be called homogeneous, although it is true that it deals with sectors sharing a common "recreational" theme and activities which are promotional or in the nature of subsidies. In fact, on another level, while tourism does relate to the industrial-economic sector, entertainment, as the expression of artistic impulses, has its own natural position in the area of cultural administration.

A negative judgment regarding the survival of the Ministry of Tourism and Entertainment is furthered by the progressive loss of powers and tasks that it has suffered in favor of the Regions. With the transfer of tourism to the Regions, the residual authority of the Ministry has been rendered so meager, indeed, that the General Directory for Tourism has been eliminated and the few missions not transferred to the Regions have devolved on the General Directory of General Operations and Personnel; moreover, the transfer of duties concerning "activities of prose, music, and cinema" to the Regions and local agencies has also been planned by recent national legislation.

In its current state, the Ministry, therefore, consists of two General Directorates: that of general affairs, tourism, and sports, and that concerning entertainment. Our attention will briefly pause on the latter.

It must be emphasized that the General Directorate concerns itself with cinema, theater, and music, each a complex discipline in many ways independent of the others. This complexity probably accounts for its great structural fragmentation. Indeed, the General Directorate for Entertainment is organized in as many as thirteen Divisions, only three of which are organized on the basis of function rather than specific art form. These three are:

I. General Operations—Cinema and Theater has responsibilities in all three sectors (especially in matters pertaining to the nomination of various committees and commissions);

II. and V. deal with cinema and the theater (theatrical and cinematographic management; theatrical and cinematographic revision).

The other Divisions have duties according to subject. For *theater:*

VI. Theatrical activities: prose, reviews, and assorted arts;

for *cinema:*

III. Activities dealing with cultural film-making in Italy and abroad and also film festivals;
IV. Production, import and export of full-length movies, movie shorts, and newsreels;
XIII. Disbursement of contributions and awards favoring film production;

for *music:*

VIII. Operatic and symphonic agencies;
IX. Operatic concerts in Italy;
X. Concert performances in Italy;
XI. Festivals, reviews, competitions, and ''groups'' (popular music);
XII. Opera and concert productions;

and finally:

VII. Circuses and traveling shows.

A number of diverse Commissions and Committees operate alongside the Divisions. Their composition guarantees a bureaucratic presence as well as the representation of the groups involved. These organs deal with theatrical and movie censorship as well as providing for the presentation of awards, subsidies, commendations, etc.

To complete this portrait of public organization in the entertainment field, mention must be made of the system of parallel administrations which, especially in this field, is an essential element within the larger design of public intervention.

In reality, the ministerial structure in this area does not have a peripheral organization. This central structure is, however, the apex of a series of agencies that operate in the three sectors of cinema, theater, and music. An attempt will be made to sketch these agencies, including the Autonomous Agency for Cinematographic Management (EAGC), which ''provides for the management of state participation in the movie sector according to cost-effective criteria''), even though this agency formally is under the Ministry of State Participations. Despite this, the relevance of this agency within the overall scheme of public intervention in the cinema ought not to be doubted. This relevance is further underscored by the presence on its administrative council and its board of auditors of representatives of the Ministry of Tourism and Entertainment.

In theater, a field which has long awaited organic legislation (being regulated on the basis of ministerial circulars or *leggine di spesa*), there are a number of assuredly public agencies as well as others whose nature is questionable and which require legislative direction. The Italian Theatrical Agency (ETI) and the National Institute of Ancient Drama (INDA) are clearly public organs.

ETI was established by law for "the purpose of promoting, within the design of instructions issued by the Ministry of Tourism and Entertainment, the growth and diffusion of theatrical activity and public entertainment within the nation and abroad." The agency also "provides for a) the nationwide coordination of movement of theatrical troupes . . . ; b) the promotion, coordination, and, as necessary, the planning and management of theatrical activities in southern Italy and the islands . . . ; c) the planning/scheduling of theatrical halls including direct management of theatrical establishments which are owned or only being used . . . ; d) the promotion of Italian theatrical activities abroad as well as foreign productions within Italy; and e) the collection and diffusion of information, news, and data related to theatrical activities, with the final goal being documentation and study."

The INDA is under the Ministry of Tourism and Entertainment in concert with the Ministry of Public Instruction. It "has the goal of recreating the dramas of the Greek and Latin period, in the Greek theater of Syracuse, the Roman theater of Ostia, in other ancient arenas, and eventually in any locality possessing a special classical mood. . . . It may also arrange for the production of open-air classical works in archaeological environments which are particularly suggestive," and, with ministerial authorization, it may exercise "supervision over the initiatives of agencies and private individuals which involve the production of works of Greek or Latin classical drama."

The public nature of the so-called "publicly managed theaters" is less clear-cut. Their juridical status is generally that of "de facto associations." However, the Communes (and/or other public agencies) are their principal sponsors, and the tasks they carry out cannot appropriately be considered to be private. They are within the system of local, rather than national, administration.

The current basic law in the area of music dates from 1967. The law declares: "The State considers operatic and concert activities of considerable general interest, because they favor the musical, cultural, and social formation of the national collectivity," and it is ordered that the operatic agencies and assimilated concert institutions "have as their goal the diffusion of musical art, the professional formation of artistic cadres, and the musical education of the collectivity." They pursue these goals through the direct management of the theaters with which they have been entrusted. These agencies are the focal point for state intervention in the musical arena.[45] The law grants them legal standing in public law and places their supervision within the Ministry of Tourism and Entertainment.

The central role played by the operatic agencies is what leads to criticism of the law. This is because the law does not give sufficient consideration to balanced distribution of these agencies throughout the country; the law recognizes eleven operatic agencies and two assimilated concert insitutions whose locations leave entire regions without any cultural/musical services, with the usual inequality regarding the South. This pattern, based "solely on the criterion of recognizing pre-existing situations resulting from the dynamics of the country's socio-economic development and ignoring any logic of programmed promotional action, institutionalizes rather than corrects the disparities that exist among geographic areas with regard to the musical cultural infrastructures."[46]

Both the Experimental Center for the Cinema and the Autonomous Agency for Cinematographic Management deal with the cinema.

The Experimental Center for the Cinema, established in 1942 and overhauled in

1977, organizes "courses designed for the cultural and professional formation of those who intend to work in the field of audiovisual devices with special reference to cinematography" and seminars for "the study of all the problems inherent in audiovisual communications" and for "professional up-dating and specialization in cinematography and television." The Center also provides for the functioning of a *Study and Documentation Section* (to promote "research and surveys that concern audio-visual communications"), a *Research and Experimental Section* (to "contribute toward the development of language and techniques of audio-visual communications"), and a *Publication Section* (which "edits periodicals, bulletins, and works pertaining to audio-visual communications"). Finally, the Center is responsible for the organization and operation of the National Movie Library, "created for the preservation of the national film patrimony."[47]

The EAGC (Autonomous Agency for Cinematographic Management), created in 1958, is under the direction of the Ministry of State Participations. It is required to provide "national cinematographic production of artistic and cultural quality." The EAGC is entrusted with "planning, management, promotion, coordination and control of the corporations which have been incorporated" into itself. The number of such corporations has varied over time. At its birth, the Agency's involvement was limited solely to Cinecittà, a corporation that had been established in 1935. In 1961, the public Istituto LUCE[48] was transformed into a joint stock company and incorporated into EAGC. Finally, in 1966, "the Agency assembled a new corporation destined to operate in the area of distribution: Italnoleggio."[49] Additional legislation in 1971 specified the tasks of each of these three corporations: to the Istituto LUCE are assigned "production duties with particular concern for didactic and specialized cinematography, as well as movies which are experimental in character and which enjoy a particular cultural relevance"; to Cinecittà is assigned "the management of cinematographic production, synchronization, processing, and editing establishments" and the promotion of "experimental research and laboratory work, as well as the modernization of cinematographic equipment"; while Italnoleggio is charged with "working in the market for the distribution of films capable of gradually elevating the public's taste," fostering the diffusion of films (either as "products of the Istituto LUCE" or as "films obtained from distributors"), and managing movie theaters.

Even though the Ministry of State Participations is outside the purpose of this study, we must allude to a basic question. "The cultural purposes of this Agency, which distinguish it from other state enterprises, . . . [and] its functional position as guardian, while indirect, of the constitutional principle of freedom of thought, . . . place the EAGC on an entirely different plane compared to other similar agencies and create no small degree of perplexity concerning the application of general principles in this sector."[50] In particular, it is inappropriate, as well as difficult, to apply mechanically a standard of "cost-effective management," as is typical in other areas of State participation where the firms and corporations involved operate according to the dictates of private enterprise. In the cinematographic field, the goals pursued by public powers "approach, to a significant degree, the role of efforts aimed toward public education—goals which would be absurd to manage according to any classic criteria of cost-effectiveness and which require instead completely different standards concerning their effectiveness."[51]

Finally, there is the Autonomous Agency "La Biennale di Venezia," which also has legal status under public law. The Agency was reorganized in 1973 as a "democratically organized institute of culture," with the goal of "promoting permanent activities and organizing international displays which focus primarily on documentation, knowledge, criticism, research, and experimentation in the field of the arts,'' so that it does not refer only to the representative arts.

Public Activity in the Artistic Sector from 1945 to the Present

The regulation of public activity in the area of the traditional arts has remained essentially unaltered from that established in the law of 1939 concerning the supervision of items of artistic and historical interest. (We have noted in the preceding section the sterility of the 1975 organizational reform, given the absence of any fundamental revision of the tutelage principles involved.[52])

Before examining the regulatory system, one must remember that in Italy, the historical artistic patrimony is not exclusively publicly owned. In fact, on the one hand, the Civil Code includes within the *public domain* ''if they belong to the State . . . real property recognized as possessing historical, archaeological, or artistic interest as defined by the appropriate laws; the collections of museums, art galleries, archives, libraries'' (Art. 822, co. 2), and among the inalienable State holdings, it counts ''items of historical, archaeological, paleo-ethnologic, and artistic interest found underground regardless of the retrieving agent or method employed'' (Art. 826). On the other hand, it also allows private appropriation of ''real and personal property of artistic, historical, archaeological, or ethnographic interest,'' even if they ''come under the jurisdiction of special laws'' (Art. 839).

Thus the law of 1939 focuses on items ''that have an artistic, historical, archaeological, or ethnologic interest'' and applies both to public agencies and to private individuals. If these items are the property of the State or of legally recognized (public or private) agencies, they are automatically subject to custodial regulation so long as they possess the ''essential quality'' of artistic or historical value and so long as they belong, or are transferred to, such agencies.[53] On the other hand, if the items belong to private parties (individuals and institutions not enjoying legal recognition)—although also in this case the *principium individuationes* considered by the law is the same ''essential quality'' of the items—the law conditions their actual subjection to the norms upon ''notification'' to the parties concerned.[54]

The custodial rules concerning objects of historical artistic interest seem to have been engineered so as to guarantee both the objects' *conservation* and their *enjoyment* by the community. These two goals are clearly related, since enjoyment mandates conservation of the item, and conservation is directly aimed toward its enjoyment.

Any discussion of the measures directed toward conservation must begin with the so-called ''direct supervision'' of items of historical artistic interest. This will highlight, on the one hand, the series of prohibitions regarding demolition, removal, modification, or repair without the prior authorization of the Minister of the Cultural Heritage, as well as prohibitions concerning the ''use of items that is incompatible with their historical or artistic character or which could jeopardize their preservation or integrity.'' These regulations apply to items without regard to whether they are public or private. In the latter case, their owner must first have been notified that the items are subject to the law. However, even if there has been no notification, it is forbidden, without the Minister's authorization, to remove ''frescos, emblems, graffiti, inscriptions, tabernacles, and other ornaments from buildings whether they are visible to the public or not.'' In order to make this series of prohibitions effective as well as to make execution of supervisory powers possible, ''projects of any type'' must be submitted to the appropriate Superintendency and authorization obtained.

On the other hand, the duty to provide for maintenance is spelled out in the law. This maintenance nearly always acquires the technical complexity of restoration work. ''In order to assure the conservation and prevent deterioration of the items,'' the Minister has the power to ''provide directly by himself for the necessary expenses'' or to ''impose the necessary measures.'' Both powers can also be exercised in matters concerning private holdings. In either case, the expenses are charged to the owner. Nonetheless, as an exception to this general principle, the law provides that in those cases where the Minister has already provided for the work and the State must be reimbursed, or in those cases where the owner has shown himself to be unable to sustain the expense imposed by the Minister, the Minister himself can ''decree that total or partial expenses be charged to the State.'' But, also, when ''the expense has been sustained by the owner of the protected item,'' the Minister can decree, without any demonstration by the owner, ''that the State share the expense up to no more than half of the amount.''

Besides ''direct supervision,'' the law provides for an ''indirect supervision'' of real estate possessing historical artistic value. It is dubbed ''indirect'' because it does not focus on the items themselves, but on items located in so-called ''zones of respect'' which are occupied by the principal objects of interest. ''Indirect supervision'' gives the Minister ''the power to prescribe distances, measurements, and other norms aimed at avoiding any harm to the integrity of the real estates . . . , and ensuring that their perspective, light, or ambient scenic conditions will not be altered.'' Even more, expropriation for the public good is allowed of ''areas and structures'' when the Minister ''recognizes such measures as necessary to isolate or restore monuments, guarantee their exposure to light, protect their perspective, guarantee or enhance their decor, as well as further the public enjoyment of them and, lastly, facilitate access.''

Shifting our attention to ''enjoyment,'' it should be noted that for a work of art to fulfil its inherent function of cultural development and the increase of spiritual values, it must be or must become an object of contemplation and study. The system of the law guarantees public enjoyment of only those items owned by the State and public agencies which can be visited. By contrast, access to private holdings is granted only in exceptional cases. Indeed, the Minister can oblige private owners to grant visits as long as details for such visits are arranged with the owner. But this rule applies only to real property and collections or series, and excludes the display of personal items.[55]

Thus, if the only possible object of State cultural policy is to provide the people with the widest possible enjoyment of the nation's historical artistic patrimony, and if, as seems incontestable, this patrimony consists of all the nation's art works (real and personal), then the provision of instruments designed to allow—by placing them in public hands—access for the general public to objects which are in private hands seems to be necessary.

The following examination of the instruments devised by the law of 1939 reaffirms such logic. According to the law, these devices are to be used not only because of fears concerning the preservation of works of art, but also, and above all, because placing them under public ownership allows the government more effectively to assure their ''enjoyment'' by the community.

Of these devices, expropriation should be mentioned first. The Minister has the power of expropriation, which may also be exercised in favor of public agencies or institutions enjoying legal recognition, over real property that comes under the purview of the law whenever such action would "respond to an important issue related to *conservation* or *expansion* of the national patrimony." It is clear that the lawmakers intended to make expropriation a generally available instrument of supervision, rather than a mere sanction as in the past.[56] Yet, expropriation is not only the extreme device established for the "conservation" of art objects. As we have seen, the State still reserves the authority to engage directly in restoration work and to impose the necessary measures. Even if expropriation therefore plays only an auxiliary role in "conservation" efforts, it still is a major instrument in the case of "expansion" of the national patrimony, making the individual work of art an actual object of public enjoyment rather than merely a potential one. Further confirmation of the claim that expropriation is primarily oriented toward promoting "enjoyment" is the fact that it can be employed against personal property also, access to which the Minister is not able to compel. Ultimately, we can say that the evaluations the Minister will have to make will be essentially political-cultural in nature, rather than simply related to the value of the art object.

The regulations governing the export of works of art should be read in a similar fashion. Exportation is forbidden if the items, whether they have been the objects of notification or not,[57] "possess such a value that their exportation would represent a substantial loss to the national patrimony." "Substantial loss" is inherent in exportation because it removes the artifact from the cultural environment that influenced its conception and realization and, even more, because it denies actual contemplation of it to the community. Thus, the determination that would lead to authorization or denial of the export license must depend more on the work's position within the national patrimony than on the artifact's own value, even though the latter is taken into consideration. However, denial of an export license does not guarantee public access, but simply preserves the possibility of future enjoyment being achieved by eventually placing the work in public hands.

A more effective instrument of cultural policy for this circumstance is the so-called "compulsory purchase upon exportation." The Minister, if he acts within a two-month time period, has the power to purchase "items that possess important value for the national patrimony" at a price that matches "that contained in the declaration." (Applicants for export licenses must declare the economic value of the items to be exported.) It is evident that the use of the power of compulsory purchase is motivated by more than a simple desire to keep an artifact within the country; that goal could be achieved simply by denying an export license. We must therefore conclude that this power is given to the Minister primarily to promote collective enjoyment of the entire historical artistic patrimony.

A similar argument can be made concerning the right of preemption. When a work of art is being sold or transferred as a form of payment, the Minister has the option of purchasing it "at the same price established in the contract." While the law granting this power does not directly specify its aims, in the context of the larger system of supervision it is not hard to see what its major function is. If conservation were the only objective, preemptive purchase would be necessary only if the prospective owner did not appear to be trustworthy. However, this would conflict with the general character given to this instrument by the law, suggesting that the true purpose is to allow pursuit of political-cultural goals.

Finally, if works that have been the object of unreimbursed state restoration are involved, the Minister has the power to purchase them at their prerestoration value. Even though the "compulsory purchase upon restoration" has the character of a sanction, we can consider it among the other instruments just examined because its effects are very similar to those produced by them. All yield an enlargement of the public's enjoyment of the national patrimony.

As has been noted, the predominant administrative activity for the representative arts is the promotion and nurture of artistic "production."

Unlike cinema and music, there is no organic law for theater. Instead, it is regulated on the basis of funding bills and, above all, by ministerial circulars which possess an "intense normative character."[58] Legislation of May 1983, which established "extraordinary interventions in the entertainment sector," provided for a simple increase in the allotments "destined to subsidize theatrical performances." Early legislation (February 1948)—which is still in effect—gives the Minister of Tourism and Entertainment the power to allocate subsidies "on the basis of the results of examination of the budgets and the artistic programs and activities carried out by each theater organization." The Minister must take the advice of a commission, whose membership is listed in the law.[59] There are no precise instructions concerning the definition of subjects and of enterprises that can be supported.

Still, subsequent legislation contains evidence of timid attempts toward greater precision. Two significant phases can be discerned. The first straddles the decades of the 1960s and 1970s. During this phase, the number of possible recipients of subsidies was extended to include those "initiatives aimed toward a greater diffusion and expansion of the theater and theatrical culture and which were promoted and organized by public agencies, university institutions, cultural committees and associations, and unions." The second phase was initiated in legislation of 1975 and 1977. This phase is characterized by the inclusion of geographical considerations among the criteria governing the distribution of funds. Particular attention was to be devoted to a "wide decentralization of theatrical activities." Indeed, the 1975 law stipulated that the distribution of funds should be oriented toward "a diffusion of these activities especially toward the central and southern regions." This stipulation, however, disappeared in the 1977 law.

These attempts did not correct the vagueness that is found in legislation governing the theater. The failure to identify activities that may be subsidized leads to perplexity. The legislative vagueness has left a substantial normative vacuum and has encouraged the routine use of ministerial circulars as a kind of remedial action.[60] In practice, this translates into assigning to the executive an enormous degree of discretionary power in the selection of recipients and the size of the government's contributions. This increases the chances that respect for the constitutional principles of substantive equality and freedom of expression will be eroded.[61] Nor can these concerns be alleviated by arguing that this lack of precision is necessary because of the constant evolution of taste in this field. Neither should one argue that such evolution requires a flexible regulatory system that can constantly adjust itself to new fashion. On this last point, no one could argue that flexibility should be maintained at the expense of constitutional principles. Rather, the one must be combined with the others.

A survey of the numerous circulars issued to date confirms the existence of this problem. Circular 4498/TCPG of July 29, 1983 can be used to illustrate the current design of public intervention in the theater sector. This is highlighted by examining the following topics: subjects and initiatives eligible for funding; types of subsidies; specific requirements for public funding; and the criteria for the allocation of public funds.

According to the circular, "publicly-managed organs of theatrical production" as well as a host of private ensembles and theater companies are fundable. Under the ministerial circular, public organs of theatrical production are "those established by territorial or local agencies, either through direct action or through associational or consortial action, as well as those institutions possessing legal standing to which the aforementioned agencies formally adhere or in whose administration they directly participate." The circular establishes numerous distinctions within the broad private sector. First and foremost, it distinguishes between privately managed companies and cooperatively managed ones. In addition, specific subsidies are anticipated for: "companies that produce musical comedies, comedies with music, and *sceneggiata*"; professional companies "of experimental theater" and those that produce "theatrical shows for young people"; drama companies "which, because of structural, project-related, and operational characteristics, are not included in the preceding [list]"; "agencies, organs, or associations involved in theatrical promotion or production"; "entities assembled by Regions, Provinces, Communes, and Consortiums of local agencies, theatrical cooperatives and other private initiatives, trade union and cultural organizations that operate within the scope of regional or inter-regional theatrical promotion and programming"; "theatrical initiatives undertaken by universities"; "festivals and reviews"; "tours abroad"; "agencies or national associations which are aimed toward a development and coordination of amateur dramatic arts troupes"; and "companies that have presented light opera or cabaret performances." The circular also allows "annual contributions toward the realization of the institutional activities" of the Italian Drama Institute and the Silvio D'Amico National Academy of Dramatic Arts.

The circular distinguishes several types of subsidies: *initial or start-up contributions* (assigned, appropriately enough, at the start of the theater season); *contributions proportional to receipts* (only for privately managed dramatic and comedy troupes and only for the presentation of Italian works); *supplementary contributions* (granted in addition to prior subsidies at the end of the season and based on examination of specific factors, such as the number of performances given); and *lump-sum contributions* (which can be awarded either at the beginning or end of the season and are awarded in place of the start-up contributions or those proportional to receipts). Of lesser importance are *bonuses*, granted "to those companies which distinguished themselves for the quality of their shows, the number of their performances, or the total employee-days," or granted to publicly managed organizations and theatrical companies "for their stimulation of national production in the area of drama," and specifically for the production of "Italian novelties" or "opera premieres." The circular also allows management grants (both start-up and final) to "individual or collective, private or cooperative enterprises that operate theaters." Finally, special provisions regulate summertime theatrical activities. Until recently, these were regulated by special circulars which provided lump-sum contributions for "festivals, reviews, and tours abroad," for theatrical productions "of an extraordinary nature," or for activities of "particular cultural, artistic, or touristic interest."

The terminology used in the circular, especially with regard to the definition of the different types of subsidies, is imprecise and results in ambiguities in interpretation. Even a careful reading does not yield a unequivocal understanding of an individual instrument, nor can any substantial difference be uncovered among different instruments. For example, the expression "lump-sum contributions" is not always used in the same manner; or the differences among the categories that can be subsidized with lump-sum contributions and those with alternative ones[62] are fleeting, especially if one considers the uniformity of the criteria used to measure the size of these contributions.

Before moving on to an examination of these criteria, it is appropriate to analyze the technical requirements for receiving subsidies. Generally, "in order to gain admission to state contributions the interested parties shall present their *program of activities* and a related *financial forecast.*" There are additional requirements for each type of theatrical organization. For example, theatrical cooperatives are required to have a minimum number of associate members in order to receive a lump-sum contribution, and privately managed companies must have a minumum number of employees if they are to receive start-up contributions.

Some of the criteria adopted by the circular for the allocation of contributions recur in almost all categories of subsidy. An example is the emphasis given to the Italian repertory. Another criterion could be called the "magnitude of the engagement" and is usually contained in such expression as "number of shows," "number of recitals," "length of activities," or "length of programming." Still another yard-stick is the ratio between production expenditures and income. If these criteria give reasonable discretionary powers to the Minister, there are others—which better characterize the system—that are distinguished by extreme discretion. These concern a variety of elements such as: the quality of shows or theatrical companies; the artistic strength and effort contained in a program; and the results attained. None of these categories are bounded by any clear-cut parameters. Evaluations based purely on merit may well be acceptable for *bonuses,* which, by their very nature may demand a subjective judgment. But when one is concerned with *contributions,* upon which the very survival of a theatrical entity may depend,[63] one must be extremely cautious because of the danger that constitutional guarantees of substantive equality and freedom of expression may be compromised. It should also be emphasized that there is no general principle to guide the distribution of funds among the various enterprises or to guide the funding's geographic distribution. Instead, it is simply stated that access to State contributions is based on the presupposition that the activity shall "*also* be qualified by an ever greater dissemination among territorial districts and locations in southern and insular Italy." As can be easily seen, everything depends upon the "competence and equilibrium" and "capacity for political and personal mediation"[64] of the individuals who run the cultural bureaucracy.

It would appear that the system of subsidies established by ministerial circulars favors undertakings that possess great economic and organizational substance. In reality, the system seems to favor maintenance of the *status quo* rather than permitting possible projects geared toward novelty.[65] This continues the familiar (one could say historic) tendency of the circulars to follow the moods of the theatrical world, merely registering them and thus allowing opportunities to formulate a better cultural policy to slip away. Responsibility for this state of affairs, as we have already emphasized, should be placed on the legislator who, by his dereliction, has encouraged the consolidation of bureaucratic power and has failed, not only to commit the bureaucracy to a precise direction, but even to specific goals.

There can be no doubt that the law governing the musical sector (L. 800/1967) has provided more coherent regulation of the music world than has been enjoyed by the theater. Still, reform is called for in the music field as well.[66]

From the very first interventions by the State, the regulations governing operatic agencies and those governing the so-called "other musical activities" were separate.

Prior to 1967, the basic regulations regarding operatic agencies dated from the Fascist era (1936), while the other activities were regulated along with dramatic theater. Regarding finance, after the war 12 percent of the taxes levied on "entertainment of any kind, including bets" was assigned to operatic agencies; on the other hand, only 4 percent was assigned to "other musical activities."

It was with Law 800 that for the first time the regulation of operatic agencies and of "other musical activities" were integrated. Two funds were established, one for operatic agencies and assimilated concert organizations and the other for "other musical activities." Both funds have been upgraded repeatedly by subsequent legislation. An additional subsidy was added to these funds in 1982 to be in large part, upon the Minister's decree, turned over to Milan's operatic agency, La Scala opera house.[67] The remainder is "turned over to other operatic agencies and assimilated concert organizations on the basis of several criteria: artistic and organizational results obtained; the increase in activity stemming from the reconstruction of theaters; the scale of activity on a multiregional basis; and the programming requirements related to the national and international importance of these agencies and institutions." A similar contribution on a larger scale was anticipated in legislation in 1983. This latter legislation, however, while on the one hand not interfering with the special provision for La Scala, decreed, on the other hand, that the remaining funds should be assigned "in favor of musical activities abroad as well as toward operatic agencies and assimilated concert organizations for their program requirements that are related to the execution of special programs in Italy, and with a special regard as well for regular programs held outdoors which have an important tourist-related role."

Thus, public intervention in the field of music takes the two forms just mentioned. *Direct* intervention takes place through the operatic agencies; it is the most highly visible public intervention and there is no reason to believe that it will be changed in the immediate future. The uneven geographic distribution of the operatic agencies necessitates a greater emphasis on *indirect* intervention: it goes to support "other musical activities." This kind of intervention is especially important because of the diffusion of musical culture, even though it involves limited expenditures.

The law dictates the administrative structure of the operatic agencies. The *President* is usually the Mayor of the Commune in which the agency is located. Aside from legally representing the agency, the President convenes and presides over the agency's Administrative Council. The *Superintendent* is appointed by the Minister on the advice of the Communal Council. The Superintendent directs the agency's activities and "arranges both the preliminary and final budgets. Along with the Artistic Director, he also plans the schedules of activities for submission to the Administrative Council." The *Administrative Council* is appointed by ministerial decree and consists of the President, the Superintendent, the Artistic Director, and representatives of territorial agencies (Commune, Province, and Region) as well as representatives of particular interests (tourism, entertainment, the arts). The Administrative Council is authorized to establish general directives and discuss the schedule of activities, the budgets, and generally any matters relating to the life of the agency. The *Council of Auditors* is appointed by ministerial decree also and consists of four members, predominantly drawn from the bureaucracy, charged with accounting control. The *Artistic Director* is not technically an administrative officer of the agency, although he cannot avoid having a decisive role in its operations. The Artistic Director is "appointed by the Administrative Council from among the most renowned musicians of proven theatrical competence. . . . He assists the Superintendent in the agency's management of the arts.'' The Superintendent is required to arrange the schedule of activities in concert with the Artistic Director, who also has responsibilities for the artistic aspects of productions.

The Artistic Director is in a potentially difficult position. On the one hand, he is subject to constant scrutiny by the Administrative Council which can, if it wishes, rescind his contract with the agency merely by expressing its displeasure with the execution of the artistic program it had decided upon. On the other hand, the Director lacks autonomous powers because he can only collaborate with the Superintendent, although his position is bolstered by the statutory requirement that the Superintendent work ''in concert'' with him. Ultimately, the Director's ability to affect artistic policy depends on the relationship between the Superintendent and the Council. When the Superintendent dominates the Council so that it merely ratifies previously made decisions, the Director has whatever freedom of action the Superintendent allows him. When the Council is ascendant, the Director must present his proposals to the Council in his role as one of its members and hope to have them approved. Thus, with regard to his influence upon artistic policy, his position is quite delicate and institutionally not very clear.

We now turn to the funding of operatic agencies and their operational autonomy in their relations with the Minister.

The State fund for operatic agencies is distributed after hearings of the Central Commission for Music.[68] The fundamental criterion for dividing the fund is based on the ''expenses sustained by each agency for the maintenance of administrative, technical and artistic personnel.'' Concerning the distribution of the sums that remain after meeting these basic costs, the law establishes additional criteria:

> a) the quality and quantity of the agency's artistic production during the preceding three years;
>
> b) the public's average attendance during the last three years. The average is set as the ratio between the number of spectators and the theater's capacity;
>
> c) the agency's program of activities . . . , considering also the activities carried out within the Region and the organization of performances of particular international interest;
>
> d) the burden of operating Professional Training Centers; and
>
> e) the quantity of support by local institutions and agencies, taking into consideration their financial resources and capacity.

As is easily appreciated, the evaluations are quite objective and one can assert that this process of funding does not result in any relevant limitation of the operatic agencies. Close examination of the criterion ''quality of their production'' does not seem particularly detrimental to the autonomy of the operatic agencies, compared with most of the criteria that are basically limited to an evaluation of objective data. Even approval of the programming (along with that of budgets) does not present occasions for discretionary decisions. Indeed, ministerial actions seem to be limited to the verification of preemptory requirements: the number of performances[69] and rough estimates of the character of the season being planned (operatic, orchestral, or ballet). Among the conditions that govern approval of an operatic agency's program, one in particular should be mentioned. This is a measure designed to protect the national repertory and the number of opportunities that are available to Italian artists. According to this regulation, programs must include ''an adequate number of operas and compositions by Italian authors of every period.'' The employment of foreign artists is allowed only ''in primary roles'' and is ''limited to one third of the total complement of choral groups employed for the length of the theatrical season.'' The ''employment of entirely foreign choral or ballet companies'' is possible only when ''the number of presentations is not greater than 5% of the number planned for the entire year's program,'' unless some exigencies of an ''exceptional order'' are recognized by the Minister.

''Aside from the activities carried out by autonomous operatic agencies and by assimilated orchestral institutions,'' the law anticipates the subsidy of ''operatic, orchestral, and ballet productions.'' They benefit from the fund ear-marked for ''other musical activities.'' At least 25 percent of this fund ''is assigned to 'traditional theaters' and to 'concert-orchestral institutions.' '' The theaters and institutions are listed in the law and their number may be increased upon the decree of the Minister and with the agreement of the Central Commission for Music. The theaters and institutions ''have the task of promoting, assisting, and coordinating musical activities that take place within the territory of their respective Provinces.''[70]

The contributions granted to these ''other musical activities'' are assigned upon decree of the Minister and agreement of the Central Commission for Music, ''which take into consideration the importance of the locality, the interests of tourism, the public's affluence, and the needs of depressed areas.'' With the exception of this last criterion, which can express the perspective of a promotional program applied uniformly throughout the nation, these legal criteria governing the award of aid do not seem to fit in with the overall goal of ''promoting the musical, cultural, and social development of the national collectivity'' which the law itself establishes as its goal.

The law decrees that the following ''other musical activities'' can be subsidized:

operatic shows;
concert, chorale, ballet shows;
operatic, concert, chorale, ballet shows to be performed abroad;
national and international festivals;
competitions, experimental activities, and reviews.

The law also reserves a specified portion of the fund to ''promote and sustain those initiatives intended in any case to spread and increase musical culture,'' as well as to provide scholarships, assistance in transportation, and contributions to bands.

Two features of the legislative rules governing these activities need to be emphasized: the types of recipients of the contributions, and the methods employed to calculate the contributions to various types of activities.

As long as they are not organized by ''traditional theaters,'' *lyric productions* can obtain the State's supplemental financial support if they are ''promoted by communal or provincial administrations, 'provincial tourist agencies,' 'sojourn, tourist, and health agencies,' musical institutions, and non-profit agencies that possess recognized legal standing.'' For the execution of these activities, these entities must make use of ''the cooperative societies and lyric companies listed in the law and of theatrical and concert-orchestral institutions managed by public agencies.'' They must also employ Italian singers and at least 45 Italian orchestra players.[71] The total subsidy is determined annually by the Minister ''for each single recital'' and, according to the ''importance of the production,'' the contribution for the ''traditional seasons'' (which are performed by the ''traditional theaters'') must be at least 30 percent more than that granted for ''ordinary seasons.'' Special incentives are established in favor of the Italian repertory.

Aside from the shows organized by concert-orchestral institutions, any other *concert, chorale, or ballet productions* must be "organized by non-profit agencies, societies, institutions, or associations" if they are to be eligible for any form of state financial aid. The amount of the contributions is based on:

> "a) cultural importance, continuity, and length of season;
> b) the number of world or Italian premieres;
> c) the number of local premieres, the number of works by a living Italian author and the number of works by an Italian author that have not been performed locally for at least twenty years; and
> d) the number and importance of collateral activities."

As can be seen, while access to supplemental contributions for lyric productions is conditioned upon consideration of the national repertory, in the case of *concert, chorale, or ballet productions,* presentation of Italian repertoire is considered only in deciding the size of the subsidies granted. It should also be noted that there are no regulations protecting Italian performers in this last field.

Of the remaining activities eligible for subsidy—"competitions in musical composition and performance, introductory and advanced professional courses in music, experimental lyric seasons and musical reviews"—the law expressly provides that eligible recipients shall be "non-profit agencies, institutes, and associations" that perform these activities "with the goal of promoting musical culture, of stimulating new lyric, concert, and ballet production, and discovering new Italian talent." The law does not specify types of recipients for funding allocated for festivals (these contributions may be granted if the enterprise possesses "particular artistic or touristic interest"). In the absence of specific regulations, it must be assumed that contributions are to be allotted according to the subject matter of the festivals, excluding, however, the operatic agencies.

The Minister provides subsidy funds for shows performed abroad after consulting with the Central Commission for Music and the Foreign Ministry. For lyric activities, subsidies can be obtained by operatic agencies, "traditional theaters," and "non-profit agencies and musical institutions with legal standing." For concert, chorale, and ballet activity, assistance may be provided for "assimilated concert institutions," "concert-orchestral institutions," and "societies, institutions, associations, and companies that have performed for at least two years in Italy or abroad, or which show themselves to be reliable on an organizational and artistic level." It is unfortunate that operatic agencies are included among those eligible to receive monies for performances abroad from the fund assigned to "other musical activities" since this policy further depletes the already meager funds allotted for such activities. According to the law, "the conductors, the first and second leads, the lead dancers, the artistic assistants, as well as the members of the concert and chorale companies must be of Italian nationality."[72] Furthermore, in calculating the size of the subsidy as well, care must be taken to "employ Italian orchestral, choral, and ballet companies" and to include in the programs "Italian operas which must have had their first Italian performance within the last thirty years or be works by Italian authors that have never been staged."[73]

With the collapse of Fascism, there was a reaction to the old regime in the movie sector that expressed itself through a sweeping series of abrogations of public intervention regulations. Legislation from 1945 affirms that "the exercise of cinematographic production is free." In reality, however, censorship remained. In the same way, "the system of credit remained intact, and so did, despite modifications, the economic incentives."[74] Of course, it was not possible to erase at one blow the entire previous structure and revert to a totally liberal system. So, propelled by various components of the cinematographic sector and gushing out of an intense debate, a series of laws was enacted in 1947 and 1949. It was thanks to these that the system of public intervention was restored, and the trend has remained unaltered since then. After modification of the 1949 norms in 1956, we arrive at the law of 1965 which declares, "The State considers the cinema as a medium of artistic expression, of cultural development, of social communication and recognizes its economic and industrial importance. The activities of film production, distribution, and programming are held to be of relevant general interest." With further modifications in 1975, the norms of 1965 correspond to current regulation.

Unlike the field of theater and music, the justification for public intervention in the cinema is rooted not only in artistic-cultural considerations, as the declaration cited above attests. The cinema presents a "double personality: the first is frankly commercial. In this regard, cinema is pre-eminently the organization, production, and exchange of economically valid activities for profit within the bounds of a free market economy . . . ; it is because of the second personality that cinema is numbered among cultural activities."[75] However, it cannot be denied that "the economic aspect has always been pre-eminent in establishing and managing public intervention." "The only interests which have never, in fact, been protected happen to be exactly the artistic ones."[76] Furthermore, the conviction that cinema must be regarded as a medium of artistic expression, regardless of its often quite questionable contents, makes it necessary to analyze the legislative regulation that contributes in no small manner to its very survival. The question of whether revision of public intervention in the cinema is desirable is another matter; and on that issue we can express our broad agreement.

The State intervenes in the sector of cinema in both a *direct* and an *indirect* way. Direct intervention is administered through public structures. We have already discussed the Experimental Center for Cinema (upon which the National Movie Library depends) and the Autonomous Cinema Management Agency (which includes three publicly controlled corporations, Cinecittà, LUCE, and Italnoleggio). The indirect instruments of public intervention operate through an interconnected system of legal provisions that assist the various operators in this field. Attention should be directed toward this second type of State intervention, which, in terms of the financial resources employed, is the most noteworthy.

The system spelled out by legislation,[77] apart from resting on a large credit apparatus, is organized along two basic lines. First is *mandatory programming* which consists of a guarantee that movies will be shown in theaters and provides for contributions to producers and allowances to exhibitors. It also includes *awards* which are given to works that have reached a certain high level of quality.

It is important to explain, preliminary to a more detailed description of the system, how the 1965 law distinguishes the various types of movies subject to legislative regulation. A full-length feature film is longer than 1600 meters; shorts are not less than 290 meters; and clips of topical interest are between 200 and 250 meters. Finally, movies "whose content is especially suited to promote the ethical, cultural, and civic development of youth below the age of 16" are deemed to be "produced for youth," regardless of their length or nationality.

With the exception of movies produced for youth, any others seeking public benefits must be recognized to be of Italian origin. The requirements to obtain Italian nationality vary according to the type of movie. Full-length movies "produced in an original Italian version'' are considered to be of Italian origin if they have ''been, for the most part, filmed in Italy by enterprises belonging to Italian citizens or by corporations that are legally situated in Italy, if they have Italian administrators and carry out the bulk of their activity in Italy. The following requirements must always be met:

a) the subject of the movie must be by an Italian author or adapted or abridged by an Italian author;

b) the director must be Italian, and the scenarists for the most part, must be Italians;

c) at least two thirds of the primary roles and at least three fourths of the secondary roles must be given to Italian actors;

d) at least three fourths of the other artistic and technical personnel used in the movie must be Italians; and

e) the remainder of the technical, executive, and labor personnel must be entirely Italian.''

Shorts ''produced by Italian firms and filmed entirely in Italy with Italian technical and artistic personnel'' are considered to be of Italian origin. Movies of topical interest are so classified when they are ''produced by Italian firms and filmed mostly in Italy with Italian technical personnel.'' Determination of nationality is made by the Ministry.

A weakening of the favoritism shown to indigenous film production is expressed by provisions which allow Italian nationality for full-length and short films produced in cooperation with foreign firms. This is also allowed for full-length films produced with the participation of foreign firms. These provisions compensate somewhat for the autarchic instincts reflected in the regulations.

The declaration of Italian nationality is an indispensable condition for the cinematographic work to be eligible for mandatory programming. But there is more. Full-length movies must demonstrate ''beyond adequate technical standards, sufficient artistic, cultural, or spectacular value.'' ''Films that vulgarly exploit sexual themes for profit'' are excluded from mandatory programming. The required elements are verified by a Commission of experts. Once the Commission has made a favorable judgment, the movie is admitted to mandatory programming. This does not, however, guarantee that the movie will be programmed. While cinema operators are obliged to ''reserve a minimum of 25 days in each trimester of projection . . . for Italian full-length features admitted . . . to mandatory programming within the last five years,'' it is not established which and how many of these films must be selected by the operators. In this matter they have full discretion.

The situation is different for shorts. Their mandatory programming depends upon either having received an award for quality or having been ''produced by the Istituto LUCE on behalf of the State Administration, public agencies, or corporations of predominant State participation'' and being judged to have ''cultural or spectacular value'' by the Commission cited above.

Only full-length movies admitted to mandatory programming enjoy additional benefits. The producer is entitled to ''13% of the gross receipts of the shows where the movie has been projected. This holds for a period of five years beginning with the movie's first public projection.'' The director and the authors of the idea and script split equally 0.4 percent of the same receipts. Theater operators benefit from all types of movies. They receive an allowance based on a percentage of the revenue taxes on receipts. This amounts to 18 percent for operators ''that show only full-length movies admitted to mandatory programming''; 3 percent goes to operators ''that show at least one of the shorts admitted to mandatory programming in addition to full-length features''; 2 percent goes to operators who ''show, in addition to full-length movies, a movie clip of topical interest . . .''; 50 percent is given to operators who have scheduled a show made up of ''either only one full-length film declared to be 'for youth,' or of a similarly designated full-length feature plus a short 'produced for youth,' or of a series of shorts all designated 'produced for youth.' ''

Mandatory programming seems to be established primarily to support entrepreneurial activity. It is through the device of awards for quality that objectives of an artistic-cultural nature are met. In fact, while it is true that for a full-length feature to be admitted for mandatory programming the ''artistic, cultural, or spectacular value'' must be weighed, the careful reader will appreciate the critical importance of the conjunction ''or.''[78] This allows even a movie of poor artistic and cultural quality to be admitted for mandatory programming solely on the basis of an ambiguous ''spectacular value.'' The issuance of awards for quality, on the contrary, depends upon certification of ''particular artistic and cultural qualities.''

Such a system of artistic promotion is, however, totally inadequate for its goals. The awards follow the completion of a work and cannot always be obtained and, therefore, ''do not stimulate or encourage a certain type of production.''[79] Moreover, the size of the award, perhaps meager from the beginning, is absolutely insufficient because it has not been up-dated since it was proposed nearly twenty years ago.

The regulations governing the awards also vary according to whether the work in question is a full-length feature or a short. Full-length features that have won a certificate of quality receive 40 million lire. The certificates, which are granted only to films admitted to mandatory programming, never total more than thirteen every six months. The Minister acts on the advice of a Commission which must certify that the film possesses those ''particular artistic and cultural qualities.'' Full-length features that have obtained this certificate secure for the theater operator who schedules them an additional allowance of 25 percent of the admissions tax that can be added to those already mentioned.

For shorts of Italian nationality, the following awards are available: ''a) two awards of 10 million lire each; b) 8 awards of 7 million lire each; c) 20 awards of 5.5 million lire each.'' These are awarded each trimester by the Minister on the advice of another Commission which must certify that ''the shorts achieve a particularly high level of technical, artistic, and cultural value.''

The system of credit for entertainment activities is not directly operated by the State. Even though it is not directed toward cultural promotion, it is important for the financial sustenance of the movie, theater, and music sectors. It is operated by two autonomous sections of the Banca Nazionale del Lavoro.

The Autonomous Section for Cinematographic Credit (S.A.C.C.) was established in 1935 and its new statute was approved in 1966. It has a regular fund plus additional funds added over time to meet special needs. The *regular fund* is used to provide financing for the production, distribution, and merchandising of films and for the operation of movie theaters, as well as to provide advances against State subsidies. Among the additional funds, the *special fund* is used for ''contributions toward the interest on loans'' obtained from the Section's regular fund or from other banks ''to finance domestic movie production.'' The *particular fund* is planned ''for the financing of movies inspired by artistic and cultural goals.'' The *intervention fund* is oriented toward financing and consolidation of production, distribution, and export of Italian movies as well as toward rendering similar assistance to technical laboratories in the cinematographic sector. It further provides "for granting of capital funds to operators and owners of movie theaters." The *sustaining fund* is assigned toward the "grant of capital funds and discount financing that favors operators or owners of movie theaters for the adaptation of structures and for modernization of equipment" as well as toward the "adaptation and renovation of small movie halls."

The Autonomous Section for Theatrical Credit (S.A.C.T.) was only established in 1967 and has little importance in comparison to S.A.C.C. It manages credit for both the musical and prose theater sectors. Its major activity is to make advance payments or provide financing based on State subsidies. It also acts in favor of theater operations or activities that do not benefit from State assistance.

Neither the authorizing legislation nor the S.A.C.T.'s statute, approved in 1969, make any mention of criteria that might govern the management of theatrical credit, so that this activity has little autonomous effect on cultural promotion. Indeed, for the most part, it simply reinforces the system of State subsidies since it is, in large part, linked to them.[80]

State Expenditures in the Artistic Sector from 1945 to the Present

In this final section, we analyze the flow of State funds to the various sectors of the arts, focusing on the budgets of the Ministry of the Cultural Heritage and of the Ministry of Entertainment and Tourism. The data are drawn from every fifth year between 1945 and 1980, plus 1981 and 1982.

Some preliminary observations will illuminate the methodology and the criteria employed in the analysis.[81]

(a) Since both of these Ministries are of relatively recent origin, we have examined the budgets of the Ministry of Public Instruction for years prior to 1975 for those items now under the jurisdiction of the Ministry of the Cultural Heritage, and we have examined the budgets of the Prime Minister's Office for years prior to 1958 for those items now under the jurisdiction of the Ministry of Tourism and Entertainment.

(b) Because of frequent changes in the headings under which expenditures are reported, the over-time analysis must be limited to gross expenditures devoted to the various sectors of the arts.

(c) The analysis focuses on two aspects of government support of the arts in Italy. First, the trend of available State funds and actual expenditures for the arts has been traced. In doing this we consider both the share of the total State budget devoted to the arts, and the breakdown of expenditures among the various artistic sectors, in order to paint a picture of State arts policy. Second, the ratio between available funds and disbursements has been analyzed. This is in order to evaluate the speed with which expenditures are actually made and, therefore, the productivity and efficiency of the procedures.

(d) Financial flows have been evaluated in both nominal and real terms, in order to control for inflation. To permit comparison in real terms, the values for earlier periods have been stated in terms of 1982 lire.

Theoretically, artistic policy should be evaluated on the basis of available funds since the eventual partial expenditure of funds may be the result either of established procedures (often slow and muddled) or of an inefficient bureaucracy (at times dull, sometimes unprepared), rather than the result of bad political choices. On the other hand, the deliberate assignment of discretion to the administrative level is very frequent. This transfers responsibility for decisions concerning expenditures to administrative organs. Thus they have *de facto* authority over arts policy. Consequently, in order to assess arts policy, it is imperative that we consider in addition the sums actually expended.

The level of actual State expenditures for the arts has definitely increased between 1945 and 1982, both in nominal and in real terms. However, while there has been constant growth in nominal expenditures, and this growth has been rather noteworthy at times (e.g., from 1975 to 1980 expenditures tripled), in real terms expenditures for the arts have not grown progressively, although there has been an overall increase. In fact, growth displays two slight pauses in the periods 1955–60 and 1970–75, plus a drop from 1980 to 1981 followed by an increase in 1982 (which did not, however, restore arts spending to its 1980 level). (See Table 1.)

Any optimism felt after this first perusal of the data is reduced upon noting the meager percentage of total State expenditures devoted to the arts—always below 1 percent. Any feeling of optimism is further dashed upon examining the curve's direction; after rising to 0.74 percent of total State expenditures in 1955, it displays a gradual drop (suspended between 1965 and 1970). The curve shows that, while it is possible to speak of an absolute increase in arts expenditures, not only has there been no relative increase but in fact there has been a steady decline since 1955 in the share of public spending devoted to the arts. (See Figure 1.)

It is interesting to look behind these general trends to the pattern of actual expenditures in the three sectors of the arts. Expenditures for the *material patrimony* grew in a noteworthy manner from 1945 to 1982 in both nominal and real terms. However, in real terms there was a pause in growth between 1950 and 1955 and a slight drop between 1981 and 1982. There was also substantial growth between 1945 and 1982 in funding for the *theater* (which includes both music and drama). Moreover, this growth exceeded that for the material patrimony. There was, however, a drop in both nominal and real terms between 1980 and 1981, with the real drop being quite significant and only partially restored in 1982. The trend for *cinema* is quite different. Nominal expenditures grew between 1945 and 1982, even though almost all of the growth occurred before 1955. In real terms, of course, State expenditures for the cinema increased greatly until 1955, but since then have declined more or less steadily. We can observe a pause from 1965 to

TABLE 1. Actual State Expenditures for the Arts*

	Nominal	*Real*
1945/46	95.032	1,885.757
1950/51	9,062.254	91,787.945
1955/56	21,875.693	183,868.481
1960,61	23,755.152	175,884.333
1965	33,907.467	198,107.766
1970	59,886.544	307,373.675
1975	100,856.869	302,187.350
1980	387,466.971	535,091.886
1981	400,914.205	466,423.586
1982	488,221.362	488,221.362

*In millions of lire.

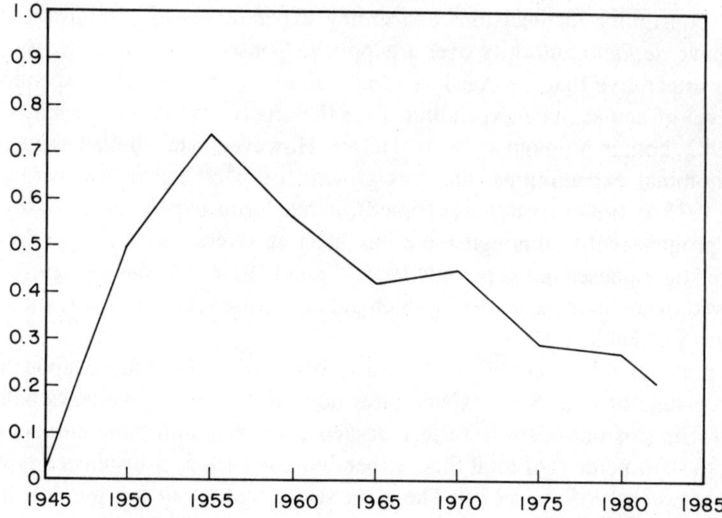

FIGURE 1. Percentage of total State expenditures devoted to the arts, 1945–82 (in nominal terms).

1970, and a slight increase in 1982, when it barely surpassed the 1980 level. (See Figures 2 and 3.)

In general, the State's pattern of expenditures for the arts appears to be not so much the product of a well conceived and carefully considered policy for the arts, as the result of having to respond to changing circumstances. In fact, the curves portraying expenditures, especially in real terms, are fairly irregular. The trend lines also are quite often in divergence among themselves. However, these diverging trend lines can be explained.

For example, if we exclude 1945, when support for the material patrimony predominated (and the sum was so meager as not to be very significant), we find that until 1965 it was the cinematographic sector that absorbed the largest part of State aid. This was because, immediately after the war, the cinema required a consistent amount of public

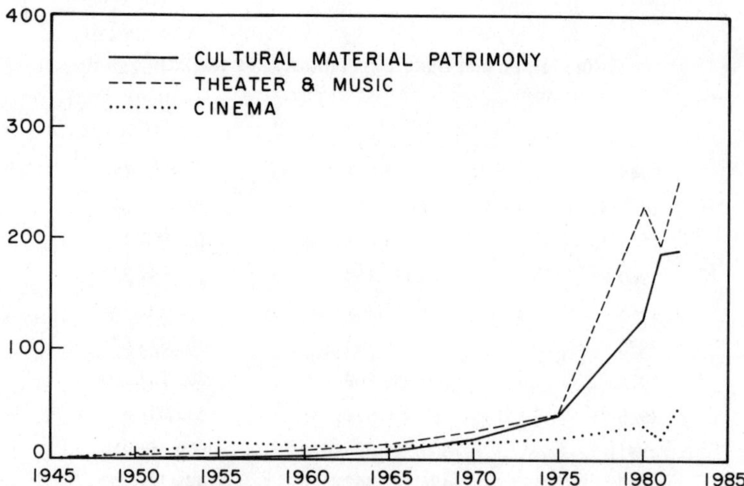

FIGURE 2. Actual total disbursements, 1945–82 (in nominal terms).

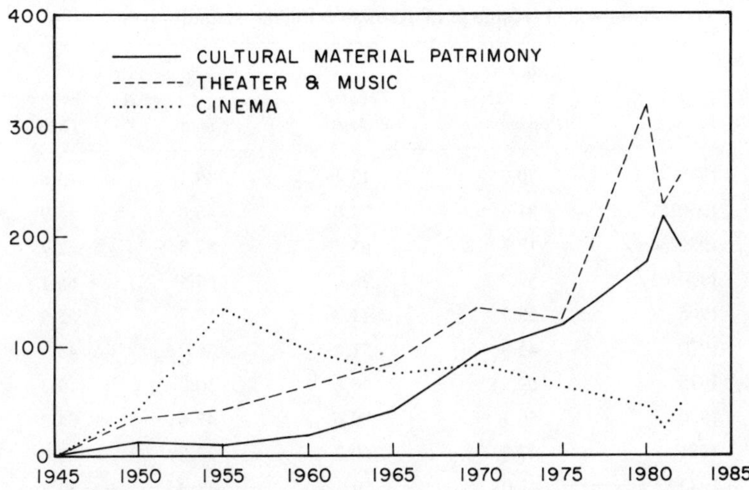

FIGURE 3. Actual total disbursements, 1945–82 (in real terms).

support. Afterwards, its own commercial vitality, which certainly exceeded that of the other arts, gave the film industry a degree of self-sufficiency.[82]

In the same way, from 1965 to 1982, the theater became the largest recipient of State funds. This was due to its growing enervation caused by high production costs that hardly ever allowed management to make a profit.

Finally, similar circumstances explain why, starting in 1970, the material patrimony obtained higher levels of support. It did so in the wake of slow but sure recognition of the importance of its special problems for the development of art (and culture in general). It was only then, indeed, that the cries of alarm and appeals for assistance of the 1960s to stem the degradation and impoverishment of the immense national historical artistic patrimony began to find a response.

To conclude, the efficiency with which government programs to aid the arts are administered in Italy deserves a comment. This requires consideration of the relationship between available funds and the actual disbursement of funds. From 1945 to 1982, only between 43.6 percent and 66.1 percent of the available funds have actually been spent. If there had been a carefully planned policy for the arts, one would have expected a pattern of gradual increase in the percentage of available funds being spent. Instead, the pattern is a see-saw of alternating ups and downs, providing additional confirmation that there is no planning for progressively accelerating disbursements. These patterns apply to all sectors. (See Table 2.)

The increase in the rate of disbursement for the theater and cinema that took place in 1980 might be regarded with a measure of optimism (respectively, they reach levels that are 40 percent and 17.6 percent above those of 1975). These increases are larger than the corresponding decrease in disbursements for the material patrimony, and produce an overall increase in general efficiency [success in spending the money] to 64.2 percent of available funds, a 20.9 percent increase over 1975. Still, prudence of judgment is advised by the data for 1981 and 1982 which, even if not quite comparable to earlier data which represented five-year intervals, may prefigure yet another drop in the rate of disbursements in 1985. It has also to be noted that the highest efficiency in the spending of available funds is achieved by the theater sector.

TABLE 2. Percentage of Available Funds Actually Spent*

	Cultural Material Patrimony	*Theater & Music*	*Cinema*	*Total*
1945/46	70.0	13.1	49.1	43.6
1950/51	81.4	74.0	46.0	57.9
1955/56	17.7	65.2	57.3	52.7
1960/61	53.7	76.0	63.5	66.1
1965	59.7	71.7	55.7	62.5
1970	45.9	51.4	36.9	45.0
1975	62.2	40.6	30.0	43.3
1980	50.1	80.6	47.6	64.2
1981	47.3	60.3	37.2	52.0
1982	42.0	59.1	48.0	50.2
Mean	53.0	59.2	47.0	53.7

*Calculated on nominal values.

The data reveal that there are some noteworthy "not disbursed funds" in public expenditures for the arts, even if sums that are actually disbursed are composed primarily of the current year's appropriations. The average percentage of the total disbursements for the arts composed by disbursed appropriations is 57.1 percent, with a low of 36.4 percent in 1955 (which is the only occasion when the figure drops below 50 percent) and a high of 66.6 percent in 1980. (See Table 3.)

Detailed examination reveals that it is again the theater that keeps the average percentage of current appropriations among total disbursements for the arts high. In the

TABLE 3. Composition of Disbursed Funds for the Arts

	Current Appropriations	*"Not Disbursed Funds"*
1945/46	56.1%	43.9%
1950/51	54.6%	45.4%
1955/56	36.4%	63.6%
1960/61	54.8%	45.2%
1965	62.8%	37.2%
1970	52.2%	47.8%
1975	62.5%	37.5%
1980	66.6%	33.7%
1981	65.4%	34.6%
1982	59.4%	40.6%
Mean	57.1%	42.9%

TABLE 4. Composition of Disbursed Funds in the Three Sectors

	Cultural Material Patrimony		*Theater & Music*		*Cinema*	
	Appropriation	*"Not Disbursed Funds"*	*Appropriation*	*"Not Disbursed Funds"*	*Appropriation*	*"Not Disbursed Funds"*
1945/46	92.2%	7.8%	95.1%	4.9%	1.0%	99.0%
1950/51	33.8%	66.2%	79.3%	20.7%	41.3%	58.7%
1955/56	76.8%	23.2%	72.1%	27.9%	22.0%	78.0%
1960/61	68.5%	31.5%	79.6%	20.4%	42.1%	57.9%
1965	42.2%	57.8%	73.2%	26.8%	69.0%	31.0%
1970	58.2%	41.8%	74.5%	25.5%	9.3%	90.7%
1975	75.1%	24.9%	70.5%	29.5%	22.5%	77.5%
1980	57.3%	42.7%	76.4%	23.6%	33.0%	67.0%
1981	51.7%	48.3%	84.0%	16.0%	15.5%	84.5%
1982	37.7%	62.3%	76.9%	23.1%	52.2%	47.8%
Mean	59.3%	40.7%	78.2%	21.8%	30.8%	69.2%

theater, in fact, this average is equal to 78.2 percent of total disbursements, against 59.3 percent in the material patrimony and barely 30.8 percent in the cinema.[83] (See Table 4.)

The extent to which the occurrence of "not disbursed funds," which is of considerable scale, is caused by the carrying over of previous "not disbursed funds" from earlier fiscal years rather than the failure to spend the current year's appropriations, remains to be explored. To find the answer it is necessary to determine the percentages of appropriations and of "not disbursed funds" available that have actually been spent in each fiscal year. The average percentage of appropriations disbursed from 1945 to 1982 is 46.5 percent of those available (with a minimum of 30.1% in 1945 and a high of 63% in 1980), while an

TABLE 5. Percentage of Appropriations and "Not Disbursed Funds" Actually Spent

	Appropriations	*"Not Disbursed Funds"*
1945/46	30.1	102.3
1950/51	48.0	77.2
1955/56	30.9	71.8
1960/61	53.2	86.5
1965	55.0	75.7
1970	40.6	51.1
1975	50.8	34.8
1980	63.0	66.9
1981	46.8	66.0
1982	46.3	56.9
Mean	46.5	68.9

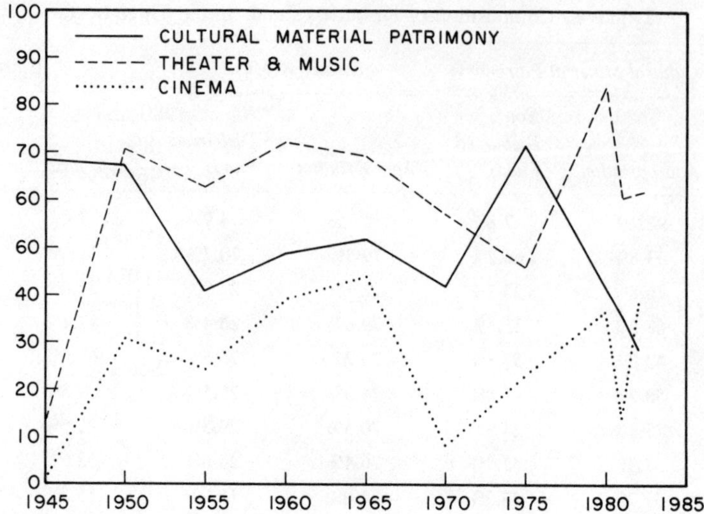

FIGURE 4. Percentage of current appropriations actually spent, 1945–82.

average of 68.9 percent of the available "not disbursed funds" has been spent (with a low of 34.8% in 1975—the only time when the figure drops below 50%—and a high of 102.3% in 1945[84]). (See Table 5.)

As we have seen, the "not disbursed funds" have been spent at a higher rate than appropriations have been spent. Therefore, despite the fact that most funds disbursed are made up of expenditures of current appropriations, the "not disbursed funds" phenomenon seems to be generated exactly by the sluggishness of the expenditures of current appropriations. This should be a source of concern because, if the inability to spend the appropriated funds in each fiscal year is not corrected, it will never be possible to reduce

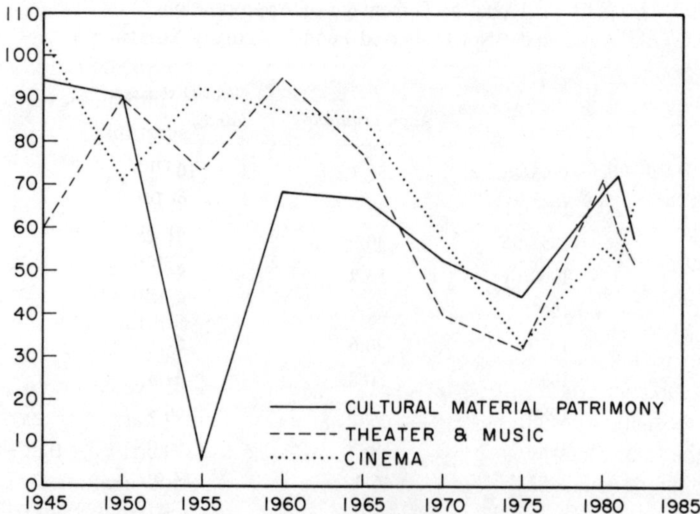

FIGURE 5. Percentage of "not disbursed funds" actually spent, 1945–82.

the existing "not disbursed funds." In fact, even if these are disbursed, they will progressively be replaced by those again produced in the current year.

Going to the details, the percentage of available appropriations that is spent is on the average higher in the theater (59.7% with a high of 84% in 1980 and a low of 12.6% in 1945) than in the material patrimony (49.8% with a high of 71.8% in 1975 and a low of 28.8% in 1982) or in the cinema (26% with a high of 44% in 1965 and a low of 0.9% in 1945). (See Figure 4.)

The average percentage of available "not disbursed funds" that is spent is instead uniformly high in the three sectors: for the cinema it is 70.5 percent (with a high 104% in 1945[85] and a low of 32.9% in 1975); for the theater it is 64.9 percent (with a high of 94.9% in 1960 and a low of 31.8% in 1975); for the material patrimony it is 62.2 percent (with a high of 94.3% in 1945 and a low of 6.1% in 1955). (See Figure 5.)

Conclusions

On the basis of the forgoing discussion, we can advance a few general conclusions:

a) With regard to the *organization* of government arts programs, it is clear that cosmetic structural reforms have been ineffective. As we have emphasized repeatedly, in the *traditional arts* structural changes in administrative organizations concerned with the arts that were not preceded by fundamental changes in the basic system of regulation of the artistic patrimony have had little effect. For the *representative arts,* ill-conceived reforms are especially illustrated by the consolidation of responsibility for entertainment with responsibility for tourism and sports in a single ministry; entertainment primarily involves the expression of artistic impulses, and cannot properly be considered as merely another form of recreation. More generally, the need remains to consolidate responsibility for both traditional and representational arts in a single structure. Finally, at the organizational level, we must emphasize once more the inequitable geographic distribution of operatic agencies, with the south being particularly disadvantaged.

b) With regard to public *activity,* in the *traditional arts* the legal measures for the guardianship of the cultural material patrimony provided in 1939 have proven useful in saving the vast Italian patrimony. Nevertheless, the complete absence of any program of subsidy for contemporary artists must be emphasized. In the *representative arts,* on the other hand, legal provisions do exist for the support of artists, although even these could be substantially improved. For example, the enormous discretionary power over the theater left to the bureaucracy must be considered unfair; the criteria specified by the law for the distribution of funds to "operatic, orchestral, and ballet productions" do not seem attuned to the stated aim of the law itself—"to promote the musical, cultural, and social development of the national collectivity"; for cinema, the system of so-called "awards for quality"—which are the only tools in this sector for the pursuit of artistic cultural goals—are inadequate and, moreover, have not kept pace with the times.

c) With regard to *expenditures,* we have shown that State spending in the artistic sector grew substantially from 1945 to 1982. On the other hand, we have also emphasized that in real terms this growth has not been constant, and that it has never reached even 1 percent of the total State budget. Moreover, it is particularly worrisome that the share of State spending devoted to the arts has declined in the period examined. The picture becomes even more negative when we consider the individual artistic fields. There has been no global planning of State intervention in the artistic field, the only goal being to respond to changing circumstances. The absence of any planning becomes especially clear in the pattern of "not dispersed funds," which instead of declining progressively, indicates a see-saw of alternative ups and downs.

To conclude, it seems that in Italy in the artistic field, rather than following a well-conceived policy, the State behaves extemporaneously—one could say in an "artistic way"—almost as if the "spontaneity" of the subject makes itself felt in its public administration as well.

[Translated by G. Falcone]

Notes

1. A. M. Sandulli, *Manuale di diritto amministrativo* (Napoli: Jovene, 1982), vol. I, p. 166.

2. L. Raggi, "L'ingerenza della pubblica amministrazione nelle manifestazioni artistiche," in *Studi in onore di C. Fadda* (Napoli: 1906), pp. 191ff., 194.

3. L. Raggi, pp. 204–5.

4. See N. Bobbio, *Politica e cultura* (Torino: Einaudi, 1955), now in "Reprints," 3rd. edition, 1980, specifically *Politica culturale e politica della cultura,* pp. 32ff, and *Difesa della libertà,* pp. 47ff. It should be stressed that, while on the one hand liberty is an indispensable precondition for any artistic manifestation, on the other hand there is an absolute necessity for public aid and public intervention—thereby legitimizing the notion of a "cultural policy"—in order to allow artistic expression which otherwise would be unable to manifest itself.

5. Among others, see P. V. Cannistraro, *La fabbrica del consenso. Fascismo e mass media* (Bari: Laterza, 1975); N. Bobbio, "La cultura e il fascismo," in *Fascismo e società italiana* (Torino: Einaudi, 1973), pp. 211ff.

6. In the vast literature on this point, see P. V. Cannistraro, op. cit.; L. Salvatorelli and G. Mira, *Storia d'Italia nel periodo fascista* (Torino: Einaudi, 1956), pp. 372ff; R. Zangrandi, *Il lungo viaggio attraverso il fascismo* (Milano: Feltrinelli, 1962), esp. pp. 120ff and 376ff.

7. P. V. Cannistraro, pp. 40–43.

8. P. V. Cannistraro, pp. 23–25; L. Salvatorelli and G. Mira, pp. 482–83; N. Bobbio, "La cultura e il fascismo," p. 241.

9. P. V. Cannistraro, pp. 22–23; L. Salvatorelli and G. Mira, pp. 498; N. Bobbio, "La cultura e il fascismo," p. 240.

10. P. V. Cannistraro, pp. 28ff.

11. P. V. Cannistraro, pp. 67ff, 101ff. The significant stages were essentially the following: (a) 1923, placement of the Office for the Press under the Office of the Prime Minister; (b) 1926, enlargement of the Office for the Press with the absorption of the Press Office of the Foreign Ministry; (c) 1934, replacement of the Office for the Press by the Undersecretariat of State for the Press and Propaganda, composed initially of three General Directorates (Italian Press, Foreign Press, Propaganda), and after some months, of two more (Cinematography and Tourism); (d) 1935, transformation of the Undersecretariat into the Ministry of the Press and Propaganda; (e) 1936, birth of two new General Directorships (Music and Theater, and Administrative Services); (f) 1937, the Ministry changes name and becomes the Ministry of Popular Culture.

12. P. V. Cannistraro, pp. 155–56. The Office of Contemporary Arts, instituted in January 1940, never went into operation, however, because of the entry of Italy into the war a few months later.

13. The current structure of state administration in the cultural sector consists of three Ministries (Public Instruction, Cultural Heritage, Tourism and Entertainment) and the Office of Literary Rights attached to the Office of the Prime Minister. We will deal later more analytically with the legislative evolution of cultural agencies after the Second World War. For the moment, one should

underscore how much this fragmentation stems from the structure originally imposed: Public Instruction and Cultural Heritage derive from the Ministry of National Education; Tourism and Entertainment and Literary Rights from the Ministry of Popular Culture.

14. F. Merusi, "Art. 9," in G. Branca, ed., *Commentario della Costituzione* (Bologna-Roma: Zanichelli, 1975), p. 435.

15. F. Merusi, p. 436.

16. V. Crisafulli, "La scuola nella Costituzione," in *Riv. Trim. Dir. Pubb.*, 1956, p. 68; for an analogous development of the question, see S. Fois, *Principi costituzionali e libera manifestazione del pensiero* (Milano: Giuffrè, 1957), which argues, on the basis of the specific regulation of liberty of art and science (and religion) with respect to the general liberty of expression of thought, that the drafters of the Constitution "intended to accord a particularly ample sphere of liberty and a particularly rigid protection" to these liberties, maintaining, that is, that they assume in comparison to other liberties, "a position which can be called 'privileged' " (pp. 45–52).

17. M. Grisolia, "Arte," in *E.d.D.*, vol. III, 1958, p. 111; G. Piva, "Cose d'arte," in *E.d.D.*, vol. XI, 1962, p. 94; G. Santaniello, "Gallerie, pinacoteche e musei," in *E.d.D.*, vol. XVIII, 1969, p. 443; G. Volpe, "Tutela del patrimonio storico-artistico nella problematica della definizione delle materie regionali," in *Riv. Trim. Dir. Pubb.*, 1971, p. 375.

18. A. M. Sandulli, "La tutela del paesaggio nella Costituzione," in *Riv. Giur. Edil.*, 1967, II, p. 74.

19. G. Berti, "Problemi giuridici della tutela dei beni culturali nella pianificazione territoriale regionale," in *Riv. Amm. Rep. Ital.* 1970, p. 619.

20. F. Merusi, p. 438. See also F. Salvia, "Cultura," in *Guida per le autonomie locali,* 1978 (p. 218) and 1979 (p. 217).

21. F. Salvia, "Cultura," in *Guida* 1978, p. 218.

22. For a list of the various laws of the Regions, see F. Salvia, "Cultura," in *Guida* 1978–83.

23. F. Bassanini, "Le potestà e le attività delle Regioni nel campo dei servizi," in *Organizzazione e diritto delle Regioni,* supplement no. 4 of the *Bollettino di legislazione e documentazione regionale* (Roma, 1982), p. 47.

24. A. Emiliani, *Una politica dei beni culturali* (Torino: Einaudi, 1974), pp. 122–23.

25. It is well known that "when one remarks on a discussion of the problem of knowing what art is, one never knows where or when one will be able to finish." H. Van Loon, *Le arti* (Milano: Bompiani, 1938), p. 8.

26. G. Palma, *Beni di interesse pubblico e contenuto della proprieta* (Napoli: Jovene, 1971), p. 353.

27. "[I]n modern society (and even more in that of the future), in which extreme technological specialization 'paralyses and atrophies all of the faculties,' art 'elevates a man from the sphere of industry to a superior sphere,' and represents the means (if not the only, certainly one of the most valid) to achieve a 'complete life.' " See G. Palma, p. 338.

28. N. Bobbio, "Libertà dell'arte e politica culturale," in N. Bobbio, *Politica e cultura,* pp. 84ff.

29. F. Merusi, "Art. 9," p. 435; G. Ghezzi, "L'intervento degli enti locali nella politica culturale," in *Pol. Dir.*, 1976, p. 462.

30. Currently, regarding the subject of this study, this Ministry is concerned only with artistic instruction.

31. M. Dallari, "Sull'organizzazione del Ministero per i beni culturali e ambientali," in *Foro Amm.* 1976, 1, 2, p. 3169; T. Alibrandi and P. Ferri, p. 61; N. Greco, *Stato di cultura e qestione dei beni culurali* (Bologna: Il Mulino, 1981), p. 105.

32. The report was published in *Riv. Trim. Dir. Pub.*, 1966, p. 119ff.

33. The report of the first Papaldo Commission was published in *Riv. Trim. Dir. Pub.*, 1970, p. 905ff.

34. M. Dallari, p. 3167. See also A. Emiliani, "Musei e muselogia," in *Storia d'Italia,* 5 (Torino: Einaudi, 1973), p. 1652; T. Alibrandi and P. Ferri, p. 11.

35. S. Cassese, "I beni culturali da Bottai a Spadolini," in *L'Amministrazione dello Stato. Saggi* (Milano: Giuffrè, 1976), p. 173.

36. D. Serrani, *L'organizzazione per ministeri* (Roma: Officina, 1979), p. 52. As the same author continues, the new Ministry seems to be "old wine in new bottles: taking from Public Instruction the General Directorates of 'antiquities and fine arts,' 'academies and libraries,' and of the 'diffusion of culture' and the peripheral organs operating in these sectors; from the Office of the Prime Minister the services relative to the State Recordings Library and a branch of the information and copyright services; from the Ministry of the Interior, the State Archives."

37. The M. S. Giannini study group relation can be found in T. Alibrandi and P. Ferri, p. 68ff.

38. D. Serrani, p. 52.

39. S. Cassese, p. 173.

40. D. Serrani, p. 52.

41. M. Dallari, p. 3183.

42. D. Serrani, pp. 52–53.

43. A. Fragola, *La legislazione italiana sulla cinematografìa* (Milano: Carisch, 1982), p. 11.

44. D. Serrani, p. 94.

45. E. Grassi, "L'intervento pubblico nel settore delle attività musicali," in *Intervento pubblico e libertà di espressione nel cinema, nel teatro e nelle attività musicali* (Milano: Giuffrè, 1974), p. 553ff; D. Giardini, "Sulla regolazione dell'attività musicale," in *Foro Amm.*, 1978, I, p. 1869ff; R. Ferrara, "L'amministrazione dello spettacolo: appunti e riflessioni," in *Foro Amm.*, 1980, I, p. 564ff.

46. E. Grassi, p. 591.

47. R. Juso, *Lineamenti di diritto pubblico dello spettacolo* (Roma: Bulzoni, 1967), p. 34.

48. LUCE became a public body in 1929 and was given a monopoly position in the production of documentaries and newsreels.

49. R. Zaccaria, "Le strutture pubbliche della cinematografìa in Italia," in *Intervento pubblico,* p. 181.

50. R. Zaccaria, p. 212.

51. R. Zaccaria, p. 216.

52. Grisolia, *La tutela delle cose d'arte* (Roma: 1952); Cantucci, *La tutela qiuridica delle cose d'interesse artistico o storico* (Padova: 1953); Geraci, *La tutela del patrimonio d' antichita e d'arte* (Napoli: 1956); Cantucci, *Le cose d'interesse artistico e storico nella qiurisprudenza e nella dottrina* (Napoli: 1968); Alibrandi and Ferri, *I beni culturali* and the numerous authors cited in Palma, *Beni di interesse pubblico* and *Il regime qiuridico della proprietà pubblica* (Torino: EGES, 1983).

53. Palma, *Il regime,* p. 225; *Beni,* pp. 247–51.

54. Truly, this notification may have no more than a declaratory value if one remembers that the procedure consists essentially of technical evaluations and in consequence there is little room for discretion. In fact, the object of the judgment would be the mere suitability of the item to represent an item of historical artistic value.

55. With regard to privately owned real property, a law of 1961 requires that ones "restored at complete or partial state expense, must remain accessible to the public according to procedures fixed on a case by case basis in conventions agreed by the Ministry and the individual owners."

56. G. Piva, *Cose d'arte,* p. 109.

57. The varying stringency of the regulations governing export relative to the stricter regulations concerning conservation can be explained with regard to the political climate characterizing the period in which the law was passed and the inherently contradictory objectives pursued: the desire to protect the precious national artistic patrimony and, at the same time, not to harm private commercial interests. The general design of the law, in fact, demonstrates a certain ambiguity. In fact, if it is true that it was established with the intention of "putting into place an adequate protective system for the monumental artistic and historic patrimony of the nation" (in the words of the *Relazione alla Camera* of Minister Bottai, *Le Leggi,* 1939, p. 892), in concrete terms it

introduced a less rigid system of export regulation, allowing even the export of items subject to notification, that is, items whose relevance to the national patrimony had already been determined.

58. R. Ferrara, *L'amministrazione dello spettacolo,* p. 559.

59. Although modified in connection with changes in structure (establishment of the Ministry of Tourism and Entertainment) and regulation (separation of musical activity from the prose theater), the composition of the commission has remained predominatly bureaucratic and corporative. R. Ferrara, p. 558; P. Caretti, "L'intervento dello Stato nel teatro di prosa," in E. Grassi, *Intervento pubblico,* p. 471; C. Zanchi, "Dove va il teatro italiano. La legislazione e le strutture," in *Città e Regione,* 3, 1978, p. 8.

60. Ferrara, pp. 558–59; Zanchi, pp. 8–9; Caretti, pp. 471, 483.

61. Ferrara, p. 564.

62. This lack of clarity may have been intentional, leaving room for the exercise of discretion by the managers of the funds, freed from rigidly established criteria.

63. Caretti, p. 484; Ferrara, p. 564.

64. Zanchi, p. 10.

65. ". . . on one side, they wanted to avoid discriminations that would have to be justified with reference to legal norms that, on the contrary, did not exist. On the other side, they succeeded only in photographing the existing situation, without any possibility of cutting through the rule to allow the survival, sometimes ephemeral, of initiatives that otherwise would be in large measure incapable of maintaining themselves in an autonomous manner." P. Caretti, p. 485.

66. R. Ferrara, *L'amministrazione dello spettacolo,* p. 564; D. Giardini, *Sulla regolazione dell'attività musicale,* p. 1893; E. Grassi, *L'intervento pubblico nel settore delle attività musicali,* pp. 569, 628ff.

67. La Scala, as the "first autonomous agency to be recognized juridically, which has assumed a position of particular international prestige," was given a "particular position as *primus inter pares*" in the words used by Minister Corona, in *Le leggi,* 1967, p. 1683.

68. The Commission is composed of 32 members who represent various Ministries, RAI, the sectors directly and indirectly interested in public aid for music and musical culture; the classification is that of E. Grassi, p. 576, who also gives a detailed consideration of the working of the Commission.

69. In this regard it is worth mentioning the duty laid upon the operatic agencies to "program at least 20% of their performances for students and workers and to provide seats for them at reduced prices, also . . . through special season tickets or by reserving a portion of the seats at every presentation."

70. The regulation seems to have been designed in this regard with the object of establishing a provincial level of public musical service. But, in the same way that the territorial diffusion of operatic agencies and assimilated concert organizations has been inadequate, so the "traditional theaters" and "concert-orchestral institutions" are also maldistributed. On this point, see E. Grassi, p. 617.

71. For seasons organized by the "traditional theaters," "in cases of proven artistic need," the Minister may authorize "the employment in the principal roles of foreign artists in numbers not greater than $\frac{1}{4}$ of the company employed during the entire theatrical season."

72. Again, in cases of proven need, limited numbers of foreign artists may be employed.

73. The other two criteria to be considered in calculating the size of the subsidy are the "number and artistic level of performances" and "the geographic position in which the performance will take place."

74. A. Orsi Battaglini, "L'intervento economico statale a favore della cinematografìa," in *Intervento pubblico,* p. 58.

75. R. Ferrara, *L'amministrazione dello spettacolo,* p. 546; A. Orsi Battaglini, p. 107.

76. A. Orsi Battaglini, pp. 107–8.

77. A. Fragola, "Il nuovo ordinamento dei provvedimenti a favore della cinematografìa," in *Rass. Dir. Cin.* 1965, pp. 175ff; R. Perez, "La nuova disciplina legislativa della cinematografìa,"

in *Riv. Trim. Dir. Pubb.* 1966, pp. 978ff; M. Ascheri, ''La incentivazione della produzione cinematografica nella legislazione vigente,'' in *Studi Senesi* 1967, fasc. 3, pp. 397ff.

78. R. Perez, pp. 1002ff.

79. A. Orsi Battaglini, p. 111.

80. P. Caretti, pp. 478–79; E. Grassi, pp. 622–23. For a fuller development, see A. Orsi Battaglini, p. 108ff.

81. A variety of other adjustments also had to be made in order to render the data comparable over time and across sectoral divisions. For full details of the methods of data analysis, see G. Palma and G. Clemente di San Luca, *L'intervento dello Stato nel settore artistico: Analisi della situazione italiana dal 1945 al 1982* (Torino: Giappichelli, 1986).

82. This characteristic of the cinematographic sector makes it always more necessary to support the ''cinema of quality.'' It seems better, indeed, not to spend public funds to sustain enterprises unable to survive in the market, just to maintain the level of employment.

83. ''Not disbursed funds'' is a technical term in Italian public finance. It refers to funds appropriated for, but not spent in, previous years and available for dispersal during the current year. In the sector of cinema, the prevalence of disbursements from the ''not disbursed funds'' instead of current appropriations, is determined by the very particular rules for supporting this kind of art. According to these rules, it is normal to disburse funds in the fiscal years following that in which funds were appropriated.

84. The quantity of ''not disbursed funds'' spent can be larger than the quantity available because, in response to extraordinary events, a law assigns special funds that, when disbursed, are counted as the spending of ''not disbursed funds,'' without being added into the total of available ''not disbursed funds.''

85. See note 84.

5

Government and the Arts: The Netherlands

PIM FENGER*

Introduction

Government support for the arts on the national level in the Netherlands dates from the nineteenth century. In 1817, after the demise of the guild system, a state scheme for art education was set up and academies of fine art were founded in Amsterdam and Antwerp, albeit without financial provision by the government.[1] In 1826, support by the central government for music education emerged, with state conservatories in Amsterdam, The Hague, Brussels, and Liege.[2] The end of the nineteenth century saw government take responsibility for museums. After 1918 support for orchestras developed,[3] but it was only after 1945 that any significant support for the theater, opera, ballet, and the creative arts followed.

In the Netherlands, traditionally, there is no coherent political vision shaping government action and steering culture in a direction considered desirable, apart from the generally accepted view that different and diverse cultural values must be given a chance of expression. The absence of an overall cultural policy may be explained partly by the pillarized political culture of the Netherlands and the political interests vested in the continuance of that culture.

Up to the mid-1960s the Netherlands was considered an ideologically pillarized society.[4] The term ''*verzuiling*'' (pillarization) is used to mean the division of Dutch society into a number of ideological groupings: Protestants, Catholics, Socialists, and, to some extent, Liberals. Each of these groups was distinct and self-sufficient, so that, for example, the whole social and cultural life of Catholics took place within the Catholic bloc: they went to Catholic schools, read Catholic newspapers, listened to the Catholic broadcasting service, participated in athletics in Catholic sports clubs, and had their own Catholic trade unions and welfare organizations. Each bloc had its own political party in a multi-party system, with no party holding a majority.[5] The blocs formed relatively self-contained networks of dependency relationships among individuals, while the political style of the elite, with its accommodating stance and readiness to compromise, helped to

*Special thanks are due to Prof. Dr. Hans van den Bergh, Prof. Dr. Hans Daudt, Hans Onno van den Berg, Berend-Jan Langenberg, Ronald Spoor, and Otto Valkman for their critical comments and suggestions on this chapter in draft form, and Paul Vincent for his translation of the draft.

form coalition governments, thus ensuring the continuation of a stable democracy of the consociational type.[6]

Next to the phenomenon of pillarization, it must be borne in mind that the Netherlands is a decentralized unitary state which, while in a legal sense centralized, strives at the same time, through constitutional, provincial, and municipal legislation, for autonomy of the various levels of government.[7] The deeply-rooted tradition of local autonomy, certainly as far as culture is concerned, is another equally important cause of the fragmented nature of Dutch society[8] that helps to explain the absence of an overall cultural policy.

The Netherlands has had, however, some experience of cultural policy, albeit of an unpleasant kind.[9] From 1940 to 1945, National-Socialist cultural policy in the Netherlands had two aims: Nazification and Germanification. It operated through a number of vehicles, such as the abominable *Kulturkammer* for writers, actors, and musicians, its own journals, its own interpretation of Dutch history,[10] and, last but not least, censorship. The resistance to National-Socialist cultural repression, which was in large part journalistic and literary in nature, made a significant contribution to developments in arts policy after the war. Initially, resistance was organized on the basis of the ideologically distinct "*zuilen*" (pillars).

During the war, a mutual understanding was reached among artists, intellectuals, and politicians of the different pillars. In the postwar period, this understanding contributed to a temporary breakthrough in Dutch political relations. Among the artists, the breakthrough manifested itself by the foundation of the Federation of Artists' Associations in 1945. The Federation, made up of artists themselves, is one of the most important pressure groups in the artistic domain.

It was in this postwar period that the principles of government involvement in the arts were formulated. This can be partly explained by the rise of mass culture in the shape of films and gramophone records, and also dance halls, which threatened the hold of the elites within the various pillars over the cultural behavior of their grass-roots supporters.[11] Legitimation of an active government policy in the field of the arts was sought by Protestants, Catholics, and Socialists alike, partly to counteract the consequences of the rising popular mass culture.

On the wings of the expanding welfare state (1960–80), with its climate of demands on and political commitments to equal distribution, its budget mechanism, and its political judgments about the trade-off of culture against economic efficiency, the modest support of the arts in the post-war "take-off period" grew into a considerable sum of money, spent by the State in numerous ways directly, or indirectly via provinces and municipalities.

Developments and Issues since 1945

1945–1960. The Thirst for Culture, Preservation, Edification, and Dissemination

The experience of the Second World War, with its dearth of cultural activities, led at its conclusion to a veritable thirst for culture in the Netherlands. In the immediate postwar period, plays, concerts, and operas were invariably sold out. In addition, less "official" forms of art and culture, such as cinema, dance halls, jazz concerts, cabarets, and operettas enjoyed great popularity. A need was felt to make up for the five lost years, and partly as a result of the outcome of the war, things American were widely regarded as superior. The widespread vogue of "popular entertainment" and the emergence of forms of artistic expression with a supposedly questionable aesthetic content, caused great concern to the majority of political parties.[12] The three confessional parties (Catholic, Protestant, and Calvinist) were worried that such coarse fare as the cinema and jazz would lead young people astray. The elite within these parties perceived a cultural threat, variously called "the film and cinema problem," "Americanization," and "the loss of moral standards."[13] The Social Democrats worried about "cultural decay." Motivated by a somewhat paternalistic, Christian-inspired view of the working class, these groups took it upon themselves to "edify."[14] Dancing, jazz, and the cinema were not calculated to achieve this aim.

The confessional parties and the Social Democrats determined the shape of Dutch politics in the postwar period, and hence also that of Dutch cultural policy. Edification of the masses and the promotion of the higher arts in order to combat coarse entertainment and nihilism were the keynotes of this policy.

The concern about moral decline and the government's view of its role in cultural preservation and popular edification echoes through the lengthy parliamentary debate held in 1950. As the first postwar debate of any consequence on the subject, it dealt with government policy on art and culture. The government presented its own views on the State's role in "artistic culture"—in abridged form—as follows:

> a. to preserve, maintain, and where possible expand the nation's artistic heritage for the benefit of present and future generations;
>
> b. to promote the presentation of that heritage and of Dutch cultural achievements to a wider section of the community, as well as to facilitate creative expression and enjoyment of art (e.g., the subsidizing of orchestras and theater companies);
>
> c. to foster important initiatives designed to make young people and adults more receptive to aesthetic experience (to educate and refine the aesthetic sensibilities of the young and of working people);
>
> d. to assist in the advancement of art and the support of artists (through the training of young artistic talent, prizes, scholarships, commissions, and the involvement of artists in the adornment and interior design of public buildings);
>
> e. to help narrow the gap between high art on the one hand and popular taste on the other (healthy popular art should be encouraged and supported alongside high art);
>
> f. to promote the showing of Dutch artistic achievements abroad in order to enhance the country's prestige and international standing; and
>
> g. to support, assist in, and initiate large-scale cultural ventures, which would not be feasible without State support (orchestras, theatrical companies, opera, exhibitions, film projects).

The government did, however, attach an important restriction to the degree to which it would perform these tasks: "As history has shown, both elsewhere and in this country, the fine arts are capable of flourishing without any impetus from government. Culture is first and foremost the responsibility of the citizens, individually and collectively. Priority must be given to individuals and to individual initiative, and to the independent organization they give to culture. Where these prove insufficient, government must lend a helping hand."

In Parliament the Social Democrats were keen to emphasize an "active cultural policy" designed to raise the mass of the population to the level of "cultural equality" (through the dissemination of culture), to "free individuals as social beings," and to improve the spiritual caliber of the nation. The confessional parties and the Liberals hesitated; large-scale government intervention might give culture an artificial character and over-involvement might easily lead to an infringement of individual freedom. There was in Parliament, nevertheless, "a general conviction that the State's responsibilities extend to art and culture," as the Minister put it in his summing-up. The Liberals' final statement "that the Minister, in view of the many expressions of encouragement, should continue on the same course and strive for the maximum allocation of funds for worthy cultural ends and for the practical and judicious support of art," met with general approval.

The arguments employed by artists themselves for support for the arts in the immediate post-war period were largely in accord with those of government. As was only to be expected, they put more stress on the socio-economic position of the artist. At the large conference of the Federation of Artists' Associations held in 1949, artists declared themselves aware ". . . that over and above their responsibility to improve their own lot they had a responsibility to further the cultural development of the Dutch people and to serve culture at the highest level." In addition, they considered that artists, "in view of their extremely important role in intellectual and social life," were entitled to a worthy position in society and to the fulfillment of among other things the following aspirations:[15]

> full recognition of their productive contribution to society;
> the right to employment befitting their professional qualifications and to remuneration commensurate with the imagined value of art to society;
> right to protection from the economic consequences of ill health, old age, and disablement for all artists, including those who are self-employed; and
> subsidies, which help to give artists greater economic security.

In the parliamentary debate there had been only incidental mention of the socio-economic position of the artist. Members did not consider it desirable "to make the artist as a skilled worker directly dependent on the State." The reluctance of politicians to place the artist himself at the center of political discussions on art can perhaps be explained by the relatively low social and professional prestige enjoyed by artists at the time. In a 1952 survey of popular attitudes on the prestige of fifty-six professions,[16] university professors came top of the list, painters in twenty-ninth place, and musicians in string orchestras in fifty-first place. In such a climate of opinion it probably made little sense to treat the artist himself as a central issue.

All in all, the outcome of the 1950 arts debate, which resulted in an appeal for more funds, was not without effect. The expenditure of the arts section of the Ministry of Education, Arts, and Sciences shows a marked expansion in relation to total government expenditure up to about 1965 (Figure 1). It must be added that the budget of the responsible Ministry itself, as a result of the policy of reconstruction, but especially because of the increase in the birthrate after 1945, showed a marked upward trend, which doubtless entailed an automatic expansion of the arts budget.

The increased resources were used above all for cultural dissemination. Local government spending increased the number of theaters and concert halls, while central government action was instrumental in expanding the number of orchestras (from 3 to 11) and in keeping the price of admission to theater and concerts low.

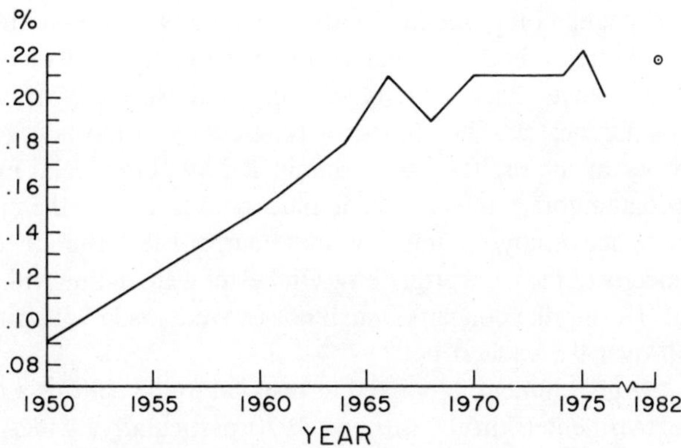

FIGURE 1. Expenditure of the Arts Section, afterwards Arts Directorate, as a percentage of total central government expenditure, 1950–1976 and 1982.
Source: Government Report on Art and Arts Policy (1976); Budget Statement 1983.

1960–1970. Changes in Cultural Orientation, but Largely Independent of Arts Policy

The most striking feature in the period between 1960 and 1970 is the shift in the basis of political justification of government involvement in cultural life. Instead of fear of mass culture and modernism in the arts, which threatened the existence of the pillars and which the dissemination of traditional culture was designed to combat, the cultural development of the individual was increasingly brought to the fore.

As in many other countries, the postwar generation had developed new sets of values, discarding tradition in the process. Provo has become the most renowned of Dutch protest and counter-cultural movements. Presenting itself in the mid-1960s not so much as a group but as an "image," Provo exerted an important influence on political culture in general and specifically on the style of artists' protest in 1969.[17] Hence the Dutch artists' protest campaign of the late 1960s was characterized by its irreverent, "fun" nature, although a grim undertone was certainly present. In the theatrical area, the protest of young actors and theater students was directed against the programs of the company which usually played in the municipal theater of Amsterdam. The action group called itself "Tomato." The name was chosen not only because of the traditional symbol of a tomato in the theater as an object with which one could show one's disapproval (actually a lot of tomatoes were thrown), but also by its color red, the color of the socialist movement. The Tomato group declared that theater must be based on new values, not only on the values of the bourgeoisie, the traditional theater-goers, but on values such as an honest distribution of goods, material as well as intellectual. Further, a theater group must share a political faith. The group sought to incorporate this common political faith into its program of performance. Theater should be a way of attacking set ideas in a society. Theater ought to be "a part of the revolution."

It is interesting to note how these demands differed from the demands in the theatrical world in the first part of the 1960s, such as restrictions on the conditions for touring, no play-doubling system, and one day off per week. At the end of the 1960s, the theme "social relevance" had replaced (temporarily) the earlier theme of more union-like professional demands.

The actions of young composers and musicians, the Nutcrackers (in Dutch we have the same word "noot" for both nut and note), had the same ideological background directed to social relevance. Their actions were directed especially toward the policy of the *Concertgebouw* Orchestra. The choice of programs was too bourgeois, they maintained. The repertory of the orchestra was dominated by commercial motives and there was no place for contemporary music. Music must be relevant for the entire society, not an aesthetic experience enjoyed only by the bourgeoisie. The disturbances of the Nutcrackers at concerts of the Concertgebouw Orchestra were in line with Provo: inconvenient but peaceful. During the concerts, small noises were made with pinch frogs, which could be heard all over the concert hall.

For its part, the government attempted to respond to the call for a new direction by setting up an "experimental kitty." Around 1970 particularly, widespread calls were made on funds available for artistic experiment. But those with the ideas, and especially the best among them, were hasty and impatient, so that the "experimental kitty," which could be drawn on only once a year, with a delay of eight months or so before one knew whether or not funds were to be allocated, did not have a really beneficial impact on new developments emerging from below. The main thrust of arts policy remained as it had been in the 1950s: the sought-for education of the population must lead to greater participation in traditional artistic forms of expression.[18]

As far as arts policy was concerned, there was as yet no question of government involvement with jazz or improvised music, let alone with pop music. Oddly enough, these areas were able to find a government-aided outlet, though not under the auspices of arts policy but in the context of youth work. Neither at the central nor the local level was there much contact between those government agencies responsible for the arts and those responsible for young people. Arts policy-makers tended to look askance at the cultural climate and artistic achievements supported by the government's socio-cultural youth policy, while on the other side arts policy was regarded as somewhat arrogant.

The *Paradiso,* which was set up in Amsterdam with the help of local and central youth-work funding, became a model for numerous other so-called open experimental youth centers. Activities were led by artists, both professional and amateur. The interest was and has remained enormous: the two largest centers in Amsterdam, *Paradiso* and the *Melkweg*—both subsidized, but not from the regular arts section budget—still draw some 500,000 visitors annually, 100,000 more than the two largest theaters in Amsterdam, the *Carré* and the *Stadsschouwburg* put together.

It is hard to escape the conclusion that the government's unstated aim was to keep young people, regarded as potentially rebellious, off the streets, and the term "repressive tolerance" was often used in this context. The channeling of supposed social and political aggression led all the same to the emergence of a flourishing network of performing arts which was especially stimulating for new forms of jazz and improvised music, and for experiments in special design, light, and sound. Similarly, it was in the youth centers in Amsterdam and the larger provincial towns, that an alternative film circuit first got under way, originally by screening scrapped but reassembled quality films which had been withdrawn from circulation for commercial reasons. After dabbling in banned (for example, "blue") films, among other things, the circuit subsequently turned increasingly to art movies considered unprofitable by commercial operators. In this way, thanks to the youth policy of central and local government, a subculture grew up quite independently of official artistic channels and of arts policy, which was of decisive importance for the artistic development of the Netherlands.

1970–1980. Government Reports, Professionalization, Government Involvement, and the Retarding Effect of Bureaucratization

In the mid-1970s the central government published a number of policy documents (*notas*) which represented a new departure in arts policy. The first of them, the *Nota Kunst en Kunstbeleid* (Report on Art and Arts Policy) of 1976, was followed quickly by individual reports on theater, orchestras, and museums. These documents were the products of policy development, both in the Federation of Artists' Associations and in the government, initiated in 1969 by the Minister of Cultural Affairs, Recreation, and Social Work, Marga Klompe, who promised an official report on the arts. The Minister's promise was one of the responses of the State to the artists' protest movements at the end of the 1960s.

In fact, the artists were a step ahead of the official report: the Federation had published its own arts report, entitled *Met verbeelding* (With a Little Imagination), in 1972. The central theme of the document was the social significance of art and creativity, both within and outside the artistic community. "By forcing themselves to take a stand on the relationship between art and society, artists are expressing a specific social responsibility which is at the same time a recognition of dependence and which may justify their appeal to society. For too long a new approach has been frustrated by one-sided thinking in terms of power, money, material progress and scientific and technological advance," declared the report. This was not so much a plea for an improved social status for the artist, as for a new social order. Society must, in the words of the report, follow the lead of the 1960s counter-culture and turn its back on the dominant direction of economic power and growth. "One may also talk of a replacement of a culture of power by a culture of personal growth, respect, wonderment and imagination," stated the artists, perhaps a little naively.

Four years later, the government's policy document on art took as its starting point the view that the need for the government to pursue an arts policy springs from society's interest in assigning art and the artistic media a clear role. The report formulated a so-called "enabling" policy, with as its main objectives:

1. the development and preservation of cultural values (the autonomy of art);
2. making cultural objects and events accessible (the availability of art);
3. the promotion of opportunities for the population to participate actively or passively in cultural manifestations (participation in art).

The new feature, compared with the tasks of government as these had been set out in 1950, was the notion that the State has a role in the development of the arts. But in other respects, too, it is possible to detect a shift in the relationship between government and the arts. In the general report, and in the subsequent individual reports, the content of art has for the first time become an object of policy. In this way orchestras and theater companies were assigned tasks in the area of the amateur pursuit of art and in artistic training, and were expected to contribute to the development of the arts. Also striking was the introduction of the term "social relevance" as a criterion for State support for the arts, on the grounds that "the social interest must underlie all policy, arts policy included." The call for social relevance issues directly from the protests of the 1960s.

Parliamentary discussion of the report was rather noncommittal and in subsequent years it was seldom referred to in Parliament. The reaction of the artistic community was different than might have been expected from their own report, *With a Little Imagination,* and, as in 1949, emphasized socio-economic demands. The first point made by the Federation with reference to the report was accordingly that artists are dependent for their income on public funds, allocated by government agencies. "An arts policy cannot exist without an incomes policy for professional artists, or a social policy establishing their conditions of employment, legal status, and job security," claimed the artists, who went on to invite the Minister to fill this gap, in properly constituted consultation.

The government report was too late to be politically effective. During the course of the 1970s, arts policy, like other sectors in Dutch society, was characterized by a certain flagging of the impulse for change.[19] Under the conditions of deconfessionalization, the emergence of television, and increased mobility, the earlier pillarized system, which in the 1950s and 1960s had led to the airing of rival views, had virtually disappeared by the end of the 1970s. The situation was dominated by increased government involvement in artistic and artists' organizations, as illustrated by the participation of government representatives on the boards of arts institutions as well as government representation on advisory bodies.[20] A striking example of increased involvement is the State financial support received by the major pressure-group, the Federation, since 1972.

A notable feature of the 1970s is the professionalization and academicization of policy. The development was noticeable on two fronts: both among the cultural interest groups and in government, an expanding guild of professionals trained in the social sciences appeared on the scene, bringing with them their own jargon and their own expertise. They came to form a sociologically based intermediary agency between on the one hand artists and traditional members of cultural institutions and on the other those politically responsible.[21] The effect of the intervention of this newly emerged class of professionals between government and its clients was a retarding one. Instead of directing their efforts primarily toward the renewal of culture, scholarship, and science, the Dutch secondary elites (the intelligentsia), Ellemers observed, appeared to be increasingly concerned with their own interests. In the field of scholarship and science, Daalder observed a comparable development at Dutch universities.[22] Preservation and expansion of the bureaucratic infrastructure, originally set up as a professional aid in articulating and coordinating the interests of artists, became ends in themselves.

1980–1984. Cut-backs, Reorientation, and Quality

Partly as a result of the economic crisis, arts policy, at the beginning of the 1980s, was caught up in large-scale changes in the whole basis of the welfare state. The means of achieving this were reassessment of collective expenditures, deregulation, and privatization. Alongside this was the reorganization of the administration itself, which helped to legitimize budget cuts.

As early as 1976, the Report on Art and Arts Policy had pointed out that the financial and economic outlook was such that public funds could not be expected in the short term to show the kind of growth that would present favorable prospects for the arts. Eighty-five percent of the arts budget consisted of staffing and material costs, which in accordance with the government's system of budgeting were adjusted annually in line with prevailing trends. It concerned mostly subsidized institutions, whose staffs enjoyed an almost civil-service status (the so-called trend-followers). Because of the application of government salary scales, in the view of the financial departments, this constituted a clearly demonstrable and recognizable salary policy. The Report gave notice that in the future development of policy, there would have to be shifts in the budget in order to meet the demands of new fields of interest (jazz, pop, fringe theater, etc.) under conditions of budgetary constraints. The exchange of "old for new" in the arts sector would be subject to constant review—no easy task, since infringement of the acquired salary rights and secondary benefits of the trend-followers is bound to meet with resistance from the complex of interests represented by trade unions, the Ministry of Home Affairs, and a sense of justice and threat in the civil service itself.

The change in the foundation of the welfare state brought about reassessment of the objectives of and motives for government involvement. In central government circles the suggestion is being voiced openly that in the coming decades there will be a development in the direction of "the State as guarantor." In such a situation, the State no longer aims to protect the citizen from himself. Government intervention outside the market sector would be confined to underwriting basic facilities. Although such prophecies are being made under a Christian-Democrat/Liberal coalition—which could be described as right of center—there are no clear indications that the largest party on the Left, the Social Democrats, has a financially viable solution which promises further expansion of the welfare state.

Besides the problems of financial viability, which force one to make choices, and so contribute whether one likes it or not to political awareness, the growing doubt about the achievements of the welfare state plays a role in the determining of priorities. In the view of some, for example, the welfare services have not succeeded in achieving their aim of making people function independently. On the contrary, many people have become more dependent than ever on a welfare bureaucracy: the supply of provisions has created its own demand instead of meeting actually existing needs.[23]

In these circumstances, how does the government see the development of arts policy in the 1980s? "Artistic and scholarly and scientific activity both determine to a large extent the quality of a society," stated the Minister of Culture in the statement accompanying his 1983 budget. In addition he observed that on the one hand, art needs room to determine for itself the direction it wants to take. On the other hand, there must be constantly renewed efforts to achieve the involvement of as large a public as possible. Policy will have to steer a middle course between these two needs. The Minister considered it acceptable that the involved public should in certain cases be a small one; the size of the public should, however, not be the result of selection on the basis of financial means. The arts will be subject to financial pressures in this time of cut-backs, but precisely because of the vulnerability of the arts in general, and of the creative arts in particular, the government has opted for a relatively small cut in the arts budget. This was by way of an exception, issuing from the agreement reached when the new government took office in 1982. The arts share with high-quality university research the honor of being treated relatively gently. The Minister sees possible savings in investigating the scope for privatization, especially in the theater.

In choosing what initiatives may or may not be eligible for subsidy, the government is anxious to make the criterion of *artistic quality* decisive. In this, one can see a parallel with research and science policy, in which the view also is taken that in future when it comes to a choice, quality must be decisive. As with the arts, the government wishes judgments of quality to be made by some agency other than itself. In cultural policy up to 1980, the case for annual increments rested especially on edification, dissemination, target-groups, and the underprivileged. In a recession situation, we see that threatened decreases were justified by reference to the notion of quality. This is an important change of course, which may have far-reaching consequences for arts policy.

Forms and Scope of Government Support

At all three levels of government—central, provincial, and local—we find various types of support for artists, artistic institutions, or artistic publics. In a number of cases, support is given through intermediary agencies and not administered by government itself. The complexity of government involvement in the arts world would be inadequately reflected if we were to confine ourselves to describing the forms of support. Within the three above-mentioned levels of government we encounter an unexpected differentiation of financial resources channeled toward the arts. This emerges forcefully in the case of the visual arts. Welters, for example, counted six ministries in the central government which provided funds benefiting visual artists by drawing on the resources of twenty departmental units.[24] Apart from all kinds of schools and creativity centers, he counted a further twenty-eight subsidized institutions, museums, and state enterprises which provide income for plastic artists. A cautious estimate of the number of similar major and minor sources of funding at all three levels would be in the region of one hundred fifty. This illustrates the pluralism of the arts support system.

The problem with this kind of quantification is that the researcher is faced with the question: what is art and who count as artists? Any distinction between art and non-art is open to question, and this has a distorting effect on official statistics. Only after forms of aesthetic expression, such as jazz, pop music, or photography, have achieved official recognition in the form of subsidy, are these forms included in the arts statistics, which does not help the comparability of the figures over a period of time. Table 1 gives the best

TABLE 1. Government Expenditure on the Arts

	× *Dfl. 1,000,000*	*(year)*
I. State Expenditure		
Ministry of Culture		
Performing Arts (including artistic training)	c. 170	(1980)
Creative Arts	c. 32	(1980)
Ministry of Education and Science		
Art Education	176.6	(1980)
1% Scheme (visual arts in new school buildings, universities, and academic hospitals)	3.4	(1981)
Ministry of Housing and Physical Planning		
1½% Scheme (visual arts in new government buildings)	3.5	(1981)
Ministry of Transport and Public Works		
1½% Scheme (visual arts in post office buildings)	0.6	(1980)
Ministry of General Affairs		
Government Information Service (films and documentaries)	c. 2	(1980)
Ministry of Social Affairs		
Visual Artists Scheme	87	(1981)
Job Opportunities within the Arts	c. 2	(1981)
Provision Fund for Artists	1.1	(1980)
Total State Expenditure	c. 478 million	

(continued)

TABLE 1 (*Continued*)

	× *Dfl. 1,000,000*	*(year)*
II. Provincial Expenditure		
Performing Arts (including training)	44	(1980)
Creative Arts	1	(1980)
Total Provincial Expenditure	c. 45 million	
III. Municipal Expenditure		
Performing Arts (including buildings and training)	503	(1980)
Visual Artists Scheme and municipal commissions	9	(1980)
Total Municipal Expenditure	c. 512 million	
Total Expenditure of All Three Levels (estimate):	c. 1035 million	
These figures may be supplemented with expenditure on museums and libraries, which gives the following picture:		
I. State Expenditure		
Ministry of Culture		
Historic Monuments, Museums, Galleries, Archives	246	(1980)
Libraries	320	(1980)
Total State Expenditure	c. 566 million	
II. Provincial Expenditure		
Museums and Art Galleries	8	(1980)
Libraries	25	(1980)
Total Provincial Expenditure	c. 33 million	
Municipal Expenditure		
Museums and Art Galleries	145	(1980)
Libraries	155	(1980)
Total Municipal Expenditure	c. 300 million	
Total Expenditure of All Three Levels	c. 899 million	
Grand Total, including Arts, Museums, and Libraries, but excluding, e.g., Youth Work and Community Centers (which provide for important performing possibilities)	c. 1,925 million	

Source: Netherlands Commission for UNESCO, 1982, and corrections on it.

possible estimate of support at the various levels of government. The three levels of government form three ''icebergs,'' of which the greater part is too complex and differentiated to be part of public political debate or subject to democratic control. This part consists of a network of joint subsidies which has evolved over the years with many intricate patterns of responsibility and financing. The provincial ''iceberg'' is smaller than that of the State or municipalities since the provinces contribute less to art and culture. Mainly because of the operation of budget mechanisms, it is estimated that more than 80 percent of government grants to the arts are ''underwater'' ones.[25] The authorities and councils have a formal say in the allocation of the funds, but this control is restricted to a minimum by mutual opposition and lack of clarity about the substance of the activities.

TABLE 2. Expenditure of the Arts Directorate of the Ministry of Cultural Affairs, Recreation and Social Work on the Arts, 1973 and 1981 (× Dfl. 1,000.-)

	1973	*1981*
Music and dance	48,201	101,220
Orchestras	26,155	46,000
Other institutions and events	4,747	11,400
Musical drama	12,294	29,000
Dance	4,338	13,300
Prizes, commissions, grants	667	1,520
Drama and mime	14,321	39,247
Theater companies	11,873	29,610
Children's and puppet theater	—	693
Incidental productions	—	1,161
Dramatic writing commissions	88	349
Mime	1,250	4,019
Institutions	1,110	3,415
Literature	2,204	6,481
Visual arts and architecture	4,646	12,611
Film	2,995	5,942
Production fund	1,640	5,200
State Academy, personnel	2,766	4,950
State Academy, equipment	811	1,261
Jan van Eyck Academy	1,153	2,150
Prix de Rome	37	26
Government study grants	613	464
Amateur arts and artistic training	11,049	18,838
Subsidies, arts, and cultural centers	—	2,466
International exchanges and Holland Festival	1,256	1,887
Dissemination of art	514	575
Non-literature journals	272	312
Foreign study	260	348
General institutions and other expenditures	2,311	5,032
Grants	834	1,175
Honorary awards	1,487	1,714
TOTAL	98,699	214,476

Source: Netherlands National Commission for UNESCO, 1982.

The part of the "iceberg" above the surface consists of commissions to creative artists, experiments, and ad hoc projects. The authorities and advisory bodies exercise far more direct control over this expenditure, and the funds are at the same time far easier to monitor and control. In order to gain a clear idea of the differentiated allocation of funds to the various arts, the expenditures of the Arts Directorate of the Ministry of Culture especially needs further analysis (Table 2).

The Organizational Structure of Support for the Arts

Spending Structure

The organizational structure of the Dutch system of subsidy for the arts is very complex and varies from art to art, and operates at different government levels. To give an overall impression, I will first look at the relationship among the central government, the provinces, and the municipalities. Table 3 gives the relative financial contribution of the three levels of government, divided into performing and creative arts. The proportions have not changed substantially over the past ten years.

From Table 3, it is apparent that central government is the principal paymaster in the creative arts. With the performing arts the breakdown is different; in this case the municipal authorities are the largest contributors. Edwards analyzed the extent to which the three levels of government emphasized the various main objectives as formulated in the Report on Art and Arts Policy.[26] His conclusion is that the central government is attaching increasing importance to such notions as development, innovation, and quality as the essential elements of its arts policy. Provinces stress their concern with the availability and accessibility of art, while municipalities are inclined to define their role in terms of the purchase of art and the promotion of participation in art. The relative emphasis put by the central government on values such as development and innovation can be explained by its task of supporting the arts in general. At the local level, there is greater resistance to supporting expressions of avant-garde art. Work by the avant-garde, which may give rise to feelings of aggression and rage, may endanger the much closer ties between officials and citizens on the local level.[27] From an analysis of seventy-seven paragraphs on arts policy in the programs of political parties in the 1982 municipal elections,[28] it emerges that professional artists come only indirectly into the picture at the local level. However, concern is expressed with the development of creativity, and amateurism is praised as a base for professional artistic activity. This position assigned to amateur art contrasts with the views of central government, which sees the professional arts as giving an impulse to amateurism.

These general observations fail to do justice to the reality of arts policy, particularly that pursued by the three cities of Amsterdam, Rotterdam, and The Hague. As far as content and scope are concerned, these cities conduct an integrated arts policy with a national and sometimes international orientation.

The expenditure per capita on the creative and performing arts shows that the three cities have a pronounced lead, both over all the rest of the country's municipalities put

TABLE 3. Average Percent Expenditure (1970–77) of Central Government, Provinces, and Municipalities on Performing and Creative Arts*

	Central Government	*Provinces*	*Municipalities*
Performing Arts**	30%	6%	64%
Creative Arts***	77%	3%	20%

*Excluding Visual Artists Scheme. Source: Edwards, 1981.

**Examples of performing arts are opera, orchestras, and theater.

***Creative arts: visual arts, writing, composing, choreography, etc.

together, and over the central government. For Amsterdam, Rotterdam, and The Hague together, expenditure per capita (1975) is Dfl. 2.61; for all other municipalities it is Dfl. 0.55; and for central government it is Dfl. 2.34. The figures on the performing arts are respectively Dfl. 49.70, 20.83, and 32.56. The relative emphasis placed on the support to creative arts at the central level versus the local level (Table 3) does not apply in the case of these three cities.

Advisory Structure

The sharp increase in government support for the arts and culture and the traditional restraint required of the government regarding the substance of policy in the field has led to the establishment of scores of consultative and advisory councils at all administrative levels, composed of experts and interested parties. On the provincial and local levels, these councils sometimes are also responsible for the allocation of the money.

Judgments concerning the substance of the artistic activities subsidized by the government are thus not made by the government itself, but entrusted to others. Though the members of the councils are formally appointed by the authority in question, the appointments are in many cases made on binding recommendations from professional artists' associations, or by means of a system of internal cooption.

The councils operate under various titles; at the national level there is the Arts Council, at the provincial level they are usually called cultural councils, and at the municipal level, cultural committees or arts committees. Amsterdam and Rotterdam maintain influential, authoritative organizations—the Amsterdam Arts Council and the Rotterdam Arts Foundation respectively—the latter having executive powers as well. It may be supposed that no two councils or committees work in the same way or have the same responsibilities.

On the national level, the Arts Council was set up in 1947 to advise the Minister. In 1956 the Council was given a legal basis obliging the Minister to seek its advice. It also may issue unsolicited recommendations. In 1979, the Arts Council Act was amended to empower the Council to act as an advisory body to the entire government, and make recommendations concerning the coordination of arts policy at central, provincial, and municipal levels. To prevent the Council from becoming a special interest group for artists, members are appointed first and foremost on the basis of their expertise, rather than their particular involvements. Most of the forty-eight members are appointed by the Crown on the recommendation/nomination of arts institutions and cultural organizations. They are appointed for two years and may be reappointed only twice. The Arts Council merely acts in an advisory capacity; decisions still rest with the Minister. The Council has enjoyed a large degree of freedom only in its working methods and organization. At present there is a Plenary Council of all forty-eight members, a central committee, three departments, and seven subcommittees. The three departments are for visual arts and architecture, music and theater, and media and literature. Each department is subdivided into committees for particular artistic disciplines.

Present Arts Policy in a Number of Areas

I shall confine myself to the policy of the central government, and within that deal mainly with the policy programs which fall within the province of the Arts Directorate of the Ministry of Cultural Affairs.

The Creative Arts in General

The extensive and differentiated package of measures for the creative arts has been described by Gerritsen in his *Money for Artists,*[29] a systematic study of official measures influencing the socio-economic position of the creative artist. Scholarships and experimental subsidies are designed explicitly for the development and renewal of the arts. To supplement these, the government has grants for further study abroad and for travel. In addition, there are commissions and prizes. A limited number of older artists of special merit, but in difficult circumstances, receive an annual honorarium. An active commissioning policy is being pursued, especially in the field of the visual arts, aimed at raising the aesthetic appeal of architecture and town planning. The awarding of commissions in other artistic fields is usually done by specialized Funds or by artistic institutions such as theater and ballet companies. Of the two hundred or so arts prizes existing in the Netherlands,[30] seven are State prizes: for the visual arts, literature, and music.

For the visual arts there are in addition loan fees for making work available to exhibitions, and rental payment for work borrowed by subscribers—most of them private individuals—from visual arts loan centers. The building of State collections, direct purchase of works of art by the Ministry of Cultural Affairs, and the commissions of various ministries (see Table 1) under the ''percentage schemes'' are further measures. The significance of these for artists should not, however, be overestimated. Muskens and Maas, in their investigation of the economic situation of visual artists, come to the conclusion that on average the State's contribution to artists' incomes is limited to 2.5 percent of the average income from sales and commissions which totals Dfl. 11,600 a year.[31] This excludes the Visual Artists Scheme, which will be dealt with below and which for about 3,000 artists generates an average gross income of Dfl. 27,000.

Lastly, the Ministry of Cultural Affairs also subsidizes the visual arts via a dozen or so organizations, some of which are its own creation, which have a promotional, intermediary, or supporting role in the arts. Good examples are the Netherlands Institute of Visual Arts, which purchases works of art and organizes exhibitions throughout the country, and the Art and Industry Foundation, which serves as intermediary between artists and industry to arrange commissions for artists and to advise corporate patrons.

The percentage schemes need some further explanation. These encourage artistic embellishment of architecture and provide an important avenue for involving artists in the design of the public environment.[32] One of the arguments for implementing the scheme was of a typical political representative character, namely to ''prove to posterity that our generation, notwithstanding its many material worries, did not fail to take care of cultural values.'' Two major State programs were created in the early 1950s which, in turn, stimulated the creation of percentage programs in cities, as well as in other government agencies, such as the Postal and Telecommunications Administration. Essentially, the central government's programs award an amount for art based upon a percentage of the construction costs of new buildings, schools, and universities. In 1951, the Government created a $1\frac{1}{2}$-percent program stating in straightforward language that important government buildings were to receive artistic embellishment. The scheme comes under the Ministry of Housing. An earlier effort to establish a state percentage program—made by Boekman in 1939, much like the French scheme initiated in 1936—failed because of the War. Under pressure from the visual artists union, the BBK, the percentage scheme has been enlarged to accommodate a variety of government subsidized constructions from water purification plants to viaducts and parking decks. In 1953, a 1 percent program for new schools followed. This comes under the Ministry of Education and Science. It applies to all secondary schools, vocational schools, and universities built with State funds. Spending State funds on the arts in this way fits well in the postwar philosophy of edification of the masses. In a letter from the Minister of Education (1953), describing the merit of the 1-percent-for-schools, new importance was attached to the need for creating aesthetically pleasing and stimulating environments and to their effect upon the youth. In the long term, "this will heighten the aesthetical consciousness of the whole population."

Special Funds

1. For Writers and Translators. In 1965, in order to promote Dutch literature by, among other things, furthering the interests of the writing profession by means of commissions, bursaries, and supplementary honoraria, the Fund for Literature (*Fonds voor de Letteren*) was set up. The Fund now operates principally within a system of work grants, which are awarded for a period of between one and twelve months on the basis of a previously submitted plan. In addition, the Fund operates a scheme of library-borrowing fees. The activities of the Fund do not constitute the sum total of support for literature. The Ministry of Cultural Affairs assists publishers with literary publications and supports such literary institutions as the scheme for visiting writers in schools and the Literary Museum, as well as literary journals and libraries.

The prelude to the setting up of the Fund was the first organized artists' protest, that of the pressure group "*Schrijversprotest*" in 1963. The Fund format was chosen because it was felt that the payment of State monies to writers could be more efficiently made by the board of a foundation than by the government itself: in that way the links between writers and the government as subsidizer become looser, and the government's responsibility for the end product less. The committee which prepared the ground, and on which the interests of writers, publishers, and the book trade were represented, considered this an advantage, and felt it to be desirable that the government should refrain as far as possible from passing judgment on individuals. It is a statutory requirement that a majority of the executive posts should be occupied by persons who are themselves practicing writers. A civil servant from the Ministry of Cultural Affairs is appointed by the Minister as secretary and treasurer, an arrangement which is generally chosen in order to create the necessary confidence in government finance departments. This governmental representation is an important political resource for the Funds, giving them access to information that is useful in formulating strategies for maximizing their budgets.

State subsidy to the Fund for Literature has risen considerably over the years (1965: Dfl. 330,000; 1975: Dfl. 1,167,000; 1979: Dfl. 2,700,000). In the period 1970–79 the national per capita income rose by 20 percent in real terms; in the same period payments to writers rose by 75 percent in real terms. Is the present contribution to the Fund then too high or too low? Particularly in the past few years, the Fund has been seeking solutions to the problem of improving the material position of artists, such as striving for a guaranteed average income for professional writers. Vleesch Dubois observes that the sums received by the Fund can be considered too low only if one takes the position that the Fund must provide writers with a guaranteed income.[33] Analyzing the functioning of the Fund, Dubois concludes that the Fund reduces its involvement in the promotion of literature to a package of social measures, because the underlying thinking behind the granting of subsidies seems to be aimed not at the furtherance of literature, but at the maintenance of writers. It is open to question whether these social aims, which were already acknowledged when the Fund was set up by including the promotion of the interests of the writing profession among its objectives, can ever be avoided. Subsidy at a certain level over a certain period of time to a particular target group or clientele easily leads to relations of increasing dependency.[34] This material dependency generates socio-economic interests that will dominate the original cultural aims.

2. For Composers. In 1980 the Fund for Creative Musical Composition (*Fonds voor de Scheppende Toonkunst*) was set up, with its aim the production and preparation for use of creative musical compositions. From the early 1960s, there had been demands from composers themselves for the establishment of such a fund which would give them some say in the carrying-out of policy in their professional area. Confidence in composers, however, turned out to be less than in writers; the government gave as the reason for its reluctance to set up such a fund the dangers and difficulties it foresaw if composers found themselves forced to be selective with regard to other composers. That a Fund for composers has now come into being is due to a rather more positive attitude by government to Funds as an instrument of arts policy. A group of composers, who had known each other since their student days at the Royal Conservatory in The Hague, have been able to articulate their demands through participation in advisory bodies and via the press. They made a spectacular splash in 1969 in the Carré Theater in Amsterdam, with the multi-media opera *Reconstructie,* with a text by prominent writers and, very much in the spirit of the times, centering on the figure of Che Guevara. But others, too, showed political agility. For example, the chairman of the Association of Composers convinced the arts officials of the Ministry that given good statutes, which provided for a regular injection of new blood into the executive board of a Fund, there need be no fear that some kind of mutual-aid arrangement would arise among musicians.

The Fund for Creative Musical Composition has now taken over the tasks fulfilled up to 1980 by the Ministry of Cultural Affairs, assisted by a special advisory committee: i.e., the granting of commissions, working bursaries, and, where necessary, other payments to composers. "These operations can be carried out more quickly and more efficiently by the Fund. In addition, it is more straightforward if those who pass artistic judgment also carry the formal responsibilities entailed," says the accompanying report on the ministerial decision to set up the Fund. The Minister appoints the board members, and the Arts Council advises him on the annual plan that the Fund submits to him with its budget.

3. For Film-makers. The Netherlands Film Production Foundation, set up in 1956, gives subsidies in the form of interest-free advances to producers of feature-length films on the basis of guarantees by recognized cinema operators. The usual ratio of private to Fund financing of such films is 40 to 60 percent, with payment to individual investors having priority. Because most Dutch films are not profitable, the Fund's loan is in many cases never repaid. The Fund is financed by the State (90 percent) and the Netherlands Cinema Association (10 percent), which incorporates cinema operators, distributors, and film producers. The influence of these free-enterprise organizations is greater than their 10 percent contribution would lead one to suppose: they occupy 50 percent of the seats on the executive, while it is a precondition of subsidy that the 40 percent share of private finance must first be provided. In practice, the 40 percent is put up by the Cinema Association, so that the latter's influence on the allocation of government money is considerable.

In all probability, the present blossoming of the Dutch feature film, reflected in the degree of public interest in the Netherlands and the quality of the films, which by Dutch standards is high, is due to the Production Fund. The budget of the Production Fund grew between 1957–79 from Dfl. 0.7 million to Dfl. 6.4 million, and the annual number of successful applications from six to eleven. Contributions to screenplays rose from two to sixteen, with the amount per screenplay increasing from Dfl. 5,500 to Dfl. 18,000. Since 1957 the Production Fund has been involved in one in every five Dutch films released, and over the period 1957–79 the total income of the Fund and the income of the films subsidized has risen, even after adjustment to the retail-price index. Besides the Production Fund, there has existed since 1983 a Fund for short artistic and cultural films, designed especially to enable young film-makers to make their debuts. The latter Fund has taken over the role of the previous direct State subsidy to young film-makers.

Complex Policy Structures

1. Theater. In the 1981/82 season the Netherlands had a total of forty partly or wholly government-funded theater companies, including a number of groups subsidized in a less formal way. This has not always been the case. The present system of subsidy began only after 1945. A characteristic feature is the sharing of funding between central and local government, the system of dual subsidies. Since 1945, there has been a sharp rise in the number of subsidized companies, a rise in the number of actors on contract, and a rise in the number of productions and performances. Audience numbers, however, have fallen (Table 4).

Besides the subsidized theater, there are a considerable number of unsubsidized more or less permanent groups and ad hoc producers: this non-subsidized theater, partly aimed at a mass audience (a gap in the market had arisen with the disappearance of a number of repertory companies after the protest against traditionalism in 1969) and partly fringe theater, performed in off-beat venues to small audiences. This theater is independent of direct government subsidy, but not of indirect government support; it benefits from guarantees which theaters are able to give because of municipal support, and in addition the venues themselves are largely financed by the municipal authorities, albeit mainly for reasons of youth policy. Moreover, the non-subsidized theater was able to develop because of the system of social provision offered by the Dutch welfare state, which made it possible for those involved to live on social benefits between engagements or during rehearsal periods.

The public reached by this non-subsidized theater should not be underestimated; the non-subsidized theater's share of the theater audience in 1980–81 was 47 percent. Thus, when we talk of the significance of government finance for the Dutch theater, we must not forget that with its approximately 50 percent contribution to the producers of subsidized

TABLE 4. Development of the Subsidized Theater in Quantitative Terms

	1947–48	*1955–56*	*1969–70*	*1974–75*	*1981–82*	*1984–85*
Number of Companies	5	6	14	16	40	48
Audience Numbers	1.2 m	1.5 m	—	—	1 m	0.7 m
Actors on Contract	166	173	250	300	450	—
Premiers/Productions	55	56	59	118	115	—
Performances	2078	2588	—	3100	4700	6200

Source: Annual Reports of the Association of Dutch Theater Companies (no complete data are available).

theater, the financial arm of central government covers only approximately 25 percent of audience members.

The subsidized theater industry is not simple in structure. Companies are subsidized according to their running deficit, which in the 1972–73 season amounted to 90 percent of the estimated costs. Municipal authorities finance theaters; central and local government jointly finance the performers. The total government subsidy per theater-goer for the 1972–73 season was estimated at Dfl. 36,[35] while for the 1982–83 season the subsidy was about Dfl. 80 per theatergoer, i.e., per occupied seat.

The arts councils play an important role in the structure of support for the theater. Chief among them are the Netherlands Arts Council, the Amsterdam Arts Council, and the Rotterdam Arts Foundation. The Netherlands Arts Council advises the Minister annually on the level of subsidies to be awarded for the theater, with the principal criterion being the standard of recent work. This advice has led over the past few years to a certain shift in the allocation of funds among companies. Sometimes a company has to trim its budget until it comes up with a more inspired and up-to-date artistic policy; new companies are admitted to the subsidy circuit; some have been able to expand steadily, while doubts as to artistic merit could in some cases lead to the termination of subsidy.

2. *Orchestras*. There are at present a total of twenty-one orchestras in the Netherlands, with approximately 1,500 musicians permanently attached to them. This includes five broadcasting orchestras, one small opera orchestra, one ballet orchestra, and one chamber orchestra. The remaining thirteen are symphony orchestras, based throughout the country. Many orchestras date back to the last century. In 1918, government assistance was begun, but extensive structural support has existed only since 1945. In 1947, the Minister of Education, Arts, and Sciences decided to guarantee 100 percent of the salaries of orchestral musicians so that the existence of orchestras became less dependent on income from concerts or donations. Next, the other running costs also became eligible for government subsidy, Subsequently, the system of dual subsidies from central and local government grew up, providing similar complex sources of funding as with the theater. Unlike the case of the theater, neither the Netherlands Arts Council nor local arts councils play any major part in determining the subsidy given to the various orchestras, and there is no annual evaluation. Because orchestras account for a large slice of government arts budgets, for years there has been resentment and frustration in chamber music, improvised music, jazz, and pop music circles.

Violent emotions flared during the artists' protest in the *Concertgebouw* in 1969. The new generation of musicians and composers stated in a manifesto, "The social position of the orchestras has not essentially changed since their creation, and they still meet the needs of the same social class for whose benefit they came into being." The activists considered the choice of repertoire too bourgeois, with not enough scope for modern work, so that the orchestras had become alienated from the younger generation. A glance at the repertoire of Dutch orchestras does not contradict this view. However, the protesting group (the Nutcrackers) was not so much opposed to the classical masters as to the atmosphere in which the music was presented and the symbolism surrounding the program.

Public interest in the large orchestras varies enormously. The national average of concertgoers is 86 per 1,000 inhabitants, but for provincial towns the average may be as low as 15 to 20, while for Amsterdam it is over 300. The same pattern applies to bigger cities like Rotterdam and The Hague, where the audience size is three times as great as in the surrounding provinces. Smit and Van den Berg come to the conclusion that the dissemination of symphonic music by means of a policy of scattered accommodations has been a failure.[36] The building of accommodations in smaller localities and the programming of symphonic performances has led to an increase in the number of concerts, but this has not resulted, given the population increase, in a growth in public interest, which has remained virtually static over the years, at approximately 1.2 million concertgoers per year.

The orchestral system has been the subject of all kinds of restructuring plans, from fusions to multi-purpose musical centers. The pressure for stimulating new developments has certainly achieved some results. In 1982, central government earmarked c. Dfl. 1,000,000 for jazz and improvised music, and Dfl. 250,000 for pop music. Still, the feeling exists that new initiatives on the alternative music scene are denied access to subsidy.[37] Smit and Van den Berg, pleading the case for a new organization in the musical field, conclude in their investigation of the actual professional performance of orchestral musicians that payment for hours worked and the fusion of regional orchestras reaching only a very small public could make room for a musical life of greater scope and better quality.[38] And indeed, besides the flourishing non-symphonic musical scene, including, for example, chamber music, there are a large number of ensembles playing alternative or improvised music, which deserve support on a reasonable scale. It is, however, questionable whether reorganizations will actually lead to reallocation of funds across the musical spectrum. The Minister finds himself forced to cut back on the arts, and money becoming available from scrutinizing the budget for established companies is easy prey.

3. The Visual Artists Scheme (Beeldende kunstenaarsregeling). Within the prevailing government allocation of funds in the visual arts world, the Visual Artists Scheme (BKR) has a predominant position. The Scheme falls within the province of the Ministry of Social Affairs and in financial terms amounts to thirteen times the expenditure of the Ministry of Culture on commissions and purchases in the visual arts sector (1983: 130 million as opposed to 10 million). The scope of the Scheme is very wide: of the approximately 10,000 living visual artists, 3,500 have made use of the Scheme at one time or another. In 1980–81, 1,800 artists could be called intensive users and 1,000 incidental users.[39]

The Scheme was introduced at the central government level in 1949, under the appropriate name "Something-in-Return Scheme" (*Contraprestatie*). The artist was eligible for a higher benefit than was provided under the existing social provisions if he was prepared in return to donate a work of art to the State. This principle was adhered to through all the successive refinements of the Scheme over the years. The aim of the Scheme was to create employment in order to combat unnecessary reliance on government help and to bolster the visual artist's sense of worth. The Scheme was not to be in the nature of salaried employment, or to lead to competition with the art trade. Mok-Schermerhorn observes that these considerations smack of a philosophy of social welfare somewhat reminiscent of the nineteenth century.[40] Welfare must not be accepted too easily or axiomatically, as if such a scheme might lead to all artists immediately queuing up to live on government help and not working any more than absolutely necessary to secure government money.

At present, all persons of Dutch nationality between the ages of 25 and 65, who are professional visual artists and have sufficient creative artistic ability and technical competence, are eligible for the Scheme. The Scheme is (still) designed to keep artists occupied, so that they can further develop their talents, thus promoting "as far as possible the earning of independent income through the execution of artistic work." The visual artist should strive to "support himself professionally without application of the Scheme." The operation of the Scheme is left by the Ministry of Social Affairs to the municipalities, which appoint advisory committees which then decide on the basis of artistic quality whether or not an artist may participate in the Scheme. The artist has to show his efforts to become self-supporting to the local authorities.

Some of the works purchased become the property of the municipalities, and some, of the State. The central government's share of the works acquired is managed by the Ministry of Culture, which uses them to form small traveling exhibitions, but principally tries to find a home for them in public buildings and in government offices. With the rise in the number of participants, from 200 in 1960 to 3,500 in 1983, the numbers of works managed in this way have multiplied considerably in recent years (total works, 1960: 15,000; 1983: c. 470,000), as have the costs (1960: Dfl. 1 million; 1983: Dfl. 130 million).

The exponential growth in the use of and expenditure on the Visual Artists Scheme led the government to set up, in 1981, an inquiry into its operation. This decision must be seen not only against the background of the necessity of cut-backs; equally important is the predicament of the Ministry of Culture, which finds it hard to bear primary responsibility for visual arts policy when it has only a fraction of the funds at its disposal.

Muskens concludes on the basis of this inquiry that the Scheme works, but not as intended.[41] He found, among others, the following causes for this:

While it is true that the Scheme does contribute to the conservation and development of creative artistic ability, this does not lead in practice to any independent earning of income, as was envisioned. This is partly due to the fact that the prices fetched on the open market are on average only one-third of those paid under the Scheme.

Anyone is in principle free to become a professional visual artist. Control of numbers by the use of qualifying rules, as elsewhere in the social security system, is lacking in the Scheme. Since the second half of the 1960s, the numbers of those wishing to take up an artistic career have increased. Valkman attributes this to three factors: (a) demographic patterns; (b) the changed attitude of parents towards professional artistic training for their children; and (c) the effect of amateur artistic activity and artistic education.[42]

The vagueness of the notions used in policy relating to the Scheme caused tensions, such as between different sections of the administration. The allied notions of artists' policy and arts policy may serve as an example. The Ministry claims to be pursuing a social policy, which links with an artists' policy. The municipal advisory committees, however, select according to artistic criteria, which points more in the direction of an arts policy, and is thus competing with official arts policy.

Past attempts to introduce modifications in the Scheme, such as a check on admission, or cuts in the budget, have led to intense political pressure from participating artists. Announced changes in the Scheme in 1969 and 1979 resulted in the occupation by artists of the famous Rijksmuseum. The decisions were subsequently reversed. In 1982 and 1983, immediately following the announcement of proposed cuts in the Scheme, the Van Gogh Museum (1982) and the Rijksmuseum (1983) were occupied. In both cases, as a consequence, the Government reopened negotiations with the artists' unions. In 1986 the

Government decided to bring the main part of the Scheme budget under the responsibility of the Ministry of Culture, and to allocate support purely on the basis of qualitative criteria.

Cut-backs

Although, as has been said, the present government wishes to go relatively easy on the arts in the process of economizing, the effects of the cutbacks are definitely becoming apparent. Briefly, the following tendencies can be discerned:

Local authorities are cutting back on the arts just as in other sectors. This has consequences for performing possibilities, not only in the theater but also in music, especially outside the large towns where the companies are based. The managements of theaters find themselves obliged to make the company share in the financial risks of performances. The package price-system (*uitkoopsommen*) whereby a company sells a performance for a set sum to a theater, which then takes on the financial risks, is on the decline. This has implications not only for geographical coverage, but can mean that under the pressure of circumstances both companies and theaters may be tempted to turn to popular programming.

The situation of the subsidized companies is not a simple one. The Ministry makes its own share in the dual subsidy conditional on the giving of a certain number of performances away from home base, in which one can recognize the central government's policy of dissemination. It is now becoming increasingly difficult to comply with this condition. The system of dual subsidies is itself now beginning to show some of its less advantageous aspects; in periods of economic growth, dual subsidies had operated in favor of the arts, offering a certain degree of security, and if one level of government was convinced of the case for expansion, then the other often went along with it.[43] Now that growth has given way to decline, there are signs that this subsidy mechanism can also have uncomfortable effects: a reduced subsidy from one side gives the other a reason for following suit.

In central government ministries other than that of Culture there is a clear tendency to cut back on the money reserved for the arts or artists, regardless of what has been agreed by the Government. In the social field an enormous cut has been announced in the Visual Artists Scheme, which, it is expected, will lead the same group of artists to try their luck with a different government department. Ministries which operate a percentage scheme for artistic decoration in new buildings are more and more inclined to give this item a low priority in their dwindling budgets.

In the Ministry of Culture the cutbacks give added impetus to three mechanisms: quality control, reorganization of financial support, and privatization. The Minister makes regular statements that his aim is to finance "top-quality art," and at least one theatrical company is being dissolved as a result of advice received on the group's artistic quality. In the orchestral fields, the Ministry of Culture is trying, by reorganizing orchestras in the western Netherlands and trimming provincial orchestras, to make larger savings than are strictly necessary, in order to release funds for newly emerged interests, such as chamber music, jazz, and pop, and to create an adequate orchestra for the new musical center, the *Stopera,* in Amsterdam. This strategy is analogous to the present economy drive in the universities. There, too, in a single process, economies are being made and funds reallocated to new developments requiring specific support. This way of proceeding has the advantage that support at least for some is maintained, thus avoiding the emergence of concerted artistic or academic opposition.

The Impact of Government Support on the Arts

Dependence and Opinions

The vast majority of Dutch artists are dependent for their livelihood on the State. There is no arts sector which is not involved in some way in the flow of subsidies from one of the levels of government. Opera, ballet, and symphonic music are 90 percent dependent on government money, theater somewhat less, while in the case of chamber music, jazz, mime, puppetry, film, and the visual arts, subsidies and government commissions make up a considerable portion of total income. Writers and composers are afforded a degree of economic security by work grants and bursaries, while even pop music receives a small fixed annual amount for rehearsal space, recording studios, and artistic projects.

Works of art and performances reach only a limited section of the population directly. Twenty-three percent of the population go at least once a year to the theater, 13 percent to a musical performance, and 35 percent to a museum.[44] These figures do not include visits to youth centers, subsidized venues where most pop music and a large part of jazz and improvised music is performed, or fringe theater. In the large towns particularly, there is a flourishing artistic life, with Amsterdam giving the lead. The relative number of art-lovers may not be very large, but there is certainly a hard core of art devotees. In the media, an increasing interest in art is noticeable. All the major newspapers have for the last ten years or so run a weekly arts or culture supplement. On TV, more and more space is given to the arts, partly under the influence of the 1969 Broadcasting Act, which obliges each broadcasting association to produce a minimum percentage of cultural programs (20 percent).

More than 1,000 million guilders are involved in the subsidy of the arts, exclusive of museums and libraries, for all government agencies put together (Table 1). This amounts to Dfl. 65 per capita. As far as one can tell, this puts the Netherlands at the top of the list of the countries discussed in this book.[45] Public opinion on government support for the arts is subject to change. In 1970, 40 percent of those questioned in a national sample were (strongly) in agreement with the proposition that the government should increase subsidies to the arts. Eleven years later, in 1981, only 16 percent of those questioned still believe that financial support by government for the arts should be increased (Table 5).

TABLE 5. Opinions of Interviewees on the Statement:
The Government Should Extend Subsidies to the Arts, 1970–1981
(expressed in percentages)

	1970	*1975*	*1980*	*1981*
(Strongly) Agree	40.8	24.3	22.1	15.8
No Opinion	23.0	23.9	19.1	16.7
(Strongly) Disagree	36.2	51.7	58.7	67.4

Source: Social and Cultural Report, 1982. n = c. 1600.

In interpreting the data in Table 5, it should be known that in the period covered, agreement that subsidies should be increased declined for almost every field. The arts, however, are in an exceptional position. Data from 1981 show that 72 percent of interviewees were in favor of a reduction in expenditure on culture and leisure activities; together with defense (73 percent), this item was at the very top of the list of items the public wants to cut.[46]

Fluctuations in the Budget

One may wonder whether public opinion on the level of arts subsidies is a relevant factor in explaining fluctuations in the arts budget. The considerable growth in the arts budget in the years 1950–65 (Figure 1) corresponds with an equally marked growth in the expenditure of the responsible ministry, Education, Arts, and Sciences. It is not implausible to suggest that the arts benefited from the political importance attached to sizable investment in education, as part of postwar reconstruction. Moreover, there is the factor of the birthrate explosion after 1945, which created its own need for education expenditure. In 1965, responsibility for the arts shifted to the Ministry of Cultural Affairs, Recreation, and Social Work. The relatively stable development of the arts budget from 1965–82 subsequently kept pace with the development of the total budget for this ministry (Table 6). The almost exponential growth of the expenditure on the Visual Artists Scheme over the last fifteen years—the Scheme fell under the Ministry of Social Affairs—correlates with the exceptional increase in expenditure on social provisions in the Netherlands in the same period (Table 6).

Looked at in this way, it would seem that fluctuations in expenditure on the arts are better explained in terms of the political fortunes of a particular ministry as a whole, following which the autonomous operation of the budget mechanism within the individual department does the rest. Within the departments, things are generally talked of in terms of incremental action and pro rata distribution, rather than considerations resulting from public opinion, political pressure, or rational choices.

TABLE 6. The Development of a Number of Categories of State Expenditure, Including Arts, Over a Period of 15 Years

	Annual Averages		
	1966–68	*1981–83*	*Growth Factor*
Expenditure minus non-tax receipts (× Dfl. 1 million)			
1. Culture and Recreation	240	1577	6.6
Arts (Arts Directorate only)	40	227*	5.6
2. Social Provisions	5105	28740	13.6
Visual Artists Scheme	c. 5	110	c. 22.0
3. Total Expenditure minus non-tax receipts	19294	97928	5.0

Sources: Budget Statements 1975; 1983.

*This is about 0.21% of total central government expenditure; see Figure 1.

Cultural Dissemination

The dissemination of culture may be regarded as the dominant objective of arts policy in the Netherlands since 1945. This means geographical and social dissemination of the cultural heritage. Initially, such arguments as popular edification and education were predominant, emanating from Socialist/Christian-inspired ideologies. In addition, the striving for cultural dissemination was in at least equal measure fueled by fears about loss of moral values, mass culture, and extremism. Knulst points out that the transmission of culture was seen above all as the dissemination of elements of a civilized way of life and should in this way contribute to the maintenance of the dominant bourgeois culture.[47] Thus a base of justification was constructed for growing public patronage of the arts. The notion of dissemination is met with later in many forms. That art needs to be subsidized because, unless it is, the less privileged cannot enjoy it, serves to this day as a justifying formula for government support.

Knulst concludes that the policy of social dissemination has made little progress. With the exception of museum attendance, public interest in theater and concerts—mainly because of the emergence of television and the record industry—has declined considerably since the Second World War. This raises the question as to who among the public benefit from subsidies to the arts.

Who Are the Beneficiaries?

Goudriaan and De Kam investigated the question of who benefited from subsidies to the performing arts.[48] On the basis of data on theater and concert attendance from a representative sample of the population, they grouped all households in ascending order of secondary income in units of 10 percent (deciles). The distribution of benefits from both the theater and the concert subsidies awarded turned out to show a striking correlation. In both cases, the best-off 30 percent of households received approximately half the benefit, 46.7 percent of theater subsidies and as much as 54.7 percent of the music subsidies. The share in the benefit of the 30 percent of households with the lowest incomes is in stark contrast to this. They received 19.5 percent (theater) and 15.7 percent (concerts).

These results suggest that socio-cultural dissemination in the sense of direct transmission of culture has had the opposite effect, since it is precisely those in the higher income brackets who benefit. It should not, however, be forgotten that the availability of these "higher" arts does have an indirect effect. It can be argued that certain expensive examples such as theater and concerts are essential elements in a culture and they could not exist on a high-quality level without government support.

Policy Coordination

The Netherlands has a reasonably well-balanced organization of government involvement in the arts.

There is a diversity of sources of finance. In the visual arts the distribution of financial sources over various ministries is striking. With the performing arts the pattern is one of a certain balance in financing at local and national levels (dual subsidies). The various moneys are channeled into private corporations (orchestras, opera, and theatrical companies) which, within the limits set by the government, such as sound financial management, reasonable productivity, and dissemination throughout the country, are free to follow an independent policy.

In the creative arts, there is an increasing tendency to switch to the Fund model, of which the most important examples at present are the Funds for film, literature, and musical composition. There are some drawbacks attached to the shifting of responsibilities and powers to autonomous administrative bodies such as Funds. Valkman points to the diminishing of parliamentary control over the policy pursued.[49] The Fund model does, on the other hand, give great scope to the government for the assertion of its political responsibility in large areas of art, for example by making choices and giving priority to "Literature," "Film," or "Creative Musical Composition" as a whole. The division of executive power between policy formation (financier) and execution of policy (the Funds) prevents too much power being concentrated in the administration.[50]

At the central government level there is one institution, the Ministry of Culture, which, supported by the Arts Council, can take a reasonable overall view of the differentiated arts policy and act as a coordinator. The formal powers available to it are:

> Money, either through complete financing of activities, or by participation in finance with local authorities and occasionally with industry, as in the case of film.
>
> (Early) information. The Ministry of Culture occupies a central position in the arts policy communications network. Pressure groups and political parties make their demands to this ministry; the Ministry is linked in an advisory capacity with other ministries which provide benefits in the arts field; the shared financing of cultural objects with local authorities automatically entails much exchange of information.

The State's formal art policy has only a limited scope. Numerous government-supported bodies have taken measures which have been of benefit to the arts, independent of formal arts policy. Within arts policy proper, the system of support does give a central position to the State, especially the Ministry of Culture.

This position, however, does not include some necessary instruments to conduct an integrated arts policy. A weak link in the coordination of involvement in the arts is the separation of responsibilities for professional artistic training (Ministry of Education and Sciences) and responsibility for the allocating of funds to professional artists (where the most important funders are the Ministries of Culture and Social Affairs). Certain centrifugal forces can be discerned in the triangle "provision to the labor market," "concern for the labor market," and "responsibilities for the arts policy."

Culture and Political Culture

In Dutch political culture, there is an aversion to direct involvement of government in the content of culture. This applies both to the arts and to the sciences. In both fields, there is a tradition of delegating substantive judgments to advisory bodies or to independent managing bodies such as Funds or foundations. As with the organization of science, there is no one dominant advisory structure, but advisory functions are spread over a number of agencies. And as with the sciences, it is largely the judgment of fellow practitioners which is dominant, which may give rise to criticism. In this way, a number of relevant interests are in danger of being excluded. Especially where it is a matter of the social relevance of an artistic achievement, there is a potential source of contention.

The fragmentation in government involvement with the arts makes it inconceivable that a uniform "State art" should be imposed by a central body. It promotes the chances of disparate views and currents finding support somewhere within the pluriform policy system. Good examples of this are provided where newly emerging interest groups in the arts, such as jazz, pop music, or fringe theater are concerned. Despite the dominant position of the established arts, these interests nevertheless succeed in finding some financial support. This is realized generally by a combination of resources: social legislation; funds for material costs (from props to amplifiers)—such as the Amsterdam Arts Fund; subsidized venues in youth centers and the increasing readiness of those concerned with arts policy to support the new at the expense of the established arts.

Notes

1. N. B. Goudszwaard, *Vijfenzestig jaar Nijverheidsonderwijs* (Assen, 1981).
2. M. Boon and A. Schrijnen-van Gastel, *Arts in Research* (Amsterdam, 1981).
3. E. Boekman, *Overheid en Kunst in Nederland* (Amsterdam, 1939).
4. A. Lijphart, *The Politics of Accommodation: Pluralism and Democracy in the Netherlands* (Berkeley, 1975), and *Verzuiling, Pacificatie en kentering in de Nederlandse Politiek* (Amsterdam, 1982).
5. H. Daudt, "Political Parties and Government Coalitions in the Netherlands since 1945," *The Netherlands Journal of Sociology* 18 (1982), 1–23.
6. Lijphart, *The Politics of Accommodation.*
7. J. van Straalen, *Decentralisatie, kunst en museumbeleid* (Amsterdam, 1981).
8. J. Goudsblom, *Dutch Society* (New York, 1967).
9. L. de Jong, *Het Koninkrijk der Nederlanden in de Tweede Wereldoorlog* ('s-Gravenhage, 1969).
10. I. Schöffer, *Het nationaal-socialistische beeld van de geschiedenis der Nederlanden* (Arnhem, 1956).
11. W. Woudenberg, "De Dreiging van een Staatsmoloch, de ARP en de Cultuurpolitiek, 1945–1955," University of Amsterdam, 1983; V. van Alem, "Katholicisme en Kunstbeleid," Catholic University of Nijmegen, 1983.
12. J. Smiers, *Cultuur in Nederland, 1945–55,* SUN (Nijmegen, 1977).
13. Van Alem; Woudenberg.
14. H. Rook "De ontwikkelingen in de kultuurpolitieke opvattingen van de PvdA," University of Amsterdam, 1981.
15. P. Ligthart, "Het Kunstbeleid in Nederland na 1945, een eerste aanzet tot een politicologische analyse," *Dokboek,* 1972–1973, nr. 3 (Amsterdam, 1972).
16. F. van Heek and E. V. N. Vercruijsse, "De Nederlandse beroepsprestige-stratificatie," in F. van Heek et al., *Socialie Stijging en Daling in Nederland,* I, 1958.
17. P. Fenger and O. Valkman, *Rotterdams Kunstbeleid, een diagnose* (Amsterdam: Boekmanstichting, 1977).
18. W. P. Knulst, "Vermanen, verheffen en Verdelen," in *Tien jaar ontwikkeling van het toneel, 1970–1980* (Amsterdam, 1980).
19. J. E. Ellemers, "The Netherlands in the Sixties and Seventies," *The Netherlands Journal of Sociology* 17 (1981), 113–35.
20. M. E. Boon, *Netwerkanalyse Beeldende Kunsten* (Amsterdam, 1975, 1976); P. Fenger, *Beleidanalyse Beeldende Kunsten* (Amsterdam, 1976), and "An Analysis of Visual Arts' Policy," in *Contribution to Sociology of the Arts* (Sofia, 1983).
21. A. de Swaan, *De Mens de Mens een Zorg* (Amsterdam, 1982).
22. H. Daalder, "The Netherlands universities between the 'new bureaucracy' and the 'new

management,' " in H. Daalder and E. Shils, *Universities, Politicians and Democrats* (Cambridge, 1982).

23. Wetenschappelijke Raad voor het Regeringsbeleid (WRR), *Herwaardering van het Welzijnsbeleid* ('s-Gravenhage, 1982).

24. L. A. Welters, *Geldstromen Overheid en Beeldende Kunstenaars* (Amsterdam, 1973).

25. Netherlands National Commission for UNESCO (NNCU), *Some Aspects of Cultural Policies in the Netherlands* (1982).

26. A. R. Edwards, *Kunstbeleid en Decentraliatie* ('s-Gravenhage, 1981).

27. O. Valkman, *Sonsbeek Buiten de Perken, II* (Amsterdam, 1973).

28. C. Smithuijsen, *Kunst van de Partij II,* Federatienieuws, mei 1982.

29. R. Gerritsen, *Money for Artists* (The Hague, 1980).

30. A. van der Brugghen, *Kunstprijzen,* Boekimanstichting (Amsterdam, 1981).

31. G. Muskens and J. Maas, "Materiële afhankelijkheid—Beroepsmatigheid—Autonomie; de Leefsituatie van Nederlandse beeldende kunstenaars," *IVA* (Tilburg, 1983).

32. Lloyd W. Benjamin, III, *The Art of Designed Environment in the Netherlands* (Amsterdam, 1983).

33. P. D. Vleesch Dubois, *Overheid, Auteur en Subsidie,* University of Amsterdam, 1981.

34. De Swaan.

35. N. van Niekerk and J. Hilferink, *Toneel ter Zake* ('s-Gravenhage, 1976).

36. S. Smit and H. O. van den Berg, *Symphonie-orkesten in Nederland* (Amsterdam: Federatie van Kunstenaarsverenigingen, 1980).

37. V. Vingerhoeds, "De Kritische Noot; de alternatieve muziekpraktijk in de jaren zeventig," University of Amsterdam, 1980.

38. S. Smit and M. O. van den Berg, *Organisatie en Bespeling van het Muziektheater in Amsterdam,* WVC, Rijswijk, 1982.

39. G. Muskens, *Sammenvattend eindverslag van het onderzoek naar het functioneren van de BKR* ('s-Gravenhage, 1983).

40. E. M. B. Mok-Schermerhorn, *Beeldende Kunstenaars Protesteren* (Amsterdam, 1983).

41. Muskens.

42. O. Valkman, *De BKR en de Crisis van de Verzorgingsstaat* (Amsterdam, 1982).

43. Smithuijsen.

44. Sociaal Cultureel Rapport (SCP), 1980, 1982 ('s-Gravenhage, 1980, 1982).

45. H. O. van den Berg, "Overheid en Kunst," in *ESB* 1-9-1982; D. Netzer, *The Subsidized Muse, Public Support for the Arts in the United States* (Cambridge, 1978).

46. G. J. van't Eind and C. A. de Kam, "Heroverwegingen van bezuinigingen op publieke uitgaven," in *ESB* 24-3-1982.

47. Knulst.

48. R. Goudriaan and C. A. de Kam, "Demand in the Performing Arts and the Effects of Subsidy," in W. G. Hendon et al. (eds), *Economic Research in the Performing Arts* (Akron, Ohio, 1983).

49. O. Valkman, *De Fondsenwet Scheppende Kunsten* (Amsterdam, 1979).

50. M. Scheltema, "Raden en Commissies als Zelfstandige Bestuursorganen," in *Adviseren aan de Overheid* (s'-Gravenhage, 1977).

Bibliography

English

Allen, J. *Theater in Europe.* Eastborne, 1981.
Benjamin, Lloyd W., III. *The Art of Designed Environment in the Netherlands.* Amsterdam, 1983.
Boon, M., and A. Schrijnen-van Gastel. *Arts in Research.* Amsterdam, 1981.

Daalder, H. ''The Netherlands Universities between the 'New Bureaucracy' and the 'New Management,' '' in Daalder, H., and E. Shils, *Universities, Politicians and Democrats*. Cambridge Univ. Press, 1982.

Daudt, H. ''Political Parties and Government Coalitions in the Netherlands since 1945,'' in *The Netherlands Journal of Sociology*, 18 (1982), 1–23.

Dorrian, F. *Commitment to Culture*. Univ. of Pittsburgh Press, 1964.

Ellemers, J. E. ''The Netherlands in the Sixties and the Seventies,'' in *The Netherlands Journal of Sociology* 17 (1981).

Fenger, P., and O. Valkman. *Protest in an Established Society: The Netherlands, Protest, Artists*. Amsterdam, 1974.

Fenger, P. ''Arts and the Political System,'' in *Studies in the Sociology of the Arts*. Vol. I. Budapest, 1980.

Fenger, P. ''Music in Cultural, Educational and Communication Policies in the Netherlands,'' in Desmond Mark (ed.), *Stock-Taking of Musical Life*. Vienna, 1981.

Fenger, P. ''An Analysis of Visual Art's Policy,'' in *Contribution to the Sociology of the Arts*. Sofia, 1983.

Gerritse, R. *Money for Artists*. The Hague, 1980.

Goudriaan, R., and C. A. de Kam. ''Demand in the Performing Arts and the Effects of Subsidy,'' in W. G. Hendon et al. (eds.), *Economic Research in the Performing Arts*. Akron, Ohio, 1983.

Goudsblom, J. *Dutch Society*. New York, 1967.

Griffith, R. T. *The Economy and Politics of the Netherlands since 1945*. The Hague, 1981.

Kempers, B. ''The Sociology of Art; a social history of ideas in the Netherlands 1967–87.'' University of Amsterdam, in press.

Ligthart, P. ''Financing of the Art Policy by the Dutch Government 1950–80,'' in C. R. Waits et al. (eds.), *Governments and Culture*. Akron, Ohio, 1985.

Lijphart, A. *The Politics of Accommodation: Pluralism and Democracy in the Netherlands*. Berkeley, 1975.

Muskens, G. ''Freedom Insured? A Survey into the Work Conditions of Visual Artists in the Netherlands,'' in *Alienation and Participation in Culture*. Ljubljana, 1985.

Netherlands National Commission for Unesco (NNCU). *Some Aspects of Cultural Policies in the Netherlands*. 1982.

Netzer, D. *The Subsidized Muse, Public Support for the Arts in the United States*. Cambridge, 1978.

Dutch

Abbing, J. R. *Economie en Cultuur*. 's-Gravenhage, 1978.

Alem, V. van. *Katholicisme en Kunstbeleid*. Katholieke Universiteit Nijmegen, 1983.

Boekman, E. *Overheid en Kunst in Nederland*. Amsterdam, 1939.

Boon, M. E. *Netwerkanalyse Beeldende Kunsten*. Amsterdam, Dl. I (1975), Dl. II (1976).

Berg, H. O. van den. *De Sociaal-ekonomische Positie van Kunstenaars*. Cenario, Amsterdam, 1981.

Berg, H. O. van den. ''Overheid en Kunst,'' in *ESB* 1-9-1982.

Berg, H. O. van den. ''De structuur van het Kunstbeleid.'' *SCP-Cahier 44*. 's-Gravenhage, 1985.

Bergh, H. van den. *Kultuur en Kwaliteit*. Alphen aan den Rijn, 1986.

Dulken, H. van. ''De cultuurpolitieke opvattingen van prof. dr. G. van der Leeuw (1890–1950),'' in *Kunst en Beleid in Nederland*. Amsterdam, 1985.

Edwards, A. R. *Kunstbeleid en Decentraliatie*. VNG, 's-Gravenhage, 1981.

Eind, G. J., and C. A. de Kam. ''Heroverwegingen van bezuinigingen op publieke uitgaven,'' in *ESB* 24-3-1982.

Fenger, P., and O. Valkman. *Rotterdams Kunstbeleid, een diagnose*. Amsterdam, Boekmanstichting, 1977.

Fenger, P. *Beleidsanalyse Beeldende Kunsten*. Amsterdam, 1976.
Goudszwaard, N. B. *Vijfenzestig jaar Nijverheidsonderwiijs*. Assen, 1981.
Heek, F. van, and E. V. N. Vercruijsse. "De Nederlandse beroepsprestige-stratificatie," in F. van Heek et al., *Sociale Stijging en Daling in Nederland, I,* 1958.
Jansen, T., and J. Rogier. *Kunstbeleid in Amsterdam, 1920–1940*. SUN, Nijmegen, 1983.
Jong, L. de. *Het Koninkrijk der Nederlanden in de Tweede Wereldoorlog*. 's-Gravenhage, 1969 e.v.
Kam, F. de. "Kunst in Nederland, Ondersubsidiering of Overproductie," in *Hollands Maandblad,* 21, 1980.
Kempers, B. "Kunst en Staat in Sienna en 's-Gravenhage," in *Tijdschrift voor Sociale Geschiedenis*. 12 jr. nr. 1, februari 1986.
Knulst, W. P. "Vermanen, verheffen en verdelen," in *Tien jaar ontwikkeling van het toneel,* 1970–1980. Amsterdam, 1980.
Knulst, W. P. *Mediabeleid en Cultuurbeleid*. WRR, 's-Gravenhage, 1982.
Leeuw, G. van der. *Nationale Cultuurtaak*. 's-Gravenhage, 1947.
Ligthart, P. "Het Kunstbeleid in Nederland na 1945, een eerste aanzet tot een politicologische analyse," in *Dokboek,* 1972–1973, nr. 3. Amsterdam, 1972.
Lijphart, A. *Verzuiling, Pacificatie en Kentering in de Nederlandse Politiek*. 4th pr. Amsterdam, 1982.
Mok-Schermerhorn, E. M. B. *Beeldende Kunstenaars Protesteren*. Amsterdam, 1972.
Muskens, G. *Samenvattend eindverslag van het onderzoek naar het functioneren van de BKR*. 's-Gravenhage, 1983.
Niekerk, N. van, and J. Hilferink. *Toneel ter Zake*. 's-Gravenhage, 1976.
Nota Kunst en Kunstbeleid. Tweede Kamer 1975–1976, 13.981, nrs. 1-1.
Oosterbaan Martinius, W. *Schoonheid, Welzijn, Kwaliteit*. Amsterdam, 1985.
Privatisering. Deelrapport 32. Heroverweging Collectieve Uitgaven. Tweede Kamer, 1981–1982, 16.625, nr. 40.
Regulering en Deregulering. Deelrapport 31. Heroverweging Collectieve Uitgaven. Tweede Kamer, 1981–1982, 16.625, nr. 39.
Rogier, J. et al. *Sociaaldemocratie en Kultuurpolitiek*. Amsterdam, 1982.
Rook, H. *De ontwikkelingen in de kultuurpolitieke opvattingen van de PvdA*. Universiteit van Amsterdam, 1981.
Scheltema, M. "Raden en Commissies als Zelfstandige Bestuursorganen," in *Adviseren aan de Overheid*. 's-Gravenhage, 1977.
Schöffer, I. *Het nationaal-socialistische beeld van de geschiedenis der Nederlanden*. Arnhem, 1956.
Smiers, J. *Cultuur in Nederland, 1945–1955*. SUN, Nijmegen, 1977.
Smit, S., and H. O. van den Berg. *Symphonie-Orkesten in Nederland*. Federatie van Kunstenaarsverenigingen. Amsterdam, 1980.
Smithuijsen, C. "Kunst van de Partij II." *Federatienieuws,* mei 1982.
Sociaal Cultureel Rapport (SCP), 1980, 1982. 's-Gravenhage, 1980, 1982.
Stellingen met betrekking tot de Kunstnota. Federatie van Kunstenaarsverenigingen, 6-1-1977.
Straalen, J. van. *Decentralisatie, kunst en museumbeleid*. Amsterdam, 1981.
Swaan, A. de. *De Mens de Mens een Zorg*. Amsterdam, 1982.
Swaan, A. de *Kwaliteit is Klasse*. Amsterdam, 1986.
Valkman, O. *Sonsbeek Buiten de Perken, II*. Amsterdam, 1973.
Valkman, O., and T. Jansen. *Muziek en Publiek*. Amsterdam, 1976.
Valkman, O. *De BKR en de Crisis van de Verzorgingsstaat*. Amsterdam, 1982.
Valkman, O. *De Fondsenwet Scheppende Kunsten*. Amsterdam, 1979.
Met Verbeelding. Kunstnota van de Federatie van Kunstenaars-vereningen. Amsterdam, 1972.
Vingerhoeds, V. *De Kritische Noot; de alternatieve muziekpraktijk in de jaren zeventig*. Universiteit van Amsterdam, 1980.

Vleesch Dubois, P. D. *Overheid, Auteur en Subsidie*. Universiteit van Amsterdam, 1981.
Welters, L. A. *Geldstromen Overheid en Beeldende Kunstenaars*. Amsterdam, 1973 (1), 1974 (II).
Wetenschappelijke Raad voor het Regeringsbeleid (WRR). *Herwaardering van het Welzijnsbeleid*. 's-Gravenhage, 1982.
Woudenberg, W. *De Dreiging van een Staatsmoloch, de ARP en de Cultuurpolitiek, 1945–1955*. Universiteit van Amsterdam, 1983.
Zijderveld, A. C. *De Culturele Factor*. 's-Gravenhage, 1983.

6

Government and the Arts in Denmark

MARIT BAKKE

Cultural activity is opposed to social organization
ALAIN TOURAINE, *The Post-Industrial Society*

Introduction

Touraine's statement is succinct and—if accepted—leaves little room for planning and organization. However, it is doubtful whether the statement can be accepted as it stands. After all, cultural (including artistic) life involves human activity which almost automatically implies some kind of social organization. Therefore, one could look at Touraine's statement as a provocative one which invites consideration of what cultural life is all about. The question is rather in what way cultural and artistic activity is and should be organized.

It is not the purpose here to deal with the social relations among the persons involved in cultural and artistic activities. Instead, the focus will be on how these activities have been established and how they have been and are financed, with private versus public support as the main dimension to be explored. More precisely, the question is to what extent the Danish government since 1945 has been involved in the arts by way of setting up organizational frameworks and offering financial support.

The chapter begins with a brief description of how the arts were supported in Denmark until 1945. This introduction also presents some characteristic traits of Danish society. The arts comprise only a part of all cultural activities. Thus, this chapter will look at: (1) the *creative* arts: literature, painting, music, crafts; and (2) the *performing* arts: theaters, orchestras, operas.[1]

A description of the relationship between government and the arts should consider three dimensions: (1) ideology, (2) politics, and (3) economics. In other words, what has been the government's *ideological basis* for its actions with respect to the arts; what kind of *organizational structure* has been established; and to what extent and in what way have the arts been *supported economically?* This chapter attempts to answer these three questions.

Historical Background[2]

The relationship between the State and the arts naturally is influenced by a country's overall organization of public affairs at a given time, i.e., each policy area will be accommodated to a general administrative order. Figure 1 shows the organizational pattern for public affairs at the national level in Denmark during two different periods. The arts' position within the organizational pattern also is included in the figure. The figure shows that ever since the Middle Ages there has been an explicit relationship between a public body and the arts in Denmark. However, Figure 2 illustrates how the most decisive public body with respect to the arts has changed over time, and how the spectrum of artistic areas supported by the State has expanded.

Until the Reformation in 1536, the Catholic Church played the role of benefactor for the pictorial arts in Denmark as in many other European countries. During 300 years of autocratic rule (1536–1849), a series of kings and other members of the royal court took more or less interest in artistic activities, Christian IV (1588–1648) being the most prominent and ardent supporter. Prince Christian Frederik was another ardent spokesman for the arts. Particularly as chairman for The Art Academy from 1808 to 1839, he managed to influence both the royal court's and the State's contributions to the Academy and to artists in general. Even during the State's severe economic crisis around 1810, he

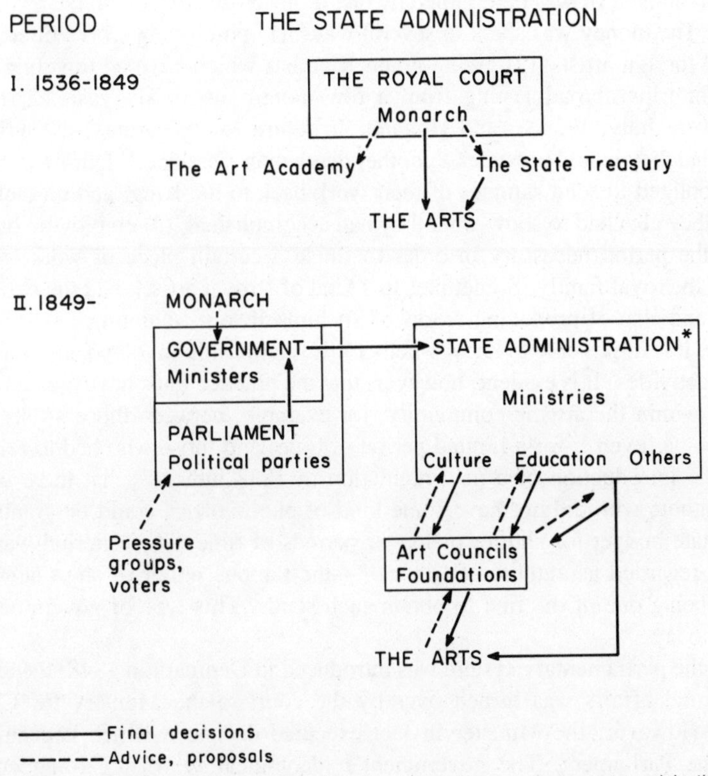

FIGURE 1. Organizational patterns for public affairs at the national level in Denmark.

FIGURE 2. The main decision-making body for public support to the arts in Denmark.

	The Arts					
Public Body	*Pictorial*	*Literature*	*Music*	*Crafts*	*Architecture*	*Other**
Church	until 1536					
The Royal Court (King)		1536–1849				
Parliament (Finance Committee)		1849–1902				
Ministry		1902–1931				
Literary Commission		1931–1964				
The Danish State Art Foundation**	1956–	1964–	1964–	1969–	1979–	1956–

*Support given to artists' widow/widower.

**1956–69, only to creative arts. From 1969 on, both creative and performing arts. Before 1969, the performing arts were supported elsewhere in the state budget.

stressed the importance of sustaining the country's cultural and artistic life: "Now we are poor and destitute. If we also become stupid, we can stop being a nation."

Depending on the King's personal interest, financial support either was granted by the monarch himself or was determined by one of his close advisors in charge of a private royal fund. The money was spent in several ways: (1) purchasing works of art from both Danish and foreign artists; (2) giving grants to artists which covered traveling and living expenses for trips abroad lasting from a few months up to six years. The preferred countries were Italy, France, and Holland. In return for the grants, the artists had to guarantee that they would not enter "another gentleman's service." During a stay abroad, they were obliged to send samples of their work back to the King, and on their return to Denmark, they also had to show what they had accomplished; (3) employing one or a few artists for the period necessary in order to finish a certain piece of work, particularly portraits of the royal family. Sometimes this kind of "royal artist" had the twofold job of buying art and also of producing works of art himself, e.g., paintings.

Today, it is impossible to know whether this relationship involved any restrictions on the artists' activities. It is evident, however, that the practice must have created some kind of division within the artistic community, for example, between those artists having an assured income (even if for a limited period of time) and those who had to rely on other sources. The introduction of a new regulation in 1838 indicates that there was such a division; authors who did not have some kind of public office could be granted support from the State budget for shorter or longer periods of time. The criterion was that they were to be regarded as authors of "merit"—the famous writer of short stories, H. C. Andersen, being one of the first to obtain such status. This type of government support still exists today.

When the parliamentary system was introduced in Denmark in 1848, the responsibility for cultural affairs was turned over by the court to the Ministry for Church and Education. However, the Minister in fact executed decisions which had already been made by the Parliament. The government's ideological views regarding cultural life therefore may be found in the parliamentary discussions, particularly those taking place within the Financial Committee.

Instead of discussing general artistic criteria, a substantial part of these discussions focused on the individual artist's personal qualities. In order to avoid this public display, in 1902 the Minister then in charge of Church and Education managed to obtain the responsibility for making a list of the artists who should have government grants. Since then, the Parliament generally has been left to comment upon the Minister's proposal, although there still is room for discussion. And sometimes there have indeed been great arguments, for example regarding a particular writer's "destructive" philosophy of life.

During the 1930s, people in government offices became increasingly aware of the need to give the artistic community more direct access to public decisions regarding the arts. Politically, this may be seen as the first sign of professional influence from the arts. This was the same development of organizational involvement in public decision-making as took place with respect to other societal issues. The Advisory Panel for Literature was established in 1931, thus moving the major decisions regarding public support for the arts away from the Ministry and Parliament.

The acceptance of such a professional body in the decision-making process indicated two things: first, that the arts were considered as a government responsibility; and second, that the issue was important enough politically to make professional assistance necessary.

The Period after 1945

Ideological Aspects

After World War II, these two trends grew stronger and formed the ideological basis for government policy with respect to the arts. But it took more than ten years before these principles became manifest in specific institutional arrangements. Until the State Art Foundation was established in 1956, the Parliament was the main public body regarding economic support, deciding once a year on a series of grants (see "Economic Aspects," below). The accompanying debates were quite similar to those which had taken place at the turn of the century and during the 1920s, more often expressing opinions about specific artists' personalities than talking about the position of the arts in general.

The often haphazard character of both the debates and decisions mobilized the artists and several Ministers for Culture and Education, Julius Bomholt being the most prominent one. They argued for moving the grant-giving procedure away from the Parliament to a more professionally competent institution. The largest manifestation of these demands occurred in 1952 when artist associations (representing drama writers, fiction writers, and composers) staged a common demonstration in Copenhagen.

When the State Science Fund was established in 1952, the artists and Bomholt, as the current Minister for Culture and Education, were encouraged to make another attempt to get a similar fund for the arts. After long discussions, the Parliament generally accepted the idea of such a fund as a political issue by setting up the Art Commission of 1954. The main question was how economic support could be provided for artistic decoration of public buildings. However, the artists' organizations argued that the Commission also ought to look at the social and economic conditions of artists in general. Public involvement should not be just a question of "rescue missions" for particular artists in acute need for support, they said.

After two years of deliberation, the Commission agreed on a proposal to institutionalize government involvement in the arts. Thus the law creating the Danish State Art Foundation was passed in Parliament in 1956. Two funds were established—one having the aim of supporting "the artistic decoration of public buildings" and the other of supporting "artists in financial need."

Among the 151 members of Parliament, eighty-eight voted for the law, six voted against it, and fifty-seven members abstained. The parties supporting the law were the Social Democrats, the Conservatives, and the Radical Liberals. Opposed were the Agrarian Liberals and the Single Tax Party. This voting pattern was in accord with the political parties' general ideological stands with respect to cultural life. Table 1 presents a summary of the positions which the Danish political parties have taken with respect to cultural life, including the arts.[3]

Thus, the table shows that the two parties which opposed the proposition—Agrarian Liberal and the Single Tax Party—always have based their cultural policy on traditional liberal principles, i.e., that government should have as little as possible to do with the arts and cultural activity. Therefore, these two parties have been placed at the bottom of Table 1, representing one end of an ideological scale. In this perspective, cultural life is regarded as an end in itself which should be performed with very limited or no interference from public authorities, leaving as much as possible to market forces.

Those parties representing the other end of the ideological scale are placed at the top of the table. In the view of these parties, cultural and artistic activity are regarded as means in an ongoing political struggle. Also, government support is viewed as a necessary prerequisite for a "just" and reasonable distribution of various facilities, institutions, and economic resources which are required for a comprehensive cultural life among different social groups.

In 1962, when the Parliament discussed minor revisions of the law on the Danish State Art Foundation, the opposition evident in 1956 had almost disappeared. The critical comments were concerned more with the way pictorial decoration of public buildings should be financed than with the question of whether government should be involved in the arts at all.

Looking at the comments made in the Art Foundation's Yearbook for the first couple of years, it is evident that the public at large knew very little about the Art Foundation. Even the intended receivers of grants—public authorities and pictorial artists—did not show great interest. In fact, during its first years, the Board regarded the distribution of information about the possibilities for grants as its major task.

The quiet atmosphere surrounding the existence and work of the Art Foundation lasted until 1964, when the Minister for Culture proposed to extend the art forms eligible for grants to include literature and music.[4] The Minister supported his proposal by saying:[5]

> There is an increasing understanding of the fact that the interplay among a country's creative forces within business, scientific research, and the arts are decisive for political, economic, and social development, and that the quantity and quality of artistic production constitute one important basis for the general evaluation of a nation's international position.

According to the new law, financial support from the Art Foundation would be of three types:

1. for talented artists in need of conditions conducive for developing evident talents, grants were given for a three-year period;

TABLE 1. Platforms of Danish Political Parties Regarding Cultural Life, including the Arts*

Party	*Stated Goal for Cultural and Artistic Activity*	*Attitude Regarding Government Support*
Communist Party	The class struggle is partly about culture, but culture is also a means in the class struggle. The arts should be integrated in everyday life: in institutions, at work, etc.	Government support to all kinds of cultural activity. Artists should be guaranteed economic security, thus being able to create independently of profit interests.
Left Socialist Party (1967)	To develop a socialist society by strengthening a socialistic culture, social networks, and aesthetics.	In the long run, cultural activity should be independent of government support.
Social Democratic Party	To break down class differences and to develop community and equality.	Government support in order to secure equal facilities for all. Alternative artistic forms should be encouraged.
Socialist People's Party (1959)	To analyze and interpret man within the surrounding society. The arts should be a means for reflecting upon man's condition.	Considerable government support, but cultural activity should be left to be performed in freedom.
Radical Liberal Party	To offer conditions conducive to individual creative activity and free choice.	Increasing government support but no involvement regarding cultural content. The arts should be guaranteed economic independence. Support for distributing arts to many different social groups.
Center Democratic Party (1973)	To strengthen traditional values, particularly in the media and in schools.	Not opposed to government support, but it should guarantee that a left-wing intellectual minority does not dominate cultural life.
Conservative Party	The individual's right to mold his own existence. Cultural supply should be comprehensive.	Government support for specific purposes, and for arts products rather than to artists.
Christian People's Party (1970)	To develop and strengthen Christian values.	Support for specific purposes of high standards. Politicized art should not be supported.
Agrarian Liberal Party	Free creative popular activity.	Limited decentralized government support.
Single Tax Party	Furthering freedom, differences, and independence.	No government support to cultural institutions and activity.
Progressive Party (1973)	To enhance individual liberty and Christian values.	No public taxes to cultural life. Government support is tutelage and contributes to a uniform culture.

*In order to give an overall view of present ideological perspectives, the table includes both the political parties represented in Parliament in 1956 (the founding year of the Art Foundation) *and* those parties founded later.

2. one-time grants to more established artists, given according to actual needs;
3. support to artists' surviving families.

The law passed without any debate in the Parliament, with 124 votes in favor and six members voting no. Thus, 1964 marks the almost unanimous acceptance of the principle that government has an obligation with respect to the arts, just like the role played by royal patrons during the sixteenth to nineteenth century.

However, the general agreement about the government's responsibility to the arts stopped at the Parliament building's front door. Trouble began with the publication in January 1965 of the list of artists who were to receive the first grants under the new law. This started a furious debate which went on for two to three months in the press and at public meetings; petitions also were delivered to the Parliament.

The protest expressed two main attitudes:[6]

1. *liberal:* stressing, on the one hand, the importance of a sound national economy, if necessary by cutting budgets, and, on the other hand, that government should not interfere in cultural affairs;
2. *social justice:* with respect to the artists, that support should be given according to actual need; with respect to the citizens, that the public at large (''the common man'') should be able to grasp the meaning of artistic products (literature, pictures, etc.).

In studies made of this protest movement,[7] these two basic ideas have been seen as characteristics of a populist ideology which made its impact not only on cultural life, but also on discussions and political decisions regarding other areas of society. By being included in the policy platforms of both the Single Tax Party and the Progressive Party, the populist ideas even became institutionalized within the party system. In fact, the protest movement's leader, Rindal, supported Glistrup when he took the first initiatives to found the Progressive Party in 1973.

The term ''populism'' suggests some of the reasons why the protest movement developed. Rapid urbanization is regarded as the main cause, giving grounds for increasing conflict between city dwellers and those living in the countryside. People in rural areas were defensive, feeling less affluent and less articulate than those in urban areas. They also felt that traditional values were threatened, values which had been an integral part of their everyday lives. We must also add the fact that via the State tax bill they contributed to a fund which was located in the capital and which—in their opinion—distributed ''their'' money to an intellectual elite whose literature, paintings, and music they did not understand. The reaction was evident: ''Why should we support such elitist crap?''

Part of the bourgeois press supported the protest movement, in part to profit from ideas and actions which appeared to be popular with ''the common man.'' The quite extensive media coverage may have given ''Rindalism'' some kind of legitimacy, thus encouraging the public expression of ideas which otherwise would have been preserved for private talk. It would be wrong, however, to make the media alone responsible for the growth of ''Rindalism.'' We have already stated that its basic ideas to a certain extent grew out of a particular structural development, namely, the manifest economic and cultural conflicts between the urban and the rural populations.

As Figure 2 indicated, since 1956 the Art Foundation has been the major government body regarding cultural life and the arts. The yearly reports from the Art Foundation may be used therefore for tracing the criteria which have been applied for the distribution of grants. Calling this the ideological significance of the Art Foundation, the economic one will be examined below (''Economic Aspects'').

First, the definition of art forms eligible for grants has become broader during the Art Foundation's existence. From 1956 to 1964, its work concerned only the decoration of public buildings. In 1964 literature and music were included as relevant art forms, in 1969 handicrafts, and in 1979 architecture was included as the last art form eligible for grants.

During the first period, when only pictorial arts were covered by the Art Foundation, the Board expressed an interest in experiments with the use of large rooms/space. It also was said that it was important for architects and artists to work together from the very beginning of the planning and designing process. For several years, the Art Foundation had to conclude that such cooperation unfortunately was lacking in most government building projects. This situation started to improve around 1970.

From 1964 on, we may compare the deliberations within the three subcommittees on pictorial arts, literature, and music, respectively.

The criteria considered can be grouped together in a set of dimensions:

young *versus* older and more established artists:
merit *versus* social welfare criteria;
current trends and interests *versus* continuity;
creative work *versus* distribution of the arts to the public;
the number of grants in proportion to the amount of money available, i.e., many and small grants *versus* few and large grants; and
geographical distribution.

During the first five years, all grants were given in order to encourage young artists who had demonstrated a flair for experimenting with new ideas and forms and were showing progression in their work. With respect to pictorial decorations, the Art Foundation strove for a reasonable geographical distribution throughout the country.

Apparently all subcommittees have regarded artistic quality as the basic factor influencing their decisions on grants. Sometimes, however, there have been discussions about the balance between social welfare criteria and artistic quality. Thus, the subcommittee on pictorial arts in 1970 made economic need the decisive criterion for grants to painters, given that artistic quality among the applicants was regarded as equal.

This demand for a certain qualitative standard involved some problems, which can be illustrated by a few examples. The first one concerns music. In an attempt to encourage modern music, the subcommittee sometimes made it possible to order compositions directly from the composers. It turned out, however, that very few composers could meet the qualitative demands set by the subcommittee, thus limiting the number of grants given.

Deliberations within the subcommittee for literature show a similar problem. In a small country such as Denmark (5.2 million inhabitants), there are very few writers who can accomplish a certain standard, thus again limiting the number of persons eligible for grants. The consequence usually has been that the same author has received support several times. Part of the literary community has criticized this practice as representing an elitist attitude. They also have claimed that it generally favors older artists who have had time to develop their talents.

The issue of artistic quality and its importance for decisions made by the subcommittees became particularly acute during the second half of the 1970s. It was especially discussed by the two subcommittees on pictorial arts and music. This was the result of two tendencies. First, quite a number of small art galleries were established particularly in order to offer exhibition facilities for nonprofessional painters. Since part of the pictorial arts subcommittee's job was to visit galleries all around the country looking for objects to buy, these new galleries made this task a difficult one. Not only were there more places to visit, but it also became more difficult to separate professional and nonprofessional art.

The other new development was the attempt to make jazz and popular music (rock, beat, etc.) acceptable as art forms which could be supported by the Art Foundation. In 1974, the subcommittee on music wrote that jazz and beat were evaluated in the same way as classical music; economic support was granted according to artistic quality. Nevertheless, when it came to the actual distribution of money, jazz and beat groups felt that they were treated unfavorably by the Art Foundation. Therefore, when the State Music Council was established in 1976, a campaign for nonclassical representation on its board was started.

The struggle partly forced this multifarious and hitherto loosely organized part of Danish music to coordinate its activities more closely. The process was further encouraged when the Ministry for Culture informally announced that money for jazz and beat had to be distributed via a formal all-encompassing association. Such an association was founded in 1981, and two years later two of the nine members of the State Music Council's board were appointed specifically to represent jazz, rock, and popular music.

Well-documented quality versus less certain experiments, young versus old, professional versus nonprofessional art—the dilemma which these dichotomies raised became more acute along with the relatively decreasing means which, due to inflation, the various subcommittees had at their disposal. "Too little money compared with the many qualified applicants and various jobs to be done" was a frequent comment included in all the Art Foundation's subcommittees' yearly reports from 1977 on. The solution usually has been to give few, but relatively large grants. This principle has been based on the argument that it is better for artists to have concentrated working periods rather than dividing the money among many persons, giving shorter periods for exclusively creative work.

The relevant question in relation to this practice is, of course, which is most conducive to creative activity. The issue of government support also contains considerations of the principles of economic efficiency and justice. Apparently, the policy of the Art Foundation has been based upon efficiency, thus trying to ensure art objects of enduring quality.

So far we have looked mainly at the support which the Art Foundation may offer to the creation of arts. Another aspect of an arts policy is to what degree and in what way the arts are used and distributed to the public. These questions particularly have been considered by the subcommittees on pictorial art, music, and handicrafts. The purchase of sculptures and paintings for public collections already have been mentioned. With respect to music, the subcommittee started considering how to finance the recording of Danish music without supporting commercial interests in 1972. One solution was to give money directly to artists, either composers or performers such as orchestras, groups, and individual musicians.

From the very beginning of its work in 1970, the subcommittee on handicrafts regarded distribution to the public as its major task. Another important job was to collect handicrafts which were made in a special way, often by particular artists, and which therefore would not be made after certain artists' death. Such artifacts were displayed at exhibitions, and later placed in study collections.

Sometimes the handicrafts subcommittee received applications for support of exhibitions abroad. Such displays offered excellent opportunities to inform the world about Danish handicrafts. At the same time, they were often part of an overall program aimed at increasing trade between Denmark and other countries. The problem was, will an exhibition mainly support the artists or business?

In this section, we have tried to identify the ideological aspects of government policy with respect to the arts on the basis of explicit statements. Ideological elements may also be deduced from organizational structures surrounding the arts and from the amount of money spent on the arts. The final evaluation of the ideological dimension therefore will be made after the next two sections, in which the political and economic factors are described.

Organizational Aspects

Government may be more or less involved in the various areas of society. What areas it can interfere in and the degree of involvement are usually stated in laws. The relevant laws with respect to cultural affairs in Denmark are presented in Table 2, showing the year of the first legislation and the goal which the law has been intended to ensure. The table also shows at what level government institutions have an implementing function.

Public legislation has gradually expanded to an increasingly broad spectrum of cultural affairs. Thus in 1986, most cultural areas are affected by some kind of public regulation.

Compared with other cultural areas, government regulations with respect to the arts appeared rather late, i.e., during the 1960s. This may be due partly to the somewhat liberal ideology which traditionally has characterized Danish society. It has, however, had a more or less strong impact on different policy areas, cultural affairs being among those where the attitude of government noninterference has lasted the longest. With respect to social welfare, e.g., nursery schools, aid to deprived groups, and the unemployed, government regulation has on the other hand been regarded as more acceptable.

Although government involvement in cultural affairs is aimed both at production and consumption, the major tendency has been to establish and support institutions which present something for individual and collective consumption. Indeed, it is only with respect to the creative arts that grants can be given directly to individuals.

Finally, Table 2 shows that most of the institutions for policy implementation are at the national level. Their job consists mainly of granting money, as the Art Foundation does.

At the local level, some institutions relevant for cultural life are prescribed by law. Public libraries are the most important ones, but local governments also grant licenses to theaters and cinemas.

Except for these institutions, local government is left alone to decide the extent to which it wants to play an active role in cultural affairs and the arts. The actual involvement depends very much upon local politicians and their views regarding how the taxpayers' money should be spent on social, economic, political, and cultural affairs.

In the section below (''Economic Aspects''), we will look more closely at the economy of the arts. Here, we will continue by describing the organizational structure which government has established with respect to the arts. Table 3 gives an historical overview, showing at what time different institutions were set up to administer the distribution of money to the arts. The table does not include institutions which primarily take care of collecting and exhibiting arts, i.e., museums and galleries.

Government money to the arts has been given in two ways: (1) a Ministry has on its

TABLE 2. Government Involvement in Culture and the Arts in Denmark

	Year of Legislation	*Goal for Policy Implementation*		*Policy-Implementing Institutions*		
		Production	*Consumption*	*National*	*County*	*Municipal*
Cinema	1922	x	x	x		x
Radio and TV	1926	x	x	x	x	
Libraries	1936		x	x		x
Recreation	1937		x	x	x	
Newspapers	1938	x	x	x	x	x
Evening classes	1942	x	x	x		x
Sports	1948	x	x	x		
Local folklore museums	1958		x	x	x	x
Music	1961	x	x	x	x	
Theater	1963*	x	x	x		x
Art museums	1964**		x	x	x	
The arts	1964	x	x	x		

*A law for the Royal Theater alone was passed in 1935.

**A law for a specific art museum was passed in 1949.

own granted money directly; or (2) a certain amount has been put at the disposal of institutions which evaluate applications and present their final proposal for grants to the Minister and the Parliament. The members of these institutions usually have a professional background in the arts.

The table shows that both practices have been and still are applied. From 1916 to 1961, the Ministry of Education was responsible for the direct grants and for the three institutions which so far had been set up. From 1961 on, a major part of these obligations was transferred to the Ministry for Culture, leaving only a small part of the fund of the Football Pools Company (which runs betting on football matches) to be administered by the Ministry of Education.

Two of the institutions in Table 3 always have been responsible for just one art form each—the Theater Council and the Music Council. Also, the State Art Foundation had a similarly restricted purpose at the time it was founded, but—as already described in the section on ''Ideological Aspects''—through the years its work has expanded to cover five different art forms. Thus, the Art Foundation and the other two institutions take care either of the arts in general or of the arts *and* other areas of cultural life, the latter being the case for the Football Pools Company. The Cultural Fund originally was founded primarily in order to encourage music, particularly in connection with performances at the Royal Theater in Copenhagen. The Fund still exists today, supporting both music and other arts. A major part is, however, spent on music and for practical reasons the administering of the money was in 1976 transferred to the Music Council.

The two Councils—for Theater and Music respectively—do not have special boards, which means that they report their decisions directly to the Minister. The other three institutions are headed by boards. Except for the Football Pools Company, all members representing government are appointed by the Minister for Culture. Board members of the

TABLE 3. Organizational Structure for the Relationship between Government and the Arts in Denmark, 1945 to 1983

		Institutions Linking Government and the Arts		
			Responsible for:	
Year	*Ministries*	*Founding Year and Name*	*In Founding Year*	*In 1986*
1848	Church and education	*1754* Art Academy		
1910	*1916* Education			
		1935 The Cultural Fund	Encourage music, particularly at the Royal Theater	Grants to the arts, particularly music
1945				
1950		*1948* The Danish Football Pools Company	*Grants to:* 1) sports 2) students, artists, scientists 3) recreation for youth 4) charity and common good	*Grants to:* 1) sports 2) culture 3) charity and common good 4) recreation for youth
1955		*1956* The Danish State Art Foundation	*Grants to:* Pictorial decoration of public buildings	*Grants to:* 1) pictorial arts 2) literature 3) music 4) handicrafts 5) architecture
		1958 The Danish State Local Folklore Museum Council (until 1976)	Advise public authorities	Responsibilities transferred to the Danish State Museum Council in 1976.
1960	*1961* Culture			
		1963 The Danish State Local Folklore Museum Council (until 1976)	Advise public authorities	Responsibilities transferred to the Danish State Museum Council in 1976
		1964 The Movie Theater Council (until 1972)	Advise public authorities	Responsibilities transferred to the Film Institute in 1972

(continued)

TABLE 3 (*Continued*)

Year	Ministries	Institutions Linking Government and the Arts: Founding Year and Name	Responsible for: In Founding Year	Responsible for: In 1986
1965				
1970				
		1972 The Film Institute	*Grants to:* Movie production. Advise public authorities	The same
1975				
		1976 The Danish Music Council	*Grants to:* 1) concerts 2) educational purposes 3) publication and distribution of music (scores, records, etc.)	The same
		1976 The Danish State Museum Council	Advise public authorities *Grants to:* 1) art museums 2) folklore museums	The same
1980				
1983				

Pools Company are appointed by four Ministers—Tax and Dues, Education, Interior, and Culture.

The professional art organizations also appoint members to the Councils and boards. An interesting question, then, is the proportions of members which represent government and the arts respectively. All board members of the Cultural Fund and the Theater Council are appointed by the government. The other three institutions—the Football Pools Company, the Art Foundation, and the Music Council—have mixed representation, but with professional artists having a majority of seats on the boards. It has not been possible to judge whether this makes any difference with respect to the institutions' general attitude toward the arts.

So far, the description of government support has focused primarily on the creative arts, especially grants given directly to creative artists. There also has been support to the performing arts and to attempts to distribute arts to the public. In the last paragraphs of this section, we will delve more specifically into these two aspects of the organizational relationship between government and the arts.

Both creative and performing artists usually have some kind of professional training. At the national level, there are educational institutions for pictorial arts, music, and architecture. All are on the budget of the Ministry of Culture.

In the performing arts, the government supports the Royal Theater in Copenhagen in addition to three regional theaters and one regional opera. Five regional orchestras also are permanently provided for in the national budget. To provide good conditions for theater performances and concerts may be regarded as an important element of support for the arts. The public's opportunity to become acquainted with the pictorial arts and handicrafts is equally important. Thus, six art galleries and museums are financed by the State. In addition, government supports approximately twenty private and municipal museums, and a series of yearly exhibitions.

Government's organizational relationship to the arts now can be summarized as comprising one direct line and two indirect ones.

1. One *direct* line from the Ministry of Culture, which grants support to the arts via the national budget.
2. One *indirect* line where government money is given to specific Councils and Foundations which quite independently grant support to various art forms. The decisions taken by the Councils and Foundations have to be confirmed by the Minister and Parliament. Usually they pass without comment.
3. One *indirect* line via institutions for the performance and distribution of the arts. Government finances the administration of these institutions which otherwise work as self-governing organizations.

In the next section, we will look at the amount of money which government transfers to the arts in these three ways.

Economic Aspects[8]

Government economic support to the arts since 1945 presents quite a complicated picture. At certain times new regulations have been introduced, while others have been dropped.

The primary purpose of this section is to put figures on some of the dimensions which are alluded to in the preceding two sections, i.e., the ideological principles and attitudes with respect to the arts, and the way government involvement in the arts has been organized. We shall look at the distribution among various grants and art forms for five-year periods, thus making it possible to compare over time.

Table 4 gives the first overview of government support to the arts in Denmark from 1945 to 1983. It includes both grants given directly from the Ministry and those given indirectly via the major separate foundation, the State Art Foundation. One evident observation is the homogeneous pattern for several years in a row, reflecting a stable organizational set up.

There are two "breaks" in the table. The first came with the budget for 1957/58, the first budget after the State Art Foundation was established. From then on, annual grants were transferred to the Art Foundation, thus reducing the number granted directly by the Ministry. Travel grants, which used to be a very important way of supporting artists, also to a great extent were made the Art Foundation's responsibility.

The absolute amount of State money to the arts increased remarkably from the 1956/57 budget to the one for 1957/58, from 328,400 Dkr. to 1.1 million Dkr. This was caused partly by inflation, but probably more by the efforts made by the Social Democratic Minister for Culture, Bomholt, to improve the status of culture and the arts in the political arena.

The second "break" occurred in 1965, when the Art Foundation was expanded to

TABLE 4. Grants to the Arts Given Directly from the Danish National Budget, 1945 to 1983 (in percent)

	Life-long Grants	*Yearly Support**	*3-Year Grants*	*1-Year Grants*	*Promising Writers*	*Purchase of Art*	*State Art Foundation***	*Travel Grants*	*Other Purchases*	*Total*	*Mill. Dkr.*
1945–49	11	64		13		7		5		100	1.09
1950–54	11	64		13		7		4		99	1.36
1955–59	3	30		3	1	2	60	2		100	4.58
1960–64	3	31	3	3	1	2	58	2	0	100	9.58
1965–69	12	20		3			66	1	1	100	31.01
1970–74	10	17		1			68	1	1	100	45.19
1975–79	10	23		0			63	1	2	100	56.92
1980–83	5	30		0			62	0	2	99	62.30

*Specified for different arts in Table 5.

**Specified for different arts in Table 6.

cover grants to literature and music in addition to pictorial arts. Another reform in 1965 was that "three-year grants," "grants to promising writers," and "the purchase of art," all were transferred to the Art Foundation.

Most remarkable was the increased proportion of life-long grants, from 3 percent to 12 percent of the total support. The fact that the number of recipients of this kind of grant increased from four to twenty-two indicates at least an attempt to satisfy demands for a more democratic arts policy. However, during the 1960s, it became more difficult to award the large life-long grants without returning to an elitist practice. Therefore, this category was dropped in the 1973/74 budget, leaving on the payroll only the artists to whom grants already had been awarded. During the entire period from 1945 to 1964, writers got a major share (between 50 and 67 percent) of the life-long grants. From 1965 on, writers and painters received an equal share (45 percent each), leaving only 10 percent to composers.

Basically, the kinds of grants included in Table 4 were intended only for creative artists. However, from 1963, there had been a residual category in the budget for "other purposes." This was used to support performing artists otherwise not eligible for state grants. This category was used mostly for actors.

Table 4 shows that most of the government money for the arts has been given in two ways: (1) yearly support from the State budget; and (2) via the Art Foundation. We therefore will look more closely at these two economic sources with respect to the distribution between various art forms. Grants from the Danish Football Pools Company also will be included in this comparison. Yearly grants directly from the national budget are shown in Table 5, grants from the Art Foundation in Table 6, and grants from the Football Pools Company in Table 7.

The overall picture which these three tables give is that fiction writers have been the main beneficiaries of grants from the national budget. From 1958/59 on, pictorial artists

TABLE 5. Yearly Support Given to Creative Artists from the Danish National Budget, 1945 to 1983 (in percent)

	Fiction Writers	*Non-fiction Writers*	*Composers*	*Pictorial Artists*	*Crafts*	*Other Cultural Purposes*	*Total*	*Mill. Dkr.*
1945–49	60	1	12	9		18	100	0.68
1950–54	59	8	12	9		12	100	0.85
1955–59	56	9	13	14		8	100	1.57
1960–64	54	9	13	20		3	99	2.79
1965–69	41*	6	14	37		2	100	6.03
1970–74	39	7	13	37	3	1	100	8.33
1975–79	38	6	13	37	6	1	101	13.12
1980–83	37	6	13	35	9	1	101	18.88
Average number of recipients per year (persons)	45–50	9	15–20	1945–77: 20 1978–83: 60	10	1945–64: 18 1965–83: 4		

*From 1965 including translators.

TABLE 6. Grants from the Danish State Art Foundation, 1957 to 1981 (in percent)

	Pictorial Arts	*Literature*	*Music*	*Crafts*	*Other Arts**	*Artists' Surviving Families*	*Exhibitions, Publications*	*Total*	*Mill. Dkr.*
1957–63	100							100	7.2
1964–69	67	18	6	0**	1	4	5	100	25.3
1970–74	58	20	10	4	2	4	1	100	31.0
1975–79	59	20	10	4	2	4	1	100	41.2
1980–82	60	16	11	5	3	3	2	100	33.7

*From 1979 specified as architecture.

**Less than 1%.

have received an increasing share of the yearly grants. On the other hand, pictorial arts have had a very strong position within the Art Foundation both with respect to percentage of money and number of persons receiving grants. In part, the reason is that the Art Foundation has been the main financial source for large decorations of public buildings. Writers have been the next largest group of grant recipients.

All subcommittees within the Art Foundation have had one common problem, an increasing number of applications has not been followed up with increasing means. The solution has been to give few grants, but big enough to ensure the recipients' good working conditions for a reasonably long period of time.

''Participate in pools betting, support the arts'' could be a slogan in Danish cultural propaganda. Since its beginning in 1948, a certain percentage of the Football Pools Company's surplus has gone to cultural purposes and the arts. The percentage has been changed by law several times, but on the average it has been around 50 percent. The share given to the arts has also been dependent upon the size of the surplus. A drastic change was made in 1976, when Parliament passed a law to the effect that from the total surplus only 7 percent should go to cultural purposes.

Until the Music Council was set up in 1976, the largest proportion of grants from the Pools Company went to music. Except for support to various cultural activities (''other

TABLE 7. Grants from the Danish Football Pools Company, 1950 to 1981 (in percent)

	Literature	*Music*	*Pictorial Arts*	*Theater*	*Other Cultural Purposes**	*Total*	*Mill. Dkr.*
1950–54	6	39	9	5	41	100	9.1
1955–59	8	41	9	7	34	99	10.6
1960–64	12	24	18	8	38	100	9.2
1965–69	11	23	15	7	44	100	10.1
1970–74	6	27	14	8	45	100	14.6
1975–79	10	8	16	12	54	100	29.8
1980–81	13	2	15	8	62	100	18.4

*Includes cultural associations, museums, local archives, publications.

purposes''), pictorial arts have also received a good share of the money available from this source for culture.

Now the question is, who benefits from the grants? The section on ''Ideological Aspects'' described some of the problems related to the criteria applied by the State Art Foundation, e.g., that they had an elitist bias. It is not possible here to look more closely at the appropriateness of this particular criticism. We may, however, state that the means available have not been in proportion to the demands. Thus we have already seen that the Art Foundation repeatedly has complained about the lack of money.

Instead of looking at possible qualitative consequences, we shall instead indicate the proportion between the number of eligible artists, the number of applications forwarded to the Art Foundation, and the grants given by it (see Table 8). The number of artists are approximate figures based on information given by artists' organizations. During the 1970s, there were between 1,700 and 1,900 writers, around 700 pictorial artists, and around 100 composers. In 1977, an organization for performing artists had registered 4,500 persons; in 1982, the number had increased to 8,675.

The figures clearly document that the Art Foundation has not been able to meet the economic demands presented by the artists' community. Generally the pictorial artists have been the most fortunate. Around 12 percent of the applications have been granted, while around 5 percent of the demands of other groups of artists have been met.

So far we have mainly looked at the creative artists. Now a few words about the professional performing arts.

A basic characteristic is that public support—be it at the central, county, or municipal level—is directed to formal institutions, like theaters, orchestras, and operas. For each kind of art, there exists a specific law which regulates organizational and financial matters.

The Royal Theater in Copenhagen is the oldest one in Denmark, dating back to 1748. However, for almost 200 years it was financed with private means. In 1935, the Parliament passed a law which changed the theater's status, making it the only one which is completely financed by the central government, i.e., any deficit automatically is covered via the national budget. This also includes expenses of a philharmonic orchestra, a ballet, and an opera, which are affiliated with the theater. During the last four years, the expenses for performances have been divided roughly between the four arts in a ratio of 10 percent to the theater, and 30 percent each to the opera, ballet, and orchestra.

Regarding the three regional theaters, a law from 1963 states that deficits will be paid by the central and local government, each covering 50 percent. In 1970, the local govern-

TABLE 8. Number of Applications to the State Art Foundation and the Grants Given. Minimum and Maximum Between 1970 and 1981 (Absolute Numbers)

	Applications	*Grants*
Pictorial arts	350–650	46–73
Literature	260–300	12–27
Music	ca. 120	4–14
Crafts	100–173	3– 7
Architecture	25– 32	1– 5

ment's responsibility was transferred to the county authorities. The effect of the 1963 law can be seen in a distinct change in the financial pattern; while the theaters were heavily dependent upon their own income in the 1950s (60 to 70 percent), the State and county government became the main financial contributors (70 to 80 percent) during the 1970s and 1980s. In 1983, the State and counties together financed 81 percent of the three regional theaters' total budgets.

The five regional orchestras are covered by a specific law from 1961. They are organized as self-governing semi-public institutions, which means that the deficit is paid automatically via the national and municipal budgets, each again covering 50 percent. According to a law from 1976, the same principle applies to the one regional opera in Denmark, that is, 50 percent is covered via the national budget and another 50 percent is covered at the county level.[9]

Overall, the performing arts obtain a greater share of the State support distributed via the Ministry of Culture than do the creative arts. Of the total support given in 1983, creative arts received 2 percent, performing arts 24 percent, and other cultural purposes 74 percent. The last category includes: museums (8 percent), educational institutions for creative and performing artists (1 percent), international contacts and information to the public (5 percent), movie institutions (2 percent), with the greatest part (58 percent) going to the public libraries in Denmark.

The various kinds of support which are described in this section all together amount to 47 percent of the total budget of the Ministry for Culture. The Ministry's part of the total *national* budget has in all years since 1961 been around 1 percent.

Conclusion

When we look at cultural life in Denmark in general, government involvement dates back to the 1920s and 1930s. With respect to the performing and creative arts, however, the Danish State became legally and economically involved rather late, i.e., during the 1960s and 1970s. During this period, government in Denmark definitely has accepted its responsibilities for cultural and artistic life.

We can identify three characteristic aspects in the relationship between government and the arts in Denmark. First, the legal framework primarily has aimed at securing *institutions* for performing and distributing the arts. Second, the *performing arts* have received a greater share of government money than the creative arts. This support also includes administrative expenses, thus leaving salaries as the kind of support which has been given directly to individual artists.

Third, when we look at the way in which government has organized its relationship to the arts, the trend has been that the government increasingly has shifted the practical responsibility for deciding who and what should be supported from the Parliamentary Finance Committee to *artistic professional bodies* appointed by the Ministry for Cultural Affairs. This development may be regarded as a tendency toward greater independence for the artistic community. On the other hand, we have seen that these professional bodies have been criticized for applying elitist standards.

The dilemma facing both government and the professional bodies seems to be that, given that support to the arts should be based on certain qualitative standards, the number of artists who may be regarded as eligible for support is rather limited in a small country like Denmark. Thus government and professional bodies must consider and choose between *equality* (support to many artists of varying quality) and *quality* (support to a few artists who definitely have demonstrated high artistic talents and standards).

So far quality has been the major criterion. The question is, of course, whether this policy in the long run supports traditional cultural values, thus leaving experiments with content, form, and presentation to more or less random private initiatives.

Notes

1. The Ministry for Education and the Ministry for Culture both have been responsible for policy areas which may be characterized as cultural, but not as creative or performing arts. Examples include public libraries, archives, museums, and cultural exchange with foreign countries. These areas are not included in this chapter.

2. This section is based on Aage Rasch, *Staten og kunstnerne* (The State and the Artists), 1968, pp. 162–92.

3. The content of the table is based upon documents obtained from the different political parties: manifestos, election programs, and special articles on culture.

4. A separate Ministry for Culture was established in 1961 when the Ministry for Education was split in two.

5. Quoted from Rasch, p. 171.

6. The paragraphs describing the protest movement are based on Anne Marie Kastrup og Ivar Lærkesen, *Rindalismen. En studie i kultursammenstød* (Rindalism. A Study of Cultural Conflicts), 1979.

7. The movement ''Rindalism'' is named after P. Rindal, a warehouse clerk from a small town in Jutland. Rindal collected the first 375 signatures for a protest petition to the Minister for Culture in 1965.

8. This section on economy could not have been written without the conscientious work of student assistant Axel Beck.

9. Because the opera company tours in various parts of the country, the county share is covered jointly by all counties.

Bibliography

Betænkning nr. 278 (1961). *Teatrene i Danmark* (Theaters in Denmark).

Betænkning no. 727 (1975). *Revision af Museumsloven* (On Revising the Museum Law).

Betænkning nr. 783 (1976). *Betænkning om Statens Kunstfond* (The Danish State Art Foundation).

Betænkning nr 943 (1982). *Filmloven* (The Film Law).

The Danish State Art Foundation, yearly reports 1961 to 1983.

Dansk kulturstatistik 1960–1977 (Danish Cultural Statistics). København, 1979.

Finansloven for årene 1945 til 1983 (The State Budget for each year 1945–1983). København.

Garodkin, Ib og John Garodkin. *Håndbog i dansk politik, 1979–80,* Mjølner. 1979.

Gravesen, Finn. *Musik og samfund* (Music and Society), København: Gyldendal, 1977.

Kastrup, Anne Marie og Ivar Lærkesen. *Rindalismen. En studie i kulturmønstre, social forandring og kultursammenstød* (Rindalism: a Study of Cultural Conflicts) København: Reitzel, 1979.

Langsted, Jørn. *Styr på teatret* (Administering Theaters), Gråsten: Drama, 1984.

Rasch, Aage. *Staten og kunstnerne* (The State and the Artists), Aarhus: Universitetsforlaget, 1968.

Wolff, Janet. *Aesthetics and the Sociology of Art,* London, 1983.

Appendix

Danish Governments since 1945 and Their Party Basis
i.e., parties which have formed the government

Period	*Party/parties*
1945–47	Agrarian Liberals (minority government)
1947–50	Social Democrats (minority government)
1950–53	Coalition government: Conservatives and Agrarian Liberals
1953–57	Social Democrats (minority government)
1957–60	Coalition government: Social Democrats, Radical Liberals and Single Tax Party
1960–64	Coalition government: Social Democrats and Radical Liberals
1964–68	Social Democrats (minority government)
1968–71	Coalition government: Conservatives, Agrarian Liberals and Radical Liberals
1971–73	Social Democrats (minority government)
1973–75	Agrarian Liberals (minority government)
1975–78	Social Democrats (minority government)
1978–79	Coalition government: Social Democrats and Agrarian Liberals
1979–82	Social Democrats (minority government)
1982–	Coalition government: Conservatives, Agrarian Liberals, Center Democrats and Christian People's Party

7

Government Policy and the Arts in Norway

MIE BERG

Introduction

Precise definitions of arts and culture are hard to find. In this chapter, I treat both concepts somewhat pragmatically, adjusting them to what has been included in the Norwegian culture and arts policies.

First, I shall outline a few facts about Norway which are important for an understanding of the amount and kind of government support in this country. A broad description of the development of cultural policy in general follows, as this constitutes the framework for the more specific arts policy. The main part of this chapter consists, however, of a discussion of the most important forms and principles of support in various fields—theaters, music, literature, feature films, pictorial arts, and support to individual artists.

Some Facts about Norway

Traditionally, Norway had all the characteristics of a peripheral and underdeveloped area: a small and scattered population, few and small centers, a lack of urban culture, industrial underdevelopment, and very limited resources. This was especially the case when the four hundred years of political union with Denmark was dissolved in 1814, and to a lesser extent when the subsequent union with Sweden came to an end in 1905. By then, industrialization and economic growth had started. Today, Norway is both a large and a small country. In terms of square miles, Norway is bigger than Italy or Great Britain, and has a varied topography. But in terms of population, Norway is a minor country in the European context. Norway has approximately 4 million inhabitants, which is half the size of London (or Sweden). A majority live in the southern part, many of them in areas relatively close to the capital, Oslo. It must also be borne in mind that only Norwegians speak Norwegian (even within the Scandinavian countries, literature is translated); and, as if that were not enough, there are two main Norwegian dialects which have the status of different languages. The political past of Norway—as a partner mostly on the periphery of Denmark and Sweden—seems to have strengthened the tension between two cultural traditions. One is more European, more elite-oriented, and represented by our union partners, notably Denmark, while the other is a specifically Norwegian culture. The division of the language into Norwegian and new-Norwegian is a typical sign of this tension. And the German Occupation of 1940–45 certainly contributed to an enthusiasm for Norwegian culture and "Norwegian-ness" (although it also opened the door for the culture of our allies, most notably the United States). This renewed national enthusiasm was also vital in the cultural climate of Norway after 1945, and consequently in the shaping of a policy for culture and arts as well. Mention also should be made of Norwegian ideals which emphasize general enlightenment of the people and a high level of education. This has applied to entertainment as well as culture, and contributed to considering art and culture as typical "merit-goods" which should be supplied collectively.

Norwegians—being only 4 million people—form a rather small potential audience for any art, and especially for art, like literature and drama, based on one of the two Norwegian languages. When these inhabitants live scattered all over a vast area, making it a costly business even to reach them, it should come as no surprise that government support of the arts is in some ways quite extensive in Norway compared to many other countries.

The Development of a Policy on Culture and the Arts

In the first part of this century (1905–45), government grants to culture and the arts were very modest, and increased less than did public expenditure as a whole. There were no sharp distinctions among science, education, and cultural activities, although personal grants to individual artists existed. In fact, this kind of support was then the strongest element in what may be identified as grants to the arts. In addition, government money paid for the education of pictorial artists and exhibitions of art. But the period as a whole is marked by a laissez-faire mentality as far as culture and the arts are concerned. It was only in the late 1930s that some theaters and orchestras began to be included occasionally in government budgets, receiving assistance for expenses. All in all, the idea of culture and the arts as a public good had not yet been recognized.

The period after 1945 offers a quite different picture. The immediate postwar years were, of course, infused with the spirit of national reconstruction. The Social Democrats held office, as they would continue to do most of the time until 1981. But the overall political climate was one of cooperation rather than conflict. This also seems to have fostered broad political agreement on a policy for the democratization of culture and cultural goods. A general policy has evolved through the alternating influence of two trends:

1. the decentralization and democratization of cultural goods; and
2. the strengthening of the professional (and often centralized and elite-oriented) culture and arts.

Democratization requires various measures. Cultural goods may be made available to new *social* classes or groups, who then will get their share of what is traditionally defined and established as culture. In Norway, however, a considerable part of such a policy of increased availability must include measures for making cultural goods *geographically* accessible. Lastly, democratization may mean the process of incorporating *new activities* into what is politically defined as culture. This also has been a trend in the cultural policy of Norway.

New activities and areas were included for the first time in the political concept of culture around 1950, signifying a greater emphasis on the national popular culture. Grants were given to leisure-time activities under the heading of "culture," notably to athletics and youth work and for the building of community centers throughout the country. Such centers in turn would become an important prerequisite for fulfilling the policy of making cultural goods geographically accessible. In fact, the key instruments in this policy were the establishment of so-called "*riksinstitusjoner,*" i.e., national, traveling, public institutions for the presentation of theatrical performances, music, art, film, and literature (the State Traveling Theater, the State Traveling Concerts, the State Traveling Gallery, the Norwegian Rural Cinema Co., and the Norwegian Authors Center).

Community centers make it much easier for the local communities to receive such visitors. On the other hand, regular grants to some theaters and orchestras also came for the first time just after the war, as did the first support arrangement to Norwegian feature films. Grants to various museums increased, and scholarships for artists were set up a little later. But support for culture and the arts suffered a relative decrease throughout the 1950s and beginning of the 1960s (see Table 3), although needs in no way had diminished. For example, the costs of theater productions increased, especially in relation to other goods, books faced new competition from media like film and television, and the entertainment industry in general posed a greater challenge to the arts.

In the 1960s, the emphasis shifted, as a considerably larger part of the budget now consisted of support to established, centralized institutions and professional arts. Here the one most significant development was the establishment of the *Norwegian Cultural Fund* in 1964. The Fund was to be administered by the Norwegian Cultural Council, and even though the Fund consisted exclusively of annual grants from the national budget, the Fund was considered to have certain practical as well as fundamental advantages over ministerial administration. First and foremost, it was set up to embody *pluralism* by avoiding a concentration of influence on cultural life by one ministerial department. But it was also intended to be a body for applying new methods in meeting the needs for innovation, experimentation, and planning. The Council has thirteen members, of whom four are appointed by the Storting (Parliament) and nine by the Government. The Council's main function is to distribute funds for special projects in the area of culture and the arts, and to support experimental projects for shorter periods. Most of the Cultural Council's activity is meant to be directed to costly once-only enterprises, in contrast to the system of regular grants covered by the national budget. If successful, an activity may be transferred to the ministerial budget after the end of the experimental period. The annual grant to the Norwegian Cultural Fund has increased from 21 million Nkr. in 1970 to 68 million Nkr. in 1983. Table 1 shows the different fields of support.

The 1970s brought new and radical elements into Norwegian cultural policy. An ambitious and systematic attempt was made to examine all aspects of cultural work together, as well as to view it as an integrated part of general social policy. The concept of culture was enlarged to include individual creativity and expression on a non-professional basis. The main points of this new cultural policy were:

a greater emphasis on cultural work in the various districts and on individual cultural activities;

a more systematic, orderly division of responsibility among the three levels of public administration in Norway: the State, the county municipalities, and the municipalities;

TABLE 1. The Norwegian Cultural Fund. Grants by Field, in Percent, 1966 to 1980

Field	*1966*	*1970*	*1976*	*1980*
Total	100	100	100	100
Literature	31	24	27	42
Periodicals	3	2	2	2
Music	7	12	8	8
Visual art/handicraft	10	11	13	12
Protection of cultural heritage	8	12	10	10
Lappish culture	—	—	2	2
Buildings	33	29	27	13
Reports and committees	—	1	2	1
General disposal	5	6	3	5
Administration	3	3	5	5

Source: Cultural Statistics, 1982.

wider distribution of art and other cultural goods to all groups in society: and considerably greater priority to cultural needs in public budgets.

As a consequence, earlier efforts toward increased availability and accessibility were strengthened and supplemented by proposals for *decentralizing* the administration of grants to culture and the arts by transferring State money to the municipalities. They then are left to decide how the grants can best stimulate local cultural activity. The degree of decentralization is indicated in Table 2.

Transfers from the national to local levels are most notable in the area of capital expenditure. Meanwhile, the cultural policy of the 1970s also contained important propositions concerning *professional artists*—the outcome of considerable political debate, as well as of actions on the part of the artists. The result has been greater State responsibility for the economic situation and working conditions of artists in Norwegian society, first and foremost through scholarships, guaranteed income, and payments for public use of their work. I will return to such specific support measures after discussing the general picture for the postwar period presented in Tables 3 and 4.

The tables show that government grants to culture and the arts have increased during the postwar period, although culture and the arts have always been present as a small part of the total activities of the Ministry of Church and Education as well as part of the total

TABLE 2. Net Public Expenditure for Cultural Purposes by Authority, in Percent

	1968	*1979*
Central government	46	40
County councils	2	4
Municipalities	52	57
	(100)	(100)

Source: Cultural Statistics, 1982.

TABLE 3. The Increase in Grants to Culture and the Arts as a Share of the Total State Budget and of the Total Budget of the Ministry of Church and Education*

	1948	*1953*	*1958*	*1963*	*1968*	*1973*	*1978*	*1982*
Total State budget (in mill. Nkr.)	2,490	4,343	5,733	9,435	15,355	30,862	70,845	111,138
Share of the State budget to the Ministry of Church and Education*	5	6	8	10	12	13	11	5*
Share of the Ministry's budget to culture and the arts	5	6	5	4	4	5	7	19*

Source: H. Roshauw, 1980; St. prp. nr. 1, 1983–84.

*From 1982 the Ministry of Church and Education was divided. These figures concern the new and smaller Ministry of Culture and Science.

State budget. There was a stagnation from the late 1950s to the late 1960s. But, in the 1970s the trend turned, and grants to culture and the arts continued to increase even after stagnation came to the government's overall budget. As for the period as a whole, the increase in grants to culture and the arts (compared to the total budget) was especially marked in the late 1940s and in the beginning of the 1970s. Then, the average annual rate

TABLE 4. Expenditure on Different Cultural Purposes under the Ministry of Church and Education in 1970, 1975, 1980, and 1983, in Mill. Nkr.

	1970	*1975*	*1980*	*1983**
General cultural purposes	—	21	63	58
The Norwegian Cultural Fund	21	30	52	68
Nordic Cultural Cooperation	—	3	8	8
Buildings	1	14	29	103
Scholarships, guaranteed income to artists	3	6	29	42
Plastic art	3	6	24	27
Music	6	20	43	70
Theater and opera	26	87	146	215
Cinema	10	26	61	81
Libraries and literature	9	41	100	106
Museums	7	25	62	82
Archives	4	18	24	29
Other cultural preservation	4	5	13	19
Youth work	2	6	21	53
Sport	1	2	4	5
Education of artists	11	33	73	116
Total	108	343	752	1082

Source: Ministry of Culture and Scientific Affairs, 1983.

*Appropriations.

of growth was nearly double in the field of culture and the arts compared to the total State budget (Roshauw, 1980). Grants in this field for 1984, however, have brought an overall stagnation and, in some areas, reductions. The main reason seems to be the policy of the conservative government, which has held office since 1981. One of its primary aims has been to reduce public expenditure. I will return briefly to the partisan division over arts policy in the 1980s in the concluding remarks.

Government Support to the Arts

The arts are labor-intensive activities, a fact that applies both to the performing and to the creative arts. A work of art or a performance today requires much the same amount of manpower it did one hundred or two hundred years ago—sometimes a little less because of modern equipment and sometimes a little more because of higher standards and expectations. This, of course, makes art, in all industrial societies, a rather costly enterprise compared to other fields of production, where it is possible to benefit from rationalization, mechanization, and automation. Consequently, the operating expenses of artists and artistic institutions are brought out of balance, so to speak, with the surrounding economy. Compared to other goods, the prices for art will be extremely high. This economic competition seems to be entangled with other kinds of competition—the struggle to gain the interest, time, and attention of the public in competition with modern media and leisure-time activities. Therefore, it is risky to trust to the law of supply and demand for the survival of artists and artistic institutions, especially in a country like Norway. This is the important background for the overall political agreement that existed through the postwar years on the need for governmental and public support of the arts. Apart from dissension on a few—but certainly important—principles, the discussion for the most part has been about the amount of support to the various arts.

In the following, I will give an account of the basic principles in the main support schemes, as well as their most obvious economic background and implications. The description covers support to both the performing and the creative arts. The main difference between these two areas is that the performing arts get their share chiefly through established institutions (like theaters and orchestras), while the creative arts get theirs mostly through individual support to artists and through government purchase of works of art and remuneration for public use.

Performing Repertory Theaters

In 1984, Norway had twelve public repertory theaters: three in the capital of Oslo, three in other main cities, five in five different regions of the country, and the State Traveling Theater (*Riksteatret*), which has its principal seat in Oslo but which for the most part tours throughout the country. No private theater exists on a permanent basis any more, but a variable number of "free groups" are active for shorter or longer periods. These groups struggle with serious economic problems and live an insecure existence, receiving only very modest public support. In addition, there are theater departments in both radio and television.

The *Riksteatret* was established in 1948. All the regional theaters started during the 1970s. The rest were founded as more or less private enterprises, but the economic responsibilities have gradually been taken over by the State. In 1980, the eight permanent theaters in the cities (the regional ones not included) gave a total of approximately 4,000 performances and sold over one million tickets (equivalent to one-fourth of the total population). Ten years earlier, they gave somewhat fewer performances (approximately 3,500) and sold a few more tickets (approximately 1.2 million), which indicates a tendency to produce more performances that fewer people attend. In 1980, the average attendance for all the theaters was 272 per 1,000 inhabitants, which is relatively high compared to other European countries outside of Scandinavia, especially considering the lack of big-city audiences and a scattered population (Theater Council, 1982). Production costs have increased drastically. From 1961 to 1972, the average increase at six of the main theaters was 461 percent. From 1972 to 1979, the corresponding figure was 239 percent (Theater Council, 1982). The reasons are to be found in the general inflation and price increase, in higher standards and expectations, as well as in employment increases, especially among technical staff, as a result of regulations through a new law on working conditions and through labor negotiations. Today, wage costs constitute about 80 percent of the total budgets.

Since 1945, there have been political reports and discussions of the theater situation in Norway approximately every ten years. Until 1962, public and governmental support was on an ad hoc basis, mostly as short-term crisis arrangements. In 1962, the first fixed support arrangement was introduced, making the support regular and predictable—which, of course, is an advantage for theater management. The support arrangement of 1962 was replaced in 1972. The new arrangement tried to adjust support to changing conditions and to previous experiences. The support scheme of 1972 still holds and its basic principle is this: the subsidy for the ordinary conduct of the theater is to be a fixed base amount plus an adjustment for price and wage increases and minus stipulated revenues. In addition, there are some grants for tours and for the maintenance of buildings. The main subsidy is to be divided between the State and municipalities according to a fixed ratio of 70 percent (State) and 30 percent (municipalities) (Theater Council, 1982).

Today, ticket revenues account for 7 to 20 percent of theaters' budgets, and this seems to have been relatively stable over the last few years. The remainder is covered by public money according to the scheme described above. Table 5 shows the development of public expenditure.

Despite this increase in grants, the theaters face a bad economic situation. Subsidy has not increased at the same pace as prices and wages, and it does not take into account the restrictions put on daily management as a result of the general law on working conditions and labor negotiations.

TABLE 5. Public Expenditure on Dramatic Art* 1970, 1975, and 1980.
In 1,000 Nkr.

	1970	*1975*	*1980*
Public expenditure total**	54,923	150,418	251,571
Local and county expenditure	27,000	65,000	93,000
Government expenditure	27,923	85,418	158,571

Source: Cultural Statistics, 1982.

*Not including expenditure on education related to dramatic art.

**Including government grants to theater buildings and grants from the Norwegian Cultural Fund to independent groups.

But in general, the fundamentals of the support scheme have been well received. The scheme avoids the danger of censorship—at least in any direct way—because grants are based on budgets and accounts and not on the repertoire. The support also has a certain automaticity which tends to keep it from being linked to the actual content of the theaters. The support is given to the theaters as institutions and enterprises, and not to productions which politicians, authorities, etc., may or may not like.

On the other hand, it is obvious that such a support scheme contributes extensively to freezing the existing structure. The permanent theaters become in a way tied up in their established patterns. And when production costs are rising, as they have been doing, it is almost impossible to establish and maintain new productions, new forms of theater, etc., without public support. When the existing institutions get so much, the practical result will be no room for new arrangements. The question is whether this eventually leads to a more conservative and less creative theater of poorer quality.

Music

Support of music bears some resemblance to theater support, and may be grouped in three categories: maintenance of the only permanent opera house in Norway; support to orchestras and musicians (including the State Traveling Concerts); and various measures like festivals and coordinating activities.

The Opera House was established in 1959. In 1983, grants were well over 63 million Nkr., thus exceeding the grant to any other single theater (St. prp. nr. 1, 1983–84). The Opera is, however, a large employer, comprising as it does both opera and ballet. Until 1983, the support scheme was in principle the same for the Opera as for the theaters: a fixed share of a basic amount covered by the State and by the municipality of Oslo. Since 1983, however, the State has taken over all obligations for the running of the Opera. The revenue from sale of tickets was, in 1982, about 10 percent of the total budget (St. prp. nr. 1, 1983–84, s. 287).

Of all the support to orchestras and musicians, about half goes to the State Traveling Orchestras (*Rikskonsertene*). This institution was established in 1968 with the purpose of bringing music of high quality to all parts of the country by giving concerts both in public and at various institutions, as well as encouraging local musical activities. Four symphony orchestras in the four main towns receive regular financial support, a mixed scheme for financing in which funds from the State, the Norwegian Broadcasting Corporation (a big consumer of orchestral music), as well as the local bodies, and the orchestras' ticket revenues are included. The distribution among them in 1982 was approximately 38, 35, 20, and 8 percent, respectively. The government grants to music increased quite sharply during the 1970s: from 6 million Nkr. in 1970 to 51 million Nkr. in 1981. In fixed terms, this means an average yearly increase of about 11 percent (St. meld. 23, 1981–82, s. 193). In the same period, concert attendance also showed a considerable increase: from approximately 200,000 listeners in 1970 to close to 1.2 million in 1980. At the same time, amateur activities are a rather strong element within the musical life of Norway compared to other art forms, and it seems that government grants may have had a more decentralizing effect here.

State Support of Literature

It is generally assumed that the increase in Norwegian book production and consumption during the 1970s was due to a number of governmental support arrangements introduced in the late 1960s and thereafter. Actually, the number of books sold per capita has been higher in Norway (and Iceland) than anywhere else in the world, including the other Scandinavian countries. The private expenditures for books, newspapers, weeklies, and magazines rose from 651 million Nkr. in 1970 to 2,344 million Nkr. in 1979. In fixed terms, sales to private persons increased by 47 percent. The increase was greatest for books (54 percent) and lowest for newspapers (38 percent) (Ministry of Cultural and Scientific Affairs, 1983).

There are various types of subsidies and support for literature: for translations of books of assumed cultural value; for publication of classics, essays, and books in minority languages (''New-Norwegian'' and sami literature); for illustration of children's books; as well as for promotion of Norwegian literature abroad.

But the main support arrangement is the so-called ''purchasing scheme,'' the primary goal of which is to enlarge the market. An example may clarify: 2,000 copies of a book is not much, but in Norway this represents one copy for every 2,000 inhabitants. An edition corresponding to this ratio in Sweden would be 4,000 (8 million inhabitants); in the Netherlands, 7,500 (14 million inhabitants); in Germany, 30,000 (60 million inhabitants); and in the U.S.A., 100,000 copies (200 million inhabitants). Considering the sharply falling curve of production cost per copy with increased print runs, it is evident that the price per book would be extremely high in Norway. The design of the ''purchasing scheme'' has been described as in Figure 1.

In Figure 1, ''the left column represents the full price of a normally calculated book, printed in 2,000 copies and with a value added tax of 20%.

''First we remove the value added tax, reducing the retail price by 16.3%, as you will see from the second column. The total exemption of value added tax—and the benefit of fixed book prices—is the basis of all public support of books in Norway.

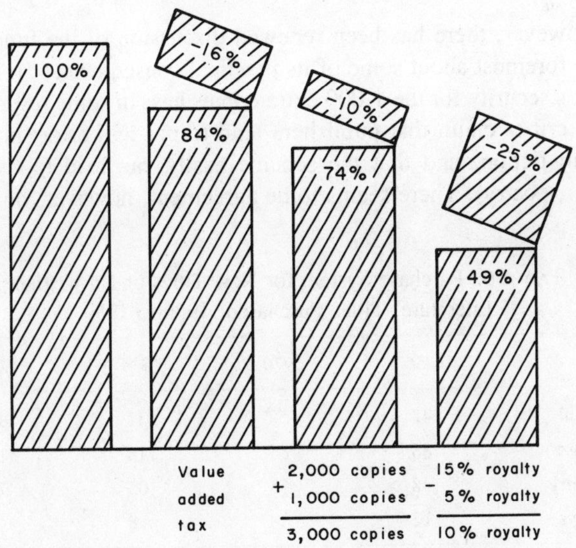

FIGURE 1. Basic principles of the ''purchasing scheme'' for books.
Source: Strømme, 1980.

"For some categories of literature, however, direct support is also needed. Therefore, the next step is the State's purchase of 1,000 copies of every new work of Norwegian literature—fiction, drama, poetry, and juveniles. By this extra purchase of books, which are distributed as an additional supply to public libraries, we can raise the printing run from 2,000 to 3,000 copies. The estimated price reduction is about 19%. (Third column)

"Finally for these books the State also contributes to the author's royalties, paying 10% for the first 3,000 copies and 5% from 3,000 to 5,000. This means that the author gets 20% royalty from the very first copy sold, but that for the first 3,000 copies only 10% have to be taken into the price calculation. The reduction of the retail price is here quite substantial, in our case approximately 25%.

"This amounts to the final result that the retail price of the book is now reduced to one half of the quite prohibitive price we started with. Norway is a high cost land, and the support must be regarded as a rescue action to secure the future of our national literature. Within this vital area of book production, which represents less than 10% of the total number of annual titles, the results have so far been most encouraging. Since the system was introduced during the sixties, it has more or less achieved the following goals:

a) reducing book prices
b) increasing the income of writers
c) extending the circulation of books
d) reducing the economic risks involved in publishing works of literary quality with minor sales potentials." (Strømme, 1980)

The scheme is administered by the Norwegian Cultural Council, but it is important to note that every book of Norwegian fiction published by members of the two publishers' associations will be purchased, without any prior evaluation by the Council. This automaticity avoids the danger of censorship or biased judgment by giving general rather than selective support. Putting it precisely, the support is given to the book rather than to authors or publishers. The number of titles purchased in 1966, 1970, 1976, and 1980 is shown in Table 6.

Recently, however, there has been renewed discussion of the fundamentals of this scheme, first and foremost about some of its practical consequences. It has been claimed that the publisher's security for the 1,000 extra copies has, in some respects, had unfortunate results. The critics claim that publishers tend to put less effort into marketing and selling Norwegian fiction, and that the scheme easily can lead to over-production in certain areas (e.g., poetry). There seems to be agreement, however, on the necessity for

TABLE 6. Purchase System for New Titles of Norwegian Literature. Titles Purchased, 1966 to 1980

	1966	*1970*	*1976*	*1980*
Total	148	158	231	194
Prose	88	85	118	113
Poetry	48	65	105	75
Plays	12	8	8	6

Source: Cultural Statistics, 1982.

some sort of "purchasing scheme," and so far no systematic plan has been put forward for changing the existing procedure.

Films

In Norway, there are grants to various institutions and activities concerned with film. For example, the Norwegian Film Institute is State-financed. In addition, subsidies are given to documentaries, children's films, the import of valuable foreign films, the writing of scripts, etc. There is also one State-owned film production company, Norsk Film A/S. The rise in total government expenditure on film has been quite extensive during the last ten years: from about 15 million Nkr. in 1972 to about 80 million Nkr. in 1983 (St. meld. 21, 1983–84, s. 18).

The support scheme for feature film production is, however, the one most discussed and with greatest relevance to this chapter. Feature films are, of course, in a special situation compared to other arts. Not only do they face the general competition for time and attention among the leisure-time activities and the new media, but they also face direct competition from foreign films running in Norwegian cinemas. During the last years, 51 percent of all films shown have been American, 11 percent British, and 6 percent French. Only 4 percent have been Norwegian productions (Film og kino, 1983, 3A). Norwegian films are, however, generally more popular than foreign films; they bring in a relatively bigger share of the total revenue than their number would suggest, well over 8 percent of the tickets and 6.5 percent of the revenues (Film og kino, 1983, 3A).

Even so, this does not remotely approach a sufficient basis for financing new productions. The market is small for a costly product like film, and most cinemas are municipally owned. That means that all revenue from general exhibition of films goes to the municipal exchequer, and none to the national film industry. Consequently, extensive support is necessary if a national film industry is to be maintained. Government support of feature film production started in the late 1940s and has existed in various ways ever since.

The last support scheme was put forward in 1964, and is still working with some adjustments. Apart from the grant to the one State production company, the basic principles of this design may be described this way: on the basis of a script, a cost estimate, and a financial plan, a special committee (*Statens Filmproduksjonsutvalg*), appointed by the Ministry, evaluates the project. Based on this evaluation, the Ministry may grant State support of up to 55 percent of the gross revenue. This, then, is intended to be a bonus arrangement, as it implies that films with high revenues get high State support also. In addition to this general support, the Ministry may give State loan guarantees to meet production costs, up to complete financing. Practically all feature films are dependent both on support and on guarantees. In fact, on account of galloping rising production costs and decreasing revenue, today practically all films are close to being fully financed by State guarantees for loans. The average yearly increase in production costs from 1973 to 1981 was around 16 percent. The average yearly increase in State guarantees has reached 20 percent (St. meld. nr. 21, 1983–84, s. 25). Hence, the evaluation screening of the applications is rather tough. Only 10 to 20 percent of the applications have been approved in recent years.

The pattern of increasing costs for feature films is similar to the situation for Norwegian theaters. However, there are fundamental differences between film support and theater support. Very little film support goes directly to institutions, i.e., film production

TABLE 7. Number of Features Produced with State Guarantees and Total Government Expenditure on Features in 1972 to 1981

	Number of films	*Total governmental expenditure (in 1,000 Nkr.)*
1972	9	5,004
1975	9	11,746
1978	8	16,210
1981	9	20,539

Source: St. meld. nr. 21, 1983–84.

companies. Most of it, on the contrary, is granted to single productions after individual evaluation by the ministerial committee, and the Ministry must in each case consent to the recommendations. Even if the appointment of members of this committee is supposed to be based on competence rather than on political or any other grounds, and while that competence should be respected by the Ministry, it is obvious that this scheme contains possibilities for censorship. Theater support, in contrast, is given to the theaters on a regular basis and as a fixed basic sum. Furthermore, it is doubtful whether present film support arrangements foster reasonably rational modes of production and the best possible utilization of resources. From the film producer's point of view, such support is not calculable, thus making it impossible to plan activity over a long period. Over the years, we have had a vast number of "one-time producers" in Norwegian film—people who have made one film and found it impossible to continue. Norwegian feature film production, therefore, has been characterized by discontinuity.

The support scheme for feature films seems to be constantly under debate. Neither the State nor the producers—for different reasons—find it satisfactory. Through the years, many film producers have argued for institutional or repertory grants to film companies rather than the single project grants. So far, these arguments have produced few results, and government concern these days seems to be concentrated on the vast increases in production costs.

Pictorial Arts

Since painters, sculptors, etc., work individually, support to *contemporary* pictorial arts and artists is channeled through institutions only to a minor extent. The largest part of government grants to the pictorial arts goes to custody and exhibitions of art in museums, national galleries, etc. Direct government aid to the pictorial arts increased from 2.8 million Nkr. in 1970 to 27 million Nkr. in 1981, which makes for a four-fold increase in ten years (in fixed terms). Grants from the Norwegian Cultural Council come in addition: 2.4 million Nkr. in 1970 and 5.7 million Nkr. in 1981.

In the 1970s, the new trend was for a larger share of the grants to be made for the purchase and exhibition of contemporary Norwegian art, thus aiming at enlarging the economic basis for living artists. In 1970, 13 percent of the total grants went to exhibitions. In 1980, this figure had increased to 37 percent (NOU 1981:45, s. 83). It is also important to note that many of the new activities to distribute pictorial arts (like galleries and different forms of exhibitions) are being administered by the artists' organizations, instead of by public museums, etc.

Parallel to the increase in exhibitions, there has been an increase in the sale of pictorial arts. Estimated sales increased from 12.4 million Nkr. in 1970 to 60 million Nkr. in 1980, and this, of course, is only registered sales (St. meld. 23, 1981–82, s. 208). This growing interest is reflected also in exhibition attendance, as the statistics from some museums, galleries, and exhibitions make clear. No systematic survey is available, however.

For the pictorial arts, also, there is an institution devoted to bringing the goods to most parts of the country: the State Traveling Gallery, established in 1952 and financed from government funds. In 1982, this major gallery, together with the central National Gallery, received about 45 percent of the total grants (of 32,079 million Nkr.). Support of exhibitions outside of these institutions took approximately 30 percent, while grants to a fund for decorating government buildings, established in 1977, got about 20 percent (St. prp. 1, 1983–84, s. 265).

New ways have been tried to decentralize the production and exhibition of pictorial arts, among them the establishment of regional artists' centers. Such experiments are being financed by the Norwegian Cultural Council, and must be added to the amounts mentioned above. There is a system of support to individual artists as well as a system of economic compensation for the public use of art exhibitions. These will be discussed next.

Grants to Artists

About 4,500 people are members of the various artists' organizations in Norway. Pictorial artists are the largest group, with about 28 percent of all the members. Next come musicians and singers with 27 percent, actors with 11 percent, authors with about 9 percent, and craftsmen designers with 7 percent. Film workers make up only about 5 percent, dancers 4 percent, and composers 2 percent of all artists registered in the artists' organizations. In all likelihood, there are also a number of people with income from artistic activities who are not members. The total number of artists is, therefore, probably between 6,000 and 7,000 people (St. meld. 23, 1981–82, s. 213).

Documentation shows that the average income level is considerably lower among artists than among other occupational groups. However, a sharp division exists between groups of performing artists like musicians and actors on the one hand, and groups of creative artists like painters and writers on the other. A majority of performing artists earn close to the average income or more, while most of the creative artists earn well below the average. This reflects their different working conditions. Most performing artists are permanently employed in theaters, orchestras, etc., while creative artists work individually rather than as regular employees.

The first government support of artists came in 1836, when the Parliament granted some travel scholarships. State-paid artist wages were granted first in 1863. Both scholarships and artist wages continued, but on an ad hoc and rather modest basis and with great variations from year to year. More regularity appeared after the Second World War, but more comprehensive support did not appear until 1963. From then on, artist wages were gradually replaced with travel and working scholarships, for which the artists' organizations (and not the Ministry) evaluate the applications and make nominations. To secure a qualified evaluation, the Ministry should be involved only formally in making the grant. In 1966, a separate committee was established to make these evaluations and nominations; its members are appointed partly by the Ministry and partly by the artists' organizations. An arrangement with scholarships for older deserving artists also came into being in 1963.

In 1963, there were 1,500 applicants for thirty travel and thirty working scholarships. The number of working scholarships gradually increased, reaching one hundred in 1969. From then on, there were no changes or adjustments until the more fundamental reform came in 1977. This reform had its background in several conditions. The most important was an accumulated need for support among the artists, as prices and wages in general had increased without any rise in grants, and because the general level of competition in the arts market seemed to have increased. This was the basis for a political campaign by artists in 1974 (*Kunstneraksjonen*), supported by a vast majority of all artists. The campaign called for: more public use of artists' work; remuneration for the public use of artists' work; and a minimum guaranteed income for all artists. Most energy was put behind the use and remuneration demands; if successful, they could make the guaranteed income superfluous. The action was met largely with sympathy. The new political climate that had brought about a more comprehensive cultural policy than ever before was certainly vital to the partial success of this action.

In 1977, a system of minimum guaranteed incomes for a limited number of artists was established, in addition to a number of working scholarships and other forms of State fellowships and grants (see Table 8). The guaranteed income, by 1981, covered 432 recognized artists. The original aim was to expand this system eventually to cover 550 to 600 artists (while a number of measures to enlarge use and remuneration, and thus the economic basis for artists, were also taken). But this scheme has not been followed up.

The guaranteed incomes are awarded on the basis of artistic merit on the recommen-

TABLE 8. Artist Grants. Government Appropriations by Type of Grant, for 1970 to 1980, in 1,000 Nkr.

Year	*Total*	*Work grants*	*Travel & education grants*	*Artist stipends to elderly deserving artists*	*Grants for establishment and materials*	*Guaranteed incomes*
1970	2,773	1,600	389	784	—	—
1971	2,869	1,605	389	875	—	—
1972	3,169	1,855	389	925	—	—
1973	3,262	1,877	389	996	—	—
1974	4,337	2,509	589	1,239	—	—
1975	4,949	2,929	589	1,431	—	—
1976	6,342	3,867	739	1,596	140	—
1977	13,784	4,751	1,200	2,204	250	5,379
1978	20,120	5,277	1,800	2,196	330	10,517
1979	26,513	5,372	2,135	2,302	425	16,279
1980	28,288	5,771	2,315	2,365	475	17,362
1981	31,631	6,167	2,450	2,497	500	20,017

Source: Cultural Statistics, 1982.

dation of professional committees appointed by the artists' organizations. The allotment is reassessed every five years, but in the normal state of affairs is meant to continue until retirement age, as long as the recipient remains an active artist. The maximum guaranteed income corresponds to the lowest starting salary in government service (approximately $10,000 per year). This income is reduced according to specific rules on the basis of the artist's other income. It is important to bear in mind that the guaranteed income grants amount to only a small portion of the grants to individual artists, as the survey in Table 8 shows.

But what makes government support to artists in Norway special and often controversial is the establishment of rights for the artists' organizations to negotiate with the State in the role of "employer," when there is no other natural or practical opposite member to be found. The idea is to put artists, as far as possible, on the same footing as other professional groups, with equal opportunities to improve working conditions, income, etc. Creative artists—authors, composers, and painters, for example—generally are not employees, and as self-employed persons they are in a very weak position with many different "employers," each of them rather marginal. For the most part, negotiations with the State deal with compensation or remuneration arrangements for the public use of art. As a result, public collective compensation arrangements in return for use are provided for to some degree in Norway. This is applied in the case where individual remuneration is complicated to administer, like the loan of library books, the copyright of books in schools, institutions, and the like. In other cases, the remuneration is individual, as for instance the painter's exhibition compensation.

The effects of such reforms, of course, are difficult to measure, especially in the short run. But many signs indicate that they have laid a basis for a greater breadth in artistic work. The possibility of an unfortunate dependence on the State does not seem to be imminent. On the other hand, the artists' organizations have developed union traits and considerable influence. Whether this is a reasonable or a worrying development in relation to, for example, artistic quality and individuality, is another discussion.

Concluding Remarks

Broadly, one may say that culture and arts policy basically concern two things: *the use of art* and cultural goods by the general public, and the premises and possibilities of *a national production of art.* As to the first point, some of the statistics cited above—e.g., the number of books and pictures sold, and orchestra attendance—indicate a more widespread access to and use of professional culture, while other figures indicate a decrease in use despite growing support (e.g., theater and film attendance). This mixed picture is confirmed when we take a closer look at the available cultural survey data. To be sure, this material is not extensive, as the first national survey was made in the middle of the 1970s. The surveys are also very general, making it difficult to pick out anything beyond very broad trends. But these confirm the general impressions above. The share of the total population having read at least one book during the last year increased from 69 percent in 1977 to 78 percent in 1980. On the other hand, the share attending a theater performance or going to a movie fell from 54 to 40 percent (theaters) and 50 to 46 percent (films) (Cultural Statistics, 1982). These decreases seem to apply to all regions and social classes.

This discrepancy is, of course, the object of political discussion, but there still is an overall agreement on the need for an arts and cultural policy much in the line of what exists today. In general, this field does not generate deep political controversies, for two main reasons.

The first is that Norway is a small country and language area. All political parties seem to realize the important differences between the situations of small and large countries in these matters. With a small public and market, it is impossible today for national culture and arts to be maintained and developed without some sort of public support. This is even more the case today, with the almost explosive development of international communication technology. There is, therefore, an overall agreement that increasing support to the arts should not be seen only as a subsidy to the consumer and as grants to non-profitable institutions and persons. It is also a basic investment in the face of the communication development—an investment necessary if any national character is to be kept and from which new art forms may benefit.

The second reason for the lack of serious conflict over the tendency toward increasing support in the face of decreasing public attendance in some areas is, of course, the relative prosperity of Norway. The country has had economic growth and a rising standard of living during most of the relevant period. Admittedly, the country has also felt the consequences of economic stagnation in the Western economy in the late 1970s and early 1980s. In fact, in the postwar period, the rate of unemployment in Norway has hardly ever been as high as in 1984. Still, Norway is a rich country, which is made richer by oil every day. In recent years, State accounts show increasing income and reserves. In 1982, there was an increase in capital of over 9 billion Nkr., and export profits as well as public and private savings increased.

But despite overall political agreement on public support of culture and the arts, it is also true that the conservative government has reduced budgets and that there are conflicting views, particularly in some areas and concerning some support schemes. This is due partly to differences over political goals and means in general, and partly to different opinions on the arts and culture. To give a brief account of the main line of division, I will, for the sake of simplicity, make a broad distinction between conservative (non-Socialist) and radical (Socialist) parties. It must be remarked, however, that at present (1986) six different parties are represented in the Storting.

The main difference between conservatives and radicals is that the conservative wing is more inclined to trust the market and is generally more suspicious of public support and expenditure. Overall, the conservatives seem to be more concerned with the cultural heritage and its protection, and with the established, recognized talents, and less concerned with the arts as an occupation, and artists as a group, necessary in modern societies.

The radicals come closer to the opposite view. They tend to see the weakness of the market rather than its strength, and to place greater importance on the general welfare and working possibilities of artists. They seem to find the welfare aspects of the grants and support schemes more important than do the conservatives.

Hence, the conservatives have been less willing to increase the size of grants and the amount of support schemes since they came into power in 1981. They have the explicit political aim of reducing public expenditure, and have proposed to increase the flow of private money into the field of arts and culture. The idea seems to be to encourage the sponsoring of concerts, exhibitions, plays, and other cultural arrangements by organizations, trade and industry, etc. But so far, this has had no great effect. In any event, the radicals fear the consequences of such a method of financing the arts and culture, especially if it will end up being a major part of the backing. They point to unprofitable art, experimental art, etc. Is it realistic to believe that private money will pay for such goods as well? Will there be venture capital for such enterprises?

Perhaps the most heated political debate on any concrete support scheme has been in connection with the guaranteed income scheme and schemes for remuneration for the public use of artists' work. This was a cornerstone of the arts policy of the Social Democrats holding office in the 1970s. In many ways, these measures introduced into politics new ways of looking at the role of the arts and artists in modern society. The welfare aspect was of prime concern, as was improving living and working conditions for artists as a group (and not only as individual talents). The resistance on the part of the conservatives to these schemes stems from the opinion that such a system gives no incentive to the production of "real" and valuable art. They also claim that the administration of such schemes gives too much power to the artists' organizations, turning arts policy more or less into union policy.

In any case, neither the guaranteed income nor the scheme for remuneration for public use have been abolished since the conservatives formed the government, even though grants were reduced. And compared to many other countries, public support to culture and the arts is likely to remain quite extensive in Norway. The problem in a small country is still, however, that this does not automatically represent a sufficient economic basis for art and artistic work.

Bibliography

Aanderaa, Johs. Norwegian Cultural Policy from the mid-70s to the present. Introductory speech at the Norwegian-American colloquy concerning cultural policy, held in Washington, D.C., April 11–12, 1983. (10 pp.)

Cultural Statistics 1982. Central Bureau of Statistics of Norway, Oslo-Kongsvinger, 1982.

Collection of data with a view of drawing up an inventory of public measures affecting the culture industries. Paper, 56 pp. Ministry of Cultural and Scientific Affairs, Department of Planning and Research, Oslo, April 1983.

Cultural policy in Norway. Paper, 24 pp. Ministry of Foreign Affairs, Oslo, June 1976.

Norwegian cultural policy. Paper, 23 pp. Ministry of Foreign Affairs, Oslo, May 1977.

Repertory of all available statistics (and indicators) relating to (1) the production of books and periodicals in Norway and (2) the cultural heritage in Norway. Division of Statistics on Culture and Communication, Report CSR-C-37, UNESCO, Paris, 1983.

Roshauw, Helene. Fra mesénvirksomhet til velferdspolitikk. Utviklingen av norsk kulturpolitikk. (From patrons of the arts to welfare.) Hovedoppgave i statsvitenskap, Universitetet i Oslo, 1980.

St. medl. nr. 21 (1983–84). Film i mediesamfunnet. (Report to Parliament: Film in a media society.)

St. meld. nr. 23 (1981–82). Kulturpolitikk for 1980–åra. (Report to Parliament: Cultural policy in the 1980s.)

St. prp. nr. 1 (1983–84) for budsjetterminen 1984, Kultur- og vitenskapsdepartementet. (Proposition to Parliament on the budget for 1984.)

Strømme, Sigmund. State Support of Literature. Paper presented at the 21st Congress of the International Publishers' Association, 15 pp. J. W. Cappelens Forlag A/S, Oslo, 1980.

Teaterrådet (the Theater Council). Teatrenes støtteordnning (Support scheme of the theaters), 121 pp. Oslo, 1982.

8

Cultural Policy in Sweden

CARL-JOHAN KLEBERG

The Concept of Cultural Policy

The definition of "cultural policy" in Sweden, as it will be discussed here, has come to be generally accepted only since the mid-1970s. Although the term was not widely used previously to that time, measures of cultural policy occurred in practice, even though they were limited mainly to the support of artistic activities, popular education, and libraries.

This definition evolved as a foundation for the new cultural policy decided on by the Riksdag (the Swedish Parliament) in 1974, following many years of inquiry. The definition also specifies the sectors to be included in the sphere of cultural policy, which is appreciably more extensive than the traditional sphere of art.

Cultural policy is defined here as an overall framework of public measures for the cultural sector. These include measures taken by the national government, municipalities, county councils, or public measures as a whole. Such a policy requires more or less specifically defined long-term goals. In order to fulfill the intentions of cultural policy, *resources, methods,* and *agencies* are needed for both planning and implementation. A fully developed cultural policy cannot be said to exist until all of these criteria have been satisfied.

Cultural policy is concerned with practical measures, and for this reason it is more appropriate to determine the range of measures of cultural policy than to define a particular concept of culture. The broader view of culture which has become increasingly noticeable in recent years is manifested in the goals and methods of cultural policy, not in the delineation of the sector itself.

The Government and Riksdag have defined the area of cultural policy as follows: State cultural policy is concerned with measures relating to cultural activities and works in written, theatrical, visual, and musical form, as well as media of communication such as the press, radio, and television. It also includes certain measures concerning popular education and associations, as well as measures for the preservation and revitalization of Sweden's cultural heritage.

Cultural policy is a policy aimed at one sector of society, similar to policies that have evolved for education, for social affairs, and for housing. Culture is one of the last fields for which such a sectoral policy has been defined. One important question to which we will have to return concerns the interaction of cultural policy with other sectoral policies and its relation to more overriding societal goals.

The Postwar Debate on Cultural Policy

The Roots of Cultural Policy[1]

Before turning to the postwar era, something should be said concerning the historical background.

A desire to assert identity was among the earliest discernible motives for measures of cultural policy. By the seventeenth century, a government office had been set up for the maintenance of archives and the care of cultural monuments, and legislation was passed for the protection of archaeological remains. Just as in present-day developing countries, Swedish cultural policy began with the defense of national identity.

The next complex of motives stemmed from the desires of the Crown and the court to have a more sophisticated and prestigious cultural establishment in the form of drama and academies. French influence played a very important role in stimulating the desire. This phase of development culminated in the late eighteenth century, partly as a result of the personal cultural interest of King Gustav III. Some aspects of royal cultural policy during his reign continued to make themselves felt until the advent of the new cultural policy of today.

The third "root" of present-day cultural policy is of a completely different kind, emanating from the popular culture which, especially during the nineteenth century, evolved parallel to, and partly in protest against, the apparatus of central government.

Many of the principal cultural events took place outside the apparatus of national government and, partly, in opposition to it. Through the religious revival and temperance and labor movements, people joined forces to campaign for their own interests. Education was given a prominent position in the work of the popular movements. The aim was to make cultural life accessible to everybody. It first took the form of lectures and subsequently changed to study circles (discussion groups). The foundation of libraries was considered a primary task for popular education.

The Debate from 1945 to 1960

Democracy was established in Sweden at the time of the First World War, but in general this did not have any immediate impact on cultural policy. During the interwar years there were many pressing social problems which had to be solved first. Some isolated but important decisions were made, however, resulting, among other things, in a nationwide touring organization, the National Touring Theater (*Riksteatern*), aimed at bringing good theatrical performances to people living outside the big towns and cities. This reform was prompted by democratic, distributive motives, and it is one of the first manifestations of the aspiration to reach out to all parts of the country. For the support of artists, an important resolution of principle was passed—allocating a certain percentage of the construction costs for State-owned buildings for the purchase of works of art.

Between 1945 and 1960, there was little debate on the practical aspects of cultural policy. Far-sighted proposals for a new cultural policy were presented in a debate book written by a number of ideologically committed Social Democrats at the beginning of the 1950s.[2] But twenty years were to pass before these ideas were translated into policy decisions.

In the field of practical policy, support for cultural workers was further improved through the introduction of compensation payments to authors for library use of their works. Inquiries were carried out by the Government and Riksdag, but the political determination required for introducing reforms was lacking. Public debate did not put heavy pressure on politicians to take practical action.

State support to culture was directed primarily toward such central cultural institutions as the two national theaters, a number of museums, and the preservation of cultural monuments. Public libraries also had been receiving support since the beginning of the century. It was at that time, too, that the municipalities had begun to support public education and cultural institutions.

1960 to 1974

The situation changed around 1960 as a result of cultural workers joining forces and forming an effective pressure group which induced the Government and Riksdag to take initiatives. The main grievances put forward were the poor earnings of cultural workers, the lack of fellowships and scholarships, and the inefficiency of art education.

The artists' arguments were accepted by the Government and Riksdag, but it took time for proposals to be drafted, because no administrative structure existed to deal with questions of this kind. Once that structure had been created, benefits were improved and the educational organization expanded.

In addition to the desire to support cultural workers, the Government also stressed the importance of cultural distribution. This led to a further development of the reform of the 1930s establishing the *Riksteatern,* with similar organizations now set up for exhibitions and music. This group of motives also was intrinsically noncontroversial.

On the other hand, cultural policy was criticized increasingly as being inadequate and incoherent. Demands were made for measures designed to activate people, to support popular culture, and to establish decentralized cultural activities, and also to support independent theatrical and musical groups. Many other demands also were put forward in the course of a vigorous cultural debate during the 1960s.

Demands for a coherent, socially oriented cultural policy led the Government to appoint, aside from a variety of specialized Commissions, a general Commission on Cultural Policy. The Commission's terms of reference included the analysis of goals, responsibilities, forms of financial support, and the State organization of culture. Ultimately, this Commission came to analyze, codify, and articulate all the demands which had been made in the course of the cultural debate.

In order to explain the link between debate and social change, a few more general remarks are needed concerning Swedish official inquiries. Inquiries conducted by Government Commissions are a very typical and important feature of Swedish national administration. These bodies publish extensive reports. They are a subject of widespread interest and public discussion, and are circulated to a large number of authorities and organizations for comment. This ensures that the decisions eventually made by Government and Riksdag are soundly based, but it is a time-consuming method of introducing reforms.

Summing up, the 1960s can be termed the decade of official inquiries into the cultural sector. During the 1970s, those inquiries bore fruit in statutory reforms.

The highly comprehensive official report on the new Swedish cultural policy published in 1972[3] was distributed to 450 different authorities and organizations. The replies ran to 5,000 pages. The press cuttings totaled several thousand. The replies were processed at the Ministry of Education and Cultural Affairs, after which the Government drafted a Bill numbering about 500 pages. The introduction of this Bill marked the opening of a detailed debate in the Riksdag and its Standing Committee on Cultural Affairs.

The Riksdag debate revealed a wide political consensus on the new cultural policy. Agreement was reached on the motives for public policy measures (see the section on the goals of cultural policy). However, differences existed among the political parties regarding the emphasis to be placed on quality in the awarding of cultural support. There were also differences of opinion in 1974, and still more later on, concerning the volume of economic support.

The Debate Following the 1974 Resolution on Cultural Policy

Among the parties, the conservative Moderate Party has been most restrained where initiatives of cultural policy are concerned. This party advocates reductions in the support given to cultural organizations affiliated with the popular movements, while on the other hand it is more favorably disposed to support for cultural institutions. Similarly, it favors the support of culture by private enterprise, a phenomenon which has not yet become very widespread.

The Liberal Party has been very much in favor of a continuous expansion of measures of cultural policy, and this expansion was in fact maintained during the six years between 1976 and 1982, when the Minister for Cultural Affairs was a Liberal. During this period, taxes were imposed on unrecorded tapes and video cassettes and the revenue thus obtained was used to finance increased cultural spending. As an opposition party since 1982, the Liberals have maintained their positive line, advocating a higher level of expenditure than the Social Democratic government. Like the Moderate Party, the Liberals take a relatively flexible view of the new mass media situation which satellites and cablevision are expected to produce during the 1980s.

The new program of cultural policy was put forward by the then Social Democratic government. In many ways, it reflected the reforming aspirations characterizing the period of several decades, ending in 1976, during which the Social Democrats held office in Sweden. The Party returned to office in 1982, but had not by 1984 established a definite profile in the new economic and political climate in which cuts in public spending are necessary. The 1974 resolution presupposed that cultural policy could be expanded continuously, as indeed it was throughout the 1970s and until very recently. One typical feature of Social Democratic cultural policy has been its heavy emphasis on the role of popular movements and independent cultural organizations. One of the important principles of the 1974 cultural policy was that national and local authorities should not engage in things which could be done just as well or even better by voluntary organizations. The Social Democrats are skeptical of cultural sponsorship by private enterprise. Instead, they are at pains to stress that cultural policy must counteract the negative consequences of commercialism.

The Center Party agrees on many points with the Social Democrats, but especially stresses decentralization.

The small Communist Party is most in favor of increasing government spending for culture and has called for legislation to augment municipal cultural responsibilities, and to reduce inter-municipal inequalities. The Communists want more vigorous action to be taken against cultural commercialism and in principle they are opposed firmly to the sponsorship of culture by private enterprise.

In sum, differences in opinion among the parties have not given rise to any major differences over practical policy; these policy differences have been due, rather, to changing circumstances, notably in the economic situation.

Party political differences to a great extent are reflected in the debate outside the political parties. Organizations of cultural workers are dissatisfied with the level of support, irrespective of the party putting forward the proposals. The expectations to which the 1974 decision gave rise have not been met. Some individuals, often those who are able to manage without grants, sometimes express concern at the element of control which any cultural policy is bound to involve and for support going to unneeded works. This type of skepticism is expressed both by pro-conservative artists and by representatives of the extreme left. In the latter case, the reason is a desire to avoid dependence on the authorities which might become hazardous in a situation of crisis. Regarding cultural sponsorship by private enterprise, there is a wide spectrum of opinions conditioned very much by varying personal experience and the prospects of managing without such support. Concerning the new media situation, there is also a wide variety of opinions. These range from a generally favorable attitude toward new technology to profound concern over its possible effects, especially on groups incapable of putting up much resistance to the expected flow of commercial influences.

The 1974 Cultural Policy

The 1974 Riksdag resolution defined the goals of cultural policy and the apportionment of responsibilities among the national government, municipalities, county councils, and voluntary organizations. It also included provisions concerning the State administration of culture and the underlying principles of State grants.

What was new about the 1974 policy resolution?

Its value lies in its holistic approach as the basis for a continuous development. The 1974 policy resolution was a point of departure that, of course, could be revised when the situation in society changes. In the absence of legislation for the cultural sector, guidelines are all the more important as a basis for further government action.

This is where the value of the extensive consultation procedure comes in. This procedure has shown that the principles affirmed by the Government and Riksdag have to a great extent been acceptable to the organizations, institutions, and cultural workers sustaining cultural life. Cultural policy in Sweden cannot be conducted by means of orders from the top. What the State can do is to sum up, back up, and encourage the ideas emerging from the cultural debate.

The Goals of Cultural Policy

The 1974 resolution on cultural policy[4] lays down that the State, municipalities, and county councils aim through their measures of cultural policy to help people satisfy their needs for experience, expression, and contact, and also to help make culture a means of exploring reality and critically appraising society. Previously, the main topics of discussion were the distribution of books, art, theater, and music, for example, to various parts of the country and the aesthetic embellishment of the external environment; this reflected a "distributive ideology" whereby finished "cultural products" were created by the few for distribution to the many.

The policy resolution rates cultural equality as no less important than economic and social equality. It is a matter of democratic equality that everybody wishing to do so can develop his resources as an active, creative individual and can be given opportunities for cultural experience. This means that cultural policy measures must be related to the situation, potential, and needs of different groups, and that cultural activities must also take place in surroundings which people frequent. Cultural policy is regarded as part of the work of improving the social environment.

Cultural policy ties in with the whole of the social environment (education, the working environment, the dwelling environment, the leisure environment, and the care environment), but it is also related to the planning and design of the external environment (physical planning, amenity planning, landscape conservation, and other aspects of environmental protection). Public cultural responsibilities relate to all cultural sectors regardless of whether they are conducted privately or publicly.

The aims of State cultural policy are summarized in eight points which have come to play an important part in the debate on cultural policy in Sweden. Cultural policy must:

> help to protect freedom of expression and create genuine opportunities for the utilization of that freedom;
>
> give people opportunities to engage in creative activities of their own and to promote interpersonal contacts;
>
> counteract the negative effects of commercialism in the cultural sector;
>
> promote a decentralization of activities and decision-making functions in the cultural sector;
>
> make more allowance for the experiences and needs of disadvantaged groups;
>
> facilitate artistic and cultural renewal;
>
> ensure that the culture of earlier times is preserved and revitalized; and
>
> promote an interchange of experience and ideas within the cultural sector across linguistic and national boundaries.

These goals have left their imprint on the measures described below, and they also have been a guiding influence in the choice among measures of different kinds. Although they are presented here in summary form, they are still relatively generalized even when quoted more fully.

But it has been on the basis of these goals that a program has been worked out to bring about their realization. No guidelines exist for weighing conflicting goals.[5]

The Apportionment of Responsibilities among States, Municipalities, County Councils, and Voluntary Organizations

One important stage in framing the new Swedish cultural policy has been to determine the apportionment of responsibilities among national and local government agencies and voluntary organizations.

The Swedish attitude rests on a very old tradition. Municipalities and county councils have extensive powers of self-determination. These are based on their independent powers of taxation, which yield considerable resources. The number of municipalities in Sweden has been reduced so as to strengthen the financial foundations of local government. In 1984, there were 284 municipalities and 24 county councils.

No legal provisions direct local governments with regard to the cultural sector.

Instead, municipalities act independently, according to their own political lights. In practice, this has resulted in all municipalities engaging, to an extent, in the cultural sector, the most widespread activity being public libraries.

Each municipality and county council decides for itself the level of its aspirations. This entails a great deal of responsibility and a considerable risk. The level of cultural input has come to vary a great deal among individual municipalities. Per capita expenditure ranges from SEK 95 to 635 (1981).[6]

The 1974 Government Bill calls municipal responsibilities for supporting cultural activities "one of the foundations of measures of public cultural policy. Many of the needs are best appraised at the local level. It is natural for municipalities to regard measures in the cultural sector as an effective means of creating a better environment."

The inquiries preceding the resolution on the new cultural policy revealed the need to entrust certain tasks—for which a municipality is too small an area—to county agencies. This applies above all to the theater, orchestras, museums, and libraries. They are autonomous institutions, supported by county councils, municipalities, and the State. At county level, there are agencies appointed by the national government known as County Government Boards. It has not been judged appropriate for cultural duties to be entrusted to these bodies. One exception to this rule is the care of ancient monuments. Responsibility for initiatives in the cultural area is vested almost exclusively in the county councils, which previously were concerned above all with medical care and certain aspects of education. The county councils have increased their efforts in the cultural sector, but at present their commitments are still relatively limited.

What, then, are the duties of the State in the cultural sector? First, there are its own institutions—the State theaters and museums and certain administrative bodies. The State has certain overriding responsibilities also, for example, for matters concerning policy objectives, certain official inquiries, and information.

The State also awards financial grants aimed at supporting certain cultural activities of local or regional relevance, popular education, and measures within various organizations. Among other things, the State is responsible for whatever legislation exists in the cultural sector, above all for the care of ancient monuments. There is also legislation relating to the freedom of the press and to copyright. Legislation, curricula, and other regulations in the educational sector provide important means of encouraging cultural activities.

Organizations of different types are active extensively in the cultural sector; some are dependent financially on the State, municipalities, and county councils. The organizations concerned here include popular education associations, cultural workers' trade unions, amateur cultural organizations, child and youth organizations, temperance organizations, trade unions, and other voluntary bodies.

These organizations would like to play a more active role in the cultural sector than they have done hitherto. In Sweden there is a long tradition of entrusting important public tasks to voluntary associations. The Government Bill on cultural policy states that the work of such organizations goes a long way toward achieving "one of the purposes of cultural policy, namely to give people an opportunity for personal development and social involvement. The organizations have greater opportunities than cultural institutions for reaching underprivileged groups. Government agencies in the cultural sector never can assume responsibility for the entire spectrum of activities which an active cultural life has to accommodate." This leads to the conclusion that the State and municipalities must give the organizations the economic resources they need in order to assume independent responsibilities within the cultural sector.

"Voluntary organizations," however, are not only those organizations whose programs include cultural activities. The term also includes the central trade union organizations. It is particularly interesting to note the growing attention paid to cultural questions in recent years by the Swedish Trade Union Confederation (LO) and the Swedish Central Organization of Salaried Employees (TCO). The 1981 LO Congress adopted a special program entitled "The Trade Union View of Culture."

The 1974 resolution did not refer to any special role for private enterprise and individual funds. Tax legislation in Sweden, unlike its counterpart in the United States, never has encouraged private enterprise to support culture financially. In spite of this, sports receive a great deal of private support, but the assistance given to culture is on a modest scale. Recently, partly under the influence of impulses from other countries, the question of the part to be played by private enterprise has come to be discussed, but the Government has not taken any initiatives to encourage private enterprise to make any more substantial contributions. The Council for Cultural Affairs finds that the most important task for private enterprise is to promote culture at and in conjunction with workplaces. Much already is being done in this respect, but efforts of this kind are distributed very unevenly.

State and Municipal Cultural Organization

National Level

The *State* cultural organization is unusual by international standards, but matches the pattern of other social sectors in Sweden. Questions of principle and finance are decided by the Riksdag. Government departments are concerned with policy-making and financial allocations, not with day-to-day administration, which is the responsibility of independent authorities. Within the cultural sector, this division of labor came into being as part of the 1974 reform of cultural policy, where a number of questions previously dealt with at the Government department level were transferred to national administrative authorities.

No cultural agencies of the national government exist at regional and local levels, except caring for ancient monuments. Responsibility at these two levels is vested entirely in local government agencies over which the State does not exert any influence.

The Riksdag, acting in response to Government proposals, makes decisions concerning goals, the organizational principle of State cultural agencies, and allocations for cultural purposes. The Riksdag has a special Standing Committee on Cultural Affairs to draft measures relating to culture and mass media. In the great majority of cases, the Riksdag adopts bills presented by the Government.

Most business is dealt with by the Government collectively, with the Minister of Education and Cultural Affairs acting as *rapporteur*. Although the Minister, formally speaking, does not himself make decisions, in practice he exerts very great influence. The collective decision-making principle finds its guarantee in discussions with other Ministers, above all with regard to the economic aspects. Cultural affairs are dealt with by two Departments at the Ministry of Education and Cultural Affairs—a Department of Cultural Affairs and a Department of Mass Media Policy. Certain questions relating to popular education are dealt with by an Adult Education Unit. The Ministry employs about thirty people to deal with questions relating to cultural affairs and mass media.

Decisions concerning the budgets of the State cultural institutions and various allocations to national authorities are made by the Government and Riksdag. The rules governing grants are laid down by the Government. A few hundred grants and allocations for grants are distributed among various institutions, organizations, and types of support. This is quite a different apportionment of responsibilities from that, for example, in the United States and Great Britain, where national cultural agencies receive a lump sum to distribute as they see fit.

At the national level, there are three main central bodies—the Council for Cultural Affairs, the Central Board of National Antiquities, and the National Archives Board—which are responsible for various major subdivisions of the cultural sector. There also are a number of autonomous bodies directly subordinate to the Ministry of Education and Cultural Affairs with more limited duties.

The *Council for Cultural Affairs* was inaugurated in 1974, the year in which the Riksdag adopted the new cultural policy. The Council is responsible at the central level for State cultural policy; its overriding task is to work for the development of that policy and the accomplishment of its objectives. In addition, the Council is responsible for State support to the theater, dance and music, literature, libraries, and cultural journals; also to art, museums, and exhibitions. Other tasks of the Council include: assessment of the State grants needed for various cultural purposes as a basis for the Government's budget proposals; distribution of State grants for cultural activities; opinion formation and the distribution of information; advisory services to municipalities, county councils, organizations, cultural workers, etc.; and investigation of questions of cultural policy.

The Council for Cultural Affairs consists of a Board and four committees for various cultural fields: one for theater, dance, and music; one for literature and libraries; one for art, museums, and exhibitions; and one for popular education. The members of both the Board and the committees are appointed by the Government.

The Board is comprised of representatives of political parties, municipalities, various organizations, cultural workers, and the chairmen of the committees. The Board decides all general issues, e.g., the budget. Comments on official inquiries, questions of principle concerning grants, and reports prepared within the Council are subject to its approval, as well.

Since the Board of the National Council for Cultural Affairs includes members of the Riksdag's Standing Committee on Cultural Affairs, the two institutions are always in close contact. This has made it easier for the Council to reply to criticisms voiced in the Riksdag. The social orientation of cultural policy, which has been so important an element in the Council's activities, has contributed to the relatively high degree of agreement on cultural matters. The Riksdag debates on cultural affairs today are both exhaustive and informed by expert knowledge. Materials presented by the Council are often used in connection with them. The close link with the central trade union organizations has made the Council known in circles where cultural issues are not so frequently discussed.

In the Riksdag, various kinds of local and regional opinions are of great importance. And the Council's policy of spreading its programs throughout the country has found support in such opinions.

The committees deal with questions arising in their special fields and general issues coming within the scope of their special qualifications. They submit proposals to the Board on all general matters, such as the budget and guidelines for committees of inquiry.

On the other hand, they have decision-making power in matters relating to their own fields.

The purpose of the widespread participation of representatives of organizations and cultural workers in the various agencies of the Council—there are a number of work groups as well as the Board and committees—is to combine decision-making with co-determination and insight, and to prevent control being left to full-time officials. Roughly 110 laymen take part in the Council's decision-making, whereas the staff number only seventy.

The general debate on cultural policy includes a great deal of discussion concerning cultural administration. Various reviews of the organization of the Council for Cultural Affairs have been undertaken, but they have not led to any thoroughgoing changes.

The *Central Board of National Antiquities* is the central authority responsible for the care of ancient monuments and cooperates with the county antiquarians attached to the State county administrations and with the regional museums.

The *National Archives Board* is responsible for the State archives described above, primarily the National Record Office and the regional archives.

Municipal Level

Ultimate decision-making powers at the *municipal level* are vested in the municipal council, especially where budgeting is concerned. Practically all municipalities have special cultural affairs committees. In some cases, there are special library committees, museum committees, etc. Cooperation with other municipal committees, such as the recreation committee, the social welfare committee, the local education authority, and the building committee, is becoming progressively more important.

As mentioned above, the *county councils* are responsible for cultural activities at the regional level. They distribute grants to the theater, music, libraries, and museums, and also to organizations. In addition, the county councils conduct cultural activities within their own institutions, mainly hospitals. Within the county councils, cultural affairs usually are dealt with by a cultural affairs committee or by a cultural and educational affairs committee.

Municipalities and county councils are in a strong economic position. They receive from the State, and can use in any manner they wish, a general leveling fiscal grant. There is a general awareness of the duty to provide, concomitantly with their right to levy taxes, a good level of social services—admittedly the inclusion of culture here is of relatively recent date. Since the State's support for culture at the local level is small, no corresponding efforts are expected. This autonomous right of municipalities and county councils to impose taxes and to incur expense makes local and regional opinion a matter of great importance. The force of good example has been extremely important for the high standards of Swedish public libraries. And individuals such as political personalities, engaged in cultural projects, also have a major effect on public opinion. The Council, too, does what it can to strengthen political opinion, regionally and locally, by providing statistics on expenditure, which are much in demand. The Council's various projects aimed at special groups are also important to local opinion, including those outside circles which have an a priori interest in culture.

The two central organizations for municipalities and county councils, the Association of Municipalities and the Association of County Councils, enjoy a very strong position within the Swedish political system. They consult with the Government concerning crucial issues, as they did on the structure of the 1974 Bill. This is why close collaboration between the Council and the local authorities' association is vital to the grass-roots application of cultural policy. In certain instances, the Council and the Association of Municipalities also make common recommendations. An inquiry into the municipalities, the State, and cultural policy is being made in close collaboration with the two central organizations. Their active support for cultural policy is most important, inasmuch as they are the municipalities' and county councils' own organs.

Efforts and Development Tendencies within Various Cultural Sectors

With reference to the goals of cultural policy, and within each subdivision of the cultural sector, organizational principles and guidelines, based on a process of interaction between municipal and regional levels, have been laid down for the financial contributions to be made by the State. By tradition, these principles differ somewhat among the various sectors. The following descriptions indicate what has been achieved, and therefore constitute a kind of evaluation. Something also can be said concerning future prospects.

Looking only at the various cultural fields, however, is insufficient to capture important aspects of the new cultural policy. Policy measures relating to such groups as children, young persons, immigrants, and the disabled—or relating to culture in various environments such as working life and housing areas—will be described therefore in another section.

Theater and Dance

On the whole, Swedish theater is publicly subsidized. The three central institutions—the Opera, the Dramatic Theater, and the National Touring Theater—are financed entirely out of State funds, over and above box office earnings. State grants provide 83 and 89 percent of the revenue of the Opera and Dramatic Theater (SEK 125m and 64m respectively in 1981/82). The National Touring Theater receives a State grant of SEK 98m. Local and regional theatrical institutions are financed by municipalities and counties and receive State grants toward wage costs. The State also makes grants to free theatrical groups and for amateur activities.

For the 1981/82 fiscal year, State expenditure totaled SEK 426m. Municipal grants for theatrical activities totaled SEK 278m in 1981. Municipalities with populations exceeding 100,000 account for the bulk of municipal theatrical performances. The county councils' grants for theatrical activities were SEK 42m in 1981.

The twenty-one regional and local theaters with permanent companies receive State grants covering a portion of wage costs for all personnel. These grants, totaling SEK 110m, varied in 1981/82 from SEK 0.6m to 21m. They are guaranteed from year to year and are adjusted automatically to offset wage movements. Theatrical activities are subjected to closer appraisal only when a real increase of the grant is being considered.

The grant for free professional theatrical and dance groups is constructed differently. The total amount in 1981/82 was SEK 12.2m. Appraisal is on an annual basis, and no group is assured of continuing grants.

What have been the results of the new State theater policy?

The 1974 resolution called for efforts to regionalize theatrical activities, above all because so much of theatrical life had come to be concentrated within the big cities. The intention was for a network of regional theaters to be built up throughout the country, under municipal and regional sponsorship and with State financial support. Today (1986) there are twenty-four local and regional theaters in Sweden. Fourteen institutions have been established since 1970/71. Despite all efforts at regionalization, theatrical amenities are still very unevenly distributed among different parts of the country.

In 1981/82, the twenty-one regional theatrical institutions receiving State grants gave a total of 7,200 performances, which was a 35 percent increase over the figure for 1970/71. The rise in the number of performances, however, has not been matched by a growth in audiences.

Private, commercial theatrical activities are of modest proportions compared with, for example, France and Britain. They do not qualify for State grants.

Dance as an art form traditionally has occupied a modest position in Sweden. It is attached to certain theaters, above all those with repertoires of music and drama. Folk dancing, on the other hand, is a widespread mass movement. Every year, 56,000 people receive instruction. Jazz dance attracts relatively large numbers of participants, almost 50,000. Roughly 15 percent of the population dance (ballroom dancing and the like included) at least once a week.

What will the rest of the 1980s signify for the theater and dance?

Increasing economic pressure can have a number of adverse effects, because the theater is so dependent on public finance. This could lead the theaters, in a necessary bid for increased box office earnings, to adopt a more mediocre, fast-selling repertoire.

Theatricals for children and young people are particularly liable to suffer, because they yield less revenue per performance than adult theater yields. Consequently, the free groups, which to a great extent cater to these very categories, are also at risk.

Much remains to be done regarding the intended regionalization of the theater. Some parts of the country still lack permanent theatricals. Many of the relatively new regional theaters are still so small that they are laboring under considerable difficulty.

If the position of dance as an art form is to be strengthened in the 1980s, this will require expenditure on a scale which seems unlikely to materialize.

Music—An Art without Boundaries

The most common way in which people come into contact with music is through the media, i.e., radio, gramophone records, or tapes. Sweden leads the world in per capita purchases of recordings (records, tapes, and cassettes).

But the Swedes also play and sing a great deal themselves, in an amateur capacity. Practically all municipalities have municipal schools of music, which are an important foundation of amateur music-making. Among them, they have about 300,000 pupils, which is roughly one-third of the compulsory school population.

Many amateur music-making associations are subsidized by government at various levels. In 1978/79, these associations organized 43,000 music circles. Many of these circles are concerned with choral singing, and it is estimated that more than 2 percent of the people of Sweden (about 200,000) are active choral singers.

For the 1981/82 fiscal year, State expenditure totaled SEK 197m. In 1981, municipal grants for musical activities (including schools of music) totaled SEK 557m; the county councils' grants were SEK 11m.

Traditionally, State support for music has gone to one particular aspect of musical life, namely occidental classical music. More recently, and perhaps above all through the advent of State cultural policy, these efforts have been broadened and have come to include other genres and forms of music, e.g., folk music, jazz and other improvisational music, pop, rock and roll, etc. Occidental classical music, however, still receives the lion's share of State assistance.

The State funds devoted to music are earmarked mainly for the following purposes:

Rikskonserter (the National Foundation for Traveling Concerts) is a State foundation concerned with music policy. Among other things, it produces concerts and other musical activities for schools, day nurseries, hospitals, and the general public. Its State grant for 1981/82 was SEK 38m.

The State Regional Music Authority formerly consisted of military musicians but has been a civilian body since 1971 and is predominantly concerned with civilian music. In the country as a whole, which for these purposes is divided into eight regions, there are just over five hundred State-employed regional musicians. The State grant was SEK 99m in 1981/82.

Professional symphony and chamber orchestras at the regional level receive, as do other regional cultural institutions, State grants (SEK 46m in 1981/82). At present, there are ten State-subsidized musical institutions of this kind.

The free music groups, i.e., freelance groups and ensembles not permanently attached to any institution, organization, or the like, have, like the free groups in other types of art, done a great deal to vitalize cultural life in the past ten years. Free groups exist for all types of music, but above all for jazz, folk music, and experimental music. Grants to the free music groups, totaling SEK 5.6m in 1981/82, are reassessed annually.

What is the outlook for music?

We are in the middle of a media explosion which will dominate cultural life during the rest of the 1980s. Where music is concerned, there is reason to suppose that recordings will become still more common as a form of contact. Live music is being hit heavily by the steeply rising costs of touring performances, for example, and may become an excessively expensive alternative for the individual consumer. One of the most important tasks of the State for the 1980s is to counterbalance this development and to give people throughout the country more opportunity to experience high quality live music in various forms.

One essential reform will be to revise the division of responsibilities between the State-financed *Rikskonserter* and Regional Music on the one hand and the municipalities and county councils on the other, in order to achieve a greater decentralization. A bill with this intent was presented to the Riksdag in 1984 and a decision was taken at the end of that year. Under the bill, responsibility for the regional music organization would be transferred to the county councils. In this way, responsibility would be uniformly distributed at county-council level. The county councils would be guaranteed State support at the same level as hitherto. The activities will be regulated by agreements between the State and each county council. Here is a new element in relationships between the State and the local and regional levels.

Public Libraries—The Most Heavily Utilized Cultural Institutions

Practically all responsibility for public libraries is vested in the municipalities. Their combined annual spending on libraries totaled SEK 1,048m in 1981, which is about 35 percent of all municipal cultural spending. State spending in the library sector, not including scientific libraries, was SEK 49m in 1981/82.

Public libraries are the most widely distributed, most frequently visited, and most heavily utilized cultural institutions. Throughout Sweden today, there are some 1,800 libraries affiliated with the central libraries of the 279 municipalities. In addition, there are about 125 bookmobiles (especially in sparsely populated areas). Loans in 1981 totaled 76.5 million volumes and the public libraries had a total of 40.2 million books and other media.

The public libraries have evolved from the popular education movement of the early twentieth century and many were founded by and for study circles. The activities underlying present-day amenities were reorganized as a municipal responsibility during the 1920s and 1930s.

There is also a network of regional libraries, and special lending centers have been set up in Malmö, Stockholm, and Umeå. Among them, municipal libraries, county libraries, and lending centers form a long-distance lending system which, in principle, makes the entire national stock of books available to every inhabitant. The regional libraries receive a State grant on the same lines as other regional institutions. In 1981/82, this grant totaled SEK 11m.

The Council for Cultural Affairs distributes the limited State support intended to eliminate differences in the service and other standards of municipal libraries. This support also is intended to promote greater decentralization and to enable new groups to participate in library activities. In addition, State grants finance the activities of the lending centers and, to some extent, those of the county libraries.

What will happen to public libraries?

In many places, steep rises in the prices of books and other media, combined with a stagnation of municipal grants and reduced acquisitions, have led to a decline in lending figures.

One serious problem concerns the inequality of library standards, not only among different municipalities but also among different parts of the same municipality.

In 1984, a commission of enquiry appointed by the Government proposed a reduction in support to local libraries and a corresponding increase to county libraries. The idea here was that this would have a leveling effect throughout each region. The National Council for Cultural Affairs will have a part to play in developing methods and taking responsibility for surveying developments. The proposals reflect the demand that reforms leave the State's costs unchanged. A much discussed proposal that a minimum standard for county libraries should be established by law has been rejected. The Riksdag considered the bill in 1985.

Support for Literature and the Press

Sweden is a small language area, which is one reason for the difficulties experienced in maintaining a wide range of literary output, especially where fiction is concerned. For this reason, special State *literature* subsidies were introduced in the 1970s. Payments for the 1981/82 fiscal year totaled SEK 26m. These subsidies are distributed by the Council for Cultural Affairs and relate, among other things, to the publication of new Swedish fiction for adults, Swedish translations of fiction for adults, classics, non-fiction for adults, literature and comic strips for children and young people, and literature in immigrant and minority languages. Most subsidies are paid *post facto,* but advance payments can be made for particularly costly publishing ventures.

Another type of subsidy in the literature sector is paid to the book trade to facilitate the distribution of State-subsidized book output. A third type of support takes the form of loans toward book trade investments. There are still great problems connected with the book trade and book distribution, and the Government therefore appointed a special commission to look into the matter. In 1984, the commission presented its conclusions. It proposed that support to literature should be retained in its present form, but supplemented in certain aspects.[7] The decision was taken by the Riksdag in 1985.

In 1977, 95 percent of the population had access to a daily newspaper, a very high figure by international standards. In 1981, the *daily press* sold 4.9 million copies to a population of about 8 million. The reason for this high rate of newspaper reading is that a differentiated daily press has been maintained successfully through substantial State subsidies.

The daily press receives extensive financial support, the figure for 1981/82 being SEK 331m. This support covers production grants, establishment subsidies, development grants, cooperation grants, distribution discounts, and loans.

The *periodical press* also receives State assistance (SEK 51m in 1981/82). Most of this money goes to journals published by organizations, i.e., membership journals, journals of nonprofit organizations, and journals ideologically connected with political organizations.

Cultural periodicals receive assistance, totaling SEK 8m in 1981/82. This money was distributed among about two hundred journals supplying civic information, engaging in economic, social, or cultural debate, or providing space for analysis and presentation of the various arts.

Museums, Exhibitions, and Art

Sweden has about fifteen central State museums, most of them in Stockholm. Several are jointly organized in groups, such as the State Museums of Art and the State Historical Museums. Grants to the State museums for 1981/82 totaled SEK 169m. The largest payment, SEK 32m, was made to the State Museums of Art. In the country at large, there are twenty-six museums receiving State grants, on the same lines as theaters, musical institutions, and regional libraries. These grants totaled SEK 25m in 1981/82, and payments varied from SEK 0.4m to 4.7m. In addition, there are a large number of municipal museums and museums of local history.

A special State organization, *Riksutställningar,* was set up in 1976 to help museums and other institutions, as well as groups and individuals concerned with exhibitions and art education, by arranging and procuring exhibitions. *Riksutställningar* also receives special funds for developing the exhibition as a medium. Its State grant for 1981/82 was SEK 15m.

The needs of the museum sector for the 1980s include an expansion of regional support. Within the museums, greater efforts are needed to improve permanent exhibitions. The documentation and care of exhibitions are also neglected fields.

Public measures in the field of pictorial art are not very well developed. The most important concerted State effort concerns purchases of art for State-owned buildings. Only in 1984 was the goal decided on in principle in the 1930s—that 1 percent of all building costs be set aside for artistic embellishment—reached. Despite an exceedingly tight budget situation, a considerable (50 percent) increase was decided on for purchases of art. The current allocation is SEK 26m. Many municipalities already have decided to allocate 1 percent or more to art purchases in connection with new buildings. It is possible the State's decision will act as a model at the municipal level, also.

There has been much discussion in recent years concerning the demand by pictorial artists for remuneration for works which they have sold to public institutions and which are shown to the general public or used in some other public manner. This question was settled by a Riksdag resolution in 1982 establishing a pictorial artists' fund for this purpose. The grant (SEK 20m in 1983/84) is used to finance fellowships and grants to individual artists.

One question in the field of pictorial art which is still awaiting a general solution concerns the reimbursement of artists for works which they make available for exhibition purposes. The State has concluded an agreement with the representative organizations of pictorial artists in this matter, but no corresponding agreement has been concluded with the municipalities and the art associations, which account for a far larger proportion of exhibition activities.

Support for individual pictorial artists is discussed in the section below entitled "Cultural Workers in Cultural Policy."

The small incomes of pictorial artists and the need to stimulate interest in art will be the main problems of the pictorial art sector in future.

Care of Ancient Monuments—One of the Few Fields with Statutory Safeguards

The care of ancient monuments now has as its aim the conservation and revitalization of Sweden's cultural heritage. Formerly, it was concerned mainly with the preservation of archaeological remains and particularly valuable buildings from bygone ages. This responsibility gradually has been broadened to include the preservation of historical continuity in the whole of the environment. At the same time, the care of ancient monuments has acquired a stronger position in social planning.

Responsibility for the conservation of historical assets is shared between the State and the municipalities. The responsibility of the State is expressed, above all, in legislation on the care of ancient monuments, while municipal responsibilities are reflected by legislation on planning and building.

State expenditures on the care of ancient monuments totaled SEK 77m in 1981/82, and municipal expenditure in this quarter during 1979 totaled SEK 75m.

The central authority for the care of ancient monuments is the Central Board of National Antiquities. The State county administration is the responsible authority at the regional level. Regional museums play a part in both State and municipal care of ancient monuments, by carrying out historical surveys and inventories and by taking part in an expert capacity in the day-to-day handling of planning and building questions, questions concerning archaeological remains, etc.

At the municipal level, the building committees are responsible for ensuring that due provision is made in planning and construction for the historical aspects of the environment.

In the archival sector, the National Record office is the central authority. There are also seven provincial archives. The National Record Office is, among other things, the repository of State public documents and the archives of central organizations. The tasks of the Dialect and Place Name Archives, the Swedish Center for Folk Song and Folk Music Research, the National Archives of Recorded Sounds and Moving Images, and the

Swedish Dictionary of Biography include the collection and preservation of material in their various fields. These authorities come under the National Archives Board.

Popular Education—Heavy Emphasis on Amateur Culture

Adult education associations were formed in the early years of the present century, mostly in affiliation with the political parties, denominational organizations, and the temperance movement. Today there are ten such associations, mainly concerned with organizing study circles and cultural activities of various kinds. The vital support given to amateur cultural activities is channeled through these adult education associations. A large number of professional cultural workers participate as leaders of circles or in other capacities in the extensive cultural activities run by the adult education associations.

The new State cultural policy allotted an important role to the adult education associations and other voluntary bodies. These organizations have a completely free hand in planning their activities, but the substantial State and municipal assistance which they receive is subject to certain conditions. In 1981/82, the adult education associations received grants totaling SEK 1,365m, of which 54 percent was provided by the State. The overwhelming bulk of this assistance went to study circles. A new State grant for cultural activities was introduced in 1981. In 1983/84, this grant totaled SEK 88m.

For 1981/82, the adult education associations reported 274,200 study circles with 2.4 million participants. On average, each circle had just over nine participants and lasted for thirty-two hours. Aesthetic subjects, e.g., music and applied arts, accounted for 100,100 circles (37 percent of the total number). Study circles apart, the adult education associations organized 73,400 cultural events with 8.8 million participants, and 20,400 group activities with 530,000 participants.

In 1976, roughly 30 percent of the population between the ages of sixteen and seventy-four attended a study circle or course of one kind or another.

The problems of popular education include mounting financial difficulties and a restructuring of activities following the radical reform of financial support introduced in 1981.

Radio and Television—Liberty by Agreement

Radio and television are managed by the Swedish Broadcasting Corporation, which is owned by the popular movements, newspapers, and various organizations. The Corporation's activities are governed by an agreement with the State. Within the Corporation there are four separate companies for television, national radio broadcasting, educational radio broadcasting, and local radio broadcasting, respectively. The new broadcasting agreement concluded in 1979 includes important provisions concerning the Corporation's cultural responsibilities. These rules are stated in general terms, but there is a great deal to suggest that they have had positive effects. Breaches in the agreement between the Corporation and the State are investigated by a special independent body, the Broadcasting Council. Its pronouncement may, but does not necessarily have to, influence the programs.

Radio and television are financed by license fee revenues. The cost of radio and TV broadcasting, estimated at SEK 2,000m for 1983/84, is not included in the State budget, although both expenditure and license fees are fixed by the Riksdag. No commercial advertisement is permitted on Swedish radio or TV.

Broadcasting plays an important part in everyday Swedish life. The average Swede spent 1 hour and 50 minutes per day in 1981 listening to the radio and almost 2 hours watching television.

On an average, the Swede watches yearly 52 hours of cinema films on TV and 157 hours of original TV drama. These figures should be compared with his 4 hours seeing films at the cinema and 1.5 hours at the theater.[8]

Apart from the broadcasting monopoly, an experimental public access radio scheme is in progress with local broadcasting in a number of small communities. These programs are entirely produced and financed by various independent associations. Public access radio has been a topic of political controversy.

The Government has appointed a Mass Media Committee with representatives from various parties. This Committee is to propose measures to be taken by the State to deal with the new media situation which will have arisen by the end of the 1980s. A Riksdag resolution was taken in 1985.

A Different Form of Public Support for Film

In most countries, the support given to the cinema occupies a special position, because it is only quite recently that film has been accepted as part of the cultural sphere of public responsibility. During the infancy of the cinema in Sweden, film provided the State with a source of income through the imposition of a special tax. Swedish film production went through a crisis during the early 1960s. This was resolved by a special agreement between the State and the film industry abolishing the tax. The Swedish Film Institute is financed by a 10 percent surcharge on box office income. The Institute also receives a surcharge from videotape rental firms for the videotapes stocked for private use. These charges are used to finance the production of Swedish films, to promote the distribution and screening of quality films, to stimulate the film industry, and for other purposes. Revenues, including the video surcharge introduced in 1982, are estimated to be about SEK 60m yearly. In addition, direct State subsidies amount to SEK 33m (1983/84). Cinema visits in 1981 totaled 22 million.

There is a great deal of uncertainty concerning the impact on cinema audience figures of the rapid growth of video consumption. In 1982, 15 percent of the population had access to a videoplayer. In the same year, a state tax was imposed on unrecorded videotapes and another on videoplayers.

Cultural Workers and Cultural Policy

One of the basic objectives of Swedish cultural policy has been to improve the living conditions of cultural workers.

Income levels vary a great deal, however, from one category of artists to another; this applies both to income from artistic work and to income from other sources. Group musicians and actors have relatively high incomes, and they derive most of their earnings from their artistic work. Pictorial artists and craftsmen have low incomes and also derive small earnings from additional occupations. Jazz musicians and other musical freelancers have small earnings, derived for the most part from their artistic work. Writers, dramatists, and dance instructors derive a large proportion of their earnings from secondary occupations.

The State is acting along the following lines to improve the situation for artists.

a. The creation of *job opportunities* through the expansion of cultural institutions, support for free dance and music groups, and purchases of art for State-owned buildings.

b. The implementation of *labor market policy* through the Labor Market Administration and a special employment service for cultural workers. Employment officers also are attached to the central agencies which have been set up by various organizations of cultural workers.

c. The *payment to authors* of "public lending right compensation," i.e., remuneration for the use of their books in public libraries. Every loan of an original work qualifies for a payment of SEK 0.37 (plus compensation for reference works, etc.). This money is paid into the Swedish Authors' Fund, which disburses part of the proceeds in the form of individual payments and applies the remainder to grants and fellowships. For 1983/84, the Fund had a total of SEK 40m at its disposal.

d. The award of *grants* to pictorial artists, actors, film makers, photographers, etc. These are distributed by various agencies in which representatives of the cultural workers concerned predominate, e.g., the Artists' Council and, for pictorial artists, the Pictorial Artists' Council. For 1983/84, these two agencies had at their disposal a total of SEK 33m (13m and 20m respectively).

e. The distribution of *income guarantees* by the Government to a limited number of artists. The number of such guarantees for 1983 was 120. The maximum payment (1983) was SEK 97,000, but there are special rules reducing this amount in proportion to the recipient's income. Writers have their own form of income guarantee. An author's benefit of SEK 42,000 is received by 180 authors, subject to deduction only for other benefit receipts.

f. *Changes in the tax system* to adapt it better to the special working conditions of cultural workers are under discussion.

An adverse economic situation means special difficulties for freelance cultural workers, and there is a great risk that the improvements resulting from the reform policies of the 1970s will be lost.

It is difficult to estimate the actual number of artistic and literary practitioners, but according to the 1980 census of population the total number was 18,000.

Measures on Behalf of Individual Target Groups

One of the main objectives of the new cultural policy is to identify the groups which have not been reached adequately by existing policy measures. To attain this goal, the interaction between cultural policy measures on the one hand and social policy, educational policy, and town planning measures on the other, have been developed more and more. For this reason, various sub-strategies were built up in the early 1980s.

Guidelines concerning measures in the field of *children's* culture were laid down by the Riksdag in the spring of 1979. The task of the State in this sector is to provide certain basic resources, but in order for anything significant to be achieved combined efforts are needed from the State, municipalities, and associations. There are State subsidies for comic strips for children and young people, for measures to promote reading, and for development work within various cultural institutions and elsewhere. In 1983, the Council for Cultural Affairs presented various reports[9] concerning ways in which culture can be integrated into preschool education. A strategy for developing culture in schools is being worked out by the Ministry of Education and Cultural Affairs in collaboration with the National Board of Education.

Demographically, Sweden remained a fairly homogeneous country until the Second World War. That has now changed. Roughly one million people, or 13 percent of the total population, are immigrants or the children of immigrants. Cultural measures on behalf of immigrants form an important part of immigrant policy. The aim is both to support the immigrants' own cultural heritage and to ensure that the cultural heritage of Sweden's minorities becomes part and parcel of the nation's general cultural life. Public efforts include measures to support immigrant organizations. The State subsidizes purchases by public libraries of literature in immigrant languages, as well as exhibition exchanges with other countries.[10]

State measures for the *disabled* have included the foundation of a talking book and Braille library to supply literature to the visually handicapped and other disabled persons. The National Touring Theater includes a professional company playing for the deaf. Easy readers are produced for the linguistically handicapped. Altogether, Sweden has about forty local talking newspapers, financed by municipalities and county councils. Cassette editions of three daily newspapers are being produced on an experimental basis.

Inmates of care institutions are isolated from the outside world. This applies particularly to those who spend time in long-term care clinics or in prison. There are many types of cultural activity in care institutions today. Hospital libraries maintain a high standard and a great deal of money is being spent on purchases of art. One very important requirement is for staff members to be made to feel responsible for cultural stimulation. The Council for Cultural Affairs has, in cooperation with the Association of County Councils, presented various reports on ways in which culture in hospitals, especially in long-term care departments, can be encouraged and based on a holistic view of human beings.[11]

One complex of questions which has been studied for a long time concerns *culture in working life*. The Council for Cultural Affairs was responsible for coordinating an international joint study which formed part of a UNESCO project.[12] This study has been followed up in a three-year experimental scheme at a number of workplaces in various parts of Sweden. The experimental scheme was conducted by the Council jointly with the central trade union organizations, LO and TCO, and their educational organizations. The experience and conclusions resulting from the project are being presented in a series of reports. Trade union organizations and employers now take more and more initiatives at the individual workplace. In addition, the Council has submitted to the Government and Riksdag a program of action outlining ways in which the State can encourage developments, for example, by means of statutory amendments or grants financed partly by an increased payroll levy.[13]

The Government has declared that stimulation of culture within the context of people's working lives should be a major priority during the next few years. A more detailed decision from the Government and Riksdag was taken in 1985.

The Council also has completed an experimental project on culture in the dwelling environment, undertaken jointly with an adult education association. What are the best methods of involving people in socially oriented cultural work? Here, as in the working life project, researchers are taking part in the evaluation process.

Evaluating Cultural Policy

A policy developed for a social sector should make provision for evaluation of that policy. When the new cultural policy was created, the Council for Cultural Affairs was given the task of evaluating its effects and, if necessary, proposing reforms. The evaluation process can assume several different guises.

(a) An annual evaluation is carried out by the Council and other cultural authorities in their budget requests. In the case of the Council, these are particularly extensive when the Government and Riksdag are being asked to increase budget allocations. In the present economic situation, rigorous definitions of priorities are being demanded by the Council and, still more, by the Government. Budget requests include long-range assessments for the coming five years.

The description already given of the various cultural sectors included some evaluation of achievements in terms of the number of institutions and the development of public participation figures. Analyses of this kind are included in the annual budget requests.

Another type of evaluation involves examining the way in which financial inputs have developed in fixed money terms, and how resources have been distributed among various fields of use. This type of economic evaluation is presented in general terms in the section headed ''How much does culture cost?''

(b) The annual general evaluation is bound to be rather superficial. More comprehensive evaluations of grant systems, organization, or problem definitions are undertaken at the instance of the Government, or sometimes of the Riksdag and the Council itself. These evaluations, which sometimes take several years to complete, often are directed by study groups or committees which include representatives of those concerned. This ensures that problems are defined realistically, but it may compound the difficulties of achieving an objective description. It is not unusual for an independent researcher to be engaged to further this end, and collaboration with universities and colleges is becoming progressively more important.

Researchers have been attached to the long-term development projects dealing with culture in the dwelling environment and in the workplace. The researchers present their own evaluations of the projects, in addition to those presented by the representatively composed study groups.

Many evaluations have been undertaken along these lines. Several evaluation projects are in progress. In 1984, committees appointed by the Government concluded their examinations of public libraries and literature subsidies. The Council has concluded in 1985 an evaluation of the overall effect of the State's, the county councils', and the municipalities' expenditures over a decade of cultural policy. Conclusions were drawn for future policy at the local, regional, and national levels.[14]

(c) The most difficult type of evaluation concerns the relationship between the goals and the effects of cultural policy. To this end, goals have to be broken down into various indicators. This is a theoretically complex task, forming the subject of a project within the Council. The usefulness of this type of goal evaluation, however, stands or falls by the statistical data available. So far this has been a weakness. A great deal has been done to improve cultural statistics and to arrange for their publication. One omnibus volume of available statistical data was published in 1981.[15] The most important sections for the evaluation of policy outcomes are those dealing with cultural habits, based on a comprehensive, continuous survey of the living conditions of the Swedish people. An interesting aspect is changes over time, and these will become discernible when we are able to make comparisons between the figures for 1976 and those from a 1983 survey.

Cultural Expenditure and the Present-Day Socio-Economic Situation

How Much Does Culture Cost?

Cultural expenditures in Sweden totaled SEK 19,700m in 1981. This included more than SEK 15,400m in private cultural spending, e.g., on purchases of radio and television sets, gramophones, records, cassettes, newspapers, and books.[16] Per capita, this corresponds to about SEK 1,850 in private consumption and SEK 520 in public spending. Thus, the greater part of cultural expenditure, just over three-quarters, is borne directly by consumers.

However, the proportion of total cultural expenditure by the *State, county councils, and municipalities* grew throughout the 1970s. (See Table 1.) Public cultural spending accounted for 14 percent of the total amount in 1970 and 22 percent in 1981. To a great extent, this rise in public spending has been due to a substantial growth of State press subsidies and of municipal expenditure. The municipalities accounted for the largest share—59 percent—of public cultural spending (SEK 4,300m) in 1981. The national government accounted for 37 percent that year, while the county councils had the smallest share at 4 percent.

Cultural spending constitutes a very small part of the running expenses of the State, county councils, and municipalities, the figures for 1981 being 1 percent, 0.6 percent, and 4.6 percent, respectively.

In nominal terms, State cultural spending quintupled between 1970 and 1981, which in real terms means that it was approximately doubled. The main real increases in State cultural spending occurred during the second half of the 1970s.

The 1981/82 fiscal year saw, for the first time, a real decrease (by about 3 percent) in State cultural spending, as a result of the general restrictions imposed on this and other national public spending. Municipal and county council cultural allocations, however, continued to rise (by approximately 2 percent and 9 percent, respectively).

But a closer study of the situation reveals considerable differences among groups of municipalities and types of expenditure.

How Is State Cultural Spending Deployed?

Let us start by considering *geographical distribution.* Just under half of all spending (46 percent) in 1981/82 was devoted to various central and nationwide activities.[17]

Support to regional and local institutions plays a vital part in cultural policy. True, it has risen by an average of 3 percent annually and accounts for just over one-quarter (27 percent) of State cultural spending. This, however, represents a decline by a couple of percentage points since 1974, which may seem surprising in view of the preoccupation of the new cultural policy with increased decentralization.

Direct State grants for local activities are of modest proportions, representing only 3 percent of cultural spending. This figure does not include funds for cultural workers, film subsidies, and literature subsidies, which cannot be distributed within these categories.

Turning to the distribution of State cultural spending *among cultural sectors,* we find

TABLE 1. State, County Council and Municipal Expenditure by Cultural Sectors and Popular Education, 1975 and 1981 SEK Millions, 1981 Level of Prices

	State		*County Councils*		*Municipalities*		*Total*	
Sector	*1975*	*1981*	*1975*	*1981*	*1975*	*1981*	*1975*	*1981*
Theater	372	426	9	42	135	278	516	746
Music[a]	185	197	4	11	457	557	646	765
of which municipal schools of music					(348)	(484)		
Museums, exhibitions, care of ancient monuments	200	286	17	38	131[b]	190[b]	348	514
Libraries	29	49	13[c]	23[c]	755	1048	797	1120
Literature and book trade	16	32	—	—	—	—	16	32
Daily press, periodicals and cultural journals	231	392	—	—	—	—	231	392
Cultural workers	64	66	1	4	5	—[d]	70[e]	70[f]
Sundry purposes	103	152	9	46	255	457	367	655
(of which pictorial art)	15	27	9	30	22	—		
archives	50	63	—	2	—	—		
film	13	27	—	1	4	—		
Total, incl. daily press	1200	1600	49	164	1738	2530	2987	4294
Total, not incl. daily press	972	1216	49	164	1738	2530	2759	3910
Popular education	763	742	96	173	317	450	1176	1365
Total	1963	2342	149	337	2055	2980	4167	5659
	47%	41%	4%	6%	49%	53%	100%	100%

[a]Incl. municipal schools of music

[b]Care of ancient monuments is included in "Sundry purposes"

[c]Not including hospital libraries

[d]Included in "Sundry purposes"

[e]Incl. municipal support to cultural workers

[f]Not incl. is municipal support to cultural workers, which for this year is included in "Sundry purposes"

that roughly one-quarter goes to the theater and about the same amount to press subsidies (SEK 426m and 384m, respectively). (See Table 1.) One-fifth goes to museums, exhibitions, and the care of ancient monuments (SEK 286m). Theater subsidies have diminished and the proportion of press subsidies has increased since 1975.

Where municipal cultural spending is concerned, grants to libraries predominate at about 41 percent (SEK 1,048m), followed by the music sector at 22 percent (SEK 557m). Theaters receive 11 percent (SEK 278m).

Culture and Spending Cuts

The socio-economic climate of the past few years in Sweden has been a far cry from the situation that prevailed when the new cultural policy was inaugurated at the beginning of the 1970s. All national authorities and cultural institutions now are required in their budget requests to present schemes for an annual savings of 2 percent. To some extent, spending cuts of this kind have been made. If they are repeated for several years, the effects will be serious, though this situation has not yet been reached. On the whole, both the Government and the Riksdag have tried to exempt the cultural sector from heavy spending cuts and economy measures. But, as mentioned above, 1981/82 saw, for the first time, a real reduction in State cultural spending. Relatively speaking, the Council for Cultural Affairs has been subjected to heavier cuts than the rest of the cultural sector. During the first years of the 1980s, the Council's administrative grant has been reduced by 16 percent, though at the same time it has received compensation for rising wage costs and prices. Even though the reduction was unquestionably a political black mark, its effects were limited, inasmuch as certain projects of fixed duration came to an end. Limitations placed on the Council's discretionary power to fill vacant positions reflect a critical attitude toward the Council on the part of those who decide the allocations.

Spending for culture in the municipalities varies. In municipalities spending declined in real terms in 1980/81. The gravest development was a reduction in spending on special initiatives apart from permanent items. In the smallest municipalities, this type of spending was halved in 1981. If this trend continues and spreads to other groups of municipalities, serious difficulties will be encountered in catering for new initiatives at the municipal level, where such initiatives are primarily envisaged.

The Council is watching the effects of spending cuts closely, and is trying, with information and the proposals contained in its own budget requests, to counteract harmful consequences for cultural life. One often hears it said that culture is the first victim of retrenchment. So far this has not been true. Other fields appear to have suffered more heavily. At the same time, the cultural sector is a relatively novel field of public effort. Its position is tenuous, and there is the risk that the work of a decade in building up cultural policy may be demolished.

Hitherto, the long and involved process of finding political support for the new cultural policy has helped the cultural sector to maintain its position, or, at the very least, to not find itself in a worse position than other parts of the public sector are in. On the other hand, should it become a question of general reductions of expenditure throughout the entire public sector, then the cultural subsector certainly will find itself under threat. The issue which most divides the parties today is perhaps their views on cultural support from industry; here the Social Democrats are extremely skeptical. And, although the Liberals and Conservatives attach greater weight to this possibility, neither expects more than marginal contributions from this quarter.

Various strategies for coping with economy measures are being discussed vigorously. One important strategy involves increasing cooperation between the cultural sector and the social sector, schools, and care institutions. Within these fields, there are resources which can be utilized for cultural purposes. In many places, there is a strong interest in developing these types of activities, not least within municipalities and county councils. In this situation, it is important to avoid regarding the representatives of the cultural sector as supplicants for help in a difficult situation. Instead, one can refer to a basic provision of the Swedish Constitution which lays down that "The personal, economic and cultural welfare of the individual must be the fundamental aims of public activity." Cultural policy will be better equipped to function in a new situation if it is regarded as one of a number of instruments for the attainment of the welfare of the people.[18]

Notes

1. An exhaustive historical analysis of the growth of Swedish cultural policy is to be found in Sven Nilsson's *Vägen till kulturpolitiken, Kulturen och samhällsförändringen,* Publica Stockholm, 1981. An English-language survey is to be found in *Swedish Cultural Policy in the 20th Century,* by Nils Gunnar Nilsson, publ. The Swedish Institute, 1980.

2. *Människan och nutiden,* Stockholm, 1952.

3. Kulturrådet, Ny kulturpolitik SOU 1972:66.

4. Government Bill 1974:28. Den statliga kulturpolitiken (The state cultural policy) was approved by the Riksdag in May 1974.

5. A report to be published within the National Council for Cultural Affairs in 1984 evaluated developments between 1974 and 1984, especially with respect to two goals—decentralization and the cultural stimulation of underprivileged groups.

6. In 1984, SEK 1 was equal to about U.S. $0.12.

7. Report from the 1982 Commission of Literature: Läs mera, Liber, 1984. Support to literature is described in greater detail in Nils Gunnar Nilsson's *Swedish Cultural Policy in the 20th Century,* p. 61 et seq.

8. "Vår fiktionskultur i förvandling, tv, biografer, teatrar, video och skönlitteratur—en jämförelse av utbud, konsumtion och publik," by Yngve Lindung, Sveriges Radio publik- och programforskning 1984.

9. *Kultur i förskolan.* Rapport från kulturrådet 1982:5.

10. A committee appointed by the Government has presented a report called Invandrar—och minoritetspolitiken, slutbetänkande av invandrarpolitiska kommittén. SOU 1984:58, proposing the cultural-political effort in this field shall be reinforced, and greater allocations be distributed over the cultural field.

11. Among other reports, *Kultur i vården; utgångspunkter, organisation, resurser.* Rapport från kulturrådet 1983:7.

12. *Culture and Working Life,* Stockholm Liber 1978.

13. *Verktyg för förändring.* Rapport från kulturrådet 1984:1.

14. A report from the National Council for Cultural Affairs was published in 1985. *Kommunerna, staten och berlten politiken.* Rapport från kulturrådet 1984:3.

15. *Kulturverksamhet, ekonomi, kulturvanor 1960–1979,* Statens kulturråd, Statistiska centrålbyran, Stockholm, Liber förlag. Some sections in English.

16. Purchases of radio and television sets, gramophones, records, cassettes and cameras amounted to about 35 percent of the private cultural spending.

17. This figure does not include the National Touring Theater, Riksutställningar and Rikskonserter, which are financed by State grants and have nationwide activities. These three bodies account for 12 percent of total spending, and their share has declined since 1974.

18. These ideas are developed at greater length in an article published in the UNESCO journal *Cultures* (33, Carl-Johan Kleberg: "Cultural objectives—empty words or practical policy?").

9

The Politics of Culture in Portugal, 1945–85: From Dictatorship to Revolution to Marketplace

ALICE E. INGERSON

Portugal has gone through three basic changes of political regime since 1945. The avowedly corporatist dictatorship of Prime Minister António Salazar (and after 1968 of his successor, Marcelo Caetano) began in 1928 and lasted until 1974. In 1974, an armed forces coup toppled this *Estado Novo,* or "new state," and began a period of socialist revolution that lasted roughly until 1976. Since 1976, various coalitions and combinations of the Socialist, Social Democratic, and Christian Democratic parties have governed Portugal, with minor participation by the Monarchists and Communists.

The relationship between government and the arts in Portugal seemed to reverse itself completely when the first provisional government after the 1974 revolution abolished the dictatorship's censorship and secret police. Despite the different political philosophies of Salazar and the 1974 revolutionaries, however, they shared some basic ideas about art and society that were not applied by the liberal and conservative governments after 1976. The post-1974 revolutionaries who most clearly detested the old regime, for example, agreed with it that artists had clear social responsibilities, although they differed from Salazar in the ways they defined those responsibilities. Many of the governments elected after 1976 opposed revolutionary socialism as adamantly as had Salazar himself. Yet these same governments defended the separation of art from politics that Salazar had attacked in 1935 as creating "amorality and art for art's sake . . . fruit beautiful to look at but unprofitable or harmful to the taste" (*Bulletin* May–June 1957:404).

The following section contrasts the political conceptions of culture defended by each of the three political regimes in Portugal since 1945. The remaining sections of this essay then illustrate these basic contrasts by describing each regime's specific policies on the arts.

Political Concepts of Culture in Portugal: Authoritarian, Revolutionary, Liberal

Following the usage of the three regimes themselves, the following analysis discusses arts policy as part of *cultural policy,* under which the various governments usually included policies on the communications media, on education, and on amateur or "recreational" arts activities, as well as on the professional fine or performing arts. In order to understand each government's specific arts policies, it is crucial to understand what each government meant by "culture" and why these governments thought it necessary to have any cultural policy at all.

As with all abstract concepts, culture was defined as much by what it was not as by what it was: under the *Estado Novo,* culture was the politically acceptable production and appreciation of the liberal, fine, and performing arts. Salazar argued that good art was that which supported his own conservative policies, without violating the natural division of labor between artists and politicians. In contrast, the revolutionary regime from 1974 to 1976 defined culture as the process of liberation from political oppression. This definition was both narrower and broader than Salazar's definition, excluding politically passive art, for example, but including political discussions and roadbuilding *within* the cultural revolution. The postrevolutionary governments after 1976 returned to a strict division of professional labor between artists and politicians and to an emphasis on "good" (as opposed to "useful" or "progressive") art. These governments often asserted that good art would promote parliamentary democracy in the end by demonstrating the advantages of a free market economy for freedom of expression. In practice, these governments often treated explicitly political (usually left-wing) art as "bad art," on the grounds that it violated this division of labor. In the process, of course, these governments ended by supporting the arts according to criteria that were less explicit but no less political than those applied by either of the two previous regimes.

In 1926, a group of generals overthrew the First Republic in Portugal and established a military dictatorship. They offered the post of finance minister to an economics professor, António Oliveira Salazar, who accepted it only on condition that he have total control of the national budget. He then maintained control of the budget and of the country until he fell fatally ill and was succeeded by his protégé, Marcelo Caetano, in 1968. Salazar dedicated his new regime to what he dubbed "the great certainties: . . . God and virtue . . . the Fatherland and its History . . . authority and its prestige . . . the family and its morality . . . the glory and duty of work" (excerpted from a 1936 speech in *Antologia* 1954:48).

Moral responsibility and nationalism were the key points of Salazar's public statements about culture and the arts. In 1935, at the awards ceremony for the first national literary prizes distributed through the new government, he spoke about the political and social responsibilities of artists under the *Estado Novo:*

> What conception of their responsibilities is held by first-rate minds in the Portugal of the present moment—those who have received a greater share in the distribution of divine gifts and therefore naturally become the leaders and examples for the rest?
>
> With unusual insistence I see them excuse their misdeeds by the oft-proclaimed sincerity of their literary, artistic or moral convictions. Is this enough? I would venture to deny it, above all because not only are the writer and the artist responsible for what they produce against their own conscience, but they are also responsible for the misuse of their own intelligence and the faulty education of their will. To be sincere is very little: we must recognize our obligation to be truthful and just.
>
> . . . those who tended to make of literature and art separate and self-sufficient worlds, bearing within themselves their own finality and justification. . . . were unaware of the deeper human realities, lost their way on the road to the great moral certainties,

> created amorality and art for art's sake, as fruit beautiful to look at but unprofitable or harmful to the taste. From even the most hopeful point of view, genius was wasted to the harm of humanity [*Bulletin* May–June 1957:404].

In 1942, Salazar summarized these views in an aphorism: "We consider the creative power of a people within the bounds of its character and personality as an element of moral defense" (quoted *Bulletin* July–August 1956:23). In short, Salazar allowed for creativity and innovation in the arts and sciences, but only "within the bounds" of what the *Estado Novo* defined as the Portuguese character. According to Salazar, that character was largely if not exclusively conservative.

Under the *Estado Novo,* the meaning of the term *cultura* varied according to the class focus of any particular policy. The *alta cultura* or high culture of the usually urban elite included the capacity for innovation, from artistic experiments to scientific discoveries to the achievements of the Portuguese explorers in sailing to India and Brazil. The *alta cultura* also included the capacity to govern the country. Professional artists' work, along with the work of natural scientists, came under the heading of *alta cultura.* However, Salazar was always careful to address both artists and scientists as workers, implying that their obligations to improve their own skills and expand the general stock of knowledge did not entitle them to run the government.

When the bureaucrats of the *Estado Novo* referred to *cultura popular* or popular culture, they meant something completely different. From 1928 to 1974, the Portuguese government defined *cultura popular* as the completely conservative preservation of custom. In many ways, Salazar saw an idyllic, almost frozen folk culture as a general model for Portuguese life and politics. One official summary of the government's views on folklore, published in 1958, could have served as both a political and a cultural apology for the *Estado Novo* itself:

> Under the stress of the hectic rhythm of innovation, the instability of customs and beliefs, the overthrowing of forms of life, modern man is finally coming to learn to love tradition . . . people give their close attention to traditional folklore, conscious as they are that they may re-discover their soul. . . . All folklore should be a bringing into the present of ancestral gestures, a prolongation of the forces of temperament or ideals defining an ethnic group. If this process is not to be reduced to the level of the automatic repetition of gestures it must preserve all the purity of its sources. . . . Only thus can the mystic message borne by folklore be preserved and only thus does it attain its maximum power of communication. Its fundamental problem is thus one of genuineness. . . . it is a difficult task indeed to sift out this genuineness in those habits that the incursion of the forms of the contemporary life tends to impoverish or distort and above all where a craving after facile picturesqueness has made them banal or commercial goods to trade with. . . . They should be restored lovingly but strictly [*Bulletin* September–October 1958:292–293].

Finally, when Salazar applied *cultura* to urban or industrial workers, the word retained some elements of both the elite *alta cultura* and the rural *cultura popular*. When corporatist bureaucrats discussed "bringing culture to the people," they meant showing them classical plays or teaching them about the achievements of Prince Henry the Navigator, not teaching welders to write poetry or make folk pottery. *Cultura* in this sense was *alta cultura,* and "bringing it to the workers" implied moral improvement or progress. Yet this progress always stopped short of conferring the rights and responsibilities of political leadership. Government cultural patronage or paternalism was supposed to make the working class more grateful to the government, rather than to provide it with the capacity to generate its own culture, artistic or political.[1]

The cultural policies of the first governments after 1974, on the other hand, were radically egalitarian. In a series of interviews granted in the fall of 1974, representatives of the Armed Forces Movement (MFA) that had overthrown the dictatorship criticized the artificially clear distinction between *alta cultura* and *cultura popular* made by the *Estado Novo:*

> Fascist cultural policy divided culture into two fields: that of the erudites, who in the end were those who had enough money to be able to study, and the so-called 'popular culture' that the fascists supported for official or touristical ends . . . with the same spirit of someone who goes to a zoo to see the monkeys jumping around. . . . Fascism was not interested and even fought against the dignifying of the Portuguese man through culture [interview in December, 1974; quoted in Correia, Soldado, and Araujo, n.d.:36].

> The fascist regime . . . forced onto the people a canned culture that served a political end, suffocating communities with its obscurantism [and fostering] the fatalistic acceptance of a non-participatory fate [interview in October, 1974; quoted in *ibid.*:17].

According to one official MFA account, "cultural dynamization became a rapidly perceived necessity" in 1974, "for involving the social strata most immobilized and conditioned by the factors of traditional obstruction to transform what began as a coup into a true revolution" (Correia, Soldado, and Araujo, n.d.:9). The MFA wanted to break down the divisions between high and popular culture and to challenge political fatalism. Some of the movement's statements came very close to defining culture as participatory democracy itself:

> . . . culture [is] an instrument that allows a people to look at itself and at the exterior reality in the sense of transforming it, which includes social, political, economic and artistic aspects . . . revolutionary transformations must be accompanied by a cultural movement [*ibid.*:11].

> We do not intend to take culture to the people, but to motivate the population to recuperate its realities [interview in October, 1974; quoted in *ibid.*:17].

> . . . cultural revitalization should lead to . . . [the Portuguese man] becoming conscious as a free man and responsible citizen, prepared to govern the life of the community to which he belongs . . . this cultural action is an integral part of the civic mission of the armed forces [interview in December, 1974; quoted in *ibid.*, n.d.:36].

At times this broad redefinition of culture seemed to include all human activity. The 1975 "Campaign of Cultural Dynamization"[2] (discussed further below) was initially "cultural" in the sense that the government employed and subsidized "film, theater, or any other means of cultural animation that might motivate the population" to support the revolution (*ibid.*:22), but it soon broadened from theater performances and literacy classes to include the building of roads and bridges.

By the end of 1975, an anticommunist backlash in rural areas, especially in the north, combined with a conservative countercoup in Lisbon to cut off all funding for the Cultural Dynamization Campaign. Nevertheless, this campaign strongly influenced the course of all subsequent cultural policy in Portugal. Those who had supported the campaign always harked back to it as the high point of socialist popular culture and popular power and used it as a standard against which to measure apolitical bourgeois art and government arts policies after 1975. Opponents of the campaign included both left-wing populists and conservatives who rejected any notion of social revolution. Both groups accused the MFA of imposing its own ideas in the name of "culture," though the two groups envisioned very different alternatives to the Cultural Dynamization Campaign; for the far left, the alternative was a popular power movement not dependent on the political vanguard of the established left wing (in effect, the Portuguese Communist Party); for the center and right, the alternative was a return to something like the pre-1974 status quo, minus only the formal apparatus of censorship.

In contrast to both the authoritarian and the revolutionary governments, the post-1976 liberal governments have had no clear political definition of culture or cultural program.[3] Government cultural policies since 1976 in Portugal have been conservative in practice, though often progressive in announced intentions. The post-1976 governments determined to distribute subsidies to theater groups, for example, not according to whether the repertory of the groups enabled their audiences to recuperate socialist realities, but according to the numbers of performances and spectators for each group. Although these criteria explicitly attempted to free art from politics, in practice they penalized those theater groups who wanted to make explicit in their performances and organization the revolutionary political principles they had been forced to keep implicit before 1974.

The law on popular education associations (number 384/76) adopted in 1976 exemplifies these avowedly nonpolitical cultural policies. Although it did not repudiate directly the principles of cultural decentralization and democracy defended by the MFA, the law considered that "it is not right to adopt a policy of aggressive intervention that might provoke the resistance of populations that have long been abandoned to a traditional and isolated way of life," and announced that "the collective organization of these populations, based on associativism, is the first step toward their own education, in a liberating perspective, and for the construction of a new democratic society." Although the "liberating perspective" and "new democratic society" of this law contrasted clearly with the "God, Fatherland, and authority" to which Salazar dedicated the *Estado Novo*, the 1976 law also contrasted with the revolutionary transformations pursued by the MFA. The new law required groups applying for government subsidies to practice "democratic management"[4] and to be formally nonpartisan. The requirement for democratic management was vague in itself but clearly was directed against the Portuguese Communist Party. The law's sponsors hoped that requiring formal parliamentary procedure in arts organizations would reduce the Party's influence there. The requirement for political nonpartisanship worked largely against the political left, both the PCP and other parties or movements that had seen cultural groups as part and parcel of the struggle to consolidate the 1974 revolution. The political right, in contrast, generally had abstained from such "cultural action" altogether, defining culture by default as the *alta cultura* and *cultura popular* already in place.

The following brief history of specific government policies on the arts attempts to illustrate the general points made above. This history uses the important changes made in the Portuguese constitution to demarcate the three periods discussed: from the constitution of the authoritarian *Estado Novo,* enacted in 1933, to the constitution of a Portugal in transition to socialism enacted in 1976, to the latest constitutional revision completed in

1982, which deleted many of the 1976 references to socialism and revolution. The contrasts among the three periods do not boil down to a simple before and after. The authoritarian regime did not share the commitment to political or cultural democracy established by the 1974 revolution and never fully repudiated by the governments after 1976. The liberal parliamentary governments, on the other hand, have rejected the explicit relations between politics and the arts defended by the dictatorship, which subordinated art to politics, and by the cultural revolutionaries, who equated good art with progressive politics.

Cultural Policy under the Authoritarian Estado Novo, 1933 to 1974

1933 to 1954: Setting Up the Regime

The 1933 constitution of the *Estado Novo* guaranteed its citizens the right to "the free expression of thought in any form" and "freedom of teaching," as long as the exercise of these rights did not "damag[e] the interests of society or moral principles." At the same time, the constitution decreed that

> [The state] shall prevent, by precautionary or restrictive measures, the perversion of public opinion in its function as a social force. . . . Public opinion is a fundamental part of the policy and administration of the country; it shall be the duty of the State to protect it against all those influences which distort it from the truth, justice, good administration, and the common weal [cited in *Bulletin* May–June 1957:327–339].

This same care to guarantee freedom of expression only to those who deserved it appeared in the constitution's only mention of the arts as such. The *Estado Novo* committed itself to "encouraging and favoring" the arts, "provided that respect is maintained for the Constitution, the authorities and the co-ordinating functions of the State." The constitution also placed "artistic, historical and natural monuments, and artistic objects officially recognised as such" under "the protection of the State" (*Bulletin* May–June 1957:327–339). This constitutional respect for works of art as monuments later emerged as a theme in the state's relations with living artists and their work. Salazar sometimes seemed to restrict the arts to the production of public monuments.[5] Government policy before 1974 often attempted to treat artists themselves as national monuments, in the sense of keeping them from saying or doing anything in the future that the state had not already approved in the past.

The censors could make cuts in page proofs at the last minute, and the law forbade silent protests such as "white spaces, crossing or blacking out, insertion of drawings or announcements, or any other indication that would permit [readers] to deduce the operation of the censor" (Rodrigues 1980:72). In self-defense, therefore, most authors and publishers attempted to anticipate the censors' decisions.[6] Graça Almeida Rodrigues points out that such self-censorship was often more restrictive than the external censors might have been. Rodrigues also argues that the lists of material censored or banned, published only after 1974, reveal the "cold and calculated arrogance with which Salazar and [the censors] addressed the Portuguese nation, entirely underestimating the intelligence of the citizens and humiliating them [as] without any power of directing their own destinies" (Rodrigues 1980:76).

A wide range of bureaucracies administered cultural policy under the *Estado Novo*. The two most important were: the government information office, in charge of censorship, literary competitions and art exhibits, folklore and tourism; and the Ministry of Education, in charge of the Institute of High Culture (for international scientific and cultural exchanges), the national and regional museums, the conservatory, and the two national schools of fine arts (in Lisbon and Porto). A few other institutions also sponsored programs for the cultural uplift of the working classes: the National Foundation for Happiness at Work (FNAT) sponsored classes in corporatist citizenship and summer camps for workers' children; the quasi-military Portuguese Youth Organization (*Mocidade Portuguesa*) organized amateur exhibitions and festivals; and both the Corporations Ministry and the information office sponsored competitions for amateur artists and traveling exhibits or performances for rural and working class audiences.

The following history relies heavily on the public and contemporary accounts of Salazar's cultural policy published by the information office. For the first decade of corporatism (after 1934), the government information office was called unabashedly the National Propaganda Secretariat and was in charge of promoting a positive image of the new regime both at home and abroad. It did so through the news media, using censorship within Portugal itself and awarding prizes for both Portuguese and foreign writers who presented the regime favorably. In addition, the Propaganda Secretariat attempted to "combat . . . the penetration into our country of any unsettling or socially disturbing ideas" by fostering "the cult of tradition [and] national regionalism," by which it meant the strict preservation of both folk art and the existing social order (Brito 1982:511–512).

In 1944 this secretariat was reorganized as the National Secretariat for Information, Popular Culture, and Tourism (hereafter referred to by its most common acronym as the SNI—*Secretariado Nacional de Informação*).[7] The substitution of an "information secretariat" for the old "propaganda secretariat" in 1944 followed Salazar's earlier realization that the Allies rather than the Axis would win World War II. In the antifascist climate that followed the war itself and preceded the Cold War of the 1950s, the SNI had to represent the *Estado Novo* as democratic, or at least as a benevolent rather than an authoritarian dictatorship. The SNI created a new press council in 1944, for example, "to assure contact between the newspapers and the State, to enlighten them as to Governmental policy, and to listen to any suggestions that may be formulated in the furtherance of their mission" (*Bulletin* November 1944:3). The enlightenment and suggestions that the SNI had in mind, of course, differed very little from what Salazar had once called propaganda.

The *Estado Novo* also attempted to incorporate artists directly into the state bureaucracy. By the 1940s, the corporatist regime had formed official unions for the graphic arts, publishers and booksellers, newspaper and theater owners, printers, journalists, and theater artists. In 1947, the SNI announced the formation of a new state-sponsored trade union for writers as if it had been an initiative of the writers themselves: the headline declared that "the literary workers are going to club together" (*Bulletin* 30 November 1947:112). The Subsecretary for Corporations proposed that writers themselves should restore "the tradition of the doctrinal leading article, signed successively by different writers, so as to demonstrate that differences of opinion are not incompatible with the existing rules of public respect" (*ibid.*:15), thus also demonstrating that the *Estado Novo* itself was not undemocratic. The writers, however, apparently ignored this suggestion.

In 1948, the SNI founded a special cinema fund "to stimulate the making of Portuguese films with a view to a progressive nationalisation of the industry and the dissemination abroad of a proper knowledge of our people and our country'' (*Bulletin* 31 January 1948:12). The SNI justified this special attention to film because ''no other form of entertainment possesses, perhaps, such a power over the mind, such educative influence or such effect as a popular cultural instrument'' (*ibid.*:11). The cinema fund thus functioned as part of the general political apparatus controlled by Salazar: it awarded prizes, subsidies, or loans only ''to films deemed to be in the national interest in the judgement of the Head of the Government,'' Salazar himself.

The *Estado Novo* also continued to support an officially frozen rural or folk culture as the ideal model for all artistic activity. Shortly after it was reorganized in 1944, the SNI opened in Lisbon the *Museu de Arte Popular,* exhibiting rural crafts. The SNI gloated over this museum, which it called ''truly poetic . . . a living museum, in which the items on show . . . speak to us with the pure and straightforward language of the very life of the people who created and used them, lovingly and with delight'' (*Bulletin* September–October 1957:565). The SNI explicitly proposed this officially sanctioned folk art as a model for all the arts, suggesting that if the Museum of Popular Art ''is put to good use, it will be a fount, a spring, of modern Portuguese art'' (*Bulletin* 31 January 1948:17).

1954 to 1964: Opening and Closing Again

Many official statements in the late 1950s and early 1960s indirectly reveal that the government faced a series of challenges in these years. In 1958, for example, the SNI opened a new press room to prevent the forces of subversion from turning ''liberty of information into a weapon against social order by distorting or mutilating information, or presenting it in a tendentious manner'' (*Bulletin* March–April 1958:111). In comparison with the ''enlightenment'' and ''suggestions'' that the government had offered when establishing the press council in 1944, this more militant announcement clearly suggested that the regime felt itself to be under attack.

The same defensiveness appeared in statements on the arts. In 1957, the director of the SNI warned that ''it is our duty to react against [such] negative tendencies'' as ''confusion of and contempt for the eternal values of humanity, anxiety and doubt in the choice of new paths to follow, forgetfulness and neglect of our own selves and our real interests. . . . we should consider restlessness an indispensable element which gives birth to new creative forms, [but] we must continue to defend [ourselves against] 'harmful restlessness' '' (*Bulletin* May–June 1957:405). In announcing a reform of higher education in the humanities and fine arts in 1958, the government insisted again that the basic problem in artistic education, as in the arts generally, was ''to seek the difficult balance between the spirit of renovation and the principles that a strong tradition has outlined for our cultural life'' (*Bulletin* January–February 1958:14–17).

In 1956, the establishment of the Gulbenkian Foundation in Lisbon dramatically changed the policy climate for the arts in Portugal. The SNI described the foundation as ''a fine and noble example of . . . the higher principle that wealth has duties of a moral order'' (*Bulletin* September–October 1956:94).[8] In later years, however, the relationship between the government and the Gulbenkian Foundation became uneasy. The Foundation competed directly with the government for the credit of supporting the arts and often sponsored artists of whom the government disapproved. Eventually the Gulbenkian's museums, ballet company, orchestra, and program of concerts outside Lisbon all outstripped the government's own programs in size and international reputation. The Foundation also established numerous fellowships and institutes in the humanities, social sciences, and natural sciences as well as the arts. Many artists and scholars had the Gulbenkian to thank for the opportunity to pursue themes during study abroad that would have been forbidden to them within Portugal. Many of these people chose to work in exile after they finished their studies and became vocal and informed critics of the *Estado Novo*.

In 1959, the SNI tacitly admitted that at least one art, that of the theater, had already been polarized between those who sought and received government help and those who largely did without it by necessity or by choice. Beyond the ideological safety zone of the official "professional" government-directed theaters in Lisbon, the SNI admitted that there were two large sectors of amateur or experimental theater: "the drama of intellectual aims . . . to satisfy artistic tastes and concepts not met by the professional theatre," and "the theatre dominated by recreational, charitable or educational purposes" (*Bulletin* July–August 1959:267–268).

The first kind of amateur experimental theater actually was staffed by professionals, some of whom enjoyed better reputations than their counterparts in the official professional theater.[9] The experiments of these semiprofessional "independents," as they were known, inevitably brought them into conflict with the government censors. The government theater fund gave some limited subsidies to a few of these groups in the late 1950s (*ibid.*:268–269). According to Luis Francisco Rebello, however, censorship of such theater groups became more aggressive after the wars of independence began in the Portuguese African territories in the early 1960s: the government made the Portuguese center of the International Theater Institute illegal, disbanded the Portuguese Society of Authors and ransacked its headquarters, and abruptly closed plays even after they had been allowed to open (Rebello 1977:30).

Perhaps abandoning hope of controlling professional artists, the SNI gave new attention to the arts as a means of political education for workers during the late 1950s and early 1960s. In 1960, the SNI involved workers actively in commemorating the Portuguese discoveries under Prince Henry the Navigator. The SNI saw the commemorations "above all [as] a means of training, educating, and teaching the vast majority of the Portuguese" (*Bulletin* November–December 1959:337). Towards this end, the state sponsored "competitions for students at the various levels of education, and also an artistic and craft competition for workers, organized in collaboration with the Social Action Board and the National Foundation for Happiness at Work" (*ibid.*:336).

After the 1960 celebrations, the SNI continued to direct new attention to the artistic appetites and production of workers. In 1962, the SNI sponsored the first annual "Cultural Competition for Workers," along with what it called a "popular art" exhibit (in this case amateur rather than folk art) (*Bulletin* November 1962:28). In 1962, the Lisbon City Council sponsored a "theatrical season for . . . poorer residents" with plays staged by the national "popular theater" company (*Bulletin* May 1962:31). In January 1963, the Ministry of Corporations approved for the *Trindade* Theater in Lisbon a new permanent program of drama, ballet, and symphony performances "intended above all for the working class" (*Bulletin* January 1963:30).

1964 to 1974: A Dictatorship Under Siege

Despite the best efforts of the corporatist bureaucracy to keep Portugal "lovingly but strictly" tied to its cultural and political past, the challenges to Salazar's politics and cultural policies from outside and from within Portugal continued to grow in the late 1960s and early 1970s. The state's cultural policies did not always pay off in greater political stability or passivity. A number of workers in amateur theater groups whom I interviewed in the 1980s, for example, recalled seeing the government's new interest in "culture for the workers" during the 1960s as an attempt to control the amateur groups rather than to encourage them.[10] In some ways, they remembered, theater groups functioned as surrogate political parties: the members read plays that they knew they would never be permitted to perform and worked out ways of transmitting forbidden political messages through approved political texts. According to José Jorge Letria, student groups and private clubs within Portugal and Portuguese professional musicians and workers abroad also supported a large body of protest music during the same period (Letria 1978).

In 1968, after forty years of Salazar's personal dictatorship, illness forced the Prime Minister to name Marcelo Caetano as his successor. The period of "Marcelismo" from 1968 until the socialist revolution that began in 1974 was somewhat more liberal than the preceding forty years of the *Estado Novo,* but often what the government gave with one hand it took back with the other. In a 1979 interview, José Oliveira Barata described the change from Salazar to Caetano as a change from "censorship by colonels" to "censorship by intellectuals"—the colonels had been relatively easy to fool by the use of double meanings, but the intellectual censors "were smarter, and much worse."[11] Two radio programs broadcast in the early 1970s permitted some limited political satire and criticism of the government, but were taken off the air in 1972 (Letria 1978:65). The Caetano government created a board of appeals to reconsider censorship decisions about theater performances, but this board almost never reversed the government's original decisions (Rebello 1977:32). João Paulo Guerra pointed out after the fact that the Caetano government, after announcing it would permit "prior examination" [censorship] . . . only in a state of emergency," then "immediately" declared an indefinite emergency (*Dossier Comunicação Social* 1981:34).

Indirectly, government policy recognized some of its own failures in the late 1960s and early 1970s. On the one hand, in 1964 the president of the official government theater council complained of "the present universal theatrical crisis" in which "the public taste for dramatic art" had "waned so much owing to contrary appeals [of] modern civilization" (*Bulletin* October–December 1964:67). On the other hand, he admitted that theater "continues to attract the attention of all audiences, and more especially those of the latest generations. This is an indisputable and irreversible fact which is deserving of the utmost consideration" (*Bulletin* October–December 1964:66). In 1971, the SNI again complained of the "public lack of interest" in the professional and national theater programs, "especially among young people, who finally turned their attention to amateur and university theater groups" (*ibid.*:25). This was as close as the corporatist bureaucracy could come to admitting that the politically critical amateur theater groups were drawing audiences away from the media closely controlled by the state.

Similar changes in the government film program in 1971 pointed in much the same direction. In 1971, the SNI reorganized the old cinema fund as the semiautonomous Portuguese Film Institute, which was supposed "to rouse the Portuguese film industry from its lethargy" (*Bulletin* 1971:29–31). In making this announcement, the SNI admitted that it never had enforced the 1948 cinema law effectively: the proportions of Portuguese and foreign films to be projected in theaters never had met the legal requirements; nor had foreign producers been forced to offer technical assistance to Portuguese film producers as a prerequisite for permission to project foreign films in Portugal. Despite the 1971 reforms, however, the majority of the Portuguese public continued to see nothing but foreign-made films well into the late 1970s (see *Com a Arte Para Transformar a Vida* 1978:113, cited in the final section of this essay).

Cultural Policy and Social Revolution, 1974 to 1976

On April 25, 1974, the Armed Forces Movement (MFA) toppled the *Estado Novo* in a bloodless coup. One hint that culture would play a central role in the Portuguese revolution was the signal the MFA chose for its first move, on the night of April 25: the playing of José Afonso's banned anthem of class consciousness, *Grandola Vila Morena,* over the state-controlled radio. From 1974 to late 1975, the MFA participated directly in the national government, and Portugal produced the first active socialist revolution in Western Europe since World War II. Millions of people marched in the major cities and towns on May Day in 1974, and in later demonstrations. Thousands set up cooperatives on estates, in apartment buildings, and in factories in a country where for almost fifty years the government had insisted that workers were not and could not become sufficiently cultured (*cultos*) to direct their own destiny. The constituent assembly elected on the anniversary of the revolution (April 25, 1975) wrote a constitution mandating a transition to socialism and a classless society in Portugal.

The governments elected under this constitution beginning in 1976, however, honored much of its socialist language more in the breach than in the observance. Whereas the constitution of the *Estado Novo* served as a useful introduction to Salazar's political rhetoric during the years after 1933, the 1976 constitution is a better guide to the events that preceded it than to those that followed it.

The 1976 constitution defined Portugal as

> a sovereign republic . . . in the process of transforming itself into a classless society. . . . a democratic state, based on the popular will, respecting and guaranteeing the fundamental rights and freedoms and pluralism of political organization and expression, which has as its goal assuring a transition to socialism through the creation of conditions under which the working classes may exercise power democratically [Articles 1 and 2].

The constitution also declared that

> Everyone has a right to education and to culture. . . . The State will promote the democratization of culture, stimulating and assuring the access of all citizens, especially the workers, to the fruit of cultural creativity, through grassroots organizations, cultural and recreational associations, the communications media and other means [Article 73].

As discussed in the introduction to this essay, the MFA and the constitutent assembly intended these statements as direct attacks on the ideology of the corporatist state, which had claimed to "represent" the aspirations of the Portuguese people but had never given the Portuguese people a chance to dispute that claim. In particular, the MFA argued that culture was not a passive inheritance from the past, preserved only by isolated peasants in villages, fundamentally threatened by the use of electricity or internal combustion engines, or properly kept under the guard of an intellectual (and economic) elite and doled out to the masses as a social prophylactic. Rather, the MFA and its allies saw culture both as the rightful present property of all the workers and as something that they had the right to change or criticize as well as preserve or revere.

In the two years after April 25, 1974, the most significant contribution of the Armed Forces Movement to changing the relations between government and the arts was the Cultural Dynamization Campaign waged mostly in rural areas in 1975. This campaign sent traveling theater troupes, dance companies, and film projectionists into the countryside to explain the program of the MFA to the population, and also mobilized large numbers of students to teach adult literacy classes and to help with farm work. Eventually, the campaign also sent out units of the armed forces to make basic public works and public health improvements: paving roads, building bridges, and digging wells.

Also during 1974 and 1975, the revolutionary governments energetically sought public participation in dismantling some parts of the corporatist bureaucracy. From September 1974 to November 1975, for example, the Directorate-General of Popular Culture and Performances (formerly under the National Secretariat of Information, the SNI) set up a Consultative Commission for Theater Activities. This commission drew up plans for government support to replace the previous censorship and competitions, and itself distributed government subsidies to theater groups in 1974 and 1975.

Luis Francisco Rebello served on this theater commission and summarized its general recommendations: theater should be considered a "public utility" analogous to public education and public health care, and theaters therefore should be nationalized just as key industries and banks already had been nationalized (Rebello 1977:46). Public ownership of the "means of theatrical production," according to Rebello, would mean that the theater "will belong to the theater workers and to the people for whom these workers are the spokesmen—and not, obviously, to the State or to the political parties" (*ibid.*:61). The commission also argued that theatrical repertory, as well as the organization of theater companies, should support popular power: theater performances should be used "for the socio-cultural promotion and political clarification of the working masses," and should express "the real problems of the Portuguese people, contributing towards the demystification of alienating, colonialist, and colonizing forms of art and culture" (*ibid.*:17, 177).[12]

The many forms of artistic and political experiment in Portugal from 1974 to 1976 outstripped any government policy. Theater in particular, as an art form requiring no special equipment beyond the human voice and body, was put to new political uses: high school students in the southern province of Alentejo staged an improved play to expose the crimes of the PIDE (secret police) before 1974; urban tenants in a northern city produced skits about confrontations with their landlords as part of a demonstration for rent control; farmworkers in the northern interior staged a play to explain to their unsympathetic and nonsocialist neighbors their occupation of the farm they worked. The neighbors then occupied the factory where they worked (owned by the same man who owned the estate).[13] Often the MFA supported these developments, providing lights and a projector for the northern farmworkers' play, for example.

Even during this period, however, not all of the government carried out the government's official policies. At the least, it is clear that the *saneamento,* or purge, of people closely associated with the Salazar regime often did little more than change official titles and the top one or two levels of personnel in many of the state bureaucracies: thus the former National Secretariat of Information and Popular Culture (the SNI) became the new Secretariat for Culture (SEC); the old paramilitary Portuguese Youth Organization

(*Mocidade Portuguesa*) became the new Fund for the Support of Youth Organizations (FAOJ); and the old National Foundation for Happiness at Work (FNAT) became the new National Institute for the Improvement of Leisure Time (INATEL). Despite changes of name and personnel at the top levels of these organizations, the lower-level functionaries could, like bureaucrats everywhere, effectively and legally tie up the funds for programs they disliked, however much the government itself may have supported those programs. Thus some local groups found themselves without funding even when they joined enthusiastically in the national dynamization or literacy campaigns.

The final effect of the cultural dynamization/revolution of 1974–75 varied according to the political affiliation of the evaluator. The Portuguese Communist Party, whose influence in the provisional governments was strongest in the first year and a half of the revolution, saw the end of cultural dynamization as an ominous sign for the revolution itself. One amateur theater activist associated with the PCP in a small northern city told me in 1979 that the "cultural dynamization campaign was the best thing that ever happened to Portugal." Those to the left of the PCP sometimes criticized the campaign for imposing a Leninist ideology on a populist (or even anarchist) peasantry; these critics wanted the revolutionary process simply to bypass the structures that the PCP had set up during its almost fifty years of clandestine opposition to the *Estado Novo*. Those to the right of the PCP argued that cultural dynamization was a kind of political propaganda whose goals as well as methods were foreign to the Portuguese people. These critics wanted to restore some semblance of the status quo from before 1974, arguing that the mass of the population already had tired of party politics (or even of elections) and valued law and order more than popular power.

The Retreat from Revolution, Cultural and Political

In the end, the cultural policies of the governments elected after 1976 aligned more closely with the conservative criticisms of the revolution than with the radical ones. After the Cultural Dynamization Campaign was closed down, for example, subsidies for the independent or amateur experimental theater groups were cut by 25 percent in August of 1975, and by 50 percent in September of 1975. The new government headed by Socialist Prime Minister Mario Soares in 1976 again cut the subsidies for these groups by 40 percent of the amount originally budgeted. During 1977, some of the most prominent independent groups were not subsidized at all. The post-1976 governments occasionally attacked funding for various arts groups precisely because such funding had begun or increased during the period of greatest left-wing influence in the government. In 1978, for example, the then Culture Secretary attacked the Portuguese Amateur Theater Association in the national assembly and proposed to withdraw its subsidy because of what he charged was a close association with the Communist Party (*A Barca* 16: December 1978).

Just as it was important to read the policy pronouncements of the *Estado Novo* as responding indirectly to a muffled or muzzled opposition, it is important to read the 1982 constitution as responding to the social and economic revolution of 1974–75. The new version of the constitution preserved or even expanded its explicit opposition to cultural inequality, but culture achieved this new prominence at the expense of references to socialism or revolution. The new constitution was drafted by a national assembly in which the Portuguese Communist Party was a definite minority, and in which the largest single party, the Socialists, tactically switched issue by issue from opposing to allying with the coalition government of Social and Christian Democrats. The most conservative architects of the new constitution had opposed the revolution and saw "cultural democracy" as a harmless phrase preferable to "classless society." Those who had supported the revolution had to settle for "cultural democracy" as a compromise between a classless society and "bourgeois democracy." The 1982 revision of Article 2, for example, changed the state's mandate from "the creation of conditions for the democratic exercise of power by the working classes" to the "realization of economic, social, and *cultural* democracy and the deepening of democratic participation" in government (emphasis added).

Article 73, on "education and culture," had required state cultural policy to promote "the progress of a democratic and socialist society" and to "guarantee to all citizens, especially the workers, access to the fruits of cultural creativity." The new Article 73, retitled "education, culture, and science," required the state to support "social progress and democratic participation in cultural life," and to guarantee cultural access "to all citizens," without any special mention of workers. The 1982 revision also added to this article a state obligation to "support and promote" scientific research, in keeping with the post-1976 government emphasis on technological modernization rather than social revolution.

The 1976 Article 78, on "cultural heritage," had merely required the state to "preserve, defend, and appreciate the cultural heritage of the Portuguese people." The 1982 revision greatly expanded this article and added to it a whole list of new state obligations:

> To stimulate and assure the access of all citizens, especially the workers, to the means and tools of cultural action, and to correct the existing asymmetries in that realm;
>
> To support initiatives that stimulate individual and collective creativity, in its multiple forms and expressions, and . . . broaden the circulation of works and objects of high cultural quality;
>
> To promote and defend the appreciation of the cultural heritage, using it to invigorate the common cultural identity;
>
> To develop cultural relations with all peoples, especially those using the Portuguese language, and assuring the defense and promotion of Portuguese culture abroad.

Indirectly, the new Articles 73 and 78 reflect effective but seldom announced changes in government policy after 1976. The phrase "especially to the workers" disappeared from the article on "education and culture" (73) and reappeared in the article on "cultural heritage" (78), in essence moving the workers away from culture as a tool of social progress (and scientific research) and linking them once again, as they had been linked under the *Estado Novo,* to a more passive concept of culture as inherited from the past. In this context, too, the use of "cultural action" as a concept only within Article 78 recalled government programs designed to "bring culture to the workers" before 1974. Rather than making cultural policy responsible to any clear political program or social constituency, the new Article 78 committed the government only to "the greater circulation of works of high cultural quality." Finally, the new Article 78 also reintroduced cultural nationalism ("the common cultural identity") as something that overrode class differences within Portugal. The MFA never had repudiated nationalism, but the revolutionaries had often criticized Salazar's nationalism as a front for class exploitation and generally sounded more internationalist than nationalist.

None of these changes explicitly renounced cultural democracy as a goal of policy. The government continued to fund adult literacy classes and cultural action as well as the professional fine and performing arts. In general, the government justified changes in policy in the name of fairness, good administrative practice, or professionalism. In 1980, for example, the coalition government announced a reorganization of the Secretariat of State for Culture in response to "successive and ineffective reorganizations" by previous governments, "many of which were . . . soon interrupted by momentary political problems" (*Decreto Lei* 59/80). The new law recited the perambulations of the culture secretariat since 1974: from the Ministry of Social Communication in 1975, to the Prime Minister's Council in 1977, to the Ministry of Education and Culture, and then in 1979 to the Ministry of Culture and Science. In administrative structure as well as in the content of policies, the Social and Christian Democrats repudiated earlier government actions as resulting from "ideological currents that attempted to impose themselves by organizing services and creating departments that did not always respond to concrete needs and that practiced no coherent or efficient administrative methods" (*ibid.*).

The legislative programs produced by the post-1979 governments' new dedication to "efficiency" were ambitious. In 1981, for example, the government published a comprehensive cultural plan, covering the cultural heritage, the creative arts, access to the arts, and education. The plan proclaimed the government's intention to improve, expand, and decentralize the national culture in all its forms. From 1980 to 1982, several governments with varying personnel, all controlled by the coalition of Social and Christian Democrats, announced the reorganization of all of the following programs and institutions: the Portuguese Book Institute; the Cultural Development Fund (in charge of distributing all arts subsidies and scholarships); the inspection of theaters and the enforcement of copyright; the national cinema archives; the Institute of the Portuguese Cultural Heritage, in charge of monuments, museums, libraries, and archives; the national television system; the theater laws; the laws governing cultural cooperatives; the Portuguese Film Institute; the system of government prizes for literature, the visual arts, and film; and the Museum of Popular Art.

The same governments in the same period also created numerous new programs and institutions: three regional delegations of the central culture secretariat; several separate regional cultural centers; special commissions for adult literacy; regional delegations for archaeology under the Institute of Cultural Heritage; an emergency plan for safeguarding the cultural heritage (in time of war, for example); a national theater museum; special social security programs for artists; a new Theater Institute (including the old Theater Fund and the theater division of the Directorate for Cultural Action); a national museum of literature (in Porto); a new headquarters for the national ballet company (established in 1977); and a national ceramics museum (in Caldas da Rainha). By 1983, the Secretariat of State for Culture also had established new programs, such as capital loans (mainly for construction) to cultural and recreational associations, and had begun to consider converting a few of the most active amateur groups into professional groups on the basis of their local success in stimulating other amateur activities and increasing local interest in the professional arts.[14] By 1982, the state also had established eight regional "cultural centers" around the country, under the direction of the Cultural Action Department of the Secretariat of State for Culture (*Intervenção*, 1 [second series] January 1982).

Yet overall, the 1982 changes in the constitution justified cultural policies to match the new governments' retreat from workers' control, nationalization of major industries, and the popular commissions and *comícios* (public meetings) that had run local governments and a significant part of the economy in 1974 and 1975. The government could justify any funding decision on the basis of cultural quality, which was difficult to measure or legislate. As long as the constitution did not specify the arbiters of high cultural quality, the government itself was the effective arbiter and could not be called to account for its standards.

In particular, these governments were careful not to restrict free market circulation, while occasionally recognizing a need for government intervention on the grounds of cultural "quality." Thus the Portuguese Book Institute was authorized in 1980 to subsidize the publication of classics no longer in circulation, but these publications were only "to protect the cultured book from the negative consequences of the market economy" (*Decreto Regulamentar* 17/80), rather than to restructure that economy itself. In 1982, the government withdrew quasi-official status from the regional "cultural centers" it had established only in 1980, redefining these as "entirely private entities that should enjoy no special privilege" (*Decreto Lei* 73/82, revoking *Decreto Lei* 219/80). Also in 1982, the government abolished its own right to collect copyright fees previously levied on works in the public domain as a means of financing government cultural programs. The 1982 government saw these fees as impeding the free circulation of such works, whose prices increased to cover the fees. Finally, the government reorganized the theater subsidies in 1982 as "contracts for theatrical creation," concluded for one year and renewable for three (*Decreto Lei* 428/82). Here, as in other reforms after 1979, the government made no reference to political or social change but justified the use of legal contracts as preserving "rigor and responsibility" in government and the "stability and security" of the theater groups themselves. The renewal of these contracts was linked to the continuity of personnel and numbers of performances in each subsidized theater group.

Yet there remained a significant or even widening gap between the governments' global planning and "efficiency" on the one hand and the actual mechanisms for awarding and distributing subsidies on the other hand. Before 1974, Salazar's and Caetano's governments had distributed subsidies according to clear and, for many artists, frustratingly stable political criteria. After 1976, however, arts organizations soon began to complain about the *lack* of any specific or consistent cultural policy and about rampant confusion and contradiction between the policies that were announced and the final appropriation or distribution of funds.[15] Many of these organizations spent much of their time learning which part of the bureaucracy considered itself responsible for funding their particular activity in any given year, as cabinet responsibilities were reorganized from one coalition government to the next. The Second National Meeting of Cultural Animators and Associations (Lisbon, December 1978), for example, concluded that "a) The cultural groups often have little idea of which organizations might support them; b) The official entities do not have a very clear status as to the activities they support; c) The conditions for obtaining support often depend on subjective (that is, political) criteria."

Although the Secretariat of State for Culture was perhaps the major institution to which these groups turned for subsidies, they also applied regularly to: the national and regional tourism boards; the Board of Rural People's Centers (*Junta Central das Casas do Povo*); the national department of education (through the Fund for the Support of Youth Activities—FAOJ); and the national department of labor (through the Institute for the Improvement of Leisure Time—INATEL). Groups could also apply for support from local government (town halls and parish councils), which received block grants from the national government for such purposes as education, sports, and culture: this money went largely to local football clubs, marching bands, choirs, amateur theater groups, and any other organization that could document its attempts to conduct adult literacy classes (see the law on popular education associations cited in the introduction to this essay, for example).

In addition, many groups also sought funding from the Gulbenkian Foundation (usually limited to the acquisition or loaning of permanent equipment, such as theater lights), from the trade unions, and from corporate sponsors. The major national trade union central, CGTP-Intersindical, had been organized in affiliation with the clandestine Portuguese Communist Party before 1974, and still was closely linked to the PCP's political positions. Direct support from CGTP, therefore, could expose groups to charges of Communist influence and endanger their chances of getting government subsidies at all after 1976. Nevertheless, many theater groups in particular sought union sponsorship of their performances, and CGTP sponsored a trade union amateur theater festival, in cooperation with the government, every two years.[16]

Each of the government funding agencies required applicants to submit plans of activity for the upcoming year and reports of activities for the past year. As a result of these reports, the plans and actions of the groups themselves were documented in much greater detail than were the plans and actions of the government policy-makers. Almost without exception, the governing bodies of the granting agencies included only career bureaucrats or political appointees and excluded any representatives of the groups receiving the grants. Without any clear public forum for the discussion of cultural policy, or any mechanism for ensuring that the bureaucracy carried out the policies announced by the national assembly or the government, funds appropriated often arrived late or not at all. Local groups outside Lisbon, who found it more difficult to remind the government of their existence than did those in the capital, complained bitterly that they could not plan their activities well enough to meet the government's own standards of formal organization precisely because the government funds promised did not arrive on time or in the promised amounts. Many local groups attributed these delays and revisions to local politics; the actual effects of national policies depended on local political rivalries.

The experience of one professional theater group in northwestern Portugal illustrates these inconsistencies: the group reported in 1979 that it received regular monthly subsidies from the Secretary of State for Culture in Lisbon; help in converting a barracks into a theater from the Civil Governor of one district and no help from the Governor of the neighboring district; virtually no help at all from the local town governments; help from the FAOJ office in one district and no help from its counterparts in two contiguous districts; and no help from the local offices of INATEL. Although an amateur group campaigned vigorously for the Socialist Party in the 1983 elections, that group found in return that their subsidies were even less regular in arriving after the Socialist victory than before. As of 1986 they attributed this to the local Socialist elite's "bending over backwards" to avoid any appearance of political favoritism (interviews, 1986).

Occasionally, the government's funding criteria provoked public debate: in 1976–77, for example, the Secretary of State for Culture proposed a new set of guidelines for the independent theater groups. The new rules would have given preference to the oldest groups by requiring a minimum number of years of professional theater experience in the group as a whole, and would have excluded automatically some of the groups formed only after 1974 (in the process excluding some of the politically more radical groups). The independent theater groups organized a massive demonstration/theater festival for twenty-four hours at the Lisbon Industrial Fair Pavilion in 1977 and reported an attendance of about 10,000 people.[17] The requirements based on years of experience were withdrawn in favor of other requirements based on the number of performances and spectators for each group in a given year. The independent theater groups accepted these guidelines but noted that the emphasis on performance and audience statistics alone effectively required them to reduce the time they spent on cultural action and animation: giving theater workshops for amateur groups, writing new plays, or setting up arts-centered programs for children (see further discussion of this issue in the conclusion). Following the government's renewed emphasis on the separation of art from politics after 1976, the new guidelines in essence encouraged actors to stay on the opposite side of the footlights from their audiences.

A PCP-sponsored arts conference brought numerous complaints against the government in 1978. José Pessoa complained of museums closed or neglected, which the *Estado Novo* and then the post-1976 constitutional governments had left without any funding or staffing for restoration or other technical services, including the museums of Contemporary Art, Ethnology, Popular Art, and Ancient Art (*Com a Arte Para Transformar a Vida,* 1978: 43).[18] José Peixoto pointed out that despite the governments' claim to be promoting cultural decentralization, 80 percent of all professional theater companies still worked in Lisbon (*ibid.*:95). The first meeting of the Association for Theatrical Decentralization (ATADT) in 1979 confirmed this pattern, pointing out that the total subsidy for all theaters in Lisbon was more than four times as large as the total subsidy for all theaters outside Lisbon, and that the official national theater received a subsidy well over ten times as large as that given to any of the independent groups "whose [high cultural] quality is well proven," even within Lisbon (ATADT 1979:8–9). Also in 1978, Henrique Leonor Pina reviewed the even lesser progress in promoting the Portuguese film industry, which had produced only 1 percent of all films shown in commercial theaters between May 1974 and April 1978 (*ibid.*:113).

A second nongovernment symposium on cultural policy in 1980 was called "What Cultural Policy?" (*Intervenção,* 16 [first series] October 1980). The participants complained that the state was leaving the nation's cultural development, by default or by intent, up to private entrepreneurs and the marketplace. António Reis complained that the government made policy for the arts largely through "confusion," "erecting barriers to action," and increasing "legal complexity" (*ibid.*). Helena Cidade Moura repeated some of the complaints from 1978, that the government had no cultural policy "other than anticommunism," and frequently had announced the opening of new institutes or museums without providing funds for their maintenance or growth (*ibid.*). José Luis Porfirio accused the government of focusing on Portugal's "moribund heritage," much as Salazar himself had done, and praised the Gulbenkian Foundation as "still the principal support of living artists" in Portugal (*ibid.*).

A controversy over the Socialist government's proposed revisions to the press law, beginning in late 1983, made it clear that politically active journalists as well as artists saw the new government as no definite improvement over its immediate predecessors. Immediately after the revolution, the government acquired a controlling interest in many newspapers when it nationalized the banks. Many of the papers were administered by workers' commissions in 1974–75 and had retained some of these structures into the 1980s. In 1983, the Socialist government suggested that the press should be treated as a regular private sector of the economy, and also spelled out the conditions under which it should be entitled to restrict freedom of the press. The journalists' union opposed these changes vehemently, arguing that they eventually would give the papers back into the hands of unscrupulous private owners and at the same time would reintroduce government censorship. The communications minister protested that it would be better to have the conditions under which the government could interfere with the press laid down in law than left vague, as they were at the time, but the journalists saw this as a plot to reduce their freedom of expression by reinstituting both private and state control of the press.

Such complaints applied across changes in the party political composition of the various governments after 1976. Even the governments themselves occasionally admitted the justice of these criticisms. When the Socialists returned to the government in 1983, for example, the government continued to make what the Minister of Culture himself, Coimbra Martins, described in May 1983 as "deep cuts" in that Ministry's budget (*Jornal de Notícias* 5 December 1983). In late 1983, Mario Soares (once again Prime Minister) affirmed in a television interview that "culture is more important than politics." Later, however, he stated matter-of-factly that "the priority of culture must be postponed in these lean times" (*Jornal de Notícias* 7 December 1983), when inflation and unemployment in Portugal both were running into double digits, and the International Monetary Fund was dictating national economic and social policy. After yet another shift from a Socialist to a Social Democratic coalition government in 1985, controversies over re-privatizing industries such as news and entertainment sharpened rather than subsided.

Politics and Culture: Which Is Cause and Which Is Effect?

The Portuguese transition from an authoritarian to a parliamentary regime, via a socialist revolution, had two potentially contradictory effects on the relations between art and politics. Certainly in comparison with censorship under the *Estado Novo,* the range of political content possible for the arts has greatly expanded since 1974. At the same time, and to precisely the same degree, the political effects attributed to art works and performances by the government's political concepts of culture have proven elusive. When politicians themselves no longer treated artists as if they could topple the government (as the authoritarian regime did before 1974), or as if they could create revolution (as the provisional governments did from 1974 to 1976), artists themselves found it difficult to have or claim either kind of political effect. The power of art to initiate or encourage resistance to the dictatorship, for example, turned out to depend closely on the government's censorship. The same plays or interpretations that were heroically antifascist when performed despite the censors before 1974 had no such clear political meanings when no one tried to suppress them after 1974. Similarly, the power of art to undermine political fatalism and "transform reality" after 1974 turned out to depend just as closely on the backing of the Armed Forces Movement and of governments that recognized "cultural action" as "integral to the civic mission of the armed forces."

In 1979, *A Comuna,* a left-wing theater group, pointed out that conditions after the revolution continually forced artists to choose between art itself ("art theater" in this case) "for a cultivated audience" and politics ("pamphlet theater" in this case) "to enlighten and mobilize the population" (*A Comuna* 2 [1979]:1). *A Comuna* wanted very much to integrate its political and artistic work into a single project. Many of the theater groups recognized this dilemma, arguing that effective cultural action depended on establishing permanent ties with their audiences, more like those enjoyed by amateur groups, ties not mediated by market or even government-subsidized ticket prices, and not limited to the one or two hours of a specific performance. Unfortunately for these groups, the government definition of culture included performances but not participant observation, the production of "works of high cultural quality" but not the production of class consciousness.

Although organization in cooperatives has changed the relations of production for some of the arts in Portugal, the relations of consumption for the arts have become more rather than less capitalist—the arts have become part of an uncensored "entertainment market." The government sometimes draws special attention to particular artistic products through censorship or subsidies, just as it regulates drugs or subsidizes basic foodstuffs, but these actions do not fundamentally change the market relations between the producers and consumers of art. To produce such change, and thus to substantiate the idea that art is essentially political in its effects as well as in its intentions, would indeed require a lasting social and economic revolution.

Appendix: Levels of Government Arts-Related Spending in Portugal

TABLE 1. Arts-Related Spending as a Percentage of Total Government Spending, 1945–83

	1945	*1955*	*1965*	*1975*	*1983*
Ministry of Education[a]	7	8	4	17	11
National Information Office (SNI)[b]	.3	.6	.4	—	—

TABLE 2. Percentage Changes in Arts-Related Spending and in Total Government Spending, 1945–83

	1945–55	*1955–65*	*1965–75*	*1975–83*
Total budget	+ 80	+288	+ 204	+800
Ministry of Education[a]	+112	+100	+1,154	+445
Directorate of National Monuments	—	+ 65	− 2	—
National Conservatory	+ 88	+ 23	+ 677	—
National Information Office (SNI)[b]	+245	+219	—	—
"Verde Gaio" (National Dance Company)	+ 30	+ 21	—	—
Cinema Fund/Institute	—	+203	+1,029	—
Theater Fund	—	+156	+ 168	—

TABLE 3. Levels of Arts-Related Spending, 1945–75[c]

	1945	*1955*	*1965*	*1975*
Secretariado Nacional de Informação[b]				
production of films	800	900	710	250
touring theater	400	800	500	1,000
touring cinema	280	220	450	800
National Cinema Fund (after 1974, Portuguese Cinema Institute)	—	3,436	10,415	117,596
National Theater Fund	—	2,726	6,992	18,731
Museum of Popular Art	500	70	200	—

(continued)

TABLE 3 (*Continued*)

	1945	*1955*	*1965*	*1975*
confidential expenses	—	851	1,710	—
censorship services	—	139	—	—
Department of the Interior				
Directorate-General of National Buildings and Monuments	35,729	121,141	200,015	342,276
Department of Education[a]				
National Academy of Fine Arts	215	327	434	—
School of Fine Arts—Lisbon	384	711	2,578	11,482
School of Fine Arts—Porto	330	795	2,444	8,064
National Conservatory	919	1,729	2,123	16,489
Conservatory of Porto	—	—	—	6,824
national theaters	1,144	9,110	9,572	40,092
museums	1,500	2,927	4,004	8,444
campaign of adult education	—	17,999	—	(See Table 4.)
Institute of High Culture				
scholarships for foreign study	585	1,079	1,799	(See Table 4.)
scholarships for study in Portugal	419	72	3,240	
scientific centers and publications	513	9	2,700	
arts education	315	405	449	
Lisbon Philharmonic Orchestra	—	180	—	
Polyphonic Chorale	—	—	50	
cultural expansion	810	1,754	3,375	

TABLE 4. New or Temporary Government Spending Related to the Arts During the 1974–76 Revolution[c]

1974	
Fund for Cultural Development	21,938
cultural diffusion	57,940
promotion of creativity	30,000
youth leisure activities	29,300
1975	
Fund for Cultural Development	28,500
Secretary of State for Culture and Permanent Education	1,012
Directorate-General of Cultural Matters	129,379
National Science and Technology Board[d]	5,099
Institute of High Culture (total)	169,057
cultural dynamization	5,032
expansion and support of cultural activities	10,000
adult/permanent education	43,519
youth leisure activities (FAOJ)	46,000

(*continued*)

TABLE 4 (*Continued*)

1976	
Fund for Cultural Development	53,126
cultural animation	12,000
Directorate-General of Cultural Action	119,917
Institute of High Culture (total)	183,850
campaigns of clarification and mobilization	2,030
special campaigns of cultural action	30,000
regional cultural centers	17,000
public opinion polls	1,900
youth leisure activities (FAOJ)	139,490

TABLE 5. Percentage Changes in Spending on "Cultural Action" from 1976 to 1983

1976–1980	– 31
1980–1983	+258

Sources: Portugal, *Orçamento do Estado* (National Budget) and *Conta Geral do Estado* (General State Accounts), 1945–75; and *Diário da República*, first series, 1980–84.

Notes for Tables

— Not available or not reported in published budgets.

[a]In 1975, changed to Ministry of Education and Culture.

[b]Abolished in 1974.

[c]All figures in contos (thousands of escudos).

[d]Assumed some former functions of Institute of High Culture after 1974.

Discussion

Changes in the categories used to report government spending on the arts in Portugal between 1945 and the present make it virtually impossible to analyze long-term trends in any detail. In addition, the political interpretation of the budget requires factoring out such variables as inflation and devaluation, an analysis too complex to include in this appendix. Tables 1 through 4 merely suggest the grossest possible upward and downward movements in government spending on the arts.

Before 1974, education and culture seemed to elicit relatively low levels of government funding, in spite of the rhetorical importance that Salazar attached to political "correctness" in the arts. Government spending on the National Information Office, which included the censorship bureaucracy, spending on "popular culture," and tourism expenditures, more nearly kept pace with the growth of the total budget than did spending on education (and apparently on the "high cultural" institutions of museums and arts schools in the Ministry of Education). The adult education campaign reported for 1955, for example, was a one-shot program that required factories to ensure that all employees could pass a minimum elementary education examination; those who could not pass, even after taking night classes, were supposed to lose their jobs (thus this program at times functioned more as a way of organizing layoffs than as a way of reducing illiteracy). The most opaque categories (confidental expenditures by the SNI, for example, or cultural expansion by the Institute of High Culture) were probably deliberately so—Salazar held himself accountable to the nation for balancing the budget in general, but not for the funding of specific programs: The figures from this period also hint at the emphasis on monuments rather than on the living arts under the *Estado Novo*.

The revolutionary governments in 1974–75 increased dramatically spending on the living arts and on education. Some of the new or temporary arts-related spending after 1974 also came under opaque headings (cultural action, animation, dynamization, diffusion), but these activities were very much public. These difficult-to-define programs were most often those that tried to break down the distinction between art and politics that was restored under the governments after 1976.

Some of the contrasts suggested by the budget figures must be qualified by considering how the figures were reported and organized. The dramatic upward shift in the level of support for the Ministry of Education in 1975, for example, partly reflects the inclusion in that ministry of a wide variety of new or temporary activities, including cultural dynamization, animation, and action. Reduced spending for such programs between 1976 and 1980, and the creation of a separate Ministry of Culture in 1982–83, similarly account for part of the relative reduction in government spending for the Ministry of Education between 1975 and 1983. On the other hand, the centralization of spending for ''cultural action'' between 1980 and 1983 increased the budget for the Directorate-General for Cultural Action (as reflected in Table 5). This apparent increase, however, may reflect the elimination of cultural programs in other government agencies, whose budgets were not reported separately in the figures available for these years (in the *Diário do Governo*).

Finally, the figures for money actually spent rarely matched those reported for original budget allocations. Before 1974, expenses were almost always under budget, but the unbudgeted ''extraordinary expenses'' in 1975 often nearly equaled the budgeted ''ordinary expenses.'' In addition, the governments after 1976 often delayed the actual payment of budgeted amounts to the point of seriously disrupting the activities of arts groups, or even of education at levels beyond elementary schooling. In 1982–83, for example, the school year in some university subjects began several months late because the government had not released the funds to pay teaching assistants. I have used the figures on expenditures in all cases, but these various gaps between theory (the budget) and practice (expenditures) make it unclear which figures reflect each government's policy intentions most faithfully.

Notes

1. One analysis of educational policy under the *Estado Novo* (Mónica 1978), for example, has demonstrated that at least some of the Portuguese corporatists argued seriously that workers, urban or rural, did not really need to read and write, much less attend plays or concerts, or understand the laboratory sciences.

2. Although ''dynamization'' is somewhat awkward in English, it is the only accurate translation for the Portuguese *dynamização*. The word means ''to render dynamic or active,'' and thus cannot be translated as the more passive ''dynamism,'' which implies that energy or activity is already present.

3. I use the term ''liberal'' here in the sense of ''liberal capitalism,'' to include all the constitutional governments that have not seen themselves as actively continuing the socialist revolution in Portugal although they have basically accepted the transition from an authoritarian to a parliamentary system; in this sense, the term includes governments of the Socialist, Social Democratic, and Christian Democratic parties, though many political observers would not consider either of the latter two parties ''liberal'' as opposed to ''conservative.''

4. In Portugal after 1976, ''democratic'' became a kind of code word for anti- or non-Communist; the coalition of Social and Christian Democrats called itself the ''Democratic Alliance,'' for example. This was a 180-degree shift from the meaning of ''democracy'' before 1974, when the Movement of Democratic Unity, for example, opposed Salazar and was allied with the clandestine PCP. I have not used the term in this essay except when it appears in direct quotes, and

in each case it should be interpreted according to its context and the group using it (before or after 1974).

5. See, for example, Pereira and Fernandes (1980).

6. At the same time, artists and audiences became very sophisticated in producing and extracting multiple meanings, as a way of criticizing the government without giving the government itself clear or legally useful evidence of their disaffection. Rodrigues lists a few examples of such double meanings: "dawn" or "morning" for socialism, "spring" for revolution, "comrade" for a political prisoner, "vampire" for policeman.

7. The main duties of the SNI were "to coordinate national activities" related to information, popular culture and tourism, and "to assure that these shall be directed and controlled by the state" (*Bulletin* November 1944:3).

8. The *Estado Novo* had always relied on private charity to supplement, or even to supplant, government spending on education and social welfare, and to some extent to supplant government spending on the arts. Since the early 1940s, the government had leased the national theater of Dona Maria II in Lisbon to a private company (Gomes 1957:431; Porto 1979). The national cinema fund established in 1948 limited subsidies to a total 30 percent of the cost of any film, requiring private capital to make up the rest (*Bulletin* 31 January 1948:12). In 1949, the SNI had even suggested that the government literary prizes were necessary only because "the taste for patronage is being lost in official business and writers are not receiving sufficient encouragement from those [private] bodies, that should look after the interest of our national literary culture" (July–August 1949:15). In the 1950s the SNI began to suggest that the drought of private patronage was over, citing numerous donations "of a social, cultural, or welfare nature" that "followed the wonderfully sound principles of Christian Unity and thereby afforded a growing number of Portuguese better welfare or new possibilities" (*Bulletin* January–February 1956:49–50).

9. Carlos Porto, writing in *Programa* (May 1979), for example, insisted in retrospect that "the discredit of the [national] company was so great that when people spoke of the 'style of the National' they were thinking of that declamatory tone used by actors whose routine turned them into mere puppets, stage designs without creativity, academic performances, without any kind of esthetic contribution, insufferably boring." Although Porto may have exaggerated, the government itself had to admit that the independent theaters attracted audiences away from the national theaters with great regularity in the later 1950s and 1960s.

10. I conducted the interviews mentioned as sources in this essay in 1979, during fieldwork in Portugal on the development of political theater since the 1974 revolution, from 1980 to 1982, during research on the responses of workers in rural northwestern Portugal to the state's ideology and changes in class relations under the *Estado Novo*, and on a brief return visit in 1986 (see Ingerson 1979, 1984).

11. Barata was the director of the student theater group in the university city of Coimbra.

12. By condemning both colonialist and colonizing culture, the commission aimed the new forms of government support for theater in Portugal against two targets: the old notion of Portugal itself as a colonial power, which had been central to the cultural policies of the *Estado Novo;* and the new invasion of entertainment from the Americas and northern Europe, including the whole range of forms previously held off by the censors, from theatrical classics and art films to soap operas, rock music, imported soft drinks, and pornography.

13. These reports are taken from interviews with people who participated in the rent control demonstrations, and from two films of the plays by the high school students (*Teatro em Borba,* by the film company Cinequipa) and the farmworkers (*Teatro Popular em Beira Baixa,* by the film company Cinequanon).

14. The one case of this transformation I know well is that of the amateur group, *Teatro Construçao,* in the district of Braga.

15. A December 13, 1983, editorial in the Porto-based *Jornal de Notícias,* for example, denounced the "total confusion" in the ministries of both education and social communication (media and information).

16. The 1982 theater law left the way open for the government to deny future subsidies to this festival by requiring subsidized theater festivals to "guarantee . . . diversity of expression" (*Decreto Lei* 428/82).

17. The film company Cinequanon documented this event in the film, *O Outro Teatro, ou As Coisas Pertencem a Quem as Torna Melhor:* "The Other Theater, or Things Belong to Those Who Make Them Better."

18. The "creation" of a museum, for example, was entirely separate from its staffing and funding. Thus the Museums of Comparative Sculpture and of Science and Technology were staffed and funded permanently only in late 1983 and early 1984, although they had been "created" much earlier (in the first case several years earlier).

Bibliography

Antologia: Discursos, Notas, Relatórios, Tèses, Artigos e Entrevistas do Sr. Dr. António Oliveira Salazar, 1909–1953. 1954. Lisboa: Editorial Vanguarda.

A Barca: Boletim da Associação Portuguesa de Teatro de Amadores. Lisboa. Various issues.

Brito, Joaquim Pais de. 1982. *O Estado Novo e a Aldeia Mais Portuguesa de Portugal*, in António Costa Pinto, et al., *O Fascismo em Portugal: Actas do Colóquio da Faculdade de Letras, Março 1980, Lisboa*. Lisbon: A Regra do Jogo.

Bulletin (official titles: 1933–56, *Portugal: Bulletin of Political, Economic, and Cultural Information;* 1956–73, *Portugal: An Informative Review*). Lisboa: 1933–44, Secretariado Nacional de Propaganda; 1944–1974, Secretariado Nacional de Informação, Cultura Popular, e Turismo. Various issues.

Com a Arte Para Transformar a Vida: Primeira Assembleia de Artes e Letras. 1978. Lisboa: ORL do PCP, Edições Avante!.

A Comuna. *Para Onde Is? Jornal do Clube dos Amigos da Comuna*. Various issues.

Correia, Ramiro, Pedro Soldado, and João Araujo. n.d. *MFA: Dinamização Cultural, Acção Civica*. Lisboa: Biblioteca Ulmeiro.

Decretos Leis and *Decretos Regulamentares*. Texts of laws and government decrees, published in the *Diário da República*, first series, (official daily gazette of the Portuguese government). Various issues.

Guerra, João Paulo. 1981. *Dossier Communicação Social*. Lisboa: Edições Avante!

Ingerson, Alice, 1979. "An Anthropological Approach to Portuguese 'Political Theater.'" Paper presented to the Seminar in Atlantic History and Culture, Johns Hopkins University.

______, 1984. *Corporatism and Class Consciousness in Northwestern Portugal*. Baltimore: Unpub. Ph.D. dissertation, Johns Hopkins University.

Intervenção: Revista de Animação Socio-cultural. Lisboa. Various issues.

Jornal de Notícías. 1983 (daily newspaper). Porto.

Junior, Redondo. 1978. *A Juventude Pode Salvar o Teatro*. Lisboa: Editora Arcadia.

Letria, José Jorge. 1978. *A Canção Política em Portugal: Da Resistência à Revolução*. Lisboa: Edições A Opinião.

Lucena, Manuel de. 1979. "The Evolution of Portuguese Corporatism Under Salazar and Caetano," pp. 47–88 in Lawrence Graham and Harry Makler, eds. *Contemporary Portugal: The Revolution and its Antecedents*. Austin: University of Texas Press.

Martins, Hermínio. 1968. "Portugal," pp. 302–336 in S. J. Woolf, ed., *European Fascism*. New York: Random House.

Mónica, Maria Filomena. 1978. *Educação e Sociedade no Portugal de Salazar*. Lisboa: Editorial Presença.

Pereira, Nuno Teotónio and José Manuel Fernandes. 1980. "A arquitectura do fascismo em

Portugal,'' in Antonio Costa Pinto, et al., *O Fascismo em Portugal: Actas do Colóquio da Faculdade de Letras, Março 1980, Lisboa*. Lisbon: A Regra do Jogo.
Programa. Grupo de Campolide (Lisboa). 1978–79.
Rebello, Luis Francisco. 1977. *Combate por um Teatro de Combate*. Lisboa: Seara Nova.
Rodrigues, Graca Almeida. 1980. *Breve história da censura literária em Portugal*. Lisboa: Instituto da Cultura e Lingua Portuguesa.

10

Tradition, Change, and Crisis in Great Britain

F. F. Ridley

Background Traditions

To understand the cultural politics of a country, one must first understand its political culture. State policies toward the arts are shaped by wider beliefs about how government ought to be conducted and what it should try to do. Britain had virtually no state patronage of the living arts before 1940. Views then changed about the proper role of the state in relation to the arts (the *what* of government), but the manner of promoting them (the *how* of government) remained consistent with earlier ideas about administration. Though the state became a major patron of the arts after the war, the arts were shielded from politics. Recent years have brought the two into closer contact. This was partly the result of government brakes on public expenditure generally, a political trend found in other countries too; partly the result of changing views about the public role of the arts themselves. Before discussing current issues in the management of cultural policy, we must therefore cast a brief look at history.

British history is different from that of many Continental countries. The English revolution saw no transition from court to state patronage. The Puritans were positively hostile to the arts, believing decorative works to be frivolous and the theater a place of debauchery, and Protestantism remained suspicious of the arts long thereafter. The interests of the ruling classes in the eighteenth and nineteenth centuries did not encourage state activity either. The landed aristocracy patronized portrait painters and purchased old masters, but their lives centered on their great houses. Culture that required a public rather than a private setting, such as theater, opera, and ballet, had only a limited place in this pattern. The rising class of industrialists and merchants purchased art works and organized exhibitions, but middle-class virtues emphasized home and family: reading novels and playing music in the domestic circle. The philosophy that life was a serious business and that leisure should be spent in morally uplifting ways meant that arts as such had no claim on the virtuous taxpayer. To this must be added the political dominance of capitalism. Unlike those European countries where capitalism came too late to destroy *étatiste* traditions, in Britain it established the "nightwatchman" state in which the functions of government were reduced to policing; "laissez-faire" applied to the arts as to all else. Commercial theaters eventually thrived, and painters probably sold more to private customers in Victorian times than they do today. National and municipal theaters were established in many Continental towns, but Britain assumed that culture, like other entertainments, should be left to compete in the marketplace.

As the functions of the state expanded, these political traditions remained a powerful force with regard to the arts. If state intervention was to be justified at all, it had to be on commercial and moral grounds, as in the Great Exhibition of 1851. Arguments for state funding came to be phrased in noncultural terms. Economic interest still plays a small part, as when the heavy subsidies for the national theater and opera are justified by reference to the tourist trade or when support of provincial theater is linked to the economic regeneration of cities. More apparent, however, is the continued emphasis on education. The mission of the Arts Council was to encourage public appreciation of the best in the arts, i.e., to raise popular taste. Although the "community arts" movement of recent years is hostile to the "elitism" of traditional Arts Council policy, which it sees as an attempt to impose bourgeois values on the rest of society, it, too, emphasizes the educational function of cultural policy. For some, the aim is to encourage latent artistic talents through activities more accessible to ordinary people, but others subordinate this to political ends, the stimulation of social change.

It hardly occurs to anyone in Britain that artists as a community deserve special support or that individual artists (be they painters, writers, musicians, or actors), however good, should receive some sort of state "pension" simply because they are artists (the Poet Laureate is an historical exception). They may benefit as exhibitors in public galleries or performers in grant-aid theaters, for example, but, with few exceptions, it is the service they provide the public that is subsidized. There is no inclination to treat artists as people different from the rest of the population. When a job creation program was established ten years ago, there was no suggestion that special provisions should be made for unemployed artists as, for example, in America's pre-war WPA. The establishment of a comprehensive social security system after the war made special arrangements unnecessary, unlike, perhaps, countries where unified social security systems do not exist or where their cover is patchy. Nor can one find any support for "art for art's sake"—subsidy of art *works* simply because great works should be created whether or not they are widely appreciated at the time, in the way that the cathedrals of the middle ages were built for the glory of God and not for the enjoyment of man.

History explains another feature of the British scene. The tradition of public museums was well established before 1940. Science museums were obviously instructional and art museums were thought to contribute to moral uplift more effectively than concerts or plays. One result is that even today central and local governments spend more on displaying "heritage arts" than on patronage of the living arts. Moreover, even collections such as the British Museum and the National Gallery came about because private owners offered them to the nation at advantageous prices; local museums were donated by philanthropic businessmen. Far from deliberate state ventures in pursuit of a cultural policy, the growth of this sector was the result of ad hoc private initiatives. This style of intervention—response rather than planning—also is characterized in the policy of the Arts Council after 1945. The shift to positive policy-making is a recent development and a call for longer-term cultural planning only now is beginning to be heard.

Another factor is worth mentioning. While elite private education produced the "cultured gentleman," the emphasis was on Latin and Greek rather than English drama. Little was made of culture in any form in the state schools which the mass of population attended. *National* culture did not (and, on the whole, does not) form part of national consciousness. Main streets are not named after great writers. That is not to say that there is no interest in the arts. The quality press covers cultural events in its columns and reports on policy issues in a generally supportive manner. The popular press, on the other hand, is largely philistine, mocking eccentric events on the fringe (e.g., a line of bricks at a Tate Gallery exhibition) and attacking the "immoral" (e.g., the simulated rape of an ancient Briton by a Roman soldier in a National Theatre production); the rest it ignores. The mass of the population is indifferent at best. Although all political parties now are committed to encouragement of the arts, there is little public support for this. Young people are not taught that culture is a "good thing," as they are in certain countries where even those relatively untouched by the arts accept considerable public expenditure as a matter of course. Nor is the state directly interested in culture as a contribution to Britain's standing in the world, unlike France, where all governments talk of her "civilizing mission." Despite the existence of the British Council and the Tourist Board, British governments do not see the arts as an element in national policy.

Although public expenditure on the arts eventually grew, earlier traditions remain important in determining the way this is administered. If cultural policy requires not just an acceptance by government that the arts as a whole should be subsidized but self-confident policy-makers who believe they know what forms of arts to promote, then British ways of thinking long exercised a negative influence. The Protestant-Liberal tradition sees every man as judge of his own good, whether in religion, politics, or leisure. As a former chairman of the Arts Council said, "One of the most precious freedoms of the British is freedom from culture." There is no belief that the pattern of cultural institutions should be directed from above, whether by politician or art administrator. This was reflected in the principle that government should find money for the arts without directing its use and that the Arts Council, responsible for allocating that money to a host of organizations, should respond to demand rather than implement a plan of its own. In so far as views are now changing, this still has more to do with the problem of rationing subsidies in a time of financial shortfall than with any positive inclination at the top to shape the cultural map of Britain.

In a democracy, personal tastes are not to be decided by policy-makers, but British reluctance to set standards goes further. Arguments about the relative merits of different art forms, like arguments about religion, are likely to end as the participants retire gracefully behind the formula "de gustibus non est disputandum." It is true that the man in the street sometimes expresses hostile views about modern art and is supported in this by the popular press, but those concerned with the allocation of funds are less likely to believe that they know what is good art or press what beliefs they have very far. This tolerant pragmatism is sometimes contrasted with the dogmatic certainties of more rationalist cultures. In practice, moreover, much of the responsibility for funding decisions is still in the hands of people who see themselves as "amateurs." One is tempted to draw a contrast here between the "generalists" of British public administration and the "technocrats" of France, very confident of their own expertise. A change in atmosphere has taken place, however. The absence of serious argument about which art forms should be promoted reflected a consensus among upper-middle-class policy-makers broad enough to embrace all forms of modernism as well as traditional schools. As new social groups involved with "popular" arts came to compete for subsidies, the Left inevitably challenged the "establishment's" emphasis on "high-arts" and brought political argument into cultural affairs. On the Right, populist moral revival movements such as the "clean up TV" campaign also entered the fray.

Development after 1945

In a single decade during and after the Second World War, British government did more to commit itself to support of the arts than over the previous century. Although it reflected the expansion of all state activities during that period, the new system of state subsidies did not involve any major change in political thought, unlike the establishment of the welfare state and economic planning. It emerged almost by accident and remained within a traditional framework of ideas.

Early in the war, the government had supported a new organization, the Council for the Encouragement of Music and the Arts. In a time of austerity, culture seemed a way of brightening the lives of factory workers, military personnel, and isolated civilian groups, thus fortifying national morale. Typically, the initiative for CEMA came from private bodies, and the government only funded the operation after it had been established. Typically, too, government support was obtained through the intervention of a small group of influential people, patrons of the arts but familiar with the corridors of power. This recognized the fact that a reform with no great popular appeal is best obtained through the "establishment" rather than the ballot box or pressure groups. The third aspect of the CEMA experiment was that it did not involve the government in direct intervention in the arts, much less in any new administrative functions. Though financed by public money, CEMA remained independent. It had an excellent record. New audiences for the arts emerged. The revival of a commercial market in entertainments after the war saw some decline in public interest but wartime experience showed what could be done.

In 1945, the Arts Council was established to continue and expand the work of CEMA. This explains why permanent government funding of the arts was accepted so easily. Without the precedent of CEMA, there would have been lengthy inquiries, probably a Royal Commission, followed by public and parliamentary debates. Conflicting views, together with the absence of any obvious party-political interest, might finally have frustrated action altogether. As it was, there was no need to make a politically controversial decision: the Arts Council appeared as a continuation of what already existed. The decision was made by the coalition government, announced by the "caretaker" Conservative government that followed, and implemented by the Labour government that won the first postwar election. Because it was created by Royal Charter, like many similar institutions, legislation was not required.

It should be added that state support of the arts was not seen as having a political function, nor is culture used today for purposes of national policy. It is true that the grant to the Arts Council takes into account its commitment to the national theaters, opera, and ballet and that the expense of these sometimes is justified in terms of national prestige, but the Council places less emphasis on this than on the excellence of the institutions and the fact that their survival depends on its support. Public discussion about the role of the Arts Council now does have a "political" character in that positions taken reflect different socio-political values, but the policy-making process has been kept out of the world of politics proper. The system of allocating subsidies to art organizations is deliberately organized in a way that prevents party-political or governmental-bureaucratic direction. This isolation of the arts has, of course, been challenged by some on the Left on the grounds that it actually leaves cultural policy in the hands of an elite which promotes middle-class values. There is a growing demand for a democratization of procedures (more participation in the decision-making process) and, a related but separate issue, for a democratization of substance (more funds for popular art forms).

Though the creation of the Arts Council marked a commitment to support the arts, the level of support was small for two decades. This period allowed the Arts Council to establish itself, however, so that it became the beneficiary when the climate changed and government spending on the arts increased. One reason for this change was the general acceptance by the political parties that state support of the arts on a more effective scale was desirable. In 1959, the House of Commons voted on a non-partisan basis for a private member's motion calling for a substantial increase in government support, while reiterating that art policy should remain free from government control. Election manifestos came to include a few sentences along these lines. Although culture was not an issue which divided the parties, however, it cannot be said that it had any electoral appeal either, so that it was unlikely that any party would push the matter very far as part of its electoral program. The question, therefore, was which government would take the initiative.

In 1965, the new Labour Prime Minister, Harold Wilson, appointed Jennie Lee (widow of Anuerin Bevan, one of Labour's great postwar figures, and a personality in her own right) as a junior Minister with special responsibility for cultural policy, the first recognition of responsibility for the arts at ministerial level. That same year, 1965, also saw the establishment for the first time of a division in the Department of Education to deal with cultural affairs. This change resulted less from concern for the arts on the part of Harold Wilson than from his interest in administrative reform, which included divesting the Treasury of responsibilities—among them grants to the Arts Council and national museums—judged incompatible with its primary functions. The status of the new division, now called the Office of Arts and Libraries, has changed several times, but the move from a ministry controlling expenditure to a spending ministry implied a more positive approach to subsidies. More important, however, was probably the appointment of a Minister. This gave the arts a defined standing within the administrative system and a spokesman within the government. Since then, there has always been a Minister with special responsibility for the arts, although his title has changed frequently and his influence has varied.

The Arts Council, which has no other source of revenue, received a grant of only £$\frac{1}{4}$ million in its first year. By 1965, this had risen to £3 million, but that year proved a turning point. Its funds (and the greater part of government aid to the arts is channelled through it) rose every year thereafter, reaching £80 million for 1981–82. In real terms, however, the rise became less spectacular after a couple of years. Between 1972–73 and 1981–82, the Council's grant only increased by a third if one adjusts the figures for inflation; 1980 was another significant year. The advent of the Conservative government, with Mrs. Thatcher's policy of cutting public expenditure, soon led to annual increases less than the rate of increase in costs. To the effects of this on Arts Council policy we shall return.

We have discussed state patronage of the arts in terms of central government so far, but something must be said about local government. Local authorities tend to play a more important role in the provision of services (e.g., education) than in many other European countries and might therefore be expected to play the major role in this field also. That is not the case, however. A number of municipal art galleries were established in the nineteenth century through the benefactions of private citizens, and some of these are of considerable distinction. They were not the result of local government initiatives, however, though they now depend on public funds for their maintenance. There were no municipal theaters, concert halls, or opera houses, in sharp contrast to much of the Continent. It has been said of Britain that the whole force of municipal enterprise was concentrated into utilitarian channels, while all the finer aspects of civil life were ignored. In addition to the historical factors that inhibited central government, however, there was a legal inhibition. British local authorities have no generalized power to operate services of public interest; authorities interested in promoting the arts therefore had to obtain special Acts of Parliament for that purpose. It was not until 1948 that all were authorized to spend a small proportion of revenue on arts and entertainments, and only in 1972 were they given discretion in the amounts they could spend. Relatively little use was made of this facility until the early 1970s when local government reform led to the establishment of the Greater London Council and Metropolitan Councils in the major conurbations. By 1981–82, local authority expenditure on the arts (excluding museums and galleries) had risen to £65m, a 50 percent increase in real terms over 1972–73.

While the political elites in London came to accept state funding of the arts, local councillors long remained unconvinced. One reason may be that they were less ''worldly'' than Members of Parliament. More important, they lacked the possibility of ''arm's-length'' patronage which the Arts Council gave central government. Allocative decisions had to be taken in local authority committees by people who did not see themselves as the proper arbiters of culture and could be subject to ridicule in the local press if they subsidized an unorthodox event. While a grant to the Arts Council could be swallowed by Parliament without debate, moreover, the British system of local government involves councillors in every item of expenditure and pressure to ''keep down the rates'' weighs more heavily on them. The relatively more ''democratic'' character of local decision-making, as compared with decisions in Westminster and Whitehall, had proved something of a drawback for the arts. It is only fair to add that post-war years saw many developments. Orchestras and theaters have been subsidized. As status symbols, they appealed to local pride. New theaters sometimes could be linked to the planning of new town centers. The establishment of Regional Arts Associations from the 1960s on also made the political situation easier because local authorities could make grants (still very small) to them, thus farming out responsibility for allocative decisions in regard to smaller clients. Several reports have urged them to go much further along this path. Even if they were willing, however, the financial restraints imposed upon them by the present government, forcing them to cut vital services, make any such move impossible.

Balance Sheet

Some attempt should be made at this stage to assess the contribution of the state to the arts in present-day Britain. What the state manages itself is mainly in the field of heritage arts. According to the Museums Yearbook, there are some 1400 museums and galleries of all sorts in Britain. Of these, 7 percent are national, 52 percent local, 6 percent military, 6 percent attached to educational institutions, while the rest are run as charitable trusts or commercial ventures. According to the Theatre Directory, there are some 400 ''principal'' theaters in Britain (ranging from over 2,000 seats to under 200 seats). Local authorities own at least 150 theaters and an equal number of halls with stage facilities. Relatively few, however, have a managerial interest in theater companies, as distinct from buildings, and in orchestras. For the rest, apart from the British Broadcasting Corporation, virtually all institutions which actually run cultural activities are to be found in the "private" sector, whether as commercial undertakings (e.g., the mass of London theaters) or as trusts or companies under charity law. An institutional survey thus reveals little in the way of state activity.

One must, therefore, turn to financial patronage: how much public money is devoted to the arts? Statistical gaps have defeated every attempt to produce comprehensive figures, though the Policy Studies Institute recently brought together all *available* data. Problems of definition often undermine the value of figures in international comparisons. Because the tendency in Britain is to talk of "the arts" rather than "culture," it is usual to omit public libraries, which some countries include in a broader category of cultural facilities. Who knows where the arts shade into entertainment? One cannot always isolate arts expenditure from the broader category of leisure activities reported by some local authorities. It is even harder to trace the contribution to the arts made by a variety of governmental agencies pursuing other primary aims.

The main central government expenditure is clear enough. In 1982–83, the relevant "parliamentary grants" to the Office of Arts and Libraries and the Ministries for Scotland and Wales came to £200m. Of this, £92m went to the Arts Council; £84m to national museums and galleries; and £24m to the British Film Institute, the Crafts Council, and other purchase funds. However, the £8m channelled to music through the Arts Council was overshadowed by the Ministry of Defense's "non-art" expenditure of £26m on military bands, an interesting reflection on British values. The British Council devoted some £2m of its parliamentary grant to events by British artists and performers abroad. One could also add the BBC here since its revenue is obtained from license fees, channelled through the Home Office, thus a form of taxation. It spent some £48m on drama and £27m on "serious" music and arts features in 1979–80.

Local government in England and Wales (the statistics exclude Scotland) spent some £116m in the same period. Of this, £50m was for museums and galleries. Since these include science museums and the like (as do the national museums above) and the money goes mainly on maintenance costs and attendants' wages, it does little for the living arts. Expenditure on directly owned and operated premises included £16m for theaters, £3m for halls with stage facilities, and £20m for the arts centers (concentrated almost entirely on the Barbican Centre in the City of London). Some £5m went to direct promotions, including a wide range of leisure facilities such as flower shows, as well as drama and music. Grants to other bodies came to £21m, of which £2m was for orchestras, £8m for theaters and drama companies, £3m for opera and dance, the rest going to the visual arts, art centers and festivals, regional and local arts associations, amateur groups, and so on. The total is far below the £276m local authorities devoted to public lending libraries—a reminder of the historical tradition that placed education (though most borrowing is now of popular fiction) well above the arts. It should be noted, however, that many painters earn their livelihood as teachers in local authority schools and Art Colleges.

A fuller picture might also take account of revenue forgone by the state as a result of tax concessions. Britain is most ungenerous in this respect compared with many other countries. Cultural activities are subject to turnover tax (VAT) at the full rate (though books are zero-rated). In 1982, a Treasury Minister informed Parliament that on a broad definition of cultural events, including commercial theater and cinema, the VAT yield to government was over £100m a year, rather more than its own contribution to the living arts. Only a few masterpieces are accepted each year in lieu of death duties: not only is the Treasury very selective, but the financial benefit to the heirs is not always sufficient to avoid a more profitable sale abroad. Gifts to cultural institutions, whether in kind or in cash, cannot be claimed as an "expense" for income tax purposes and thus do not reduce the donor's tax liability—a concession which in some countries effectively subsidizes benefactors of the arts. Beneficiary organizations (all charities) may obtain a "refund" from the Inland Revenue equivalent to income tax at the standard rate in respect of cash donations received under covenants, i.e., promised over a number of years, but the maximum permitted is low. Business sponsorship of the arts is limited by the fact that it is only tax-deductible if "wholly and solely" incurred to promote a business interest (i.e., can be treated as advertising). In other words, the more positive attitude to government spending traced earlier is not yet shared by the Treasury, which has firmly resisted all pressures to allow a special status to the arts. One "guesstimate" is that tax concessions cost the Exchequer £10m in 1980, a small sum, much of which probably relates to heritage arts.

Figures such as the above need to be placed in some perspective if the significance of state patronage is to be assessed. International comparisons sometimes are made on a per capita basis because this allows one to take into account the different size of countries. The difficulty is that such figures are based on incompatible definitions of public expenditure and of the arts. Britain nevertheless appears to rank quite low compared with many countries of western Europe. Central and local government between them spent some £6 per head of population, taking into account the figures discussed above. This covers considerable variations between local authorities, however. By counties (two tiers of authority), it ranged from 496 pence in London and 139 pence in Manchester to an average of 74 pence, with one county falling as low as 6 pence. Another way of looking at the relative importance of arts expenditure is to consider it as a proportion of total public expenditure. In 1981–82, this came to 0.25 percent for central government and 0.45 percent for local government, surprising figures which put a better face on art patronage.

It is even harder to assess what proportion of total spending on the arts from all sources public subsidies provide. Private corporate "patronage" (distinguished from "sponsorship" by the absence of any commercial benefit to the donor) is marginal. Individual benefactors are rare. Britain has fewer millionaires than America, and those alive today that seek to immortalize their name over the portals of an art gallery or concert hall can be counted in tens rather than thousands. Small-subscriber associations such as the National Art Collections Funds and the "friends" of various galleries contribute a little to the acquisition of paintings, but often only as a "pump-priming" exercise to release much larger sums from public funds. The arts, however, live in a mixed economy and consumer spending dominates overall. The Arts Council believes that the public spends £15m a year on first sales of contemporary British art, which is less than grants to exhibitions (most non-selling) and quite overshadows the purchase of works by living painters with public money. Theater, opera, ballet, and concerts, on the other hand, take around £125m at the box office, far more than the grants they receive. It must be remembered, however, that London is especially rich in commercial theaters: provincial theater, regional orchestras, and opera rely heavily on subsidies to cover their operating costs. Survey of a sample of companies in 1980–81 showed that box-office receipts only accounted for 34 percent of income for opera, 35 percent for music, and 49 percent for drama; the remainder came from the Arts Council and local authorities, with only 1 or 2 percent from donations and sponsorship. All three groups are thus extremely vulnerable not only to changes in Arts Council policy but to changes in local government where, on the whole, it was a few major authorities that contributed 10 percent of drama companies' revenue and over 20 percent of orchestras'.

The picture is also disturbing if one looks at the geographical distribution of public subsidies and the implantation of the performing arts throughout the country. A considerable part of the Arts Council's funds are devoted to the great London-based companies. Although it now contributes to a wide and widespread range of activities, it is in no position to support more than a few resident companies elsewhere. Local government expenditure also is heavily concentrated in London. Of the £65m it contributed in 1981–82, £42m is accounted for by the Greater London Council and the London Boroughs. The Metropolitan and District Councils of the six other great English conurbations accounted for a further £10m. Most towns of any size have a theater and some of the larger towns have several, but there are probably only forty resident repertory companies. Opera, ballet, and music are far worse served. There are only five regional symphony orchestras in England (Manchester, Birmingham, Liverpool, Newcastle, and Bournemouth), while the six conurbations can muster only one opera company (Leeds) and one for ballet (Manchester) among them. For these activities, as indeed for the best in drama, the provinces thus depend on occasional tours (including those of the national companies of Scotland and Wales, not mentioned above).

Probably few would disagree with the verdict of a former chairman of the Arts Council that "the public contribution to the arts is pitifully inadequate for a civilized nation." In real terms, the grant to the Arts Council has been stable for some years and is now declining a little. This has led to a crisis. As a result of the "revolution of rising expectations" in earlier, more prosperous times, and because new organizations representing new art forms have emerged, the potential demand for funds has grown enormously. New developments are being stifled. Less open-ended than the question of unmet "needs" is whether established institutions are secure. The evidence is that many are gravely underfinanced, their programs may have to be cut, and some may collapse altogether. Even in the limited perspective of maintaining the status quo, in other words, state funding is now inadequate.

The Role of Government

Although there has been a Minister for the arts since 1975, the status of the post has fluctuated, largely as a result of the different political standing of the men appointed. It has generally been held by junior Ministers of various ranks subordinate to the Secretary of State for Education and Science, though in 1970 it fell for a time to a senior member of the Conservative Party with a longstanding interest in the arts and member of the Cabinet as Paymaster General. Until 1979, however, no separate administrative unit was established and the civil servants concerned remained within the Department of Education. In 1979, responsibility was again entrusted to a Cabinet member, Mr. St. John-Stevas, Chancellor of the Duchy of Lancaster and leader of the Conservative Party in the House of Commons. He had sufficient influence with Mrs. Thatcher to insist on making the Office of Arts and Libraries independent and, psychologically important, moving it to premises of its own in Berkeley Square. In 1981, however, he was dismissed from the government because of his public criticism of the Prime Minister's economic policies and the unit was reintegrated in the Department of Education. When Mrs. Thatcher formed her new government after the 1983 election, the situation changed once more. Lord Gowrie, writer, poet, and former arts dealer, a youthful junior Minister outside the Cabinet, technically subordinate to the Lord President of the Council, combined responsibility for the arts with responsibility for management of the civil service; the Office of Arts and Libraries became a free-standing unit again, though at a less prestigious address. Much of the time, therefore, Britain has had a Minister for the Arts but no separate ministry for the arts, and it was on the Education budget that government expenditure on the arts was carried. The most obvious disadvantage of this arrangement is its relative weakness: a ministry in its own right can negotiate more vigorously with the Treasury and a senior Minister can defend the interests of the arts in the Cabinet. More than that, an autonomous administration symbolizes the status of the arts in government affairs generally. It can be argued, on the other hand, that as things stand there is not really enough work for a proper ministry. This is reflected in the unit's title even now.

The functions of the Minister and his services are to negotiate the annual grant for the arts with the Arts Council on the one hand and the Treasury on the other; to supervise national museums and the British National Library; to coordinate national policy for the arts; and to hold a watching brief with regard to the public libraries of local government. In all this, there are virtually no executive functions because the Office runs nothing itself, and even its supervisory functions are limited given the independence of the Arts Council and the fact that the national museums form autonomous units with their own trustees. Nor is there much scope for policy-making. The only controversial legislation in which the Minister's services have been involved has related to the payment of royalties to authors of books borrowed from local libraries. Its budget of £193m for 1982–83 was spent as follows: Arts Council £85m; eleven national museums in London £50m; British Library £43m; British Film Institute £7m; Museums and Galleries Commission £2.2m; Local Purchase Grant Assistance £1.9m; Crafts Council £1.5m; Government Art Collections £0.1m.

Responsibility for cultural policy in its broadest sense remains dispersed. The Treasury is responsible for taxation policy, the field which offers the greatest possibilities of encouraging private patronage of the arts. The Foreign Office is responsible for the British Council which represents British culture abroad. The Department of the Environment is concerned with historic buildings and itself administers some of those that belong to the state (e.g., Hampton Court Palace with its large collection of paintings). The Scottish Education Department and the Welsh Office carry the grants to the national museums in those countries. Radio and television fall within the purview of the Home Office. Art education in schools and Art Colleges, the direct responsibility of local government, interests the Department of Education. Art organizations may receive subsidies from the British Tourist Board, an independent agency like the Arts Council but funded by the Department of Trade, which is also responsible for the film industry. The Manpower Services Commission, an independent agency funded by the Department of Employment, may support temporary employment in community arts as part of its job creation program. Community arts also may be helped by the urban aid programs administered jointly by central and local governments in certain deprived areas. Local authorities manage their own galleries and may contribute to the cost of theaters and orchestras, but the authorities themselves come under the general supervision of the Department of the Environment. Examples could be multiplied. There have been calls for a much broader based ministry of cultural affairs, even of arts and leisure. The point here is that the Office of Arts and Libraries is somewhat skeletal in character and that Britain still lacks anything like a real

Ministry of Culture. Even if it took in some responsibilities from other departments, the system of intermediaries described below would leave it with few powers to intervene directly in the world of the arts.

In what follows, we concentrate on the Arts Council as the main distributor of state funds to art organizations. It falls into a British tradition of farming out responsibility for certain fields of activity to independent bodies. These "quangos," as they have come to be named (quasi-autonomous non-governmental organizations), are not "public institutions" as a European administrative lawyer would understand that term: they are not agencies of the state in law and do not see themselves as part of a state system. Among them (also redistributors of state funds) we find the British Film Institute, which dates from 1931, and the Crafts Council, not established till 1980. The Independent Broadcasting Authority supervises private sector radio and television companies. Unlike the ministers responsible for the public corporations that run the nationalized industries, including the BBC, the Minister for the Arts has no legal powers of direction, nor has governmental practice led to the less formal intervention on matters of policy that is now common in public enterprise.

The formal powers of government are limited to fixing the annual grant and to the appointment of members of the Council. The powers of Parliament are limited to voting the annual grant: in Britain, unlike other countries, departmental estimates are voted without amendments, however, and usually without debate. Because public money is involved, the activities of the Arts Council may nevertheless be scrutinized by parliamentary committees and its accounts are subject to audit by the Comptroller and Auditor General. The size of the annual grant—the crucial point of interaction between the government and the Council—does not depend on the government's cultural policy, for there is none, but on its reaction to the Council's estimate of needs. Although there will be discussion between the Council and the Office of Arts and Libraries about those estimates, it is the government's attitude to public expenditure that is decisive. The Minister for the Arts has sometimes been able to persuade the Treasury or the Cabinet to be a little more generous than it would otherwise be: Mr. St. John-Stevas, for example, was relatively successful in protecting the arts budget in the early days of the Thatcher government. That his successors could not do this is less a reflection on them, however, than on the ever harsher policy of cutting public expenditure.

It is a firm principle (stated in the government's White Paper on the arts of 1965, for example) that the Arts Council retains full freedom to allocate the money made available to it. Lord Melbourne's dictum as Prime Minister in 1835, "God help the minister that meddles in the arts," still holds good. The Council may spend the grant voted by Parliament almost entirely as it thinks fit, regardless of the estimates upon which it based its original request and the fact that these may have influenced the total agreed. This underlines the principle that Ministers and civil servants should not intervene directly in its activities. Behind-the-scenes "discussions" and "influence" are another matter, but so far as is known they never amount to irresistible pressure. Ministers resist all parliamentary and public pressures to intervene officially (such criticism is usually sparked off by an activity which appears morally distasteful, politically biased, or simply ridiculous to the layman, but is marginal to the main thrust of the Council's subsidies). As a result, they will not take parliamentary responsibility for the way the grant is spent and will not answer questions about individual cases except, perhaps, to pass on information obtained from the Council itself. Since cultural policy in the British system tends to be made through such allocative decisions, this effectively means that the government opts out of the substance of cultural policy. When public outcry forced the Minister to inquire about the impact of a Council decision in 1982 to withdraw its subsidy from a number of organizations in order to make its own ends meet, he was careful to add: "In no way would I wish to intervene in the individual decisions made by the Arts Council within the total sum available to it *nor* [our italics] the strategy which lay behind them." Of course, Ministers may influence the broad direction taken by the Arts Council through the appointment of its members. Moreover, since it depends on the good will of the Minister and his civil servants for negotiations about the size of its annual grant, there is further scope for influence. In a period of financial cuts, as at present, this becomes more important: the government may threaten to subsidize certain activities directly (the national companies, for example) if the Arts Council does not allocate a sufficient proportion of its grant (in government eyes) to them, cutting the Council's grant pro rata. Since this process takes place outside the framework of democratic responsibility through a Minister to Parliament, the Arts Council effectively is "irresponsible." The traditional argument is that this is necessary to protect the freedom of the arts but some now think that "democratization" of one sort or another is necessary.

The secrecy which surrounds such informal contacts is typically British. Private discussions take the place of defined powers, formal procedures, and recorded decisions. This has something to do with the limited role of law in the structure of British administration. There is little belief that the relations between government and other bodies are improved by formalizing their interaction or that organizations work better if their internal procedures are regulated. This makes it hard to trace the influence of Ministers, civil servants, Council members, staff, and other notables in the arts world. It is doubly difficult because of the network of personal relations between the people concerned. The chairman of the Arts Council, for example, invariably has contacts in high places. The chairmen of the great national theater and opera companies are members of the same network. One critic refers to "the incestuous world of opera house politics." Ties of class (including the old school ties of Eton), family and business connections, overlapping committee membership, shared experience around Whitehall, and the circuit of London social life link many of the decision-makers in the arts. Matters can be discussed at opening nights, at dinners, in clubs, or by "old boy" telephone calls. This is also part of the British tradition. Some left-wing observers therefore conclude that whatever the apparent independence of the Arts Council, it forms part of a ruling elite and has the values of that class, so that there is no need to direct it because it goes along acceptable paths anyway. There is some truth in this, but to pursue the argument further would involve discussion of theories of the political system that use the concept of hegemonic ideas to explain power structures.

The fact remains that Ministers and politicians respect the principle of nonintervention. Officials probably have few strong views of their own, in any case, and those they have are hidden in accordance with the principle of civil service anonymity. Just as Britain lacks technocrats in other fields of government, so it lacks cultural technocrats in the ministry responsible for the arts. Ministers, though always well disposed towards the arts, have not pushed their views very far either. The one left-wing Labour Minister who actually wanted to democratize the whole system of art administration, Hugh Jenkins, found himself isolated within his ministry; without real powers, he had no way of influencing an Arts Council hostile to his philosophy. The Arts Council, therefore, is a device to enable the state to encourage the arts without the need for direct intervention on its part, the "arm's-length principle" as it is called, a happy solution for governments which had no cultural policy of their own and saw little political dividend in having one.

This situation may change if a left-wing Labour government committed to a shift from "elitist" to "popular" arts were elected. The example of the Greater London Council under the leadership of "Red" Ken Livingstone pointed the way. The chairman of its arts committee was clear that all art is political and that arts policy must serve a political purpose. He shifted funds towards popular activities (including fireworks displays on the Thames) and community groups, encouraged activities that would bring "ordinary" people to the South Bank's Festival Hall, and threatened to withdraw support from prestige institutions like the National Theatre. Note, however, that, like the Minister for the Arts, he did not attempt to censor GLC clients. Such an attempt *was* made by the previous Conservative leader of the GLC who announced (though later was forced to retract) that he would stop the National Theatre's grant because of indecency in "The Romans in Britain." Other local authorities, some Conservative-led, have made similar threats, sometimes implemented, on political as well as moral grounds. A substantial (though decreasing) part of the Arts Council's resources may go to traditionalist art forms, thus indirectly supporting the established socio-economic order, but it does protect art organizations against the direct political censorship that sometimes is found in other countries of Europe.

There are fields, of course, in which the government has to make its own decision. The protracted debate about the building of the National Theatre was an example. Direct intervention also occurred when large sums were needed to save privately owned masterpieces from sale abroad and supplementary budgets had to be presented to Parliament. In general, however, decision-making is farmed out. While encouragement of the living arts is mainly left to the Arts Council, many other bodies are concerned with the preservation of the nation's cultural heritage. The British Museum, National Gallery, Tate Gallery, and now the Victoria and Albert Museum have their own boards of management and are virtually autonomous. The V. & A., earlier administered on a loose rein through the Department of Education, has a fund which helps local authorities purchase important works for their own galleries. The Commission on Museums and Galleries advises the government on the placement of art works accepted by the Treasury in lieu of death duties. The Committee on the Export of Works of Art decides whether privately owned masterpieces may be sold abroad. A recently established National Heritage Fund, independently administered, can use its funds to save private collections for the nation. Other examples could be quoted. Taken together, they form a complex network of intermediaries between the state and the arts.

The Arts Council

The chairman and members of the Arts Council—approximately twenty—are appointed for a fixed term by the Minister for the Arts. Members are chosen for their personal standing in public life or the arts, not as nominees of other organizations, though it has been custom to include someone active in local government and now a member of an ethnic minority. Selection is by the same mysterious process which characterizes appointment to most committees in Britain: individuals may be known personally to the Minister or his advisers, or known by repute, or their names may have been mentioned by someone else at an appropriate moment. Random selection of a group of people to pursue their own judgment in some field of public life is very much part of the British tradition. This introduces an element of chance into policy-making but such people are also likely to show greater independence of mind than political appointees or representatives of specified interests, a freedom further enlarged by the very broad definition of the Arts Council's functions in its charter.

The chairman has always been someone who has occupied important positions in public life. Until recently, there was no suggestion that such appointments served a political purpose, though personal contacts with politicians explain most choices. Lord Goodman, for example, was Harold Wilson's solicitor and confidant. The immediate past chairman, Sir Kenneth Robinson, another Labour appointee, had been Minister of Health in a previous Labour government. A change seems to have occurred under Mrs. Thatcher, whose famous "is he one of us?" has politicized top appointments in many fields. The Minister for the Arts did not reappoint Richard Hoggart to the Council at the end of his first term because "No. 10 doesn't like him," although his fellow councillors had elected him vice-chairman only two years previously and he could therefore have expected a second Council term. Her personal selection for chairman in 1983 was Sir William Rees-Mogg, a traditional "establishment" figure (editor of *The Times* from 1968 to 1981, vice-chairman of the BBC, and a director of General Electric) but also an outspoken supporter of her policies.

There is a staff of several hundred persons, though this includes all staff levels, not just administrators. At its head stands the Secretary General. When Sir Roy Shaw, whose earlier career was as a professor of adult education, retired in 1983, Rees-Mogg imposed Luke Rittner on a reluctant Council and a very hostile staff. A student of drama and stage management, he became director of the Bath Festival, then first director of the Association for Business Sponsorship of the Arts (whose revenue he had increased from £½m to £8m). At thirty-five, he was just the sort of dynamic young man with free enterprise contacts that suited the Thatcher era. His deputy had been a civil servant in the Department of Education and the Treasury before joining the Council in 1979.

The Council is served by a system of specialized committees for art, drama, music, dance, art films, literature, housing the arts, regional affairs (which include art centers, festivals, community arts, and touring groups), and training, some with more specialized sub-committees. Subject to the Council, they determine policy within their fields and make allocative decisions. This brings a large number of additional personalities into the decision-making process. Though the Council advertises its interest in receiving nominations, the selection of members is privately done, largely by committee chairmen and senior officials. Within the Arts Council of Great Britain, there are largely autonomous organizations for Scotland and Wales, with their own Councils, offices, and staff in Edinburgh and Cardiff. Blocks of money are allocated to the Councils for the two countries and the Arts Council of Great Britain takes direct responsibility for clients in England. This reflects arrangements in British government, where there are special Ministries for Scotland and Wales while English affairs are managed by the whole range of UK ministries.

The Arts Council's main function, measured in financial terms, is the allocation of grants to other bodies. Some 95 percent of its income is redistributed. It manages very little itself: the Hayward and Serpentine galleries, the Wigmore Concert Hall, and an arts bookshop, all in London, and some touring exhibitions. Much staff time is spent, however, in providing support services for other organizations, advice on marketing to theaters, for example. There are publications, press and research sections, and a useful library.

Recently, an education liaison officer has been appointed. The Arts Council is thus a facilitator of cultural activities rather than a provider.

The estimate of expenditure for the financial year 1983–84 assumed that the Arts Council would receive £92m. Of this, it passed £11.1m to Scotland and £6.5m to Wales. The rest was to be divided as follows: the national companies £25.1m; drama £11.8m; music £6.1m; art and film £3.7m; dance £2.8m; literature £0.9m; touring £7.1m; arts centers and community projects £1.1m; housing the arts £1.1m; training and education £0.7m; regional arts associations £10.4m; administration £4m. The list of subsidies awarded each year includes more than a thousand items. The four great London-based institutions, the "national" companies (a misleading term since these are not public institutions as the term would be understood elsewhere in Europe) which still take an important share, are the English National Opera, the Royal Opera and Ballet, the National Theatre, and the Royal Shakespeare Theatre. Quite a number of other organizations receive substantial support: among those with more than £250,000 in 1982–83 were the London Festival Ballet and the Ballet Rambert, the Kent and Glyndebourne Opera, the Manchester Hallé and Liverpool Royal Philharmonic Orchestras, and the Bristol Old Vic and Sheffield Crucible Theatres. Numerically, however, the list was dominated by relatively small grants. Some were operating subsidies for art galleries, performing companies, art centers, literary magazines, and so on; others were contributions to the cost of specified activities such as exhibitions, tours, festivals, and on-off publications. Something like 165 drama, 75 music, and 40 dance groups obtained grants. The cost of purchasing works of art for display in public places was shared with several local authorities, hospitals, and universities. "Artists in residence" were employed for a year in a few towns and educational institutions. Bursaries were awarded to writers, actors, and musicians and training grants given to art administrators and technicians, but grants are not otherwise made to individuals. The list is bewildering in its range.

A rough analysis of the 1981–82 accounts for England shows that £62m was distributed as follows: £22m (35 percent) to the four national companies; £13m (21 percent) in 23 grants over £250,000; £6m (11 percent) in 93 grants over £100,000; £7m (11 percent) in 93 grants over £10,000; £5m (8 percent) divided among 320 items plus bursaries to individuals; £9m (14 percent) to the regional arts associations which, of course, redivided it into a mass of small grants. The large number of small grants (quite a few less than £1,000) involved a considerable burden of work. Although it would be administratively easier to concentrate on major clients, this spread ensures variety and experimentation. It remains questionable, nevertheless, whether so much should be decided in London and whether it would not be administratively rational, as well as politically desirable, to decentralize some of these decisions. A move in this direction is the increasing sums allocated to the twelve Regional Arts Associations which cover the country since the 1960s: independent bodies with their own committees (on which local authorities are represented) and their own staff, each with a somewhat different constitution. Decentralization is now a topic of debate, but there are limits. Regional associations, for example, would be reluctant to fund the overhead costs of touring companies which only visit them occasionally. If made responsible for funding a regional orchestra or major provincial theater, they might find this an embarrassingly large proportion of their total budget. There is also the possibility of political intervention in decision-making by local councillors who sit on their executive committees and are subject to greater pressures by their electorate than appointed notables meeting in London.

The Arts Council divides its annual budget among the sectors listed above, leaving many individual decisions to its committees. Although the "legitimation" of committee members is sometimes queried, it is hard to see how the committees could be "democratized." Whom should they represent: client institutions, those employed in the arts (e.g., a musicians' union), associations to which supporters of the arts belong or the public at large (perhaps through Parliament or local councils)? How could they be elected? Appointment of a cross-section of persons interested in the arts avoids this difficulty, but it does mean that the funding of a particular activity may depend on the chance balance of tastes in a particular committee. The assessment of individual applications seems often to have depended on impressionistic judgments. This accords with the British style of administration which avoids formalized procedures wherever possible. It is difficult to formulate criteria in fields where value judgments predominate and difficult to weigh the various elements now taken into account, such as artistic quality, regional spread, box-office demand, financial support from other sources, and educational benefit.

The secrecy of the decision-making process also has been subject to criticism. Applicants are not present during committee discussions and until recently were informed of the outcome by sketchy explanations rather than full minutes. Some felt that their case had not been properly considered and occasionally suspected bias, a situation aggravated by the absence of appeal procedures. Growing unease about the system came to a head a few years ago when the Arts Council was forced to end its support of forty organizations in order to balance its budget. The resulting outcry had its effect. Noting in its annual report that public goodwill depended on greater openness, the Council began to explain its decisions more fully and to publish policy papers on issues affecting the arts for public discussion. This fitted into growing demands for more "open government" in Britain.

In their internal affairs, clients remain independent of the Arts Council, just as the Arts Council remains independent of the government. The major national companies receive subsidies based on their overall operating needs on the one hand, on what the Council thinks it can afford on the other, with no attempt to control their programs. The same applies to other organizations, which determine their own policies and receive grants in response to their own proposals. They may plan with the reaction of the Arts Council in mind, and in consultation with its officers, but in that they are doing no more than when they try to anticipate box-office demand. In any case, the Council generally funds only part of their costs and other sources of subsidy exist: the regional associations, local authorities, the job creation and urban aid programs, foundations, private enterprise. Pluralism of funding has, indeed, become a major political theme, with a recent parliamentary committee advocating more from local government and Thatcherite Conservatives urging more business sponsorship. The limiting factor, of course, is the state of the economy.

Freedom of the arts also is ensured by the Arts Council's long refusal to have a cultural policy of its own, preferring to be "guided by events." In the first decade of its life, it avoided an "active" role altogether and simply responded to good applications (the word "response" was central to its vocabulary). It divided its budget between cultural sectors less in accordance with its own view of their needs than by trying to balance the claims made on it. Its committees tended to take each application separately, judging it largely on artistic merit. Applications were not matched against a predetermined plan, nor even against any clear view of the direction in which the arts should go. This is the tradition of British pragmatism, less favorably described as "muddling through."

The Council has moved to a more positive approach in recent years, developing clearer ideas about the priorities against which to assess applications and encouraging the sort of applications it wishes to see. In comparison with its earlier history, it could be said to have become more interventionist. By comparison with a real planning agency, however, it remains remarkably noninterventionist. It does not specify in advance, except in broad categories, the particular activities it will fund and it does not direct its clients in their management of those activities.

Although artistic criteria are still important, there has been a change of approach. An immediate cause has been financial: the public expenditure cuts of the Thatcher government. In previous decades, new developments could be funded through the regular increase in its grant; now they can only be funded if something else is cut. This makes it much harder to "muddle through" and more thought has to be given to priorities. At the same time, past success in encouraging the arts has added to the Council's problems because the number of potential clients has multiplied: the "revolution of rising expectations" born in the years of financial optimism has led to demands far beyond its resources. The cake has to be divided among more claimants, many of which have also become better organized as pressure groups. All administrations face new procedural problems in a period of financial restraint, and existing methods of allocating money are bound to be increasingly challenged everywhere as the number of unsatisfied claims rises.

Other developments also explain the Council's greater concern with priorities. Growing public discussion of cultural policy and a changing climate of ideas have influenced its thinking. New priorities can be related to wider political debates and to that extent have a "political" dimension. The argument about the balance of expenditure between prestige institutions in London and activities elsewhere is closely related to wider concerns about the distribution of wealth between capital and provinces. Arts Council expenditure on the great nationals dropped from 55 percent of its budget in early days to around 30 percent now simply as a result of its increasing grant, but the positive emphasis on regional development and the encouragement of tours is relatively new. Wider demands for political decentralization are reflected in increased financial support of the regional arts associations and current talk of a new "partnership." These associations also fit into wider demands for public participation in government: they bring more local people into decision-making; they are closer to client organizations and facilitate the pressure-group politics which is part of the democratic process. Support for ethnic art reflects a growing awareness of the problems of race in Britain and marks a shift from the previous philosophy of absorbing immigrants into the British way of life to a belief that they should be encouraged to maintain their own cultural identity. Growing support of community arts similarly reflects national concerns: the Council now speaks of encouraging artists who contribute to the rehabilitation of depressed inner-city areas, for example. An even newer interest in educational activities must be seen against the background of national worries about youth. Community and ethnic arts have also been helped by the emergence of vocal pressure groups. In a general way, moreover, the background of those actively involved in cultural affairs at the grassroots level has changed. A growing number are paid, full-time professionals who see themselves as rooted in the working class. They differ from the unremunerated elites which tend to fill the decision-making levels of the Arts Council and from the middle-class people who traditionally ran local art activities on a voluntary basis. To that extent, social change in Britain has not been without influence on cultural policy.

At the same time, a certain shift in the Council's self-perception of its role may be noticed. Although it liked to describe itself until recently as essentially a grant-making body, there is a growing interest in questions that fall outside its immediate control, i.e., cannot be handled by any strategy it may devise itself but are matters of national policy. It has organized debate and published reports on such topics as education in art, youth and the arts, community arts and the inner city, arts and tourism. To that extent, it is trying to influence the climate of ideas in fields in which it will play only a small funding role.

Though innovations are significant as indicators of change, they still tend to be at the margin of expenditure and have not reduced support for the traditional arts. The Arts Council has simply widened its scope. It has not promulgated an official doctrine about what forms of cultural activity are socially desirable. It has drawn up no "plan" in which these forms have their balanced place. There is no blueprint "cultural map" of Britain in its offices. It reacts to grant applications, judging these in the light of values that are themselves a reaction to public debate. This, of course, may not be the view of dissatisfied applicants who periodically accuse the Council of cultural bias. Any system of allocating scarce resources is bound to leave some groups unsatisfied and these may well explain their rejection by conspiracy theories. As critics are now found on the right and on the left of the political spectrum, just as they have always been found on the traditional and modern ends of the aesthetic spectrum, it seems clear that policy remains eclectic.

Crisis in the 1980s

Like many other Western countries, Britain is now facing an "end of government growth," the joint product of economic recession and ruling ideologies. In times of expansion, new developments could be financed out of new money. That flexibility has gone. New developments mean a cut in subsidies to existing clients, many of whom have ongoing commitments. Even when the Arts Council only covers part of their costs, a small margin may be crucial to survival. Attempts to meet the challenge of change while protecting established institutions havc aroused more opposition to the Council in the last few years than it met over the 25 years of its earlier life.

For the financial year 1982–83, the Arts Council received an increase over its previous year's grant that did not quite match the rate of inflation. To avoid sharing out misery, spreading its subsidies so thinly that many funded clients would nevertheless be at risk because their costs were rising faster than the general price index, and to give a little extra to those which had shown particular vitality, it decided to eliminate some clients altogether. Forty organizations lost their grant, some fringe activities but including well-established institutions like the National Youth Theatre and Orchestra (saved by sponsorship through an oil company) and the New Shakespeare's open-air program in London. The £1m saved this way went to support regional orchestras, northern repertory theaters, and touring dance companies for which there is a growing audience. The anger of the losers was intensified by the absence of prior warning or possibility of appeal. It was suspected that off-the-cuff comments by one or two prejudiced committee members were responsible for chopping the D'Oyly Carte Gilbert and Sullivan operas (though in justification it could be said that productions had become tired and were "commercial theater" anyway). Protests were orchestrated. The Arts Council promised that its decision-making process would be more open in the future, though it was hard to see, even then, that any system of rationing which involved cuts could avoid such conflict.

There were subsequent reports that the Arts Council was considering more withdrawals. Among those thought in danger were two smaller London theaters, nine provincial theaters, and five touring companies. A senior officer explained that "in the economic straits imposed by the government, the Arts Council would rather support fewer companies than many at subsistence level.'' A phrase much used was that ''one should not spread the jam so thinly that no sandwich tastes good.'' For 1982–83, however, the Arts Council compromised. Given its rejection of a ''thin jam'' policy, it could not make equal reductions all round. On the other hand, it now declared that a further client-dropping exercise really needed a more radical change in priorities than could be undertaken on the spur of the moment—a not unexpected reaction to earlier waves of protest. It economized, instead, by reducing its own activities, e.g., touring exhibitions and the purchase of contemporary art. A ''longer-term strategic view'' of its commitments was promised.

In submitting the Council's estimate of needs for 1983–84, the chairman wrote to the Minister that it represented the sum required to obtain the best use of existing resources by those clients in whom the Council had already invested. ''Not an expansionist exercise,'' it nevertheless came to £111m, a considerable increase over the previous year's grant of £85m, indicating the extent to which clients had already been forced into damaging cutbacks. He stressed the desirability of raising standards in provincial theater companies and encouraging the growing interest in dance; the need to help regional arts associations reach new audiences in the socially disadvantaged inner cities; the case for encouraging ethnic arts. Realizing that the figure was unrealistic, however, the Council had undertaken a second exercise to identify a minimum level of funding—£98m—required to ensure the survival of established clients, some of whom had accumulated dangerous deficits. The chairman spelt out that anything less would force the Council to withdraw the entire grant from one of the great national companies; or decimate the ranks of the next largest clients—regional orchestras, major repertory theaters, and dance companies; or keep all clients on short rations and see who collapsed. This was no rethinking of priorities, more an attempt to blackmail the government into maintaining the status quo.

Meanwhile, the Thatcher government was screwing down public expenditure ever tighter and seeking marginal savings in every quarter. Its response was to offer £92m, an increase of 7 percent over the previous year, about the expected rate of inflation, and the Arts Council decided once more that it would not drop any clients. A short time later, as part of yet another round of public expenditure cuts, the government reduced its original offer by 1 percent. This was denounced by the chairman, only recently appointed as a favorite of Mrs. Thatcher, as an unprecedented breach of faith, doubly embarrassing because the Arts Council had already committed the full £92m and had informed its clients of their allocation. It had no choice but to pass on the cut on an equal basis to all, thereby breaking its own word to its clients. Financial pressures thus make it hard to do anything but continue muddling through—perhaps until bankruptcy breaks the mold. Crisis is sometimes thought to be conducive to a revaluation of priorities, but it is just as likely to harden existing patterns as established institutions struggle for survival.

If the Arts Council *is* really feeling its way towards a ''strategy,'' applicants have a right to know what its priorities are, as, indeed, does the public. Until recently, officers seem to have justified their recommendations to committees by ''the drift of Council opinion over a period,'' but 1983 saw some clarification. When the Council invited its clients to submit their estimates for 1984–85, so that it could prepare its own submission to government, it sent them an extensive list of criteria against which they would be assessed. Since it did not explain how these criteria would be weighed against each other, however, it cannot be said that it had really defined priorities (since that requires some rank-ordering of criteria).

How is artistic quality to be assessed and how can very different types of activity be ranked in terms of artistic merit? How is this to be balanced against other criteria listed, e.g., the fullest practicable use of facilities and the widest provision of arts to the community; education policy in relation to the artistic programs; the employment and other opportunities extended to ethnic minority groups; box office and attendance returns; the balance between London and other regions—plus overall value for money; success in raising local authority support and other income; efficiency in the use of available resources; urgency of financial problems? How can these be evaluated and what weight should attach to each? If one believes that a body dispensing large sums of public money should be publicly responsible, the continued ambiguity of principles, the informality of their application, and the secrecy in which business is conducted make it impossible to monitor the decision-making process effectively. While procedure could be made more transparent, there is no way a policy-making body could set out clear rules, capable of "objective" application to individual cases. Does that mean such decisions must be left to impressionistic judgments by appointed committees which represent no one? While judgment of artistic merit may well be entrusted to persons experienced in the arts, so long as they include a spread of aesthetic schools, some of the other criteria mentioned above are essentially "political" in character. It is on those grounds that the argument for democratizing committees becomes important.

It becomes even more important as regards the policy-makers at the top of the Arts Council. Although arguments for democratization are sometimes made in procedural terms (democracy is a "good thing" in itself), what usually underlies them is a concern with matters of substance, notably with "who gets what." Most of those who challenge the present organization really want a shift in funding from what they describe as elitist art to more popular forms. One's views about the power structure are likely to be colored by one's view about the purpose art should serve. Reform thus seems unlikely unless a left-wing Labour government comes to power. Proposals that the Arts Council should be made more responsible (to government, Parliament, interest groups, or public) remain on the agenda, however, and are likely to be further debated as it becomes ever harder for it "to foster the best in the arts" because of growing disagreement about what is best and for whom.

Debate about the nature of art and its social purpose is sharpening. This is partly because the growing strength of community arts coincides, almost fortuitously, with a period of scarce resources, so that their claim for a larger share of the existing cake depends on attacking traditional art forms. Equally important, however, is the growing critique of bourgeois art by "marxisant" intellectuals, reflected in a literature (including an Open University course) previously scarce in Britain—and forcing traditionalists to reply. In the Art Council's view there is no such thing as "class art" and its task is to make "the best" available to "the most"—best being defined in artistic terms rather than by reference to popular taste (which it is its duty to raise) or purposes other than appreciation of the arts. Even its support of ethnic and community arts is predicated on this. Though its supporters might not like the description, this is essentially a "highbrow" view. Some of its opponents are simply populists who want to bring the arts to groups outside charmed circles of the middle-class at levels they can enjoy, even if some sacrifice of standards is the result. They want artists to work in and with the community (murals, street theater, participatory events, workshops). Others, though their activities are very similar in form, have a socio-political orientation. Community art is seen as a way of helping the underdogs of society to critical awareness, group identity, and political action. Yet others are educationalists and see the arts as a means to personality development. It is because the Arts Council is the major funder of the arts in Britain that advocates of community arts see it necessary to set their activities against more traditional forms. They would be more appropriately funded on budgets related to education, social work, and inner-city rehabilitation, however, as indeed they sometimes are. Perhaps the Arts Council should restrict itself to the role for which it was established, thus avoiding a confusion of purpose which is bound to increase the difficulties of policy-making. If there were any serious attempt to divert resources from the great national companies to less prestigious activities, moreover, governments might well reduce its grant and fund those companies directly. If too much is spent on art with a political content, it is hard to see a Conservative government maintaining the grant at its present scale. In the longer run, some other ways of funding community arts on an adequate scale should be found, perhaps through a parallel agency.

We have touched on other questions requiring a government solution. One agenda item is a better spread of cultural facilities throughout the country. Despite a proud tradition of local government, policy-making in Britain is as dominated by London as it is said to be by Paris in France. Prestige institutions are concentrated in London and so, for example, are the commercial galleries that sell contemporary art. History again: unlike Germany, England has not inherited a number of cultural capitals from days of princely rule. The difference between what is available in the depressed north and the prosperous south-east is becoming more apparent as the structure of the economy changes. The demand is for some redress of balance. This cannot be achieved by a readjustment of Arts Council spending alone, nor through the regional arts associations. The parliamentary committee that reported in 1982 on the funding of the arts proposed that local authorities should have a duty to support the arts, and should assume the major responsibility for theaters, orchestras, opera, and dance companies in their area. Since the Thatcher government is cutting local government expenditure, this seems wishful thinking. Nor can one be sure that local politicians would be reliable trustees of this role. Nevertheless, any major expansion of cultural activities in the provinces is unlikely without some real decentralization of power.

Another balance that needs redressing is between public and private patronage of the arts. There is no way that box-office receipts can meet the costs of national opera, regional orchestras, or provincial theaters. Community projects, for their part, cannot charge at all if they are to attract the socially underprivileged hitherto strangers to the arts. So long as the economy is stagnant and government ideologically committed to limiting public expenditure, other sources of money need to be tapped. Not surprisingly, the Conservative Party pins great hope on organizations such as the Association for Business Sponsorship of the Arts. Business support is growing and has saved some institutions but remains marginal to total needs. If private patronage—individual and corporate—is to expand seriously, more is required of government than kind words. Financial contributions to the arts must be tax-deductible, another recommendation of the parliamentary committee, and cultural activities should be relieved of turnover tax. Although the Treasury will not forgo these sources of revenue in the present climate, in the longer run tax relief, which does not require a positive spending decision by government, is a relatively painless way of encouraging the arts. Britain has much to learn from other countries in this respect.

Finally, there is the "machinery of government" issue. At the national level, responsibility for cultural affairs is dispersed among too many ministries. This weakens the voice of the arts in the scramble for funds and prevents government from taking a broad view of the nation's cultural health. Since 1945, there has been an almost continuous reorganization of departments, but all that has been achieved in the cultural field is the Office of Arts and Libraries—with limited functions, a skeletal organization, a relatively small budget and, for most of the time, sub-ministry status. Despite recommendations by the parliamentary committee that a Ministry of Arts, Heritage and Tourism should be established (and proposals by the Labour Party, for example, for a Ministry of Arts and Leisure), it is hard to predict such a reform. It would be administratively sensible, but the idea of a Ministry of Culture, however named, is as alien to British traditions as that of a Ministry of Justice. It still raises fears of excessive government intervention in matters it should not seek to determine.

Arguably, however, the time has come for a more positive approach to planning the arts if resources are to be used rationally and new needs met. The parliamentary committee believed that the ministry it envisaged should cooperate with local authorities in formulating a twenty-year program to improve the distribution of cultural facilities. One hopes that such planning, were it to come about, would concentrate on finance and leave the arts themselves, the programs on offer for example, to client organizations. The present system of response to initiatives encourages diversity and allows for experimentation. In the last resort, it is also a guarantee of freedom. There is always the danger that a planning machine will gather its own momentum, expand its role, and stifle vitality at the grass-roots; the danger, too, that it will end in censorship—a not uncommon feature of state intervention in other countries.

The parliamentary committee's call for a substantial increase in public expenditure on the arts as a matter of urgency is bound to fall on deaf ears at present. Can one hope for a more positive commitment from future governments? The years 1945 and 1965 were turning points in state funding. The Prime Ministers of the time, Clement Attlee and Harold Wilson, had no personal enthusiasm for the arts, however, any more than Margaret Thatcher is hostile to them. What matters in the end is government attitudes to public expenditure generally. One can but hope that Thatcherism is a brief interlude in this respect.

Storm Signals 1983

The analyst of current affairs is always likely to be overtaken by events before his account is read, but especially in turbulent policy times like the present. Developments towards the end of 1983 not only left the future uncertain (it is always that), but suggested that the next years would see a major shift in the way public subsidies are allocated, a marked change in the cultural map of Britain, and deepening crisis for the arts.

The backdrop was an expected 5 percent increase in the Arts Council's grant for 1984–85, not a drastic cut for a government vigorously pruning expenditure in all fields, but a drop in real income when adjusted for inflation nevertheless. Total available funding from central and local governments was unlikely to rise over the next few years.

In October 1983, members of the Arts Council engaged in a fundamental rethinking of policy at a two-day meeting in Yorkshire. They were stimulated, no doubt, by financial pressures, but also by the growing realization that one could not go on muddling through as in previous years—brought to a head by the appointment of a new, strong-willed chairman and a dynamic new Secretary General. A press release in November announced "a major review of policies and the allocation of subsidies which will provide the basis for a development strategy and more flexible modes of operation better suited to the demands of the 1980s and beyond." A wide consultation exercise was to take place and existing grants were to be reviewed immediately; the Council would determine its development strategy (the word "plan" still was avoided) early in 1984; and consequent decisions on funding would take effect from 1985.

The Council explained that over recent years it had been "locked in to an increasingly restrictive framework"—its commitments to established clients took up its entire grant, leaving it no room for maneuver. If money were to be found for new developments, in other words, there would have to be matching cuts in current grants. Putting a good face on this, Luke Rittner stressed the positive side: "The arts, like seeds, need room to grow if they are to blossom. Some of the seeds we have nurtured over the years are bursting to grow but are being held back by lack of nourishment. The strategy will help thin out the seed-bed to give more room for them to develop and for new seeds to be planted."

It was not clear what the criteria for weeding out would be. The only indication of the Council's priorities was its statement that "in developing its strategy, it will continue to have regard for the maintenance of the highest standards throughout the arts; to the importance of providing adequately for the new and developmental as well as the established; and, of course, to the geographical spread of arts provisions." It was hard to tell whether the ordering of these considerations was significant, but Sir William Rees-Mogg is a Conservative believer in "the best," not a Socialist advocate of the popular or socially relevant. He declared: "We have got ourselves in a position where we are not able to respond to excellence." Should a national strategy for the arts rank-order grant applicants according to their artistic standards? Some provincial theaters may fall below "the highest" standards, but the geographical distribution of facilities is just as important if the arts are to be accessible throughout the country. The Arts Council can only free resources on any scale by withdrawing its support from a number of major institutions as well as a host of smaller ones. Unless these can find other sources of revenue, an unlikely prospect for all but a few in the present economic climate, a fair number seem likely to close sooner or later. "Thinning out the seed-bed" may thus leave parts of the garden without any large blossoms at all.

All client organizations were asked to indicate how they would respond, both "artistically" and "structurally," to a substantial increase or decrease in public funding from all sources. Since the Council had hardly set out clear-cut tests for the assessment of their replies, they were left far more confused than in the past. Whether the promised strategy would define and rank-order criteria more clearly remained to be seen. It was also too early to tell if the strategy would consist simply of priorities against which applications are judged (thus still in the tradition of response to initiatives) or come to resemble a plan, with the Arts Council indicating in some detail what activities it intends to fund and where.

The Merseyside Regional Arts Association undertook a similar exercise, albeit on the much smaller scale of its own budget, in order to establish a development fund for new activities. Experience showed how difficult it is to work out priorities for the future and seriously assess the performance of existing clients at the same time. That process was made doubly difficult by the political pressures brought to bear as threatened clients mobilized their lobbies. Since the Arts Council's review was to threaten better known and better connected institutions, it could hardly avoid a political storm. The objectivity of its assessment techniques was also likely to be questioned, so that both its "technical" capacity and its democratic legitimacy would be challenged even more loudly than before.

The Prime Minister, apparently appalled by the mounting deficits of the Royal Opera House and the Royal Shakespeare Company, doubtless hoping that wasteful expenditure would be uncovered, instigated efficiency reviews of the two companies. Clive Priestley, recently retired head of the efficiency review teams in the civil service (the "Rayner scrutinies," named after the managing director of Marks and Spencer who served Mrs. Thatcher as adviser on management in government), produced two lengthy reports. They contained many managerial recommendations which were well received by the companies whose standard of performance he praised highly. Priestley found that the Arts Council had failed to assess their cost structures in sufficient depth, partly because it lacked the requisite analytical techniques—a significant criticism given the Council's forthcoming fundamental reassessment of all its clients. More important, he suggested that the viability of the two companies should be assured by larger subsidies and that government should take direct responsibility for their funding.

Others have made the same suggestion in respect of all the great national companies. The consequence for the Arts Council would be a cut in its own grant, but it would be freed from a responsibility it cannot meet as costs escalate and from the counter-accusation that it already puts too large a share of its resources into a few elitist activities. The changes in local government structure discussed below also strengthened the case for direct funding. This would certainly be a major departure from the "arm's length" tradition of state patronage and bring the companies into direct contact with civil servants in the determination of their budgets. It would also mean ministerial responsibility to Parliament, making it much harder for the Minister for the Arts to resist pressure to intervene if programs aroused strong criticism. Remembering the interventions of the Greater London Council in recent years, it was the National Theatre which was hostile to such a move, while the others seemed more favorable.

A coincidental development was the Government's announcement that it would introduce legislation abolishing the Greater London Council and the six Metropolitan Councils (the upper-tier authorities in the major conurbations) as of 1986. These politically motivated reforms were bound to add to the troubles facing the arts over the next years.

In a White Paper of October 1983, the Government made some proposals for the transfer of County functions. The British Museum and the Victoria and Albert Museum would be invited to administer the Horniman, Jeffreye, and Kenwood Museums in London; the Tate Gallery to take over Liverpool's Walker and Newcastle's Laing Galleries. In the performing arts, additional government funds (presumably earmarked for the first time) would be made available to the Arts Council for a small number of organizations "of national and international standing" which it already supported together with the Counties: the National Theatre, National Opera Company, London Festival Ballet, and London Orchestral Concert Board (which redistributes funds to London's orchestras), the Hallé Orchestra and Royal Exchange Theatre in Manchester, the Royal Liverpool Philharmonic Society, the Birmingham Symphony Orchestra, and Opera North in Leeds. An independent board of management answerable to the Arts Council would take over the South Bank Complex (the GLC operated the Royal Festival Hall and associated concert halls, and acted as landlord to the National Theatre, the National Film Theatre, and the Hayward Gallery). As regards the rest, the government looked to the District Councils to take over most of the Counties' responsibilities in the arts, possibly through voluntary cooperation among several authorities and, for smaller items, through the Regional Arts Associations. The White Paper declared that the liabilities assumed by the Districts would rank for block grant, the all-purpose grants central government makes to local authorities.

These were hasty proposals, off-the-cuff solutions to the unpremeditated consequences of a political vendetta against the Counties. How well could the Tate administer Liverpool's gallery, 200 miles away and with masterpieces that fall outside the orbit of its own collection? How effective are local authority consortia where no one authority feels special responsibility for an institution? Even if block grants were increased to allow for new responsibilities, they are not earmarked for particular activities: would local authorities, currently obliged to cut social services through government-imposed limits on expenditure, be willing to spend their money on new commitments in the arts?

A considerable number of organizations were, in fact, involved. In Liverpool, to take only one example, the County managed the Empire Theatre, the only auditorium suitable for opera and ballet on tour, and it contributed to the city's two repertory theaters as well as the Royal Philharmonic. The Greater London Council contributed some £9m in 1981–82 to more than 400 organizations, ranging from the National Theatre, Sadler's Wells Ballet, and the London Dance Company to the open-air theater in Regent's Park, arts centers, and community and ethnic arts. It was hard to believe that the hard-pressed London Boroughs could pick up all these tabs. Coupled with the Arts Council's threatened reassessment of clients, the impending reform of local government was likely to place many established companies in double jeopardy and could lead to a spate of closures. Political opposition mounted, however. The Conservative spokesman for the arts on the GLC resigned to join the campaign against government policy, sharing a platform with the left-wing chairman of the GLC's arts committee. Similar common fronts between the parties emerged in the Metropolitan Counties. The arts were thus, for the first time, being dragged into a primarily political debate.

Storm Unabated 1986

Statistics are notoriously liable to partisan interpretation and politicians find ways of presenting figures to show themselves in a favorable light. Whatever gloss the Thatcher government puts on state support of the arts, however, it has not kept up with rising costs in recent years. Changes in local government brought further pressure on financing of the arts, largely through the abolition of the most important funding authorities but also through government-imposed restrictions on local expenditure generally. The Thatcher government's predeliction for privatization is reflected in the emphasis it places on business sponsorship as a substitute, and the Arts Council's Conservative chairman now plugs this theme also. Business sponsorship, estimated at £17m for 1985/86, is certainly growing, aided by a modest government scheme to match certain payments. The Inland Revenue's rule that tax-deductible sponsorship must be commercially justified, i.e., a public relations exercise, still means that directors cannot use company funds as simple patronage of the arts. Business thus tends to support the safe and popular, preferably blockbuster exhibitions in London and performances which enhance the corporate image. Though this has saved some activities, it is little help to the less prestigious. The brightest event in recent years has been John Paul Getty's promised gift of £50m, starting with £20m to the National Gallery, seven times the government's annual purchase grant: but there are few such American fortunes in Britain.

Overshadowing the last two years was the impact of the abolition of the Greater London Council and the six Metropolitan Counties in 1986. The government's original intention was that the lower-tier Districts should take over most County functions. Individually too small, collectively unable to agree, with severe financial problems of their own, and with priorities in housing and social services, they finally offered spotty support to the arts, a fraction of their predecessors'. Abolition raised another sort of problem in addition to funding, a legal and organizational one: what to do with the institutions managed directly by the defunct authorities.

The GLC's South Bank complex, as originally proposed, was vested in the Arts Council, which thus became responsible for a cultural center of international standing on the bank of the Thames. The Council's Deputy Secretary General was appointed director and a board was named, with provision that the whole might eventually form an independent trust. Elsewhere the situation was less easily resolved, notably in Merseyside. The government discovered belatedly, for there was no mention of it in the original White Paper, that the County Council possessed an important museum and was involved in the ambitious development of a further maritime museum as part of Liverpool's dockland regeneration strategy. Amalgamated with the equally important Walker Art Gallery, this complex became a national trustee museum (i.e., funded directly by Parliament and staffed by civil servants, though with an independent board of trustees to manage its affairs)—the only national museum in Britain outside the three national capitals of London, Edinburgh, and Cardiff. Even so, it left in limbo Croxteth Hall, previously attached to the County museum. The Office of Arts and Libraries could not be shaken from its bureaucratic ruling that this large country house with its vast parkland, an important tourist asset now totally surrounded by urban development, did not fall within its terms of reference and so could not form part of a complex funded through its parliamentary vote. The example is quoted as another illustration of the anarchic consequences of Mrs. Thatcher's political decision to eliminate Metropolitan Counties. Eleventh-hour rescue attempts are being made. Similar last-minute measures had to be taken to save the County-managed Philharmonic Hall, home of the Royal Liverpool Philharmonic Orchestra, which is being transferred to a new trust. While the Arts Council was willing to subsidize the orchestra through additional money received from the government, its declared policy is to subsidize performing companies rather than receiving theaters. Some fudging allowed an indirect contribution to the building's running costs, and District authorities are making some contribution, but the future is not yet secure. Nor is there yet a solution to the large County-managed Empire Theatre in Liverpool, which has no drama company of its own but is the only venue suitable for opera tours. The story, thus, is one of muddling through in permanent crisis.

The Arts Council's grant for 1986/87 included an earmarked sum of £25m, half for the South Bank complex, to compensate for subsidies lost as a result of abolition. This sum was well below the actual expenditure on the arts by the defunct authorities. The frequently repeated ministerial statements that the District authorities should pick up the remaining tabs were always unrealistic. So, more generally, is the Arts Council's frequently repeated view that funding partnership with local government generally should be substantially strengthened. The City of Liverpool, for example, with a population of only 500,000, could not afford to meet the deficits of the Royal Philharmonic and various theaters, with considerable out-of-town audiences, even in the unlikely event of these being given a spending priority by its extreme left-wing Council. Voluntary cooperation with the other Districts of the former County, on the other hand, is almost impossible to obtain for political reasons. Since the subsidies offered by the Arts Council were only half what the County had given, these institutions remain in crisis. The crisis is just as bad for a host of smaller institutions whose County grants, often quite small, were nevertheless essential to survival. While the Arts Council took—albeit inadequate—responsibility for the larger institutions, it left the funding of the smaller ones to the Regional Arts Associations which were thus, in turn, faced with almost impossible internal problems.

The Arts Council, for its part, was also subject to impossible pressures during this period. It continued to struggle with conflicting interests and insufficient funds. Its policy review led to the publication in March 1984 of a policy document entitled "The Glory of the Garden"—a reference to the blossoming of cultural activities throughout the country, which led to many caustic comments. Described as "the first major strategic review in the Council's forty years of existence" and a "ten-year development strategy," it put a seal to the Council's changed role discussed earlier. Its thrust was the development of activities in the less-favored provinces. As a result, it faced several sorts of cross-pressures at the same time: notably the balance between new activities and established clients, but also between sharing necessary real-term cuts among many clients and hitting a smaller number more heavily. Its problems were aggravated by the consultation process which had preceded "The Glory of the Garden," when Regional Arts Associations were asked to submit development plans. Much work went into these and since few of the proposals could then be funded, given the government's financial constraints, irritation was inevitable. The Arts Council nevertheless committed itself to a shift of resources. It obtained a derisory £1m addition to its grant from the government for new developments and earmarked a further £2m of its existing grant (matched by the relevant local authorities), which it could only find by squeezing established clients still further.

The government announced an Arts Council grant of £136m for 1986/87. Though this looks like a substantial increase over previous years, it was £25m below what the Council had asked for—under a Conservative chairman favoring cuts in public expenditure—as the minimum needed. Moreover, this figure included the sum earmarked to compensate for abolition of the Greater London Council and the Metropolitan Counties. The remainder was clearly inadequate to meet established needs, leave aside new developments that could make a real impact on the cultural map of Britain. The 1985/86 subsidies to the great national companies had not kept up with inflation, much less with actual costs, which in labor-intensive sectors like music and drama tend to rise more steeply than the retail price index. This caused serious difficulties, with activities cut and repeated threats of closure. Their future looks no better.

Recent years have thus seen a politicization of the arts world in the sense that conflicts have become more open, more bitter, and have taken on political tones. The Arts Council is under almost continuous attack, not just for its distributive decisions but also for its stance in relation to the government. The chairman, Sir William Rees-Mogg, likes to say that he is doing his best and that too strong an attack on government miserliness would be counterproductive. It is difficult for him to live down his past support of Mrs. Thatcher's economic policies even when, as recently, he does publicly criticize the level of government support for the arts. Many client organizations have come to feel that the Council has betrayed them by its failure to lead a real crusade for adequate state funding and by its unrealistic declarations that the shortfall should be made up by business and local authorities; many also consider the energy it now devotes to chasing business sponsors improper. An indication of the new mood was a recent meeting of the directors of London's subsidized theaters, led by Sir Peter Hall of the National Theatre, which issued an unprecedented declaration of no confidence in the Arts Council and accused it of having become "an instrument of government." The Council meanwhile soldiers on. It has firmly said that it will stick to its strategy of encouraging new developments and this, in its own language, means encouraging new blooms at the cost of weeding out old ones. Opposition from the weeds is bound to grow, while inadequately watered new blooms are unlikely to be loudly grateful.

The outcome of all this is unpredictable at the time of writing. Is the government stumbling almost by accident towards a system of earmarked grants to the Arts Council or even towards direct funding of major arts institutions? What effect will the Arts Council's new strategy have on the cultural map of Britain over time? What new activities will be seen and what old friends may we lose? How will the arts fare if they become involved in wider-ranging confrontation? Will attacks on the Arts Council finally destroy confidence in it? A further period of turbulence seems to lie ahead. Things may get worse before the pendulum swings back to expansionist economic policies. One can only pin one's hope on a change of climate. That is bound to involve a new government, and Opposition parties have reform proposals at hand. More generous funding of the arts may then be matched by institutional changes making our account of the present system past history.

Bibliography

Books

Baldry, H. *The Case for the Arts* (Secker & Warburg, 1981).
Braden, S. *Artists and People* (Routledge & Kegan Paul, 1978).
Harris, J. S. *Government Patronage of the Arts in Great Britain* (University of Chicago Press, 1970).
Hutchinson, R. *The Politics of the Arts Council* (Sinclair Browne, 1982).
Jenkins, H. *The Culture Gap: An Experience of Government* (Marion Boyars, 1979).
Minihan, J. *The Nationalization of Culture: The Development of State Subsidies to the Arts in Great Britain* (Hamish Hamilton, 1977).
Pearson, N. *The State and the Visual Arts: State Intervention in the Visual Arts in Britain, 1760–1981* (Open University Press, 1982).
Pick, J. *Art Administration* (Centre for the Arts, City University/E. & F. N. Spon, 1980).
St. John-Stevas, N. *The Two Cities* (Faber & Faber, 1984).
White, E. W. *The Arts Council of Great Britain* (Davis-Poynter, 1975).

Reports, Papers, Articles, etc.

Abercrombie, N. *Cultural Policy in the United Kingdom* (UNESCO, 1982).
Arts Council of Great Britain. *Annual Reports* and *Arts Council Bulletin* (ACGB).
Arts Council of Great Britain. *The Glory of the Garden: The Development of the Arts in Britain: A Strategy for a Decade* (ACGB, 1984).
Barratt, P. C., et al. "Corporate Donations and Sponsorship as Sources of Income for Arts Organizations in Great Britain," in *Charity Statistics 1980–1981* (Charities Aid Foundation, 1981).
Brough, C. *As You Like It: Private Support for the Arts* (Bow Group/Conservative Party, 1977).
Central Office of Information. *The Promotion of the Arts in Britain* (HMSO, 1975).
Chartered Institute of Public Finance and Accountancy. *Leisure and Recreation Statistics* (CIPF).
Clark, R. R. *The Arts Council: An Examination of National, Regional and Local Policy* (Centre for Leisure Studies, University of Salford, 1980).

Conservative Political Center. *The Arts: The Way Forward* (Conservative Party, 1978).

Elsom, J. *Change or Choice* (Liberal Party, 1979).

Green, M., and M. Wilding. *Cultural Policy in Britain* (UNESCO, 1970).

House of Commons: Education, Science and Arts Committee. *Public and Private Funding of the Arts: Report, Minutes of Evidence and Appendices* (3 vols., HMSO, 1982).

Labour Party. *The Arts and the People* (Labour Party, 1977).

Liberal Party. *The Arts, Artists and the Community* (Liberal Party, 1980).

Marshall, A. H. *Local Government and the Arts* (Institute of Local Government Studies, University of Birmingham, 1974).

Myerscough, J. *Facts About the Arts 2: 1986 Edition* (Policy Studies Institute, 1986).

Nissel, M. *Facts About the Arts: A Summary of Available Statistics* (Policy Studies Institute, 1983).

Office of Arts and Libraries. *Public and Private Funding of the Arts: Observations by the Government in the Report of the Education, Science and Arts Committee* (HMSO, 1984).

Pick, J. (ed.). *The State and the Arts* (Centre for the Arts, City University/John Offord Publishers, 1980).

Redcliffe-Maud, Lord. *Support for the Arts in England and Wales* (Gulbenkian Foundation, 1976).

Ridley, F. F. "Patronage of the Arts in Britain: The Political Culture of Cultural Politics," *Social Science Information,* 17/3/1978.

Trades Union Congress. *The Arts* (TUC, 1976).

Travis, A. S., and others. *The Role of Central Government in Relation to the Provision of Leisure Services in England and Wales* (Centre for Urban and Regional Studies, University of Birmingham, 1981).

For new publications, see Arts Council of Great Britain, *Arts Documentation Monthly* (ACGB).

11

Government and the Arts in Ireland

ANNE KELLY

In a turbulent history, Ireland has had a rich and varied, although interrupted, artistic tradition, and the relationship between art and politics has, from time to time, been a difficult one. In 1922, the birth of the new state coincided with the end of a remarkable late nineteenth-century cultural flourishing which reflected less the twentieth-century political revolution than the social upheavals which had gone before. Many reasons have been put forward for the artistic decline. Censorship (a Censorship of Publications Act was passed in 1929), the role of the Church, the need to impose official cultural standards (in particular Irish cultural standards), and the unwillingness of the new bourgeoisie to see itself portrayed truthfully, all have been cited. Economic factors certainly were relevant. But in the view of writer Mervyn Wall,[1] there was also a lack of a tradition of public art support—the feeling that government had a duty to support the development of arts institutions. In this respect, Ireland differed from much of the rest of Europe where there is a virtually unbroken tradition of art patronage, from Church and royal sources at first, but with municipal patronage beginning after the Renaissance. Another factor which helps explain the cultural inertia was the homogeneous nature of Irish society, which, without the six Northern and largely Protestant counties, was Catholic, conservative, predominantly rural, and increasingly inward-looking. Art was considered to be the preserve of the elite, a luxury which could be done without, but perhaps worst of all, un-Irish or even anti-Irish.

As might be expected in such a climate, even institutions which were well established in Irish life, such as the National Gallery, the National Museum, and the National College of Art and Design, suffered in the early decades of the new state. The National Gallery had 24,723 visitors in 1941, a figure which is startling when compared with the attendance figures when the Gallery first opened in 1864–167,698 for the first ten months, with attendance figures for the next three years of 89,943, 109,605, and 128,680.[2] By the early 1950s, the Gallery was described as being "in a stagnant, if not moribund condition"[3] with a grant-in-aid of £3,000 annually. Also in poor financial state was the Royal Hibernian Academy, whose membership had included every notable painter, sculptor, or architect practicing in Ireland since its foundation in 1823. In 1947, the Academy formally petitioned the Government for a building grant of £50,000. Not only was this refused but a long-standing annual state subsidy of £300 was withdrawn.[4] The Abbey Theater, which first received a government subsidy of £800 in 1925[5] had this increased to £8,000 per annum by 1952, with a further £3,000 for productions in Irish.

This partly reflected the Government's aspiration towards restoring the Irish language, an aspiration described by one Irish American in 1963 as "a declared government policy of restoration combined with an obvious anaemia in its enforcement."[6]

The Development of Public Policy in the Arts

The urgent need for positive public policy in the arts was first outlined in detail in 1949. At this point, it is worth mentioning some aspects of Irish political culture, which often determine the way political initiatives develop. A direct personal approach to a member of Parliament, or a Minister, or even to the Taoiseach (the Prime Minister) is a common occurrence and is always possible in a small society such as this, where most politicians conduct political "clinics." The face-to-face relationship between politician and client is important and is underpinned by the electoral system, and the multi-seat constituency, which encourages competition, not just between political parties but between members of the same party. The system of public interest group lobbying is a relatively recent phenomenon in Irish political life and was not common in the 1940s and 1950s. In 1949, it was the friendship between the Taoiseach, John A. Costello of the Fine Gail party, and Dr. Thomas Bodkin, a former director of the National Gallery, along with a feeling that economic times were right, which initiated the first Arts Act. Dr. Bodkin had worked at the Barber Institute in Birmingham and was familiar with Britain's Committee for the Encouragement of Music and the Arts (CEMA). This undoubtedly influenced the shape of subsequent developments in the arts in Ireland, where Dr. Bodkin had this to say: "We have not merely failed to go forward in policies concerning the Arts, we in fact regressed to arrive, many years ago, at a condition of apathy about them in which it had become justifiable to say of Ireland that no other country of Western Europe cared less, or gave less, for the cultivation of the Arts. It might almost have been assumed that any sense of responsibility for the welfare of Art had faded from our national tradition."[7] Bodkin was retained to report on the arts in Ireland. His report was published in September 1949 and reflected the state of disarray and neglect of the arts institutions at that time, the lack of aesthetic taste, the poor quality of design in industry, and the underdevelopment of art education. It mobilized the Government into some action, however limited, and finally made the arts as a whole the subject of public policy.

The purpose of the Arts Bill introduced in 1951 was "to stimulate public interest in, and to promote the knowledge, appreciation and practice of, the arts, and, for these and other purposes, to establish an arts council."[8] Prior to this, the small number of arts grants which were sanctioned by the Government, such as that to the Abbey Theater, had been administered by the Department of Finance. "The arts" now were specifically defined as covering painting, sculpture, architecture, music, drama, literature, design in industry, and the fine arts and applied arts generally. The initial state subsidy to the Arts Council was £10,000, representing a cost of $1\frac{1}{2}$ old pence per head of population. This compares with the sum of £3,000 which was granted to the National Gallery for the purchase of pictures and £1,500 which was received by the National Museum. As far as the arts were concerned, the main emphasis still was being placed on the restoration of the Irish language, and in 1953 almost £46,000 was granted for publications in Irish, including Irish drama, and for the Irish Folklore Commission.[9]

The Arts Council was to be "a small body which will be as far as possible autonomous, which will be entitled to work on its own, free from the trammels of Civil Service procedure."[10] There is an interesting distinction here which concerns the apparently deliberately protective nature of the Bill. The proposed Arts Council was to be "subject merely to the Government," and not under the authority of any particular Minister except that it should report through the Taoiseach to the Government. The Bill was designed "to give this body [the Arts Council] as far as possible freedom from bureaucratic control."[11] Thus in both wording and in spirit there is an obvious attempt to distance the arts from the bureaucracy and allow them comparative freedom. An alternative interpretation is that the Government were unwilling to place the arts on a firm official footing. This would have had the effect of institutionalizing a new expenditure heading, which in the nature of things it might be in the interests of the civil servants concerned, and people involved in the arts, to see increasing in line with government expenditure generally.

What the Arts Act expresses is the Government's feeling of goodwill towards the arts and their anxiety to make some response to the Bodkin Report. They were unwilling, however, to make the kind of structural changes in relation to the arts institutions which the report recommended. One suggestion was that a body be set up to coordinate and administer the arts institutions. This was not acted on and the institutions continued to decline, the Arts Act being largely irrelevant to them. Attendance at the Dáil debate was poor and frequently reflected the anti-intellectualism of the time. One opposition deputy expressed regret that Dr. Bodkin had not been asked "to say a word about the radio, the pictures [films], the newspapers" and other elements which debased what standards the Irish had. There was nothing to be ashamed of in Irish standards, which were old and "our own" as well as "honest and decent, perhaps simple and homely," although they might not have pleased "intellectuals." However, the principle of State involvement in the arts, limited as it was, went unchallenged.

In 1951, a change of government meant that the first Arts Council was appointed by Eamon de Valera of Fianna Fáil, the new Taoiseach, and its Director was a Fianna Fáil member of the Dáil, Patrick J. Little. This was the first and only time that a politician was appointed as Director of the Arts Council, which was by definition to be an autonomous body free from political interference. Mr. Little's position, however, was a non-executive one and there is no indication that he politically abused his role in any way. In Mervyn Wall's rather cryptic terms, he was "a good, honest, pleasant man," who tried to promote music, "a safe art not dangerous to faith or morals. He frowned on literature which he thought dangerous to both."[12] There were ten other members of the Council—six ordinary members appointed by the Taoiseach and four coopted members—all of whom had an interest in the arts. All were appointed for a five-year term of office. By 1964, Arts Council expenditure on music amounted to 21.6 percent of the total available funds while drama received 20.1 percent, and painting 18.1 percent. Expenditure on industrial design is said in the 12th annual report to have been noteworthy because of the limited role the Council had played in its earlier years in promoting good design in industry. With the new emphasis on export-led industrial expansion, the problem of poor design in industry had to be tackled.

The deficiencies in design in industry had been outlined in the Bodkin Report in 1949, which concluded that Irish industrialists had shown little enthusiasm in this area. In 1960, eleven years later, the Government gave Coras Trachtala (C.T.T.)—the Irish Export Board—the main responsibility for improving standards in industrial design. This effectively ended the Arts Council's direct involvement in the design area, although some small grants continued to be given for design purposes. Because of their achievements in design, C.T.T. approached the Scandinavians for assistance, and a Scandinavian Design

Group visited Ireland in April 1961 to make a study. Their report,[13] published in February 1962, stressed the importance of education in the development of aesthetic taste and suggested that the Irish school child "is exposed in a much lesser degree to drawing and the manipulation of materials than his Scandinavian counterpart. . . . [T]he Irish school child is visually and artistically among the most under-educated in Europe."[14]

A recent study of the place of the arts in Irish education (the Benson Report),[15] helps to put the problem in its historical perspective. It points to the narrow emphasis (on reading, writing, and arithmetic) which was part of the "minimum education for all" policy which began in 1872. While this changed in 1900 to a more "child-centered" approach, the new state again narrowed the curriculum. Drawing and physical education were dropped as obligatory subjects and the main emphasis was placed on the restoration of the Irish language. In 1961, the Scandinavian designers felt that it would be impossible for Ireland to make progress in design without a radical change in the existing educational institutions. The National College of Art, while having adequate facilities and space, was found to be using methods of education which were completely out of date, and in the opinion of the design team the College could not "as presently constituted" be the "starting point for the education of people in the different crafts or indeed for the education of painters, sculptors or designers."[16] The report made many criticisms of the state of design in Ireland and recommended how this might be improved, but it took a period of student unrest before conditions improved, and the College was granted partial autonomy from the Department of Education in 1971.

Most of the major educational recommendations in the Scandinavian report were not taken up by the Government, but action was taken to improve the quality of Irish design. In 1965, the Kilkenny Design Workshops (K.D.W.) were established; their main purpose was to be the advancement of good design in industry and among consumers. At last, design was recognized by the state as an essential element of economic development. Just as Bodkin's report had given birth to the Arts Council, Kilkenny Design, which grew out of the Scandinavian report, was to make an important contribution to the arts in Ireland, although each development was only a partial response to a deeper need. Public policy in the arts was extended, but it was not until 1971 that this extension was to attempt to cover crafts with the establishment of the Crafts Council of Ireland, state-aided through the Industrial Development Authority, and helped also by the Royal Dublin Society. K.D.W. advises the Minister in matters relating to design as well as conveying the design needs of industry to the relevant educational authorities. In conjunction with the European Social Fund, it provides designer training, and the 1981 Training Scheme gave practical work experience to twenty young graduate designers.[17] K.D.W. also funds Designer Development awards which enable Irish designers to benefit from experience and training abroad. In 1981, the magazine of Britain's Design Council held Kilkenny Design up as "a model of state intervention in design."[18] Its success is all the more praiseworthy when one considers the low base from which K.D.W. began, with poor standards of design education and very little public awareness of good design.

The 1960s were happier times for the National Gallery also, although not because of a more benevolent attitude on the part of the State. The annual state subsidy was still small, but George Bernard Shaw, who died in 1950, left a third of his estate to the Gallery, which meant that for fifty years after Shaw's death the Gallery would receive one-third of the royalties from his published works. An unlikely source, the box-office hit *My Fair Lady* (based on Shaw's *Pygmalion*), brought the income to an undreamed of sum of £70,000 annually for the next few years.[19] In 1962, the Government sanctioned a sum of £277,000 for the building of an extension to the Gallery—an extension which first had been requested eleven years before. The period is referred to by Homan Potterton, the present Director, as a "golden age" for the Gallery, with attendance figures increasing to 68,137 in 1964, and reaching an all-time record of 506,678 in 1977.

The Arts Council's fortunes also were changing. In 1956, a new Council was appointed in accordance with the provision in the Arts Act, and the writer, Sean O'Faolain, was appointed Director, although he retired before his term expired. It was O'Faolain's view that while great progress had been made with little money, the Arts Council ran the risk of trying to do too much with such a small budget. This now stood at £20,000. O'Faolain felt that it might be wiser "to concentrate on fewer things of the very first rank in order to establish standards of excellence"[20] and that future policy should reflect this. He prepared a report for the Taoiseach on the working of the Arts Council and requested an increase in the state subvention. By the end of the 1960s, and in line with a general economic improvement, the state subvention had been increased to £70,000 per annum. Along with the more traditional funding of arts events, a scheme was developed to encourage local authorities to purchase paintings, sculpture, and stained glass by Irish artists for public display. The Arts Council contributed half the cost in each case and by 1964 either had bought for their own collection or had contributed half the purchase price of over 300 works of art.[21] In 1966, the Arts Council was empowered by the Government to establish and administer a fund called Ciste Cholmcille out of which annuities could be paid to creative workers in the arts who were old or in ill-health.[22] However, while the state was willing to honor such artists, it was not to be out-of-pocket in any way, for the Arts Council cannot use any part of its annual state endowment for the Fund, the financing of which must depend on public subscription. The cash position of the Fund stood at £19,085 in 1981 and it has had "some limited success" in assisting artists.[23]

The Finance Act of 1969 portrays the Government in a rather better light in relation to the arts. It is one of the most exciting and innovative developments in the relationship between the state and the arts in Ireland. The Fianna Fáil Minister for Finance at that time was Charles J. Haughey, and he has always indicated a personal commitment to the arts. When, in later years, Mr. Haughey became Taoiseach, he appointed the writer Anthony Cronin as his cultural adviser, the first appointment of its kind in Ireland. The 1969 Act reflects Mr. Haughey's commitment, rather than the work of an arts lobby, and is generally regarded as a progressive piece of legislation as far as the arts are concerned. Section 2 of the Act provides exemption from income-tax and surtax for earnings from "original and creative work" having "cultural or artistic merit." This work may be a book or other writing, a play, a musical composition, a painting or other picture, or a work of sculpture. The Revenue Commissioners may seek outside advice, including that of the Arts Council, on the cultural or artistic merit of works on which exemption is claimed. The artist who benefits from the exemption must be resident in Ireland and this provision has brought many artists, and particularly writers, to live in Ireland. The purpose of the measure subsequently was said by Mr. Haughey to be to halt the intellectual drain from Ireland and to underline the importance of the artist to the community, and of the contribution he makes. Its purpose is therefore more to acknowledge the role of the artist than to give him any great financial benefit, although the benefit could be substantial in the case of a very successful writer.

Whether Mr. Haughey's purpose has been achieved is a matter of some debate today. It is difficult to understand how the role of the artist can be acknowledged when this is done in private negotiations between the artist and the Revenue Commissioners. The measure may encourage artists to take up residence in Ireland whose work is not of a quality to benefit Irish culture. There is some evidence that the Revenue Commissioners have problems in assessing the artistic merit of some work, and that they are not always prepared to listen to the advice of the Arts Council in the matter. Furthermore, nothing is required of the artist in the way of benefit or service to the state and it would seem that the question of cultural impact should be a consideration when exemption is being claimed over a number of years. For example, the Revenue Commissioners might take into account the artist's willingness to participate in the various educational schemes now run by the Arts Council.

Out of 1,646 applications, the Revenue Commissioners granted 1,145 tax exemptions between 1969 and March 1982: 47.5 percent of these were for writers, 26 percent for painters, 13.5 percent for playwrights, 7.5 percent for sculptors, and 5.5 percent for composers.[24] It is not known how many of these are native Irish and how many are foreigners who have come to live in Ireland because of the tax-exemption. Criticism of the measure was expressed in the European Parliament in 1977 and subsequently in the Dáil,[25] but the Arts Council defended the measure and, in view of the state's previously negative attitude to the arts, Mr. Haughey's concession was undoubtedly a positive and well-intentioned measure at the time.

The 1960s thus may be seen as a time of reviving fortunes for the arts. Nevertheless, by the mid-1960s the Arts Council was the center of a growing controversy. The Director, Father O'Sullivan, a liberal although autocratic figure, indicated his willingness to serve another term and was reappointed at a time when there was a general feeling that change was necessary. There were no overt political moves but Mr. Haughey was made directly aware of dissatisfaction in the artistic community, as were some senior civil servants in the Taoiseach's department, and discussions took place on the need for change. One criticism was that the Arts Council might be developing into a coterie which was interested mainly in established artists, and particularly in the visual arts. When the new Arts Act finally was introduced in 1973, the danger of cliquishness, staleness, and disillusion creeping in when people held offices for long periods was brought up in the debate. Father O'Sullivan was not replaced when he retired in the summer of 1973 and this led to the expectation that the Arts Council might be reconstituted.

In the new Arts Act, the Arts Council was now to consist of sixteen members, all appointed by the Taoiseach. It was thought that this was preferable to the previous method of coopting some members, a practice which had led to charges of cliquishness in previous councils. The Opposition felt that the new Act heralded the end of artistic freedom, but this method of appointment is similar to that adopted for other semi-state bodies, and to date no government has used the Council in a political way. Defeated members of the Dáil have not been given places on the Council and the larger Council represents all the arts. A part-time Chairman is appointed by the Taoiseach, and a full-time chief executive, or Director, is appointed by the Council, subject to the sanction of the Taoiseach. Before this, the Director had been part-time. Another new and important provision was one enabling a local authority to assist the Council, with money, or in kind, or by the provision of services or facilities. The Act also extended the Council's activities by including film among the arts for the first time.

The new Act introduced a changed atmosphere in the Arts Council. An increase of 50 percent in the grant made the financial future seem brighter, although the funding was still short of the standard set elsewhere. The new Council, which included the poet Seamus Heaney and playwright John B. Keane, proposed "that literature and drama should be fostered more deliberately and to a greater extent than heretofore'' because these were the art forms ''in which in modern times Irishmen have caught and continue to catch, the attention of the whole world.''[26] But this emphasis did not mean that the visual arts were to be neglected, and, following a brief suspension because of lack of funds, the Council in 1974 again began purchasing paintings and sculptures, both for its own collection and for institutions, on a shared-purchase basis. The emphasis of the Council now began to change, and fostering creativity through various educational and training schemes was seen to be at least as important as giving grants to institutions. This was significant in light of the absence of a coherent arts education policy. Regional arts development also was given priority. In order to counteract what was felt to be an indication of some bias in favor of arts activities in Dublin, the Council undertook to correct the imbalance and ''to encourage regional development of the arts as a matter of urgency.''[27] Lack of finance was still a problem, however, with Arts Council expenditure at 50 pence per head of population, comparing unfavorably with the per capita expenditure in Northern Ireland of 78 pence, England 89 pence, Scotland £1.14, and Wales £1.41.[28] It was not until 1979 that a relatively dramatic increase in funds meant that for the first time action could be taken in relation to the improvement and maintenance of arts buildings, mainly theaters. The increase largely reflected a general improvement in Irish economic circumstances rather than any upsurge in public arts lobbying, which continued to be weak and sporadic. However, another factor may well have been the private lobbying role of the Arts Council itself, particularly in the light of its revitalized image as a national body.

Funding from Departments of the Central Government

The passing of the 1973 Arts Act means that the organizational structure of government support for the arts now involves three main areas. Support comes from central government, through the various Departments of State; from local government; and from the Arts Council. However, while the Arts Council is the source of imaginative policies on a relatively low budget, some of the arts institutions suffer not only from lack of funds, but also, in the absence of an overall cultural policy, from a lack of political initiative to deal with the serious problems they face.

Following the appointment in 1982 of a Junior Minister for Arts and Culture at the Department of the Taoiseach, responsibility for the major arts institutions is now centralized at that department. However, like the Arts Council, the National Gallery has a separate vote of funds from the Government, but a rather anomalous position regarding departmental responsibility. The Gallery was established by an Act of Parliament in 1854 and is run by a Board of Governors and Guardians, with executive decision in the hands of a Director. The works of art are vested in the Board, which has exclusive control, but ministerial responsibility lay, until the recent transfer, with the Department of Education. This Department had no power to run the Gallery, and in this sense the Department's position was quite different from its position in relation to the National Museum. Nevertheless, Gallery staff salaries are linked to civil service salaries and the Director of the Gallery is unable to take on staff without the approval of the Department of the Public Service, which imposes staff restrictions on the Gallery, as it does in other areas where it has direct responsibility.

Financial stringency also applies to the Gallery. In 1980, the grant allocated to the

Gallery by the state for purchases amounted to £24,700.[29] This compares with expenditure of £140,000 from the Shaw fund in the same year. The state grant was increased to £25,900 in 1981, and £105,000 was spent from the Shaw fund. The state grant compares with Dublin Corporation's grant of £30,000 to the Municipal Gallery for purchases in 1982, and the sum of £150,000 annually which the British government gives to the City of Manchester Art Gallery. Furthermore, the National Gallery is obliged to pay value added tax (VAT) on works of art which it purchases. Notwithstanding all of these problems, the Richards Report on provision for the arts in Ireland said of the Gallery in 1976 that it "stands ahead as a center of art activity, and in the efforts it makes to engage public interest, especially the interest of the uninitiated and of children."[30] All the main European schools of painting are represented in the Gallery's collection, as well as an important display of Irish painting and of icons, and a room devoted to American painting. The Gallery has had the benefit of the Shaw fund, which can be used only for the collection, including the acquisition of new work. It also has benefitted from progressive Directors. The present Director, Homan Potterton, continues to press the Government for an increase in the purchase fund, and feels that while the Gallery could and should be run like a business, there is little incentive to do this because of the danger that the Government grant will be cut accordingly.

The relative autonomy of the National Gallery is in stark contrast to that of the National Museum, the nucleus of which was formed in 1732 by the Royal Dublin Society. The Museum reflects an almost complete lack of public policy, if not wilful neglect on the part of successive governments. Much of the explanation for this lies in the historical unwillingness on the part of government to tackle cultural problems in a fundamental way. Responsibility for the Museum lay until recently with the Minister for Education, and the Museum has for many years been the subject of strong criticism, initially in the Bodkin Report and then in the Richards Report "for its conservative policies, boring display, and the general inadequacy of the service it provides."[31] The Reports of the Board of Visitors (set up to make annual reports to Parliament) from 1976 to the latest available one, for 1980, if anything paint an even bleaker picture of its condition.

Some of the collections in the Museum are of unique importance in art history, because many of the items were being made while the rest of Europe was in the Dark Ages. "Scholars from Gaul and Germany came to learn from the Irish teachers and theologians; and in the monastic schools of the island, craftwork, and particularly the art of illumination, reached a standard in its own idiom and within its limits, which far surpassed that of contemporary work on the Continent. . . . This Celtic Art was to be exceedingly fruitful, and to exert its influence, not only over the neighboring island, but over many of the countries of Europe during the succeeding centuries."[32] What little remains of the manuscripts and metalwork of the golden age of Irish art is thus a valuable and irreplaceable link in the artistic chain, for which no prototypes exist in Europe. But because of the neglect of successive governments, many of these objects are housed in the most deplorable conditions. The Museum building itself is grossly inadequate, and the Board of Visitors Report for 1977–78 refers not only to the inadequacy of space but to "dry rot fungus rampant in the Rotunda and probably elsewhere, as there are leaks in most of the downpipes in the interior of the building."[33] Rainwater had already caused serious damage to Museum material. Now, many years later, the majority of rooms are closed to the public while the dry rot is still being dealt with. Meanwhile, the various collections are being stored in nine different locations, some of them remote. The Museum has no conservation laboratory; there is no national education service from the Museum and no training in Ireland for museum personnel. The Museum library is for staff use and has no librarian. There is no shop for catalogues and replicas, and no organized official guided tours, like those in the National Gallery. Most museums use voluntary helpers for guide work and sales, but, perhaps because of union problems, voluntary workers are not used in the National Museum. Neither is the Museum given adequate media coverage. There is no growth policy for the Museum and no national policy agreed between the different political parties. Each government starts afresh, and the problems are being tackled now by the Minister for Arts and Culture who proposes to transfer part of the collections to the newly restored Royal Hospital at Kilmainham, which is to become a national center for culture and the arts.

The Board of Visitors has no fiscal functions and has no power to make decisions on the administration of the Museum. One of the recommendations in the Richards Report is that the National Museum should be given the same degree of autonomy as the National Gallery. This would have the effect of removing the Museum from the direct responsibility of a government department, and the present Government is committed to introducing legislation to bring about this change. A committee also exists, the aim of which is to interest and inform the public outside Dublin about the national collections. This committee organizes travelling exhibitions to different parts of the country. A National Heritage Bill proposed by the previous Government would have given responsibility for the Museum to the Department of the Public Service. The Heritage Council, which the Bill proposed to set up, was envisaged as a semi-state body of fifteen people, similar to the Arts Council, which would administer the Museum, national monuments, and some national gardens and parks. However, the present government has not proceeded with the Bill.

Like the Museum, the National Library does not have the same degree of autonomy as the National Gallery, and the Richards Report suggests that a strong case can be made for such autonomy. The Library is still administered by the Department of Education and is a deposit library which acquires, as far as possible, all material published by Irishmen or related to Ireland. The unique character of the collection is in its Irish manuscripts. The grant-in-aid for the purchase of books stood at £75,000 in 1982—an amount which has doubled since 1976. However, the Library building itself is not in very good condition; there are space problems as well as financial and staff problems, none of which is likely to be solved in the short term.

Another important departmental source of funding for the arts now comes from the Department of Labour through the Teamwork and Social Employment schemes. These schemes, although short-term, have generated considerable cultural activity particularly among young people. The involvement of this Department is a recognition of the employment potential of the arts, a potential often underestimated by governments even in times of high unemployment.

Ireland's image abroad is regarded as important, but no financial provision whatever was made for the development of cultural relations between Ireland and other countries until 1947, when a grant of £10,000 was voted for the establishment of an Advisory Committee on Cultural Relations at the Department of External Affairs (now Foreign Affairs). This Department continues to set aside an annual sum to be spent on the development of cultural relations with other countries. Cultural Relations received a grant of £150,000 in 1982 and this remained the same in 1983. A breakdown of Cultural Relations expenditure in 1981 indicates that almost 32 percent of the budget was spent on lectures, symposia, and congresses, with 25.26 percent being spent on exhibitions and the visual arts. Music, theater, dance, summer schools, and literature also were subvented.[34]

With many Departments of State involved in the arts, a lack of cohesion exists, and it has been suggested that a separate Department of Culture would bring all the arts under one umbrella. The Taoiseach's Department, which is now the central focal point for public policy in relation to arts and culture, recently had responsibility for the Irish Film Board transferred there from the Department of Industry and Energy. A Film Board Bill, passed in 1980, established a seven-member board, appointed by the Minister for Industry and Energy, with a four-year fund of £4.1 million. The purpose of the Board is to fund film-making, and its role was seen by the Department of Industry and Energy as being more concerned with industrial promotion—getting a self-sustaining industry off the ground—than as a cultural body. The Bill received a mixed reception from those involved in film in Ireland, and the Arts Council's view was that to continue the policy of funding major foreign film productions acts to the detriment of indigenous Irish film-making. However, the Council's fears in this regard were premature, because the Film Board sees its own function as one of promoting an indigenous film industry through helping the commercial low-budget film-maker. The Board has also expressed consciousness of the need to establish high standards both artistically and commercially.

The Film Board, the Kilkenny Design Workshops, and the Department of Labour schemes are examples of how positive public policy can benefit both industrial development and job creation, as well as contributing to general aesthetic development. They also highlight the fact that Irish governments are prepared to be generous to the arts as long as they can see a return in terms of industrial development, but are unwilling to provide adequate assistance to an institution like the National Museum where the return for money is less tangible. However, there is no doubt that as well as being an immense educational and national asset, a revitalized National Museum could be an important tourist attraction which ultimately would repay the state's investment. This is especially relevant in a country like Ireland, which depends heavily on income from tourists. An Bord Fáilte (the Irish Tourist Board) played a major role in direct funding of cultural events until 1980, when the Board decided that tourism criteria were no longer appropriate in assessing grants for arts activities. These grants are now dealt with by the Arts Council. However, the case of the National Museum provides an example of how a particular economic policy—that of attracting tourists—can have an active cultural dimension. The highly successful "Treasures of Ireland" exhibition, first mounted in the United States and later touring Europe, is evidence of this potential. Whether such unique and irreplaceable treasures should be permitted to travel outside Ireland is a matter of some controversy, but the success of the exhibition contrasts sadly with the low level of basic standards in so many areas of the Museum.

Funding from Local Government

The second major public source of funding for the arts is local government, and while the financial provision is not very large, the development of structures has begun which should be of great future benefit, given the essential local commitment from the different areas.

One of the really important changes in the 1973 Arts Act was to grant permission to local authorities to be involved in the arts. In Ireland there are eighty-seven local rating authorities which administer a healthy, dynamic library service. A survey of their involvement in the arts for the financial year 1973–74 indicates that most local authorities regard the Arts Council as the national authority on the arts.[35] Perhaps the most important development has been the establishment, with the cooperation of the Arts Council and the Regional Development Organizations, of five regional arts committees. These Committees include members of local authorities and each committee has appointed an Arts Officer. Arts Council grants to the Regional Arts Committees amounted to £50,417 in 1982.[36] The Arts Council is the main source of funds but limited funding also is provided by the Regional Development Organizations and by the local authorities. The Committees themselves are not granting bodies, the local authorities retaining a "reserve function" in relation to Arts Act Grants. The Arts Officer can make a recommendation to the individual County or City Council, which the Council then may or may not accept. In practice, the system is making slow but sure progress. Local authorities are beginning to seek professional arts advice and this is seen in increasing public awareness and higher standards of art in public places.

As usual, finance is the main problem in local government expenditure on the arts. The Arts Act allocation by four County Councils in the comparatively well-off Mid-West Region for 1981 was just under £9,000.[37] In comparison, the relatively deprived area of the Donegal County Council provided an arts allocation of £25,000 in 1982.[38] The degree of local authority support for the arts cannot be measured by the wealth of the area being served, but probably reflects the commitment of a few individuals. However, the development of the Regional Arts Committees has meant that structures have been set up which ultimately will benefit the arts in all the regions. Each region develops its own policy. For example, it is part of Mid-West arts policy to assist local authorities to develop their interest in the arts, so that "eventually all the local authorities should give greater funding to the arts, should seek advice on application for funds, should increase their arts budget annually and should operate systems encouraging initiative."[39] This is being implemented by contact with County Councillors and officials, and also by encouraging the setting up of cultural committees in local authorities and by liaison between arts groups and local authorities.

The larger City corporations also are involved in the arts and have displayed some progressive arts policies in recent years, as well as funding local authority museums. Dublin Corporation has shown itself to be aware of its duties towards the arts, as well as having responsibility for the Municipal Gallery of Modern Art. A purchasing fund was introduced at the Gallery in 1970 and the provision made increased from the scarcely believable initial sum of £200 per annum to £30,000 for 1982.

Dublin Corporation also has responsibilities under the Arts Act which it meets through the Arts Act Grants Fund first introduced in 1976. In 1982, the Corporation allocated £100,000 to the arts,[40] almost 50 percent going by direct vote to the theater. The Dublin Theater Festival is now the largest city function drawing annually on the fund. A Bursary Scheme for individual awards also has been introduced, along with other smaller grants.

The Corporation of Cork, the second city of Ireland, since 1974 has made grants to groups and organizations promoting the creative arts in the City.[41] Here the estimate for the arts has increased from £1,000 in 1974 to £50,000 for 1981, and while there was no increase on this figure in 1982, there is an obvious improvement in the funding of the arts by the Corporation.

Funding from the Arts Council

The third and most important source of funding for the arts is now the Arts Council. The Oireachtas grant-in-aid to the Council for 1982 stood at £4,082,000. By far the largest slice of the grant—£1,831,461—goes to drama, with £1,068,125 going to the Abbey and Peacock Theaters. For this reason, it is worth examining in some detail.

Drama and theater traditionally have occupied an important place in Irish cultural life, and amateur drama is widely spread and strong. The theater, which exemplified democracy in Athens, has had an important political role in Irish life, and it was on the stage of the Abbey that many of the past battles between art and politics were fought. Yeats, whose name is synonymous with the Abbey and whose crusade was to create a new literature as well as a new nationalism, wanted to maintain the artistic independence of the theater. But the dramatization of ideas, instead of being a source of inspiration, frequently provoked rejection by the audience. The Abbey experienced riots in 1907 with the production of Synge's *Playboy of the Western World* and again in 1926 when Sean O'Casey's *The Plough and the Stars* was presented. Having survived the days when any denial of the idealized national stereotype was liable to incur a riot, the Abbey's influence on theater has been worldwide. To the inspiration of the Abbey has been attributed the start of the Little Theater movement in the United States, including the Washington Square Players, which became the American Theater Guild, and the Provincetown Players which introduced Eugene O'Neill to world theater.[42] The Abbey is thus an important institution in Irish cultural life, and cultural life worldwide, a fact recognized even by people with no interest in theater.

Today, the Arts Council is responsible for funding the Abbey, having taken over from the Department of Finance in 1976, and it sees its role as one of trustee for the public, although at "arm's-length" rather than directly. The question of artistic conflict between the Council and the Abbey artistic staff does not arise, the Abbey Board adopting or modifying the artistic policies of its own Director. However, this is an area of some controversy in recent years. From the Arts Council's point of view, an external organization such as the Abbey states its objectives, and the Council judges how successful the organization is in achieving these objectives. Thus, for example, the Council feels it important to have a balance between new Irish work and revivals. It may note that there are fewer new Irish plays, the Abbey perhaps balancing the cheapness of revivals against the risk involved in new work. Here the Council would have a view, and would provide what former Director, Colm O'Briain, described as "a forum for informed dialogue."[43] Furthermore, a public failure would not necessarily be a failure in the eyes of the Arts Council, which would base its judgment on whether or not the objective on which public funds were spent was a valid one.

The problem of financing an institution such as the Abbey is a matter of some concern, and it raises the question of how support for established companies can be balanced against the need to support innovative programs. The emphasis of the Arts Council today is on encouraging creativity and developing the conditions conducive to art, despite a climate of increasing fiscal stringency. Thus, while it sees the major institutions as essential to the development of the arts in Ireland, their maintenance does not necessarily increase creativity, while it does consume much of the available budget. As the Arts Council itself has stated, "the task of having to choose between the maintenance of the institutions where creative work can be performed or developing the conditions for the creation of art is an invidious one which would be resolved by adequate funding.''[44] To anticipate increased funds in the present economic climate is unrealistic, and the Council seeks instead to make the best use of available resources. It has introduced and administers an Independent Theater Management Scheme, described as a flexible system of funding whereby managements may apply for assistance, for example, to advance royalties to a playwright when a new play is being commissioned, or for grants towards production expenses.

The area of theater has, however, involved the Arts Council in some controversial decisions, particularly one in 1982 to drop the grant (of £278,000 in 1981) to the second biggest state theater, the Irish Theater Company. This group was set up as a touring company in 1974, and in 1980 gave a total of 161 performances in twenty-one venues in Ireland and three in Britain.[45] The Irish Theater Company also gave school lectures, public readings of new plays, and workshops in many of the areas they visited, and the withdrawal of funds reflects an Arts Council policy shift in relation to theater outside Dublin. The Department of the Taoiseach intervened in the affair and provided temporary ''ticking over'' finance for the ITC following ''total rejection'' of the disbanding proposal by the ITC Board and representations from Irish Actors' Equity to the leaders of the three main political parties. The Arts Council now operates its own touring scheme, the Arts Council Theater Touring Scheme (ACTTS), as well as providing guarantees to a new agency, the National Touring Agency, which provides management services to those using the Council's touring scheme. However, problems remain in the area of touring theater.

Larger arts institutions must rationalize and cut back on expenditure in these hard times; it seems that the taxpayers' money goes further in a small company like the excellent ''Druid'' in Galway, whose grant in 1982 was £56,300. By way of contrast, the Arts Council in Britain recently defended their level of support for the larger national arts bodies on the grounds that few professional artists would exist without them. In the words of the Chairman of the Council, Sir William Rees-Mogg, ''national companies radiate out advantage to the rest of the arts.''[46] The ITC debate, however, also raises the question of the power of the Irish Arts Council to bring into effect radical policy changes, especially when such changes mean the disbanding of an existing national institution. The intervention by the Department of the Taoiseach indicates the limitations of the Arts Council's autonomy in issues such as this, and while the Council ultimately succeeded in changing touring policy, the issue remains a controversial one.

The Arts Council was involved in another theatrical controversy in 1982, this time in relation to the Dublin Theater Festival, which is a major annual event in the arts. The Council threatened to withdraw from future funding of the Festival because the 1982 Festival had been changed from a three-week to a two-week event by the financially reduced organizers. The Council funded the 1983 Festival, but its policy in relation to funding festivals, including theater festivals, is undergoing change at present.

Other important Irish theaters also are assisted by the Arts Council. The Gate, founded by Micheál MacLiammoir and Hilton Edwards, dates back to 1928, and has been state-subsidized only since 1971. It now puts on its own productions for eight months of the year and during the other four months the theater is available to outside companies which automatically benefit from an Arts Council subsidy of £3,500 per week. The subsidy to the Gate amounted to £228,835 in 1982. The Peacock Theater, which is housed in the same building as the Abbey, originally was meant to divide its attention between plays in the Irish language and "experimental" theater. In practice, it generally also puts on plays for children, as well as new plays and lunch-time theater.

Literature, visual arts, dance, music (traditional and otherwise), opera, and film all now receive Arts Council aid. The Council also continues to operate the Joint Purchase Scheme for works of art, as well as funding arts centers, which received £228,047 in 1982. The growth of arts centers has been significant, and the whole notion of community arts is particularly important because (to quote Lord Redcliffe-Maud), "it signifies a special *process* of art activity rather than any special *product*—a process which seeks to involve action by the local population as a whole rather than passive interest of that minority (often estimated at some five percent of total population) which regularly attends performances of serious music, opera, ballet and drama or visits art exhibitions."[47] Art as process is thus an essential part of cultural democracy.

Study awards and travel grants also are funded by the Arts Council, and a studio in Milan is available for Irish artists to work in. Arts Councils, North and South, have combined to develop the Tyrone Guthrie Center at Annaghmakerrig, Co. Monaghan, as a retreat where artists can work in peaceful surroundings. The Center also has benefitted from grants totalling £170,000 from the Special Border Areas Program Fund. This Fund was established as part of the European Economic Community Regional Development Program and the Center is regarded as a good example of practical cooperation between people, North and South. In spite of the political problems, it is now also an established practice for the Irish Arts Council and the Arts Council of Northern Ireland to meet annually in joint session.

In recent years, the Arts Council has subsidized individual artists through the bursary schemes and the Aosdana. The bursaries, expenditure on which was £103,987 in 1982, are competitive and are open to specific categories of artists. They were designed to help towards the completion of a specified work, or to allow the artist time to work. The Aosdana is an association of artists engaged in literature, music, and the visual arts whose members (not to number more than 150) can apply for a "cnuas"—funding of £5,000 a year over a five-year period. A scheme to honor artists was first discussed by the Council in 1978. In 1979, a proposal was made by the Council to the Government and with the help of Anthony Cronin, the Taoiseach's Cultural Adviser at that time, Aosdana was born. The "cnuas" is awarded by the Arts Council to members of Aosdana on the basis of need, established by the artist, and the scheme is regarded as a very important development because it creates the circumstances which allow artists to work. It thus ensures that the artist's creative potential is not taken up in making a living in areas other than through his art, with a consequent cultural loss to the life of the community.[48]

In 1978, an Arts Council survey of the living and working conditions of artists found that most artists, both "interpretive" and "creative," "rely, for the majority of their income, on money earned at activities other than their art."[49] Many have inadequate access to social welfare because they have not built up the necessary level of contributions, and most do not have pension plans. Their aspirations tend to be modest—more work, or to own a house or a studio. Aosdana thus goes some way towards improving the lifestyle of the Irish artist, and brings this country into line with the UNESCO recommendation that governments should help to create and sustain not only a climate encouraging freedom of artistic expression but also the material conditions facilitating artists' work.[50] Aosdana has been the subject of some criticism, but what is important is that an imaginative scheme has begun, which will greatly benefit artists and the arts.

The Council's bursaries to individuals first were awarded in literature, but as the writer needs a publisher, and the publishing industry has been relatively underdeveloped, the Council now gives grants and interest-free loans to organizations such as the Irish Book Publishers Association (CLE) and Irish Bookhandling Ltd. This is an important development in a country where the lack of publishers in past years meant that Irish writers had to be published abroad. Along with the distinctly unfavorable intellectual climate, this is said to have been one reason why so many writers left Ireland in the period up to the late 1950s.*

A system of "Writers in Schools" is operated by Arts Councils, North and South. On invitation, writers make short visits to schools to read from and discuss their work, and it is hoped "that by introducing living writers to young audiences, both the appreciation and practice of creative writing will be encouraged."[51] A somewhat similar program operates in the visual arts at primary school level. This is a mural scheme, "Paint on the Wall," through which an artist spends two weeks in a school, working on a mural with the pupils. The objectives of this scheme are "to increase visual awareness of pupils of color, texture, shapes and to stimulate their creative ability."[52] This program, used by over one hundred schools each year, should assist in the development of children's visual abilities in an area where there has been a traditional educational weakness. However, no study to judge the impact of the scheme has yet been undertaken, and the Council is reassessing its educational projects at present. The Council also assists with funding theater in education by subventing TEAM Educational Theater Company.

Arts Council policy covers a wide area of the arts, with support for both amateur and professional programs. Decisions on who or what qualifies for funding are made by the members of the Arts Council acting in council. The Council has an initiating role as well as a monitoring role in a financial sense. It is, nevertheless, in the former Director's view, "unrigid in the flow of money."[53] Problems in grant-aided organizations tend to be known in advance to Arts Council staff, so a viewpoint can be expressed by the Council before the problem gets out of hand. However, the ITC and the Dublin Theater Festival controversies seem to indicate that this does not always work in practice.

In general, with the major exception of ongoing expenditure on national institutions such as the Abbey, what remains of the Arts Council budget is spread out rather than centralized either geographically or with respect to art form.

Arts Council policy also includes participatory programs such as those outlined for Irish education. The Council feels that the question of the arts and education is the single most important problem facing it. "The neglect of the arts in Irish society has its roots in the low status of the arts within our education system. An increase in arts activity cannot be sustained unless it can rely on a public that has learned how to enjoy, appreciate and participate in the experience."[54] While the Council has no statutory responsibility for education, it commissioned the Benson report on the place of the arts in Irish education, which was published in 1979 to coincide with the International Year of the Child. The report concluded that "the peripheral role which the arts have traditionally played in Irish education has been perpetuated" in the educational changes which have occurred in the last decade, and suggests that the Department of Education itself must conduct a "search-

*In the words of Yeats, who also left but returned,

Out of Ireland have we come
Great hatred, little room
Maimed us from the start.

ing examination of its own provisions for the arts in education.''[55] In 1980, the Department published its White Paper on educational development, which for the first time in any education White Paper contained a separate chapter on the arts, with the suggestion that a departmental committee should be established to examine the extent to which artistic and creative activities are being catered to in second-level schools.[56] Music, in particular, has suffered and the position of music in the educational system must now be regarded as a national disgrace. A Curriculum and Examinations Board appointed by the present Government has recently published a discussion document on the arts in the educational system, and it remains to be seen if positive action will follow.

The Current Crisis

The state is now the most important patron of the arts in Ireland, although there are still areas which receive little attention. Perhaps one of the most positive developments in recent years has been the contribution made by privately financed national groups such as An Taisce, the Heritage Trust, the Architectural Archive, the Irish Georgian Society, the Historic Irish Tourist Houses and Gardens Association, and the Irish Museums Trust. The growth of such organizations is related directly to the limited interest taken by the state in some particular areas, such as the architectural heritage, and the benefit to the arts of such private effort has been immense.

However, with some notable exceptions, the individual private patron has not played a major role in the arts in Ireland since the seventeenth century and the end of poetic patronage. During the period 1200–1600 A.D., noble Irish families acted as patrons by maintaining in their houses hereditary poets. At the peak of his career, the poet enjoyed the permanent patronage of the king or lord and was endowed with land and property which he could bequeath to his descendants. Colonization brought an end to this system and in modern times we have had no Medicis or Mellons to call on. At a rather different level, the National Gallery has had the benefit of generous patronage from such benefactors as Lady Milltown, Hugh Lane, Chester Beatty and, of course, Shaw. Institutional patronage also has been important, for example, from the Royal Dublin Society whose schools also were vitally important for artists in the past. Edward McParland[57] shows that the Bank of Ireland has had a tradition of enlightened patronage of the visual arts dating back to 1783. In recent times, the Bank has built up an extensive collection of modern Irish art—a collection which, in McParland's view, exceeds in importance that of any other public or private collection of contemporary Irish art in the country.

The best possible solution to funding the arts is a combination of state and private patronage. The state's involvement sets up essential structures which provide a guarantee of continuity of patronage, and private enterprise is then in a position to take an innovative interest in specific projects. However, such a balance needs to be encouraged actively by the state, and this is not happening. The present position regarding taxation does not provide an incentive for private investment in the arts. Unlike the situation in the United States, where all donations to the arts are tax-deductible, in Ireland tax relief on gifts is at the discretion of the Department of Finance. Section 32 of the Finance Act 1984 provided the basis for a system of tax-allowable private support for the arts. Through it gifts of amounts between £100 and £10,000 to certain nominated bodies which promote the arts could be deducted from the sponsor's tax liabilities. However, the Department of Finance still maintains its discretionary position in relation to which arts bodies may benefit from this. So far a limited number have been sanctioned and it seems that a very narrow interpretation is being applied.

This position would seem to present an insuperable obstacle against a combination of state and private funding of the arts, and must inevitably mean more direct demands on the state purse. Ireland has a relatively narrow tax base and the Department of Finance must ensure that it takes in sufficient funds to meet essential expenditure. It thus jealously guards its position and is unwilling to weaken its own discretionary powers. The result is likely to be a continuation of the serious under-funding of the arts. This position is accentuated in the present period of economic recession when the trend is towards increasing the taxation burden rather than on tax relief. For example, the report by the Commission on Taxation in 1981 suggested replacing the tax exemption for creative artists and recommended taxing the "cnuas" of £4,000 granted under the Aosdana scheme. However, in spite of rumors that these changes were to occur, the tax exemption remains and the "cnuas" is still untaxed.

The main financial burden of the arts thus falls directly on the state, and the health of the arts depends largely on the level of state generosity. However, although the state gives financial aid in the form of grants and subsidies, it also receives back revenue from the arts in the form of the various taxes on income and expenditure. As well as receiving income tax from all those involved in the arts, the state extracts 5 percent (until recently 23 percent) value added tax on theater tickets, a burden that threatened many theaters with closure. This position indicates how little the state provides in real terms for the arts. Persistent under-funding has meant that capital expenditure is now urgently needed for the maintenance of buildings and for the provision of new arts facilities—for example, the many new housing estates of the larger cities where no such facilities now exist.

Ireland is a poor country by European standards and support for the arts must be seen in the context of housing, health care, and other essential social needs. Yet even when seen in this context, the level of state aid is low, and the present recession means that there is little hope of a dramatic improvement in funding in the immediate future. Because of the institutional nature of its funding, the Arts Council budget increases annually, although not always in line with inflation. The level of increase also depends on the strength with which the Arts Council makes its case to the government. The budget for 1982 was only 2.4 percent over the previous year. With inflation at over 20 percent, this meant a drop of about one-fifth in real terms. This inevitably meant cutbacks and the withdrawal of Arts Council grants to some organizations. The cuts resulted in the birth of Action '82, a group representing most professional arts organizations in the country (about seventy-five in number), which requested the government for an urgent increase in the level of financial support. However, in Ireland arts lobbying tends to be relatively weak, responding to particular arts crises and therefore by nature temporary.

The cutbacks in 1982 also led to accusations that the Arts Council used the shortage of funds against some arts organizations with which the Director and his staff had little sympathy.[58] One of the most notable victims of the difficult times was the Douglas Hyde Gallery at Trinity College, which in June 1982 had its Arts Council grant withdrawn and ceased to function as a professionally run center. The Hyde Gallery is Dublin's only fully equipped center for temporary visual arts exhibitions and is visited by 50,000 people annually. Its grant was withdrawn because the Gallery was running up a deficit, and its staff of three became redundant. A rescue package was worked out between the Arts Council and Trinity College, the effect of which was to give the Arts Council a deeper involvement in the running of the Gallery—a development which some critics felt was what the Arts Council had in mind in the first instance.

Criticism of the Arts Council is relatively common and inevitable in the light of the number of arts organizations which seek assistance, some of which must be disappointed, either for failing to receive a grant or at the level of the aid. The system by which the state distributes its limited largesse is bound to be imperfect but the Arts Council has achieved a good deal of success. One problem which has been raised concerns the danger that the administration of the Council is developing into an unmanageable bureaucracy. The problems of bureaucracy are particularly relevant to the arts, where flexibility is essential if imagination and creativity are not to be stifled. There is also some evidence that a move towards greater democracy and visibility in the Arts Council now might be appropriate. This is particularly necessary when sensitive decisions are made in private on who or what is eligible for an arts grant, or indeed for an arts cutback. Changes such as these would go some way towards a greater degree of public accountability in relation to expenditure on the arts.

One recent change is the appointment by the Government of a Junior Minister with responsibility for the arts. Opinion is divided on the benefit for the arts of such a change, and a central question it raises concerns the autonomy of the Arts Council. This autonomy is guarded jealously by the Council, which sees itself as a buffer between government and the arts, ensuring that ministers cannot be used to intervene in specific areas. The Arts Council always has been free from political interference, although there is evidence that in the early years some unsuccessful attempts were made by politicians to influence Council policy. The clientelist political culture means that a member of the Dáil spends a good deal of his time doing favors for his own constituents. In this situation, it is useful to have a buffer between the arts and the state patron. A Department of Culture might well change this position and the benefits of coordinating the many arts interests under one umbrella, and of having a Minister arguing the case for the arts at the cabinet table, may well be outweighed by the dangers of political interference in the arts, and by the increased bureaucracy. The appointment of a Junior Minister has created an obvious focal point for arts interests and one which will be used by some who feel their case is not being adequately dealt with by the Arts Council. This situation may mean a critical weakening of the Arts Council, and, ultimately, the politicization of the arts.

As the intervention of the Department of the Taoiseach in the ITC affair indicates, the autonomy of the Arts Council is by no means absolute. The Department of the Taoiseach keeps a very watchful eye on the Council, and the impression remains that the Council must tread carefully. The changes which led to the 1973 Arts Act, far from being initiated from within the Council, were spearheaded by the Department of the Taoiseach. Confrontations and controversy of the kind I have indicated are dangerous for the Council, and are unlikely to be regarded with much sympathy or tolerated for long. Indeed, the present position in relation to the appointment of a Junior Minister for the arts, while part of government policy, may well signify the desire on the part of the bureaucracy to bring the Arts Council under a greater degree of control. The position of the Arts Council was weakened by the decision to place the administration of the new National Concert Hall, now the home of the RTE Symphony Orchestra, outside its jurisdiction. The Concert Hall is run by an independent Board which reports to the Department of the Taoiseach. The Council always has emphasized its need for wide scope and a strong integrated public policy in the arts, and this move was seen by it as a potential threat.[59]

It thus can be seen that the Arts Council by no means has things its own way under the present system, but there is a grave danger that it could become an impotent body under a Minister for Culture. Some distance from the bureaucracy has been shown to be healthy for the arts in Ireland, and those bodies which have a degree of autonomy—for example the Arts Council, the Kilkenny Design Workshops, and the National Gallery—are in a much better position than those under direct departmental control. It is tempting to think that a Department of Culture would remove all the problems that beset the arts in Ireland today, and it is conceivable that the arts could flourish under a progressive Minister working with an enlightened department. However, the risks involved in such a development cannot be underestimated, particularly if the move is made only as a means of centralizing arts administration and without consideration of the deeper questions of cultural policy—questions which concern not just the arts but the nation's whole way of life. "The arts" in Ireland, as in many other countries, have been separated from other social experience instead of being defined in broader cultural terms which involve the total development of man in his social environment.[60] Until such time as politicians are prepared to consider the arts within this context and government policy reflects this, no new department or Minister can bring about more than superficial change for the arts. For this reason, the Government's proposed policy "White Paper" on arts and cultural development is eagerly awaited.

Conclusion

Some progress has been made in the area of government and the arts in Ireland, but much remains to be done. Inequality of access to the arts is still a problem and the Arts Council's stress on the importance of education is supported by a recent survey[61] on participation in the arts in Ireland, which suggests that the main obstacle to increased participation is a cultural one. People's attitudes to the arts tended to be negative and audiences do not appear to be expanding over the last decade, in spite of increased expenditure since the mid-1970s. Perhaps the most important task now to be faced is to reintegrate the arts within a broadly defined concept of culture, so that the arts no longer are associated only with leisure, and arts policy is no longer a matter of waiting until economic times improve but instead is seen in the context of cultural policy and cultural democracy. In this way, the arts can be an active ingredient in defining the kind of society we want and how best this can be achieved.

A culture is, as Raymond Williams says,[62] essentially unplannable, because culture is a process of natural growth. It is therefore essential that a movement towards cultural democracy is community-based, coming from the people to the politicians. Here, the Regional Arts Committees could have an important role to play. But education also is vital in helping to develop the creative capacities of life, which have not in the past been given the attention they deserve. We can see all around us the disadvantages of the relatively rapid economic expansion of the 1970s, which occurred without an adequately growing cultural base. Our cities are monuments to disastrous planning and much development in the countryside tells the same tale—a lack of sensitivity to environment which is having consequences not just for cultural development, but for social and economic development also.

Increased financial aid to the arts, involving bigger grants to the Arts Council and greater allocations of funds to the arts institutions, as well as a degree of autonomy, is only part of the solution. A re-thinking of arts educational policy must also occur if increased expenditure is to have lasting benefit and do more than add to the present state of inequality of access to the arts. Widespread arts participation and equality of access cannot come about without such a policy change. Neither does widespread participation imply a lowering of artistic standards. As Ciaran Benson has said, "what is needed is not a stooping of the arts to the level of common accessibility, but a fundamental altering of those factors which pre-empt a greater intellectual and aesthetic popular consciousness."[63]

The cold economic and political facts of life in the 1980s are beginning to raise questions about the self-definitions and the political choices which we in Ireland have made in the past. The current cultural crisis indicates that alternative choices might be made in the future—choices which take into account not just particular aspects of development processes but those which emphasize man's common cultural progress towards true freedom.

Appendix

Arts Council State Endowment 1952–1983

1952–1953	£10,000*	1971–1972	£80,000
1953–1954	£11,400	1972–1973	£85,000
1954–1955	£19,150	1974	£113,000**
1955–1956	£18,889	1974–1975	£200,000
1956–1957	£17,000	1975–1976	£990,000***
1957–1961	£20,000	1976–1977	£1,200,000
1961–1963	£30,000	1977–1978	£1,565,000
1963–1964	£35,000	1978–1979	£2,340,000
1964–1967	£40,000	1979–1980	£3,000,000
1967–1969	£60,000	1980–1981	£3,750,000
1969–1971	£70,000	1981–1982	£4,082,000

*First full year
**New Arts Act
***Responsibility for Theater taken on

Notes

1. Mervyn Wall, "An Address to the Annual Meeting of the American Committee for Irish Studies," April 1980, in *Journal of Irish Literature,* January-May 1982, p. 64.

2. Figures from the introduction to *National Gallery of Ireland Summary Catalogue of Paintings* (Dublin, 1981), p. xviii. The Catalogue is edited by the Gallery Director, Homan Potterton.

3. Thomas Bodkin, *Report on the Arts in Ireland* (Dublin, 1949), p. 19.

4. *Ibid.*

5. For a good account of the Abbey Theater subsidy debate, see James Meenan, *George O'Brien, a Biographical Memoir* (Dublin: Gill and Macmillan, 1980), pp. 115–122. George O'Brien was the first government nominee on the board of the Abbey Theater.

6. Gearoid O'Tuathaigh, "Language, Literature and Culture in Ireland since the War," in J. J. Lee, ed., *Ireland 1945–70* (Dublin: Gill and Macmillan, 1979), p. 110.

7. Bodkin, *Report on the Arts*, p. 8.

8. Dáil Debates, 21 February 1951.

9. Figures from Estimates for Public Expenditure for year ending 31 March 1953.

10. Dáil Debates, 24 April 1951.

11. *Ibid.*

12. Mervyn Wall, "An Address to the Annual Meeting . . . ," p. 70.

13. K. Franck, et al., *Design in Ireland*, Report of the Scandinavian Design Group in Ireland, The Irish Export Board, April 1961.

14. *Ibid.*, p. 49.

15. Ciaran Benson, *The Place of the Arts in Irish Education* (Dublin: The Arts Council, 1979), p. 16.

16. *Scandinavian Report*, p. 45.

17. *Kilkenny Design Workshops Ltd.*, Report and Accounts, 1981.

18. *Ibid.*

19. *National Gallery of Ireland Summary Catalogue of Paintings*. All Gallery figures from this source.

20. Letter from Sean O'Faolain to *The Irish Times*, 29 December 1956.

21. Arts Council 12th Annual Report, March 1964.

22. *Ibid.*, March 1967.

23. *Ibid.*, 1980.

24. Figures supplied by the Revenue Commissioners.

25. Arts Council Annual Report, 1977.

26. *Ibid.*, 1974.

27. *Ibid.*, 1976.

28. *Ibid.*, 1977.

29. *National Gallery of Ireland, Recent Acquisitions 1980–1981* (introduction).

30. J. M. Richards, *Provision for the Arts* (Dublin: The Arts Council, 1976), p. 49.

31. *Ibid.*, p. 35.

32. Elfrida Saunders, quoted in the introduction to the *Bodkin Report*, p. 7.

33. *Report of the Board of Visitors to the National Museum*, 1977–78, p. 3.

34. Breakdown of figures from the Department of Foreign Affairs.

35. Richards, *Provision for the Arts*, p. 13.

36. Arts Council Annual Report, 1981.

37. Letter from the Regional Arts Officer, Mid-West Region to the Arts Council, 4 November 1982.

38. Survey (unpublished) on Local Authority expenditure on the arts, conducted in March 1982 by Jerome Hynes, Druid Theater Company, Galway.

39. Mid-West *Three-Year Plan for Developing the Arts*, October 1982.

40. *Contributions to the Arts 1979*—leaflet issued by Dublin Corporation's Cultural Committee, and letter from the City Manager to the Cultural Committee, 8 November 1982.

41. Information on Cork Corporation's arts activities from the Corporation, November 1982.

42. Gerard Fay, "The Abbey Theatre," in *Ireland of the Welcomes*, Vol. 15, No. 2, 1966.

43. Conversation with Colm O'Briain, 1 October 1982.

44. Arts Council Annual Report, 1980.

45. *Ibid.*

46. "Report to the Nation," Channel 4 TV, 9 January 1983.

47. Quoted in John Lane, *Arts Centers—Every Town Should Have One* (London: Elek), p. 20.

48. Letter from Colm O'Briain, 13 October 1982.

49. Survey: *Living and Working Conditions of Artists*, The Arts Council, 1980.

50. Report: *The Status of the Artist*, UNESCO, 1980.

51. Directory: *Writers in Schools,* The Arts Council, 1981.

52. Leaflet: *Paint on the Wall,* The Arts Council, 1981.

53. Conversation with Colm O'Briain, 1 October 1982.

54. Arts Council Annual Report, 1978.

55. Ciaran Benson, op. cit., p. 126.

56. Arts Council Annual Report, 1980.

57. Edward McParland, "The Bank and the Visual Arts 1783–1983," in F. S. L. Lyons, ed., *The Bank of Ireland: Centenary Essays* (Dublin, 1983).

58. Fintan O'Toole, "The Brightest and the Best," profile of Colm O'Briain, *The Sunday Tribune,* 29 August 1982.

59. Interview with Colm O'Briain, 1 October 1982.

60. Herbert Marcuse writes of one-dimensional man and of the tendency in modern industrial society towards living and acting in the single dimension of adaptation to reality and not in the dimension of transcending that reality. Lucien Goldmann, writing in 1968 (Cultural Creation), suggests that the fundamental problematic of modern societies is no longer at the level of poverty (although poverty remains) or even at the level of limited freedom. It lies now, he feels, entirely in the contraction of the level of consciousness and in the tendency to reduce the fundamental human dimension of the possible.

61. R. Sinnott and D. Kavanagh, *Audiences, Acquisitions and Amateurs: Participation in the Arts in Ireland,* The Arts Council, March 1983.

62. Raymond Williams, *Culture and Society 1780–1950* (Pelican, 1976).

63. Ciaran Benson, "The Art of Policy and Policies of Art in Irish Education" in *The Crane Bag,* Vol. 6, No. 1, p. 102.

12

Cultivating the Bushgarden: Cultural Policy in Canada[1]

JOHN MEISEL AND JEAN VAN LOON

Introduction

In fashioning their cultural policies, governments inevitably respond to universal forces prevailing in a variety of countries as well as to the particular idiosyncratic ones they find at home. In this chapter, emphasis is placed on the latter which, however, cannot but at least occasionally reflect world-wide trends. In Canada historical antecedents, demographic conditions, the physical setting, and socio-political and economic realities, all provide the limits constraining the fertile minds of even the most daring cultural policy-makers. We shall therefore begin by briefly scanning the setting within which Canadian governments fashioned programs and policies affecting the country's artistic and cultural life.

Canada was inhabited by Indians and Inuit when the first European settlers arrived in the seventeenth century. The bitter struggle between the British and French for what Voltaire had called *quelques arpents de neige* was won by the former but left a legacy of an ethnically and culturally mixed society. To what later came to be known as "the founding races" (a term characteristically applied to the first European settlers and not to the natives) there were soon added immigrants from other lands so that the originally overwhelmingly British and French ethnic character was gradually altered. At the present time people whose origins are in the United Kingdom constitute a bit less than half of the population, whereas those of French and other background each make up a little over one-quarter of Canadians. Almost two-thirds of Canadians report English as their mother tongue, a quarter French, and the remainder (a little over three million) spoke other languages as children.

In size, Canada is the world's second largest country, but its population is small—twenty-five million largely scattered along a very thin inhabited sliver hugging the southern (United States) border. Because of the immense size, there are numerous climatic and other environmental differences which account in part for the presence of significant regional variations. These find expression in intense local loyalties which sometimes conflict with strong national attachments.

Political arrangements reflect some of these conditions. Because of the British origins of Canada, the country was created in 1867 by an Act of the Parliament at Westminster which united a number of British colonies into the framework of a federal state. Canada's political system thus combines the centralizing features of the parliamentary and cabinet system with the centrifugal elements of a rather loose federation.

The last key factor relevant to cultural policy to be noted here concerns the country's proximity to the United States. The physical presence of its powerful and exuberant neighbor, the fact that about 80 percent of Canadians speak English, and the deep economic penetration of the United States in Canada pose very special problems for Canadian culture and hence for cultural policy. The matter is exacerbated by the fact that although Canadians for the most part do feel themselves to be different from Americans, and like to preserve their regional and national characteristics, many do share certain aspects of a common North American culture. Inside every anglophone Canadian, therefore, there is an American. The same phenomenon can be observed in the case of francophones, but to a lesser extent.

The popular and more rarefied arts usually subsumed under the term culture, as used in the present volume,[2] are everywhere an absolutely vital element in human experience, touching on the fundamental values by which men and women guide their lives. They concern the ends, and not only the means of existence and so are of unrivalled significance to every individual. In the light of the factors sketched above, the cultural dimension is even more important in Canada than in other communities. This special significance in Canada arises from the role cultural activities play in giving expression to many of the collective experiences of populations and from the fact that the bonds that hold individuals together and bind them into coherent collectivities are to an important degree fashioned by cultural activities. The latter encourage the sharing of the felt, emotional dimensions of the human condition. Common memories, exploits, traumas, activities, and interests unrelated to the mundane drudgeries of everyday life are imbedded by cultural experiences in the hearts and minds of members of various human collectivities, including particularly members of national communities and nation states.

The extraordinary importance of culture to a place like Canada becomes clearly evident when one compares it and, say, France. In the latter country, whose population is linguistically and ethnically pretty homogeneous, and which has fought many wars against common enemies, a strong national feeling exists irrespective of its current cultural life. National cohesion would be great even if Marianne, the Marseillaise, or Molière had not enhanced Gallic pride and group cohesion. Canada, on the other hand, has never faced a serious, immediate foreign threat, has had no dynastic, religious, or national enemies, and is at the same time, as we saw, very disparate in its demographic and geographic characteristics. In this situation, a national anthem, emotionally laden emblems, shared pride in Glenn Gould (or Wayne Gretzky), and a common perception of its northern landscape as portrayed by the Group of Seven (the country's earliest distinctive and most widely known school of painters[3]), all play a very special role in creating the socio-political cohesion necessary in a modern state.

Incentives to Policy-Making

Since the end of the Second World War, Canada, like many other countries, experienced an exponential growth in its cultural activities. This growth occurred partly because of general changes in Canadian society and partly because governments adopted specific policies designed to foster a more vigorous creative life in the arts and related fields. Among the legacies of the war were a growing feeling of Canadian consciousness and nationalism and the acceptance of large-scale and vigorous activities on the part of the state. The latter change in attitudes and in the behavior of the government had been given an early impetus by the need to confront the ravages of the Depression and was then reinforced by the exigencies of a massive war effort. Widespread acceptance in government circles of Keynesian economics further enhanced the emergence of a positive state. Although Lord Keynes's keen interest in the arts certainly had no direct impact on Canadian cultural policies, his theories emphasizing the heavy involvement by governments in offsetting the vagaries of the economy created a climate conducive to the intervention of the state in various fields, including that of culture and the arts.

The Second World War was a significant agent in the metamorphosis of Canada from colony to nation. Although in 1939 the country was to all intents and purposes a completely independent Dominion, there were still significant links with Britain, many of them of an emotional kind, particularly on the part of those whose origins were in Britain. The strong, highly distinctive contribution of Canada to the war, Britain's decline as a world power, massive immigration from the European continent, and the awakening of Quebec nationalism, all contributed to a major economic and psychological reorientation. In a sense Canada was beginning to feel her oats not only politically but also economically and culturally. The United Kingdom was still, to be sure, the major influence, inspiration, and source of most of the cultural life in English Canada, but there were unmistakable signs of indigenous stirrings in many of the performing arts and other cultural and aesthetic initiatives.

French Canada had cut most of its cultural ties with Europe much earlier and had in fact also been less involved in the war than the rest of the country. Although the immediate war experience had less impact on cultural growth, other developments led to a national awakening and to the birth of numerous cultural initiatives on the part of the Quebec government. The so-called "Quiet Revolution" after the early 1960s—the transformation of Quebec into a modern, energetic community—was accompanied by a vigorous cultural flowering. The inspiration for the widespread burst of creativity came from deeply felt traditions and a sense of community the Quebecers had developed ever since the departure of the French in 1760. In the two hundred years that followed, the descendants of the small number of settlers developed a very high level of cohesion and a vigorous indigenous culture. Until the 1960s their nationalism was essentially inward looking and isolationist, but all this changed in the course of the Quiet Revolution, when world-wide currents in all aspects of human experience, including the arts, acted as a liberating force on Quebec society.

The postwar years were followed, in Canada as in many other parts of the world, by far-reaching social, economic, and political changes. These had a direct impact on the cultural life of the country.

Work hours decreased for large numbers of people whose incomes were nevertheless generally rising. They therefore had more time and money to devote to leisure activities. Among these, cultural pursuits played an increasingly important part. At the same time the growing prosperity and expansionist tendencies of governments resulted in more resources becoming available from public funds. New programs were launched making previously unknown or neglected pastimes and activities accessible to large numbers of people.

Demographic changes also contributed to the rising interest in cultural affairs. For some years there was a massive increase in births with appreciable effects on the demographic pyramid. Younger age cohorts created new demands and required new services.

Educational systems had to adapt to the changed circumstances and did so in part by offering courses which were deemed suitable for generations which would enjoy more leisure than had been given their parents and grandparents. Community colleges and similar institutions, offering non-academic and vocational courses, attracted large numbers of students and introduced many of them to subjects about the very existence of which many had never even dreamed. Arts and crafts courses proliferated and attracted large numbers of students. Even though many of these may never have actually plied the trades they were taught, they often became avid consumers of cultural experiences inspired by their education. There was also a substantial growth in the number and size of universities which professed fields of study in culture and the arts. Thus universities, community colleges, and their equivalents played a major role in providing cultural opportunities as well as keen consumers anxious to enjoy them. Canada, like many other countries, saw the expansion of universities go hand in hand with the expansion of cultural activities. Universities and colleges often became major centers of cultural life, particularly in smaller and medium-sized cities.

It was not only the so-called "baby-boomers" who contributed to the substantial expansion of cultural life. Successive waves of immigrants from the United Kingdom and the European continent brought with them a strong traditional interest in the arts and folk cultures. They also introduced an exciting ethnic mix which, added to the long-established presence of both anglophones and francophones, created a climate encouraging to the expression of national distinctiveness through both folk and high arts.

A less potent contributing factor, but one worth mentioning, concerns the role of tourism. This industry has always been important in Canada, largely because of the country's varied topography and climate and its great scenic attractiveness. It became increasingly valued as the Canadian economy encountered mounting difficulties and problems in exporting many of its manufactured goods. Cultural events, such as festivals, widely known performing arts companies, and other entertainment opportunities, came increasingly to be seen as relevant not only to the aesthetic but also the economic well-being of the country, both from the domestic viewpoint and that of the balance of payments.

We have already noted that the general expansionist and interventionist style of Canadian governments after the Second World War included an increasing involvement with the arts. A very special circumstance in Canada ascribed a particular significance to these inititiatives. Being a new and post-colonial community, Canada lacked a strong tradition of royal, aristocratic, and even private patronage of the arts. In the United States the populist and post-colonial legacy was compensated for by lavish private support of the arts by owners of huge fortunes, including the so-called robber barons. Canada, because of its economic dependence and late industrial development, produced almost no financially well-endowed individuals or clans comparable to those of the United States and western Europe who could or would subsidize cultural causes. And even when huge profits from various commercial and industrial enterprises were eventually being created, this occurred at a time when heavy personal and corporate taxes slowed and diminished the accumulation of massive fortunes. Under these circumstances it became particularly important that public agencies become involved in supporting the arts.

Other dynamic forces contributed to a more interventionist stance of governments. Among them, Royal Commissions and other similar special inquiries played a major role. Several of these were instrumental in shaping the Canadian broadcasting system—a major factor in cultural policy.[4] Even more central to our concerns are two inquiries with an even broader mandate. The Massey Commission, established in 1949, and the Applebaum-Hébert Committee which sat in the early 1980s surveyed virtually every nook and cranny of the country's artistic landscape.[5] Among the towering achievements of the former was the recommendation of the creation of the Canada Council, patterned roughly after the British Arts Council, which, as we shall see, became the single most important instrument in Canada's cultural policies during virtually all of the period under review.

A brief look at the way in which the Canada Council was established will prove revealing. Political forces were gathering strength in support of the creation of a granting agency supporting universities and the arts. Agitation by intellectuals and artistic communities, the work of the Massey Commission, reasonably encouraging economic conditions, and the commitment of a few individuals converged to create an environment conducive to the launching of a national arts council. But the caution and tastes of the Prime Minister (''I've never been much in favour of ballet'') left the whole matter in doubt until a couple of ingenious officials and politicians persuaded the Prime Minister that the matter could be presented to the public in an engaging form if it were connected to some windfall revenues from the succession duties collected from the estates of two recently deceased entrepreneurs. Louis St. Laurent, the Prime Minister, finally went ahead with the project when he was persuaded that he could link the creation of the Canada Council and the establishment of its endowment fund to the unexpected receipt by the government of about $100 million from the succession duties on the estates of Isaac W. Killam and Sir James Dunn. There is no question that the project would have gone ahead sooner or later in any event, but the demise of the two tycoons enhanced the political milieu in which the project could be presented to Parliament.[6]

Policies and organizations launched as the result of the various public inquiries ultimately assumed a life of their own and dominated the cultural scene until quite recently, when a subtle change began to be evident. We shall deal with it towards the end of this chapter. Here, the important point to note is that a number of individuals who, either as politicians or as officials, found themselves at the center of cultural policy-making, came to assume a particularly critical role in the evolution of Canada's cultural life.

Bureaucracies, like other organizations, often develop the habit of vigorously promoting the fields which they administer both because they believe in them and because their organizations acquire a vested interest in their ''turf'' being generously supported by large votes of funds. Cultural bureaucracies are no exception. If anything, they tend to attract arts enthusiasts who have much more than a routine commitment to the programs for which they are responsible. As a result, in a brokerage society in which decisions are increasingly made as the result of the interplay of numerous interests, bureaucracies themselves become involved in the game of pressure politics which is crucial in the allocation of societal resources. During the period from 1945 to the present, arts and cultural bureaucracies grew from a handful of individuals into thousands of officials operating at the federal, provincial, and municipal levels, at each of which they strengthened pressures for governmental policies favoring the arts.

More conventional lobbies have also encouraged the evolution of large-scale programs. Among the factors which led to the creation of the Massey Commission was the pressure brought to bear after the war by artists in various parts of the country concerned about the future of their craft and art. It is noteworthy that the first major public presence of the artistic community in a lobbying context occurred when the Canadian Arts Council presented a brief to the Turgeon Committee which was conducting a major inquiry into the problems of Canada's postwar reconstruction. This Council—not to be confused with the Canada Council, the major granting agency—was to turn into the Canadian Conference of Arts—the umbrella organization which has become the most powerful and effective cultural lobby in the country. It is, interestingly, financed to an important degree by the government department now primarily responsible for cultural matters.

Yet another incitement for a lively governmental involvement with culture is found in what we might term "competitive federalism."[7] This rather bizarre Canadian phenomenon was triggered in the first instance by separatist tendencies in Quebec. All of that province's recent governments have followed strongly nationalist policies ranging from the repudiation of many federal initiatives, particularly in the field of culture, to outright calls for independence or something called "sovereignty-association"—a formula involving economic association but political sovereignty. The Canadian constitution clearly assigns education to provincial jurisdiction, and culture is considered by most provinces to be so intimately related that the provinces must have unchallenged responsibility and primacy. Since Quebec is the only province in which francophones are in a majority, its government has assumed that it is the protector of French culture in Canada and that it must have all the means available to discharge this role.

Ottawa, however, believes that it also represents Quebecers and, in addition, francophones who live outside the province. For most of the period of concern to us, Quebecers sent huge majorities backing the Liberal governments which have dominated Canadian politics since the mid-1920s. At any rate, intense rivalry developed between the two governments which, more often than not, involved cultural issues. Politicians and officials in both jurisdictions vied with one another with respect to cultural initiatives, and this intense competition led to greater government involvement at each level than would have been likely had competitive federalism not become part of the Canadian scene.

This federal-provincial rivalry was certainly most acute in so far as Quebec and Ottawa were concerned, but it was by no means confined to these two players. Other provinces also resented what they saw as Ottawa's intrusion into areas under their jurisdiction. The strong sense of regionalism in Canada further encouraged provinces to launch programs strengthening local cultural life. All of them now operate extensive programs aiding the arts. These both supplement and compete with those of the federal government.

The final cluster of factors prompting extensive governmental involvement in culture to be noted here can best be characterized as idiosyncratic elements. For example, a number of individual Secretaries of State (Ministers under whom cultural matters fell for a good many years) played a particularly central role. In the 1960s and 1970s Maurice Lamontagne and Gérard Pelletier in particular provided strong leadership both with respect to their subordinates and, more important, within the cabinet where the fundamental policy decision had to be made and where the funding of major projects had to be approved. It is perhaps no accident that both were members of a small group of Quebec intellectuals who were lured to Ottawa by Prime Minister Lester Pearson in his efforts to strengthen French-English relations in the country. Previously, the individuals who were instrumental in the founding of the Canada Council also played a seminal role in official arts policies. To some extent, the evolution of major federal policies, at the times they evolved, can be ascribed to the fortuitous presence in the government of Ministers and some officials with very strong commitments to the arts.

Another fortuitous circumstance was the celebration of Canada's Centennial in 1967 and the holding of the World's Fair—Expo—during the same year. These events not only liberated substantial sums of money, a fair proportion of which was allocated to cultural projects, but they also engendered an atmosphere of optimism and confidence which was conducive to the launching of bold programs. As well, they pointed to the importance of symbolic aspects of the human experience and hence of the artistic imagination. The importance of Expo and of the Centennial to the evolution of cultural policy in Canada is therefore a useful reminder that serendipity often plays an important role in the evolution of policy goals and practices.

Some ongoing programs also had unintended consequences for the arts in Canada. Schemes to support the activities of the so-called "other" ethnic groups, for example, often provided funds for artistic endeavors. Similarly, various initiatives intended to deal with the problems of native people led to the establishment of cultural programs. The creation of Inuit cooperatives producing remarkable works of sculpture and prints is a good example. The role of the federal government was of critical importance in the evolution of these activities. The impetus for them was social, not aesthetic. Similarly, programs intended to provide work for young people and to help various local projects during periods of high unemployment quite unexpectedly turned out to funnel impressive resources into cultural activities. Some of these later became the basis of professional endeavors of artists who were able to receive assistance from the Canada Council under its ongoing programs of support for plastic and performing artists.

Disincentives

There were, of course, also some obstacles to the free flowering of cultural life and to government involvement in this domain. The country's historical antecedents, for one, left a legacy which was not always encouraging to cultural pursuits. The puritanical tradition of many settlers in English Canada, the harshness of the climate and of the pioneering life, economic and social challenges confronting those who arrived more recently and settled in the towns and cities, and the effort and energy required of citizens as well as governments to develop a new land, all tended to inhibit the easy and rapid flowering of many of the arts.

In the 1970s and 1980s economic difficulties imposed the necessity of severe governmental spending restraints which had particularly deleterious effects on cultural programs. When belts have to be tightened, it is usually the arts that are first to engage in slimming. This is caused in part by the lingering sense among many that the arts are a frill and in part by the very nature of much of artistic and cultural activity. Experimentation, the exploration of the subconscious, and attempts to amuse the public by means of satire, all of which are frequently integral to the artistic experience, create antagonism and fear. Many forms of artistic expression, although of course by no means all, tend to question the status quo and to mock political, social, and economic establishments. The artistic community is therefore often suspect in many circles, and thus an easy target when spending cuts are in the air. It is also the case that occasionally, although by no means always of course, cultural ventures are inefficiently administered and that the creative impulse behind them banishes respect for the "bottom line."

By far the most serious obstacle to the free flowering of Canadian culture, and indeed a major reason for dynamic governmental involvement, is the presence of American cultural products. As a British colony and Dominion, Canada was, during much of its formative period, under the cultural domination of its mother country.[8] While English Canada undoubtedly benefited from the cultural links with Britain, they retarded the development of many indigenous initiatives and the training of Canadians capable of doing first-class work in the arts.

Just as the British influence was declining, Canada fell under the massive economic and cultural spell of the United States. It was and still is often much easier, cheaper, and more commercially attractive to import American cultural goods than to produce Canadian ones. This retards or stultifies the growth of local talent and exposes the consumers of the imported fare to the preoccupations of a society other than their own. Canadian artistic efforts expressing Canadian realities and dreams have, for this reason, had a very hard time to materialize and so could not readily be enjoyed.

In concluding this sketch of some of the principal factors encouraging and impeding the colossal growth of cultural life and the massive contribution of governments to it, we must note that no one seems to have hatched a grand design or master plan guiding Canada towards a richer artistic experience. It was rather the convergence of numerous factors, some of them quite fortuitous, which cohered into the rich landscape we shall deal with below.

Support Instruments

The diverse means employed by Canadian authorities to effect their cultural objectives can conveniently be classified according to two criteria: first, whether they are permanent fixtures or ad hoc creations. The former are infinitely more important; the latter will, therefore, be given short shrift here. We have already mentioned some of them: bodies and policies to create or support special cultural projects in relation to, say, Canada's Centennial celebrations and similar provincial occasions, Expo 1967 or 1986, or the Olympic or Commonwealth Games. Another example is the administrative machinery created to mark Canada Day (the national holiday) or St. Jean Baptiste Day (the national celebration of French Canadians).[9] Despite the magnitude of some of the ad hoc projects, such as support for the construction of performing arts centers to mark the anniversaries of cities or provinces, the long-term impact tends to be much less marked than that of on-going programs which operate year after year.

Second, governmental instruments must also be distinguished on the basis of whether they actually function as operating cultural agencies, whether they merely provide financial and other support to individuals or organizations in the arts, or whether their primary concern is to do research, plan policy, or administer cultural projects. These functions cannot always be clearly separated; some official structures or projects touch on more than one of the categories just noted.

Operating Bodies. Among the operating bodies, the most important are the Canadian Broadcasting Corporation (CBC), the National Film Board (NFB), various national museums including the National Gallery, the National Arts Centre (NAC), and the Public Archives and the National Library. Some provinces have created analogous institutions. There are educational radio and television systems in Ontario, Quebec, Alberta, and British Columbia, for instance, and many provinces operate museums and galleries, as well as centers for the performing arts.

Supporting Institutions. By far the most important of the supporting institutions is the Canada Council, the federal cultural granting agency which, however, as we shall see, does a great deal more than offer financial assistance. Another of the supporting agencies is Telefilm Canada (formerly known as the Canadian Film Development Corporation). Again, similar bodies operate on a smaller scale at the provincial level, particularly in the larger and wealthier provinces.

Administrative and Policy-Making Machinery. Here the two most important instruments at the federal level are the Ministry most preoccupied with culture—at present this is the Department of Communications (DOC)—and the Canadian Radio-Television and Telecommunications Commission (CRTC). The inclusion of this body in our list suggests that regulation, through an independent regulatory agency, is one of the means available to governments for the implementation of cultural policies. Also important, but to a lesser degree, are certain branches in ministries other than the DOC, such as the Department of External Affairs, Public Works, or Canada Post, and organizations like the Canadian Commission for UNESCO.

As we have already noted, provincial governments have created organisms which perform at least some of the functions discharged by the agencies just listed, although in most instances, if not in all, they are individually smaller in scale and have been created more recently than their federal counterparts. Nevertheless, as we shall see when we examine the sums of money spent by the three levels of government on the arts, the involvement of what is usually thought of as the more junior jurisdictions is very impressive. At the municipal level, it is not only the very large cities like Toronto, Montreal, Vancouver, and Edmonton which have launched important studies and programs but smaller places as well.

Within the confines of a single chapter it is quite impossible to describe and analyze all the instruments listed above. So as to relieve the conscientious reader of a deserved feeling of deprivation prompted by this state of affairs, however, a short sketch of some of the players will be provided.

Operating Bodies: CBC, NFB, NAC

CBC. It was recognized in the early days of radio that the propinquity of U.S. broadcasters and their thirst for markets threatened the cultural integrity of Canada. A path-breaking Royal Commission[10] (the first of many on broadcasting) recommended the creation of a publicly owned broadcasting system. A powerful campaign by interested citizens and organizations, the Canadian Radio League, was mounted in support of this policy and the Canadian Radio Broadcasting Commission (later to become the CBC) was established in 1932. A telling argument for choosing a public corporation was made by R. B. Bennett, the Conservative Prime Minister:

> . . . this country must be assured of complete Canadian control of broadcasting from Canadian sources, free from foreign interference or influence. Without such control radio broadcasting can never become a great agency for communication of matters of national thought and ideals, and without such control it can never be the agency by which national consciousness may be fostered and sustained and national unity still further strengthened . . .[11]

Bennett expressed a concern which has continued to preoccupy Canadians ever since, and not only with respect to broadcasting but also in relation to virtually all of the country's cultural life. The CBC, although increasingly confronted by vigorous competition from the private sector, became a major force in the evolution not only of Canadian broadcasting but also of the country's musicians, writers, poets, and actors. For many years now, it has provided two national radio services (AM and FM) in both of the official languages as well as a television service for each of the linguistic groups. In addition, it covers the debates in the House of Commons and runs a short-wave international service as well as offering special programming in the North, much of it in the Inuktitut language. It provides programs for francophone majorities outside Quebec and to remote areas. Long before there were any significant government programs encouraging the arts, the CBC regularly organized talent festivals and writing competitions as well as commissioning works by Canadian playwrights, composers, and all sorts of people with other creative talents.

The Canadian Broadcasting Corporation's radio services are widely acclaimed as being among the best in the world, but the very high cost of television production has caused profound problems. Parliament (for which read the various federal governments of the day) has been reluctant to provide long-term predictable funding and to enable the Corporation to manage without commercial revenue. The CBC must therefore rely on advertising (on television only) and so play the ratings game. This has led it to become a major purveyor of American programming on Canadian television. It is the CBC which gives Canadians *Dallas*.

Still, without the publicly owned network, which includes private affiliates, there would be mighty little Canadian programming available, particularly in the most watched categories. If all English TV stations are taken together, it is found that of all the time Canadians spend on television during the day, 65 percent is devoted to American shows. The corresponding figure for the evening hours is 71 percent. On the other hand, the audiences watching the CBC take in a much larger proportion of Canadian shows. From 2 p.m. to 6 p.m., two-thirds of the viewing is Canadian, and from 7 to 11 p.m., three-quarters.[12]

Where the difference between the private and the public sector is really staggering, however, is in the field of drama. Here the economics of television makes it extremely difficult for Canadians to compete with American productions, largely because of the disparities in the sizes of the two markets. Canadian commercial broadcasters have therefore done very little indeed to provide their viewers with original Canadian dramatic presentations. The CBC has tried to make up for this and has produced some highly successful Canadian shows, but the costs prevent enough of these being made to give Canadian viewers a real choice between domestic and imported television drama. At the present time, the "CBC is only able to offer the Canadian English viewer less than two hours of original Canadian drama in an average week."[13]

It is therefore not surprising that the cost of public broadcasting (quite apart from the provincial educational services) is extremely high. For 1984–85, the Corporation foresaw expenditures of more than a billion dollars. Of this amount, over $800 million was voted by Parliament. Even this substantial sum, however, represented a reduction of $60 million in its parliamentary vote. There have been drastic budget cuts and the President of the Corporation has warned that continued reductions in the Corporation's government grant would destroy the CBC.

It appeared to many that the CBC and cultural agencies generally had been singled out by the newly elected Conservative government of Brian Mulroney when it tried, after its stunning victory over the Liberals in 1984, to reduce the extremely high national deficit. The CBC plays an important and ambiguous role in the Canadian psyche. It is both loved and hated, and there are few who do not have strong views about it. The massive budget cuts, while obviously pleasing to some, including many Conservative Members of Parliament, on the other hand provoked a fierce reaction among cultural nationalists and other friends of public broadcasting. As a result, the knife paring down the Corporation's vitals was blunted and a Task Force was appointed in 1985 to make recommendations to the Minister of Communications on an industrial and cultural strategy "to govern the future evolution of the Canadian broadcasting system through the remainder of this century."[14] The place of public broadcasting generally, and of the CBC in particular, is obviously the major issue confronted by the Caplan-Sauvageau Committee, as the Task Force is known. At the time of writing, the Task Force gives no indication that it will seriously tamper with the very special place given to the CBC in Canada's broadcasting system.

The CBC is run by a President who is appointed for a fixed term by the cabinet. It is virtually impossible to remove him during this period for anything but the most serious reasons. The President reports to a board, also appointed by the government for a fixed term. The CBC is therefore independent of the government to all intents and purposes and operates at an arm's length distance from it. It reports to a Parliamentary Committee annually but in practice this is largely something of a formality. The state-owned broadcaster has, therefore, been free of political interference. It is certain that the Caplan-Sauvageau Task Force will leave this feature of the landscape untouched.

NFB. As the cultural spending estimates presented elsewhere in this chapter show, the National Film Board absorbs fewer resources than the national museums. We have, however, selected the Board for additional comments because a publicly owned experimental film industry is rare.

Among film *cognoscenti* throughout the world the NFB is well known, for it has won thousands of international prizes including some in the commercial sector. Its films have been nominated for fifty Hollywood Academy Awards and won eight Oscars. Created in 1939 primarily as an instrument for building up and maintaining morale in wartime and interpreting Canada to Canadians and others, it became one of the world's most productive and experimental film studios. A board of governors, appointed by the cabinet, is responsible for the management. Its nine members comprise a government film commissioner who is chairman, three members of the public service, and five outsiders. Like most of the cultural agencies, it reports to Parliament through the Minister of Communications.

The NFB has created at least 4,000 films; in 1978–79 its cumulative audience reached a billion viewers of whom a quarter were Canadian. It has consistently experienced difficulties in having its productions shown in Canadian moviehouses because these, belonging to multinational chains, excluded the exhibition of films made by others than the large foreign companies who had a tie-in with the Canadian distributors. Even the CBC has on occasion been less than cooperative in showing NFB productions. But even despite these inhibitions, the NFB has succeeded in having its distinctive fare viewed by a wide selection of people. A non-commercial, almost underground network of fans has emerged, utilizing the NFB's own distributing centers throughout Canada and abroad. The NFB was the first institution ever to have an exhibition of its work in New York's Museum of Modern Art (1985). Schools, universities, clubs, film councils, libraries, even in some instances local cable systems have utilized the searching and innovative films produced by the Board.

Cinematographically, the NFB has made major original contributions to emerging conventions of the art: pioneering forms of social documentaries, daringly new modes of animation, documentary drama, and direct cinema have been some of the areas in which the NFB has made its mark on the dominant art form of the twentieth century.

But despite its artistic achievements, the Board has encountered severe criticism. At various times it has been accused of being oblivious to certain fundamental changes occurring in society, notably the new relationships emerging between anglophones and francophones in Canada, between men and women, and between the native population and those of European descent. The Board managed to respond creatively to these criticisms and launched vital productions in both of Canada's official languages. After a slow start, it contributed much to the development of talented *cinéastes* who played a key role in the emergence of a highly successful Quebec cinema. Similarly, the creation of the famous Studio D, which concentrates on exploring issues redefining gender roles, and which is run and operated by women, redressed previous neglect of this dimension of the human experience. A certain imperviousness to the needs of the native population was followed by the creation of production facilities enabling Canada's original inhabitants to develop their own cinematic production.

The NFB has been at the center of numerous controversies. Its productions are sometimes seen as being altogether too self-indulgent; some have seen it as a hotbed of communism; questions have been raised about the propriety of publicly owned enterprise providing competition to the private sector. Its effects have been compared unfavorably with that of the Canada Council whose budget is lower. The Applebaum-Hébert Committee proposed that it be converted into a film school. At the time of writing, the Board is once again under strong public attack, but the noises being made by government spokesmen suggest that in the crunch this controversial element of the country's cultural policy is not likely to be abandoned or crippled.

Late in 1985 the NFB released a plan proposing a major reorganization in its structure and operations. It restated its mission as being

> to produce films and videos of quality, which can compete in the marketplace, but which never lose sight of the NFB's ongoing preoccupation: to create authentically Canadian films and videos, social and cultural in character, and profoundly cinematic in nature.

The Board also intends, in cooperation with the private sector, to become a center for applied technical research "to advance the art and technology of audiovisual communication in Canada, and to engage in a large training program for people both within and without its own organization."[15]

NAC. The National Arts Centre, although not the most expensive of Canada's operating public arts institutions, also deserves a brief note; the controversies surrounding some of its activities nicely encapsulate some of the general concerns affecting arts policy in the country.

This glittering performing arts showcase in the heart of Ottawa was the major centennial project of the federal government. It was to have cost $9 million but the bill exceeded $46 million by the time it opened with a performance by the National Ballet in 1969. The objects of the corporation running it are to operate the theater complex, to develop the performing arts in the capital region, and to assist the Canada Council in developing the performing arts elsewhere in Canada. The coordinating role is underlined by the composition of the Board, which must include not only the mayors of Ottawa and Hull, the capital's two principal municipalities, but also the President of the CBC, the government Film Commissioner, and the Director of the Canada Council. Nine other members are chosen by the Governor in Council (the cabinet).

In addition to operating three theaters of different sizes and types, the Centre also maintains two restaurants and reception and exposition space. At the height of its activities it supported two permanent theater companies (one in each language), the National Arts Centre Orchestra, and annual opera productions for summer performances. Its companies play primarily in Ottawa but also go on tours.

When the federal government felt compelled to make economies, the NAC was one of its targets. Its parliamentary appropriation accounts for about 55 percent of its income, and it has observed that this part of its revenues has been shrinking by about 2.5 percent annually during the past five years, when it is measured in constant dollars. For 1984–85, half a million dollars was taken from it and reallocated to job-creating projects, a redistributive measure that affected other government programs as well. Its other revenues were also curtailed because, under a federal anti-inflation program during the early 1980s, it was compelled to limit increases in its ticket prices to levels below those of the annual rises in the cost of living. These pressures compelled the NAC to suspend its annual opera productions and some of its other activities.

Although deemed an undisputed asset to Canada's capital, the NAC has received considerable criticism. It has been accused of being inadequately concerned with cultural life outside Ottawa. Its touring efforts have been found to have been meager. More important, cultural organizations throughout the country have resented the fact that substantial federal funds (over $14 million annually) were, in their eyes, taken out of their own pockets to support the Ottawa Centre and its lackluster companies. The money, they argue, might be better spent on orchestras or theater groups throughout the country. Furthermore, the NAC is sometimes seen as being too elitist. Its stages are not always available to lesser known theatrical groups in greater need of exposure than the National Ballet or Canadian Opera companies and other widely known Canadian or foreign artists.

These charges have been strenuously denied by the Centre which challenges what it sees as parochial and self-serving arguments. The symbolic significance of a national center of excellence at the seat of Canada's senior government has usually been ignored in these controversies, as has the significance for the hundreds of companies and individuals performing there each year of appearing in a magnificent theater situated in a nationally and often internationally visible milieu. The NAC's experience thus reflects stresses seen throughout Canadian arts policy arising from tensions between centers and peripheries, and between professionalism of the highest order and less exalted or even amateur efforts.

Among the policy proposals for the Centre which aroused the most vigorous debate, few can rival the brouhaha wrought by the Applebaum-Hébert Committee. While highly complimentary about many of the NAC's activities, its Final Report proposed that the Centre "should forego in-house productions of theatrical and operatic works in favour of co-productions with other Canadian companies." The NAC Orchestra was, however, to be exempted from this pruning.[16] Not surprisingly, the NAC repudiated these suggestions and seriously undermined the argument of the Committee by showing that a number of the observations it had made about the Centre were not correct. It also questioned the logic of recommending the abandonment of theatrical productions but not those of the Orchestra.[17] The Applebaum-Hébert recommendations with respect to the Arts Centre, like most of its other ones, have not yet been acted upon by the present government or its predecessor. A committee was established by the Minister of Communications early in 1986 to review the NAC's activities and make recommendations about future policies relative to it. There can be no question that recent Canadian governments have failed to relieve the financial difficulties encountered by Ottawa's performing arts showcase.

Supporting Institutions: The Canada Council and Telefilm Canada

The Canada Council. Canada's first and largest general public support agency to the arts is also the most crucial. The Canada Council set the tone for many of its provincial counterparts. Its Annual Reports contain a succinct sketch of its basic features:

> The Canada Council was created by an Act of Parliament in 1957. Under the terms of the *Canada Council Act,* the object of the Council is "to foster and promote the study and enjoyment of, and the production of works in, the arts." It offers a wide-ranging program of financial assistance and special services to individuals and organizations. The Council also maintains the secretariat for the Canadian Commission for UNESCO and has some responsibility for promoting Canadian culture abroad.
>
> The Council reports to Parliament through the Minister of Communications, and is called from time to time to appear before parliamentary committees, particularly the are implemented by a staff headed by a Director and an Associate Director, both appointed by the Government of Canada. The Council and its staff rely heavily on the advice and cooperation of . . . Disciplinary Advisory Committees, and artists and arts-related professionals from all parts of Canada, who are consulted both individually and in juries and selection committees. . . .
>
> The Council reports to Parliament through the Minister of Communications, and is called from time to time to appear before parliamentary committees, particularly the House of Commons Standing Committee on Communications and Culture. Its accounts are audited by the Auditor General of Canada and reported to Parliament.
>
> Annual grants from Parliament are the Council's main source of funds. These grants are supplemented by income from a $50-million Endowment Fund established by Parliament in 1957. The Council also has received substantial amounts in private donations and bequests, usually for specific purposes.[18]

Two amplifications are required to this pithy official description. The Director and Associate Director are appointed by and hold office at the pleasure of the Governor in Council. This means that they can be removed by the government of the day at any time. Secondly, the original endowment of $50 million was made so as to ensure the Council's complete independence of the government. At the time, this nest egg was the sole source of income. It was only later, when the financial need exceeded the revenues derived from the endowment, that Parliament resorted to annual grants as a supplement to the Council's original income. The sums voted annually by Parliament now constitute about 85 percent of the Council's income. In 1985–86 this came to $72,044,000—a reduction of about half a million (in current dollars) compared with the previous year.

The Council's programs are geared mainly to supporting professional artists and arts organizations. Table 1 indicates the level of financial support allocated to each group of programs. Only the "Explorations" competition is open to anyone with a project which is likely to contribute to "Canada's cultural knowledge and development." This program, however, as the table shows, accounts for only 3 percent of the budget. About four-fifths of the total budget goes to the support of professional arts organizations. Arts Awards, the category of programs offering assistance to individual artists, covers the disciplines of

TABLE 1. Canada Council: Allocation of Funds, 1980–81, 1984–85*

Programs	In Millions (Percentage of Arts Budget) 1980–81	1984–85
Arts Awards Service	$4.9 (11%)	$8.4 (12%)
Writing and Publishing	$6.1 (14%)	$9.5 (14%)
Music	$9.3 (21%)	$13.3 (19%)
(Operating grants to orchestras & operas)	($6.9)	
Theater	$9.6 (22%)	$14.4 (21%)
Dance	$4.9 (11%)	$8.4 (12%)
Touring Office	$2 (4%)	$3.55 (5%)
Visual Arts	$4.6 (11%)	$4.6 (7%)
Media Arts	—	$3.3 (5%)
Arts Bank	$ .6 (1%)	$ .9 (1%)
Explorations	$1.4 (3%)	$2.4 (3%)
Multidisciplinary and other	—	$2.9 (3%)

*The Canada Council, *News Release,* March 1984

architecture, arts administration, and arts criticism, as well as interdisciplinary work and the six main disciplines of dance, music, theater, visual arts, media arts (including film and video), and writing. Programs are available which offer living expenses to established or developing artists during the conduct of an approved work program, project costs, and travel to important artistic events.

The forms of aid to professional arts organizations vary by discipline. In all fields, grants are available for the annual operating costs of professional groups. In the case of writing, these grants take the form of aid to periodicals and block funding to Canadian publishing houses for their Canadian publishing programs. Similarly, there are grants within all disciplines for travel and exchange among artists in Canada. In the field of literature, a series of special programs offers encouragement to writers enabling them to visit the United States, Scotland, and Wales. Most of the disciplinary programs also include support for certain workshops or similar events and for the costs of special projects.

With respect to the media and writing, there are programs designed to facilitate access to, and recognition of, artistic works. These promote short-film distribution, promotional tours by writers, writing festivals, promotions, and prizes. Programs here also include direct purchases. Books are bought from Canadian publishers and offered, free of charge, to public non-profit groups in Canada and abroad. The Art Bank purchases works which are then rented to federal government departments and agencies.

The programs of the Council's Touring Office go beyond offering assistance for tours by Canadian and foreign artists. Grants are available for apprenticeship and career development of artists and for tour management, and a Performing Arts Venture Capital Fund provides investments in theatrical, musical, or dance properties by independent or non-profit Canadian producers.

Since 1975, the real value of Council grants has declined in most programs. For example, in 1976, the Council provided an average 20 percent of funding for the major symphony orchestras. By 1983, the proportion was reduced to 14 percent. From 1970 to 1983, six major theater companies saw Council grants decline by 20–30 percent. Support for performing arts tours, some of the visual arts, and the Council's Explorations program has also declined.

There are few in Canada interested in the arts who do not applaud the wide-ranging contribution the Council has made, and is making, to the cultural experiences and opportunities of Canadians. It is probably no exaggeration to say that Canada would be a much poorer country had it not been for the Council. For all of its successes, however, the Council has not escaped criticism. Among the failings attributed to it from time to time have been bureaucratic heavy-handedness, insensitivity to the requirements of certain regions or groups (notably francophones and those living outside the central provinces), snobbery with respect to non-professional artists and activities which lie at the borderline between the arts and crafts, and the awarding of grants to inappropriate and even shocking projects. At a 1985 meeting of Canada's ministers responsible for cultural policy, several of the provincial participants accused the Council of bias and canvassed the possibility that its funds might better be given to the provinces for their cultural programs. Culture, as we have noted earlier, is often seen as being closely related to education—a provincial matter.

For its part, the Council has vehemently repudiated these charges and proposals. It has consistently consulted widely among the artistic community throughout the country and has usually justified its decisions on the grounds that it cannot compromise its strict adherence to excellence and the highest levels of professionalism. It has also been critical of the government's failure to keep its grants up to suitable levels. More recently, it has, in addition, expressed concern about the government's commitment to keeping itself at an arm's length from cultural agencies. This is a complex matter to which we shall return. For the time being we must note, however, that during the last years of the Trudeau government, the Department of Communications increasingly engaged in activities which were the responsibility of some of the independent cultural agencies like the Canada Council. A telltale sign here was the increasing budgetary provisions for the DOC programs helping the arts, while the budgets of the agencies themselves were being restrained. This process gained momentum after the Conservatives came to power in 1984. A comparison of the increases in cultural expenditures of the Canada Council and those of the DOC is revealing. The former's budget, in current dollars, increased by 176 percent between the years 1974–75 and 1985–86, whereas the latter's rise in the same period amounted to 551 percent.[19] We shall return to this issue.[20]

Telefilm Canada. This agency is small and confined to relatively modest goals compared with those of the Canada Council. It was created in 1967 by Parliament under its original name—the Canadian Film Development Corporation—"to foster and promote the development of a feature film industry in Canada" with an original budget of $10 million to operate as a loan fund available to Canadian film producers.

In its earliest period it invested in a number of low-budget films considered of high cultural value but eventually took a more commercial orientation. The agency's efforts, aided by another governmental initiative—the Capital Cost Allowance—ultimately led to a large growth in the Canadian film industry, large-scale private investment in productions, and a substantial increase in the number of films produced in the country. Its mandate was, however, not only "to foster and promote the development of a feature film industry in Canada," but also to promote the making of films with "significant Canadian creative, artistic and technical content.''[21] It was much more successful in realizing the former than the latter goal.

The Capital Cost Allowance, which allowed investors to deduct from taxable income 100 percent of their stake in certain kinds of films, and the CFDC's policies, resulted in the production of large numbers of films (67 features were being made in 1979), the vast majority being of very low quality. Many of them were never even shown, partly because of the nature of the Canadian distribution system and partly because of their lack of appeal. Furthermore, a great many of these films were made specifically for the American market and, given the latter's rather parochial tastes, obliterated anything in them that might possibly be identified with Canada. Canadian creative talent tended to play a minor and subservient role in many of these productions. Of the $26 million put up by the CFDC during its first ten years, only five million was earned back. The results of these film policies were therefore rather mixed, although they helped create the base for a competent, diversified film-production industry.

Many of the difficulties and errors of the CFDC had been eradicated by the advent of the 1980s when a new, more successful era dawned for the agency. In 1983, the Minister of Communications introduced a new Broadcasting Policy which included provision for the establishment of the Canadian Broadcast Development Fund, to be administered by the CFDC.[22]

This new venture made a substantial sum of money ($34 million in the first year, to rise to $60 million in its fifth year) available for certain kinds of Canadian television programs that met certain conditions. Applicants had to raise two dollars elsewhere for every one received from the fund, and they had to have a commitment from a broadcaster that their shows would be aired. The scheme was ultimately altered and the name of its administering agency changed, but there is little doubt about its success.

In less than the first two years of its operation, the fund provided over $80 million to Canadian producers which, given the leverage of the program, produced substantially more for the production of original Canadian drama, children's programming, and variety shows. Although the private broadcasters have steadily increased their use of the fund, it has been the CBC which has benefited most, although this was not intended to be the case. The Corporation reported that a $28 million investment on its part generated $120 million in production.[23]

Telefilm's production fund is being singled out for comment because it constitutes a unique approach of the Canadian government, in many respects quite different from others it has adopted. In the first place, to finance this scheme, the government instituted a tax on cable companies, arguing that cable, which pays nothing to program originators, should contribute to the cost of Canadian production. Second, the fund relied less on regulating the content of broadcasts than on encouraging the production of attractive Canadian shows capable of competing with American programs. This, as we shall see, is an important complement to the heretofore dominant strategy of broadcast regulation in Canada.

Administrative and Policy-Making Machinery: DOC and CRTC

DOC. Such responsibilities as Canadian governments have from time to time assumed in relation to the arts used to be discharged by a bewildering and improbable array of ministries. The Department of Agriculture, for instance, used to be hospitable to various enterprises, including such items as the public archives.[24] No effort has ever been made to establish a federal Ministry of Culture, partly no doubt because such a move would have aroused a good deal of controversy on substantive grounds, and partly because of the jurisdictional ambiguity of this domain in the context of the distribution of powers between the federation and the provinces. In the early 1960s the Department of the Secretary of State however became a *de facto* cultural ministry, although it was also given some other responsibilities. A Ministry of Communications was created subsequently and in 1980 it took over the cultural concerns of the Secretary of State.[25]

The Cultural Affairs Program within the DOC serves two areas: cultural policy (arts and heritage, film, sound recording, and publishing), and cultural support programs which include such items as the Special Program of Cultural Initiatives, the Movable Cultural Property Secretariat, and the Film Festival Bureau. In its 1985–86 Estimates the objectives of the Cultural Policy Branch are identified as follows:

> To formulate Canada's national cultural policy in support of cultural activities: to support or manage select artistic and cultural programs as the government may, in special circumstances determine: to advise the Minister on the implementation by cultural agencies of programs consistent with national cultural policy issues arising from the application of cultural, communications, space, and information technologies.[26]

Although many of the cultural policies are being administered by independent agencies (Table 4 below lists the major programs and their respective expenditures), the Minister of Communications is more than a disinterested observer of their activities. He or she is the link between the agencies and Parliament, and under the Financial Administration Act must sign certain documents pertaining to their expenditures. It is also the Minister who makes recommendations to the cabinet on persons who are to be appointed to the boards of the agencies and who are to be their heads. In discharging these duties and generally occupying him- or herself with cultural issues, the Minister obviously relies on analyses and advice tendered by the departmental staff. These facts have serious implications for the arm's length principle which is deemed to be of critical importance in the satisfactory application of cultural policies. Departmental officials often become involved in matters which are under the jurisdiction of the agencies, and conflicts thus inevitably occur.

Another complication affecting the arm's length relationship is that the Minister is held responsible by his or her cabinet colleagues for the cultural life of the country, including broadcasting, and for the government's cultural policies. When budget allocations or cuts are being discussed, it is the political head of the DOC who advises the cabinet on what should be done. The Minister is therefore closely involved in decisions which are of vital importance to the agencies, irrespective of the degree of independence they enjoy. The artistic community, for its part, sees in the Minister either their foe or defender, depending on the Minister's relations with it. The controversies surrounding the relationship between the Minister and his or her government and the cultural agencies are therefore never simple: we shall return to them below.

As cultural issues have come to assume an increasingly important place in Canadian life, Ministers of Communications have sought to devise new policies and to seek appropriate advice from sources both within and outside their Department. Thus, David MacDonald, and later Francis Fox, launched and enlarged the famous Applebaum-Hébert Committee, noted above. Francis Fox, in the early 1980s, initiated several policy reviews and attempted to chart a number of new courses. The Canadian Broadcast Production

Fund noted above was one of these.[27] His successor, Marcel Masse, confronted by the government's desire to reduce the country's deficit and by other turbulent conditions in the arts, similarly commissioned a number of fundamental reviews of the options available to him and his colleagues. The Film Industry Task Force reported in November, 1985;[28] copyright issues and strategies for the appropriate funding of the arts are also subject to examination and the latest probe into the future of broadcasting (the Caplan-Sauvageau Task Force, to which we have already referred) is expected to present its critically important report in 1986. Flora MacDonald, who succeeded Masse in the summer of 1986, just as this book was being edited, was confronted with no less than nine reports guiding her toward policy revision.[29]

Both the budgets and the activities of the Cultural Branch have in recent years been expanding. The annual expenditures, apart from payments made to the Post Office to cover lower rates for certain kinds of printed matter, have in recent years ranged from $70 million to somewhat under $100 million. In addition to cooperating with the Post Office, DOC is involved with a number of other government departments in running the Canadian Film Certification Program and the Cultural Statistics Program, and in providing services related to heritage questions and foreign cultural relations.

The CRTC. Another major policy-making and regulatory organism is the Canadian Radio-Television and Telecommunications Commission. As with the other instruments of government policy discussed above, no attempt is made here to provide a complete picture; only a few salient points relevant to the immediate purposes of this chapter are noted.

The Broadcasting Act of 1968—still the basic charter in this domain—not only defines the goals of the Canadian broadcasting system but also provides for the creation of an organism responsible for seeing that the objectives are realized. The CRTC is this organism. In charging it with the supervision of the whole broadcasting system, Parliament has made the CRTC responsible for radio, television, cable casting, and some aspects of satellite communication. It is appointed by the Governor in Council and consists of nine full-time and ten part-time members, and a Chairman and two Vice-Chairmen, also named by the cabinet. Like some of the other agencies we examined, it is not under any Minister but reports to Parliament through the Minister of Communications. Under certain well-defined conditions, the cabinet can issue directives to it, and appeals are also possible from its decisions to the courts and to the cabinet. It has the powers of a court of record and is a quasi-judicial body.

Among other things, the Broadcasting Act specifies that the Canadian broadcasting system should "safeguard, enrich and strengthen the cultural, political, social and economic fabric of Canada," and that the programming should be of high standard, "using predominantly Canadian creative and other resources." The CRTC endeavors to ensure the realization of these and other goals by three mechanisms: (1) it issues licenses and renews them; this way it can to some extent influence the quality of broadcasters; (2) it can attach conditions to each license, specifying, for example, what kind of programming it expects; and (3) it can make regulations, which have the force of laws, binding all broadcasters to certain kinds of behavior. It has specified, for instance, that 60 percent of each day's programming on Canadian television stations must be Canadian. As conditions of license, it has identified the proportion of the gross revenues that certain pay television licensees must spend on the acquisition of Canadian programs.

For a great variety of reasons, the Commission has fallen far short of bringing about the kind of system envisaged by the drafters of the Broadcasting Act. But it has nevertheless had some successes. A regulation it made some years ago, stipulating that 30 percent of music on AM stations had to be Canadian, resulted in the establishment of a successful Canadian record industry. Its constant harping on the need, on the part of Canadian television licensees, to try to increase Canadian programming has had some effect and its insistence that cable companies of a certain size provide local community channels has borne fruit. It has also so far succeeded in ensuring that the process of awarding licenses has been free of partisan political interference.

The Commission has nevertheless often been criticized and it has on occasion antagonized the government. Legislation was introduced by the Trudeau Liberals which would have substantially enlarged the cabinet's powers of direction. The measure died on the order paper when the Liberals were defeated, but their Conservative successors have reintroduced it and it is likely to become law.[30] These developments will make the Commission more susceptible to political pressure and may endanger the independence of the licensing process.

Levels of Support

So far we have concentrated almost exclusively on the federal level. There are good reasons for this: the Ottawa government provided leadership in modern methods of supporting the arts. Many of the institutions have served as models to the provinces and most of the issues relevant to the evolution and application of cultural policy are well manifested at the national stage. But it would be quite misleading to assume that the activities in the other two jurisdictions are unimportant. On the contrary, as we shall see shortly, in terms of sheer numbers of dollars, Ottawa appears to contribute less than the provinces. We use the term "appears" because in cultural statistics it is inordinately difficult to be sure exactly what expenditures are counted. Provincial data often include the costs of youth and recreational activities and federal figures normally reflect allocations to libraries and scholarly endeavors which may have little to do with the arts.

The latest data available are for 1983–84. They illustrate, among other things, how important it is to understand the composition of one's data if one wishes to arrive at a sure sense of reality. Expressing our sums in millions of dollars, we find that Ottawa spent on culture $1,547.1, the provinces $990.7, and the municipalities $580. This means that the federal government was responsible roughly for half the cultural pie, the provinces for almost a third, and the municipalities for a little less than a fifth. But the more than one billion and a half spent by Ottawa includes its contribution to the CBC. When this sum of over one billion dollars is subtracted, it becomes apparent that the provinces together spend more on culture than does the federal government. A closer look at the provincial data shows, however, that sums reported as being destined to culture do not necessarily aid the arts. Thus, of the provincial total of nearly $991 million, almost half went to libraries, one-fifth to heritage programs, 13 percent to broadcasting, and only 8 percent to the performing arts.[31]

Table 2 presents cultural expenditures for each of the ten years between 1972–73 and 1982–83. It is based on definitions and calculations made by the Canada Council which differ from those applied by Statistics Canada, which we used for 1983–84 in the preceding paragraphs. The federal contributions to the CBC (and, where applicable, provincial

TABLE 2. Cultural Expenditures by Jurisdiction 1973–74 to 1982–83*

		1973–74	*1974–75*	*1975–76*	*1976–77*	*1977–78*	*1978–79*	*1979–80*	*1980–81*	*1981–82*	*1982–83*
Millions of Current Dollars	Total	325.2	427.4	493.2	538.2	670.1	751.5	825.7	983.8	1,089.4	1,212.9
	Federal	87.4	126.1	161.3	154.7	222.7	265.2	245.7	314.5	353.0	335.3
	Provincial	91.2	116.2	154.7	167.2	210.5	233.4	288.6	323.5	349.1	438.5
	Local	146.6	185.1	177.2	216.3	236.9	252.9	291.4	345.8	387.3	439.1
Percent of Total Government Cultural Expenditure	Total	100	100	100	100	100	100	100	100	100	100
	Federal	26.9	29.5	32.7	28.8	33.2	35.3	29.8	32.0	32.4	27.7
	Provincial	28.1	27.2	31.4	31.1	31.4	31.0	35.0	32.9	32.0	36.2
	Local	45.1	43.4	36.0	40.2	35.3	33.6	35.3	35.2	35.5	36.2
Percent of Gross General Expenditure	Total	.6	.6	.6	.6	.6	.6	.6	.6	.6	.6
	Federal	.4	.4	.4	.4	.5	.5	.4	.5	.4	.4
	Provincial	.4	.4	.4	.4	.5	.5	.5	.5	.5	.5
	Local	1.3	1.4	1.1	1.2	1.1	1.1	1.2	1.2	1.2	1.2

*Drawn from the Canada Council, *Tri-Level Cultural Expenditure Data Base Technical Tables,* Ottawa, Fifth Edition, June 1986, pp. 1, 3, 4.

Numbers may not add owing to rounding.

expenditures on educational broadcasting, as well) are excluded, as are provincial outlays on recreation; archives, museums, historic sites, and libraries are, however, covered.

One of the interesting features of the ten-year overview is that the relative importance of the local contribution has declined. The federal expenditure almost reached one-third of the total in 1977–78 but has slipped slightly since. The table covers only a ten-year period and consequently does not permit long-term comparisons. If the 1970s and 1980s are compared with the late 1960s, however, it becomes apparent that the federal proportion of cultural expenditures has been growing relative to those of the other jurisdictions. A striking insight provided by the table is that although cultural expenditures of governments are sizeable in actual dollars, they represent only a tiny fraction of total government expenditures. During the decade under review they never reached even 1 percent of total expenditures at all levels and, even for municipalities, the most lavish cultural spenders of the three, they never attained 1.5 percent of total outlays.

Table 3 compares the per capita expenditures of the ten provinces. Local spending has been included on the grounds that most Canadian municipalities derive a substantial portion of their revenues from provincial transfers. Differences between the provinces are revealed to be quite substantial, with the big spenders allocating twice as much or more to culture than the less generous ones allocate. The table indicates that in most parts of the country provincial spending has, during our decennial span, for the most part leveled off or even declined slightly. But if we go back again to 1969–70, the first year for which the Canada Council produced its tri-level comparisons (table not provided), we see that there has been a substantial growth in the degree to which the provinces have made financial commitments to the arts. The per capita expenditure in Prince Edward Island, Canada's smallest province, increased sevenfold, in Quebec by a factor of three, and in four provinces—Newfoundland, New Brunswick, Saskatchewan, and Alberta—it at least doubled. The last-named province reached almost astronomical heights in 1982–83, compared to its sister provinces, as shown in Table 3, but it remains to be seen whether it can sustain this giddy level. But even if it cannot, it is without question the leader in the amount of money each province spends on the arts per citizen.

Three provinces—Prince Edward Island, Quebec, and Manitoba—are revealed by Table 3 to have reduced their spending in the ten-year period under review. While this is the case, one should not overlook the substantial increases which have occurred in their contributions since the late 1960s, which we noted above, or other circumstances brightening the picture conveyed by our lifeless table.[32]

Before leaving our examination of per capita expenditures for each of the provinces it will be useful to consider the federal and overall picture. Ottawa's outlay for each of its citizens during our decennial period ranged from a low of $2.74 in 1972–73 to a high of $5.37 in 1978–79, after which it declined. In 1982–83 it stood at $4.14. Overall, the combined allocation of the three levels of government has in recent years been around $15.00.

The expenditures reported in Tables 2 and 3 do not include the proceeds of government-run lotteries. Since a 1970 amendment to the Criminal Code made lotteries legal, both federal and provincial governments have resorted to this mechanism for raising funds, and in many cases a portion of the receipts, or the receipts from a particular "game," are earmarked for the support of the arts. It has been estimated that in 1979 at least $40 million in provincial lottery revenue was spent in support of the arts.[33] Although exact figures are not available, it is extremely likely that that sum is quite a bit higher now. The federal government has vacated the field of lotteries, after a rather bitter dispute

TABLE 3.* Cultural Expenditures by Province, Constant (1971) Dollars Per Capita, Provincial and Local 1973–74 to 1982–83

	1973–74	*1974–75*	*1975–76*	*1976–77*	*1977–78*	*1978–79*	*1979–80*	*1980–81*	*1981–82*	*1982–83*
Nfld.	5.03	7.95	8.20	7.53	6.25	6.23	6.74	6.54	6.69	5.99
P.E.I.	7.02	6.09	5.13	5.93	8.40	8.26	8.20	7.32	6.50	6.50
N.S.	6.09	6.16	5.98	6.63	6.72	8.00	8.55	6.86	8.02	7.16
N.B.	4.17	5.96	10.23	9.90	12.43	8.58	8.53	10.07	8.05	8.44
Que.	8.18	8.51	7.48	5.95	7.15	7.92	8.28	9.30	8.50	8.02
Ont.	11.77	12.85	11.92	12.60	12.47	12.05	13.09	12.28	12.03	12.29
Man.	8.23	7.75	9.07	10.27	7.98	6.01	6.42	6.73	7.89	7.64
Sask.	7.96	8.89	9.92	9.01	11.55	12.62	12.72	12.72	11.05	11.24
Alta.	11.42	10.16	7.71	8.38	10.51	11.60	13.78	15.69	14.22	20.22
B.C.	6.91	8.50	8.47	9.61	9.20	8.26	9.12	8.48	8.45	9.06

*Drawn from the Canada Council, *Tri-Level Cultural Expenditure Data Base Technical Tables,* Ottawa, Fifth Edition, June 1986, p. 5.

about the matter with the provinces. It receives some funds from the provinces annually, as a result, of which about $13 million (indexed) is set aside for Special Cultural Initiatives.

Table 4 enables us to see how the federal government and the independent agencies allocate public funds to various arts and other cultural endeavors. At first glance the table suggests that the Cultural Affairs Branch in DOC has more to spend than the Canada Council, but this impression is misleading. The Cultural Affairs item includes the substantial sums DOC transfers to Canada Post. When these are deducted, the Cultural Affairs expenditures for 1983–84 and the two subsequent years are (in thousands) $43,010, $55,650, and $55,183.

The two most striking features of Table 4 are that it shows in stark contrast how very expensive it is for Canada to operate its public broadcasting system and how relatively little is spent on the Canada Council. The former point needs to be weighed in relation to the very extensive mandate of the CBC. It is about ten broadcasting systems rolled into one, responsible for a number of functions undertaken in the national interest and not always in relation to economic criteria. The comparative position of the Canada Council shows that its importance, relative to some of the other agencies and particularly to the DOC, is declining. This means that a larger proportion of sums allocated to the arts is under the direct control of Ministers, and therefore subject to political influence.

Table 4 excludes expenditures on cultural affairs of a few government departments which have some involvement with the arts. Of these, the Department of Public Works (responsible for federal buildings), the Canadian International Development Agency, and the Department of External Affairs are the most important. The latter, which is most pertinent to our purposes, spends about $11 million a year on international cultural relations, of which 95 percent is devoted to bilateral programs with other countries. Of this total about a quarter subsidizes the performing arts; a fifth, arts bursaries and leave fellowships; a quarter is devoted to Canadian studies programs abroad; and 12 percent to the maintenance of a few cultural centers in foreign countries. The visual arts and cinema, literary exchanges, and the "exchange of persons" together account for another 15 percent.[33]

TABLE 4. Cultural Spending Estimates for 1983–84, 1984–85, 1985–86
Cultural Affairs Program and Cultural Agencies ($ thousands)

	1983–84	*1984–85*	*1985–86*
Cultural Affairs	75,068	90,904	94,592
Canada Council	65,581	69,614	72,044
Canadian Broadcasting Corporation	819,966	895,735	846,847
Canadian Film Development Corporation	4,764	54,764	65,290
Canadian Radio-television and Telecommunications Commission	24,620	25,545	25,396
National Arts Centre	14,427	14,832	14,574
National Film Board	58,439	62,530	62,928
National Library	29,829	29,759	32,857
National Museums	66,220	69,517	74,864
Public Archives	36,109	39,437	41,877

The Main Issues in Arts Policy

We have now seen enough of the relationship between governments and the arts in Canada to be able to make a few general observations about them. In this section, we shall identify some of the main issues which have arisen in the delicate interrelationships between the muse and the polis; the concluding part, which follows, shall briefly consider some of the principles which underlie Canadian arts policy.

One of the questions which has had to be resolved over time is how cultural policy should be handled administratively. Since for a very long time the efforts of governments were minor, their arts bureaus had to be housed with those responsible for other concerns. We noted earlier that in Ottawa, the Department of Agriculture had at one time been involved, although many other ministries also got into the act at one time or another. In the recent era, as we have seen, arts policy and citizenship were combined in the office of the Secretary of State until culture and communications became the responsibility of the Minister of Communications.

At the provincial level, the involvement of governments in culture has often been related to their activities in the field of recreation. Thus culture and sports have frequently been the responsibility of the same administrative organ. Sometimes these domains have been linked to youth programs. More recently support for the arts has been seen as fitting in with projects preserving or restoring historical monuments and other artefacts and practices growing out of the community's heritage. These shifts are nicely illustrated in the organizational pilgrimage of the relevant administrative body in the province of New Brunswick. The Cultural Development Branch was created in 1975 within the Department of Youth. Two years later handicrafts and library services were moved from the Departments of Tourism and Education respectively to this ministry, renamed the Department of Youth, Recreation and Cultural Resources. Then, in 1982, the Historical Resources Administration and the Cultural Section of this department were combined to form the Department of Historical and Cultural Resources.

Decisions have had to be made not only about the best administrative arrangements for arts policy but also about the relative weight and priorities to be attached to youth, sports, arts, and heritage programs. The first two tend to have a much wider mass appeal than the last two. It is probably also the case that among politicians jocks are by and large better represented than culture vultures. It has therefore been easier to find resources for recreation, youth, and sports than for the arts. But the data we have seen on the growth in public expenditures on cultural activities show that, whatever the administrative structures and linkages serving the recreational and artistic pursuits of the citizens, the arts have not done too badly at all three levels of government. They have often in fact benefited from being lumped together with more widely acceptable spending programs.

An issue somewhat related to administrative proximity of culture and youth, sports, and recreation concerns the alleged narrow appeal of the arts. It is often thought, and occasionally stated, that cultural activities engage only the few and that governmental programs in this area are therefore elitist. Why should the taxpayer subsidize the few who like that sort of thing, particularly since those who benefit most from governmental programs in the arts are usually the better off, better educated, and otherwise favored members of society? Governments in Canada have, as we have seen, generally not allowed this argument to stand in the way of developing substantial cultural programs. The reasons for this are varied. For one thing, cultural attendance has risen rapidly. Thus from 1971 to 1981, the figures in the performing arts more than doubled.[35] One of them is that the political decision-makers themselves constitute an elite and so tend to identify the public good with the interests of their own class. Furthermore, there has been a growing tendency to see in the arts a creator of jobs.

The idea that the arts deserve being pursued for their own sake has in recent years been supplemented by one which sees them as part of what is usually termed cultural industries. This notion has given rise to a certain amount of ambiguity and controversy. There is no doubt at all that the number of Canadians making their living in the cultural area has been growing, and growing faster than those for most other sectors of the economy.[36] In a period of what appears as steady high unemployment, cultural enterprises thus assume an economic significance quite apart from their intrinsic worth. Some champions of the arts have therefore argued that governments should provide aid to the so-called cultural industries as part of their efforts to create more jobs. Few enterprises, it is argued, are as labor intensive as the arts. The Minister and officials in the Department of Communications have themselves made this argument, no doubt in part so as to be able to pry greater resources from the overall governmental kitty. It has not always been easy for the artistic community to disparage what seems a powerful support for their cause, but the matter has also raised a lot of controversy. The arts, it is argued, are worth supporting for their own sake, and must be considered on their own merits. To view them primarily as job-creators is to run the risk of distorting them and the policies aiding them and so reduce, in the long run, the total benefit a society can derive from its cultural life. The cultural industries concept might aid some of the arts but injure others, irrespective of their merits. To plead for arts support on employment grounds should, therefore, not be used to gain short-run strategic advantage since the long-run consequences might be harmful not only to the arts but to everyone.

Another issue arising from what can be termed the utilitarian perspective relates to the nation-building potential of cultural activities. We noted earlier that the Broadcasting Act includes the strengthening of Canadian identity among the objectives of the broadcasting system. But other art forms are also perceived as being important elements in enabling Canadians to see and understand themselves better. Thus the strengthening of the country's cultural life is expected to foster the national cohesion and self-awareness of Canadians. There are those, however, who see a danger in this argument and in policies growing out of it. Again, the intrinsic, universal value of art is feared for, as is the possibility that some types of artistic expression might be favored over others on grounds which have nothing to do with their respective intrinsic worth.

Something of a battle has in fact been raging between the cultural nationalists, who seek a great variety of measures intended to strengthen Canadian cultural production and consumption, and those who believe in a laissez-faire approach in which Canadian artists would have to take their chances in open and unfettered competition with the works of others, particularly, of course, Americans. The "protectionists" argue that without some assistance, the country's culture cannot compete effectively with that of its southern neighbor because the disparity in the size of the two countries makes fair and reasonable competition impossible.

This tendency is exacerbated when some of the Canadian cultural efforts can only reach a wide public through foreign-owned distributors. Such is the case, for instance, in part in the book-publishing, magazine, and film industries. Similarly, in the field of television drama, which is exceedingly expensive to create, American programs, having amortized their high costs in the huge American market, are offered to Canadian broadcasters at bargain-basement prices. Canadian shows cannot possibly, under these conditions, compete with the imports and could not be offered to the public without some government assistance. The commercial broadcasters are not likely to pay very high prices for Canadian drama when they can obtain well-tried American programs for a tiny fraction of the cost of the indigenous product.

We have seen that Canadian content regulation by the CRTC is one means whereby the forces of the market, in this situation, are offset by the application of a national policy. The subsidization of the creation of Canadian shows by Telefilm Canada is another means used to pursue the national interest in this particular cultural domain. Efforts to prevent the publishing industry from being dominated by foreign companies are another way of achieving the same end in a different field. In these and many other such nationalist policies, the authorities are trying to enable Canadian artists to speak to their compatriots on terms equal to those available to their neighbors.

Since the election of the Conservative Mulroney government in 1984, the issue of cultural nationalism has appeared in a particularly virulent form. The Conservatives undertook to negotiate new trade agreements with the U.S.A., seeking what they called "enhanced trade." Many see this term as merely a euphemism for "free trade." Whatever the name, at issue is the free, unfettered trade and investment between the two countries, at least with respect to certain sectors of the economy. Since a number of irritants have arisen in the relation between the two countries over cultural matters, the U.S.A. sought to have certain cultural items "put on the table" for negotiation. One of the bones of contention is a Canadian law preventing Canadian advertisers from being able to deduct from their taxes the cost of advertising on American TV stations or in American magazines. Not to have its book-publishing industry owned by foreigners is another irritant. Cultural nationalists, who constitute a significant majority of the artistic community, have mounted a determined campaign to prevent this matter from being included in any general bargain on Canada–U.S.A. trade relations. Others, including the government, have insisted that nothing should be excluded from the talks. At the time of writing, the whole issue is still unresolved. If nothing else, however, it has thrust the question of cultural policy into the consciousness of everyone.

One issue which has aroused lively controversies in a number of countries, including the U.S.A., has left Canadians rather unconcerned. Despite the American and British example, Canadians have shown very little interest in withdrawing from UNESCO. Perhaps because of the country's economic and cultural dependence on the U.S.A., Canadians have tended to show considerable understanding for the position adopted on many international cultural issues by the Third World. While a number of developments within UNESCO have received criticism, there have been no serious efforts to abandon the world body. On the contrary, the Canadian government has emphatically expressed its resolve to continue its membership and seek redress from within.

A totally domestic issue generated considerably more heat than the future of UNESCO. It concerns the way in which the state generally—not its cultural agencies—deals with its artists. A major ruckus erupted in the early 1980s over the manner in which the Department of National Revenue treated Canadian academics, painters, and other creative, self-employed individuals. The episode is instructive because it tells us quite a lot about general attitudes to artists, the nature of these, and the growing importance of the cultural community. Officials in the taxation offices, at first probably quite unthinkingly, applied the regulations in a manner seriously damaging to people making their living as writers or artists.

Among the vexing ways in which regulations were applied was the practice of preventing artists from deducting from their income expenses incurred in the production of their works before these had actually been sold. They also tried to tax unsold inventories of paintings and prints in the possession of their makers. One highly successful West Coast painter—Toni Onley—whose oeuvre is worth considerable sums, was told by a tax official that some manufacturers escaped this tax by destroying their excess production. Onley took his cue from this enlightened suggestion and threatened to burn his works in a public demonstration. This flamboyant gesture focused widespread attention on a cause that the Canada Council and arts lobbies, including the CCA, had been fighting for some time. The government finally capitulated; income tax rules no longer discriminate against artists and writers.

Among the lessons from this episode is that officials for a long time reflected the widely shared insensitivity to the life and concerns of practising artists but that as the role of the latter changed, official reaction had to accommodate itself to the new conditions. Second, the issue only became "hot" because the importance of writers and artists had increased to a point when they no longer were an insignificant minority but a component of the population with which governments had to reckon.

Another even more torrid controversy arose as the result of efforts by governments to reduce their expenditures on the arts. The Canadian economy, like that of many other countries, ran into heavy weather after the dramatic increase of prices by OPEC. Furthermore, seemingly uncontrollable government spending was responsible for the national debt reaching totally unacceptable levels. Its servicing alone took a sizeable bite out of the tax dollar. The Liberals under Trudeau made a number of attempts to reduce their spending which of course affected the budgets of the cultural agencies. We saw above how the real income of the Canada Council suffered; the latter's plight was fairly typical although certain new expensive projects with enough political clout managed to be approved. Thus, in 1982 the government announced that it would finance the construction, at an estimated cost of $165 million, of a new National Gallery and a new National Museum of Man. Apart from such exceptional items, however, there were unmistakable cutbacks which reduced the means available to a great many arts organizations to maintain their previous level of activity.

These cutbacks, however, had some other effects. They were instrumental in mobilizing the cultural community, which became increasingly effective in presenting its case to the public and to the government. A vocal and influential voice, the 1812 Committee, published a hard-hitting Manifesto attacking budget cuts aimed at the arts. The Committee, which attracted national attention in 1978, was composed of thirty-six of the country's cultural associations from the association of designers to the Writers' Union. In addition to such ad hoc bodies as the 1812 Committee, the Canadian Conference of the Arts became increasingly active as the focal point and facilitator for political action by arts groups from coast to coast. It played a key role in the 1978 campaign.

It is highly likely that the organizational and lobbying ventures of various arts groups in the 1970s and early 1980s were responsible for the fact that the spending rollbacks proposed by the newly elected Conservatives, in 1984 and 1985, ultimately were less far-reaching than was originally feared. The new Minister of Communications, Marcel Masse, at first appeared to be somewhat capricious and insensitive to the needs of the arts community. He was blamed for the fact that the government appeared to have singled out culture for especially harsh treatment—a particularly odious distinction in the eyes of the arts community which noticed, for instance, that almost $36 million were found for the purpose of changing the uniforms of the armed forces.

It was widely believed by arts groups in English Canada that Marcel Masse's difficulties emanated in part from his having spent virtually his whole life in Quebec. The conventions guiding arts administration in that province are quite different from those in English Canada and at the federal level. Governments there have always dealt more directly with arts organizations than those elsewhere in Canada. The arm's length principle is less common, and ministerial involvement expected. Masse, by behaving according to the folkways of his province, caused considerable alarm among the members of the cultural community. But he soon adapted to the new circumstances and ended up being seen as a defender of and powerful spokesman in cabinet for the arts. There is every indication that in Masse the arts community has in fact found a champion who sees his role as that of protecting Canadian cultural interests both domestically and with respect to the United States. But he was moved to another portfolio, as we saw. The arts community regretted his departure but was generally favorably disposed to Flora MacDonald who had a record of being friendly to cultural endeavors. It is impossible to say, at the time of writing, whether further cutbacks are likely. The future will, in part, depend on the contents of the various inquiries which will report in 1986 and 1987.

The one area in which doubts still persist among the cultural community is that of the independence of the agencies from political intervention motivated by partisan or other "non-professional" motives. The question is not, of course, as simple as some believe.[37] On the one hand, it is indisputably the case that decisions about who should receive grants, capital aid, and other assistance are best made by peer assessors, making judgements within the scope of clearly established and known guidelines. Political influence, special pleading, factors extraneous to artistic considerations should have no place in the matter. It is not surprising, for instance, that the Director of the Canada Council should have been scandalized by the fact that when his budget was cut by $3 million, agreements between the federal and provincial authorities would make almost ten times as much available for new or expanded cultural establishments (like the Montreal Museum of Art, for instance) without any consultation of experts and without any provision for operating grants ensuring that the new facilities could be used effectively. The relative decline of the Canada Council budget and increased resources available to DOC grants, we noted earlier, indicate that the politicization of funding is occurring on a substantial scale.

On the other hand, no one can seriously expect public funds to be spent without there being any formal and realistic accountability and without the governments of the day having some say in the broad policy guidelines within which grants are administered. It is not unreasonable of governments to expect some congruence between their goals and the decisions of agencies spending public funds. A government which wishes to develop and apply cultural policies must have the means available to implement them. The trick, of course, is to combine the use of unassailably professional, independent agencies with a broad policy milieu guiding all the decision-makers towards a reasonable level of coordination. There is no evidence that this desirable state of affairs exists in Canada at the present time or has in recent decades.

One reason for this must be sought in the aggrandizement of the DOC and the accompanying relative decline of the so-called arm's length agencies. This has occurred as the result of the convergence of interests between the political heads of the Department and some of its key officials. Another factor of central importance is the federal nature of the country and the perennial pull between the center and periphery.

Tensions between the central provinces (Ontario and Quebec) and the more outlying ones have been endemic in Canada. Much of the political life and that of the party system has been greatly influenced by them. It is therefore not surprising that a field so sensitive to its regional context as culture should also be affected by the conflicting interests of Canada's regions. On the contrary, the clashes can be expected to be more intense here; it is a universal tendency for artistic life to drift towards the great metropolises and to concentrate in the largest urban agglomerations. This often leads to the resentment of the less favored sites, whose inhabitants feel neglected and deprived. In Canada, the cultural centers of Toronto, Montreal, and Vancouver have been powerful magnets attracting artists and providing jobs for them; there has therefore been a weakening of the other parts of the country, making life there all the more difficult for artists who do not wish to move to the largest cities. The concentration of a good deal of artistic activity in these cultural "poles" has of course meant that there has also been a certain concentration of grants and arts funds in them; this has given rise to discontent and to accusations of bias. It should nevertheless be noted that despite the obvious strong pull of metropolitan areas, cultural life in Canada has flourished throughout the land, with theater groups, galleries, and orchestras functioning well in a large number of smaller places.

Provincial ministers responsible for cultural matters have nevertheless complained bitterly about the absence of even-handedness on the part of the Canada Council and about its failing to cooperate with provincial governments and agencies. Demands are therefore beginning to be heard, as we noted earlier, suggesting that federal funds which now go to the Canada Council be provided to the provinces for their own best use, as they see it.

The Mulroney Conservative government has shown itself to be much more conciliatory towards the provinces and is less centralizing than its predecessors. It has also had some disagreements with some of the cultural agencies. There may therefore be some disposition to meet some of the requests of the provinces. At the time of writing it is not clear how the matter is likely to be resolved. One factor likely to impede a major shift toward the provinces is the self-interest of the Minister of Communications and of his or her officials; they are not likely to wish to abandon activities in which they have placed such hope and confidence and which add to their power.

A certain division of labor has developed, at least in part, between the federal and provincial granting agencies. It would therefore be highly undesirable to reduce the scope of either. To do so would diminish the variety of arts programs available. It is interesting, for example, to note the manner in which the approach of the provincial granting agencies often differs from one another and from that of the Canada Council. We have seen that the latter is austerely professional and disinclined to compromise its adherence to the achievement of the highest standards of performance. The former of course also aspire to funding the best possible work but they sometimes pursue other goals. Among the goals identified by the Manitoba Arts Council, for instance, are youth-oriented and rural and northern-oriented programming and the possibility of developing schemes creating more opportunities for minority groups.

A brief summary of the activities of the well-endowed Ontario Arts Council (its 1985 budget was around $23 million, constituting about 40 percent of the Ontario government's spending on the arts) shows both the similarities with and the differences from the Canada Council. The OAC's activities are devoted primarily to encouraging professional artists and performing arts organizations in dance, film, photography, video, literature, music, theater, and the visual arts. Certain programs, like those fostering school performances and arts activities based in schools or those supporting community and regional arts councils, and support for touring events, are designed to broaden public interest in, and knowledge of, the arts. Musical training support, assistance to non-profit arts schools, and an array of programs intended to foster Franco-Ontario artistic expression are also supported by the Council. Some of these areas would not be supported by the federal granting agency which, in turn, does a number of useful things which are not, and could not be, duplicated by its provincial homologue.

Principles Underlying Arts Policy

There is no single source to which a curious, scenting culture hound can run when tracking down cultural policy in Canada. Nor is there any hallowed tablet enshrining the principles underlying the government's approach to the arts. There are several reasons for this, the chief of which being that no explicit, consciously defined cultural policy actually exists. That is not to say that no such course of action is in place but merely that its rationale has never been defined, and possibly perhaps never even perceived.[38] Cultural policy in Canada did not spring ready-made from Athena's or Athlone's[39] brow but developed slowly, almost imperceptibly, not only like the British Empire in a fit of absent-mindedness, but also to some extent, in a philistine fog of lacking interest. Cultural activities were for a long time considered to be well beyond the bounds of the government's responsibilities and were accorded a low priority in the scheme of things generally. The pioneer past and the inexorable claims on most people's energies of the harsh material world left little time for what was often seen as a frill.

Another reason, and an enduring one, for the absence of a cultural policy lies in the federal nature of the country. Although a greater degree of coordination than exists now between the three levels of government, particularly the two senior ones, is desirable and even likely, it is inconceivable that a community so heterogeneous, whose governments compete on so many fronts, is ever likely to come up with a single cultural policy. There will always be cultural *policies* in Canada. One of the realities of which policy-makers must always be aware is that no jurisdiction can, in the cultural domain, have it its own way. No one can quite go it alone.

During most of the period of Liberal domination of federal politics (from the 1930s to the late 1970s), Ottawa tended to pursue its goals largely independently of the provinces, in part because at first the latter did relatively little, and in part because of the political style of a party become accustomed to weak opposition. But since the days of Expo, the Centennial, and subsequently, closer contact with the provinces was inevitable. Political changes in the 1980s, which have installed new governments not only in Ottawa but also in several of the provincial capitals, augur well for a new climate affecting cultural politics. One of the emerging principles of cultural policy-making in Canada is in fact that each element must now be considered in relation to others, some of which fall within several jurisdictions.

One condition shared by all governments—and it is central to the whole cultural enterprise in Canada—is that, whatever applied in the past, they are now all completely committed to pursuing effective policies with respect to the arts. If, indeed, one were to identify a single pivotal principle of arts policies in Canada, it would be that the arts are of public concern and therefore within the jurisdiction of public policy.

This conscious involvement is animated by several motives. One of them is the recognition of the importance in human affairs of culture and the arts: that the arts are worth pursuing because of what they are and what they contribute intrinsically to the individuals and collectivities making up Canada, its provinces, and its municipalities.

What might be called the "art for art's sake" principle is, however, supplemented by others which add to the complexity of the case. For other imperatives drive governments toward the cultural field. One of these, as we have seen, is the "cultural industries" argument, which considers the arts as an increasingly important factor in the employment situation.

Another—one which has been of paramount importance to policy-makers both in Ottawa and Quebec—is the relation between the arts and a sense of national identity. Nation-building and province-building imperatives have provided powerful incentives for public expenditures on the arts and other cultural pursuits—not least the currently growing preservation of the national, regional, and local heritage. This element reveals that increasingly, cultural pursuits are seen by citizens and governments as integral elements in the fabric of everyday Canadian life. The occasional linkage of cultural programs to such concerns as language policy or aid to ethnic minorities confirms this tendency.

A principle related to the one noted in the preceding paragraph is of particular relevance to Ottawa but is not totally absent from the provincial sphere. It grows out of the recognition that the arts are an important factor in Canada's defence of its sovereignty. In so far as the Americanization of the country depends on more than just economic and political developments but also on cultural ones, policies dealing with the latter are perceived as an element in national and regional efforts to preserve the distinctiveness of Canada vis-à-vis the United States. We have seen how clearly and unequivocally this matter is recognized in the Broadcasting Act and in policies applied under its guidance. But other artistic enterprises are often seen within this context and derive some of the support they receive as a consequence.

The posture of governments vis-à-vis the arts is nowadays dominated by the perception of the artistic community as a legitimate and worthwhile element of society, not merely, as was the case earlier, as an infinitesimal minority of somewhat eccentric individuals. The arts, artists, and their followers have become part of the Canadian mainstream and are recognized as such. This change has occurred in part because of the growing importance of arts lobbies and interest groups.

It is probably to some extent because of the acceptance of the arts as part of the mainstream that governments are less tolerant of the independence that arts organizations and agencies once enjoyed. The sums of money spent in support of the arts (which are constantly growing) and the steadily increasing number of people involved in them actively or passively attract the interest and attention of governments. In this perspective, the seeming partial attrition of the arm's length principle can be seen as a manifestation of the changing importance attached to cultural life.

Finally, the new status of the arts, and their political mobilization, have given the cultural community an unprecedented political clout. Particular parties and governments may vary in the degree to which they wish to support the arts. But whatever their ideological hue in this respect, aesthetic power, as organized in associations like the Canadian Conference of the Arts, can now exert an appreciable influence on decision-making. Eloquent proof was provided just as the last revisions were being made to this chapter toward the end of February 1986. In a deficit-reducing budget drastically cutting government expenditures, the government of Canada *increased* its proposed spending on culture by $75 million. In a pluralist, bargaining, consensus-seeking society like that of Canada, cultural interests have become players whose voices must be taken into account. The fact that this access to the seats of power has been achieved in part as the result of government aid does not diminish its political effectiveness. Nor is it likely that its future power role will be diminished by the likely partial shift of financial aid to the arts from public to private sources—which is a possible outcome of current political realignments. It is the arts which have created the metaphor of the sorcerer's apprentice and it is the arts, organized politically, which, in the manner of the sorcerer's apprentice, are now likely to continue an independent political (as well as aesthetic) existence, irrespective of their erstwhile patron.

Notes

1. In naming one of his books *The Bush Garden: Essays on the Canadian Imagination,* Northrop Frye "pilfered," as he said, the title "from Margaret Atwood's *Journals of Susanna Moodie,* a book unusually rich in suggestive phrases defining a Canadian sensibility." For the title of this chapter, we could not resist doing some pilfering of our own from Frye, who is one of the most perceptive observers of the arts in Canada. We gratefully acknowledge the splendid research assistance of Mary Louise McAllister and the generous response to requests for information from the Canada Council, Statistics Canada, the Department of Communications, the Canadian Conference of the Arts, and provincial cultural agencies and departments.

2. In this chapter "culture" embraces all the arts as well as such closely linked aspects of popular culture as broadcasting and film.

3. D. Reid, *The Group of Seven,* Ottawa, National Gallery of Canada, 1970; P. Mellen, *The Group of Seven* (Toronto: McClelland and Stewart, 1970).

4. The (Aird) Royal Commission on Radio Broadcasting, 1929; The (Fowler) Royal Commission on Broadcasting, 1957; The (Fowler) Committee on Broadcasting, 1965.

5. The title of the former reveals its scope: Royal Commission on National Development in the Arts, Letters and Sciences. Its *Report* appeared in 1951. The more recent inquiry, while still vast, had a more modest scope. It was called the Federal Cultural Review Committee and was presided over by Louis Applebaum and Jacques Hébert.

6. For details of the creation of the Council, see Bernard Ostry, *The Cultural Connection* (Toronto: McClelland and Stewart Ltd., 1978), 64–72; and The Canada Council, *The Canada Council 25th Anniversary Dinner, Château Laurier, Ottawa, June 14, 1982,* n.d. The quotation from Louis St. Laurent is on p. 23 of this collection of speeches in which various individuals instrumental in founding the Council reminisced about the early days.

7. For general analyses of this phenomenon see Albert Breton, "Supplementary Statement," in Royal Commission on the Economic Union and Development Prospects for Canada, *Report,* Ottawa, Department of Supply and Services, 1985, Volume 3, pp. 486–526, and Alan C. Cairns, "The Governments and Societies of Canadian Federalism," *Canadian Journal of Political Science,* Vol. X, No. 4 (December 1977), 695–725.

8. French Canada was, as we have noted, cut off from France. Much of the secular role originally played by the French administration was taken over by the Catholic Church which, cut off from France during and after the French Revolution, presided over the spiritual and worldly needs of the population and to some extent performed functions elsewhere assumed by the state. Most of the cultural life of French Canada, and hence of Quebec, was, until the advent of the Quiet Revolution, therefore closely linked to the Church.

9. For a while in the 1970s and 1980s, an intense rivalry had in fact developed between the Federal and Quebec governments with respect to the lavish sums each made available for the appropriate celebration of "its" holiday—a competition which was of benefit to audiences and performers generally but added little to the dignity of the sponsoring governments.

10. The Royal Commission on Radio Broadcasting was chaired by Sir John Aird. Created in 1928, it reported in the following year.

11. Cited by Frank W. Peers, *The Politics of Canadian Broadcasting: 1920–1951* (Toronto:

University of Toronto Press, 1969), p. 101. This is the definitive study of the origins and development of public broadcasting in Canada. See also *idem, The Public Eye: Television and the Politics of Canadian Broadcasting 1952–1968,* (Toronto: University of Toronto Press, 1979).

12. Canadian Broadcasting Corporation, *TV & Radio: Figures That Count,* (Ottawa: CBC, 1985), 20.

13. Pierre Juneau, President of the CBC, in an address to the Canadian Club in Winnipeg, February 7, 1985.

14. Department of Communications, *Fact Sheets,* "Review of the Canadian Broadcasting System," n.d., "Task Force to Review the Canadian Broadcasting System," n.d.

15. The National Film Board, *News Release,* "The National Film Board Begins Implementing New Operational Plan Reconfirming Its Role as a Public Producer and Distributor," November 25, 1985. The cited passages are on pp. 3 and 5.

16. *Report of the Federal Cultural Review Committee* (Ottawa: Department of Communications, 1982), 351.

17. National Arts Centre, *Annual Report 1982–1983,* 1–4.

18. *The Canada Council 28th Annual Report 1984/85* (Ottawa: The Canada Council, 1985), 4.

19. The DOC's figure does not include the subsidies paid the Post Office, noted below.

20. Relevant comments on the Canada Council case are in Mavor Moore, "Unholy Alliance Jeopardizes Cultural Agencies," *Globe and Mail,* July 13, 1985; Matthew Fraser, "Is Arm's Length Principle in Jeopardy?" *ibid.*, December 8, 1984; Matthew Fraser, "Masse Asserts Role in Cultural Policy," *ibid.*, September 23, 1985. For a detailed, succinct exposition of the chief salient facts about the Council, see The Canada Council, *The Canada Council: Mandate, Structure, Programs & Administration—A Summary,* 1982. This is one of a very large number of useful analyses published by the Council's Research and Evaluation Unit.

21. *Report of the Federal Cultural Policy Review Committee,* 254–55.

22. Department of Communications, *Towards a New National Broadcasting Policy* (Ottawa: Department of Supply and Services, 1983).

23. Cited in "Telefilm Funding Sparks Quarter Billion Dollar Biz in Third Year," *Canadian Communications Reports,* Vol. 12, No. 17, September 15, 1985.

24. Bernard Ostry, *The Cultural Connection* (Toronto: McClelland and Stewart Ltd., 1978), 33. See also John Meisel, "Political Culture and the Politics of Culture," *Canadian Journal of Political Science* VII, No. 4 (December 1974), 603–4.

25. André Fortier and Paul Schafer, Développement et croissance des politiques fédérales dans le domaine des arts, 1944–85 (Ottawa: Department of Communications, unpublished document), *passim.*

26. DOC, *1985–86 Estimates,* Expenditure Plan (Ottawa: DOC), 55–59.

27. DOC, *Towards a New National Broadcasting Policy,* 1983; *Building for the Future: Towards a Distinctive CBC,* 1983; *The National Film and Video Policy,* 1984; *Copyright and the Cultural Community,* 1984.

28. *Canadian Cinema: A Solid Base,* Report of the Film Industry Task Force (Department of Supply and Services, 1985).

29. Their mandates (and presiding officers) were: (1) A general review of issues of culture and communication under a government-wide scheme of examining expenditures and government performance (the Nielsen Report); (2) Broadcasting (Caplan-Sauvageau); (3) Funding of the arts (Bovey); (4) National museums (Richard-Withrow); (5) National Arts Centre (Hendry); (6) Cultural industries; (7) Status of artists (Gelinas-Siren); (8) Film industry (Raymond-Roth); and (9) Non-theatrical film industry (Macerola-Jensen).

30. The Thirty-third Parliament, 1984–85, "Bill C20, An Act to Amend the Canadian Radio-television and Telecommunications Commission Act, the Broadcasting Act and the Radio Act," Ottawa, House of Commons, 1984.

31. Statistics Canada, *Arts and Culture: A Statistical Profile* (Ottawa: Ministry of Supply and Services, 1985), 34.

32. Thus Manitoba, for instance, started incredibly strongly. In 1969–70 it spent the highest per capita amount in Canada, over $10.00, more than two dollars ahead of the next highest spender, Ontario. Prince Edward Island's expenditure for each citizen in 1969–70 was less than $1.00. It has made quite amazing strides. As for Quebec, it now ranks a close second to Alberta as the biggest provincial spender.

33. The Canada Council Research and Evaluation Branch, *Lotteries and the Arts: The Canadian Experience 1970–1980*. July 1982.

34. Department of External Affairs, *International Cultural Relations, Statistical Summary of Activities for 1984/85*, Ottawa, 1985, pp. 1, 11.

35. In 1971 over 3.9 million attendances were recorded. By 1981 this had risen to more than 8.8 million. Claire McCaughey, *A Survey of Arts and Audience Studies: A Canadian Perspective 1967–1984* (Ottawa: The Canada Council, 1984), 17.

36. The total labor force increased by 39 percent between 1971 and 1981. The arts labor force grew by 74 percent. The Canada Council, *Selected Arts Research Statistics,* 5th Edition (Ottawa, 1984), 61.

37. For useful background see Canada Council, *The Arm's Length Principle and the Arts: An International Perspective* (Ottawa: The Canada Council, 1985).

38. Several efforts have actually been made in the recent era to provide studies which would have enabled the formulation of some coherent policies, at least with respect to specific jurisdictions, but they have never produced the optimum political follow-up. We have referred to some of them earlier. The principal works are the reports of the Massey Commission and the Federal Cultural Review Committee and such provincial inquiries as Jean Paul L'Allier, *Pour l'évolution de la politique culturelle,* Document de travail, Mai 1976, Quebec City, Editeur officiel du Québec, 1978 (two volumes); *Report to the Honourable Susan Fish, the Minister of Citizenship and Culture, by the Special Committee for the Arts,* Toronto, Spring 1984.

39. Alexander Augustus Frederick William George Cambridge, Earl of Athlone, was the Governor General from 1940 to 1946.

13

Government and the Arts in the United States

KEVIN V. MULCAHY*

Historically, government support for the arts in the United States has been very limited. However, such public patronage never has been completely absent. The Smithsonian Institution, chartered by Congress in 1846 as a non-profit corporation, has grown from the "nation's attic" to a vast holding company of museums and special collections. States and localities administer and support a variety of art, historical, and natural science museums as well as commemorative sites and "cultural parks." Since the nineteenth century, national copyright laws have protected individual artistic creators while subsidized postal rates have dramatically enhanced the publication and fund-raising activities of cultural organizations. More recently, the federal government has sponsored international cultural exchange programs. The federal government also allows tax deductions for individuals and corporations making donations to cultural organizations and localities typically exempt these organizations from paying property taxes.[1]

Significant as this support for the arts has been, until recently its impact was indirect, episodic, and largely marginal. No public arts agency existed on the national level comparable to the British Arts Council, let alone to the state-run cultural institutions found in either East or West Germany. The principle of public subsidy was also the subject of harsh partisan and ideological debate. It is difficult to disagree with Milton Cummings that for the arts in the United States before 1965, "there was no large-scale and continuous tradition of direct subsidy by the government, such as was common in Europe."[2]

Government support for the arts in the United States has developed since the 1960s with the political legacy of the New Deal arts program of the 1930s still uppermost in the minds of policy-makers and the interested members of the public.[3] The political controversies that resulted from the cultural projects of the Works Progress Administration served to dramatize the dangers as well as the benefits for the arts that might come with an official embrace. Public arts agencies have been very sensitive to any charges of ideological or aesthetic biases and, in both their organizational structures and programmatic policies, have sought to prevent their occurrence. As America's preeminent public patron, the National Endowment for the Arts (NEA) has been particularly aware of these prece-

*I wish to acknowledge the invaluable assistance provided by Peter Zwick, Cecil V. Crabb, Louise Rosenzweig, and Brian Mirsky in the preparation of this chapter.

dents and problems and has sought to develop a model of public patronage that would avoid previous political pitfalls. In the discussion of public support for the arts that follows, certain major themes will recur that reflect the ongoing concern with political acceptability and popular approval.

First, public patronage and public arts agencies have played a highly circumscribed role in the nation's culture. The NEA has not functioned as a national "ministry of culture"—that is, a Cabinet-level department responsible for comprehensive cultural policy-making and for administering the nation's artistic activities—but has promoted the arts in strictly limited ways.

Second, the NEA, while a highly circumspect public patron, has developed close relationships with state arts agencies. These "little NEAs" have complemented the federal agency in supporting a broad range of national cultural policies including increased public funding.

Third, the delimited nature of federal commitment to the arts has been underscored by the limited public funding that has been made available. Not only have appropriations for the Arts Endowment and related agencies remained small, but the federal government has chosen not to provide operating subsidies, assume responsibility for artistic production, or become the guarantor of a national cultural heritage.

Fourth, the history of past cultural controversies has led the NEA to adopt a political strategy that avoids extremes both in funding and in programming. The guiding decision-making principle has been a commitment to "cultural pluralism"—that is, a definition of the arts capacious enough to allow broadly distributed support for a diversity of cultural expressions.

Overall, the Arts Endowment has sought to build a broad base of public support, from within the arts world and without, while also broadening the nation's cultural base in both its variety and availability. Public support has come to be associated with greater access to and awareness of the arts, even as the NEA has sought not to become identified with particular aesthetic values. On the other hand, the NEA's record has also been cause for much criticism; government support for the arts has proven no more immune from political controversy than other public policies.

National Patronage of the Arts

Public Law 89-209 created the National Foundation for the Arts and Humanities in 1965; this enabling legislation defined the arts broadly as including but not limited to:

> . . . music (instrumental and vocal), dance, drama, folk arts, creative writing, architecture and allied fields, painting, sculpture, photography, graphic and craft arts, industrial design, costume and fashion design, motion pictures, television, radio, tape and sound recording, the arts related to the presentation, performance, execution, and exhibition of such major art forms, and the study and application of the arts to human environments.

While this discussion is almost exclusively about the NEA, some observations should also be offered about the National Endowment for the Humanities (NEH). The Arts Endowment's administrative twin, the NEH, provides public support for studies in the following academic disciplines:

history, philosophy, languages, linguistics, literature, archaeology, jurisprudence, history and criticism of the arts, ethics, comparative religion, and those aspects of the social sciences employing historical or philosophical approaches.

The creation of the Arts and Humanities Endowments represented the first permanent commitment by the federal government to support cultural programs. (The WPA projects were only "emergency relief.") Yet, the role of the federal government was to be limited and indirect, lest it become a state-imposed culture at odds with the American pluralist tradition.[4] As grant-making agencies (similar to the National Science Foundation or the National Institutes of Health), the Endowments normally provide only discretionary funding on a competitive basis to underwrite partially the costs of specific projects undertaken by private or locally supported cultural institutions.

The NEA is involved primarily with execution, exhibition, and performance while the NEH places greater emphasis on aesthetic criticism and philosophy. More important, the NEH may be seen as an agency of the major research universities in the United States while the NEA is closely related to the major arts organizations. Although the political and budgetary fates of the NEA and NEH have been closely linked, the Humanities Endowment has had a more difficult time in creating a public identity and solidifying political support. The enabling legislation provided for a Federal Council on the Arts and Humanities as a coordinating agency, but this council largely has been inactive, and the two Endowments have functioned as separate administrative entities.

In addition to the Endowments, there are other public cultural agencies of somewhat lesser importance. (See Table 1.) Prominent are the museums located in Washington, D.C., whose operations are directly underwritten by the federal government even if they are technically autonomous institutions. These are the National Gallery of Art and the Smithsonian complex, the latter receiving a larger appropriation than the NEA. The Institute of Museum Services, an independent Executive branch agency, is endowed with

TABLE 1. Appropriations for Major Federal Cultural Agencies, 1983–1985 (in Millions of Dollars)

Recipient	*FY 1983 Appropriations*	*FY 1984 Appropriations*	*FY 1985 Appropriations**
National Endowment for the Arts	143.875	162.000	175.000
National Endowment for the Humanities	131.247	140.000	145.000
Institute of Museum Services	11.520	20.150	27.000
Smithsonian	195.756	174.803	198.599
National Gallery of Art	33.137	34.639	35.603
Commission of Fine Arts	.319	.340	.379
Historic Preservation Fund	26.000	26.500	27.000
Corporation for Public Broadcasting	137.000	130.000	130.000
TOTALS	678.854	688.432	738.581

Source: Congressional Arts Caucus.

*House Appropriations Committee recommendations of June 28, 1984 except for the CPB appropriation which represents "forward funding."

a small budget to provide museums nationwide with technical and management assistance. The Interior Department supports historic preservation efforts in cooperation with the (private) National Trust for Historic Preservation and maintains the National Register of Historic Places. Interior's Park Service also maintains a number of commemorative sites and historic monuments.

The Corporation for Public Broadcasting (CPB) serves as a conduit for federal funds to the various not-for-profit radio and television stations around the country that provide noncommercial cultural and public affairs programming. These stations may either be privately run or operated by local governmental authorities such as state departments of education or public universities. These stations form a loose "network" with locally supported member stations providing the bulk of the programs. CPB itself is a government-owned corporation, yet is not a government agency; however, since funds are appropriated by Congress, that may be a fine distinction.

This summary of the federal government's involvement with culture does not include government programs that are involved with cultural matters, but as ancillary activities. The Library of Congress and the National Archives are important cultural institutions; however, the former is at root a legislative reference service and the latter is a document-preservation arm of the General Services Administration. In one of the few examples of direct patronage by the national government, the General Services Administration commissions art work to decorate federal buildings. The United States Information Agency (USIA) supports international cultural and educational exchange programs, which along with informational activities such as Voice of America and Radio Marti, export American arts and artists to audiences abroad.

For all this, there is no ministry of culture in the United States. The cultural programs of the federal government are highly fragmented, located in a variety of administrative agencies, overseen by different congressional committees, supported by and responsive to a variety of interests, and articulating the policy perspectives of discrete segments of the cultural constituency. This institutional fragmentation reflects both the diffuse nature of artistic activity in the United States and a fear of the effects that a unified cultural bureaucracy might have on artistic expression. The United States has eschewed the idea of establishing an official culture in which the state would act as the sole or even the most influential patron of the arts. The government has seen itself as a minority stockholder in the nation's culture. Consequently, public spending on the arts in the United States remains small. Despite a major spurt in the 1970s, funding remains at approximately $688 million out of a 1984 federal budget of $853 billion for the federal arts agencies listed in Table 1.

The National Endowment for the Arts, while but one of the arts agencies of the federal government, is the paramount actor in cultural policy-making. No other public arts agency enjoys its prestige in the arts world or exercises comparable influence on cultural institutions. Though not a cabinet department, the NEA as an independent agency reports directly to the President and enjoys considerable political prestige. Its chief administrative officer is its Chairman (see Figure 1), appointed by the President for a four-year term upon Senate confirmation. The Chairman is responsible to a twenty-six member National Council on the Arts appointed by the President, and confirmed by the Senate, to staggered six-year terms. The Chairman may appoint any such subordinate officials—for example, Deputy Chairmen—as is deemed necessary, and administrative arrangements have varied with different incumbents. At the same time, the basic building blocks of the NEA's administrative structure have remained the various program areas that embody the legisla-

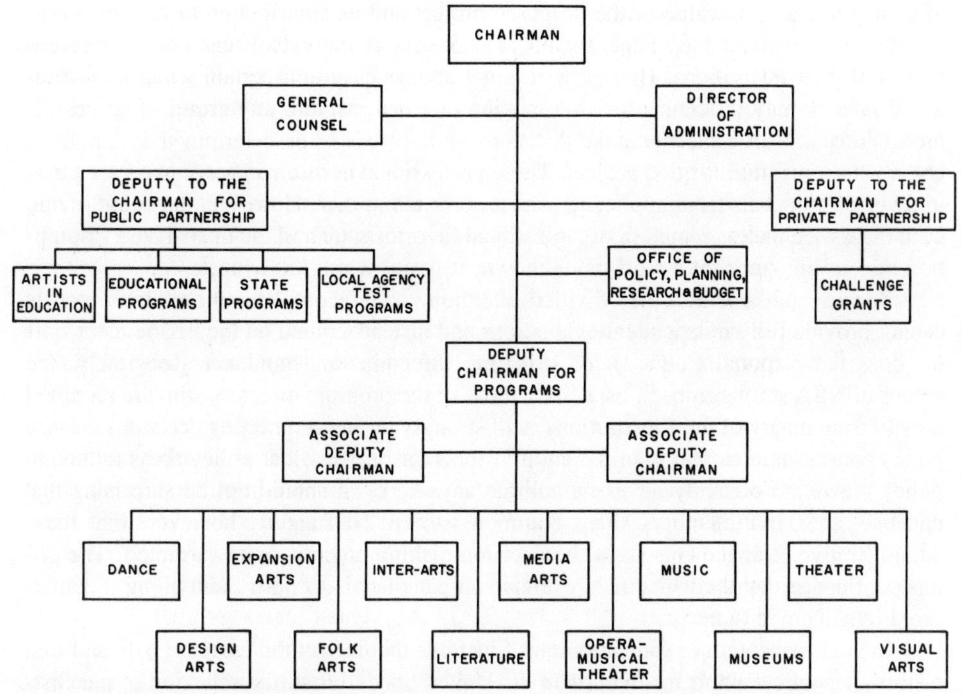

FIGURE 1. Administrative organization of the National Endowment of the Arts.
Source: Adapted from the NEA Staff Directory, October 1983; updated, September 1984.

tive intent of PL 89-209. It is the program personnel—staff and advisory panelists—who largely determine the NEA's grant-making decisions and create its cultural guidelines.

By statutory provision all grant-making decisions are made by the Chairman; while this means that the NEA Chairman may approve or disapprove grant applications at will, this has occurred only rarely.[5] Each of the NEA's program areas advises the National Council and the Chairman about grants to be awarded on the basis of recommendations provided by specialized panels. (As will be discussed more fully in the section on the arts budget, each of these programs—for example, music, museums, opera, theater, expansion arts, artists in education—represents a major interest in the cultural community.) The panels are, in many ways, the bedrock of the Arts Endowment's administrative organization. Panel members are appointed by the NEA Chairman for terms of up to four years on the recommendation of the NEA staff, arts lobbyists, cultural administrators, Council members, elected officials, and other concerned parties from the cultural community. On one level, these advisory groups serve to provide expert, and presumably disinterested, evaluations of the grant proposals submitted to the program areas into which the Endowment is organized. On another level, the panels represent an effort to minimize "cultural porkbarrelling" and to keep "politics" out of the grantmaking process. More basically these panels serve as the principal means for insulating the NEA from adverse criticism about the wisdom of having made a particular grant.

As is typical of groups of outside consultants, the panels cannot be convened more than five or six times a year and for periods of only a few days. Although proposals are distributed to panelists in advance, the average panel has about eleven days a year in which it must evaluate perhaps 1,000 grant applications. The bases for making a grant are, of course, the artistic value of the proposed project and its contribution to the community's cultural development.[6] Panel members also serve as individuals and not as representatives of their institutions. However, it is not always easy to ascertain when an institutional interest may influence decision-making or when, as with any group of successful professionals, NEA panelists make decisions on the basis of predetermined assumptions about what constitutes a good project. These professional norms may serve to create a bias in favor of proposals from applicants whose work is familiar. However, the cause of any such biases seems less rooted in organizational favoritism than in the unanalyzed assumption that, if an applicant's work is unknown, it is not worth knowing.[7]

Because of lack of time, divided attention, and incomplete information, panels cannot provide fully independent evaluations and instead depend on the Endowment staff (as does the National Council) for structure, direction, and guidance. Inevitably, the values of NEA staff members, especially those of the program directors who are recruited largely from major cultural institutions, will strongly influence granting decisions.[8] Since policy consensus is as strong in the cultural sphere as it is in other policy areas (although policy views are certainly never monolithic anywhere), it should not be surprising that panelists and staff members share common values. To suggest, however, that these administrative arrangements skew the decision-making process, is unwarranted. The primary influence that staff members exercise on panelists is to push them along a demarcated bureaucratic path.

In sum, panels serve four important functions that reflect the current goals and past history of public support for the arts in the United States. First, the selection of panelists allows for the representation of relevant interests from the arts world in the process of cultural policy-making. Second, the panels are important assurances that government support for the arts is not "politics as usual," but represents an effort to allow merit and need to determine grant decisions. Third, by actively involving artists and arts administrators in the grant-making process, the NEA secures a large measure of legitimation for its decisions and also emphasizes the "partnership" goal of its funding arrangements. Fourth, the panel system helps to protect the Arts Endowment from political interference and censorship. It allows the Chairman to justify his opposition to such intrusions as deferring to the considered judgment of a group of experts rather than asserting the superiority of his own opinion or that of the NEA staff.

Given the criticism of the New Deal arts projects as unrepresentative of community preferences, ideologically motivated, politically unaccountable, and in need of censorship, the administrative procedures of the Arts Endowment reflect a good sense of bureaucratic politics. Whether the NEA's political tactics are to be judged a success depends ultimately on one's assessment of the cultural outcomes. Nonetheless, it cannot be overemphasized that the policies and programs of the National Endowment for the Arts are not simply an administrative convenience. These arrangements reflect the realities of American politics. In particular, the history of cultural politics in the United States strongly suggested the advisability of a grant-making agency with limited authority and indirect responsibility rather than a comprehensive cultural department with direct responsibility for artistic production.

State Arts Agencies

Eighteen state arts councils existed before the creation of the NEA, but with the distinct exception of the New York State Arts Council, these public arts agencies were not particularly active. Following the NEA's creation, the number of these councils quickly grew to include each of the states and territories. Now all states serve as official patrons of the arts, and have departments responsible for the administration of a cultural budget. The impetus for this spectacular growth came from provisions of the Endowment's enabling legislation that required the existence of a state arts agency as a condition for receipt of federal funds and provided for a once-only basic grant of $50,000 to establish an arts agency if none existed. While this sort of an organizational requirement may seem like an administrative formality, it did lay the foundation for a locally-based NEA constituency and stimulated state arts appropriations.

State arts agencies range considerably from the New York State Arts Council, which until the mid-1970s outspent the NEA, to the councils of Nevada and most of the territories whose budgets remain below $100,000 per year. Most states administer their cultural programs according to the following model: an independent agency with a small staff; a council or commission with an average of fifteen members appointed by the Governor to staggered terms to formulate policy; and advisory panels to review grant applications and recommend awards.[9] Seven states have some form of cabinet-level department of cultural resources with responsibility for the arts council and a variety of other cultural activities such as historic preservation, public broadcasting, and a state library.[10] The Arts Task Force of the National Conference of State Legislatures has recommended that all states have a unified cultural department both to enhance coordination of activities among cultural agencies and to increase the political visibility of the arts. Decisions about awarding grants typically are made by the appointed members of the state arts councils acting on the recommendations of advisory panels whose members are experts in particular art forms. Most states also provide for direct representation of professionals from the visual, literary, or performing arts on their councils.[11]

Nineteen state arts agencies delegate responsibility for grant distribution to local entities. This administrative decentralization is advocated because of the ability of local agencies better to assess audience demand and to identify deserving projects. Moreover, local arts agencies, by accepting responsibility for making certain grants, may serve to deflect criticism from the state agency in controversial allocations. Locally oriented arts agencies sometimes are criticized for funding programs that are decidely "amateur," if not actually "hobbies." On the other hand, these programs may provide the only cultural activities that further community participation and identification. This debate has raged at all levels of public cultural funding and has led to the criticism that public arts agencies are subsidizing artists and audiences where few actually exist. Yet, the dearth of opportunities outside of major metropolitan areas is precisely the situation which state and local arts agencies are seeking to correct. Dick Netzer, who is not uncritical of the funding decisions of public arts agencies, makes the following observation:

> In the last decade hundreds of thousands if not millions of Americans have discovered through publicly supported programs some form of the arts and found it so fascinating that continuing experience with that art form—at some level—will be part of the rest of their lives. The emphasis of the public funding agencies on wider availability has made ordinary Americans more familiar and comfortable with the arts than their counterparts in other large countries seem to be. And this development may in time result in significant audience expansion.[12]

From its inception, the NEA envisioned active participation by the states in the grant-making process. Indeed, not less than 20 percent of the Arts Endowment's budget must be distributed to the states with no state (or territory) receiving less than $200,000. These funds then are distributed by the state arts agency as the "federally-mandated conduit."[13] Total spending by the states and territories in 1983 amounted to $125,732,153; the average appropriation by the fifty-six legislatures in 1983 was $2.3 million. (See Table 2.) These appropriations ranged from the highest spending states on a per capita basis, Alaska, New York, and Hawaii, to the lowest spending states, Nevada, Idaho, and Tennessee. In dollars, the Northern Marianas spent $10,000 compared to New York's $35 million. The uniqueness of the New York State Arts Council cannot be overemphasized. The second-ranked state in spending was California, yet its appropriation of $20,000,000 was only about 60 percent of New York's. Forty-three of the fifty-six states and territories appropriate more funds for the arts than they receive from the NEA.

In distributing funds, most states follow the NEA's decision-making model—that is, they are grant-making agencies in which councils act after reviews of advisory panels. Twenty states, however, have "line-item" appropriations for one or more of their arts institutions. This direct legislative support varies from authorizing bonds for a specific capital project (such as a performing arts center) to underwriting the operating expenses of a cultural institution (such as a symphony or museum). Clearly, line items in the state budget are welcomed by institutions as more stable and predictable sources of financial support than those provided by the grants programs of the various state arts agencies. For many arts administrators, however, these direct appropriations violate the council and panel review system that was designed to ensure the allocation of arts funds based on

TABLE 2. State Arts Agencies Legislative Appropriations, Fiscal Year 1983

	Per Capita (¢)		*Appropriations ($)*
	Rank	*1983*	*1983*
Alabama	48	15.3	600,000
Alaska	1	1207.7	4,975,800
American Samoa	6	146.6	47,500
Arizona	49	15.0	419,100
Arkansas	31	33.1	759,731
California	20	44.9	10,864,488
Colorado	35	28.7	851,586
Connecticut	36	28.6	897,034
Delaware	12	74.0	442,400
District of Columbia	7	123.0	784,100
Florida	26	41.2	4,190,664
Georgia	37	28.2	1,573,221
Guam	11	86.6	91,652
Hawaii	3	161.6	1,585,509
Idaho	55	10.8	103,300
Illinois	39	25.0	2,866,600
Indiana	40	23.7	1,294,169
Iowa	51	12.9	374,176

(continued)

TABLE 2 (*Continued*)

	Per Capita (¢)		Appropriations ($)
	Rank	*1983*	*1983*
Kansas	43	17.9	425,623
Kentucky	30	36.4	1,332,700
Louisiana	19	45.1	1,940,758
Maine	42	19.2	217,039
Maryland	25	42.5	1,810,603
Massachusetts	9	95.3	5,500,000
Michigan	14	61.0	5,617,200
Minnesota	23	43.1	1,766,100
Mississippi	45	17.5	441,955
Missouri	16	52.8	2,607,672
Montana	44	17.6	139,456
Nebraska	32	30.2	475,504
Nevada	54	11.2	94,282
New Hampshire	47	16.2	152,078
New Jersey	18	48.5	3,589,842
New Mexico	28	39.2	521,100
New York	2	200.8	35,340,000
North Carolina	21	44.2	2,629,575
North Dakota	41	19.9	131,067
Northern Marianas	15	59.3	10,000
Ohio	17	48.5	5,230,906
Oklahoma	13	61.8	1,914,567
Oregon	51	12.9	342,460
Pennsylvania	27	40.0	4,758,000
Puerto Rico	4	152.1	5,020,620
Rhode Island	24	42.7	406,716
South Carolina	22	44.1	1,395,227
South Dakota	33	29.0	199,201
Tennessee	56	10.4	481,600
Texas	53	12.2	1,803,313
Utah	10	87.2	1,324,200
Vermont	29	36.8	190,000
Virgin Islands	5	150.9	150,858
Virginia	38	27.2	1,474,700
Washington	50	14.4	607,161
West Virginia	8	102.9	2,008,504
Wisconsin	46	17.2	817,600
Wyoming	33	29.0	142,902

Source: The National Assembly of State Arts Agencies.

cultural need or value rather than due to political pressure. Allegations of "playing politics" with public culture are particularly intense if an arts organization's line-item appropriation constitutes a disproportionate share of the arts budget, or if a line item has been sought to override a decision by the state arts agency.[14] These budgetary decisions raise the specter of a "line itemization" of the arts budget and an end to decision-making autonomy. Opponents of the line item prefer that the legislature appropriate an overall amount for all cultural spending and allow the state arts agency to decide which institutions to fund and at what level.

State arts agencies support a variety of programs and in general these follow the guidelines established by the NEA for its programmatic divisions. The majority of states have programs such as the "Arts in School" or "Arts in the Community." Dance, theater, and music touring groups are supported widely as are major, private arts organizations. Public cultural institutions such as state museums or state libraries usually have established budgets and separate administrative organizations. States also provide significant support for local arts agencies—some of which, like the San Francisco Arts Council, and the New York City Cultural Affairs Commission have national significance. Many states and localities have also instituted special devices to support the arts such as hotel/motel taxes, income tax checkoffs, dedicated portions of sales taxes, special assessment districts, and in Massachusetts a state lottery for the arts.[15]

State arts agencies came into existence reflecting a wide variety of legislative intentions usually expressing vague, broad-based goals such as the "cultivation of arts appreciation" and the "nourishment of artistic quality and creativity." Typically, state legislation provides little specific programmatic guidance; moreover, many state arts agencies originally came into existence simply to qualify for NEA funds. Given the absence of a tradition of arts administration in the states in the early years, the Arts Endowment became the source of guidance about policies, programs, and administrative organization. These agencies functioned in effect as "little NEAs" in their close association with the national arts agency and its cultural goals.

As state arts agencies have developed their own cultural identity and administrative autonomy, friction between them and their national parent over policy questions has increased. Nonetheless, the NEA realizes important political goals through its close partnership with the state arts agencies. Endowment officials are able to recite the specific local uses of cultural funds when testifying before congressional committees with specific mention of NEA-supported institutions in the districts of the committees' members. The cultural institutions funded, with their administrators, boards of trustees, and clienteles, constitute a constituency base for the Endowment. These arts advocates, disproportionately well-off and well-educated, are able to articulate concerns about the nation's cultural condition while focusing on specific issues and local concerns. In sum, state arts agencies, with an understandable instinct for bureaucratic self-preservation, have become institutionalized advocates for the NEA's general policies and the principle of continued public funding.

The Arts Budget

The administration of New Deal Arts projects involved the government in a variety of allocational, supervisory, employment quota, and subject matter conflicts which left a negative association with government support for the arts. Given the government's role as direct patron of the relief artist, this may have been inevitable, but it nevertheless served to involve these projects in debilitating political controversies. The Arts Endowment, by contrast, operates on the principle of indirect sponsorship through matching grants (up to 50 percent of the cost) for special projects to be undertaken by private cultural institutions and state and local arts councils. The NEA ordinarily does not subsidize the operating costs of cultural institutions, make grants to individual artists, or commission works of art.

Great as its impact on the arts has been, the NEA has chosen to insulate itself by working through intermediaries and to avoid a permanent commitment to particular arts organizations. Avoiding direct patronage has not completely spared the NEA from being tarred by the brush strokes of controversial projects. However, sharing responsibility with cultural institutions in the private sector and relying on the panel system for grant-making has helped the NEA avoid the political criticism that undermined the effectiveness of the New Deal arts program.

By the end of Richard Nixon's tenure in office, the basic contours of the cultural budget had been established as the Arts Endowment successfully passed through its "initial survival threshold." A sign of having navigated this passage is the allocation of enough resources so that an agency "can rapidly expand to meet the needs its members have long been advocating."[16] Table 3 shows the appropriations, and the rates of yearly change, for the NEA and NEH from the end of the Nixon Administration to Ronald Reagan's second budget (1974–84). In this decade, the Endowments reached an appropriations plateau of over $100 million. Over much of the past decade, the Endowments (with the NEH just behind the NEA) have enjoyed a regular, steady upward increase in appropriations that only recently has been slowed in the face of efforts by the Reagan administration to impose sharp budgetary cutbacks.

As noted earlier, the Arts Endowment is organized administratively according to its major programmatic activities. Table 4 shows the allocation of the 1981 NEA budget (its last "normal" budgetary year in the outgoing Carter administration) among these programs by amount and as a percent of total program funds. These budget figures illustrate

TABLE 3. Budget Growth (in Millions of Dollars) of the National Endowments for the Arts and Humanities, 1974–1984

Year	*Arts*	*% Change*	*Humanities*	*% Change*
1974	$ 64	—	$ 54	—
1975	80	20	79	31
1976	88	9	85	7
1977	100	12	99	14
1978	124	19	121	18
1979	149	17	145	17
1980	154	3	150	3
1981	158	2	151	9
1982	143	−10	131	−15
1983	144	1	130	−1
1984	162	13	140	8

Source: National Endowments for the Arts and Humanities

TABLE 4. Comparison of NEA Spending by Clusters of Programs, Fiscal Year 1981 (in Millions of Dollars and Percent Shares)[a]

Program	$	%
Traditional Arts		
Dance	9.0	8.4
Museums	13.0	12.1
Music	16.2	15.1
Opera/Musical Theater	6.2	5.8
Theater	10.7	9.9
Literature	4.8	4.5
Visual Arts	7.5	6.9
Media Arts[b]	12.4	11.6
Cluster Total	79.7	73.3
Outreach Activities		
Education	5.0	4.7
Design	5.2	4.9
Expansion Arts	8.6	8.0
Folk Arts	3.0	2.8
Special Projects	5.7	5.3
Special Constituencies	.4	.4
Cluster Total	27.9	26.1
Ancillary Services		
Research	1.2	1.1
Evaluation	.3	.3
Partnership Coordination	.6	.6
International Fellows	.4	.4
Cluster Total	2.5	2.4
Total Regular Program Funds: $110.1		

Source: National Endowment for the Arts

[a]These figures exclude the 20 percent of appropriations mandated by Congress to go to the states as well as administrative costs. Challenge grants, most of which were awarded to major art institutions, are also excluded. Total percentages add up to over 100% because of rounding.

[b]A significant segment of this program spending is used to support the filming and broadcasting of traditional art forms.

some major characteristics of the NEA as a public agency. First, there is a decidedly strong emphasis on support for traditional art forms and major cultural institutions. Almost three-quarters of the 1981 cultural budget went to a cluster of programs made up of museums, music, theater, visual and media arts. Second, the programs that are popular with broad segments of the cultural community (such as folk art) and which represent explicit ''outreach'' efforts (such as artists-in-schools) account for almost 25 percent of the budget. (The commonality in these programs is their orientation to developing support for, and an awareness of, the arts.) Third, a small percent of NEA funding is allocated for ancillary services (such as research and evaluation). It may also be noted that this pattern of distribution among programs has stayed almost the same over the past decade.

The budget cuts, which were announced in 1981 by then Director of the Office of Management and Budget (OMB) David Stockman, were perhaps a healthy shock to an overly complacent cultural community that had come to expect steady increases in the cultural budget and strong presidential support—regardless of party. OMB proposed cutting the 1982 appropriations for the Arts Endowment almost in half—from $158 million to $88 million and the Humanities Endowment from $155 million to $85 million. Stockman's proposed budgetary reductions were "premised on the notion that the (Reagan) administration should completely revamp federal policy for arts and humanities support." The Arts Endowment was sharply criticized for "promoting the notion that the federal government should be the financial patron of first resort for . . . artistic and literary pursuits." OMB's working paper on the NEA further observed:

> This policy has resulted in a reduction in the historic role of private individual and corporate philanthropic support in these key areas. These reductions would be a first step toward reversing this trend.[17]

In assessing the probable reaction to the drastic cuts that it would propose, OMB officials forecast (correctly) that there would be a strong opposition.

> The Arts and Humanities Endowments have broad and articulate public constituencies, ranging from university presidents to museum directors to individual artists and scholars. In addition, most artistic and cultural institutions maintain strong ties to business and corporations through honorary appointments on boards of directors.[18]

The cultural constituency indeed had become a very well-connected group, and members of the NEA's National Council, like Beverly Sills, were very vocal in their opposition to the proposed cuts.

The Endowment itself took a different approach. Instead of arguing against the cuts in the arts budget on normative grounds, NEA officials emphasized "dollars and sense" consequences. Chairman Livingston Biddle disputed David Stockman's assertions that public support for the arts militated against private funding. "I think that, from the very outset, Congress envisioned that very role of the Endowment as a catalyst. Corporate support for the arts has grown from $22 million in 1966 to more than $435 million today." Representative Sidney Yates (D-Ill.), chairman of the Appropriations subcommittee responsible for the NEA, also attacked the OMB Director's assumptions about cultural philanthropy.

> Mr. Stockman says that the Endowments have hindered business from contributing to arts organizations. He doesn't understand how it's worked in the past. The Endowments have been trailblazers for contributions from business, not the other way around. I think if the Endowment cut its contributions, so will business.[19]

But the Arts Endowment was not to rely on rhetorical argument alone. It introduced a "worst case" budget that implemented the OMB's mandated cuts in such a way that Congress would reinstate lost funds. This occurred in the reconciliation stage of the budgetary process when the NEA appropriation was set at $143 million—a reduction of 10 percent rather than Stockman's recommended 50 percent. Moreover, the funds allocated to each program stayed at the same relative magnitude (if reduced actual amounts) as in the 1981 Carter budget. In sum, the cultural community and its congressional colleagues had managed to fend off a major offensive in the battle for the 1982 budget and, while accepting monetary losses, had kept the NEA's programmatic structure intact. By 1984 the NEA succeeded in raising its appropriations to a higher level of funding (albeit uncorrected for inflation) than had existed at the end of the Carter administration.

In its strong showing in the budgetary struggle, the cultural constituency had established itself as a force to be reckoned with. The arts proved to be not only "politically saleable," but politically potent as well.

Politics and Culture

Despite the Arts Endowment's tiny budget when compared with overall federal government spending, the NEA Chairman has strong symbolic powers and represents a vocal constituency. While the demonstration of intense conflict over so small an agency may seem incomprehensible, NEA bureaucratic politics has been anything but the civilized affair that one might expect of a public arts agency. Indeed, President Carter was said to have quipped that he was devoting more time to the appointment of an NEA Chairman than he was to the Strategic Arms Limitation Talks. Administratively, the Chairman sets the tone for the Endowment. Politically, the NEA Chairman is widely viewed as the cultural community's official spokesman in national policy-making.

The power of the Chairman, and the role of the NEA in cultural policy-making, was largely shaped by Nancy Hanks who held the position from 1969 to 1977. During the tenure of her predecessor, Roger Stevens (1965–69), the NEA budget stayed at about $8 million. During the Hanks chairmanship, the Arts Endowment's budget grew from $8 million to over $82 million—a tenfold increase. (The appropriations actually doubled each year from 1970 to 1972.) She also mustered support for the arts from the culturally unsympathetic Nixon White House through her friendship with presidential assistants Leonard Garment and Frank Shakespeare. As someone with a background in Republican politics (among other things as an arts consultant to Nelson Rockefeller), she was able to ensure that an agency closely associated with Democratic party principles would be acceptable to the new administration. Most important, Nancy Hanks forged a strong political constituency in support of the Arts Endowments that included well-placed congressional allies and a well-organized network of grassroots supporters. As was evidenced during the Reagan administration, this network could be orchestrated to give voice when NEA programs were challenged and to provide evidence of strong local appeal. Above all, the Hanks era saw the Arts Endowment achieve national visibility and the principle of government support for the arts recognized as an established public policy.

The first rumblings of a "Kulturkampf" (or cultural fight) were heard during the Carter administration over the issue of "cultural elitism."[20] It was probably inevitable that once tax revenues came to be spent on the arts in a major way, political controversies would arise. A commitment to support for the nation's culture has come to be accepted as a public responsibility—but slowly, sometimes grudgingly, and not without debate. As art goes public, citizens and their elected representatives are invited to become art critics. When the battleground is the gallery or auditorium and the combatants are bohemians and the bourgeoisie, the struggle remains fairly localized. But when the artists and arts institutions struggle with elected officials and interest groups for control of the arts budget, the consequences of cultural warfare loom larger.

Few public policies attract unanimous political support; issues of arts policy, however, seem to generate a disproportionate amount of dissension. For one thing, the act of making grants requires establishing guidelines about what standards of cultural judgment should prevail—for instance, artistic excellence or social utility. Another problem involves the primary purpose for NEA funding: is it to make artistic production easier for the artist or to make art more available to the public? Yet another problem is what modes of artistic production would be supported. The arts were defined in the statutory provision cited earlier to include (among others) music, dance, drama, creative writing, painting, design, sculpture. But is this listing meant to include classical whistling, mime troupes, street theater, amateur poetry, and graffiti—let alone distributing six perfectly rounded stones about Hartford, Connecticut's town square or a serenade for the whales migrating along the California coast?

A related question is the extent to which the NEA should have a metropolitan, as distinct from a localistic, emphasis—that is, whether public funds should be used to subsidize companies with a national orientation or those with a regional importance. The first Endowment Chairman, Roger Stevens, was disposed to support large institutions with established reputations; Nancy Hanks looked with favor on neighborhood and community-oriented groups. Her successor, Livingston Biddle, wanted to help both types of organizations; Reagan's NEA Chairman, Frank Hodsoll, would force a choice between the two. The metropolitan emphasis is popular with the major cultural institutions and well-organized arts groups; the localistic emphasis is popular with grassroots cultural groups and their congressional representatives. Neither emphasis, however, addresses the question of what cultural policy objectives are best for a public arts agency. This would require specifying the relationship between the social and aesthetic goals of a public arts policy.

On the other hand, much of the NEA's political and budgetary success in the 1970s can be attributed to the bureaucratic style of Nancy Hanks, which avoided overly specific formulations of policy goals. Where her counterpart at the National Endowment for the Humanities, Ronald Berman, could be characterized as a bureaucratic "zealot" concerned with the correctness of a narrow policy viewpoint, Mrs. Hanks was an "advocate" concerned with broad goals and agency growth.[21] Berman was a forthright, outspoken, and often combative defender of what he saw as the classical values of the liberal arts. He regarded this defense as a sacred trust, and he remained loyal to that policy in the face of strong congressional criticism of the Humanities Endowment for its elitism and unrepresentativeness.

Senator Claiborne Pell (D-R.I.), Chairman of the Subcommittee on Education, Arts and Humanities and a longtime supporter of public culture, was particularly opposed to a "mandarin culture" that concentrated NEH grants in a few prestigious universities. Senator Pell saw this as "elitist" and out of touch with the public that the Endowment was supposed to serve. In fairness, it should be noted that the NEH usually does not fund projects that enjoy either visibility or popularity. Despite exceptions (like the Tutankhamen exhibit), most NEH grants go to support scholars engaged in specialized, even esoteric, studies. Compared with the NEA's funding of the performing and visual arts, these scholarly pursuits may seem less defensible as claimants for public support. Regardless, Berman's persistence in defending such a culturally rarefied and politically isolated position was a major factor in the denial of his reappointment. His policy also severely compromised the NEH's political standing among its congressional supporters.

The controversy concerning the allegedly elitist policies of the Humanities Endowment points up some important lessons for cultural policy-making. By making a cult of culture, not touching bases with congressional critics, and failing to cultivate broad grassroots support, Ronald Berman got into a battle that he could have avoided and was bound to lose. Culture in general, and "high culture" in particular, cannot hope to survive politically by claiming historical necessity, educational correctness, or aesthetic superiority. Nor should so staunch and invaluable an ally of public arts programs as Claiborne Pell (a principal author of PL 89-209) have become so critical. In effect, Berman was the victim of his own misplaced, if deeply felt, zealotry. From an intellectual standpoint, his position was defensible, although still debatable; from a political standpoint, it was administratively self-defeating.

Nancy Hanks stood in sharp contrast to Ronald Berman: the cultural advocate as opposed to the cultural zealot. Rather than lecture congressmen on their moral obligation to support Western civilization with the taxpayers' money, she would remind them of the economic benefits that the arts brought to their districts. She also developed a strong cultural constituency that would lobby in support of NEA programs. In classic advocacy fashion, Mrs. Hanks built a public arts agency engaged in supporting a wide range of artistic activities and having broad political support from within the cultural community and the culturally conscious public. Her goal, as she put it, was to preside over "a concerted effort by all elements of our society—private and government alike—to assure that the arts can make the contribution of which they are capable to the quality of life for all Americans." Whatever one might think of the wisdom of the policy, from a political standpoint it was inspired. The Endowment went through a period of dramatic growth in its size, appropriations, political esteem, cultural impact, and public support. Indeed, the last two Chairmen of the Arts Endowment, Livingston Biddle and Frank Hodsoll, can be characterized as administrative "conservers" seeking to retain the levels of bureaucratic power, resources, and prestige achieved during the Hanks era.[22]

For all the Endowment's success, however, it has not been immune from criticism within the cultural community that the arts have been "politicized" as a result of NEA policies. Of course, the Arts Endowment, like any other bureaucratic agency, has been involved with politics. It should not be surprising that Frank Hodsoll was an aide to Reagan's chief-of-staff James Baker; or, that Livingston Biddle was the staff director of Senator Pell's subcommittee that oversees the Arts Endowment. Furthermore, the major criticisms of the NEA have concentrated on its programmatic goals not its administrative leadership. Representatives of diverse ideological viewpoints have expressed disfavor with the current state of public culture and the NEA's adopting, or failing to adopt, particular cultural policies. What is "politicized" policy for one ideological camp is good policy for another. The question of politicization has proven particularly fractious where there have been charges that aesthetic excellence was sacrificed to considerations of geographic dispersion, ethnic and racial representation, or artistic diversity.

On the other hand, many of the policies for which the NEA stands accused of politicization have an old and respected basis in democratic theory. The practice of geographic dispersion, for example, makes good sense in a democracy where support for public programs often is related to the availability of any public goods that are provided. This argues for a policy of spreading cultural funds among as many different constituencies as possible rather than concentrating in a few. A similar argument may be made in terms of political accountability. For example, to what extent do arts institutions that are granted public subsidies bear an obligation to make access more available to those in the public who could not afford their normal ticket prices?[23] In fact, the NEA has long advocated policies that would increase public accessibility and promote cultural responsiveness.

The NEA has also emphasized the user or consumer of the arts, and has sought to promote cultural products that meet diverse constituent demands. This approach argues that, since the arts mean different things to different people, public cultural programming should include "populist" art forms (attractive to lesser-developed cultural constituencies) as well as "elitist" fare (emphasizing the established fine arts). As a public arts agency operating without official aesthetic guidelines, such a latitudinarian cultural policy can be defended in terms of political equity as well as political expediency.

The Record of Public Support for the Arts

The recent attacks on public subsidy have been concerned less with its content (populist or elitist) or its emphasis (local or metropolitan) than with the very fact of subsidy itself. In *Policy Review,* a publication of the Heritage Foundation, Ernest van den Haag spoke in opposition to cultural subsidies and argued that the arts must demonstrate some special justification to qualify for public support. An adequate argument for federal support of the arts must show, according to van den Haag, that they yield indivisible collective benefits. Only if the arts yield such benefits, and of a sufficient magnitude, is the government justified in levying taxes to provide support.[24]

The NEA has also been criticized for pursuing a "middle-brow" cultural policy. Ronald Berman describes such artistic fare as follows:

> The models are the Kennedy Center and Wolf Trap Farm, large establishments heavily supported by government, corporations, and foundations, and offering a combination of mass-audience programs and enough adversary culture to stay ahead of the media.[25]

Yet, what programming alternative does a public arts agency have in the United States where there is broad cultural heterogeneity, little history of official sanction for a special cultural canon, and even less popular deference to any claims of a social class to cultural superiority? If the Arts Endowment restricts its patronage to the established repertory, it is attacked as culturally imperialist. If it subsidizes non-traditional art forms, it is condemned for pandering to cultural populism.

The NEA has responded to these criticisms by emphasizing that it is forbidden specifically from producing art and that its concerns are with fostering, maintaining, and disseminating the nation's cultural heritage. The NEA also would cite the greater numbers of arts organizations, the growth in audience size, and the increase in private support of the arts. Some examples will suffice.[26]

> In the decade prior to the Endowment's establishment, private support for the arts rose three percent; since 1965 this support has shown a 13-fold increase (corporate giving grew at the fastest rate—a 20-fold increase).
>
> In 1965 there were about one million tickets sold for dance performances, principally in New York; today, there are about 16 million ticket buyers, 90 percent of whom live outside of New York; the orchestral audience has risen from 10 million to 23 million; annual museum attendance has risen from 22 million to over 43 million.
>
> Since 1965, the number of professional arts organizations has grown by almost 700 percent. Professional orchestras have increased from 58 to 145; professional opera companies from 31 to 109; professional dance companies from 35 to 250; professional theater companies from 40 to 500.

This is an impressive record of cultural growth—even if the question of quality is not answered by numbers alone—and the NEA rightly can claim credit for contributing to this success. Some critics of public arts agencies dismiss these programs for draining off funds needed for elite arts organizations by subsidizing mass entertainment. Put crudely, but not untypically, the NEA has been funding "cultural clambakes" at the expense of "national treasures." The NEA responds that for the past decade "6.2 percent of the nation's arts organizations received 51.6 percent of the Endowment's dollars."[27] (Such an admission will doubtless fuel the fires of the Endowment's populist critics.) Overall, the NEA has sought to realize two broad objectives: supporting established institutions (while also funding touring and satellite companies to serve grassroots cultural constituents); and promoting the wide dissemination of quality cultural resources (thus aiding the creative activities of artists and expanding cultural equity).

A primary goal of Endowment policy has been to get the arts to the people. Government support for the arts cannot be characterized simply as a "transfer payment for the upper-middle class," nor as a form of "cultural imperialism" that threatens the artistic autonomy and cultural vitality of "non-high cultural taste publics."[28] Critics of the NEA's outreach efforts might note the following survey findings describing the condition of culturally less-developed respondents.

> The responses of those without high-school diplomas to cross-sectional survey questions indicate that a sizable group of Americans are, in fact, cultural dropouts, individuals with no apparent artistic or cultural interests. . . . Cultural deprivation then is not a matter of choosing performances or hobbies that diverge from upper-middle class norms; rather, it consists of having no creative or expressive pastimes, enjoying no performances of any kind, and being equally immune to the claims of galleries, zoos, or public parks.[29]

It is this unrepresented cultural constituency to whom the Endowment has addressed much of its efforts through nontraditional programming and support for community-based cultural activities. The NEA thus seeks to reconcile high culture with mass publics and to gain the broad support that is necessary for such a specialized public policy. It also bears repeating that small, nonestablishmentarian arts groups will be badly, if not mortally, wounded by substantial reductions in public support. The major orchestras, opera companies, dance troupes, and museums will continue to operate regardless of public subsidy. Rich patrons and large corporations could still guarantee their basic operating expenses even if public funding were abolished or dramatically reduced. Less likely to survive are community-based and minority-oriented institutions that depend almost solely on NEA, or NEA-generated, funds. Many of the needs of these special cultural constituencies are being addressed by local arts agencies; however, these agencies are themselves heavily dependent on NEA funds. The result of drastic cuts in the arts budget would be a step back from past public commitments to artistic pluralism and cultural democratization.

Government support for the arts in the United States always has shown a good return on the investment—politically as well as culturally. Nancy Hanks and Leonard Garment made this pragmatic argument for public subsidy in a memorandum to President Nixon:

> For an amount of money which is minuscule in terms of the total federal budget, you can demonstrate your commitment to "reordering national priorities to emphasize the quality of life in our society."
>
> The amount proposed . . . would have high impact among opinion formers. It is on the merits, justified, i.e., the budget for the arts and humanities is now completely

> inadequate. Support for the arts is, increasingly, good politics. By providing substantially increased support for cultural activities, you will gain support from groups which have hitherto not been favorable to this administration.[30]

Even some of the more doctrinaire members of the Reagan administration, who were disposed towards a negative appraisal of the Endowment's performance, have come to believe that the case for public subsidy is stronger than they originally had thought. Consequently, they have "not fundamentally altered the agency's philosophy or mission or its standards for awarding grants."[31]

In all the controversy about the Endowment's programs and the Reagan budget cuts, it is very easy to lose sight of the magnitude of the issue in monetary terms. The NEA's budget amounts to less than one-tenth of 1 percent of total federal spending; moreover, public funds from all sources account for only about 15 percent of the operating expenses of arts organizations in the United States. Nonetheless, this makes the Endowment the biggest single source of support for the arts in the nation and means that it exerts an influence vastly greater than the dollar amounts would suggest. Since the importance of NEA support is in inverse proportion to the size of the institution, public subsidy sometimes can determine whether a small arts institution will survive. Yet, even for the large arts organization, public support often may determine the hours that a museum can be open or what a symphony orchestra's scheduling arrangements will be like.

Besides the financial margin of survival that the NEA sometimes provides, it is possible to identify three qualitative contributions provided by government support for the arts. First, an NEA grant constitutes an imprimatur for the smaller and newer arts organizations, that is, it provides a respected and recognized, official seal of approval. In the amorphous arts world, this can be particularly helpful in generating funds from foundation and corporate sources. Second, an Endowment grant often allows cultural institutions to do what they otherwise would be unable to consider. Public support, for example, can make possible low-cost concerts for groups outside the usual subscription clientele; allow exhibitions and performances in smaller communities, at the workplace, shopping malls, health-care facilities, and custodial institutions; and, promote the development of younger and nontraditional artists through commissions and sponsorships. Third, as a public arts agency, the Endowment properly has addressed itself to concerns of cultural equity that cannot be addressed by a private arts institution. The Endowment's policies have sought to further the accessibility of culture to people of different socioeconomic and ethnic backgrounds than have usually constituted the culture-consuming public even as it continues its support for elite, standard-setting arts institutions.

The Endowment's goal of cultural democratization would make the arts more accessible than is possible under exclusively private patronage while respecting the autonomy of the individual artist and the independence of arts organizations. Such a goal does not, of course, mean that the record of public culture has been without reproach. For example, the Arts Endowment has yet to develop a set of guiding principles for public patronage. If any guideline exists, it has been the negative injunction: avoid the experience of the New Deal arts programs. As was discussed, this judgment is not based on an analysis of the cultural value of the Treasury and WPA projects. Rather, it is a warning against supporting any project that may result in political controversy or run the risk of giving public offense.[32] In a democratic system, these are not bad things to avoid, but they do not amount to a cultural policy. This would require public arts agencies to specify which arts were to be promoted, what types of institutions were to be funded, and whose taste preference would receive official sanction. In effect, this would mean guaranteeing some commonly accepted minimum of cultural awareness and participation as part of the general quality of life. For a nation as heterogeneous as the United States, such a policy would hardly be uncontroversial even if successfully formulated.

These criticisms may be unfair to cultural policy in holding it up to standards of judgments that are higher than those usually applied to other policy areas. How many public policies can be characterized by specificity and selectivity? Moreover, there is the danger that an overly defined cultural policy could become an "official culture," that is, one propogated by the State to serve its interests and legitimate its activities.[33] For the government to favor a particular style or mode of expression is to risk the public enshrinement of that cultural form. By contrast, government programs that encourage "grass-roots" and "outreach" efforts by major cultural institutions are principally concerned with who is to have access to culture rather than the content of the culture itself. The public policy goal is more procedural than substantive. Government acts as a benefactor to broaden access, to create greater cultural equality, to insure diversity and representation. In sum, the government's role in arts policy-making is to foster equity in the distribution of cultural opportunities.

There is nothing new or unusual in an approach to public policy-making that is essentially pluralist in its administration and benefits. Cultural policy in the United States may be pluralism by default—that is, an inability to define a public cultural interest—as its detractors maintain. On the other hand, if it is recognized that the public interest is not served by defining the content of culture, there is a strong argument for a pluralism of choice as most appropriate for a heterogeneous democracy. A pluralistic cultural policy can seek to ensure that the broad range of artistic heritages in this country is recognized and supported while also respecting the autonomy of art organizations and the individual artist. Public arts agencies also might promote subcultural programming, as advocated by Herbert Gans, through increased funding for arts programs that are sensitive to audiences of different ethnic backgrounds, social classes, educational levels, ages, and places of residence.[34] What has been realized over the past two decades of public patronage is a commitment to the principle that the survival of cultural institutions, greater accessibility to arts activities, and the preservation of aesthetic pluralism is a public good that merits government support. This cultural commitment has come under periodic attack but, unlike the New Deal programs, the National Endowment for the Arts (and its administrative "cousins") has had strong enough constituency and congressional support to ensure the continued survival, and relative prosperity, of public patronage in the United States.

Notes

1. See Alan L. Feld and others, *Patrons Despite Themselves: Taxpayers and Arts Policy* (New York: New York University Press, 1983). In this Twentieth Century Fund Report, the authors argue that two-thirds of public support for the arts comes in an indirect form, principally through federal income tax deductions and local property tax exemptions.

2. Milton C. Cummings, Jr., "To Change a Nation's Cultural Policy," in Kevin V. Mulcahy and C. Richard Swaim, eds., *Public Policy and the Arts* (Boulder, CO.: Westview Press, 1982), 142.

3. See William F. McDonald, *Federal Relief Administration* (Columbus: Ohio State University Press, 1968); Jerre Mangione, *The Dream and the Deal* (Boston: Little Brown, 1972); Richard McKinzie, *The New Deal for Artists* (Princeton: Princeton University Press, 1973); Jane DeHart Mathews, *The Federal Theater, 1935–1939* (Princeton: Princeton University Press, 1967); Law-

rence Mankin, *The National Government and the Arts: From the Great Depression to 1973* (unpublished doctoral dissertation, University of Illinois, 1976); Karal Ann Marling, *Wall to Wall America: A Cultural History of Post Office Murals in the Great Depression* (Minneapolis: University of Minnesota Press, 1982).

4. Kevin V. Mulcahy, "The Rationale for Public Cultures," in *Public Policy and the Arts,* 52–55.

5. Margaret J. Wyszomirski reports that in Frank Hodsoll's first year as NEA chairman, he exercised a "chairman's veto" on 20 out of a total of nearly 6000 panel-endorsed applications. Yet such an action was considered highly unusual. "Hodsoll's predecessor, Livingston Biddle, could not remember one instance of his overruling either a panel or Council recommendation during his entire four-year tenure." See "The Reagan Administration and the Arts, 1981–1983," paper prepared for presentation at the Annual Meeting of the American Political Science Association, Chicago, 1–4 September 1983, p. 14.

6. For a discussion of the panel system, see Committee on Appropriations, House of Representatives, *Report on the National Endowments for the Arts and Humanities,* U.S. Congress, House, 96th Congress, 1st Session, Vol. 1, pp. 865–1041; also Michael Straight, *Twigs for an Eagle's Nest: Government and the Arts, 1965–1978* (Berkeley: Devon Press, 1980), 77–80.

7. For a contrary view, see Michael Macdonald Mooney, *The Ministry of Culture* (New York: Wyndham Books, 1981), 330–74, but one should be advised that his discussion is often widely off the mark. See Kevin V. Mulcahy, "Public Culture and the Public," *Western Political Quarterly,* 34 (September 1981): 461–70.

8. These characteristics of the panel system reflect the observations of the various NEA staffers interviewed by C. Richard Swaim for the "National Endowment for the Arts" in *Public Policy and the Arts,* 169–204. This writer reached similar conclusions during the time in which he has served as a panelist for the Louisiana Council on the Arts and for the Arts and Humanities Council of Greater Baton Rouge.

9. Arthur Svenson in Kevin V. Mulcahy, "Government and the Arts: A Symposium," *Journal of Aesthetic Education,* 14 (October 1980): 36–7. See also Arthur Svenson, "State and Local Arts Agencies" in *Public Policy and the Arts,* 200.

10. Not all states with a "cultural department" include all of these cultural agencies under the departmental umbrella. See *Arts and the States* (Denver: National Conference of State Legislatures, 1981), 41–42.

11. *Ibid.,* 42.

12. Dick Netzer, *The Subsidized Muse: Public Support for the Arts in the United States* (New York: Cambridge University Press, 1978), 162.

13. "The Interrelationship of Funding for the Arts at the Federal, State, and Local Levels," *Report by the Committee on Government Operations,* U.S. Congress, House 98th Congress, 1st Session, pp. 14–15.

14. *Arts and the States,* 47.

15. "The Interrelationship of Funding," 32–33.

16. Anthony Downs, *Inside Bureaucracy* (Boston: Little Brown, 1966), 9.

17. Quoted in U.S. House of Representatives, Democratic Study Group, "Special Report: The Stockman Hit List," mimeograph, 7 February 1981, p. 35.

18. Quoted in *ibid.*

19. *Washington Post,* 2 February 1981, Sec. B, p. 5.

20. This discussion is adapted from Kevin V. Mulcahy, "Cultural Policy and '*Kulturkampf*'" in "Government and the Arts: A Symposium," *Journal of Aesthetic Education,* 14 (October 1980): 48–53.

21. On the meaning of the term "zealot" and "advocate," see Downs, *Inside Bureaucracy,* 88–89, 101–11.

22. For a discussion of administrative "conservers," see *ibid.,* pp. 96–101. For a detailed discussion of the Arts Endowment under Livingston Biddle, see Lawrence Mankin, "The National

Government and the Arts: The Biddle Years,'' paper presented at the Annual Meeting of the American Political Science Association, Chicago, 1–4 September 1983.

23. Douglas M. Fox, ''Government Support for the Arts: A Review Essay,'' *Public Administration Review,* 36 (July/August 1976): 451–54.

24. Ernest van den Haag, ''Should the Government Subsidize the Arts?'' *Policy Review,* 10 (Fall 1979): 72.

25. Ronald Berman, ''Art v. the Arts,'' *Commentary,* November 1979, p. 49.

26. The following data are from ''Advancing the Arts in America,'' *Cultural Post,* 7(September/October 1981): 20. (This is a summary of a report submitted by the Presidential Task Force on the Arts and Humanities.)

27. *Ibid.,* 22–23.

28. For a discussion of different taste cultures and the aesthetic preferences involved, see Herbert Gans, *Popular Culture and High Culture* (New York: Basic Books, 1979); also see Herbert J. Gans, ''American Popular Culture and High Culture in a Changing Class Structure,'' in Judith Bafe and Margaret J. Wyszomirski, eds., *Art, Ideology and Politics* (New York: Praeger, 1985), 40–57.

29. Paul DiMaggio and Michael Useem, ''The Arts and Cultural Participation,'' *Journal of Aesthetic Education,* 14(October 1980): 65.

30. Quoted by Swaim, ''The National Endowment for the Arts'' in *Public Policy and the Arts,* 185.

31. *New York Times,* 6 July 1983, p. 8. See also the ''Report on the National Endowment for the Arts,'' in Charles L. Heatherly, ed., *Mandate for Leadership* (Washington, D.C.: Heritage Foundation, 1980), pp. 1051–56.

32. Gary O. Larson, *The Reluctant Patron: The United States Government and the Arts, 1943–1965* (Philadelphia: Univ. of Pennsylvania Press, 1983), 29.

33. Any form of patronage, private as well as public, can limit aesthetic freedom as artists are sensitive to the perceived preferences of potential patrons. For example, there was a tendency of artists seeking public commissions during the New Deal period to ''paint Section,'' that is, to produce art work that would be acceptable to the officials of the Treasury Department's Section on Fine Arts. The ''official cultures'' found in ideological systems (such as Nazi Germany and the Soviet Union) make such peculiar demands on their artists as to warrant separate analyses. See, for example, Kevin V. Mulcahy, ''Official Culture and Cultural Repression: The Case of Dmitri Shostakovich,'' *Journal of Aesthetic Education* 18 (Fall 1984): 69–83.

34. Gans, *Popular Culture and High Culture,* 142.

14

Government and the Arts in Contemporary Japan

THOMAS R. H. HAVENS

Seiji Ozawa once complained that "one of the defects of Japanese society is that ordinary citizens do not feel proud of the arts and contribute to them."[1] Until recently this has been equally true of their government. Neither individual, corporate, nor foundation giving is substantial; only in the 1970s and 1980s has the national treasury offered significant subsidies. Since 1983 the official Agency for Cultural Affairs has had an annual budget of roughly $200 million, 60 percent of it for historical preservation and the rest for the arts broadly defined. Of this sum, the aid to commission fresh works is just under $6 million.[2] Assistance from prefectural and local governments for both access and innovation is proportionately smaller.

Direct patronage in the form of public or private subsidies is still underdeveloped, but market support for most forms of serious music, dance, theater, and visual art is very substantial. Most genres are thoroughly commercial, obtaining their revenues from ticket sales, advertising, recording, radio and television, the sale of products and services, and income from teaching. This is equally true of traditional arts and the modern ones derived from Europe, for popular arts as well as those with more defined clienteles.

Three times as many artists earn a living in Japan today as in 1955, the year Japan recovered from the economic collapse caused by defeat ten years earlier. The principal features of patronage since then have been the systematic cultivation of selected private audiences by arts leaders in each genre and the recent large increase in subsidies from the state. There is little general public for the arts in Japan, especially for genres that often seem high-brow. Instead audiences group themselves into private noncompeting clienteles, patterned after the structure of a family, which are composed of relatives, friends, classmates, and others with whom the artists have concrete bonds. Nearly all social relations in Japan are based on small-group affinities, not on identity with classes or occupational groups. For this reason the audience identifies mainly with the individual artist or performing company, not with the overall art form. Nearly all who attend are there because they know the artist—usually as their teacher in the neighborhood studio. Revenues from instruction of millions of middle-class children (and often their mothers) are the key financial underpinning of many art forms.

Although Japan is now wealthy and corporations can easily afford to help the arts, the tax laws do little to encourage business contributions to nonprofit organizations of any sort. Companies may write off donations to any charitable corporation as business losses for tax purposes, up to 0.125 percent of their capital including reserves plus 1.25 percent of their net profit for the year. Few companies have taken advantage of even this small opportunity to help arts groups. A more basic reason for the poverty of corporate patronage is that the idea of private philanthropy has very shallow roots in Japan. Instead there is the common view that the government, not private enterprise, should aid the arts because they are a national resource. Many foundation executives believe that Japan's tax laws help to assure that the authorities can control nonofficial charities, not encourage them. Moreover, big business until the early 1970s was preoccupied with postwar recovery, then reinvestment and expansion, leaving little surplus for charitable activity. Only a handful of Japan's 16,000 foundations make grants to the arts, and several hundred companies make small gifts for current operations to arts institutions. There is no reliable estimate of the overall sum that foundations and corporations give each year to the arts because few of them report their grants. Total corporate contributions to private nonprofit groups of all kinds total less than $150 million annually, only a small percentage of which goes to the arts.[3]

As in other countries, private industry supports the arts as consumer of their offerings. Theater parties at the Kabuki and free tickets to a flossy art show are favorites because these amenities are good for business. The leading newspaper companies and major Tokyo department stores also help the arts by sponsoring major exhibits of foreign and classical Japanese art. Only within the past decade have the national museums, backed by public monies, begun to match the newspapers and department stores in putting together blockbuster exhibits. The stores and newspapers continue to mount huge shows because it helps to improve their images, confers respectability, and usually raises sales and circulations. A King Tut show, backed by the *Asahi* newspapers, drew 1.3 million spectators to a Tokyo museum in 1965 (compared with 1.2 million for a slightly different show in New York that was on display twice as long in 1979).[4] Commercial tie-ins of various sorts provided some badly needed patronage, especially during the 1950s and 1960s when state aid was meager, but their real value was probably in making the arts much more accessible to the public than ever before.

The State as Patron

The Japanese government has built museums and libraries and preserved important cultural monuments ever since the Meiji state was established in 1868. Museums and libraries were put under the supervision of the new Ministry of Education in the early Meiji period, and an official school of art was opened in 1876 "to study the new realistic styles in order to make up for the short points of traditional art."[5] The state soon hired foreign instructors in painting, sculpture, music, opera, and ballet to teach the new styles from abroad. The Tokyo Academy of Music was officially founded in 1879 and the Tokyo Academy of Art eight years later. They merged in 1949 to form Tokyo University of Fine Arts, the premier institution in Japanese arts education today. Historical preservation became another duty of the education ministry when the Diet passed the ancient shrines and temples protection law in 1897. Ten years later the ministry sponsored the first of its annual art shows, which continue today in private hands under the name Nitten, the largest open-entry art exhibit in the world. An Imperial Art Academy was established in 1919 to recognize outstanding achievements, and the state began awarding cultural medals in 1937, the year the art academy was broadened to take in literary and performing artists. Still the arts existed before 1945 almost entirely through the efforts of private associations and troupes formed by the artists themselves, aided occasionally by generous benefactors or by commercial backing—such as the Kabuki and Bunraku theaters, aided by entrepreneurs like the Shōchiku and Tōhō enterprises.

Artistic innovation and dissemination became official responsibilities of the education ministry only in 1949. Beginning the next year, the national authorities funded the annual autumn arts festival that today continues to confer nonpareil prestige on those who take part. The next step was to subsidize federations of artists. The first state aid directly to arts groups came in 1959 from the education ministry. By the time the Agency for Cultural Affairs was formed nine years later, $375,000 was being spent annually to subsidize new works, send artists overseas, aid local organizations, and supply performances for young people. Still this sum was just 2.7 percent of the agency's first budget, which totaled $13.7 million; in 1980 these same programs took up 11.6 percent of its $200.1 million budget. About $80 million of the latter budget was devoted to the traditional and contemporary arts as a whole. The cultural agency's total budget grew 574 percent between 1968 and 1978 (the national budget rose 489 percent at the same time) and went up another 19.8 percent from 1978 to 1980.[6] The figure has been virtually frozen since.

Why did this astounding increase in public spending on the arts occur? Like many governments, the Japanese authorities in the late 1960s discovered that culture was in "the public interest at home and national interest abroad."[7] They set up two main organizations to promote these interests, the Agency for Cultural Affairs within the Ministry of Education (1968) and the Japan Foundation, an autonomous nonprofit public corporation established by legislative act (1972). The former is mainly concerned with domestic cultural matters, whereas the Japan Foundation is responsible for cultural relations abroad. Both of these units were creatures of Japan's ambition, first expressed in the late 1960s, to become a country of the first rank in arts and culture as well as industrial output. By then the number of professional artists in Japan had doubled compared with 1955, and the scale of productions had outgrown the capacity of private audiences to support them all. Yet only when national economic prosperity began to seem permanent in the mid-1960s did arts federations, as well as politicians in culture-poor localities, dare to lobby openly for sizable government aid. The demands from the arts groups were persistent but low-keyed, a bow to the reality that for two decades the state had starved welfare and other public services in favor of quick industrial expansion. Elected officials grew more outspoken on behalf of the arts in the mid-1960s, aware that culture—especially the traditional Japanese arts—was good politics in their home districts. As with all requests for more funding from the national budget, the lobbying was targeted on the appropriate policy groups in the administrative bureaucracy, not parliamentary committees because these Diet bodies have little power to alter the executive branch's budget. Still it seems that the government's desire for Japan to become a cultured country like the major Western states was even more decisive than domestic pressures in creating the cultural agency in 1968 and increasing its funding throughout the 1970s.

The Agency for Cultural Affairs took shape in June 1968 through the merger of two former bureaucratic units, the Cultural Affairs Bureau of the Ministry of Education and the National Commission for the Protection of Cultural Properties. It is a semi-independent body unconnected with the five bureaus that carry on the main work of the education ministry. The agency consists of a secretariat, a Cultural Affairs Division, and a Cultural Properties Protection Division. Its staff numbers about 200. From the start, the new agency pleased arts administrators because the unified entity gave them more weight inside the government. Priests of the temples and shrines receiving preservation funds were happy for the same reason. The change also satisfied Satō Eisaku, the prime minister, who was then trying to consolidate bureaucratic units whenever he could. Satō knew from visiting the United States that the National Endowment for the Arts, established in 1965, had soon become popular with politicians and the public. Most importantly, the cultural agency gave arts leaders a forum in the national government, and representatives of both the traditional and modern arts have been generously sprinkled on its advisory boards ever since 1968.[8]

Since its beginning, preservation, innovation, and access have been the main goals of the Agency for Cultural Affairs under a general mandate to "promote and spread culture and preserve cultural properties."[9] In American terms, the agency is expected to be both a National Endowment for the Arts and a National Trust for Historic Preservation. About two-thirds of its resources are tied up in the latter function. Other public units, from the Japan Foundation for international activities and NHK (the public broadcasting network) to prefectural and local governments, have helped boost public patronage of the arts to levels many times greater than the total of private gifts.

The main programs supported by the cultural agency have changed very little since 1968, but the government began spending much more for outreach after 1971 and for new national facilities after 1975. The outreach programs were intended partly to enrich the notably skimpy arts offerings of the public schools but mainly to respond to local political demands. The investments in facilities were more likely prompted by overseas models, although city and prefectural bodies also vied to outdo one another with new museums and concert halls out of long-standing feelings of competition or simple civic pride.

The chief arts-related items listed under cultural preservation in the cultural agency's budget are subsidies for the national theater and the national museums. The theater outlays include aid to Kabuki, Bunraku puppet theater, and the other traditional stage arts. The national theater, overlooking the imperial palace in downtown Tokyo, today absorbs about $11 million of the agency's budget. The three national general museums now receive roughly twice this sum, but their acquisitions grants were frozen in 1980 at just under $2 million. Preservation as a budget category rose more slowly than the cultural agency's overall budget after 1975 because of the sizable new allocations for bricks, mortar, and especially concrete.

A second category of programs since 1968 has been innovation. Grants to stimulate artistic creativity, nearly all of them in the modern arts, increased hardly at all during the early 1970s and grew by only 55 percent during 1975–80, a time when the agency's budget as a whole rose 89 percent. The 1980 total of $7.1 million included $560,000 for the agency's arts festivals and prizes, and another $760,000 to help individual artists get further training at home or abroad. These individuals must undergo a fierce national competition, but otherwise Japan relies on peer review far less than Great Britain or the United States in deciding how money for innovation should be spent. Instead funds are usually distributed more or less equally to each of the several federations representing artists in the various genres. In this way the state avoids having to choose among claimants, acknowledging the need to preserve harmony and avert confrontation among splintered social groups in the arts as in most other areas of Japanese life. The usually balkanized arts federations each determine which of their constituent members receive the public funding—not always according to criteria of artistic promise. National aid to arts organizations for commissioning new works started off at $56,000 in 1968, reached $2.3 million in 1975, and rose another 70 percent in yen terms to the 1980 plateau of $5.7 million; there has been little change since. In the cultural agency's overall budget, no arts category has grown more slowly since 1968 than the program to encourage creative activity.

The third basic policy objective involves access to the arts: schemes to spread both traditional and modern arts beyond the biggest cities, to aid national art museums, and to construct a new cultural complex in Tokyo. Part of the subsidy to the art museums also helps painters, sculptors, print-makers, and others by providing for the purchase and exhibition of their works. In this third category the government raised its total spending on national art museums and related facilities by 71 percent in yen terms between 1975 and 1980 to $13.3 million. Money for acquisitions in this third program increased 79 percent, to just over $2 million in 1980, and the subvention for exhibits went up 111 percent, to $1.2 million. As in other countries, the aid to museums went mainly to stanch the chronic deficits that arose from keeping the buildings open so the public could visit.

The main outreach efforts have gone toward extending the arts to people outside the half-dozen biggest cities. This program grew fast during 1972–75, under Adachi Kenji, the commissioner of cultural affairs, and expanded another 87 percent in yen terms between 1975 and 1980, when its allotment totaled $16.2 million. A bit more than half the annual grants for outreach were used to help prefectural and municipal leaders build new museums, theaters, concert halls, and cultural centers. The balance went to subsidize plays for children and teenagers, to aid touring arts festivals, and to help local arts organizations with deficits. Some of these monies ended up subsidizing big-city troupes, orchestras, and dance companies, supplementing the basic $5.7 million provided each year in the early 1980s to stimulate creative activity in the performing arts. Outreach funds also helped to support traditional performing-arts groups based in the cities. The outreach project was the cultural agency's most vigorous arts program in the 1970s and early 1980s, and it was also a magnet for private patronage, which sponsored even more events for children and high-school youths around the nation.

A final category that boosted the arts starting in the late 1970s was government aid for new national theaters and concert halls. In 1975 the cultural agency was spending $130,000 per year to plan new facilities; by 1980 it was paying out $10.4 million annually to construct halls for Nō, Bunraku, and the modern performing arts. Even though no other arts-related component of the agency's budget grew as fast during 1975–80 as the overall budget itself, the new theaters and concert halls, including state support for their inevitable deficits, are a major benefit to every arts group using them.

Despite the major push after 1971 to spread the arts to cities and towns all over the country, cultural activities are still concentrated in the major cities. The cultural agency heeded warnings to this effect in the late 1970s, but its budget virtually stopped growing in 1980—and with it the chance to shore up soft spots in its programs. As so often seems the case elsewhere, the cultural agency is the lowest priority in the government's politically weakest ministry—and grants to encourage the modern arts are perhaps the least favored program within the agency. Just 3 percent of its budget goes for commissioning creative activity.

Preserving the Traditional Arts

Premodern arts like the regal Nō drama, the riotously colorful dance-dramas of Kabuki, classical Japanese dance, and traditional instrumental music now belong to all Japanese. Shorn of their specific class origins, they are now available to everyone, at home and abroad (often at government expense). About 7,000 objects of art are protected from export, and another 10,000, including buildings, are classed as important cultural properties and eligible for preservation funds. About a tenth of the latter are considered national treasures. Forty individuals and groups in the traditional arts and about forty-five others in crafts are honored as living national treasures and receive modest yearly stipends for life.[10]

Bunraku and Kabuki have benefited most from state aid to traditional stage arts. Since 1966 the help has come from the national theater, a special corporation funded by the cultural agency. It is a showcase for eight runs of Kabuki each year and four of Bunraku puppet-dramas. Bunraku became a ward of the state in 1963 when Shōchiku, a private entertainment company, could no longer prop it up. The city and prefecture of Osaka helped the education ministry and the national broadcasting network NHK bail it out. Starting in 1970 the national theater began training about ten new performers a year in both Kabuki and Bunraku and started free summer workshops for high-school students to develop future audiences. Bunraku has recently moved back to a new theater in its original home, Osaka, built at public expense. The national theater continues to supply it with the greatest financial security it has enjoyed in a century and provides marketing expertise to maximize income and minimize the public subsidy.[11]

The national theater building itself was built in Tokyo in 1963–66 at a cost of $10.8 million. Its large hall holds 1,746 and the small hall 630. Bunraku remains its only resident company—and that part-time—but the producers have kept the stages bright with a mix of traditional arts events, while still renting them out for a number of private performances in classical Japanese dance, traditional music, and Nō drama.[12] Kabuki is the chief magnet, drawing more than half the theater's 650,000 customers each year. Opening the new theater in 1966 benefited both Shōchiku, which leases its actors to the national theater, and Kabuki in general. Instead of cutting into audiences at the commercial theaters, events at the national building have lifted overall attendance at Kabuki by about a third.[13] Kabuki also profits from NHK broadcasts, touring arts festivals sponsored by the cultural agency, and overseas trips on behalf of the Japan Foundation.

As the government's flagship for the traditional arts, the national theater receives aid from the cultural agency that has risen from $1.2 million to more than $10 million today (this constitutes about three-fifths of its annual revenue from all sources).[14] The agency decided in 1975 to start work on the new Bunraku facility at Takatsu, Osaka, which opened in 1983 at a cost of $28.5 million. The state also erected a new national Nō theater at Sendagaya, Tokyo, completed in 1982. Originally considered aristocratic arts, Nō and its comic accompaniment Kyōgen have adapted to an age of middle-class audiences. Studying Nō has become a mark of refinement for women as well as men in white-collar families. Thanks to fees from more than a million pupils each year, Nō has thrived without much state aid, but the new theater in Tokyo adds a welcome facility in a city with only five other Nō stages and a fitting monument to the world's oldest continuously practiced dramatic form.[15] Even though only a minority of the cultural agency's budget for preservation goes to the traditional arts (much of the rest is used to protect religious institutions), few theatrical performers could deny by the 1980s that the government's aid made a great deal of difference to their art.

Safe Innovations

Traditional Japanese artists rarely prized creativity for its own sake, preferring to vary received patterns, and even today they carefully regulate who may alter a time-honored script, technique, or piece of choreography. The premodern arts have evolved steadily since the Edo period (1603–1868), Japan's late feudal age, yet it is mostly their claim to continuity across epochs that makes them so attractive today.[16] As an absolute, creativity is a foreign idea, imported from Europe as a cardinal aesthetic value only in this century. It had little following among Japanese artists until after World War II. Instead, innovation has more often meant testing the limits of familiar techniques and concepts, often by bridging native and Western elements. Like other artists, Japan's postwar painters, sculptors, print-makers, playwrights, composers, and choreographers have needed the past in order to rebel against it, and their creations have often revealed their debt to tradition even more clearly than their departure from it.

Yet it is true that commissioning new works in the modern arts was one of the first activities of the education ministry when it began subsidizing artists through their federations in 1959. The main programs to help creative artists were in place by the late 1960s and have grown very little since. In Japan as elsewhere, it is axiomatic that foundations and governments help the visual arts less systematically than the performing arts because most visual artists work alone, outside the umbrella of a troupe or company to which grants can be easily made.

Most government support for the visual arts "is confined to classical Japanese art," according to Inumaru Tadashi, who directed the cultural agency from 1975 to 1980 and now heads the national theater. The state has been buying new works by contemporary artists since 1959 at the minuscule rate of about ten per year, a very modest investment for the world's most productive art country. The cultural agency sends the works on tour and then gives them to the national art museums. A few visual artists win government funds each year to study abroad.[17] Until recently, the national museums have been reluctant to sponsor Japan's artists by exhibiting or commissioning their works, preferring a course of caution that favors safe works by dead or elderly individuals.

The government has also sponsored a weekly TV broadcast, *In Quest of Beauty,* since 1972 to help publicize art shows of all kinds. In that same year the cultural agency began making grants of $33,000 each to ten film-makers per year to help produce good movies. Since 1976 the agency has spent $25,000 annually for each of five animated films prepared for children's television.[18] Otherwise the government has done little to enhance creativity in the mass media, although it operates a national film center as a part of the Tokyo National Museum of Modern Art.

The cultural agency's annual autumn arts festival became the main vehicle for public aid to the performing arts in the 1950s. Throughout the 1950s and 1960s the festival prospered in the number and quality of works performed because its awards, bearing the cachet of official approval, soon became the most prestigious in the nation. Yet as late as 1969 the government supported it with a grant of just $84,000. Then in the early 1970s the cultural agency turned the festival into a three-month-long production, quadrupling its support and bringing many more participants into each of its ten divisions. Since 1975 the agency's grant for the festival has run between $500,000 and $600,000 per year.[19] This sum pays for about a dozen commissioned works, more than sixty-five prizes in various categories, and the excess costs of production beyond the income from ticket sales, program advertising, broadcast fees, and miscellaneous sources.

The festival as it has taken shape in the 1970s and early 1980s is still centered in Tokyo and now includes divisions for film, radio, television, and recorded music as well as the live performing arts. About 260 productions are offered each year, some of them several times. Participating entries are quite evenly divided among dance, popular entertainments, music, and theater (including Nō).[20] The traditional arts, in which public competition is usually discouraged, have been less active in the autumn festival than the modern ones. Prestige and publicity are the main incentives to the many hundreds of artists who appear each year, usually selected by their respective federations if they are well-established but otherwise by juries in each genre. The festival has usually managed to balance excellence with access: quality productions have been mounted (despite incomplete objectivity in choosing the performers) for large audiences at various levels of taste. Whether the same funds would yield even greater inventiveness if they were distributed directly to the artists cannot be known. But the cultural agency answers to the public, which has an interest in being entertained as well as in creativity, and the arts festival for more than a decade has managed to avoid lapsing into either elitism or pandering.

Even more important for bringing new art to the public may be the government's fellowships for further training at home and abroad. The first state grant of any sort for this purpose was made in 1959 for activity abroad by individual artists, administered through their federations. When the cultural agency was founded nine years later, it spent $121,000 annually to send Japanese artists abroad, mainly to observe and practice, but sometimes to exhibit or perform. By 1975 the outlays for foreign training reached $415,000 and then rose another 22 percent in yen terms to their present level of roughly three-quarters of a million dollars.[21] With this program the cultural agency superseded both the Tokyo American Cultural Center and the Fulbright program in exchanging performing artists between Japan and the United States. Since 1968 the agency has picked about eighteen fellows each year for foreign training in various genres, usually for a year but (beginning in 1974) sometimes for two. More seasoned artists started receiving three-month grants in 1979. The numbers chosen in the visual arts, music, and theater (including stage design and film) have been roughly equal, slightly larger than the total for dancers.[22]

Equally useful is a program, started in 1977, for thirty artists a year to receive stipends for advanced training within Japan. Performing artists are especially pleased with this home-front opportunity because a long stay overseas can become counterproductive. Going abroad polishes their art and ornaments their curricula vitae, but it also ruptures the harmony of their performing groups and weakens their connections for side jobs, which they need to survive when they return. Visual artists are more independent and less ambivalent about foreign study, having so little to lose and much to gain from the chance.[23]

Neither festivals nor further training have brought new works to the stage so systematically as a third major program: government subsidies to artists' federations in each of the major genres. The first grants were awarded in 1965 and totaled $12,500. After the cultural agency was formed, the aid went up from $372,000 in 1968 to $2.3 million in 1975. Five years later it was fixed at $5.7 million, a rise of 70 percent in yen terms between 1975 and 1980.[24] In some cases the money ends up covering deficits, especially for professional orchestras, but even they are expected to use the sums to commission and perform new works by Japanese composers. Once a grant is received, the federation decides which constituent members receive the outlays—often by criteria of longevity, connections, or near bankruptcy rather than merit as it might be objectively judged by open peer review.

As of 1980, eight regional orchestras and four more in Tokyo were receiving $100,000 to $150,000 each, and the other Tokyo orchestras without separate public backing have been included in the payouts since 1981. Certain orchestras also get varying amounts to travel under the cultural agency's outreach program for children, youths, and touring arts festivals.[25] Smaller grants for performances of new instrumental works are made each year to federations of composers in both traditional Japanese and classical Western music.

At the head of the grant list each year is Tokyo's Nikikai Opera Company, a reminder that art forms with the smallest audiences often get the biggest awards. Nikikai's allotment doubled between 1977 and 1980, to $500,000 per year, not merely because the group is politically ingratiated but also because its 330 members make Nikikai the largest performing arts company in Japan and a funnel for state aid to opera as a whole. The cultural agency has also supported an opera school run by Nikikai. The government subsidizes opera partly to create jobs for voice majors who graduate each year from public universities (there are no dance majors at these institutions, and the state feels less obligation toward their art). Above all, opera is something a cultured country ought to have, the government believes, and it is determined to help Nikikai become a respectable company. The national subsidy covers about a sixth of Nikikai's annual budget.[26] The group uses the funds to produce new operas by Japanese composers, but the bulk of its offerings are works from abroad.

Ballet is another art form favored at the cultural agency. Each year it grants about $200,000 to the Japan Ballet Association, representing most of the major companies, and slightly larger sums to the Japan Ballet Council, a funnel for receiving state aid formed in 1977 by four big Tokyo companies that split from the balkanized Japan Ballet Association. Each federation decides which of its member groups will get shares for staging productions of new works in both the fall and the spring seasons. Until the late 1970s ballet received far more help from the national treasury than either classical Japanese dance or contemporary dance, even though both have as many students as ballet and despite the fact that creativity is the very essence of the latter.[27]

The cultural agency each year gives more than a quarter of its funds for creative activity to professional orchestras and about 15 percent to opera companies. Another 5 percent goes to other musical groups, including composers and performers in traditional Japanese as well as classical Western music. Dance gets about 10 percent, nearly all of it for ballet and (to a lesser degree) contemporary dance. Theater receives most of its public funding for productions through the agency's various outreach programs, but nearly 10 percent of the budget for fostering creative activity is used each year for overseas tours by Japanese mime, puppet, and youth dramatic groups, for visiting performances by foreign companies, and exhibits, lectures, research, and publications on modern theater of all types.[28] Most of the balance goes for similar international events, publications, and off-stage services in music or dance, but a part of it helps to pay for three or four art shows of contemporary works at home and abroad each year. The creative-activity budget is a catchall for aiding arts organizations of many sorts, some of them amateur and most of them in modern genres. A slight majority of its funds are used for live productions by professional performing groups.

Nearly everyone agrees that the cultural agency is more adept at preserving and providing access to the arts than at stimulating them to innovate. Part of the difficulty is a universal bureaucratic preference for making grants to federations of artists rather than to individuals.[29] It is customary to give something to every recognized federation that applies, shirking judgments about their relative merits. Visual artists suffer the most, since they are shut out from the creativity grants to arts institutions. The government's policy of caution, with its preference for such familiar encouragements to innovation as festivals, study fellowships, and grants to reliable arts organizations, is so well established that a big jump in the currently static budget will be needed before the cultural agency can gamble on creativity where it is often concentrated: among individuals and the avant-garde.

Access to the Arts

Like Paris or London, Tokyo dominates the nation's cultural life so overwhelmingly that ever since 1949 the authorities have tried to spread the arts to the 80 percent of the public living outside the capital region. The explicit aim has been to create a real public where almost nothing existed before but private audiences with tangible connections with the artists. The result is more traveling by metropolitan performing groups, more activity by local arts organizations, and more deference to Tokyo's tastes and policies. In cases where the arts cannot be taken out-of-town, greater throngs have packed into Tokyo to take advantage of what is there.

Outreach programs run by the national government have brought exhibits, concerts, and productions to every prefecture and nearly every community in the country, involving artists in both traditional and modern genres. At present the cultural agency spends about $1 million each year on live performances for children and nearly $2 million each on productions for high-school students and touring arts festivals.[30] Most are deliberately held in smaller cities and towns. The agency also distributes about $1 million to local sponsors to help cover deficits for performing arts events of their own, and it grants another $10 million for erecting and maintaining local arts facilities. The first outreach grants were made by the education ministry in 1957. When the cultural agency began in 1968, the allocations were just $138,000, but they jumped to $5.8 million by 1975—mostly because the state began helping localities build new arts centers in the early 1970s. The current figure for outreach is nearly $17 million.[31] Although TV blankets the country, the government clearly believes that seeing exhibits and attending live performances are experiences worth making available to everyone.

A mixture of moral uplift and practical economics has tinted the touring arts programs for teenagers since they began with twenty-five performances in 1967. The presumption is that encounters with expressions of beauty are ethically instructive, especially for pupils whose school curriculums are weak in the arts. Road performances are also useful ways to support stage artists, and they help to cultivate fresh audiences for the future.[32] The teenagers in the audiences seem to prefer the modern arts. Because attendance in most genres is very much an age-group phenomenon, it is easy to imagine that the three-to-one ratio by which young people choose contemporary arts will shift significantly as they grow older. The experience of previous generations in the twentieth century has been that many in the young audiences are women who drift away from the theater or concert hall when they have families, then choose traditional performances when they return in middle age.

The biggest of the cultural agency's out-of-town performing programs is the most diffuse and probably the most artistically satisfying: the touring arts festivals that have been held every year since 1971 to put on traditional and contemporary performing arts "in every nook and cranny of the country."[33] Tickets to the 170 performances each year are one-third the normal cost, and attendance at each event runs about 1,000. Although audiences are older than in the high-school series, the share of performances of traditional genres is the same, about a third.[34] Still the 330 performances sponsored each year by the cultural agency, drawing about 350,000 people, represent only a fraction of the local arts activity that takes place. Most events are locally produced, often financed commercially but sometimes with funds from the agency.[35]

The costliest element by far on the government's agenda for extending the arts has been aid for building community museums and arts centers. Many are monuments to architectural ingenuity, but a few are bureaucratically banal. As the economy matured and the largest cities stopped growing so fast in the 1970s, prefectural capitals and other smaller centers began sharing more evenly in national commerce, manufacturing, and education. Building cultural facilities expressed local pride; the result was that the number of public art museums and performing-arts centers doubled between 1970 and 1980. Part of the aid came from Tokyo, but most of the funds were supplied by city governments.

Many of the new art museums own very little art and mainly display local amateurs, but at least three dozen of Japan's hundred local and prefectural public art museums support contemporary Japanese artists through purchases, exhibits, educational programs, and publications.[36] Occasionally a local museum attains instant notoriety by purchasing a Cézanne or a Picasso (Millet's *The Sower* cost Yamanashi prefecture nearly $1 million in 1977), but more typically the museums acquire art by committee, a safe approach that often follows the lead of the national museums or the recommendations of major Tokyo galleries. Traveling shows sent around by the cultural agency and private art associations, together with special exhibits put on by local art groups, are the main events in most of the new public museums.[37]

The largest construction boom has come in the form of multipurpose performing-arts centers, of which the paragon remains Tokyo's splendid Metropolitan Festival Hall, opened in 1961. The education ministry began helping local governments put up theaters and concert halls in 1967, and by the early 1980s the national aid to local public museums and cultural complexes, including construction and maintenance, surpassed $10 million per year. When the cultural agency began operating in 1968, there were 233 public centers in Japan with theaters or concert halls holding at least 500 people. By 1979 the number had grown to 509, and more have opened since.[38]

Far more impressive than the cultural agency's outlays for buildings are prefectural and local expenditures on new facilities. As recently as the mid-1960s, almost no prefectural or city construction for the arts was taking place. By the late 1970s, prefectures were spending about $140 million annually on arts facilities and municipalities another $130 million, each from its own tax revenues.[39] The boom slackened somewhat after that, but there is no question that regional and local governments have been the major patrons of construction for the arts in the past fifteen years in Japan—even though many of the facilities are also used for popular music and events unrelated to the arts. By one estimate, prefectures and municipalities spent $450 million on new cultural facilities in the late seventies, and governments at all levels invested another $17.9 million each year in direct payments to promote the visual arts, theater, dance, and serious music in public museums, cultural centers, and school auditoriums.[40]

Because access includes drawing people to metropolitan arts institutions as well as sending the arts around to the people, the Japanese government began very slowly in the 1970s to transform the national art museums into living expressions of the contemporary imagination. It also started planning for a second national theater building just west of Shinjuku (Tokyo), to house the modern performing arts. The new complex, opened in 1987, brings the same entrepreneurial skill to the contemporary stage and studio arts that the national theater has provided the traditional ones since 1966.

Japan has three national general museums, each dating from the late nineteenth century, and four national art museums built after World War II. The combined national subsidy for these seven facilities is about $35 million per year, but acquisitions (including nonartistic materials for the three general museums) run only $4 million and have not grown since the late 1970s.[41] The keystone of the group is the Tokyo National Museum of Modern Art, built in 1969 with a $3.5 million gift from the Bridgestone tire magnate, Ishibashi Shōjirō. Its annual budget of $4 million leaves only $500,000 for acquisitions each year, even though the museum is the nation's leading depository of modern art. Only four living artists, all very elderly, are represented in its collection, meaning in effect that Japan has no public institution of contemporary art.[42] Yet changes in the museum's programs at last seem to be under way.

The new $100 million cultural complex outside Shinjuku includes a concert hall and three theaters, as well as archives, rehearsal space, meeting rooms, and a study center for the stage arts. Orchestras and choruses appear in the large concert hall, and the theaters serve opera, ballet, modern drama, contemporary dance, and recitals of instrumental and vocal music.[43] Perhaps it is fitting that the new center for the contemporary arts is located near ultramodern Shinjuku, whereas the original national theater, which patronizes the traditional arts, overlooks the feudal castle moat of the imperial palace.

To people living in Japan since the 1950s, the most noticeable public patron of the arts has been neither the cultural agency nor municipal governments but NHK (the state broadcasting network). To residents of foreign countries, the most visible sponsor of the Japanese arts abroad has been the Japan Foundation since it began in 1972. These two independent, nonprofit public corporations, along with a few other government-authorized organizations and international agencies, aid the arts with cash and give them exposure far beyond those who can attend Japanese galleries, theaters, or concert halls.

NHK, which collects subscriber fees from 28 million households each year, is a consumer service that breaks even on its budget of $1.5 billion. Its main support for the arts goes to music, which benefits from payments for live performances and through broadcasts on FM and television. The corporation grants about $1.5 million to cover the deficit of the NHK Symphony Orchestra, a world-class group formed in 1926. It also spends at least that much each year on weekly TV concerts of semiclassical music by the Tokyo Philharmonic Orchestra.[44] Through the orchestras it aids, NHK encourages fresh works by Japanese composers, who are also hired directly to produce music for television programs. NHK also stages full-length productions of familiar modern plays, such as *A Streetcar Named Desire* and *Death of a Salesman,* soon after modern drama companies present them live. Like its commercial counterparts, NHK imports talent from the major movie and commercial drama corporations, Shōchiku and Tōhō, or turns to the modern drama companies. In this way the government provides indirect, if often impecunious, sustenance to Japan's large corps of actors and actresses.[45]

The foreign ministry, like those in many countries, began sending traditional performing-arts groups overseas in the 1950s as instruments of cultural diplomacy.[46] When the Japan Foundation was created in 1972 with an endowment from the national treasury of $13.9 million, it inherited the job of international arts exchange. The foundation's main purpose was to make foreign nations more aware of Japan by promoting its culture abroad.[47] Today about $3.5 million of its $17 million annual budget goes for art exhibits and live events in the performing arts. Part of the $7.6 million paid each year for the exchange of individuals supports artists as well. Although the foundation is small by international standards, it has cooperated closely with the cultural agency and foreign ministry to send a great many traditional and contemporary Japanese artists all over the world and invite foreign performers and exhibits to Japan.[48]

An Official Culture?

In concert with the Japan Foundation, NHK, and localities, the Agency for Cultural Affairs operates a system of public aid to the arts that is more centralized than is true for most other countries. It coordinates nearly all of Japan's tax-supported programs affecting the arts, in much the same way that the central bureaucracy provides policy guidance in most other areas of national life. Japan entered the 1980s spending about $3 per capita in public funds each year on aid to the visual and performing arts.[49] In constant terms, the per capita figure climbed rapidly in the 1970s because of heavy governmental payments for new art museums and cultural centers outside the biggest cities. Public patronage of the arts in Japan was mostly a dream before the mid-1960s but a fact ten years later. When so much public cash flooded the financially parched world of the arts, some persons feared that an official view of culture would soon begin to take root. Through the practice of letting arts federations decide how to allocate grants to their members, the cultural agency has erased most of the fears that it would try to control the arts by playing favorites or selecting specific works for production. In other countries it seems that when state support grows large enough to be divided among a number of arts organizations, the threat of official manipulation vanishes.[50] But the more subtle fear is that the federations will reward their most well-established members, not necessarily those with something to say artistically. All too often this fear is a reality—and avant-garde companies outside the federations are sometimes excluded entirely. Handy as it may be to make the federations take responsibility for allocating the grants, there is the familiar suspicion that they use the funds not to encourage the most dynamic of their members but to prop up the feeblest.

Bureaucratism is the enemy of artists no less than other professionals. The authorities in the national government unquestionably agree on a definition of accredited Western culture that begins with Bach and ends with the School of Paris, but it is not clear how much they officially impose this outlook, or how much they need to, since artists and citizens seem to share it so widely anyway. The repertoire that visiting artists can present is sharply restricted by which "approved" works their Japanese hosts think audiences will turn out for.[51] Yet the public's preoccupation with famous names and fashionable artists seems at least as tyrannical as bureaucratism in enforcing a definition of what constitutes acceptable art. The problem seems circular: the cultural agency selects big-name performers for its touring festivals in order to attract audiences, and yet the great weight of official prestige borne by a state-supported exhibit or performance means that any activity sponsored by the agency is almost always presumed to be worthwhile. Like fashion, politics is a poor but all too common substitute for aesthetics in reaching judgments about art.[52] Less ambiguous or exceptionable is the government's attempt to export official culture through the Japan Foundation. Art-for-nation's-sake is politically useful, yet the Japanese authorities fortunately seem aware that it cannot be asked to surrender its essential character as art.

A second major issue in current arts patronage in Japan is indifference. Adachi Kenji, now head of the Tokyo National Museum of Modern Art, has pointed out that "there is not really an official view of culture in Japan, but there are officials' views. In general the arts are not greatly favored by the political or economic establishments. . . . performing artists, especially contemporary creative artists, see the establishment as heedless, perhaps even opposed, to their art."[53] Although Adachi probably overstates the oppression of accredited culture because it is taken so much for granted in Japan, there is little question that nothing discourages an artist more than being ignored. Recognizing the role that art has come to play in Japanese life, an official government task force in 1977 trumpeted "an unprecedented rise" in public expectations of the arts.[54] Three years later a blue-ribbon study by Yamamoto Shippei and others, known as the Age of Culture Report, recommended a 500 percent rise in the budget of the cultural agency and a series of measures to make the 1980s the age of culture. By 1986 it was clear that the age of culture was starved for cash, so the government commissioned the first really comprehensive study of the state of the Japanese arts. An advisory council responded in late July 1986 with recommendations for improved arts education, more support from the private sector, and a restoration of cuts meted out to the cultural agency's budget in the mid-1980s.[55]

Government units at all levels were spending about $18 million a year in the early 1980s on outreach programs, and private sources contributed a few million more for the same purpose. Nearly fifteen times this amount was being spent as of 1980 to erect new public facilities for the arts throughout the country, but the outlays for construction have since shrunk. Japan lags well behind the United States and most European countries in the proportion of national income collected as taxes and social security premiums, and its budget in the early eighties was strained by vast deficits. New programs have already been adopted to increase national spending on defense, social welfare, and energy research. For these reasons, the corporate world, not government, seems the most promising vein to tap for fresh contributions to the arts. Companies will offer more support as they come to appreciate art for its inherent worth, not just as entertainment—a lesson already apparent to many of their middle-class shareholders and customers.

Through the policy of giving aid to nearly every recognized group seeking it, the government has carefully avoided choosing between traditional and modern art forms or between Western styles versus those that are native. Most art practiced in Japan today, as elsewhere, is thoroughly contemporary: performances of Kabuki seem just as premodern to Tokyo audiences as Shakespeare seems in London. But the Japanese art world has not fallen victim to some bland international style in any important genre since World War II. Sculpture, architecture, contemporary dance, and new musical compositions often show effects of their Japanese environment. The degree of nativism versus internationalism, like the extent of traditional versus contemporary idioms, varies considerably in dance, music, theater, and the visual media. The cultural agency's preservation programs protect ancient paintings, sculptures, and works of architecture as well as supporting Kabuki, Bunraku, and other traditional stage arts. Its outreach efforts assist both traditional Japanese arts and contemporary styles, with about two-thirds of its funds for these programs devoted to the latter. The agency's subsidies for creative work go almost entirely to the modern arts—but innovation claims only a tenth of its total budget for the arts. Although few artists working in contemporary styles feel shut off from public funding, they almost uniformly believe that government officials prefer to use tax monies to promote the art of old Japan. Yet whatever the nativist instincts of career civil servants, the government is clearly committed to developing opera, ballet, and classical Western music to reinforce Japan's standing as a cultured country.

To some degree the government is spared having to choose between aiding the traditional Japanese arts and supporting the modern ones because so many of the former are largely self-sustaining. Kabuki is a commercial success, and Nō theater, classical Japanese dance, and traditional Japanese music are financed through fees from instruction. (To a lesser degree, the same is true of Western-style instrumental music, ballet, contemporary dance, and even some visual-art media.) The most important social group boosting the arts in Japan is the family itself. The patronage of millions of middle-class families has been the single biggest help in establishing art as a worthy profession since World War II, through formal schooling but especially through private lessons. Their interest in studying the arts is partly a product of fashion, like seeing the latest art show from abroad or hearing a famous recitalist on tour. Yet art also serves the social system not merely as an index of snobbery but also as a moral exemplar. Many families believe that taking lessons helps to build selfhood and inner strength among the young, and the arts have become something of a secular church for people of all ages by acting as sources of value in an era of otherwise privatized goals.

The greatest problems facing dance, music, theater, and the visual media in Japan today are not ideological, organizational, or financial but instead artistic: the relative dearth of open competition and scantiness of frank criticism. The clubby nature of instruction in the traditional arts is only the most arresting example. Even where criticism could be best applied, neither schooling in the modern arts nor the ubiquitous recital system in dance and music offers the artist many real critiques, since each minimizes head-to-head rivalry and rewards faithfulness more than imagination. Museum directors and theater managers equally take a tack of caution, selecting safe works and shirking critically promising but potentially controversial ones. Even teaching dulls the competitive appetite for many artists by making them economically secure without having to show their talents in the gallery or onstage. The habit of avoiding confrontation and criticism is deeply embedded in Japanese social structure and reinforces the group solidarity that undergirds all the arts. As the nation enters its age of culture, it seems likely that the arts will serve society best by thriving freely and openly, nurtured by the state, big business, and the family system but standing on their own aesthetic merits.

Notes

1. Ozawa, quoted in Kimura Eiji, ''Nihon no geijutsu josei wa kokkakei ka minkankei ka,'' *Ongaku geijutsu,* November 1980, p. 52. Except for Ozawa, all Japanese names in the text are listed with surname first.

2. Bunkachō, *Bunkachō yosan jimu teiyō, Shōwa 55nen* (Tokyo: Bunkachō, 1980), 22–23.

One U.S. dollar is calculated as 360 yen during 1945–1971, 300 yen during 1972–1976, 250 yen in 1977, 220 yen during 1978–1979, and 200 yen since 1980.

3. Japan Center for International Exchange, *Philanthropy in Japan* (Tokyo: Japan Center for International Exchange, rev. ed., 1978), 7; *''Kigyō no shakai kōken'' shiryōshū, 1980* (Tokyo: Sanken, 1980), passim.

4. Asano Shōichirō, ''Asahi no tenrankai,'' *Asahijin,* August 1980, p. 85; *New York Times,* July 30, 1979.

5. Michiaki Kawakita, *Modern Currents in Japanese Art,* trans. by Charles S. Terry (New York and Tokyo: Weatherhill/Heibonsha, 1974), 38.

6. Bunkachō, *Bunkachō* (Tokyo: Bunkachō, 1980), 1; Bunkachō, *Bunkachō yosan,* 22–25; Bunkachō, *Bunka gyōsei no ayumi* (Tokyo: Bunkachō, 1978), 62, 69, 111–12; Nobuya Shikaumi, *Cultural Policy in Japan* (Paris: UNESCO, 1970), 36.

7. Roy McMullen, *Art, Affluence and Alienation: The Fine Arts Today* (New York: Praeger Publishers, 1968), 24.

8. Adachi Kenji, *Bunkachō kotohajime* (Tokyo: Tōkyō Shoseki, 1978), 6–8; Machida Yutaka interview, October 29, 1980.

9. Bunkachō, *Bunkachō,* 1. Budget details in the next seven paragraphs are taken from Bunkachō, *Bunkachō yosan,* 22–25; Bunkachō, *Bunka gyōsei no ayumi,* 62.

10. Japan, Office of the Prime Minister, Bureau of Statistics, *Statistical Handbook of Japan 1980* (Tokyo: Bureau of Statistics, 1980), 135; Bunkachō, *Bunka gyōsei no ayumi,* 169; Sōrifu Tōkeikyoku, *Nihon tōkei nenkan* (Tokyo: Sōrifu Tōkeikyoku, 1980), 631; Adachi, *Bunkachō,* 74–76.

11. Asahi Shinbunsha, *Asahi nenkan 1971* (Tokyo, Asahi Shinbunsha, 1971), 705; Bunkachō, *Bunka gyōsei no ayumi,* 83–84; *Asahi Evening News,* February 20, 1981; *Japan Times,* February 21, 1981; Minoru Tanaka, *Foundations in Japan* (Tokyo: Japan Center for International Exchange, 1975), 6, 17–18; Koshimura Sadanao interview, November 5, 1980.

12. Kokuritsu Gekijō, *Kokuritsu Gekijō jūnen no ayumi* (Tokyo: Kokuritsu Gekijō, 1976), 42; Nihon Engeki Kyōkai, *Engeki nenkan '77* (Tokyo: Nihon Engeki Kyōkai, 1977), 57–65; Bunkachō, *Bunka gyōsei no ayumi,* 217.

13. Ōkōchi Takeshi interview, November 19, 1980; Asian Cultural Centre for UNESCO, *Report on Traditional Forms of Culture in Japan* (Tokyo: Asian Cultural Centre for UNESCO, 1975), 28–29.

14. Shikaumi, *Cultural Policy,* 22; Bunkachō, *Bunkachō yosan,* 22–25; Machida interview, October 29, 1980.

15. Adachi, *Bunkachō,* 117–123; *Asahi nenkan 1979,* 630; Inumaru Tadashi interview, November 5, 1980; *Japan Times,* February 22, 1981.

16. See J. Thomas Rimer, *Modern Japanese Fiction and Its Traditions: An Introduction* (Princeton: Princeton University Press, 1978), 5–6.

17. Inumaru interview, November 5, 1980; Bunkachō, *Bunka gyōsei no ayumi,* 12, 104; Bunkacho, *Bunkachō,* 9–12.

18. Bunkachō, *Bunkachō,* 12, 39; Bunkachō, *Bunka gyōsei no ayumi,* 110–11, 132–33; Adachi, *Bunkachō,* 137–40, 246; *Asahi nenkan 1967,* 724; *1970,* 700; *1971,* 700; *1972,* 695; Shikaumi, *Cultural Policy,* 25.

19. Bunkachō, *Bunkachō yosan,* 22–25; Shikaumi, *Cultural Policy,* 33–34; Adachi, *Bunkachō,* 126–31; Bunkachō, *Bunka gyōsei no ayumi,* 11–12, 105–9.

20. Bunkachō, *Bunka gyōsei no ayumi,* 106–9; *Japan Foundation Newsletter,* February-March 1980, p. 12.

21. Bunkachō, *Bunkachō yosan,* 22–25; Bunkachō, *Bunka gyōsei no ayumi,* 12, 112.

22. Shikaumi, *Cultural Policy,* 18; Bunkachō, *Bunkachō,* 33–34; Bunkachō, *Bunka gyōsei no ayumi,* 102–3; Adachi, *Bunkachō,* 125.

23. Ebara Jun, *Nihon bijutsukai fuhai no kōzō* (Tokyo: Saimaru Shuppankai, 1978), 127; Bunkachō, *Bunka gyōsei chōki sōgō keikaku ni tsuite,* (Tokyo: Bunkachō, 1977), 25–26.

24. Bunkachō, *Bunka gyōsei no ayumi,* 112; Adachi, *Bunkachō,* 126; Bunkachō, *Bunkachō yosan,* 22–25.

25. Nihon Ensōka Kyōkai, *Shōwa 45-51nen geijutsu kankei dantai hojokin kōfugaku ichiran* (Tokyo: Nihon Ensōka Kyōkai, n.d. [1978]); Bunkachō, *Bunkachō yosan,* 22–25.

26. Nihon Ensōka Kyōkai, *Shōwa;* Machida interview, October 29, 1980; Adachi, *Bunkachō,* 113; Kawachi Shōzō interview, December 3, 1980.

27. Ogawa Ayako interview, November 21, 1980; Nihon Ensōka Kyōkai, *Shōwa;* Adachi, *Bunkachō,* 126.

28. Nihon Ensōka Kyōkai, *Shōwa;* Bunkachō, *Bunkachō yosan,* 22–25; Shingekidan Kyōgikai, *Kaihō,* no. 57, July 1980, pp. 1, 3.

29. Adachi, *Bunkachō,* 60, 124; Ohara Shigeo interview, November 20, 1980.

30. Bunkachō, *Chihō bunka gyōsei jōkyō chōsa hōkokusho* (Tokyo: Bunkachō, 1980), 11.

31. Bunkachō, *Bunkachō yosan,* 22–25; Bunkachō, *Bunka gyōsei no ayumi,* 14, 112.

32. Bunkachō, *Bunka gyōsei chōki,* 10.

33. Gendai Buyō Kyōkai, *Gendai buyō: Bunkachō idō geijutsusai gendai buyō kōen* (Tokyo: Gendai Buyō Kȳokai, 1980), 1.

34. *Ibid.*, 1, 14; Adachi, *Bunkachō,* 135–36; Bunkachō, *Bunkachō,* 14.

35. Shingekidan Kyōgikai, *Kaihō,* no. 57, July 1980, pp. 1, 3; Kurabayashi Seiichirō interview, November 11, 1980.

36. *Asahi nenkan 1975,* 702; *Japan Times,* January 9, 1981.

37. *Asahi nenkan 1979,* 615; *Japan Times,* January 9, 1981.

38. Bunkachō, *Bunkachō,* 16; Adachi, *Bunkachō,* 133–34; Bunkachō, *Bunkachō yosan,* 22–25; Bunkachō, *Chihō,* 129–33, 162–82; Bunkachō, *Bunka gyōsei no ayumi,* 134–35.

39. Bunkachō, *Bunkachō yosan,* 22–25; Bunkachō, *Chihō,* 9, 11–12.

40. Projected from figures in Bunkachō, *Chihō,* 11. For detailed calculations, see Thomas R. H. Havens, *Artist and Patron in Postwar Japan* (Princeton: Princeton University Press, 1982), 87, note e.

41. Adachi, *Bunkachō,* 93–95; Bunkachō, *Bunka gyōsei no ayumi,* 115–18; Bunkachō, *Bunkachō yosan,* 22–25.

42. Ebara, *Nihon bijutsukai,* 77–78, 131; Bunkachō, *Bunka gyōsei no ayumi,* 75; *National Museum of Modern Art, Tokyo* (Tokyo: National Museum of Modern Art, 1978).

43. Bunkachō, *Bunka gyōsei no ayumi,* p. 120.

44. Masui Keiji, ed., *Dēta ongaku Nippon* (Tokyo: Min'on Ongaku Shiryōkan, 1980), 135; Hase Takao interview, October 14, 1980; Matsuki Shōgo interview, October 14, 1980.

45. *Asahi nenkan 1977,* p. 713; Takeishi Hideo interview, October 29, 1980.

46. Shikaumi, *Cultural Policy,* 12; Bunkachō, *Bunka gyōsei chōki,* 36.

47. Kokusai Kōryū Kikin, *Kokusai Kōryū Kikin nenpō, Shōwa 54nendohan* (Tokyo: Kokusai Kōryū Kikin, 1979), 9.

48. *Ibid.*, pages 9–18.

49. See detailed computations in Havens, *Artist and Patron,* 101, note q.

50. Anthony Phillips, "The Arts, Economics and Politics: Four National Perspectives," in Aspen Institute for Humanistic Studies, *The Arts, Economics and Politics: Four National Perspectives* (New York: Aspen Institute for Humanistic Studies, 1975), 17.

51. See Phillips, "Arts," 15–16; *Asahi nenkan 1977,* 713. I am indebted to Donald Richie (interview, October 6, 1980) for comments on this point.

52. Adachi, *Bunkachō,* 132.

53. Adachi Kenji interview, October 22, 1980.

54. Bunkachō, *Bunka gyōsei chōki,* 3.

55. *Japan Times,* August 2, 1986, p. 4.

15

Government and the Arts in the Modern World: Trends and Prospects

MILTON C. CUMMINGS, JR., AND RICHARD S. KATZ

As the preceding tour through western Europe, North America, and Japan makes abundantly clear, since World War II there have been two conflicting tendencies in relations between government and the arts. On the one hand, there has been enormous variety in the specific arts policies individual governments have pursued. Yet on the other hand, there have been certain broad trends and common patterns in arts policy-making by governments; and these general trends have been reflected in nearly every industrialized country in the West.

The most outstanding overall trend has been that government activity and government support for the arts have expanded tremendously since 1945. Although this explosion started earlier and from a higher level in many continental European countries than it did in Britain, North America, and Japan, by 1986 even those nations that had a long tradition of state support for culture were spending many times what they spent before the War and had vastly expanded the range of activities included in their programs. In the countries without a major prior public commitment to the arts, strong programs had taken root by the 1980s so that government support in those countries now has a significant impact on the arts.

In many countries of continental Europe, government ministries with responsibility for the arts already were firmly established by the 1930s. Elsewhere, public agencies for the arts were only established in the 1940s (Great Britain), 1950s (Ireland, Canada), or 1960s (United States). Since then, the level of government involvement has increased manyfold, often starting slowly in the 1940s. Expansion began to pick up speed in the 1950s and crested in some countries in the 1960s and in others in the 1970s. Triggered by the economic dislocations of the oil shocks of 1973 and 1979, between 1975 and 1985 this virtually uninterrupted growth came to an end, and arts advocates encountered or were threatened by serious reductions in government support. The pain caused by these cuts was sometimes acute, but in most countries, most of the higher levels of funding that had been attained remained in place—far more than had been dreamed of in 1945, or even in 1955. Moreover, in every country surveyed, by 1986 an extensive public involvement in the arts seemed to be a permanently established government responsibility.

Variations in Arts Policies

Philosophers and lovers of the arts often assert that a vital artistic life is essential for a full and rich human existence. Government programs for the arts, however, usually have far more concrete and less elevated purposes in addition to enhancing the quality of human life. Even the humanistic objectives of arts policies can have differing emphases. Moreover, the more mundane purposes have been dictated by a variety of circumstances and historical experiences, and thus reveal wide variations from country to country.

Culture is an expression of national identity, and the governments of all the countries surveyed here have been concerned with the fostering and maintenance of a distinctive national cultural identity. The positions from which they start vary widely, however, as do their specific policies and objectives. Depending on the nature of their existing cultural heritages, government programs vary in the degree to which they emphasize the preservation of the national patrimony versus the creation of something new. Countries with a strong cultural self-identity (France, Japan) or a massive physical patrimony (Italy) usually emphasize preservation. Countries without a long independent cultural history (Ireland, Norway, Canada) try to foster cultural development. In addition, fears of the "cultural imperialism" of larger or more powerful neighbors may make cultural defense an important aim of government policy (France, Canada).

These concerns refer to a single national culture. Another objective of cultural policy, however, often has been the preservation of diverse cultural strands within the same nation. This tendency has been particularly pronounced in Canada and the United States as nations of immigrants with many ethnic traditions; but even in traditionally unitary systems like Britain or France, increasing attention is being given to the cultural needs of peripheral minorities.

A second set of objectives that governments have pursued through support of the arts has been economic rather than cultural. Often, the "cultural industry" has been seen as a part of a larger industry of tourism or entertainment. In these cases, support of theaters, for example, has been viewed as a means of ensuring patronage for the restaurants providing "pre-theater dinners," the hotels providing lodging for out-of-town audiences, and the taxis carrying people from airport, to hotel, to restaurant, to theater, and back. This certainly has been a primary objective of the arts support given by American cities, but it also has been significant in European countries for which tourism is an important source of foreign exchange credit. More broadly, development of cultural institutions has been a device for bringing people back into otherwise decaying urban centers, and thus a stimulus and support for projects of urban renewal. The Barbican Centre in London and Lincoln Center in New York were both intended to revitalize run-down areas.

Some government arts policies have been special cases of more general policies to promote social welfare or employment (while in other cases, the arts have been particular beneficiaries of social programs not specifically designed for them). The importance of this objective is reflected by the frequently imposed requirement that the recipients of state arts support primarily or exclusively employ citizens of the country giving the support.

Although rarely a concern of the first order, governments have also supported the arts for their intrinsic value to the fulfillment of the human potential of their citizens. Art and culture are, from this perspective, essential elements of a life that is worth living, and therefore providing access to artistic and cultural expression is a state responsibility equal to the state's responsibility to provide for the citizens' physical needs. One aspect of this objective is to demand an aesthetically satisfying environment. Programs earmarking a portion of money spent on the construction of public buildings for their decoration reflect the judgment that art is valuable, and worth paying for, in its own right. Another aspect has been the encouragement of personal participation in artistic expression, rather than mere passive appreciation of the expression of others.

Finally, some arts policies have been pursued to provide a political advantage for prominent political or governmental leaders. Use of the arts for the political advantage of the prince has a long history, as anyone who is familiar with the buildings of the Medici will appreciate. In the United States, Richard Nixon supported the establishment of the National Endowment for the Arts as an inexpensive way of currying favor among important groups that were not notable for their support of him or his other policies. In Great Britain, Harold Wilson's support of a major expansion of British arts programs under the direction of Jennie Lee enabled the Prime Minister to reward the widow of a major leader (Aneurin Bevan) of a prominent faction within his party. In both these cases, support of the arts became a strategic device in the enduring process of government coalition building.

As this discussion has made clear, nearly every program of cultural support has had multiple objectives. Different people will support the same program for different reasons. Conversely, each supporter of government involvement in the cultural field is likely to have more than one objective in mind. The Pompidou Center in Paris was built to symbolize the glories of French culture, to stimulate the redevelopment of the Beaubourg section of Paris and its tourist trade, to provide a cultural mecca for the enrichment of popular taste, and as a monument to the second President of the Fifth Republic. At the same time, Monsieur DuPont (the French "John Doe") may have supported the project because of his love of the arts, while not forgetting that his construction company would benefit from a large public works project.

This variety of objectives is reflected in the enormously difficult problem of how "art" is to be defined in order to determine eligibility for state support. Three questions are involved here. First is the perennial question "what is art?" Second, which particular forms from among those accepted as true arts will the government support? Third, within those artistic fields, what kinds of activities will be supported?

The definition of art per se has been one of the most vexing problems confronting arts policy-makers. At the core, there are some activities and objects, crudely describable as "high culture," that virtually everyone recognizes as being art. Among these are Beethoven's symphonies, George Balanchine's dance creations, the paintings of Claude Monet, and the novels of James Joyce: music, dance, painting, literature. But, are the compositions of the "Sex Pistols" art? Is the performance of a rhythmic gymnast or a strip-tease artiste art? Are the "sofa-sized original oil paintings" advertised on television art? Are the novels of Harold Robbins, or comic books, art? Each of these may be enjoyable, and indeed in some terms valuable, but at some point a line is crossed that divides "art" from "popular entertainment" or "sports."

Even if an activity is generally recognized as falling within the legitimate definition of art, this does not guarantee that it will fall within the scope of government arts policies. Nor need all art forms included within the scope of these programs be treated equally. Most governments support the disciplines at the core of the traditional conception of art, although even here different governments may favor one form over others. Other art forms have been accepted as legitimate objects for public support more slowly and less universally. Established programs for the support of jazz, for example, only began in the

United States in 1970, five years after the National Endowment for the Arts was founded and began supporting classical music. Similarly, craft design, at the center of Irish arts support programs, is not a major concern of Italian cultural programs at all.

Within those fields that the government decides to support, there remain important distinctions with regard to the particular kinds of activities the government chooses to emphasize. Here again is the familiar choice between preservation and creation. Should the emphasis be on quality or quantity of artistic activity? Given the limited number of truly brilliant artists, a related question is whether to support a few individuals or organizations, who will naturally tend to concentrate themselves in one or two "cultural capitals," or to stress geographical dispersion of artistic support, even if it means supporting less illustrious artists and organizations at the expense of quality. Likewise, should support be concentrated on the relatively few professional artists and companies or channeled to support the many, many amateurs? Finally, is it better to encourage new or extraordinary activities (starting a new performing arts company, mounting a special exhibition, etc.), or to underwrite the ongoing costs of established institutions?

Moving from the question of what to support to the question of how to support it, what is truly amazing is the tremendous diversity, range, and ingeniousness of the means employed in different countries. In broad terms, these programs differ along two dimensions. The first concerns the way in which the funds available to artists and arts organizations are increased or their expenses reduced, while the second concerns the diversity of the sources of funds, especially the proportion of the total funds provided by governments.

In their efforts to provide financial support for the arts, governments can employ a variety of specific mechanisms. They may give money directly to arts organizations or individual artists, either as flat grants or according to a proportional matching formula. Governments may also provide indirect or concealed subsidies, through publicly constructed theater buildings, programs of social insurance, cheap postage rates, and "tax expenditures" in the form of tax exemptions for artists or arts organizations and tax incentives for private donors.

The second dimension along which the financial situation of the arts varies among countries concerns the diversity or concentration of their sources of support. There is first the question of the mix between public and private support. The proportion of total expenses for the arts that are borne by government varies dramatically. For example, one set of estimates suggests that public subsidy pays 84 percent of the costs of theater in Germany but only 35 percent in Canada, and substantially less in the United States.[1] Within the public sector, there is also great variation in the degree to which support comes from one or several levels of government.

Why the government role in financing the arts varies is an intriguing question. First there were different patterns of expectations and needs, based on the distinction, discussed earlier, between those countries that established traditions of state support under monarchic regimes in the eighteenth and nineteenth centuries (or even earlier) and those in which what cultural life there was was supported by private individuals. Moreover, having developed independently, many of the arts institutions in the latter countries were fearful that government control would accompany massive public financing, and so have themselves supported strategies that would limit the proportion of funds coming directly from the state.

There also are striking differences in public opinion in different countries about the importance of culture. What Frederick Dorian once called the "dense cultural life" of Germany reflects the conviction there that the arts are important and thus deserving of lavish public support. At least until the early 1960s, one reason there was no solidly established national program of direct support for the arts in the United States was that many Americans did not feel that the arts were important enough to merit the spending of public tax dollars.

The availability of funds from other sources also has had an effect on the level of government aid. Where there have been no massive private fortunes, large government programs have been necessary if there were to be any cultural institutions at all. Likewise, given that many of the costs of artistic production are independent of audience size, the limited size of the market often has been a factor impelling greater government support in the smaller countries.

Governments also vary widely in the ways in which they organize and administer their programs of arts support. As discussed in the introduction, there are three basic models for structuring the administration of cultural programs: the "Ministry of Culture" model; division of responsibility for culture among several ministries; and the "quasi-independent arts council" or "national endowment" model—with the "government as impresario" model as an occasional fourth possibility.

Three main factors appear to have influenced the choice of organizational structures for the arts. First, the organizational structure of arts programs tends to follow the way the government is organized and does its business in all fields. Second is the extent to which there is a general fear of state involvement in communications and the arts; where such fears were strong, the framers of government arts policies turned to the arts council/national endowment model to insulate their programs as much as possible from the normal political and administrative process. Finally, the choice of administrative structure reflects the importance accorded to the arts by the government. On one hand, creation of a separate cultural ministry may reflect the actual magnitude of arts programs and funding, while on the other hand, such a move may also be symbolic, reflecting a moral rather than a fiscal commitment.

The preceding discussion has focused on the national administration of arts policy. In fact, however, at least in monetary terms, the arts activities of regional and local governments often exceed those of the national government. Moreover, the organizational structure employed at the national level may not be reproduced at lower levels.

There are striking national differences in the balance between the central government and local governments as sources of financial support, although the fact that subnational governments provide a major share of public arts spending does not necessarily mean that they have substantial autonomy. Among the larger countries, one extreme is represented by Italy, where in 1983–84 some 68 percent of public expenditure for the arts and culture came from the national government. At the other extreme is the Federal Republic of Germany. There, only 2 percent of total public art and culture expenditures came from the national government.[2]

Even in those countries in which the central government dictates most of the content of local government arts programs, there may be a substantial disparity between the organizational structures employed at different levels. In the United States, the arts council model is reproduced at the state level, and often at the local level as well. In Great Britain, on the other hand, while the arts council model is employed nationally, local arts programs are usually organized as regular governmental functions exactly like education. Overall, the smaller the governmental unit, the more likely it is that the arts will be treated as a normal governmental function under the jurisdiction of a department with broader responsibilities, be they for education, parks and recreation, tourism, or sports and entertainment.

At the national level of government, and sometimes in subnational units as well, there is some variability in the extent to which governments have relied on "panels" of artists or art experts in deciding how government funds are to be divided among individual artists or institutions. At one extreme are the countries in which panels play a strong, sometimes an overwhelming, role in the evaluation and selection of specific applicants for support. For example, while the amount of money to be spent on the visual arts in the Netherlands is decided by Ministers in consultation with their bureaucrats, panels of artists actually view thousands of individual paintings and decide which ones the state will buy. At the other extreme, all decisions would be made by bureaucrats on the basis of their own judgments. While no country goes to this extreme, the Italian system closely approximates it. In between the "pure panel model" and the "pure bureaucratic model," is the hybrid possibility of the "bureaucrat with advice."

Countries also vary enormously in the degree to which the details of cultural policy are embodied in the national budget, and therefore are in fact determined in the budgetary process. The range here is between the "block grant," which specifies neither the recipient nor the specific purposes for which the money is to be spent, all the way to very detailed appropriations which allocate funds to particular institutions to be used for specified purposes. The undifferentiated block grant to the Arts Council of Great Britain typifies the former possibility, while the Italian grant ear-marked for the regular season of the *Teatro alla Scala* approaches the other extreme.

In fact, specificity with regard to recipient and specificity with regard to purpose are separable. Support for Washington, D.C.'s National Symphony Orchestra was in 1986 a specific line-item in the federal appropriations bill for the Department of the Interior and Related Agencies, but the Orchestra was free to spend the money as its board saw fit. On the other hand, the National Endowment for the Arts is given an appropriation with a specified amount tied to its Dance Program, but is free to allocate those funds among dance activities and companies it selects.

Most of our discussion so far has been in terms of what governments do for the arts and how they do it. Of equal importance, at least potentially, are the things governments can do *to* the arts. Censorship, of course, is one possibility. Alternatively, rather than prohibiting artists from doing something—publishing, displaying, or otherwise disseminating their work—government can shape artistic development by providing bribes (less pejoratively, incentives) for artists to do what the government wants. One of the most common examples of this is the conscious attempt that most governments have made to promote a geographical dispersion of artistic activity.

There are many other ways in which governments may take an activist role in shaping cultural development. Many governments give heavy emphasis to arts education, thereby trying to enlarge the size of the appreciative audience for the arts. Creation of incentives for arts organizations to do "outreach" or to provide programs that will appeal to larger-than-usual audiences are further examples. Critics of such programs, however, may feel that they run the risk of lowering standards to meet the level of popular taste even as they try to raise that level.

At the very least, activities that receive government support are made more likely to occur, often at the direct expense of activities that are not supported. This kind of program may stimulate activity in a broadly defined sector, or its target may be extremely narrow.

In the past, for example, the National Endowment for the Arts has had specific support programs for the presentation of opera in English, much to the discomfort of some opera companies that had a tradition of performing in the original languages. Active direction of arts life may go even farther, as the "Cultural Dynamization Campaign" of the Portugese MFA illustrates.

The events since 1945 in Portugal also illustrate another dimension on which relations between governments and the arts may vary—there have been major differences in the extent to which artists themselves have played an activist role in the political struggles of their countries and have served as forces for governmental change. The arts community of Portugal was in the vanguard of groups critical of the Salazar regime and played an important role in propagandizing for the regime that replaced it. In the United States, artists played a substantial role in the growing protest movement against the Vietnam War. The public rejection of President Johnson's invitation to the White House Festival of the Arts by the poet Robert Lowell in 1965 was an early and much publicized indication that there was growing opposition to the President's war policies. Political activism in a more directly cultural sphere is exemplified by the Dutch Provo movement, and particularly by the theater group "Tomato."

Common Trends in the Arts

As our discussion thus far makes clear, there are many possible ways in which governments may play an active role in the development of culture. These possibilities are amply reflected in the variety of programs and relationships that have actually emerged in western Europe, North America, and Japan. At the same time, one cannot help but be struck by a number of common trends in relations between governments and the arts that are apparent in nearly all industrial nations.

One specific manifestation of the trend toward greater support for the arts, and one found in almost every country surveyed, is that there has been a great expansion in what might be called "housing for the arts." A particularly striking feature of this building boom is the scale of the enterprises involved. Critics may extol the virtues of a "natural" and sometimes scattered development of buildings to house the arts, but there seems to have been a worldwide explosion in the construction of brand new "cultural centers"—large-scale complexes featuring several concert halls, theaters, or opera houses, with sometimes museums and other art spaces included as well. With the Barbican Centre and National Theatre complex in London, the Pompidou Center in Paris, a new contemporary arts complex in Tokyo, the National Centre for the Arts in Ottawa, and, among the largest of all, Lincoln Center in New York as leading examples, new theaters, concert halls, alternative performance spaces, new wings for existing museums, and even wholly new museums have become common throughout the Western world.

Of course, the same money that paid for one monumental project could have bought several smaller facilities, but a nearly universal preference for the massive and the attention-commanding is apparent. Governments tend to prefer demonstration projects, which they think have a specific end date for their costs, rather than projects entailing a continuing commitment. Often, demonstration arts projects are tied to larger demonstration projects of urban renewal. Moreover, while one could pay for several smaller arts centers with the money spent on one large center, once a commitment to "several" centers has been made, an irresistible pressure arises to build "several more."

A second reason for this preference is the practical recognition that it is easier to get people excited about a "world-class project," one that will make an international splash. This makes it easier to get private and corporate financial support, and it makes it easier to get individual political leaders to take on the project as a cause. Great cultural centers also may be monuments for the philanthropists and political leaders who make them possible. It is not coincidental that President Georges Pompidou played a major role in pushing the massive arts center that now bears his name through the governmental and bureaucratic labyrinth of France.

Two other trends in the building of these cultural centers appear to be almost universal. Like most large-scale government construction projects, nearly every one of the postwar cultural centers has cost far more than originally estimated. Nearly every one also has opened months and usually years after it was supposed to.

An analogous tendency that is broadly apparent is a preference for support of one-time blockbuster events and exhibitions, rather than less glamorous and eye-arresting arts programming. For example, the Tutankhamen exhibition that toured from Egypt cost enormous amounts of money and attracted correspondingly enormous media attention. The Vatican's shipping to the New York World's Fair of a single work of art, Michelangelo's *Pietà,* was greeted with all the fanfare that would accompany a royal progress.

Blockbuster events have their pluses and minuses. They enable large numbers of people to experience works of art, normally scattered throughout the world, that they could never afford to go to see. Moreover, the media coverage and hoopla surrounding such exhibitions bring the arts into the consciousness of vast numbers of people and encourage people who would otherwise be unlikely to attend an art exhibition nonetheless to attend the "event." They may, thereby, "get used" to going to a museum. On the other side, however, the very success of such exhibitions in attracting crowds lessens the aesthetic experience of those who view them. In addition, blockbuster exhibitions can only go to a few large urban centers, although they draw on the limited resources available for the arts everywhere. Finally, many arts professionals fear that a concentration on blockbuster events may unbalance their programming, leaving them less time and fewer resources to devote to less glamorous, but potentially more important activities.

Many people in the arts world seem to believe that the assertion that the arts are "a good thing" ought to be adequate to ensure government support. That is not the way things work in modern democracies. There are more "good things" competing for the government's limited resources than can possibly be supported to the extent that their advocates think desirable. Government support has grown in country after country because a remarkable process of coalition building has taken place by which members of the arts community have expanded the number of other citizens and interest groups who feel they have a stake in government aid for the arts. In some cases, coalitions have been built at the initiative of advocates of government support; in other cases, arts supporters have been forced by government to accept a broader definition of eligibility for arts funding, only to realize later how valuable a broadening of their base of political support could be.

An important lesson the advocates of support for "high culture" had to learn was that it is politically advantageous to expand the definition of culture to include more popular art forms and activities. Nothing has altered the fact that devotees of symphonic music, opera, abstract painting, etc. are a tiny minority of the population. Often, programs that started out supporting only traditional arts activities were able to expand their support for those activities only after the range and depth of the programs was extended to include additional art forms and companies with a less "high brow" orientation. This has taken place in two ways. Specific programs such as support for the theater have expanded so that *Kiss Me Kate*, for example, as well as *The Taming of the Shrew*, becomes eligible for support. And the total scope of government arts programs has grown as "new" fields like jazz, folk art, and ethnic arts have been added to the more traditional programs. Each expansion has increased the political constituency for government arts programs.

Another vivid example of the importance of coalition building is the support the arts often have gained by forging an alliance with the education community. There is a natural affinity between education and the arts, but the artistic community has been able to do many things to strengthen its links with education and to enlist the vastly more influential groups supporting education to support the arts as well. By providing art experiences for school children and services for teachers, cultural organizations have given the education people a stake in securing more arts funding. At the same time, by supporting arts education programs in the schools, the potential audience has been enlarged and popular support for the arts increased.

Coalition building for the arts also occurs when programs become more widely distributed throughout a country. One of the clearest trends is that the expansion of government arts programs in the cultural capitals is almost always accompanied by political pressures for these programs to be expanded geographically as well. In a number of countries, pressures have been growing for funds to be channeled directly to the periphery. Often the established arts organizations have resisted government programs that bow to these pressures as unwarranted yielding to political expendiency. However, often they have come to find that the vast network of organizations and individuals that thereby become political allies more than compensates for any short-run costs stemming from a wider sharing of the government arts budget.

Notwithstanding the tremendous expansion in government programs to support the arts in comparison to those that were in place in 1945, cultural programs still represent only a minuscule portion of the total national budget. This has meant that there has been great scope for individual leaders to play an enormous role in shaping and expanding their government's arts programs. John Maynard Keynes played a decisive role in the original establishment of the Arts Council of Great Britain. Julius Bomholt played a similar role in the development of Denmark's cultural policies. And in the United States, Nancy Hanks combined great personal charm with an extraordinary political perspicacity to bring about a remarkable increase in political support for the principle of government funding of the arts.

Sometimes people who are initially perceived as "enemies" of government programs to support the arts turn out to be valuable "friends." In 1981, many arts people in the United States feared that the appointment of Reagan campaign adviser Frank Hodsoll to head the NEA foreshadowed an attempt to decimate the agency. As it turned out, however, Hodsoll became a firm supporter of nearly all the agency's programs and it was highly useful for the arts people to have Hodsoll, whom Reagan trusted, speaking for them in the councils of the administration. Apparently it is the case for arts agencies, as it is known to be more generally, that once a politician assumes control of a government department, he often develops an incentive to support its programs and position within the total governmental structure, no matter what he may have thought of the department before.

Two other common trends emerge from our survey of arts policy development. The first is that the arts often are affected in a major way as an unintended consequence of policies that are enacted to achieve objectives that have little or nothing to do with the arts.

National broadcasting systems, originally conceived as passive channels of communication, often have become major supporters of the arts by purchasing the work of performing artists on a massive scale, by developing audiences for live performances, and sometimes even by making direct grants to artistic organizations. Moreover, television and radio have become major vehicles for delivery of the arts. Audiences of undreamed-of size are able to enjoy the performing arts without ever entering a theater. Social security and unemployment compensation systems in nearly every country help make the common artistic pattern of intermittent employment and "resting between engagements" supportable.

Second, basic, complete statistics on the arts seem to be in short supply everywhere. It is hard to get a clear picture of such a simple thing as how much government aid there is for the arts, even at the national level, and in country after country local government aid for the arts is almost a terra incognita. One reason for this is that government aid is tucked into many different agency budget lines, and merely to find them all and count them up entails enormous amounts of work and ingenuity. Even worse are measures and statistics on the *effects* of government aid programs for the arts. It is relatively easy to count the number of people who attend a play. But it is far harder to tell how many would have come in the absence of government programs that fostered appreciation of the theater and lowered the price of tickets, and far harder still to tell what benefits the audience received by being there.

Explanations and Evaluations

In the preceding section, we identified a number of common trends in arts policy. It remains to explore why these developments have taken place and to evaluate some aspects of government programs that have affected the arts.

It is clear that arts programs are subject to the same political pressures that affect all government policy-making. Although arts advocates sometimes claim that their programs, because of their sensitive character and dependence on individual creativity, ought to be totally free of any oversight or control by government even as they receive public money, and although some countries have gone to great lengths to insulate detailed policy-making from partisan pressures, complete insulation from "normal" politics has not happened, will not happen, and, in the opinion of many of the politicians who make the financial decisions upon which government programs depend, should not happen. The idea of giving a block grant of support to an arts council, with no framework restrictions on how the money is to be distributed, is virtually unique to Britain, and even there the government has exercised informal pressure to influence the distribution of funds. Moreover, we must remember that Arts Council members are government officials in fact, if not in form. "Politics" has a bad name among those who want unrestricted access to the public treasury, but as one congressman observed, discussing the assertion by the American Corporation for Public Broadcasting that it should be exempt from political oversight, "politics" is the way the people make decisions concerning the spending of their money in a democracy. At the very least, it is entirely proper for the elected representatives of the people to set the broad parameters and objectives of arts policies—to decide what forms of art they want to support, how they want their money distributed, and whether the greater emphasis should be on quality or quantity.

In considering arts as a public policy area, the most important fact to bear in mind is that even in countries where culture is supported "lavishly," all cultural programs taken together account for only 1 or 2 percent of the total national budget. Not only does this fact explain many developments in the field of arts policy, but it is ironic that the relative unimportance of the arts has been a political asset much of the time.

One consequence of the relatively minuscule size of arts programs is that it is hard to justify the idea of an independent senior Ministry of Culture. Some arts advocates have argued for the creation of one central ministry to coordinate arts programs, to represent the arts in government circles, and to dramatize the importance of the arts. Their assumption often is that this will also lead to greater funding for culture. The fact is, however, that the greatest increases in public funding for the arts often have occurred when the arts were part of a larger non-arts ministry that was growing for other reasons. Dutch arts programs housed in the Ministry of Education were able, for example, to "ride up the escalator" during a period when the government was increasing its support for education. Moreover, advocates of a separate ministry also tend to assume that this will give the arts more effective representation in government decision-making. In fact, given the actual size of government cultural programs, the best the arts could usually hope for is a very junior minister. The arts usually are better off with part of the attention of a senior minister than with the full-time attention of a "political lightweight."

The small size of the arts budget also has the curious effect of increasing the political effectiveness of the outcry which proposed budget cuts elicit from the arts community. Particularly because of their special access to the media, their ability to mobilize celebrities, and their emerging organizational strength, arts advocates are able to mount a protest and have it heard. They can therefore impose on political leaders costs that are likely to outweigh the relatively small absolute potential savings involved. Thus, for political officials, "arts bashing" is often not worth the cost.

Notwithstanding that small size can frequently be turned to the advantage of the arts, it can also have its drawbacks. Occasionally, the arts may be caught in the middle of larger political controversies that its advocates have very little ability to control. In April 1986, for example, the seven British metropolitan county councils were abolished. The major impetus for this move by the Conservative government of Prime Minister Margaret Thatcher was the defiance on the part of Labour-dominated councils of national directives concerning public housing and public transport. The abolition of these councils, however, had serious consequences for the arts. Several of the councils, most notably the Greater London Council, were major supporters of the arts; but at the time they were abolished no provision had been made to replace the funds that were lost.

The emergence of democratic governments as a major force in the funding of the arts, less than creating new problems, has confronted the arts with many of the same problems faced in earlier times, albeit in a somewhat different form and perhaps in sharper relief. There is a misperception that there once was a "Golden Age" when artists lived like princes and were able to do their creative work without the need to cater to anyone's taste but their own or to worry about how to support themselves. The example of Haydn profiting from the inspired patronage of Prince Eszterhazy is often cited as a normal occurrence in this "Golden Age." However, for every Haydn, there were numerous artists or would-be artists for whom life was a much darker, harder struggle. Mozart, one of the transcendent geniuses of the world of music, died penniless and was buried in a pauper's grave.

Artists in this so-called "Golden Age" depended on patrons, whether princes or private citizens, for much of their livelihood. But an artist who depends on a patron must satisfy that patron if his patronage is to continue. The taste of the patron has always made a difference; and this applies to modern governments, when they become patrons, as well.

Patronage of the arts by modern democratic governments, however, brings with it problems that the older patronage by private donors did not face. Earlier patrons were responsible only to themselves. Democratic governments, however, are responsible to the people who elect them. But the concept of "responsibility" has two aspects. One is that officials should pursue a course of action that is desired by the people. But another is that officials should use their own judgment to do what is best for the people. In the field of art and culture, the first aspect of responsibility implies catering to public tastes and supporting popular art forms with mass appeal; the second, however, may require governments to support activities which many citizens neither understand nor approve. As in most policy fields, what is required is a balancing act. If public tastes are offended too often, it may contribute to popular removal of the current administration, and with it its arts policies. If only mass opinion is considered, there is the danger that only the most commercially viable arts activities will be supported and the fine arts will be left to languish.

Once governments begin supporting the arts, they inevitably face complex and difficult questions of choice and taste. Otherwise, cultural policy becomes an indiscriminate and open-ended commitment to support anything and everything that anyone calls "art." If the government is not to be indiscriminate in its cultural patronage, then it has to make choices. How can this be done, without stifling creativity and the free flow of artistic imagination? Inevitably, this means making judgments of taste. To discharge this difficult responsibility, governments have used combinations of three basic devices—allocations by bureaucrats, choice by "panels of experts," and the "privatization of allocative decisions" through such devices as tax incentives and matching grants. Each approach has its own strengths and its own weaknesses.

Allocation of support by bureaucrats is a clear-cut exercise of public power by public officials. There are clear lines of political accountability, and in general citizens are able to know who is responsible for deciding what. In countries which rely on the bureaucratic model for allocating government support, there is also usually less discretionary authority; conditions that will entitle an artist or organization to receive aid, not just conditions that must be met in order to be eligible to be considered for aid, are generally specified by law. Even with this model, however, some discretion is almost always left to administrators. The potential disadvantages of the bureaucratic model are that bureaucratic administrators may be cut off from vital new currents in the world of the arts. They may be conservative and unimaginative, and often epitomize the staid middle-class values that some artists find abhorrent. Placing arts decisions in the hands of bureaucrats may also magnify the dangers of centralized power.

Panels also have their advantages and disadvantages. On the plus side, panels with rotating membership increase the possibility that decision-makers will be in touch with new developments in the arts. They offer a way to bring experts on particular art forms to the service of government. They also provide insulation from potential political interference by allowing politically vulnerable administrators to disclaim responsibility for unfortunate decisions. Finally, the use of panels has the potential to introduce greater flexibility and daring into government decision-making. On the minus side, however, panels of artists can act as a kind of mutual admiration society. They may share the notable unwillingness of most professional groups to make negative judgments about their peers. The community of leading artists, the pool from which panelists are commonly drawn, may develop its own inbred standards of taste. Panels may be as intolerant of any activity that is not in their current mindset as the often criticized ''booboisie.''[3] Finally, while insulating individual decisions from political pressure, use of panels also fuzzes lines of accountability and makes it difficult for the people to know who is responsible for the way their money is being spent.

In a sense, all of the problems of both the bureaucratic and the panel models are avoided by privatizing the allocative decisions. This may be done through government policies that encourage and multiply private support through such devices as tax incentives, and especially by some types of matching grants. A commonly cited advantage of this model is that it decentralizes allocative decisions; tens of thousands and even millions of individual citizens are encouraged to be private patrons of the arts. Moreover, this system ensures that public funds will go to activities and organizations with public support and substitutes the judgment of the public for that of bureaucrats or panelists. It also encourages artists and arts organizations to develop strong roots in their communities. On the other hand, the privatization of allocative decisions in the arts suffers from the same problems as all market-oriented decision processes: ''Them that has, gets.'' While tax incentives and matching grants multiply the value of private donations, they still leave the greatest power in the hands of those who can donate the most. And, until they are well established, it is hard for individual artists and arts organizations to attract donations at all.

The countries in our survey differ not only in the extent to which they rely on decisions by bureaucrats, decisions by expert panels, or privatized decision-making for the allocation of public money for the arts. They also differ in the extent to which they provide steady, massive institutional support for arts organizations, or the extent to which they emphasize grants for specific projects—and provide grants which usually make up a much smaller proportion of an art institution's total budget. In Germany, France, Italy, Sweden, and several other continental European countries, major arts institutions like *La Fenice* in Venice or the *Comédie Française* regularly receive half or more of their total operating budgets from the government,[4] and singers, actors, and other performing artists in such institutions may actually be government employees. In Great Britain, Canada, and the United States, by contrast, the more common pattern is for arts institutions to be private or semi-private organizations, and in the United States, with very few exceptions, direct government appropriations do not come close to providing half of the organizations' annual budgets.

These two patterns of arts support also have their pluses and minuses. An institution with an assured financial base is better able to undertake long-term planning and also freer to experiment with more venturesome programming which runs a greater risk at the box office. At the same time, this model of arts support may have certain drawbacks. There may be a disadvantage to having all of one's eggs in one basket. Massive direct government funding clearly makes arts institutions more dependent on the government's financial well-being and on government decision-making; if there are major government budget cutbacks the effects on dependent arts institutions may be severe. This model also does not provide an institution with the incentive to control expenditures or to develop new audiences. Arts institutions in countries that lack a steady source of major institutional support may face a precarious existence. But the situation in those countries tends to create a resourceful and tenacious group of arts institutions.

In country after country, there has been a natural tendency for the arts to concentrate themselves in a few major population centers, while government programs, especially in recent years, have attempted to promote a greater geographic dispersion. For centuries, French artistic life has tended to be concentrated in Paris. London has been the natural cultural capital of Great Britain, just as New York has been the arts center of the United States. Many government programs developed since World War II have sought to bring about a greater distribution of arts activities nationwide. There has sometimes been resistance to channeling "too large" a proportion of the national government's total cultural budget into the already established arts centers. There have been determined attempts—by government-funded touring programs, for example—to get art collections and art companies out into the country; and there has sometimes been a premium for supporting new and developing arts activities in the provinces rather than in the nation's arts capital.

In many countries in recent years there has been a major flowering of arts activities in areas outside, and sometimes very remote from, the older established arts centers. This flowering of the arts on the periphery might have occurred to some extent even without government programs, but the acceleration of wider public access to the arts is one of the signal accomplishments of government aid in the postwar years.

Finally, another word or two needs to be said about censorship and state control of artistic expression. In the years since World War II, one is impressed by the extent to which democratic governments have attempted to limit state censorship and state control imposed on the arts. Strong efforts, often backed by constitutional guarantees, have been made to assure a free artistic life. Yet, even in countries with deeply entrenched traditions of artistic freedom, censorship and state control of artistic expression are, to some extent, matters of degree. Political control of the arts to protect the government of the day from criticism, as occurred in Portugal under Salazar, would find few approving supporters in the West. But, few democratic governments are immune from pressures to control some forms of expression—often forms of expression that are presented as being "art." Should governments try to control pornography, which often is presented as a form of "art"? And how is government to define where valid artistic expression ends and "pornography" begins? Should governments try to censor sexually explicit lyrics in popular songs that command a vast audience of adolescents? And should government-aided film institutes show movies that portray the assassination of a political leader in countries where the nation's own chief executive has been shot? These are just some of the issues involving questions of taste, judgment, or potential censorship and control that democratic governments that support the arts have actually wrestled with. The practice in the countries in our survey has been to give a quite wide latitude to free artistic expression. But, at some point on a continuum between complete government control of artistic expression and complete freedom for anything which is claimed to be artistic expression, most governments are likely to intervene.

The importance of state aid to the arts also raises questions about the meaning of censorship. In the days of private patronage, the question was relatively simple; censorship was a positive action by government to prevent publication, production, or display of a work that would otherwise have been available to the public. Today, however, many works can be produced or displayed only if they have not just the acquiescence but the positive support of government. To cite an extreme case, there is essentially no private market for monumental sculpture at all. Some would claim that this creates an affirmative obligation for government to support their work. Similarly, they argue that if a work is produced with government support or commissioned for a public space, it is "censorship'' for the government not to display it. But other observers take a different view. Here, they say, the state is not acting as regulator but rather as the agent of the people as purchaser. Surely, they add, once a work is purchased, the people through their government have the right to do with their property, whether a work of art or not, what they will—including relegating it to the ''attic'' where they will not have to see it.

Arts Support in an Era of Retrenchment

As has been noted, government financial support for the arts was expanding almost everywhere in the 1960s and 1970s, often at a spectacular rate. This dramatic growth of cultural spending was part of a much larger explosion of government spending for social programs generally, often financed through government borrowing. In the 1980s, however, the long-term costs of massive deficit financing of social programs became obvious and the expectations of permanent unbridled growth in social spending came abruptly to an end. For the arts, this new need to adjust thinking to an era of retrenchment has been extremely uncomfortable. Problems and choices that could be fuzzed over in an era of expansion now present themselves with new clarity and urgency.

By now, these choices are familiar. Which art forms should be supported, and in what measure? What balance should be struck between supporting the preservation of the nation's existing cultural heritage and traditions, and the fostering of its creative expansion? To what extent should government resources be concentrated on support for professional arts activities versus support for amateur participatory programs? To what extent should government support be concentrated on the more ''elite'' arts activities rather than those with a more ''populist'' appeal? What should be the balance between stimulating a greater geographic dispersion of the arts versus emphasizing aid for the established artistic centers?

In the ''good old days,'' the question was one of relative growth. Even those activities that were not favored in the balance struck could nonetheless expect increasing absolute levels of support. To lose the financial battle simply meant to grow more slowly. Now, however, losers may suffer cuts in absolute terms, not just slower growth. In some cases, indeed, to lose in the competition for public support may mean extinction. The case of the D'Oyly Carte Opera Company is the best known, but not the only example of a long-established artistic institution killed by the withdrawal of government support.

The prospect that a government's allocative decisions may be a matter of life or death of an institution can make it more difficult to maintain a unified political constituency for the arts. When overall government support was expanding and everyone could be a winner, compromises and accommodations among arts institutions and constituencies were easy to reach. Everyone was willing to accept a slightly smaller increase in order to preserve a united front. In an era of retrenchment, the question is potentially different. No one is willing to go out of business just to maintain a united front. To date, the level of cuts imposed usually has been relatively modest. Even in the one case in which a large number of programs were cut off entirely, Britain in 1982–83, the absolute level of the government appropriation had actually increased, although at a lower rate than the rate of inflation.

The Arts Council of Great Britain announced its decisions abruptly, without advance notice, and with no right of appeal. There seems to have been no time or occasion for the losers to attempt to press the relative merits of their claims over those of other Council clients, and unanimity in the protests from the arts community could be maintained. Were institutions to suspect in advance that some of their number would be eliminated, as would be the case if the absolute government appropriation were to be substantially reduced (if, for example, the American NEA budget were to be cut by the 50 percent that President Reagan proposed in 1981 rather than the 10 percent cut that was made), then the prospects for internecine warfare would increase dramatically.

One defensive strategy by larger and stronger institutions which has emerged in some countries is to seek to separate their grants from general arts funding decisions. In the United States, for example, major cultural institutions such as the New Orleans Symphony Orchestra have sometimes obtained a line-item appropriation in their state government's budget. This means that public money goes directly from the Louisiana state government to the state's leading orchestra. The orchestra thus avoids the need to compete for funds in the advisory panels of the Division of the Arts which distributes state funds to most other Louisiana cultural institutions. In the short run, the line-item appropriation is likely to be neither more nor less than the funds which would have been granted to the New Orleans Symphony anyway (with the Division of the Arts' budget correspondingly reduced), so that this procedure may make little difference to the actual levels of support received either by the New Orleans Symphony or by other artistic organizations in the state. In the longer run, however, it may tend to remove the orchestra and its powerful backers from the coalition supporting the general appropriation for the state's Division of the Arts.

Another strategy that the arts community has attempted to pursue in some places is to separate the entire question of arts funding from the government's regular appropriations process by obtaining a special ear-marked tax, the proceeds of which go directly to support the arts. In this way the level of arts funding is determined by the tax receipts rather than by explicit government decisions. This is an alternative behind which the arts community has been able to unite. In particular, it has appeared attractive where the yield from the dedicated tax is relatively impervious to the forces that have caused general government retrenchments, thus insulating the arts from them. The Norwegian practice of dedicating a portion of the takings of football pools is a long-standing example of such a funding arrangement. More recently, San Francisco has had a tax on hotel receipts which is divided between the city's convention and tourism office and the arts.

Conclusion

The overriding conclusion that emerges from this survey is that government support for the arts is here to stay everywhere in the industrialized world. There has, of course, been a long tradition of state support for the arts on the continent of Europe. What has been the striking development of the postwar years is that state support now appears to be a firmly entrenched component of the political traditions of Great Britain, Ireland, North America, and Japan, as well. Government involvement has grown impressively at all levels. There has been a growing recognition that the artistic community is a legitimate and worthwhile element of society, as deserving of governmental assistance as are the many other groups that are aided by the state.

To be sure, the 1980s have witnessed threatened and actual cutbacks in government support for the arts. Especially in those countries in which the tradition of state support is relatively new, these developments have naturally raised fears in some quarters that arts support might be cut out altogether. In fact, arts support has continued at impressive levels despite general government retrenchment, and what is most impressive is that often the cuts proposed for the arts have actually been less than those proposed for much longer established government programs. Of course, no program is immune from the possibility of elimination at some time in the future, but as of 1986, government programs to support culture and the arts appear to be permanent public responsibilities.

Both a cause and a consequence of this institutionalization and growth of cultural programs has been the tendency for culture to become a policy field in which the normal rules of the political process apply as in other fields. While some people decry this development as leading to the "politicization" of the arts and fear the possibility of political interference, becoming a "typical" policy area rather than a "unique field of human endeavor" is an inevitable accompaniment to becoming a significant item on the government's agenda.

Greater politicization is well-nigh inevitable when the sums of public money become larger, and political leaders as well as the general public see the arts as a more important field. Politicians are not likely to spend much time on matters that everyone feels are insignificant, and neither are they likely to allocate public resources to them. The arts have often benefited when major political leaders have taken a direct interest in their funding and development, whether because of personal interest or because of perceived political advantage. But, of course, these politicians have had their own ideas about how cultural policy should operate, and their involvement heightens the political character of the arts support process.

A parallel development is that the organizations of artists, arts institutions, and art lovers have evolved into interest groups that speak for the arts community in the governmental arena, much like the lobbying organizations of other sectors of society. In fact, in using some of their "stars" to command the attention of the media, the arts groups have sometimes used techniques that could serve as lessons to some of the old-line lobbying groups. In short, there has been a rather remarkable increase in the political sophistication of the constituency for the arts.

There are some consequences of this tendency to equate culture with other policy areas. Political leaders have come increasingly to see the arts as yet another service to the community. At least some artists, however, tend to take a different view of the proper role of public policy as it affects the arts. Is the primary function of cultural policy to be service to the community? Or is it to be service to the artists? The former conception implies emphasis on expanding access to the arts for the public and providing those artistic services that the public wants or would directly benefit from. It also may entail a capacious conception of the government's role in shaping the development of the arts. On the other hand, if programs are designed primarily to benefit the artists, emphasis will be placed on freeing artists from the restraints of the box office and mass taste and allowing them to do what they want to do with fewer budgetary strings attached. In this conception, there is a much more limited role for government planning, and government is supportive but reactive rather than directive in the evolution of the nation's artistic and cultural life.

The central point is, however, that by and large arts organizations seem to have been able to come to terms with both kinds of governmental arts programs. They have learned how to accommodate themselves to the strictures imposed by government support, but also how to mitigate and indeed shape those strictures to their own advantage. They have learned how to play the political game with enviable skill. Most important, they have demonstrated an ability to adapt and to survive in the political marketplace.

The political pressures and economic forces that shape cultural policies are broadly similar throughout the industrialized democracies. Moreover, once established, programs of cultural support seem to spawn any number of specific pressures that further shape arts policy, and which have been relatively constant as well. The result is that there has been a noteworthy tendency for the cultural policies of the nations we have considered to become more and more similar over time—in short, there has been a convergence of arts policymaking in these nations. Two aspects of this process of convergence merit reemphasis here.

The first is the strong tendency for the definition of culture, and correspondingly the range of activities supported, to expand. Programs that originally were designed to support only "high culture" have been broadened to include more popular or populist activities as well. Programs that were designed originally to support one art form in particular have been broadened to include virtually all art forms. Programs originally for professionals have been broadened to include amateurs; those concentrated on a few artistic centers now extend nationwide.

The second tendency has been for governments to develop packages of support programs containing many diverse elements. This focus on the concept of a total support system for the arts includes programs to stimulate private and corporate giving, tax concessions and other indirect subsidies, as well as direct government grants. The result is that the distinctions between countries that emphasized direct support and those that emphasized indirect support are becoming less pronounced as all countries do a bit of everything.

In these respects, governments are coming to take a middle road, both between those that want to support only "high culture" and those that think that popularity is the only standard by which government support can be justified in a democracy, and between those that want government to free totally the arts from the harsh world of economic reality and those that think that the market is the only valid standard of value. In fact, the middle road is probably the best road. In this way, the arts may avoid the twin dangers of excessive dependence on commercial considerations that can destroy the arts and render them just a branch of the entertainment industry and, on the other hand, an excessive insulation from the market that leads to profligacy and a widening gap between artists and their audiences.

One final point remains to be made. When advocates of arts programs begin to assess their success, they often apply unrealistic standards, and thus are too hard on themselves. They lament the fact that many individuals in their society do not avail themselves of all the cultural opportunities that government programs have sought to make available. In particular, they lament the fact that audiences remain overwhelmingly middle-class, and that many art forms are not patronized by large segments of the population. If the objective is "cultural democracy," they ask, shouldn't audiences reflect a broad representative cross-section of the population? True cultural democracy includes the right not to like high culture, as well as to enjoy it. The objective is not to force people to attend operas and music recitals. Rather, it is to afford to all, regardless of social class or economic position, the opportunity to develop a taste for these art forms and the opportunity to indulge that taste once it has been developed. The real accomplishment is to keep the arts at their highest level alive and accessible to all. In the democracies discussed, government programs for the arts have done precisely that, and they have also brought about a substantial broadening of the audience. That is enough.

Notes

1. Deutscher Buhnenverein, Bundesverband Deutscher Theater, *Theaterstatistik 1982/83*, pp. 102–3; The Canada Council, *Selected Arts Research Statistics,* 4th. ed., September 1984; William Baumol and Hilda Baumol, "The Future of the Theater and the Cost Disease of the Arts," paper presented at the international colloquim: "L'Economie du Spectacle Vivant et l'Audiovisuel," Nice, France, 15–17 October 1984.

2. J. Mark Davidson Schuster, *Supporting the Arts: An International Comparative Study,* Department of Urban Studies and Planning, Massachusetts Institute of Technology, March 1985, p. 43.

3. The word was coined by H. L. Mencken to describe the bourgeoisie.

4. In the case of *La Fenice* in one recent year, 96 percent of operating funds came in the form of government subsidies. David Cwi and Michael Quine, "Public and Private Arts Support in North America and Europe: Income Data for 32 Cultural Institutions," Department of Arts Policy and Management, City University (London), 1985.